Health Status Index: Rajasthan

By the same author

- **Human Development Index : Rajasthan**
  (Spatio Temporal and Gender Appraisal at Panchayat Samiti/Block Level—1991-2001)

About the Author

Prof. Hemlata Joshi, a faculty in Geography, Mohanlal Sukhadia University, Udaipur (Rajasthan), is at present on deputation at the Institute of Development Studies, Jaipur. She obtained her B.A. (Honours), M.A. and Ph.D. Degrees from the University of Rajasthan, Jaipur. Her areas of specialization are Human Development Studies, Industrial Geography and Remote Sensing. She has completed research projects on "Fertilizer Industry of India" (UGC), "A Geographical Appraisal of Textile Mill Industry—Banswara District" (UGC), "Fairs of Vagad Region" (TRI-Udaipur), "Education Development Index of Panchayat Samities, Rajasthan, 1991-2000", "Economic Development Index", "Health Status Index" and "Human Development Index-Spatio-Temporal and Gender Appraisal at Panchayat Samiti/Block Level" (all of IDSJ). Besides, having contributed articles to various journals of repute, Prof. Joshi has many books to her credit including *Fertilizer Industry of India, Bhartiya Suti Vastra Udyog, Janjation Ka Bhaugolik Adhyayan, Perspective in Industrial Geography—A Case Study of Sugar Industry of Rajasthan, Geographical Appraisal of Textile Mill Industry, Jansankhya: Ek Bhaugolic Adhyayan, Vastra Udyog: Ek Bhaugolic Vishleshan, Education Development Index: Rajasthan* and *Economic Development Index (Spatio-Temporal & Gender Appraisal at Panchayat Samiti/Block Level).*

Health Status Index: Rajasthan

Spatio-Temporal Appraisal at Panchayat Samiti/Block Level

Hemlata Joshi

Published for

Institute of Development Studies, Jaipur

by

CONCEPT PUBLISHING COMPANY, NEW DELHI-110059

Cataloging in Publication Data—DK
Courtesy: D.K. Agencies (P) Ltd. <docinfo@dkagencies.com>

Joshi, Hem Lata, 1956-
Health status index, Rajasthan : spatio-temporal appraisal at panchayat samiti/block level / Hemlata Joshi.
p. cm.
Includes bibliographical references (p.
Includes index.
ISBN 8180693899

1. Health status indicators—India—Rajasthan. 2. Health surveys—India—Rajasthan. 3. Rural health services—India—Rajasthan—Statistics.
I. Title.

DDC 614.425 44 22

ISBN 81-8069-389-9

First Published 2007

Published and Printed by
Ashok Kumar Mittal
Concept Publishing Company
A/15-16, Commercial Block, Mohan Garden, New Delhi-110 059
for
Institute of Development Studies, Jaipur

Phones : 25351460, 25351794
Fax : 091-11-25357103
E-mail : publishing@conceptpub.com

Dedicated to

My Beloved

Mother Late (Mrs.) Bakhtawari Devi Sharma

and

Father Mr. Sampat Raj Sharma

PREFACE

The first Human Development Report brought out by United Nations Development Programme (UNDP) in 1990 started with a simple but far-reaching statement: "People are the real wealth of a nation. The basic objective of development is to create an enabling environment for people to enjoy long, healthy and creative lives. Human development is a process of enlarging people's choices." Since then, UNDP has been bringing out Human Development Report (HDR) every year by adding additional criteria for the measurement of human progress and well-being of the people of various nations. In 1997, it introduced Human Poverty Index (HPI) which is a multi-dimensional measure of human deprivation. In addition, other indicators like Gender-related Development Index (GDI) and Gender Empowerment Measure (GEM) were also introduced and countries were ranked accordingly. India with HDI value of 0.602 is placed at the 127th rank amongst 177 countries of the world (HDR, 2005).

Though global in their perspective, the HDRs have encouraged the preparation of about 275 national HDRs in some 135 countries. In a few cases, HDRs have been prepared at sub-national level. Rajasthan is the first state in India to prepare an HDR at Panchayat Samiti level. The report of the first and the second phases of this work covering educational and economic aspects of human development are already published (IDSJ, 2003 & 2005). The present report covers the health aspect of human development.

This report thrusts on spatio-temporal appraisal of Health Status Index at Panchayat Samiti (block) level during 1991-2001 period in Rajasthan. This report presents the kind of analysis that is at the core of health development. It examines the facts and interprets a wide variety of data through geographic information system (GIS) and statistical techniques. It is believed that the information contained herein would help in the proper planning and future growth of health status and in the removal of regional disparities in the state. I hope that this research would prove to be a milestone in the health development agenda for the state.

I am indebted to Professor Sarthi Acharya (Director, IDSJ), Professor V.S. Vyas (Chairman, IDSJ) and Professor S.S. Acharya (former Director, IDSJ) for their intellectual advice, motivation and for extending all facilities as well as gracious support throughout the course of the present investigation. I am deeply indebted to my father Mr. Sampat Raj Sharma for his constant inspiration and moral support in the successful completion of this comprehensive study. My husband Professor C.P. Joshi (Former Cabinet Minister of Education, Rural Development and Panchayati Raj, GoR) and brother Mr. B.N. Sharma (IAS, Finance Secretary, GoR) deserve a special mention for the intellectual encouragement, constructive criticism and assistance during the critical phases of this study inspite of their demanding political and administrative involvements respectively. My son Himanshu Joshi deserves a special mention for his dedicated and valuable help during the tenure of the research.

I would like to acknowledge with great appreciation the dedicated, untiring and valuable support of Mr. Nitin Bhatia (Research Assistant) throughout the course of the research.

I am extremely thankful to Mr. Ashok Mittal (Concept Publishing Company, New Delhi) for taking keen interest to publish this work. I am also grateful to Dr. P.R. Binda (Cartographer, Department of Geography, UoR, Jaipur) especially for preparing meticulous "ISOHSI" map using latest GIS (Geographic Information System) technique.

I would like to acknowledge with great appreciation the intellectual encouragement and constructive criticism of the IDSJ faculty especially Professors: Surjit Singh, Sunil Ray, Vidya Sagar, M.S. Rathore and Pradeep Bhargav.

My sincere thanks and grateful acknowledgement are also due to Mr. R. Harikishan (Joint Director, Census Department), Professor H.S. Sharma (Department of Geography, University of Rajasthan, Jaipur), Mr. Harish Sharma and Mrs. Jyoti Luhadia (Assistant Directors, Census Department), Mr. G. Fernandes and Mr. Roy (Sr. Investigators Grade-I, Census Department), Mr. M.I. Khan, Mrs. Puspa Kriplani, Mrs. Asha Tekchandani and Mr. G.G. Rajan (all of IDSJ), Mrs. Rashmi Chaturvadi (Principal, Kanodia College), Dr. D.P. Jaroli (Zoology Department, UoR, Jaipur), Mr. Narayan Paliwal (Statistical Officer, FWD), Mr. Pankaj Mathur, Mrs. Lata Suresh (Librarian, IIHMR), Mr. Rocky Bhargava, Mr. Suresh Saini, Mrs. Rekha Bhatia and Mr. Manish Dadhech who assisted me in various ways.

Jaipur **Prof. (Mrs.) Hemlata Joshi**

CONTENTS

LIST OF FIGURES

LIST OF TABLES

LIST OF MODELS/CHARTS/BOXES

MODELS

CHARTS

BOXES

LIST OF ANNEXURES

ABBREVIATIONS

ABER	Annual Blood Examination Rate	DEMO	Demonstrator
ADB	Asian Development Bank	DES	Directorate of Economics and Statistics
AIDS	Acquired Immunity Deficiency Syndrome	DFID	Department For International Development
AIIMS	All India Institute of Medical Sciences	Dg	Dungarpur District
AIR	All India Radio	DGHS	Directorate General of Health Services
Aj	Ajmer District/Division	Dhaul	Dhaulpur District
ANC	Ante-natal Care	DHO	District Health Officer
ANCD	Annual New Case Detection	Distt./Distts	District/Districts
ANM	Auxiliary Nurse-Midwife	DM & HS	Director of Medical and Health Services
ANMTC	Auxiliary Nurse-Midwife Training Centre	DMHS	Directorate of Medical and Health Services
API	Annual Parasite Incidence	DoFW	Department of Family Welfare
ARI	Acute Respiratory Infection	DOTS	Directly Observed Treatment Short Course Chemotherapy Strategy
ASST	Assistant		
Bans	Banswara District	DP	District Panchayat
BH	Behaviour Surveillance	DPC	District Planning Committee
Bha	Bharatpur District	DRDA	District Rural Development Agency
Bhil	Bhilwara District	Ds	Dausa District
Bk	Bikaner District/Division	DY. DIR.	Deputy Director
Bln	Billion	EAG	Empowered Action Group
Bmr	Barmer District	EmOc	Emergency Obstetric Care
BPL	Below Poverty Line	EMR	Emergency Medical Relief
Brn	Baran District	EPI	Expended Programme of Immunisation
Bun	Bundi District	ETCT	Enhancing Training Competence of Trainers
CBR	Crude Birth Rate		
CHC	Community Health Centre	FHAC	Family Health Awareness Camping
Chitt	Chittaurgarh District	FICCI	Federation of Indian Chamber of Commerce and Industries
Chu	Churu District		
CII	Confederation of Indian Industries	FPAI	Family Planning Association of India
CINI	Child In Need Institute	FRU	First Referral Unit
CM & HO	Chief Medical and Health Officer	FW	Family Welfare
CMO	Chief Medical Officer	FWD	Family Welfare Department
CNAA	Community Needs Assessment Approach	FWFW	Family Welfare Field Workers
CSB	Central Supervisory Board	FWTRC	Family Welfare Training and Research Centre
CSSM	Child Survival and Safe Motherhood		
CTP	Comprehensive Training Plans	FYP	Five Year Plan
CuT	Copper T	GA	General Annex
DANIDA	Danish International Development Agency	GDI	Gender-Related Development Index
DCO	Directorate of Census Operation	GDP	Gross Domestic Product
DDP	Drug De-abdicate Programme	Gg	Ganganagar District

GoI	Government of India
GoR	Government of Rajasthan
GOVT.	Government
GP	Gram Panchayat
GW	Guineaworm
GWEP	Guineaworm Eradication Programme
H	High Level/Group
HA(M)	Health Assistant (Mate)
HDI	Human Development Index
HDR	Human Development Report
HFWTC	Health and Family Welfare Training Centre
HMIS	Health Management Information System
Hn	Hanumangarh District
Hos	Hospital
HQ	Headquarter
HRD	Human Resource Development
HSDM	Health Sector Disaster Management
HSI	Health Status Index
ICDS	Integrated Child Development Scheme
ICMR	Indian Council of Medical Research
ICPD	International Conference on Population and Development
IDA	International Development Association
IDSJ	Institute of Development Studies, Jaipur
IEC	Information, Education and Communication
IIM	Indian Institute of Management
IIPS	Indian Institute of Population Science
IIT	Indian Institute of Technology
IMA	Indian Medical Association
IMR	Infant Mortality Rate
IOD	Index of Deprivation
IPD	Integrated Population and Development
ISM	Indian System of Medicine
ISOHSI	*See* Terminology
IT	Information Technology
IUD	Intrauterine device
Jais	Jaisalmer District
Jhal	Jhalawar District
Jhun	Jhunjhunu District
JL	Jalor District
JM	Jan Mangal
Jodh	Jodhpur District/Division
Jp	Jaipur District/Division
JT. DIR.	Joint Director
Kg	Kilogram
Kr	Karauli District
Kt	Kota District/Division
kWh	Kilowatt-hour
L	Low Level/Group
Lakh	100 Thousand
LEC	Leprosy Eliminations Campaign for Urban Area
LEM	Leprosy Eradication Monitoring
LHV	Lady Health Visitor
M	Medium Level/Group
MCH	Mother and Child Health
MCW	Mother and Child Department
MDT	Multi Drug Therapy
MEM	Mass Education and Media Wing
MIS	Management Information System
MLEC	Modified Leprosy Elimination Campaign
Mln	Million
MNGO	Mother Non-Government Organisation
MO	Medical Officer
MOHFW	Ministry of Health and Family Welfare
MPW	Multipurpose Worker
MPW(M)	Multipurpose Worker (Mate)
MSS	Mahila Swasthya Sangha
MTP	Medical Termination of Pregnancy
Mtrs	Metres
MVA	Manual Vacuum Aspiration
NA	Not Available/Not Applicable
NACO	National AIDS Control Organisation
NACP	National AIDS Control Programme
NDC	National Document Centre
NFHS	National Family Health Survey
Ng	Nagaur District
NGO	Non-Government Organisation
NHDR	National Human Development Report
NHP	National Health Policy
NIC	National Information Centre
NID	National Immunization Day
NIFP	National Institute of Family Planning
NIHFW	National Institute of Health and Family Welfare
NIRD	National Institute of Rural Development
NNF	National Neonatology Forum
No.	Number
NPSF	National Population Stabilization Fund
NPSP	National Polio Surveillance Project
NPVP	National Polio Vaccination Programme
NSPCD	National Surveillance Programme for Communicable Diseases
NSV	Non-Scalped Vasectomy
NYK	Nehru Yuvak Kendra
OPV	Oral Polio Vaccine
ORG	Organization

ORT	Oral Rehydration Therapy
PC,VD	Personal Computer, Video
PDS	Population and Development Strategy
PHC	Primary Health Center
Pl	Pali District
PM	Prime Minister
PMGY	Pradhan Mantri Gramodaya Yojna
PMSSY	Pradhan Mantri Swasthya Suraksah Yojana
PMTCT	Prevention of Mother To Child Transmission of HIV
PNDT	Prenatal Diagnostic Techniques (Regulation and Prevention of Misuse)
Pop	Population
PPI	Pulse Polio Programme
PR	Prevalence Rate
PRIs	Panchayati Raj Institutions
PS\PSs	Panchayat Samiti\ Samities
R&D	Research and Development
Raj	Rajasthan
Rajs	Rajsamand District
RCH	Reproductive and Child Health
RFWC	Rural Family Welfare Center
RHS	Rapid Household Survey
RHTC	Rural Health Training Center
RSICO	Rajasthan State Industrial Development Corporation
RNTCP	Revised National TB Control Programme
RRC	Regional Resource Center
RRTs	Rapid Response Teams
RSACS	Rajasthan State AIDS Control Society
RSBTC	Rajasthan State Blood Transfusion Committee
RTI/STI	Reproductive Tract Infection/Sexually
SAP	Structural Adjustment Programme
SAPEL	Special Action Project for Elimination
SC	Scheduled Castes
SCOVA	Standing Committee on Voluntary Action
SET	Survey, Education and Treatment
SEWA	Society for Empowerment of Women
SGHS	State Government Health Services
SHC	Sub Health Center
SHEB	State Health Education Bureau
SHG	Self-Help Groups
SIDA	Swedish International Development Authority
SIFPSA	State Innovation in Family Planning Services Agency
SIHFW	State Institute of Health and Family Welfare
Sk	Sikar District
SM	Sawai Madhopur District
S. Madhopur	
SNA	System of National Accounts
SOHS	School of Health Sciences
SPR	Slide Positive Rate
Sr	Sirohi District
SRS	Sample Registration System
ST	Scheduled Tribes
STD	Sexually Transmitted Disease
SWAPs	Sector-Wide Approaches
TAG	Technical Advisory Group
Targ.	Target
TB	Tuberculosis
TBA/DAIS	Trained Birth Attendant
TFA	Target Free Approach
TFR	Total Fertility Rate
Tk	Tonk District
TOT	Training of Trainers
Ud	Udaipur District/Division
UIP	Universal Immunization Programme
UNDP	United Nations Development Programme
UNESCO	United Nations Educational Scientific and Cultural Organisation
UNFPA	United Nations Funds on Population Activities
UNICEF	United Nations International Children Education Fund
UPE	Universalisation of Primary Education
USAID	US Agency for International Development
UT	Union Territory
VCTCs	Voluntary Counselling and Testing Centers
Vg/Vgs	Village/Villages
VH	Very High Level/Group
VHAI	Voluntary Health Association of India
VL	Very Low Level/Group
VPDs	Vaccine Preventable Diseases
WHO	World Health Organisation

TERMINOLOGY

Age Specific Fertility Rate (ASFR). The number of live births per 1000 women of a particular/specific age group in a given year (Number of births to woman of a given age group per 1000 women in that age group).

Age Specific Marital Fertility Rate (AMFR). The number of live births per 1000 married women of a particular/specific age group in a given year.

Births attended by skilled health staff. The percentage of deliveries attended by a doctor, nurse or midwife or trained traditional birth attendant.

Contraceptive prevalence. The percentage of married women aged 15-49 who are using, or whose partners are using, any form of contraception, whether modern or traditional.

Crude Birth Rate (CBR). Number of live births per 1000 population in the given years. The CBR depends on both the level of fertility and age distribution of population.

Crude Death Rate (CDR). Annual number of deaths per 1000 Population.

Cumulative Percent Marital Fertility. It is defined as the ratio of the age specific Marital fertility rate to total Marital Fertility multiplied by 100.

Full Immunisation. BCG, Measles and Three Doses Each of DPT and Polio Vaccines.

General Fertility Rate (GFR). Number of live births per 1000 women in the reproductive age group (15-49 years) in a given year.

General Marital Fertility Rate (GMFR). Number of live births per 1000 married women in the reproductive age group (15-49 years) in a given year.

HIV/AIDS, people living with. The estimated number of people living with HIV/AIDS at the end of the year specified.

Human development index (HDI). A composite index measuring average achievement in three basic dimensions of human development—a long and healthy life, knowledge and a decent standard of living.

Improved Drinking Water. Based on the improved water sources, drinking water supply has been classified as 'Improved' or otherwise. If the household has access to drinking water supplied from a tap or hand pump/tube well situated within or outside the premises it is considered as having access to 'improved drinking water source'. However, the concept of improved drinking water is state specific and this is to be considered accordingly.

Infant Mortality Rate (IMR). Annual number of deaths of infants under one year of age per 1000 live births. More specifically this is the probability of dying between birth and exactly one year of age.

Lakh. 100 thousand.

Life expectancy at birth. The number of years a new born infant would live if prevailing patterns of age specific mortality rates at the time of birth were to stay the same throughout the child's life.

Low-birth Weight. The percentage of infants with a birth-weight of less than 2,500 grams.

Maternal Mortality Rate (MMR). Annual number of deaths of women from pregnancy related causes per 1000 live births.

Neo-natal Mortality Rate (NNM). Annual number of infants dying within the first month of life (technically 4 weeks, i.e. under 28 days) per 1000 live births.

Oral rehydration therapy use rate. The percentage of ill cases of diarrhoea in children under age five treated with oral rehydration salts or recommended home fluids, or both.

Panchayat Samiti. Elected body responsible for local government at the block level.

Peri-Natal Mortality (Peri-NM). Death of foetus after seven months of Conception and death of Infants with in seven days of birth.

Post-Neo-Natal Mortality (Post NNM). Infants Dying after one month and before one year of life. (NNM + Post NNM = IMR).

Probability at birth of not surviving to a specified age. Calculated as 1 minus the probability of surviving to a specified age for a given cohort.

Probability at birth of surviving to a specified age. The probability of a new born infant surviving to a specified age, if subject to prevailing patterns of age-specific mortality rates.

Sex-Ratio. The number of females per 1000 males.

SFR. Slide Falciparum Positivity Rate.

SPR. Slide Positivity Rate

Total Fertility Rate. The average number of children a woman would bear if age-specific fertility rates remained unchanged during her lifetime. Average number of children that would be born to a woman if she experiences the current fertility pattern throughout her reproductive span (15-49)

Total Marital Fertility Rate (TMFR). The number of children that would have been born alive per married woman during her life time, if she were to pass through her child bearing years and bear children at each age in accordance with prevailing age-specific fertility rates. Average number of children that would be born to a married woman if she experiences the current fertility pattern throughout her reproductive span (15-49).

FORMULAS*

$$\textbf{Crude Birth Rate (CBR)} = \frac{\text{Number of live births during the year}}{\text{Mid-Year Population}} \times 1000$$

$$\textbf{Total Fertility Rate (TFR)} = \frac{5 \times \sum_{15-19}^{45-49} \text{ASFR}}{1000}$$

$$\textbf{General Fertility Rate (GFR)} = \frac{\text{Number of live births in a year}}{\text{Mid-year female pop. in the age-group (15-49) years}} \times 1000$$

$$\textbf{Age-Specific Fertility Rate (ASFR)} = \frac{\text{Number of live births in a particular age-group}}{\text{Mid-year female pop. of the same age-group}} \times 1000$$

$$\textbf{General Marital Fertility Rate (GMFR)} = \frac{\text{Number of live births in a year}}{\text{Mid-year married female pop. in the age-group (15-49) years}} \times 1000$$

$$\textbf{Age-Specific Marital Fertility Rate (ASMFR)} = \frac{\text{Number of live births in a particular age-group}}{\text{Mid-year married female pop. of the same age-group}} \times 1000$$

$$\textbf{Total Marital Fertility Rate (TMFR)} = \frac{5 \times \sum_{15-19}^{45-49} \text{ASMFR}}{1000}$$

Mean age at effective marriage = Average age at which females start living with their husband

$$\textbf{Crude Death Rate (CDR)} = \frac{\text{Number of deaths during the year}}{\text{Mid-Year Population}} \times 1000$$

$$\textbf{Infant Mortality Rate} = \frac{\text{Number of infant deaths during the year}}{\text{Number of live births during the year}} \times 1000$$

$$\textbf{Maternal Mortality Rate (MMR)} = \frac{\text{Number of maternal deaths to women in the age group 15-49}}{\text{Number of live births}} \times 100{,}000$$

* Compedium of India's Fertility and Mortality Indicators, 1971-97, Based on The SRS, RGI, New Delhi, 1999, pp XXVII.

Age-Specific Mortality Rate (ASMR) $= \dfrac{\text{Number of deaths in a particular age-group}}{\text{Mid-year pop. of the same age-group}} \times 1000$

Neo-natal Mortality Rate (NMR) $= \dfrac{\text{Number of infant deaths of less than 29 days during the year}}{\text{Number of live births during the year}} \times 1000$

Early Neo-natal Mortality Rate $= \dfrac{\text{Number of infant deaths of less than 7 days during the year}}{\text{Number of live births during the year}} \times 1000$

Gross Reproduction Rate (GRR) $= \dfrac{5 \times \sum_{15-19}^{45-49} \text{ASFR for female live births}}{1000}$

Late Neo-natal Mortality Rate $= \dfrac{\text{Number of infant deaths of less than 7 days to less 29 days during the year}}{\text{Number of live births during the year}} \times 1000$

Post Neo-natal Mortality Rate (PNMR) $= \dfrac{\text{Number of deaths of 29 days to less than one year during the year}}{\text{Number of live births during the year}} \times 1000$

Peri-natal Mortality Rate (PMR) $= \dfrac{\text{Number of still-births and infant deaths of less than 7 days during the year}}{\text{Number of live births and still births during the year}} \times 1000$

Still-Birth Rate (SBR) $= \dfrac{\text{Number of still-births during the year}}{\text{Number of live births and still-births during the year}} \times 1000$

1

IMPORTANCE AND METHODOLOGY

The Human Development Index (HDI) developed by United Nations Development Programme (UNDP) is often regarded as an alternative to income based measure of welfare. It is based on three indicators: longevity, education and standard of living. Thus merely rising income is not the central concern of human development.

The first Human Development Report, 1990 started with simple but far-reaching statement: "People are the real wealth of a nation. The basic objective of development is to create an enabling environment for people to enjoy long, healthy and creative lives. Human development is a process of enlarging people's choices."

Since then, UNDP has been bringing out Human Development Reports (HDRs) every year by adding additional criteria for measuring human progress and well-being of the people of various nations. In 1997, it introduced Human Poverty Index (HPI) which is a multi-dimensional measure of human deprivation. In addition, other indicators like Gender-related Development Index (GDI) and Gender Empowerment Measure (GEM) were also introduced and countries were ranked on these bases. India with Human Development Index (HDI) value of 0.602 is placed at the 127th rank amongst 177 countries of the world (HDR–2005).

Though global in their perspective, the HDRs have encouraged the preparation of about 275 national HDRs in some 135 countries. In a few cases, HDRs have been prepared at sub-national level too. It is being gradually recognized that socio-economic issues of importance at macro, meso and micro level could be effectively addressed by human development profile of spatial units such as district/panchayat samiti/village. In India, NCAER undertook a comprehensive exercise in this area. Amongst states, MP, Karnataka and Rajasthan have done pioneering work. Other then these attempts not much work has been done in India in the field of human development and at panchayat samiti (block) level it is almost negligible. Now, Rajasthan is going to become the first state in India to prepare a HDR at panchayat samiti level.

Panchayats have been the backbone of Indian villages since the beginning of recorded history. Gandhiji's dream of every village being a republic and panchayats having powers for local governance has been translated into reality with the introduction of the three-tier Panchayati Raj System to enlist people's participation in rural reconstruction. April 24, 1993 is a landmark day in the history of Panchayati Raj in India. On this day the 73rd Amendment Act, 1992 of the Constitution came into force to provide constitutional status to the Panchayati Raj Institutions (PRIs). With the growing thrust on decentralised planning and devolution of development functions and financial resources to PRIs at different levels, there is a need for evolving objective criteria for directing resources to most deserving areas (with the need of various micro administrative and planning units). Due to wide ranging disparities amongst districts and amongst panchayat samities within the same district, there is an urgent need for constructing HDI for all the three levels of PRIs viz. districts, Panchayat Samities and Gram Panchayats. The second step for assessment of human development at disaggregated level is to measure the levels of development in different panchayat samities.

Rajasthan is not only India's largest state, but also among the poorest. More than 61 per cent area of the state falls under harsh desert and semi-desert region which is known as the Great Indian Desert, *'The Thar'*. The state with its meagre water resources and perilous dependence on scanty, low and uncertain rainfall is highly vulnerable to drought and famine conditions.

Drought is synonymous with Rajasthan, as the state has experienced the pangs of thirst for 40 out of 49 years of its existence since 1956. Fortunately, with concerted efforts of the state government, various financial institutions, NGOs etc., the state became the fastest mover in agriculture and education amongst 19 major states in India (Table 1.1). These states were evaluated on 46 parameters across 8 categories. (as per the research carried out by *'India Today'*, May 19, 2003).

TABLE 1.1: Improving Performance of Rajasthan Amongst Major Indian States 1991-2001

S. No.	*Particulars*	*Rank in India*		
		1991	*2001*	*Change*
1.	Agriculture	18	12	6
2.	Law and Order	7	5	2
3.	Education	18	17	1
4.	Infrastructure	14	13	1
5.	Health	14	14	0

The committee of the Planning Commission in its report praised Rajasthan highly for its achievements in human resource development. The report had assessed the overall progress of states in the last three decades. It said that Rajasthan, which was at 11th position among the 15 developing states, has scaled up to the 9th position.

Keeping this in mind an attempt has been made to present an indepth study of health aspect of human development at panchayat samiti level in Rajasthan. Studies on educational aspect (phase I) and economic aspects (phase II) have already been carried out and published by the author.*

Various geographical factors viz. physical, economic, human, historical, technological, political etc. affect health status of an area. There are three essential components of the health status paradigm namely, Equity, Sustainability and Empowerment as depicted in Model 1.1.

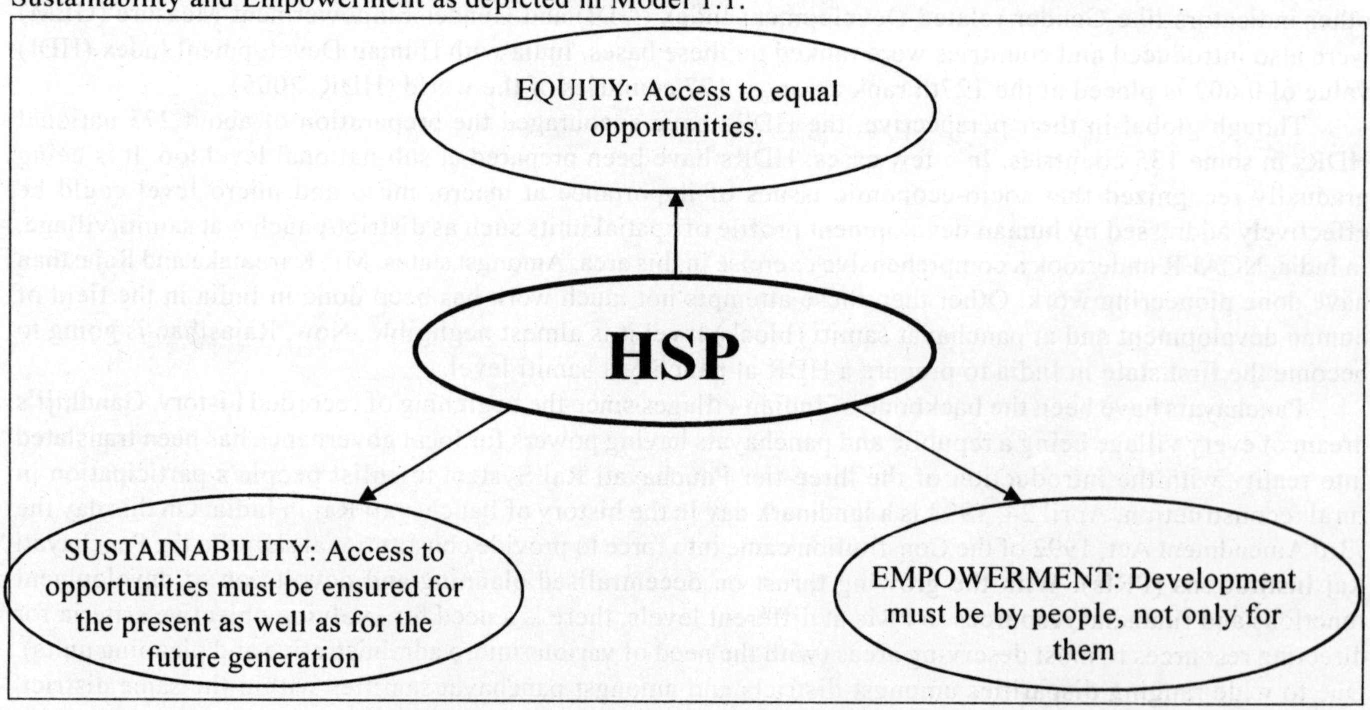

MODEL 1.1: Components of the Health Status Paradigm (HSP)

* Hemlata Joshi, *Educational Development Index-Rajasthan and Economic Development Index, Rajasthan (Spatio-Temporal Appraisal and Panchayat Samiti/Block Level)*, (Published Research Projects, Institute of Development Studies), UBH, Jaipur-(2003 and 2005)

Health care facilities include Prevention and Cure of Diseases, Control of Commuinicable Diseases, Family Planning and Care of Mothers and Children, Health Insurance, Nutrition, Safe Drinking Water, Sanitation etc. (Model 1.2).

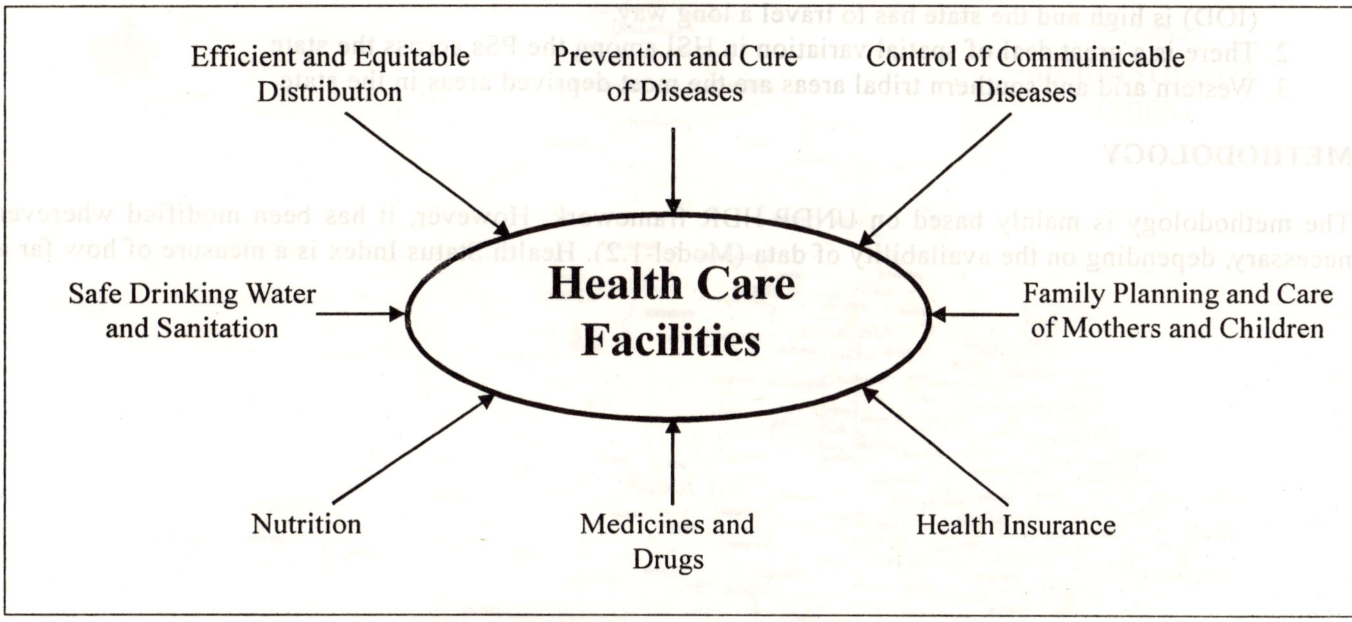

MODEL 1.2: Health Care Facilities

THE STUDY REGION

The present research entitled 'Health Status Index: Rajasthan (Spatio-Temporal Appraisal at Panchayat Samiti/ Block Level 1991-2001)'. The study covers all the 237 Panchayat Samities (PSs) of Rajasthan (India) which are spread over 32 districts and 6 divisions (Fig. 1.1 and Fig. 1.2).

OBJECTIVES

The main objective of the research is to present spatio-temporal appraisal of health status Index of 237 panchayat samities of Rajasthan. The specific objectives of the study are:

1. To present Health Status Index (HSI), of Panchayat Samities in two points of time viz. 1991 and 2001,
2. To interpret spatial distribution pattern of HSI during the period,
3. To study changed relative status of Panchayat Samities in HSI,
4. To present Growth Trends, and
5. To present Plan of Action.

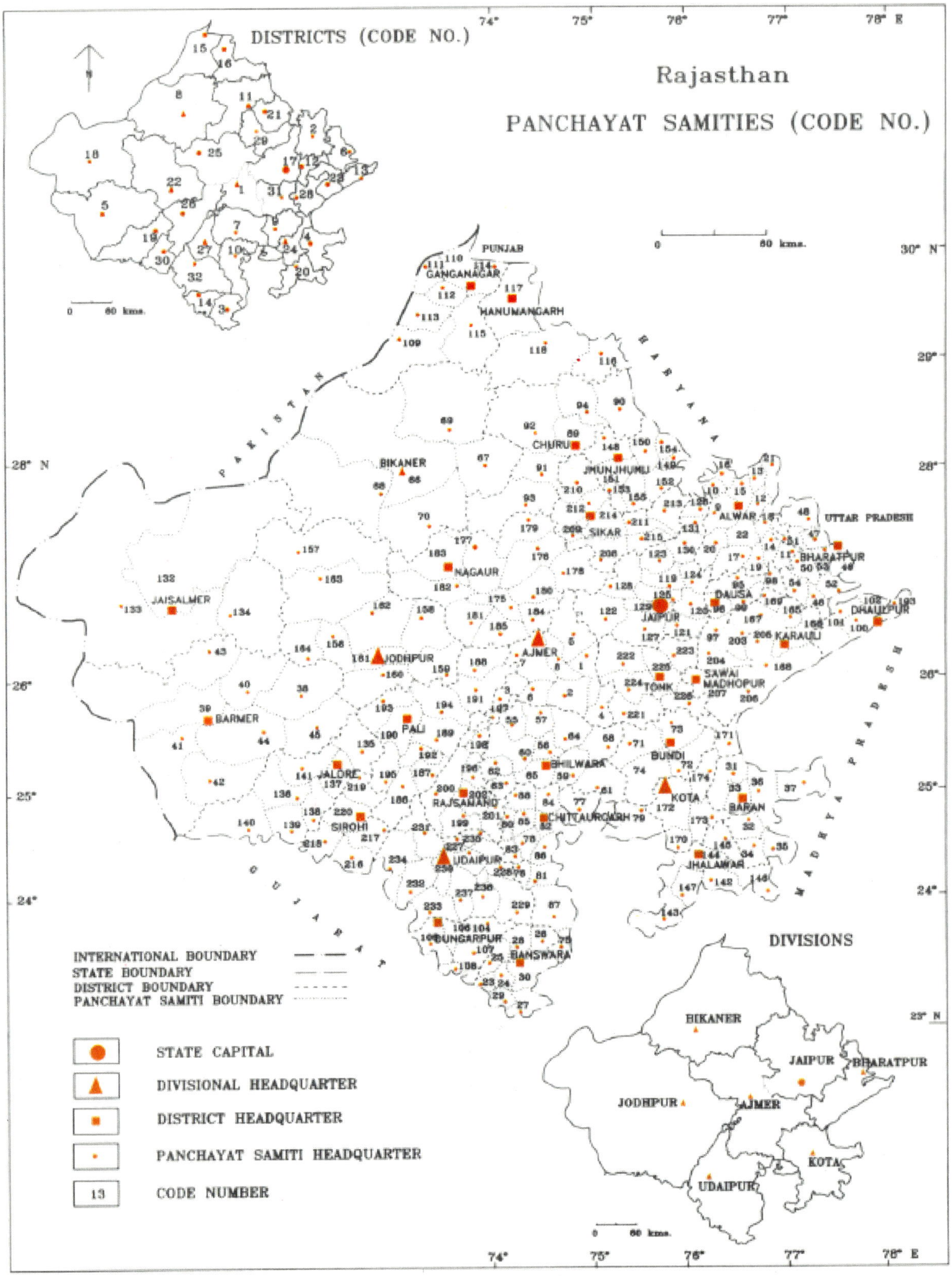

Note: Dungargarh Panchayat Samiti (Code No. 67) Shifted from Churu to Bikaner District on 1st April 2001.

FIG. 1.2

panchayat samiti (PS) has travelled from a minimum level of achievement in health status and how far it has still to travel.

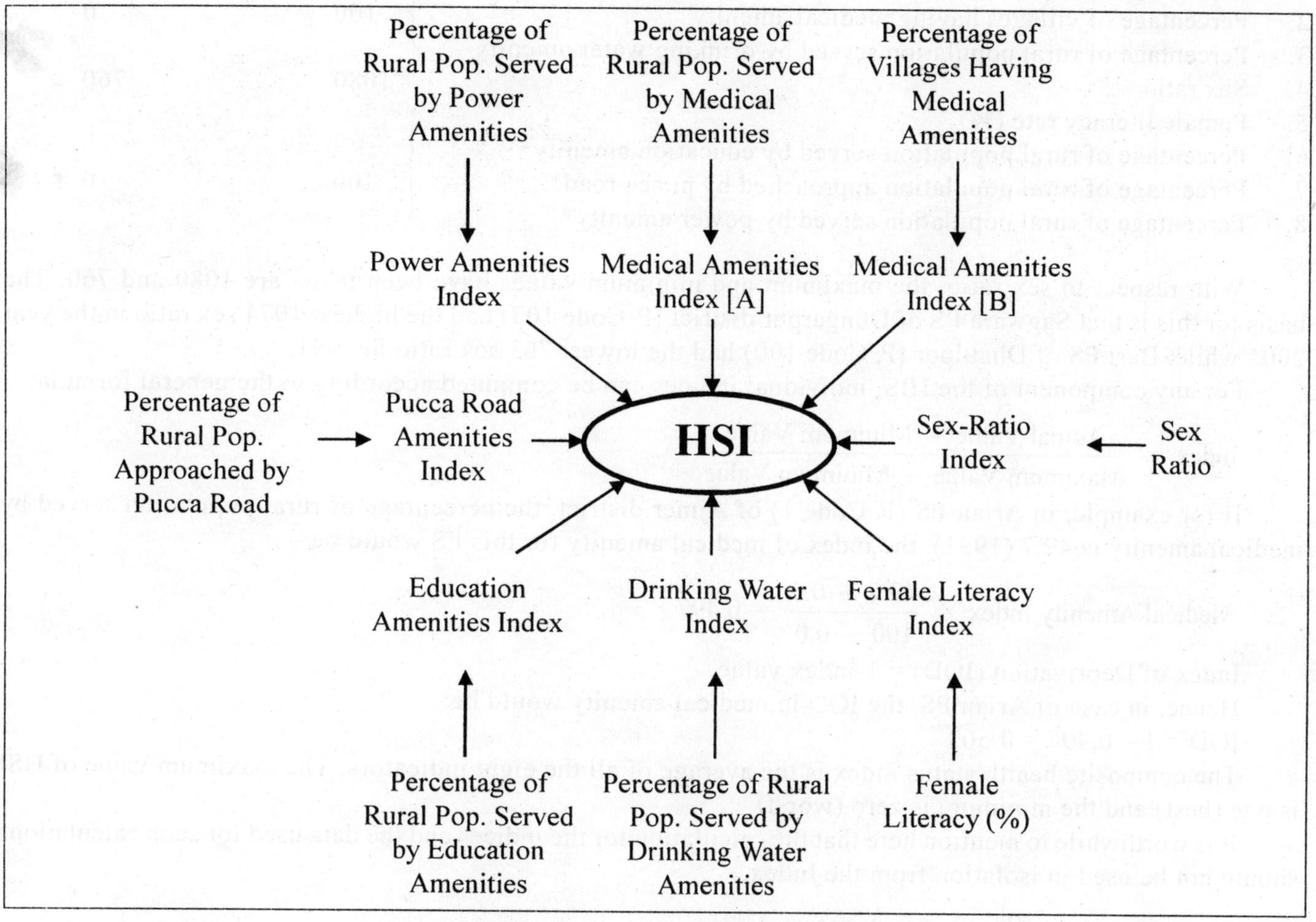

MODEL 1.3: Calculating Health Status Index

The Health Status Index (HSI) is a composite index comprising 8 parameters/ variables namely, percentage of rural population served by medical amenity (V1), percentage of villages having medical amenity (V2), percentage of rural population served by drinking water amenity (V3), sex-ratio (V4), Female Literacy Rate (V5), percentage of rural population served by education amenity (V6), percentage of rural population approached by pucca road (V7) and percentage of rural population served by power amenity (V8).

LIMITATIONS OF THE METHODOLOGY

It is worth while to mention here that the UNDP has used 'life expectancy at birth' for assessing the level of health status in human development index. Since, data related to life expectancy at PS level is not calculated or estimated in Rajasthan as well as India, HSI in the presented study is based on the available data at PS level for both the census years 1991 and 2001 viz. medical and other related amenities (having direct bearing on health status), female literacy rate and sex-ratio.

GOALPOSTS FOR CALCUTING THE HSI

To construct the index, maximum and minimum values have been established for each of the following indicators:

	Variables	Maximum Value	Minimum Value
1.	Percentage of rural population served by medical amenity		
2.	Percentage of villages having medical amenity	100	0
3.	Percentage of rural population served by drinking water amenity		
4.	Sex ratio	1080	760
5.	Female literacy rate (%)		
6.	Percentage of rural population served by education amenity*		
7.	Percentage of rural population approached by pucca road*	100	0
8.	Percentage of rural population served by power amenity*		

With respect to sex ratio, the maximum and minimum values have been taken are 1080 and 760. The basis for this is that Sagwara PS of Dungarpur district (P. Code 107) had the highest 1074 sex ratio in the year 2001 while, Bari PS of Dhaulpur (P. Code 100) had the lowest 763 sex ratio in 1991.

For any component of the HIS, individual indices can be computed according to the general formula:

$$\text{Index} = \frac{\text{Actual Value} - \text{Minimum Value}}{\text{Maximum Value} - \text{Minimum Value}}$$

If for example, in Arian PS (P. Code 1) of Ajmer district, the percentage of rural population served by medical amenity is 49.7 (1991), the index of medical amenity for this PS would be:

$$\text{Medical Amenity Index} = \frac{49.7 - 0.0}{100 - 0.0} = 0.497$$

Index of Deprivation (IOD) = 1-index value

Hence, in case of Arian PS, the IOD in medical amenity would be:

IOD = 1 – 0.497 = 0.503

The composite health status index is the average of all the eight indicators. The maximum value of HSI is one (best) and the minimum is zero (worst).

It is worthwhile to mention here that the calculation for the indices and the data used for such calculations should not be used in isolation from the Index.

SOURCE OF DATA

This study is mainly based on secondary data, which are compiled from the following sources:

1. Directorate of Medical and Health, GoR, Jaipur.
2. Directorate of Census Operations, Jaipur.
3. Census of India 2001, Series 9, Rajasthan, Final Population Totals.
4. 'Primary Census Abstract, Rajasthan', Series-21, 1991.
5. District Census Handbooks (all districts), Rajasthan, 1991.
6. Directorate of Economics and Statistics-DES, GoR, Jaipur.

It may be pointed out here that in 1991, there were 237 PSs distributed in 27 districts. After 1991 census, five new districts viz Baran, Dausa, Rajsamand, Hanumangarh and Karauli have been created. Hence, for temporal appraisal of HSI of the PSs of these new districts for the year 1991, data of the concerning PSs has been taken, from the parent districts namely, Kota, Jaipur, Udaipur, Hanumangarh and Sawai Madhopur respectively.

* Infrastructure Related Indices having direct bearing on Health Status.

CODE NUMBERS

The code number of 32 districts and 237 PSs are given as follows:

I. Alphabetical coding of 32 districts that existed in the year 2001.
II. District-wise alphabetical coding of the PSs of these 32 districts.

It is worthwhile to mention here that these code numbers of districts and PSs (Fig. 1.2) are different from the census code numbers. **Annex 12.14** reveals both the code numbers for the planning purposes.

ORGANISATION

The present volume is divided into twelve Chapters.The first three introductory Chapters are devoted to Importance of Research and the Methodology Adopted, Geographical Profile of Rajasthan and Health Status of Rajasthan in India. Chapter fourth deals with Health Scenario during Five Year Plans Period while Chapter fifth and sixth represent Health Programmes/Schemes and Health Organization. Key Data from NFHS and SRS are presented in Chapter seventh. Next two Chapters discuss Medical and Other Related Amenities for the year 1991 and 2001 respectively.

Health Status Index (HSI) at Panchayat Samiti Level for the year 1991 and 2001 has been presented in Chapter tenth and Chapter eleventh respectively. The Main Findings, alongwith Challenges Facing Rural Rajasthan, Suggested Strategy and Action Plan are discussed in the twelfth and the last Chapter.

2

GEOGRAPHICAL PROFILE OF RAJASTHAN

Rajasthan is the largest state of India with 10.4 per cent of the geographical area. It constitutes 5.5 per cent of the country's population and occupies 8th position among the states and union territories. It is located between 23°3' and 30°12' North latitudes and between 69°30' and 78°17' East longitudes. The Tropic of Cancer passing through the southern-most tip of the state places the state into sub-tropical and tropical zones of the Northern Hemisphere.

The state is situated in the north-western part of the Indian Union covering the complete Arid 'Great Indian Desert' and parts of semi-arid climatic zone. Rajasthan is delineated by Punjab, Uttar Pradesh, Haryana and the union territory of Delhi in the north; part of Uttar Pradesh and Madhya Pradesh in the east; Gujarat and Madhya Pradesh in the south and Pakistan in the west. Its location in the western fringe of the Indian landmass has placed the state on the route of hot western winds during summers and mediterranean cyclones during the winters. The state streches 826 kms from north to south and 869 km from east to west. The overall length of the state boundary is 5920 kms, of which 1070 kms is the international boundary, separating India from Pakistan on its western flank. Thus, the state has a special status in the matters of defence, political interaction and security arrangements.

Administratively, the state comprises of 6 divisions, 32 districts, 188 sub-divisions, 241 tehsils, 237 panchayat samities/blocks, 9189 gram panchayats and 41353 revenue villages (Table 2.1 and 2.2). It is

TABLE 2.1: Rajasthan At A Glance

S. No.	*Items*	*Particulars*	*S. No.*	*Items*	*Particulars*
1	Area* (Lakh sq kms.)	3.42	6	ST pop. (Million No.)	7.10 (12.56%)
	Population*			Number of	
2	Total (Million No.)	56.51	7	Divisions**	6
	Male (%)	52	8	Districts**	32
	Female (%)	48	9	Sub-Divisions**	188
3	Rural (Million No.)	43.29 (76.6%)	10	Tehsils**	241
	Male (%)	52	11	Municipalities**	183
	Female (%)	48	12	Towns*	222
4	Urban (Million No.)	13.21 (23.4%)	13	Panchayat Samities**	237
	Male (%)	53	14	Village Panchayats**	9189
	Female (%)	47	15	Revenue Villages*	41353
5	SC pop. (Million No.)	9.69 (17.16%)	16	Inhabited Villages*	39753

Source: 1. Census of India, Series 9, Rajasthan, DCO, Jaipur. 2. *Economic Review*, 2004-05, DES, Jaipur.
Note: Figure in brackets shows %age of total population. * for the year 2001; ** for the year 2003.

worthwhile to mention here that after the 1991 Census, five more districts have come into existence namely: 1. Hanumangarh carved out of Ganganagar district, 2. Dausa from Jaipur and Sawai Madhopur districts, 3. Rajsamand from Udaipur district, 4. Baran from Kota district, and 5. Karauli from Sawai Madhopur district. Thus, the total number of districts in the state has gone upto 32. Similarly, 28 new tehsils have been created by the state government after 1991, raising the total number of tehsils to 241. The number of revenue villages has also increased from 39810 to 41353 during the decade. However, the number of urban units has remained the same at 222.

TABLE 2.2: Administrative Structure: Rajasthan

S. No.	*District*	*Sub-Divisions*	*Tahsils*	*PSs*	*Gram Panchayats*	*Villages*
1	Ajmer	6	9	8	276	1038
2	Alwar	12	12	14	478	1994
3	Banswara	3	5	8	325	1504
4	Baran	6	8	7	215	1207
5	Barmer	4	8	8	380	1941
6	Bharatpur	9	10	9	371	1472
7	Bhilwara	8	12	11	381	1745
8	Bikaner	5	8	4	189	778
9	Bundi	5	5	4	181	849
10	Chittaurgarh	8	13	14	391	2395
11	Churu	5	6	7	279	979
12	Dausa	5	5	5	225	1058
13	Dholpur	4	5	4	153	802
14	Dungarpur	3	4	5	237	858
15	Ganganagar	6	9	7	320	3014
16	Hanumangarh	7	7	3	251	1905
17	Jaipur	13	13	13	488	2131
18	Jaisalmer	3	3	3	128	637
19	Jalore	5	7	7	264	706
20	Jhalawar	5	7	6	252	1600
21	Jhunjhunun	5	7	9	339	1063
22	Jodhpur	5	6	8	288	859
23	Karauli	5	6	5	224	798
24	Kota	5	5	5	162	892
25	Nagaur	9	10	11	461	1500
26	Pali	6	9	10	320	949
27	Rajsamand	4	7	7	205	987
28	Sawai Madhopur	4	7	5	197	794
29	Sikar	6	6	8	329	992
30	Sirohi	3	5	5	151	462
31	Tonk	7	7	6	231	1093
32	Udaipur	7	10	11	498	2351
	Total 32	**188**	**241**	**237**	**9189**	**41353**

Division-wise distribution of districts and Panchayat Samities (PSs) is presented in Table 2.3. Jaipur is the biggest division comprising of 7 districts and 61 PSs while, Bikaner is the smallest division with 4 districts and 21 PSs.

TABLE 2.3: Division-wise Distribution of Districts and PSs: Rajasthan

S.No.	*Division*	*Included Districts*			*PanchayatSamities*	
		No.	*%*	*Name*	*No.*	*%*
1	Jaipur	7	21.88	Jaipur, Dausa, Alwar, Bharatpur, Dhaulpur, Sikar and Jhunjhunun	61	25.74
2	Bikaner	4	12.50	Bikaner, Ganganagar, Hanumangarh and Churu	21	8.86
3	Ajmer	4	12.50	Ajmer, Nagaur, Bhilwara and Tonk	36	15.19
4	Jodhpur	6	18.75	Jodhpur, Jaisalmer, Jalore, Barmer, Sirohi and Pali	42	17.72
5	Udaipur	5	15.63	Udaipur, Rajsamand, Banswara. Dungarpur and Chittaurgarh	45	18.99
6	Kota	6	18.75	Kota, Bundi, Jhalawar, Baran, Sawai Madhopur and Karauli	32	13.50
	Rajasthan	**32**	**100.00**		**237**	**100.00**

BOX-2.1: Peculiar Geographical Characteristics of Rajasthan

- Two-third area of the state comes under arid, semi-arid and under hilly region. These vast tracts coupled with sparce population renders the task of development of health infrastructure very costly.
- Great spatial variation in physical and cultural environment.
- High fertility, mortality and morbidity indicators. The situation is very grave in tribal, backward and remote areas and in vulnerable groups.
- Very high percentage of rural population (77%).
- Very high population growth rate (28.33) during 1991-01.
- Children below 6 years constitute approximately 17 per cent of the total population.
- High percentage of SC (17.16) and ST (12.56) population.
- Low female literacy rate (44%).
- Low female work participation rate (38%).
- Very low CPR (43%).
- Very low child sex-ratio (909) and total population sex-ratio (922). Decreasing trend of child sex ratio further worsening the situation (Table 12.12).
- Dominance of small villages.
- Great gender disparity (Very low status of girls and women).
- Rajasthan is one of the highly guineaworm endemic states, contributing more than 68 per cent of total affected villages and 78 per cent of total cases in India.
- The prevalence rate of blindness is very high 2.24 per cent as compared to national average 1.49 per cent.
- 70-75 per cent birth in Rajasthan happen out-side hospitals.
- Low female age at marriage. Around 25 per cent females are married in 10-14 age group in rural Rajasthan.
- Percentage of never married males are higher than females in both rural and urban areas.
- 78 per cent rural households are deprived of tap water amenity*.
- 69 per cent rural households are without hand pumps facility*.
- 56 per cent rural households are deprived of electricity amenity*.
- 51 per cent villages are without road connectivity*.
- 40 per cent rural households are deprived of safe drinking water amenity*.
- 76 per cent rural households are deprived of bank account*.
- 47 per cent rural households are deprived of specified assets*.

* Rapid Households Survey under the RCH Programme 1998-99, Ministry of Health and Family Welfare, GoI, New Delhi.

Table 2.4 shows classification of districts on the basis of number of Panchayat Samities (PSs). Both Alwar and Chittaurgarh districts have the highest (14 each) number of PSs followed by Jaipur (13); Bhilwara, Nagaur, Udaipur (11 each); Pali (10) etc. respectively. On the otherside, Jaisalmer and Hanumangarh districts have the lowest number of PSs (3 each).

TABLE 2.4: Classification of Districts on the Basis of No. of PSs: Rajasthan

No. of PSs	*Districts*	
	No.	*Name*
14	2	Alwar and Chittaurgarh
13	1	Jaipur
11	3	Bhilwara, Nagaur and Udaipur
10	1	Pali
9	2	Bharatpur and Jodhpur
8	5	Ajmer, Banswara, Barmer, Jhunjhunun and Sikar
7	4	Ganganagar, Jalore, Baran and Rajsamand
6	3	Churu*, Jhalawar and Tonk
5	7	Bikaner*, Dungarpur, Kota, Sawai Madhopur, Sirohi, Dausa and Karauli
4	2	Bundi and Dhaulpur
3	2	Jaisalmer and Hanumangarh
237	32	

Note: * Dungargarh PS shifted from Churu to Bikaner district on 1st April 2001.

Rajasthan, meaning "the abode of the rajas," was formerly called 'Rajputana, the country of the Rajputs (sons of rajas)'. In 1947, when India achieved independence from British rule, it comprised of 18 princely states, two chieftainships, a small British-administered province of Ajmer-Merwara, and a few pockets of territories outside the main boundaries. After 1947, the princely states and chieftainships were integrated with India in stages, and the state took one the name of Rajasthan. It assumed its present form on Ist of November 1956, when the act for the reorganization of the Indian states came into force.

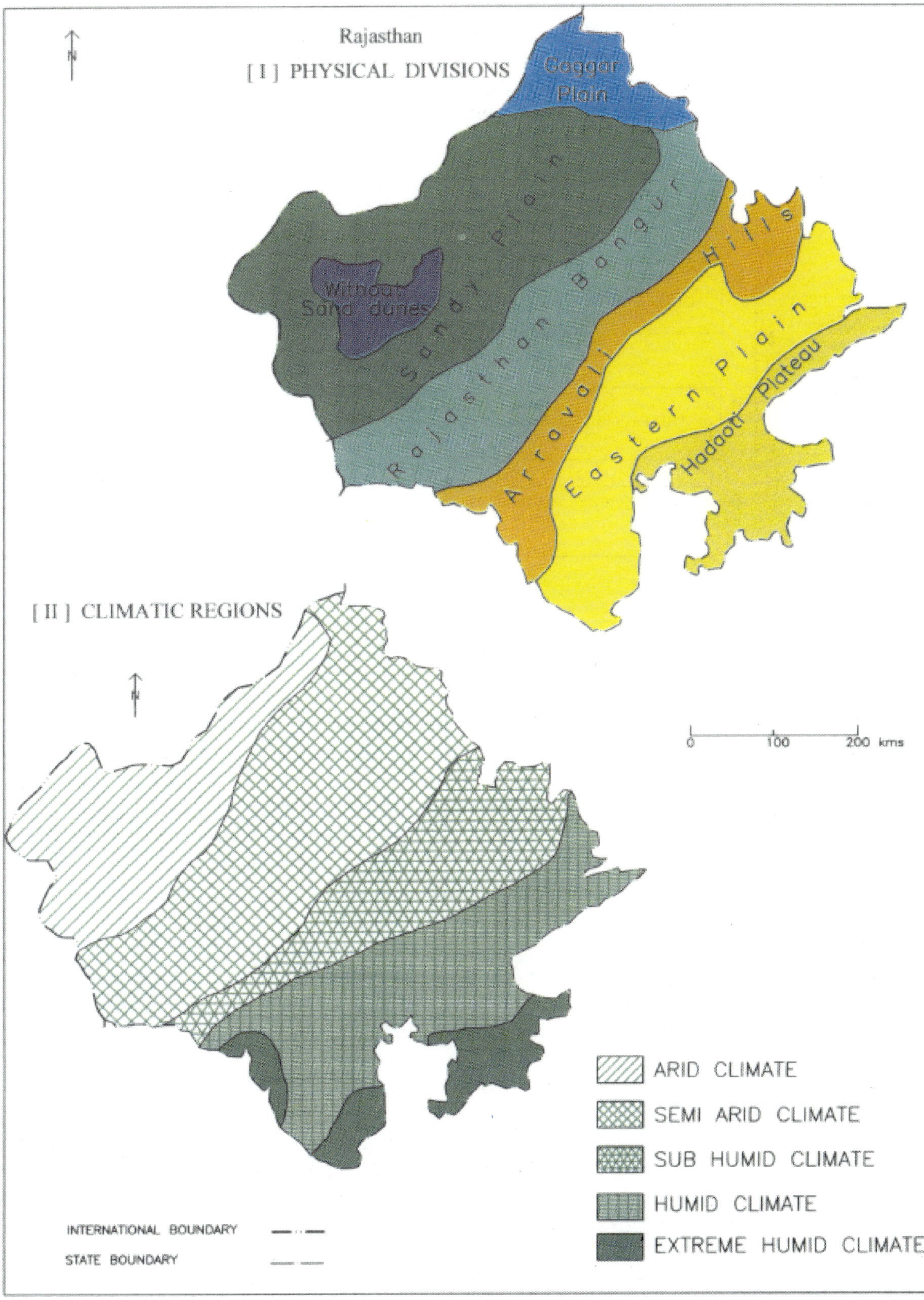
Rajasthan
[I] PHYSICAL DIVISIONS
Gaggar Plain
Sandy Plain
Without Sand dunes
Rajasthan Bangur
Arravali Hills
Eastern Plain
Hadaoti Plateau
[II] CLIMATIC REGIONS
0 100 200 kms
ARID CLIMATE
SEMI ARID CLIMATE
SUB HUMID CLIMATE
HUMID CLIMATE
EXTREME HUMID CLIMATE
INTERNATIONAL BOUNDARY
STATE BOUNDARY

FIG. 2.1

Rajasthan was the first state to start 'Panchayati Raj' in India. The dream of democratic decentralization was materialized with the inauguration of the 'Panchayati Raj' by the then Prime Minister, Pandit Jawahar Lal Nehru at Nagaur on 2nd Oct., 1959. Presently, the Panchayati Raj is a well knit system organised into 32 Zila Parishads, 237 Panchayat Samities (Development Blocks) and 9189 Gram Panchayats.

Physiographically, the state is divided into 4 major and 11 meso divisions as shown in Fig. 2.1 and Chart 2.1

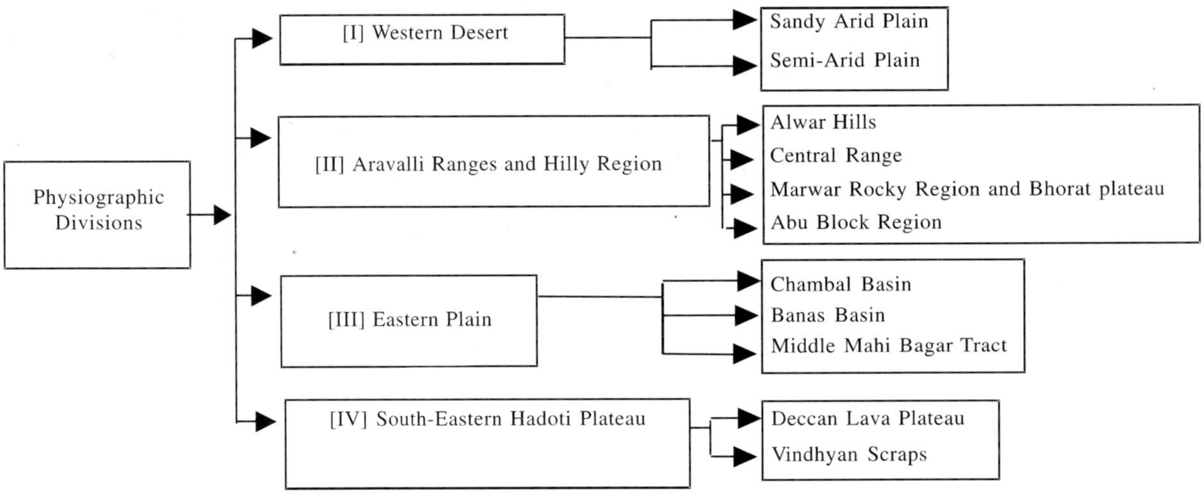

CHART 2.1

The western desert accounts for 58 per cent of the total area and 40 per cent of the population of the state. It comprises of 12 districts viz. Jaisalmer, Barmer, Jalor, Pali, Jodhpur, Nagaur, Jhunjhunun, Churu, Sikar, Bikaner, Hanumangarh and Ganganagar.

The Aravalli range of hills, one of the oldest mountain systems of the world, is the most conspicuous physiographic feature of the state. It consists of parallel hills with high dimensions of folds, stretching diagonally across the state from south-west to north-east direction over a distance of about 690 kms. This division comprises of 9 districts, namely, Sirohi, Banswara, Dungarpur, Chittaurgarh, Udaipur, Rajsamand, Ajmer, Jaipur and Alwar. The Aravalli ranges divide Rajasthan into two natural divisions viz., the northwest, which comprises of about three-fifths of the state, and the south-east, which covers about two-fifths.

The eastern plain accounts for 24 per cent of area and 42 per cent of the total population of the state. It is mostly tabular to plain ground surface through which flow the important river courses of the state like Banas, Berach, Gambhiri, Chambal, etc. This region comprises of Bharatpur, Dhaulpur, Karauli, Dausa, Sawai Madhopur and Tonk districts and plainy areas of Jaipur, Alwar, Bhilwara, Kota and Bundi districts.

The south-eastern Hadoti plateau region comprising of Kota, Jhalawar, Baran and Bundi districts contains 9.6 per cent of the area of the state. The tableland has a very diverse topography, broad depressions and level stretches of deep black soil.

As per Census 2001, Rajasthan has recorded a population of 56.5 million (5.5% of India) with an addition of 12.5 million persons to the population of 44 million in 1991 Census. Out of the total population, 52 per cent are males and remaining 48 per cent are females. Rural-urban population ratio in the state is 77:23. Similarly, the percentage of SC and ST population to total population is 17.2 and 12.6 respectively.

The percentage decadal growth rate of the state has declined from 28.44 in 1981-91 to 28.41 in 1991-2001 (Table 2.5). The trends at the district level reveal that the border districts of Jaisalmer, Bikaner, Barmer apart from Jaipur and Jodhpur have attained the highest percentage decadal growth rates of 47.45; 38.18; 36.83; 35.10 and 33.77 per cent respectively. Among these districts, Jaisalmer, Barmer and Jodhpur have shown increasing trend in growth rates from 1981-91 to 1991-2001, whereas, Jaipur and Bikaner have shown a declining trend.

TABLE 2.5: Growth of Population in Rajasthan

S.No.	*Year*	*Population (million No.)*	*Decennial Growth (%)*
1	1951	16.0	15.20
2	1961	20.2	26.20
3	1971	25.8	27.83
4	1981	34.3	32.97
5	1991	44.0	28.44
6	2001	56.5	28.41

Source: *Economic Review*, 2004-05.

The density of the population is only 165 persons per sq. km. The state presents a peculiar case in terms of population distribution among its districts. Jaisalmer district accounts less than 1 per cent of the total population but have 11 per cent of its area and recorded lowest density. On the other hand, Bharatpur has highest density, accounts for 4 per cent population but has less than 1.5 per cent area.

The Balai, Raiger and Bairwa are the major scheduled castes while, the Bhil, Meena and Sahariya are the important scheduled tribes. The highest concentration of scheduled castes is found in Ganganagar district, while scheduled tribes are concentrated in Udaipur, Banswara, Dungarpur and Sirohi districts.

The sex-ratio in the state is highly adverse i.e., 1000 male to 922 female whereas, for the country as a whole it is 933. Except Dungarpur, Banswara, Udaipur, Sirohi, Sikar, Nagaur, Jhunjhunun and Churu districts, the state is continues to be a male dominated state. This is an important indicator of gender status. Obviously, there is neglect of the girl child. There are various structural and institutional dimensions, which have created inequality between male and female in Rajasthan. The *purdah* system, child marriage, widowhood, dowry and *sati* practices have been responsible for the low status of women in Rajasthan.

The human settlement in the state is scattered. Low density of population, vast area and segmented pattern of human settlement are some of the constraints in the development of the state's health status. Besides, higher initial investment for creating infrastructural facilities, the state requires higher per unit expenditure for providing basic services and necessities.

The Chambal is the only large and perennial river of the state. Similarly, the Luni and a large number of tributaries originating in the Aravalli ranges form drainage of the arid region. The Mahi and the Sabi river systems have dissected the southern region into a maze of innumerable valleys. The drainage of the lower area in the south-east of the Aravalli is through various rivers and rivulets flowing in the north-easterly direction. The Berach drains itself into Banas which later joins the Chambal. While the south-eastern region is watered by rivers like Kalisindh, Ahu and Parbati, the north-eastern part has a number of rivers like Banganga, Gambhiri and Sabi. These are swell basins of interior drainage, the most important of which is that of 90 sq. miles of Sambhar lake.

Recurring drought and scarcity of water are the characteristic features of the state's climate. Rajasthan, with its meagre water resources and perilous dependence on scanty, low and uncertain rainfall, is most vulnerable to drought and famine conditions. The state has an amalgamation of arid, semi-arid and sub-humid climates. As mentioned earlier, western Rajasthan has arid climate. Here rainfall is low and varies highly year after year, creating inhospitable living conditions for both human and livestock population. True desert conditions prevail in the extreme western part of the state. The semi-arid region includes the districts of Alwar, Jaipur, Bharatpur, Ajmer, Tonk, Sawai Madhopur, Bhilwara, Bundi, Kota, Chittaurgarh, Udaipur, Sirohi, Dungarpur and part of Jhalawar. While, the sub-humid region covers parts of Jhalawar and Banswara districts of the state.

A short spell of monsoon with low, erratic and scanty rainfall has made Rajasthan the most water-deficient state in the country. The climate of the state with a large variation from region to region is, thus, the driest in the country. The average rainfall in the state is 57.5 cms which is not only meager but also varies significantly from year to year and from one place to another place led to frequent droughts.

Till now, 37,680 villages and all the 222 cities have been covered under safe drinking water supply. Besides, drinking water has also been made available to about 56,057 *dhanies*. During the year 2004-05 (upto December 2004), 7,416 habitations were benefited with the drinking water facility.

The state is predominantly an agrarian state where about 70 per cent of the population depends on agriculture as a source of livelihood and about 32 per cent of the Net State Domestic Product (NSDP) is generated by primary sector. Water resources in the state are decreasing gradually. Agriculture is essentially rainfed and continues to be susceptible to the vagaries of monsoon.

In the year 2004-05, total cultivable area and agricultural production in the state was 25.4 million hectares and 28.02 million tonnes (excluding 6.5 lakh bales of cotton) respectively. Principal crops cultivated in the state are barley, jowar, millet, maize, gram, wheat, oilseeds, pulses, cotton and tobacco. Cultivation of vegetables and citrus fruits such as orange and malta has also picked up over the last few years. Other crops are red chillies, mustard, cuminseed, methi and *hing*.

There are four major sources of irrigation viz. canals, tanks, wells and tube-wells. In the year 2002-03, the gross irrigated area in the state was 5.27 million hectares which was only 32.4 per cent of gross cropped area. Out of this gross irrigated area, 73.7 per cent was irrigated by wells and tube-wells, 25.6 per cent by canals, 0.1 per cent by tanks and remaining 0.6 per cent by other sources.

The state has rich deposits of zinc concentrates, lead, emerald, garnet, gypsum, silver ore, asbestos, felspar, mica, salt, rock phosphate, marble, red stone, beryl, quartz, tantanite, lime stone, sand stone and copper. The first Export Promotion Industrial Park (EPIP) of the country has been established and made operational at Sitapura, Jaipur.

Rajasthan is the first state in India to have restructured its entire power sector in one phase. The reforms changed it all. Power generation increased mainfold, transmission and distribution losses came down and revenues shot up sharply. The installed capacity of power in the state up to Dec. 2004 was 5278 MW. Kota and Suratgarh Thermal Power Plants, Mahi Hydel Project, Bhakra, Beas, Chambal and Satpura Projects are the main sources of power supply to the state. Besides, Rajasthan Atomic Power Plant, Singrauli, Rihand, Anta, Auraiya, Narora, Dadari Gas, Unchahar Thermal and Tanakpur, Salal, Chamera and Uri Projects in central sector are also sharing power with the state.

Despite the abundance of natural resources, Rajasthan is still to emerge as an industrially developed state. Efforts are being made for speedy industrial development in the state. The state government launched the Industrial Policy 1998 with the aim of rapid industrialisation and for making Rajasthan a preferred destination for investment in the identified sectors so that it might ultimately achieve global competitiveness. Major industries identified for this purpose are: textiles and woollens, sugar, cement, glass, oxygen, vegetable dyes, pesticides, zinc, fertilizers, railway wagons, ball bearings, water and electricity metres, sulfuric acid, television sets, synthetic yarn and insulating bricks. Around 220 thousand industrial units were registered with a total investment of Rs. 31000 million and one million persons were employed therein. Some of the important central undertakings are: Zinc Smelter Plant at Debari (Udaipur), Copper Plant at Khetri Nagar (Jhunjhunun) and Instrumentation Limited at Kota.

Rajasthan is an under-developed state in respect of transport and communication. In the absence of internal waterways and inadequate expansion of railways, roads provide a major infrastructural link in the state. The total road length in the state is 1.64 lakh kms as on March, 2005.

The total length of railway routes in the state by the end of March, 2002 was 5894 kms (9.4% of India). Out of the total railway route length in the state, 51 per cent was under broad gauge, 47.4 per cent under meter gauge and 1.5 per cent under narrow gauge. Regular air services connect Jaipur, Jodhpur and Udaipur cities with Delhi and Mumbai.

Rajasthan is one of the most attractive destinations in India for both domestic and international tourists. Many forts and palaces, heritage hotels and the attraction of travelling on the 'Palace on Wheels' have been the unique selling propositions for tourists coming to the state. Visitors also appreciate the colourful fairs and festivals. The different ethnic culture of the people has proved to be a major attraction for the visitors, alongwith the unique desert environment in western Rajasthan. The total arrival of tourists in Rajasthan were 13.2 million (95% domestic and 5% foreign) in the year 2003.

The state has made impressive gains in education, rural development, energy and infrastructure. Literacy has gone up to 60.4 per cent and is showing an upward trend. More children have been enrolled in rural schools this year than ever before. It is a mater of great pleasure that the state was awarded by 'Decade Literacy Award' and Decade Female Literacy Award on National Literacy Day-2001. This is in recognition of the state's excellent performance in literacy reflected in the recent census 2001 report that indicates that the literacy rate for all persons has increased by 21.8 per cent (38.6% to 60.4%) and the rate of female literacy by 23.5 per cent (20.4 to 43.9%) during the last decade.

A 2002 survey by Shiksha Darpan reveals that out of 23 lakh children, 16 lakh are on the schools rolls. It is heartening to see 7.7 million village kids being served a modest meal of *ghughri* under mid day meal scheme.

There are total 33266 primary, 25057 upper primary and 9383 secondary/senior secondary schools functioning in the state (2003-04). CTS (Child Tracking System) has been introduced in the state to achieve cent percent enrolment and retention of children in the age group of 6-14 in school.

The State Government had worked out a new concept of linking drought relief works with development and utilised the funds on the construction of roads in villages. This helped lakhs of drought victims to secure employment. It also helped in connecting hundreds of villages in the State by link roads.

The National Highway Authority of India (NHAI) has completed work for making the 93 km long Jaipur-Kishangarh (National Highway No. 8) into a 6 lane highway and 431 km long Kishangarh-Chittaurgarh-Udaipur-Ratanpur Highway into a four lane highway. Similarly, work on 641 km long East-West corridor Pindwara-Udaipur-Chittaurgarh-Kota, Baran-Shivpur highway into 4-lane highway will be completed by May 2007.

Upto Dec. 2004, sanction of Rs 17.4 billion has been received from the GoI under PMGSY (Pradhan Mantri Gram Sarak Yojana) for connecting 4015 villages by constructing 14 thousand km BT (Black Top) roads against which 2643 villages have already been connected by constructing 9205 km BT roads.

Almost 4,000 km of new roads are being built in nearly 1,200 villages at a cost of Rs. 4 billions. This is besides up-gradation and renewal of 24,000 km of older roads and four-laning of Delhi-Mumbai Highway at a cost of over Rs. 15 billions by NHAI through Rajasthan.

Various benefits have been provided to diversify rural livelihoods especially in the non-farm sector. Over 24,000 small shops have been constructed under the Swarn Jayanti Gram Swarojgar Yojna (SJGSY) and 23,000 have been allotted to BPL beneficiaries, who, with an infusion of credit and subsidy, are running their shops.

Today there are over 84 thousand self-help group (SHGs) in the state with a membership over 8 lakh. About 60 per cent of these groups are of women and 32 per cent groups are of BPL families. Under the Swaran Jayanti Gram Swarojgar Yojana provision has been made to set up at least two self-help groups at each gram panchayat area.

A computer revolution that will make the e-government dream possible is recently started in the villages of Rajasthan. With STD and ISD rates slashed, the focus is now to provide additional services. Similarly, with the introduction of net telephony, tele-density has been increased significantly.

The State Government in a major drive launched *'Prashasan Gaon Ke Sang Campaign'* (administration at the doorsteps of the villages) in rural areas, benefiting over 7 million population. It has played a vital role in identifying and solving the rural problems. In the rural areas of the state more than 25 centrally and state sponsored schemes are being implemented to eradicate poverty, generate additional employment opportunities, develop basic amenities and to remove regional disparities.

3

HEALTH STATUS OF RAJASTHAN IN INDIA

Despite concerted efforts made by the state as well as central government, health status of Rajasthan remains appalling. The position is more alarming in rural areas. Fertility, Mortality and Morbidity indicators in the state continue to be higher than the national average. An indepth incisive look at the tables 3.1 to 3.6 indicates that Rajasthan continues to remain among the worst in most of the health indicators in India.

BOX 3.1: Health Status of Rajasthan in India

[I] Unsatisfactory		
Health Indicators are Higher than National Average	*Health Indicators are Lower than National Average*	*[II] Satisfactory*
• IMR • CBR • GFR • GRR • Rural TMFR • Neo-natal mortality rate. • Percentage of currently married women with any reproductive problem.	• Life expectancy at birth. • Female age at effective marriage. • Percentage of live birth receiving ante-natal care. • Percentage of live birth receiving 2 doses of TT vaccine. • Percentage of live birth receiving iron/folic tablets. • Percentage of birth delivered in medical institutions. • Percentage of deliveries assisted by health professionals. • Percentage of children age 12-23 months receiving full immunization. • CPR • ANC. • Sex-ratio (more particularly of 0-6 pop.). • Female literacy rate. • Access to safe drinking water in rural areas.* • Percentage of households having electricity within house in rural areas.*	• Still- birth rate in rural areas. • CDR. • Peri-natal mortality rate in rural area. • Percentage of Neo-natal deaths to infant death. • Achievement in immunization programme (under 20-point programme). • Achievement in villages covered under drinking water facility (under 20-point programme). • Access to safe drinking water in urban areas*. • Percentage of households having electricity within house in urban areas.* • Male literacy rate, 2001. • Percentage increase in female literacy and total literacy rate during 1991-01.

Note: * Infrastructure related indices having direct bearing on health status.
Source: Table 3.1 to 3.6

TABLE 3.1: Key Indicators of Health Development: Rajasthan *vis-à-vis* India

Item		*Rajasthan*	*India*
Sex Ratio (2001)	(i) Total Population	922	933
	(ii) 0-6 Population	909	927
Life Expectancy at Birth (2001-06)	(i) Male	62.17	63.87
	(ii) Female	62.8	66.91
Infant Mortality Rate (per 1000 live births, 2002)	(i) Male	75	62
	(ii) Female	80	65
	(iii) Total	78	63
	(iv) Rural	81	69
	(v) Urban	55	40
Crude Death Rate (per 1000), 2002 (P)	(i) Rural	8.0	NA
	(ii) Urban	6.4	NA
	(iii) Total	7.7	8.1
Crude Birth Rate (per 1000), 2002 (P)	(i) Rural	31.9	26.6
	(ii) Urban	24.2	19.9
	(iii) Total	30.6	25
Literacy Rate 2001		60.4	64.8
Access to Safe Drinking Water (%, 2001)	(i) Rural	60.4	73.2
	(ii) Urban	93.5	90.8
	(iii) Total	68.2	77.9
Female Age at Effective Marriage, SRS, 2002	(i) Rural	19.1	19.4
	(ii) Urban	20.5	21.1
	(iii) Total	19.3	19.8
GFR (General Fertility Rate), SRS, 1998	(i) Rural	142.8	115.2
	(ii) Urban	97.8	79.2
	(iii) Total	134.2	106.5
TFR (Total Fertility Rate), SRS, 2000	(i) Rural	4.4	3.5
	(ii) Urban	2.9	2.3
	(iii) Total	4.1	3.2
TMFR (Total Marital Fertility Rate), SRS, 2000	(i) Rural	5.2	5.0
	(ii) Urban	4.1	4.2
	(iii) Total	5.0	4.8
GRR (Gross Reproduction Rate), SRS, 2000	(i) Rural	2.1	1.7
	(ii) Urban	1.4	1.1
	(iii) Total	2.0	1.5
Neo-natal Mortality Rates, SRS, 2000	(i) Rural	52	49
	(ii) Urban	32	27
	(iii) Total	49	44
Peri-natal Mortality Rates, SRS, 2000	(i) Rural	40	44
	(ii) Urban	30	26
	(iii) Total	39	40
Still Birth Rates, SRS, 2000	(i) Rural	6	9
	(ii) Urban	9	7
	(iii) Total	6	8
%age of Neo-natal Deaths to Infant Deaths, 2000	(i) Rural	63.1	65.8
	(ii) Urban	54.4	63.0
	(iii) Total	62.2	65.5
%age of households Having Electricity Within House, 2001 Census	(i) Rural	44	44
	(ii) Urban	90	88
	(iii) Total	55	56
%age of Live Births by Various Maternal Care Indicators, NFHS-2, 1998-99			
• % Receiving Antenalal Care		48	65
• % Receiving 2 Doses of TT Vaccine		52	67
• % Receiving Iron/Folic Tablets		39	58
• % of Births Delivered in Medical Institutions		22	34
• % of Deliveres Assisted by Health Professionals		36	42
%age of Children Age, 12-23 Months who Received Full Immunisation, ** NFHS-2, 1998-99		17.3	42
CPR (Couple Protection Rate), NFHS-2, 1998-99		40.3	48.2
ANC (Ante Natal Care), NFHS-2, 1998-99		47.5	65.4
%age of Currently Married Women with any Reproductive Health problem, NFHS-2, 1998-99		43.2	39.2

P = Provisional, ** BCG, Measles and Three Doses Each of DPT and Polio Vaccines.

Source: 1. *Economic Review*, Rajasthan 2004-05, DES, Jaipur. 2. *Economic Survey* 2004-05, GoI, New Delhi. 3. 'NFHS-2', Oct. 2000, IIPS, Mumbai. 4. *'Statistical Report'*, 2000, SRS, RGI, New Delhi 5. *'SRS Bulletin'* Oct 2002 & 2003 Vol. 36 & 37, No. 2, RGI, New Delhi 6. Vital Rates in India-1995, Based on the SRS, Tables 7. *Census of India*, Data Product No.: 00-28-cen-CD Tables on Houses, Amenities & Assets. 8. *Health Monitor*, 2004, Foundation for Research in Health Systems, Ahmedabad.

TABLE 3.2: Rank of Rajasthan in Key Indicators of Health Development (India)

Rank in India	*Indicators*
	(A) Basic Health Indices
2	GFR (SRS, 1998)
3	Female Infant Mortality Rate (2002)
	Birth Rate (2002)
	TFR (SRS, 1998)
	GRR (SRS, 1998)
4	Male Infant Mortality Rate (2002)
	Total Infant Mortality Rate (2002)
	Rural IMR (2001)
	Rural Neo-natal Mortality Rate (SRS, 1998)
5	TMFR (SRS, 1998)
7	Death Rate (2002)
	Rural Peri-natal Mortality Rate (SRS, 1998)
10	Infants Immunised Under 20 - Point Programme
11	Female Age at Effective Marriage (SRS, 1998)
12	Percentage Decadal Growth of Population (1991-01)
	Life Expectancy at Birth Male (2001-06)
	Life Expectancy at Birth Female (2001-06)
	Rural Still Birth Rate (SRS, 1998)
	Percentage of Neo-natal Deaths to Infant Deaths-Rural (SRS, 1998)
19	Sex Ratio (2001)
22	Percentage of Currently Married Women with any Reproductive Health Problem (NFHS-2, 1998-99)
24	Density of Population Per sq. km. (2001*)
25	Percentage of Deliveries Assisted by Health Professionals *
28	Percentage of Live Births Delivered in Medical Institutions, (NFHS-2, 1998-99)
	Percentage of Live Births Receiving 2 Doses of TT Vaccine, (NFHS-2, 1998-99) *
29	Couple Protection Rate (NFHS-2, 1998-99)
32	Percentage of Children Age 12-23 Months who Received full Immunisation, ** (NFHS-2, 1998-99)
33	Percentage of Live Birth Receiving Iron/Folic Tablets (NFHS-2, 1998-99)
34	Percentage of Live Births Receiving Antenatal Care (NFHS-2, 1998-99)
	(B) Infrastructure Related Indices having direct bearing on Health Status
9	Percentage of Electrified Villages to Total Villages (2003)
	No. of Registered Primary Schools (2002-03)
16	Total Road Length Per 100 sq. km (1999) *
17	PCI at Current Prices 2002-03
24	Access to Safe Drinking Water in Rural House Holds, 2001
27	Percentage of Rural Households Having Electricity Within House (2001)
25	Female Enrolment Ratio, (Class I to V, 6-11 Yrs., 2002-03)
32	Female Enrolment Ratio, (Class VI to VIII, 11-14 Yrs., 2002-03)

* Rank Amongst Major States. ** BCG, Measles and Three Doses Each of DPT and Polio Vaccines.
Source: Same as Table 3.1.

TABLE 3.3: Immunisation Under 20-Point Programme: Raj/India (Apr., 04-Jan. 05)

	Infants Immunised			*Rank of Rajasthan in India*
	Target (million No.)	*Achievement*		
		No. (million No.)	*As % of Target*	
Rajasthan	1.46	1.32 (6%)	92	X
India	21.41	22.25	104	

Note: Figure in brackets shows percentage of Rajasthan in India.
Source: Compiled from Monthly Review of Rajasthan Economy, Centre for Monitoring India Economy Jaipur, May, 2005.

TABLE 3.4: IMR: Fluctuating Position of Rajasthan in India (1991-02)

	1961			*1981*			*2002 (P)*		
	Male	*Female*	*Person*	*Male*	*Female*	*Person*	*Male*	*Female*	*Person*
Rajasthan	114	114	114	94	79	87	81	55	78
India	122	108	115	74	79	77	69	40	63
Rank of Rajasthan in India	6	5	6	7	11	7	4	3	4

(P) Provisional from SRS.
Source: 1. *Economic Survey,* 2004-05, GoI, S-113.
2. SRS, 2002.

TABLE 3.5: Villages Covered Under Drinking Water Facility (Under 20-Point Programme): Rajasthan, India

	Villages Covered			
		Achievement		
	Target	*No.*	*As % of Target*	*Rank of Rajasthan in India*
Rajasthan	6900	8007 (19.6)	116	XI
India	57397	40888	71.2	

Source: *Economic Survey,* 2004-05, GoI, S-113.
Note: Figures in brackets show percentage of Rajasthan in India.

TABLE 3.6: Access to Safe Drinking Water in Households: Deteriorating Rank of Rajasthan in India (1981-01)

	Tap/Handpump/Tube-well								
	1981			*1991*			*2001*		
	Total	*Rural*	*Urban*	*Total*	*Rural*	*Urban*	*Total*	*Rural*	*Urban*
Rajasthan	27.1	13.0	78.7	59.0	50.6	86.5	68.2	60.4	93.5
India	38.2	26.5	75.1	62.3	55.5	81.4	77.9	73.2	90
Rank of Rajasthan in India	21	24	13	17	19	14	25	24	15

Source: *Economic Review,* 2004-05, GoI, New Delhi, S-114.

4

HEALTH SCENARIO DURING FIVE YEAR PLANS (1951-2005)

Inspite of being developing state with weak socio-demographic indicators, Rajasthan registered remarkable achievements in health status during the Five Year Plans (FYP) period. Since the commencement of the first FYP in the year 1951, a multifold increase is registered in government investment in health sector (1022 times), total number of medical institutions (30 times), number of doctors (7.4 times), beds (580 times), patient treated etc. Health infrastructural facilities have been strengthened and both qualitive and quantitative improvement is achieved in health services. Various national and state level health programmes and schemes are being launched in the state. Special schemes have been also launched for the arid/semi-arid, tribal, backward and remote areas. Concerted efforts are being made by the state as well as central government for the availability of health services to people at their door-steps. As a result, life expectancy at birth increased significantly while sharp decline is registered in fertility, mortality and morbidity indicators.

Similarly, as a result of improvement in the health infrastructural facilities, number of population served per bed and per institution came down from 2792 to 1454 and from 38208 to 4468 respectively during 1951-04 period; and number of population served per doctor came down from 22132 to 9149 during 1955-04 period.

Prior to the formation of Rajasthan in 1949, medical and health services were confined to a few larger towns and capital cities of the erstwhile princely states. With the introduction of planning, health programmes were taken up and directed mainly for control/eradication of major communicable diseases, provision for curative, preventive and promotional health services, augmentation of training facilities for medical and para-medical personnels and strengthening of PHCs in rural areas.

The state government has giving special thrust to strengthen the Ayurvedic, the indigenous system of medicines. At the time of formation of Rajasthan, the state had only 346 ayurvedic hospitals and homeopathic hospitals with a total bed-strength of 100. By the end of 2000-01, the number has gone up to 3733 hospitals and dispensaries with a total bed strength of 1186. Besides these, the state has 6 mobile dispensaries, 3 ayurvedic colleges (including two private colleges) and 2 training centres for para-medical staff. The National Institute of Ayurved (NIA) is also located at Jaipur.

A brief description of changed health scenario during FYP period is presented in this chapter.

First Five Year Plan (1951-52 to 1955-56)

In 1951-52, the first year of the I FYP, there were total 418 medical institutions (234 hospitals, 156 dispensaries and 24 MCW centres) in Rajasthan. The number of beds in government hospitals were 5720. The total health budget and per person health budget was Rs. 11.2 million and Rs. 0.64 respectively. Similarly, the population served per bed was 2792 and per institution was 38208.

TABLE 4.1: Changing Health Scenario During FYPs: Rajasthan (1951-04)

		I FYP	*II*	*III*	*3 Annual Plans*	*IV*	*V*	*VI*	*VII*	*2 Annual Plans*	*VIII*	*IX*	*X FYP*			
													Annual Plan	*Annual Plan*	*Annual Plan*	*Annual Plan*
S.No.	*Descripition*	*1951-52*	*1955-56*	*60-61*	*65-66*	*68-69*	*73-74*	*79-80*	*84-85*	*89-90*	*91-92*	*96-97*	*2001-2002*	*2002-03*	*2003-04*	*2004-05*
1	*2*	*3*	*4*	*5*	*6*	*7*	*8*	*9*	*10*	*11*	*12*	*13*	*14*	*15*	*16*	*17*
1	Hospitals (Community Health Centers)	234	261	264	320	348	140	171	186(25)	208(57)	214(68)	219(72)	219(72)	219(95)	215*(95)	215*(95)
2	Dispensaries	156	210	237	211	229	551	989(262)	1083(280)	756(279)	275	278	268	268	209	209
3	Mother & Child Welfare Centers	28	45	63	76	76	92	98	111	117	118	118	118	118	118	118
4	Primary Health Centres (Upgraded PHC)	—	12	142	230	232	232	232(18)	348(51)	1059(133)	1373(148)	1616 (189)	1674(191)	1674(191)	1675(202)	1677(203)
5	Urban Primary Health Centres	—	7	—	—	—	—	—	—	—	—	—	29	29	29	29
6	Sub Centres	—	—	—	690	696	1624	2140	3790	8000	8000	9400	9926	9926	9926	10387
	Total No. of Medical Institutions	**418**	**528**	**706**	**1527**	**1581**	**2639**	**3630**	**5518**	**10140**	**9980**	**11631**	**12234**	**12234**	**12172**	**12635**
7	Family Welfare Centres	—	—	71	287	292	292	370	390	384	384	384	293	293	293	293
8	Beds	5720	6798	9459	12241	13415	15450	17397	21916	28867	32195	36967	37918	38018	38687	38873
9	Doctors	—	830	1300	1737	1855	2022	2840	3476	4388	5194	5932	6252	6381	6125	6176
10	Population (in million No.)	15.971	18.37	20.65	22.65	24.46	27.864	31.52	36.823	41.925	43.83	44.006	56.473	56.473	56.507	56.507
11	Budget (in million Rs.)	11.2	16.721	39.399	66.453	108.402	177.568	333.679	949.306	2022.812	2842.566	6287.095	10223.07	10550.064	11285.093	11448.928
12	Per Person Budget (Rs.)	0.64	0.91	1.91	2.93	4.43	6.37	10.59	25.78	48.25	64.85	142.87	181.02	186.81	199.71	202.61
13	Population Served Per Bed	2792	2702	2183	1850	1823	1803	1812	1680	1452	1361	1190	1489	1485	1461	1454
14	Population Served Per Doctor	—	22132	15885	13040	13186	13780	11099	10593	9554	8439	7418	9033	8850	9226	9149
15	Population Served Per Medical Institution	38208	34792	29249	14833	15471	10559	8683	6673	4135	4488	3784	4611	4611	4637	4468

Note: 1. Since Fourth FYP, definition of hospital has been changed from earlier having 1 bed to 10 beds. * excluding 4 ESI hospitals
2. No. of CHCs decreased from Seventh FYP due to their conversion into upgraded PHCs.
3. In Ninth FYP, some dispensaries are upgraded and converted into urban PHCs.
Figures in brackets show No. of CHCs

Source: *'Pragati Prativedan'*, 2004-05, Directorate of Medical and Health, GoR, Jaipur.

TABLE 4.2: Improvement in Health Indicators: Rajasthan (1985-02)

Year	*Indicators*			
	BR	*DR*	*IMR*	*CPR*
1985	39.7	13.2	108	19.8
1991	35.0	9.8	79	28.9
2001	31.1	8.0	80	38.0
2002	30.6	7.7	78	38.2

Source: *Pragati Prativedan,* 2004-05, Directorate of Medical, Health and Family Welfare Services Raj., Jaipur.

TABLE 4.3: Achievements of FWPs: Rajasthan (1985-04)

(*'000 No.*)

S.No.	*Year*	*Sterilisation*	*IUD Inserted*	*OP Users*	*Nirodh Users*
1	1985-86	267.9	95.6	13.6	178.0
2	1991-92	173.3	158.6	60.2	275.5
3	1995-96	168.2	168.2	125.2	519.0
4	2001-02	252.1	239.0	502.3	1038.1
5	2002-03	285.9	242.2	606.8	1277.9
6	2003-04	300.1	265.8	713.7	1459.8
7	2004-05 (Upto Jan. 05)	233.1	226.2	399.3 (New Users)	446.0 (New Users)

Source: *Pragati Prativedan,* 2004-05, Directorate of Medical, Health and Family Welfare Services Rajasthan, Jaipur.

There was only one medical college in the state at Jaipur which was established in the year 1947. Two para-medical centres one each for male and female nursing training were also established at Jaipur in the year 1951-52. National Malaria Control Programme was also launched in the year 1954-55.

In the year 1952, family planning programme was launched in the state as a 100 per cent centrally supported scheme. Clinic based approach was adopted and focus was laid on providing FP advice, services, supplies through various clinics already existing at that time and those which would be established in future. Rhythm and conventional contraception methods were advocated during the period.

During the First plan period, adequate infrastructure has been created in rural areas. Determined and continued efforts made by the state government to provide better coverage has resulted in achieving the following:

	Increase/ Improvement*
No. of Hospitals	27
No. of Dispensaries	54
No. of MCWs	17
No. of PHCs	12
Total No. of Medical Institutions	110
No. of beds	1078
No. of doctors	830
Health budget (million Rs.)	5.52
Per capita health budget (Rs.)	0.27
Decrease in number of population served per bed*	90
Decrease in number of population served per institution*	3416

Source: Computed from Table 4.1

Second Five Year Plan (1955-56 to 1960-61)

There were total 528 medical institutions (261 hospitals, 210 dispensaries, 45 MCW centres, 12 PHCs), 6798 beds and 830 doctors in the year 1955-56 (commencing year of the Second FYP). Total health budget was of Rs. 16.72 million while per capita budget was of Rs. 0.91. Now the population served per bed came down at 2702, per doctor at 22132 and per institution at 34792.

The first Medical Surgical Unit of the state was established at Jaipur in the year 1956. Similarly, National Malaria Eradication Programme (NMEP) was launched in 1958. In the year 1959, the second medical college of the state was established at Bikaner.

In this FYP, to control population growth, thrust was laid on extension of FP services, establishment and maintenance of training centres and on sex education. Free of cost sterilization was introduced with 100 per cent central assistance.

The achievements during this FYP is presented below:

	Increase/ Improvement*
No. of Hospitals	3
No. of Dispensaries	27
No. of MCWs	18
No. of PHCs	130
Total No. of Medical Institutions	178
No. of FWCs	71
No. of Beds	2661
No. of Doctors	470
Health budget (million Rs.)	22.68
Per capita health budget (Rs.)	1
Decrease in number of population served per bed*	519
Decrease in number of population served per doctor*	6247
Decrease in number of population served per institution*	5543

Third Five Year Plan (1960-61 to 1965-66)

In the beginning year of the third FYP (1960-61), the total number of medical institutions rose to 706 (264 hospitals, 237 dispensaries, 63 MCW centres and 142 PHCs) 71 FWCs. The number of doctors and beds were 1300 and 9459 respectively. Similarly, total health budget was of Rs. 39.4 million while per capita budget was of Rs. 1.91. Now, the population served per bed decreased to 2183, per doctor to 15885 and per institution decreased to 29249 in comparison to 1955-56 (beginning year of Second FYP). In the year 1962 and 1965, the 3rd and 4th medical colleges of the state were established at Udaipur and Jodhpur respectively.

In the year 1963, Family Planning Programme was recognized as Family Welfare Programme (FWP). The plan stated that Family Planning Education, being a part of education for better life, has to be interwoven with other constructive activities, especially the work of the primary health centres, community development blocks, voluntary development block and voluntary organizations. Information was to be made available on the largest possible scale and conditions created in which individuals could freely resort to family planning practices.

The central feature of the plan was the integration of family planning with the normal medical and health services, specially those services might also be made available through centres maintained by voluntary agencies, mobile units and industrial and other establishments.

The plan stated that in addition to birth control, the family planning programme should include sex and family life education and advice on such other measures as may be necessary to promote welfare of family.

The strategy during the Third Plan was revised from the 'clinical based apporach' to 'extension approach', which meant educating the people and providing knowledge and information about various aspects of family planning through the family planning workers approaching them at their door-steps.

Introduction of the intra-uterine contraceptive device, (IUCD) popularly know as "Lippe's loop", as a contraceptive method was a great achievement of this FYP. The concept of payment of incentive money to Family Planning services acceptors was introduced in the year 1963.

During this FYP, central assistance had been offered to the State Government for starting one sub-centre for every 10,000 population. The reorganized Family Planning Programme was integrated with the Maternity and Child Health Programme from the very beginning. It was decided that in the areas entering the maintenance phase, there would be one sub-centre for every 10,000 population, with one Auxiliary Nurse Midwife (ANM) and one basic health worker. In order to have effective supervision, family planning and health assistants were provided on the scale of one for every two sub-centres. For communication activities at the block level, the post of the Extension Educator (FP) was created.

The changed health scenario during this FYP is given below:

[A] Increase/Improvement*

No. of hospitals	56
No. of MCWs	13
No. of PHCs	88
No. of SHCs	690
Total No. of Medical Institutions	821
No. of FWCs	216
No. of Beds	2782
No. of Doctors	437
Health budget (million Rs.)	27.05
Per capita health budget (Rs.)	1.02
Decrease in number of population served per bed*	333
Decrease in number of population served per doctor*	2845
Decrease in number of population served per institution*	14416

[B] Decrease

No. of dispensaries	26

Three Annual Plans (1965-66 to 1968-69)

In the year 1965-66, the total number of medical institutions increased to 1527, (hospitals 320, dispensaries 211, MCW centres 76, PHCs 230 and SHCs 690) and FWCs to 287. The number of doctors and bed became 1737 and 12241 respectively. Similarly, total health budget rose to Rs. 66.45 million while the per capita budget rose to Rs. 2.93. As a result, the population served per bed (1850), per doctor (13040) and per institution (14833) also came down in comparison to the year 1960-61 (beginning year of the Third FYP).

In the year 1966-67, Family Planning Programme was made target oriented and time bounded. Similarly, in the year 1967-68, Family Planning Department (FPD) was formed in the state.

The changed health scenario during this FYP is presented as under:

[A] Increase/Improvement*

No. of hospitals	28
No. of dispensaries	18
No. of PHCs	2
No. of SHCs	6
Total No. of Medical Institutions	54
No. of FWCs	5
No. of beds	1174
No. of doctors	118
Health budget (million Rs.)	41.95

Per capita health budget (Rs.)	1.5
Decrease in number of population served per bed*	27
[B] Decrease/ Deterioration**	
Increase in number of population served per doctor**	146
Increase in number of population served per institution**	638

Fourth Five Year Plan (1968-69 to 1973-74)

In the first year of the Fourth FYP, there were 1581 medical institutions (348 hospitals, 229 dispensaries, 76 MCW centres, 232 PHCs and 696 SHCs), 292 FWCs, 1855 doctors and 13415 beds in the state. Budget of Rs. 108.4 million was earmarked for health sector with per capita budget of Rs. 4.43. Whereas population served per bed (1823) came down in comparison to the year 1965-66, population served per doctor (13186) and per institution (15471) increased during the same period.

In the year 1970-71, National Leprosy Eradication Programme was launched in the state. Similarly, in 1970, Hospital Post-Partum programme was started. Like-wise, in 1973, new medical college was established in Ajmer.

With regard to Family Planning programme, thrust was laid on stepping up targets for sterlisation and IUCD insertion and to widen the acceptance of oral and conventional contraceptives. The plan provided for immunization of infants and pre-school children with DPT, immunization of expectant mothers against tetanus, prophylaxis against nutritional anemia for mothers and children and nutritional programme for control of blindness caused by vitamin 'A' deficiency among children implemented through family planning centres.

The achievements of this FYP are presented as below:

[A] Increase/Improvement*	
No. of dispensaries	322
No. of MCWs	16
No. of SHCs	928
Total No. of Medical Institutions	1058
No. of beds	2035
No. of doctors	167
Health budget (million Rs.)	69.17
Per capita health budget (Rs.)	1.94
Decrease in number of population served per bed*	20
Decrease in number of population served per institution*	4912
[B] Decrease/ Deterioration**	
No. of hospitals	208
Increase in number of population served per doctor**	594

Fifth Five Year Plan (1973-74 to 1979-80)

During the Fifth FYP, the main accent was on increasing the accessibility of health services to rural areas, as a part of minimum needs programme and to develop referral services by providing for specialists' attention to common diseases in rural area.

The concept of minimum needs programme was introduced in the year 1974-75. The broad strategy to this programme during the plan period has been conceived within the framework of targets and scale of facilities suggested by the planning commission under the Revised MNP. Augmenting the health services, correcting regional imbalances, filling in the gaps and strengthening health infrastructure are the main objectives of the programme. Opening of new SHCs, upgradition of PHCs, establishment of subsidiary health centres, provision of requisite staff, drugs and equipments to PHCs and SHCs, and construction of buildings for the existing SHCs have been given priority.

In the year 1973-74, there were total 2639 medical institutions (140 hospitals, 551 dispensaries, 92 MCW centres, 232 PHCs and 1624 SHCs) and 292 FWCs in the state. The number of doctors were 2022 and beds were 15450. Total Rs. 177.57 million were earmarked for health budget with Rs. 6.37 per capita budget. Whereas, population served per bed (1803) and per institution (10559) decreased in comparison to the year 1968-69 (starting year of the Fourth FYP), population served per doctor (13780) increased during the same period.

Besides, five medical colleges and 29 institutions for training in various para-medical courses, there were 1057 allopathic hospitals and dispensaries with 16475 beds at the close of 1977-78. One PHC in each PS was also functioning. To provide special types of medical facilities, 26 TB clinics and sanotoria, 93 MCW centres and 5 clinics for veneral diseases were existing.

During the plan period, 8 PHCs were upgraded to 30-beded referral hospitals and 200 SHCs were established along with 334 dispensaries and aid-posts in rural areas.

The state has achieved the target of providing at least 2 dispensaries and 1 aid-post in each PS in addition to the PHC and SHCs. A State Health Bureau (SHB) and State Nutrition Bureau (SNB) have been established during the plan period.

In the year 1975, ICDS (Integrated Children Development Scheme) programme was launched in the state. Similarly, in the year 1975-76, NMEP (National Malaria Eradication Programme) was merged with the general health system and changed from unipurpose to multipurpose functioning. Multi-purpose worker scheme was also started in the same year.

In the year 1976, National Blindness Control Programme (NBCP) was started in the state. Like-wise, in the year 1977, Revised National TB Control programme, National Health Guide Scheme and Community Health Volunteers Schemes were started in the state.

Family Planning became a concurrent subject with effect from January, 1977. This facilitated providing assistance to the family planning programme to the states. Contraceptives were distributed free and also sold at subsidized rates through the social marketing channels. In 1979, the distribution of oral pills was also introduced through trained paramedical staff. The mass education and motivation activities, were planned and coordinated by the Mass Education and Media Wing of the Family Planning Bureau at the State and district levels.

In this FYP, family planning was integrated with the minimum needs programme. The communication approach adopted was to obtain optimum results from the view point of demographic effectiveness and cost effectiveness. For this purpose, the concentration of efforts was on promoting family life education before marriage and intensive motivation of high parity couples in the age group of 25-35 years and the recently married couples.

The changed health scenario during this FYP is presented as below:

[A] Increase/Improvement*

No. of hospitals	31
No. of dispensaries	438
No. of MCWs	6
No. of SHCs	516
Total No. of Medical Institutions	475
No. of FWCs	78
No. of beds	1947
No. of doctors	818
Health budget (million Rs.)	156.11
Per capita health budget (Rs.)	4.22
Decrease in number of population served per doctor*	2681
Decrease in number of population served per institution*	1876

[B] Decrease/ Deterioration**

Increase in number of population served per bed**	9

Sixth Five Year Plan (1979-80 to 1984-85)

There were 3630 medical institutions (171 hospitals, 989 dispensaries, 98 MCW centres, 232 PHCs and 2140 SHCs) 370 FWCs, 2840 doctors and 17397 beds in the year 1979-80. Total budget for health sector was of Rs. 333.68 million, while per capita budget was of Rs. 1059. In comparison to the year 1973-74 (beginning year of the Fifth FYP), the number of population served per doctor (11099) and per institution (8683) came down significantly, but the population served per bed (1812) stepped up marginally.

The first phase of UNFPA assisted area project was launched in 4 districts of the state in the year 1980-81. Similarly, Revamping Scheme was started in slum areas of cities having population one lakh or above in 1984-85.

Family Welfare was included as one of the main points of 20-Point Programme in this FYP. It was emphasized that all methods of contraception have to be promoted simultaneously stressing the need for motivation, persuasion and IEC with better focus. The role of education, particularly of females was underlined. Like-wise, role of extension education, motivation for voluntary acceptance of small family and involvement of voluntary agencies, Panchayati Raj Institutions, local bodies etc. were also stressed in the strategy for implementation of the programme. The plan also favoured an integrated approach to the problem of public health and proper coordination of achieves in different family planning fields.

The achievements in health sector during this FYP are as below:

Increase/Improvement*	
No. of hospitals	15
No. of dispensaries	94
No. of MCWs	13
No. of PHCs	116
No. of SHCs	1650
Total No. of Medical Institutions	1888
No. of FWCs	20
No. of beds	4519
No. of doctors	636
Health budget (million Rs.)	615.63
Per capita health budget (Rs.)	15.19
Decrease in number of population served per bed*	132
Decrease in number of population served per doctor*	506
Decrease in number of population served per institution*	2010

Seventh Five Year Plan (1984-85 to 1989-90)

In the beginning year of this FYP, there were 5518 medical institutions (186 hospitals, 1083 dispensaries, 111 MCW centres, 348 PHCs and 3790 SHCs), 390 FWCs, 21916 beds and 3476 doctors. Rs. 949.31 million were

TABLE 4.4: Seventh FYP: Expenditure Incurred on Medical and Health

Particulars	*Expenditure (Million Rs.) Descending order*
1. Allopathy	
A. Other than M.N.P.	429.96
B. M.N.P.	382.21
C. Medical Education	277.52
D. E.S.I.	4.73
E. Mobile Surgical Unit	1.52
2. Ayurved	120.04
Total	**1215.95**

Source: Draft Eighth FYP, Vol. I, 1992-97, Planning Department, GoR, Nov., 1991, Jaipur.

earmarked for health budget with Rs. 25.78 per capita budget. In this year, the number of population served per bed was 1680, per doctor was 10593 and per institution was 6673, which was lower than the year 1979-80 (starting year of the Sixth FYP).

On 15th November 1985, National Immunization Programme was started. Similarly, in the year 1987, AIDS Inspection Center was established at SMS hospital Jaipur. FP Incentive Schemes for Panchayati Raj bodies were also started in the same year.

The changed health scenario during this FYP is presented as below:

[A] Increase/Improvement*

No. of hospitals	22
No. of MCWs	6
No. of PHCs	711
No. of SHCs	4210
Total No. of Medical Institutions	4622
No. of beds	6951
No. of doctors	912
Health budget (million Rs.)	1073.51
Per capita health budget (Rs.)	22.47
Decrease in number of population served per bed*	228
Decrease in number of population served per doctor*	1039
Decrease in number of population served per institution*	2538

[B] Decrease

No. of dispensaries	327
No. of FWCs	6

With respect to FWP, this FYP stressed the need for inter-sector coordination and cooperation and the involvement of voluntary agencies in the implementation of the programme. Thrust was also laid on to adopt a strategy of consolidation of the infrastructure already available, focus attention on younger age groups couples, reorganize the management structures at the district level and the need to promote the entire range of contraceptives available and not only sterilisation. Late marriage and the social enforcement of this programme were also greatly emphasized in this FYP.

Two Annual Plans (1989-90 to 1990-91)

There were total 10140 medical institutions (208 hospitals, 756 dispensaries, 117 MCW centres, 1059 PHCs and 8000 SHCs), 384 FWCs, 28867 beds and 4388 doctors in the year 1989-90. Health budget was increased to Rs. 2022.81 million and per capita budget to Rs. 48.25. In this year, the number of population served per bed (1452), per doctor (9554) and per institution (4135) decreased in compression to year 1984-85 (beginning year of the Seventh FYP).

The changed health scenario during this FYP is presented as below:

[A] Increase/Improvement*

No. of hospitals	6
No. of MCWs	1
No. of PHCs	314
No. of beds	3328
No. of doctors	806
Health budget (million Rs.)	819.75
Per capita health budget (Rs.)	16.6
Decrease in number of population served per bed*	91
Decrease in number of population served per doctor*	1115

[B] Decrease/ Deterioration**

No. of dispensaries	481
Total No. of Medical Institutions	160
Increase in number of population served per institution**	353

Eighth Five Year Plan (1991-92 to 1996-97)

In the year 1991-92, there were total 9980 medical institutions (214 hospitals, 275 dispensaries, 118 MCW centres, 1373 PHCs and 8000 SHCs), 384 FWCs, 32195 beds and 5194 doctors. Rs. 2842.57 million were earmarked for health budget and per person budget was Rs. 64.85. In comparison to year 1989-90 (commencing year of the Seventh FYP), there was decrease registered in persons served per bed (1361) and served per doctor (8439) but increase registered in persons served per institution (4488).

The main thrust laid during the eighth plan period was on improving, consolidating and modernizing the existing health care delivery system and to correct the imbalances both in rural as well as in urban areas.

A sum of Rs. 3109.49 million was proposed for eighth plan period for medical and health sector, which included modern medicine, mobile surgical unit, medical education, ESI and Ayurved. Provision of Rs. 318.5 million had also been made for medical college, Kota.

TABLE 4.5: Eighth Five-Year Plan: Outlay for Medical and Health

Particulars	*Million Rs. (Descending order)*
1. Allopathy	
A. M.N.P.	1346.18
B. Medical Education	900.00
C. Other than M.N.P.	607.41
D. Mobile Surgical Unit	9.74
E. E.S.I.	7.47
Total (Allopathy)	2870.79
2. Ayurved	238.70
Total	**3109.49**

Source: *Draft Eighth FYP*, Vol. I, 1992-97, Planning Department, GoR, Nov., 1991, Jaipur.

In the year 1992-93, Jan-Mangal and Social Security Schemes were launched in the state, Amendment in Panchayati Raj Act was also made for elected members of panchayats and municipalities to boost FWP in the state.

On 1st April 1994, World Bank funded Cataract Blindness Control Project (CBCP) was launched in the state. Similarly, on 26th Nov., 1995 Medicare Relief Society was established.

With respect to FWP, stress was laid on involvement of Panchayati Raj Institutions and couples in the younger age group, adoption of integrated multi media approach and communication policy, strengthening of infrastructure, integrated family welfare programme approach and on welfare of women and children.

The improved as well as deteriorated changed health scenario during this FYP is as under:

[A] Increase/Improvement*

No. of hospitals	5
No. of dispensaries	3
No. of PHCs	243
No. of SHCs	1400
Total No. of Medical Institutions	1651
No. of beds	4772
No. of doctors	738
Health budget (million Rs.)	3444.53

Per capita health budget (Rs.) 78.02
Decrease in number of population served per bed* 171
Decrease in number of population served per doctor* 1021

[B] Decrease/ Deterioration**

Increase in number of population served per institution** 704

Ninth Five Year Plan (1996-97 to 2001-02)

In the commencing year of this FYP, there were total 11631 medical institutions (219 hospitals, 278 dispensaries, 118 MCW centres, 1616 PHCs and 9400 SHCs), 384 FWCs, 36967 beds and 5932 doctors in the state. Similarly, health budget was of Rs. 6287.1 million and per capita budget of Rs. 142.87. Like-wise, population served per bed came down to 1190, per doctor to 7418 and per institution to 3784 in comparison to year 1991-92 (starting year of the Eighth FYP).

TABLE: 4.6: Ninth FYP: Outlay for Medical and Health (Rajasthan)

Particulars	*Million Rs. (descending order)*
Minimum Need Programme (including BMS)	4473.19
Rajasthan Health Care (EAP)	2112.50
Medical Education (including Medicity)	1379.76
Other than MNP	1014.87
Population Control and Family Welfare	276.80
Ayurved	159.68
Mobile Surgical Unit	29.22
ESI	13.01
Total	**9459.01**

Source: *Draft Ninth FYP,* Vol. I, 1997-02, Planning Department, GoR, Jaipur.

In the year 1996-97, target approach in FWP was ended in the state. On 25th January, 1998, medicare relief societies were established in 100 beded government hospitals and CHCs. In the same year, Rajasthan AIDS Control Society was constituted. In April 1999, CNNA approach was adopted in RCH programme.

Chief Minister Jeevan Raksha Kosh (CMJRK) and Medicare Relief Society Schemes in the state were launched in the year 1999. Similarly, National Cancer Control Programme was started in the year 1999-2000. During the Ninth FYP the sum of Rs. 3769.5 million was spent on Medical and Health Department.

On 20th June 2001, amendment in the act related to recruitment into government services and for government servants was made to encourage FP. In August 2001, compensation amount failure of FP operation was raised from Rs. 50 thousand to Rs. 2 lakh if unfortunately a woman died within 30 days of the operation.

The changed health scenario during this FYP is given below:

[A] Increase/Improvement*

No. of PHCs 58
No. of SHCs 526
Total No. of Medical Institutions 603
No. of beds 951
No. of doctors 320
Health budget (million Rs.) 3935.98
Per capita health budget (Rs.) 38.15
Decrease in number of population served per bed* 299
Decrease in number of population served per doctor* 1615
Decrease in number of population served per institution* 827

[B] Decrease

No. of dispensaries	10
No. of FWCs	91

Tenth Five Year Plan (2002-07)

The first annual plan of the Tenth FYP accounted 12234 medical institutions (219 hospitals, 268 dispensaries, 118 MCW centres, 1674 rural PHCs, 29 urban PHCs and 9926 SHCs), 293 FWCs, 37918 beds and 6252 doctors. In this year, total budget allocation for health sector was of Rs. 10223.07 million and per person budget was of Rs. 181.02. Unfortunately, population served per bed (1489), per doctor (9033) and per institution (4611) was higher than the year 1996-97 (beginning year of the 9th FYP).

TABLE 4.7: Tenth Five Year Plan: Outlay for Medical and Health Services: Rajasthan (2002-07)

S.No.	*Item*	*Outlay (million Rs.) Descending Order*
1	Health Development System (EAP)	2250.00
2	Minimum Needs Programme (Including PMGY)	1374.61
3	Medical Education	1081.16
4	Other than MNP	1032.12
5	Population Control and Family Welfare	275.00
6	Ayurved Department (Including College)	203.03
7	Health Service (EFC)	164.04
8	School Health Care in Tribal Area (EAP)	151.10
9	Population Mission	54.30
10	ESI	24.29
11	Mobile Surgical Unit	19.60
	Total	6529.25

Source: Draft Tenth FYP (2002-07) Vol. I, GoR, Planning Department, Jaipur.

TABLE 4.8: Revenue Expenditure on Medical, Public Health and Family Welfare: Rajasthan

(Million Rs.)

S.No.	*Particulars*	*Accounts (2003-04)*	*Revised Estimates (2004-05)*	*Budget Estimates (2005-06)*
(A)	*Allopathy*	5955.25	6770.05	7302.10
1	Direction & Administration	105.14	115.85	124.09
2	Medical Relief	4657.75	5276.27	5607.43
3	Tribal Area Sub-Plan	220.03	288.05	331.68
4	Medical, Education & Training	768.92	873.69	1010.81
5	Employees State Insurance	193.31	204.98	215.86
6	Medical Stores Depot	10.09	11.21	12.24
(B)	*Other Systems of Medicines*	1483.46	1635.52	1783.92
1	Ayurvedic	1318.91	1466.20	1581.35
2	Tribal Area Sub-Plan	73.32	75.72	87.70
3	Homeopathy	42.05	46.98	60.07
4	Unani	31.67	34.98	42.86
5	Other Systems	17.52	11.65	11.94
(C)	*Public Health*	657.53	790.10	1487.03
(D)	*Family Welfare*	2042.61	1818.35	1986.96
	Total	**10138.85**	**11014.01**	**12559.99**

Source: Budget Study, 2005-06, Directorate of Economics & Statisticas, Rajasthan, Jaipur.

An outlay of Rs. 195.44 millions has been proposed for the Directorate of Ayurvedic and Rs. 7.59 millions for the government ayurvedic college, Udaipur during tenth FYP period. A sum of Rs. 35.54 millions has been proposed for Ayurvedic department.

TABLE: 4.9: Tenth FYP: Outlay for MNP, Other than MNP and Medical Education

Particulars	*Outlay (Million Rs.)Descending Order*
Minimum Needs Programme	
Opening of 300 SHCs	244.20
Construction of 400 SHCs building	160.00
IEC Activities	60.00
SIHFW	49.60
For the working of PHCs	38.90
Renovation and modernization of rural institutions	31.45
METP	25.00
To provide 51 ambulances	20.40
To provide x-ray machines to CHCs	15.64
Disaster management	6.00
Telephone at Dy. CM & HO's office	4.72
Strengthening of SHCs	3.45
200 Calory metres in CHCs	3.00
Other Than Minimum Needs Programme	
Straightening of general nursing training centres	180.63
Jeevan Raksha Kosh	50.00
Renovation and modernization of hospitals building	41.09
Bio waste management	34.30
Medical technology in district hospital	27.70
Strengthening of drug lab	19.34
METP	18.49
Construction of district hospital building	1.00
Medical Education	
Medical College, Kota	354.00
Medical College, Jaipur	231.83
Medical College, Jodhpur	200.00
Medical College, Bikaner	113.30
Medical College, Ajmer	96.80
Medical College, Udaipur	85.25

Source: Draft Tenth FYP, Vol. I, 2002-07, Planning Departmen, GoR, Jaipur.

TABLE 4.10: Budget Provision for Medical and Health under MNP and Other Than MNP: Rajasthan (2004-05)

(Million Rs.)

S. No.	*Particulars*	*Budget Provision*		
		Original	*Revised*	*Final Revised*
1.	Minimum Need Programme (MNP)	157.03	157.03	214.71
2.	Other Than MNP	206.90	212.74	214.74
	Total	**363.93**	**369.77**	**429.51**

Source: *'Pragati Prativedan'*, 2004-05, Directorate of Medical and Health, GoR, Jaipur.

TABLE 4.11: Budget Estimates 2005-06 and Revised Estimates 2004-05: Family Welfare, Rajasthan

(Million Rs.)

Name of Scheme	*Budget Estimates*		
	2004-05		*2005-06*
	Consolidated	*Revised*	
State Plan	106.80	120.00	109.43
Non-Plan	264.75	247.56	268.20
C.S.S.	1445.14	1418.27	1541.16
Total	**2073.1**	**1801.9**	**1750.7**

Source: *'Pragati Prativedan'*, 2004-05, Directorate of Medical, Health & Family Welfare Services, Rajasthan, Jaipur.

TABLE 4.12: Family Welfare: Budget Estimates 2005-06 and Revised Estimates 2004-05 (Non-Plan)

(Million Rs.)

Name of Scheme	*Budget Estimates*		
	2004-05		*2005-06*
	Budget Estimates	*Revised Estimates*	
Direction and Adm.-State F.W. Bureau (Hq.)	0.45	0.48	0.52
Laproscopic Training	7.46	7.84	8.44
RFWS- at PHC	176.07	167.74	178.74
MCH Centre	72.47	71.50	80.50
Total	**264.75**	**247.56**	**268.20**

Source: *'Pragati Prativedan'*, 2004-05, Directorate of Medical, Health and Family Welfare Services, Rajasthan, Jaipur.

In the year 2003-04, voluntary blood testing centres were established in 26 district hospitals. Similarly, various incentive and compensation schemes to promote FP were launched in the state. Incentive schemes of cash payment for FP operation and for NGO and for private hospitals started. In compensation scheme, provision was made that a woman will be given Rs. 5000 in cash and free MTP facility in case of failure of FP operation.

TABLE 4.13: Family Welfare: Budget Estimates 2005-06 and Revised Estimates 2004-05 (Plan)

(Million Rs.)

Name of Scheme	*Budget Estimates*		
	2004-05		*Budget Estimates*
	Budget Estimates	*Revised Estimates*	*2005-06*
Direction and Administration			
State F.W. Bureau (IEC)	5.7	4.0	4.5
Compensation			
Population Control Measure	69.0	83.9	71.2
Mass Education (Jan Mangal)	32.1	32.1	33.7
Grand Total	**106.8**	**120.0**	**109.4**

Source: *'Pragati Prativedan'*, 2004-05, Directorate of Medical, Health & Family Welfare Services, Rajasthan, Jaipur.

TABLE 4.14: Budget Estimates 2005-06 and Revised Estimates 2004-05: Family Welfare (CSS)

(Million Rs.)

Particulars	*Budget Estimates*		
	2003-04		*Budget Estimates*
	Budget Estimates	*Revised Estimates*	*2004-05*
State Sectt. Cell	0.7	1.7	1.8
State F.W. Bureau	14.1	14.1	15.3
District F.W. Bureau	105.4	97.9	107.8
Regional Health and FW Centre	7.5	7.5	7.6
ANM Training Centre	63.3	72.8	71.8
Rural FW Centres at Sub-Centres	820.9	787.7	879.7
Urban FW Centres	50.0	52.6	56.6
Urban FW Centres Run by Vol. Org.	2.0	1.2	1.2
Externally aided CSSM Project (kind)	180.0	180.0	180.0
POL & Repairs	4.7	5.4	5.9
State Health Trans. Org.	0.5	1.4	1.4
Compensation (IUD, Vasectomy & Tubectomy)	96.0	96.0	112.0
Conventional Contraceptives GoI (kinds)	100.0	100.0	100.0
Total	**1445.1**	**1418.3**	**1541.2**

Source: *'Pragati Prativedan'*, 2004-05, Directorate of Medical, Health & Family Welfare Services, Rajasthan, Jaipur.

BOX 4.1: CHRONOLOGICAL HIGHLIGHTS

1947	: **First Medical College of Rajasthan Established at Jaipur.**
1948	: **Malaria Control and Eradication Programme** started.
1951	: **2 Para Medical Centres** started at Jaipur (one each for male and female nursing training)
1952	: **Family Planning Programme** was launched in Rajasthan.
1954-55	: **National Malariya Control Programme** was launched.
1956	: **Mobile Surgical Unit** started
1958	: **National Malariya Eradication Programme** was launched.
1959	: **Medical College at Bikaner** established
1962	: **Medical College at Udaipur** established
1963	: **Family Planning Programme** was recognized.
1965	: **Medical College at Jodhpur** established.
1966-67	: **FP Programme** was made target oriented and time bounded.
1967-69	: **Family Planning Department** was formed.
1970	: **Hospital Post-Partum Programme** launched.
1970-71	: **National Leprosy Eradication Programme** started in Rajasthan
1973	: **Medical College at Ajmer** established
1975	: **Integrated Child Development Service (ICDS) Programme** launched
1975-76	: **NMEP was Merged** with the general health system and changed from unipurpose to multipurpose functioning.
1975-76	: **MPW (Multipurpose Worker) Scheme** was started.
1976	: **National Blindness Control Programme (NBCP)** started in Rajasthan.
1977	: **Family Planning** was made a concurrent subject.
1977	: **Rural Health Scheme** launched
1977	: **Revised National TB Control Programme** started in Rajasthan.
1977	: **Village Health Guide Scheme** started.
1977	: **Modified Plan of Operation (MPO)** in Malariya eradication was started.
1977	: **Community Health Volunteers (CHV)** Scheme was started in Selected PHCs.
1978	: **FP Programme was renamed as ' FWP'**
1979	: **Distribution of Oral Pills** was introduced in FWP.
1980-81	: **I Phase of UNFPA Assisted Area Project** started in 4 districts.
1984-85	: **Revamping Scheme** launched in the slum areas of cities having population one lakh or above
19th Nov. 85	: **National Immunization Programme (NIP)** started
1987	: **AIDS Inspection Center** was established at SMS hospital, Jaipur
1987-88	: **FP Incentive Scheme** for panchayati raj bodies started
1992	: **Amendment In Act** was made for elected members of panchayats and municipalities to boost FWP
1992-93	: **Jan-Mangal Scheme (JMS)** started
1992-93	: **Social Security Scheme** started
1st April, 94	: **World-Bank Funded Cataract Blindness Control Project (CBCP)** started
26th Nov, 95	: **Medicare Relief Society** established
1996-97	: **Target Approach in FWP** was ended
1997	: **TFA has been renamed as CNAA**
1998	: **Rajasthan AIDS Control Society** was constituted
25th Jan 98	: **Medicare Relief Societies** established in govt. hospitals (100-beded) and CHC
Mar. 1999	: **Chief Minister Jeevan Raksha Kosh (CMJRK) Scheme** started
April 1999	: **CNNA** approach was adopted in RCH programme
Nov. 1999	: **Medicare Relief Society Scheme** started to encourage FP.
1999-2000	: **National Cancer Control Programme** started in Rajasthan.
20th June, 01	: **Amendment** in the act related to entry into govt. services and for govt. servants was made to encourage FP.
Aug. 2001	: **Compensation Amount in FP Operation was Raised** from Rs. 50 thousand to Rs. 2 lakh if a woman died within 30 days of operation
2003-04	: **Voluntary Blood Testing Centres** established in 26 district hospitals.
4th Mar. 04	: **Compensation Scheme** started in FP. In case of failure of FP operation woman will be given Rs. 5000 in cash and free MTP facility.
13th Apr.04	: **Incentive Scheme of Cash Payment** for family planning operation started
17th May 04	: **Incentive Scheme for NGO and Private Hospitals** started to promote FWP
24th Aug. 04	: **'Rajasthan Health System Development Project' (RHSDP)** was launched
Sep. 2004	: **'Sanjivini' Health Programme** was launched
4th Oct. 04	: **Mother And Child Health Day Scheme** started
1st Dec.04	: **'Jeevan Jyoti', Rajasthan's First Community Service Center for AIDS** started at Jaipur
Feb. 2005	: **'Revised Sanjivini' Health Programme** was started
2005	: **New Blood Bank** is being opened at district hospital Dausa.
2005	: **Model Art Blood Banks** are being opened at Jaipur and Udaipur medical colleges.
12th April 05	: **National Rural Health Mission was launched.**
12th April 05	: **New Standards for CHC were announced by GoI.**
4th May 05	: **Rajasthan High Court directed the Indian Railway Board to Provide medical teams in long distance trains.**
5th July 05	: **'Free Medical Facility to Journalist Scheme' announced by GoR.**
25th Aug. 05	: **Rajasthan's First Community Eye Bank was established at Jaipur by 'Eye Bank Socitiey of Raj.' in Collaboration with Orbis International of USA.**

TABLE 4.15: Number of Ayurved and Other Institution: Rajasthan (upto Dec. 2004)

No.

S.No.	*Name of Pathy*	*Hospital (Beded)*		*Dispensary*		*Total*		*Grand*
		Rural	*Urban*	*Rural*	*Urban*	*Rural*	*Urban*	*Total*
1.	Ayurved	25	58	3308	174	3333	232	3565
2.	Homeopathy	—	2	50	63	50	65	115
3.	Unani	—	3	45	43	45	46	91
4.	Naturopathy	—	2	1	2	1	4	5

Source: *Economic Review*, 2004-05, DES, Rajasthan, Jaipur, PP 74.

With respect to medical education, 6 medical colleges are already imparting graduate and post-graduate education in all the major specialties at Jaipur, Jodhpur, Udaipur, Ajmer, Bikaner and Kota. Reorganisation of medical education is also being expanded during the period.

The improved as well as deteriorated health scenario during this FYP upto 2004-05 is presented below:

[A] Increase/Improvement*

No. of PHC	3
No. of SHCs	461
Total No. of Medical Institutions	463
No. of beds	955
Health budget (million Rs.)	1225.86
Per capita health budget (Rs.)	21.58
Decrease in number of population served per bed*	35
Decrease in number of population served per institution*	143

[B] Decrease/ Deterioration**

No. of doctors	76
Increase in number of population served per doctor**	116

'Jeevan Jyoti', Rajasthan's first community service center for AIDS was also started at Jaipur in the year 2003-04. Like-wise, Rajasthan Health System Development Project (RHSDP) and Mother and Child Health Day Scheme were also started in the same year. In February 2005, 'Revised Sanjivini' health programme was started in the state. Model art blood banks are being opened at Jaipur and Udaipur medical colleges.

5

PROGRAMMES AND SCHEMES

Various Health and Family Welfare Programmes/Schemes at national level as well as at state level are launched in Rajasthan to tackle the menace of communicable and non-communicable diseases. Coverage of disease surveillance programme is also being extended to prevent outbreak of infectious diseases. Various institutions and organizations engaged in health care, medical education and research are continuously being strengthened to tackle the emerging diseases. Rural health forms part of the MNP and Basic Minimum Services Programme and nearly 3/4th of the total provision of health plan has been made for rural health in the State.

Under the medical and health department, major programmes include: National Rural Health Mission (NRHM); National Programme for the Control/Eradication of Maleria, Leprosy, Blindness, AIDS, TB, Cancer, Cholera and Guineaworm; Chief Minister Jeevan Raksha Kosh/Sahayata Kosh; Rajasthan Health System Project; Sanjivini Scheme and National Surveillance Programmes (Chart 5.1).

CHART 5.1

Health Programmes and Schemes (Rajasthan) →

- National Rural Health Mission (NRHM)*
- National Malaria Control/Eradication Programme
- National Leprosy Control Programme
- National Programme for the Control of Blindness
- National AIDS Control Programme
- National/Revised National TB Control Programme
- National Cancer Control Programme
- National Cholera Control Programme
- National Filaria Control Programme
- National Goitre Control Programme
- Guineaworm Eradication Control Programme
- Chief Minister Jeevan Raksha Kosh (CMJRK)
- Chief Minister Sahayata Kosh (CMSK)
- Medicare Relief Card (MRC) Scheme
- Rajasthan Health System Development Project (RHSDP)
- Sanjivini Scheme
- National Water and Sanitation Programme
- National Surveillance Programme for Communicable Diseases

Note: * For Recentaly Launched "NATIONAL RURAL HEALTH MISSION (NRHM)", Please see Box 12.1.

Similarly, various Family Welfare Programmes have been launched in the state. These are: Reproductive and Child Health (RCH), Universal Immunisation Programme (UIP), Special Pulse Polio Scheme, Pilot Project on Hepatitis-B Vaccine, UNICEF Assisted Women Health Project, UNFPA Assisted Projects, Jan Mangal (JM), Raj Laxmi (RL), Vikalp Yojana, Minimum Needs Programme (MNP), National Motherhood Benefit Scheme (NMBS), Integrated Child Development Services (ICDS), Social Security Scheme etc. (Chart 5.2).

Objectives

The main objectives of these programmes/schemes are as under:

1. To reduce mortality, morbidity and fertility indicators.
2. Population stabilization.
3. To improve the quality of life.
4. To reinforce the delivery of primary, secondary and tertiary health care.

CHART 5.2

Family Welfare Programmes and Schemes (Rajasthan)

- Reproductive and Child Health Programme
- Expended Programme of Immunization (EPI)/Universal Immunization Programme (UIP)
- Special Pulse Polio Scheme (SPPS)
- Pilot Project on Hepatitis-B Vaccine
- UNFPA Assisted Area Project (UAAP)
- UNFPA Assisted Integrated Population and Development (IPD) Project Phase II
- UNICEF Assisted Women's Health Programme
- European Commission Assisted Health and FWP
- Post-Partum Centre Scheme
- Pariwar Seva Sansthan (PSS)
- Pariwar Kalyan Pension Yojana (PKPY)
- Jan Mangal Scheme (JMS)
- National Rural Health Mission*
- Rajasthan Health Care Project (EAP)
- Vikalp Yojana
- National Motherhood Benefit Scheme (NMBS)
- Raj Laxmi Scheme (RLS)
- Minimum Needs Programme (MNP)
- Integrated Child Development Services (ICDS) Scheme
- Employees State Insurance Scheme (ESIS)
- UNICEF Assisted Border Districts Community Strategy Project
- Static and FRU Center Scheme
- Revamping Scheme
- Village Health Guide Scheme (VHGS)
- Social Security Scheme (SSS)

Note: * For Recentaly Launched "National Rural Health Mission (NRHM)", Please see Box 12.1.

The national programmes are vertical programmes and are sponsored by central government. These programmes are generally initiated with the international collaborations which provide financial and technical assistance alongwith equipments support. These programmes are being implemented by state government through the network of primary health centres. In this chapter a brief description of important health and family welfare programmes/schemes is presented.

BOX- 5.1: National Health Policy, 2002

The upsurge in health care development coincided with the National Health Policy formulated in 1983 with the objective of achieving 'Health for All by 2000 AD' in Rajasthan. The basic objective of the National Health Policy-2002 is to achieve an acceptable standard of good health amongst the general population of the country. This covers all aspects of health care and contains policy prescriptions covering various issues including, inter alia, financial resources, equity, delivery of national public health programmes, public health infrastructure, education of health care professionals, health research, role of various stakeholder-NGOs, civil society, enforcement of quality standards for food and drugs, women's health etc.

Source: Health Report, 2003, GoI, New Delhi.

National Rural Health Mission (NRHM)

- Launched in Rajasthan: On 6th June 2005 (12th April, 05 in India) at a state level consultation meet.
- For the first year, a budget of Rs. 2642.6 million has been set aside for the state and was likely to appreciate in the following years.
- The nationwide mission, which will last till 2012, will focused on 18 states with low human development indices (HDI) including Rajasthan. For details please see Box 12.1.

NATIONAL MALARIA CONTROL/ERADICATION PROGRAMME AND ENHANCED MALARIYA CONTROL PROJECT (NMCP/NMEP/EMCP)

NMCP launched in	:	1954-55, (2 units established at Ajmer and Jalor)
Funded by	:	100 per cent by central government
NMEP launched in	:	1958
Expenditure share	:	GoI : GoR 50 : 50

Objectives

- Government of India provides material assistance in form of insecticide i.e. DDT, Malathion (Technical), larvicides and drugs. The state governments bear all other expenses of programme implementation.
- Eradication of malaria (total ending of transmission of malaria).
- Elimination of reservoirs of infection.
- Prevention of re-establishment of malaria.

Administrative Set-Up

Additional Director (RH & Malaria) ↓ Joint Director ↓ State Entomologist	State Level
Joint Director ↓ Dy. Director ↓ Zonal Entomologist	Zonal Level
Dy. Chief Medical and Health Officer (Malaria) ↓ Assistant Malaria Officer	District Level
Medical Officer ↓ Malaria Inspector ↓ Laboratory Technician	PHC Level
↓ Sector Supervisor	Sector Level
↓ MPW	SHC Level

Activities

- Surveillance and radical treatment of the detected cases fortnightly.
- Active surveillance involves collecting blood slides from fever cases during house to house fortnightly visits by the MPW at the villages level.
- Passive surveillance entails taking blood slides from fever patients from hospitals/PHC.
- Indoor residual spray with insecticides (DDT) twice a year.
- Anti larval operation.

Structural/Functional Changes

In 1975-76, integrated with the general health services at the grassroot level with the implementation of multipurpose worker scheme. However, at the state and district level, the programme maintained its vertical identity.

Modified Plan of Operation (MPO) launched in April 1977

Components

- Interruption of transmission by residual spray of insecticides in the areas having annual parasite incidence (API) more than 2.
- Reduction of reservoir of human infection by case detection through surveillance mechanism and treatment.

OPERATION MALARIA CONTROL MOVEMENT (OMCM)

Started from August 2004

Centres established for:

Free distribution of medicines	:	27156
Fever treatment	:	2541
Fever treatment sub-centres	:	11163
Malaria clinics	:	1514
Mobile groups	:	45

Malaria Crash Programme

Implemented through district collector

Stage I	:	1st Jan. to 14th May, 2004
Stage II	:	15th Oct to 30th Nov., 2004

Enhanced Malaria Control Project (EMCP)

Launched in	:	Sept. 1997
Period	:	Sept. 1997 to March 2005
Funding agency	:	World Bank. Material assistance in terms of insecticides, drugs etc. as well as cash assistance through State and District Malaria Control Societies.
Districts covered	:	12 (10 + 2*) mainly hard core pre dominantly tribal (Banswara, Baran, Bhilwara, Bundi, Chittaurgarh, Dungarpur, Jhalawar, Rajsamand, Sirohi, Udaipur, Barmer* and Jaisalmer*)
Block PHC covered	:	38 (34 + 4*) mainly hard core pre-dominantly tribal blocks
Population of PHC covered	:	5 million
Cities covered	:	2, Jodhpur and Bharatpur (high risk urban areas)

Components

- Early case detection and treatment,
- Selective vector control and personal protection,
- Capacity building and
- Epidemic planning and rapid response.
- IEC activities

The project facilitated strengthening of surveillance including malaria microscopy and introduction of rapid diagnostic kits to ensure early case detection. Newer medicines like Artemisinine derivatives have also been introduced in the programme for management of severe and complicated malaria besides use of alternative new generation safer insecticides like synthetic parathyroid, biological control agents and insectides treated mosquito nets.

The project also facilitated capacity building for epidemic preparedness and response as well as manpower development at various levels of programme implementation. Progress has also been made in intensifying IEC activities and establishing computerized management information system with World Bank support.

Under the project, State Malaria Society has been constituted and orientation of state level functionaries have also been undertaken.

Fund allotted : Rs. 54.7 million
Expenditure incurred : Rs. 46.5 million

TABLE 5.1: Malaria Epidemiological Situation, Rajasthan (1981-2004)

Year	*Blood Slides Collected ('000 No.)*	*Maleria Cases ('000 No.)*	*Plasmodium Falciparum (PF) Cases ('000 No.)*	*Annual Blood Examination Rate (ABER)*	*SFR*	*Slide Positive Rate (SPR)*
1981	3991.7	100.7	14.8	11.0	0.4	2.50
1991	3178.4	77.6	16.1	7.2	0.5	2.40
2001	6745.2	129.2	17.4	11.9	0.3	1.92
2002	5691.3	68.6	5.3	10.1	0.1	1.21
2003	7832.1	142.8	16.4	13.9	0.2	1.82
2004	7236.1	104.2	7.3	—	0.1	1.47

Source: *'Pragati Prativedan'*, Various Issues, Department of Medical and Health, GoR, Jaipur.

NATIONAL ANTI-MALARIA PROGRAMME (NAMP)

Dengue/Dengue Hemorrhagic Fever (DHF)

Dengue/DHF a viral infection is also widely prevalent in Rajasthan as well as in India. Since, 1996 Dengue/ DHF is being monitored under NAMP.

Monitoring Strategy

- Surveillance for disease and vector.
- Early diagnosis and prompt cases management.
- Vector control through community participation and social mobilization.
- Capacity building.

TABLE 5.2: Dengue Causes and Deaths: Rajasthan Vis-à-Vis India (1997-02)

	1997		*1998*		*1999*		*2000*		*2001*		*2002***	
	Cases	*Deaths*	*Cases*	*Deaths*	*Cases*	*Deaths*	*Cases*	*Deaths*	*Cases*	*Deaths*	*Cases*	*Deaths*
Raj.	18	1	2	0	1	0	0	0	1452	35*	163	5
India	1177	36	707	18	944	17	622	7	3278	53	748	15

Source: Health Report, 2003, GoI, New Delhi.
* Suspected Deaths,
** Up to Oct. 2002.

BOX 5.2: Medicare Relief Societies (MRS) Rajasthan

- *Constituted on* 26th Sep. 1995.
- *Total No. (up to Nov. 04)*: 320.
- *Objectives*: To provide modern health testing facility and medical treatment to patients.
- *Established at*
  * Medical Colleges and hospitals at zonal and district headquarters
  * Also established at 100 beded govt. hospitals and CHCs from 25th Jan. 1998
- *Margin money allotted*: Rs. 42.1 million, during 1995-97 period
- *Norms*
  * 25 per cent of earned amount should be utilized for providing free medicines to medicare relief card holders and their families.
  * Free of cost medical treatment facility should be provided to widows, orphans, accidental patients, prisoners and old persons.

BOX 5.3: Population Policy and Rajiv Gandhi Population Mission: Rajasthan

(A) Population Policy:

Objectives
- Bringing fertility rate at 2.1 by 2011.
- Ensuring minimum age of marriage of girls at 18 years, by 2010.
- Promoting couple protection rate to 65 per cent by 2011.
- Complete immunization of 90 per cent children by 2007.
- Polio eradication; control on diarrohea, dysentery and pneumonia, nutritional improvement.
- Promoting male participation in family planning.
- Ensuring 100% safe delivery by trained personnel by 2005.
- Raising level of institutional deliveries to 50 per cent by 2011.

Strategy to be adopted are
- Ensuring pre-natal and post-natal effective services.
- Child health.
- Adoption of effective methods for couple protection and ensuring male population.
- Ensuring marriage at the legally permissible age.
- Encouraging responsible parenthood.
- Safe delivery services.

(B) Rajiv Gandhi Population Mission
Set up on July 5, 2001

Objectives
Population Mission aims at tackling the problem through 'Mission Approach', with a time bound frame.
- To bring down birth rate from 31.1 per thousand to 18.4 by 2011.
- To bring down Infant Mortality Rate (IMR) from 81 per thousand of live births, to 56 by 2011.
- To reduce death rate from 8.4 per thousand to 7.0 by 2011.
- To bring down TFR at 2.1 by 2011.
- Rising contraceptive prevalence rate at 68 by 2011.

Strategies to be adopted are
- Creating demand for reproductive health and family welfare services.
- Expanding outreach or reproductive health and family welfare services.
- Concentrating on unmet need of reproductive and child health and family planning services.
- Effective implementation of laws and acts.
- Effective inter-regional coordination.

Source: Rajiv Gandhi Population Mission, Rajasthan, Jaipur.

NATIONAL LEPROSY CONTROL/ERADICATION PROGRAMME (NLCP/NLEP) RAJASTHAN

NLCP Launched in	:	1970-71, as a 100 per cent centrally aided programme.
NLEP Launched in	:	1980-81, jointly run by the State and the Central Government
NLEP II Phase Launched in	:	June 2001
• Funding by	:	World Bank
• Period	:	3 years

Main Objective

To eradicate leprosy in the state through:

- Detection of the leprosy patients.
- Quick treatment of detected patients.
- Preventing and limiting disabilities.
- Health education and rehabilitation.
- Integrating leprosy services with existing health care systems

District Covered : 32 (all)

Strategy

- Integration of leprosy services with general health care system.
- Leprosy training of health functionaries.
- Surveillance for early diagnosis and prompt MDT, through routine and special efforts.
- Intensified IEC using local and mass media approaches.
- Prevention of disability and care.
- Monitoring and evaluation on regular (monthly/quarterly/annually) basis as well as with special efforts such as independent evaluation, Leprosy Elimination Monitoring (LEM), annual survey and validation of elimination etc.

Functioning

- Supervised and controlled by state leprosy officer and district leprosy officer at state and district level respectively.
- Implemented through an independent state leprosy control unit supported by:

Zonal leprosy units	:	7
Leprosy control units	:	6 (Bharatpur, Bundi, Jhalawar, Udaipur, Ganganagar and Baran)
Urban leprosy control centres	:	5 (Jaipur, Jodhpur, Udaipur, Kota and Jaipur)
20 beded leprosy wards	:	In all the general hospitals affiliated to Jaipur, Jodhpur, Udaipur and Bikaner colleges
Leprosy hospitals	:	Jaipur and Jodhpur
District leprosy skeleton units	:	22 (Ajmer, Alwar, Barmer, Banswara, Bhilwara, Bikaner, Churu, Chittaurgarh, Dausa, Dhaulpur, Dungarpur, Hanumangarh, Jaisalmer, Jalor, Jhunjhunun, Pali, Karauli, Rajsamand, Sikar, Sirohi, Sawai Madhopur and Tonk.
Involvement of NGOs	:	NGO serving in NLEP are given Rs. 200 per bed per month.

Survey, Education and Treatment (SET) Centres

Above 75, attached to PHC/dispensaries/hospitals in rural areas.

Modified Leprosy Elimination Campaign (MLEC)

With the package of teaching/training, intensified IEC, special efforts for case detection and prompt MDT were put together and implemented to facilitate efforts toward leprosy elimination. While involving the general health care staff, district technical support teams (DTSTs) and community volunteers, intensive campaigns have been carried out by the state government.

Intensive Media Campaign

For generating public awareness through television, radio, press etc. IEC activities are frequently implemented across the state.

Multi Drug Therapy (MDT)

- Launched in all the 32 districts of Rajasthan by GoI.
- Districts having very low leprosy prevalence rate (<1) are 30
- Districts having low leprosy prevalence rate (1 to 2) are 2 (Jaipur and Baran)
- I Stage completed in Sep. 2000
- II Stage completed in Mar. 2004. Mobile leprosy units are functioning under all the district leprosy eradication committees headed by respective Zila Pramukh.

TABLE 5.3: National Leprosy Eradication Programme, Rajasthan : Achievements (1999-04)

Year	*Detection and Treatment of New Leprosy Patients*			*Patients Cured*			*Leprosy Prevalence Rate*
	Target	*Achievement*	*%*	*Target*	*Achievement*	*%*	*(Per 10,000 Pop.)*
1999-2000	2500	2689	108	12000	6977	58	1.08
2000-2001	1200	2033	169	7000	3679	53	0.82
2001-2002	1200	2390	199	5000	2409	48	0.76
2002-2003	800	2212	277	5000	2791	56	0.66
2003-2004	800	2111	264	5000	3555	71	0.38
2004-2005*	—	957	—	264	1079	—	0.36

* up to Dec. 04.

Source: *'Pragati Prativedan'*, 2003-04 & 2004-05, Department of Medical and Health, GoR, Jaipur.

Total leprosy cases detected up to Dec. 2004	:	54,535
Patients cured	:	52,396
Patients presently under treatment	:	2,139

NATIONAL PROGRAMME FOR CONTROL OF BLINDNESS (NPCB)

Launched in 1976 as a 100 per cent centrally sponsored programme.

Objectives

- To reduce blindness up to 0.3 per cent, by the year 2000 A.D.
- To provide comprehensive eye care through primary health care.
- Increase ophthalmic services in the state through extended eye camps.
- To strengthen infrastructural facilities.

World Bank Funded Cataract Blindness Control Project

- Launched in : 1994
- Period : 1st April 1994 to 30th June 2002.
- Presently sponsored by GoI, through supply of materials, machineries, instruments and appliances. Subsidy is given to NGOs to perform eye operations.

Objectives

- To reduce blindness through identification and treatment of blinds.
- To develop eye care facilities in every district.

- To develop human resources for providing eye care services.
- To improve quality of service delivery.
- To secure participation of voluntary organisations in eye care.

Plan of Action for X FYP Plan (2002-07)

- Strengthening of infrastructure for eye care including facilities of Intra Ocular Lens (IOL), human resource development and free service delivery of the poor.
- Identification and treatment of bilateral blind person.
- Strengthening of the follow up of operated cases for provision of corrective glasses.
- School eye screening programme for detection and correction of refractive errors and eye banking services.
- Prevention and control of childhood blindness.

Administrative Set-up

Joint Director (Ophthalmic Cell) ↓	← State Level
Consultants (Medical Colleges) ↓	← Apex Institution
Specialists (Regional Mobile Eye Units) ↓	← Zonal Level
Specialists (District Mobile Eye Units) Specialists (District/Sub-District Hospitals) ↓	← District Level
Ophthalmic Assistants (Primary Health Centres)	← Block Level

Achievements (1994-2004)

- Rajasthan blindness control committee is formed and registered.
- District blindness control committees are formed and registered in all the 32 districts under the chairmanship of District Collectors.
- Ophthalmic department of all the 6 medical colleges are strengthened.
- 19 district hospitals and 228 PHCs are strengthened.
- Imparted training to 160 eye specialists (of medical colleges and district hospitals).
- *School eye screening programme*: Children are being screened by trained teachers. After confirmation by ophthalmic assistant, glasses are prescribed or provided free of cost to the poor.
- *Collection and utilisation of donated eyes*: Hospital retrieval programme envisages motivation of relatives of terminally ill patients, accident victims and other patients having grave diseases to donate eyes. Eye donation fortnight is organised from 25th August to 8th September every year to promote eye denotation/ eye banking.
- *Commodity Assistance*: Major equipments viz. operation microscope, slit lamp, anterior vitrectomy unit, keratometer, scan binometer, yag laser and indirect ophthalmoscopes were supplied under World Bank assisted project:
- Eye camps having all facilities with free of cost are organised for cataract operation for the people of remote areas with joint efforts of NGOs, district blindness control committees and district mobile surgical units.
- Huge quantity of vitamin-A solution is distributed among children.
- NGO are paid Rs. 500 per operation and Rs. 750 per lens transplantation.
- Static centres established at 75 places to perform eye operations on scheduled dates.
- 44 operation theatre, 44 wards each with 20 beds and 211 dark rooms are constructed.
- Refractive and other eye care facilities are also made available across the state.

Financial Provision Made During 2004-05

Particulars	*Amount (in million Rs.)*
State Ophthalmic Cell	0.8
19 District Mobile Units	11.0
Assistance to NGO	8.0

BOX 5.4: Medicare Relief Card (MRC) Scheme

- *Launched in Nov. 1999*
- *Objective*: to provide free of cost medical treatment facilities to BPL families and persons who are suffering from chronic diseases.
- Medical Relief Card are given to identified BPL families in rural as well as in urban areas. Card holders are entitled to free medical facilities in all government hospitals of the state.

Table 5.4: Medicare Relief Card Scheme, Rajasthan Achievements: (1999-04)

Year	*Beneficiaries (Lakh No.)*	*Expenditure (Million Rs.)*
1999-2000	1.28	1.9
2000-2001	3.69	9.2
2001-2002	7.52	37.5
2002-2003	8.26	39.2
2003-2004	11.72	29.2
2004-2005*	6.12	17.5

Source: *'Pragati Prativedan'*, 2003-04 and 2004-05, Deptt. of Medical and Health, GoR, Jaipur.
* up to Nov. 04.

NATIONAL AIDS CONTROL PROGRAMME (NACP)

NACP I Stage : 1992-99
Financial Assistance By : World Bank

Achievements

- Licensing of blood banks
- Remarkable achievement in blood safety by making compulsory testing of 4 diseases viz HIV, Hepatitis-B, Malaria and VDRL.
- Strengthening of 14 STD clinics (one each at 6 medical colleges and 8 district hospitals)
- Treatment of STD made free of cost.
- State AIDS control society established (SACS) in Dec. 1998.

NACP II Stage (1999-2004)

Project Amount : Rs. 866.2 Million
Funding Share (%): WB : GoI, 85 : 15
Implemented Through: State AIDS Control Society (SACS)

Objectives

- To stabilize the infection level of HIV/AIDS in the general population.
- To reduce the blood borne transmission of HIV to less than 1 per cent of total transmissions.
- To attain awareness level up to 90 per cent among the youth and others in reproductive age group and
- Strengthening states resources to fight AIDS.
- Use of condom to be increased up to 90 per cent in truck operators, commercial sex worker and among migrants.

Implementation

For the expeditious implementation of the programme, the GoR constituted State AIDS Control Society. NACO (National AIDS Control Organisation) is providing adequate support including technical, managerial and financial resources to the SACS for the implementation of the programme components. Government of India has approved the National AIDS Prevention and Control Policy and National Blood Policy with the aim to adapt a more holistic approach towards prevention and control of HIV/AIDS. The policy envisages effective containment of the infection levels of HIV/AIDS in the general population in order to achieve zero level of new infection by 2007.

Achievements and Facilities Developed

Sentinel Surveillance

- Based on the HIV prevalence rates in adult population in States/UTs estimated from National Sentinel Surveillance round 2001. Rajasthan state is included Group III where the HIV infection in any of the high-risk groups is still less than 5 per cent and is less than 1 per cent among ante-natal women.
- Targeted interventions aimed at groups at high risk are being implemented across the state. These interventions provide a package of services comprising behaviour change, communication, counselling provision of health care services such as STD treatment and creation of enabling environment.
- Sex workers, intra-venous drug users, men having sex with men, truckers, migrant labourers and street children.

Treatment and Control of STD

- 38 STD clinics are working.
- 33 STD clinics (32 district clinics + 1 Janana hospital, Jaipur) are identified by National AIDS Control Organisation (NACO) and are being strengthened.
- Free treatment of STD is being provided at these STD clinics.
- Consumable medicines worth Rs 1 lakh per annum is provided to these clinics. Fifty per cent amount is for female patients.

Blood Safety

- The government adopted the National Blood Policy in April, 2002 and put in place a dynamic action plan to operationalise this NBP with significant revitalization of the existing blood transfusion services.
- HIV-free blood is being provided to AIDS patients through 66 blood banks (43 govt + 23 pvt) in the state.
- NACO selected 40 blood banks (8 major + 31 district level) for modernization.
- Consumable medicines worth Rs. 3 lakh per annum is provided to each major blood bank.
- Consumable medicines worth Rs. 1.25 lakh per annum is provided to each district blood bank.
- New blood bank is going to be established at district hospital Dausa.
- Model art blood banks are going to be established at Jaipur and Udaipur medical colleges.
- More than 1.42 million blood samples were tested (from 1987 to Dec. 2004):
- Percentage of HIV inflected (eleza reactive) was 0.32.

Voluntary Consultancy and HIV Testing Centres (VCHTS)

- Established at microbiological department of all the 6 medical colleges.
- In the year 2003-04 these centres were also opened at 26 district hospitals.
- Total 5282 patients were inspected (1999 to Dec. 04).
- 770 (14.6%) patients were found HIV positive.

Family Health Awareness Campaign (FHAC) Swasthya Youwan Mela

- It is an effort to address the management of STDs and HIV/AIDS by generating awareness amongst rural and urban slums by social mobilization through community participation. Early diagnosis and treatment of these infections are achieved by involving health functionaries by training them in syndromic management of STDs and providing drugs for treatment of such infections.
- In 5 stages, door to door contact has been made to people in the age group of 15 to 50.
- Awareness campaigns have been organised in rural areas as well as in urban slum areas.
- During 1999-2004 (up to Mar.) 11.38 million people were contacted and 49.2 thousand AIDS patients were treated.

School AIDS Education Programme (SAEP)

- The programme reinforce family values and respect for the opposite sex. The activities include training of teachers and poor educators amongst students, role-playing, debates and discussions question box and access to referral services. A training module called *"Learning For Life"* has been prepared and distributed. University talk AIDS show is also financed by NACO. NSS and Nehru Yuvak Kendras are also actively involved.
- Provision of Rs. 4 million has been made for the year 2003-04.
- Students of 2146 schools were educated in the year 2004-05 while students of 584 secondary and senior secondary schools were educated about AIDS in the year 2003-04.

Prevention of Mother to Child Transmission of HIV (PMTCT): By using anti-retroviral drugs like AZT

AIDS workshop held for

- 23 district-level head masters.
- 13 district-level pear teachers and pear educators.
- 9 others.

AIDS projects run by NGO: 7
New project to be launched soon: 10
AIDS patients treated (up to Dec. 2004).

Total: 1221
home state: 1133
neighbouring states: 88
percentage of males: 78

Information Education and Communication (IEC) Activities

- Through school programme
- Through cultural programme
- Hospitals, blood banks and NGO performing remarkable work have been awarded on AIDS-day (1st Dec.) every year.
- Public awareness on AIDS through hoardings and other publishing materials at bus stops, railway stations, hospitals, fairs etc.
- 100 condom vending machines are being installed in high risk areas of Jaipur.
- On 17th Jan. 2005, Rajasthan state AIDS control society organised a workshop on HIV/AIDS and calls for inter-department cooperation to fight AIDS.
- *'Jeevan Jyoti'* state's first community service center for AIDS started at Jaipur in 1st Dec. 2004.

- Facilities for serological screening for AIDS antibody by Elisa technique is available at SMS medical college, Jaipur.
- Anti-discrimination cell has been established to protect AIDS patients from stigma and discrimination.
- Under Chief Minister Sahayata Kosh (CMSK) more than 11 million rupees have been sanctioned to 47 patients belong to BPL families and 300 others for the treatment of AIDS.

TABLE 5.5: National AIDS Control Programme, Rajasthan: Achievements (1999-04)

Year	*Blood Bank Samples*		*Substance Prepared Through Blood Segregation*	*Voluntary Blood Centres*		*No. of Patients Treated in STD Clinics*	*Family Health Awareness Campaign*	
	Examined	*Sample Found Reactive*		*Examined*	*Sample Found Reactive*		*Information Given to ('000 No.)*	*No. of AIDS/STD Patients Treated ('000 No.)*
1999	119219	492	6388	—	—	5783	1733.7	72.6
2000	130851	410	13145	162	56	6365	3213.2	96.8
2001	156159	453	60176	1640	217	10040	2135.6	89.1
2002	181736	427	65932	1163	118	11474	2257.9	114.1
2003	184369	419	59147	1266	228	13459	2135.2	491.9
2004	192082	524	88604	1898	306	32970	—	—

Source: *'Pragati Prativedan'*, 2003-04 & 2004-05, Deptt. of Medical and Health, GoR, Jaipur.

BOX 5.5: Management of Bio-Medical Waste: Rajasthan

- **Nodal agency:** State Environment Control Board
- **Norms:** Compulsory at all hospitals, nursing homes and health centres having 10 beds or more
- **Rs. 70.69 million allotted** to health centres, during 2003-04 by deptt. of Medical & Health
- **Rs. 57.82 million utilized**
- **Provision of Rs. 93 million** has been made under PMGY in the year 2004-05

NATIONAL CANCER CONTROL PROGRAMME (NCCP)

Launched in : 1999-2000, as a Central Sponsored Scheme
Districts covered : 10 (Sikar, Bundi, Baran, Dungarpur, Banswara, Barmer, Jalor, Ganganagar, Nagaur and Churu

Objectives

- Primary prevention of cancer by health education.
- Secondary prevention i.e. early detection and diagnosis of common cancer such as cancer of cervix, mouth, breast and tabacco related cancer by screening self examination methods.
- Tertiary prevention by strengthening of the existing institutions for comprehensive therapy including palliative care.
- To impart training to doctors and para-medical staff.

Financial provision

Rs. 15 million. Central assistance is providing to hospitals for augmenting cancer diagnostic and treatment facilities for establishing cobalt therapy and mammography units and for development of oncology wing.

Expenditure incurred

- Rs. 3.39 million in 2000-01
- Rs. 0.62 million in 2001-02
- Rs. 3.48 million in 2002-03
- Rs. 5.63 million in 2003-04

TABLE 5.6: Details of Cancer Patients Treated in Govt. Hospitals (1998-2002)

Year	*Cancer Patients*					
	Outdoor ('000 No.)		*Indoor ('000 No.)*		*Deaths*	
	Male	*Female*	*Male*	*Female*	*Male*	*Female*
1998	31.3	29.4	3.8	4.7	302	153
1999	42.2	36.6	8.0	7.8	306	168
2000	28.5	26.4	5.2	6.5	315	157
2001	31.5	30.9	5.7	6.3	453	209
2002	27.0	30.9	4.2	4.7	317	123
2003	31.8	39.0	6.7	8.2	486	256

Source: *'Pragati Prativedan'*, 2003-04 & 2004-05, Deptartment of Medical and Health, GoR, Jaipur.

NATIONAL / REVISED NATIONAL TB CONTROL PROGRAMME (NTCP/RNTCP)

NTCP launched in : 1966
Funding (%) : GoI: GoR 50: 50
Revised NTCP launched in : 1997 as a pilot project of Directly Observed Treatment Short Course (DOTS), at Jaipur.
Funding agency : WB (through soft loans)
Technical guidance : WHO
Assistance by : GoI-TB Deptt.
Functions : Planning for organizing case findings, providing treatment, BCG immunisation, supervision and monitoring

Objectives

[I] Long Term:
- To reduce TB in the community.

[II] Short Term:
- To immunize neo-natal and infants with BCG vaccine.
- To detect new cases of tuberculosis.
- To provide treatment to sputum positive cases.
- Follow up of cases under treatment and persuade the defaulters to continue with the treatment.

Administrative Set-up

Additional Director (Rural Health)
↓
Joint Director (Rural Health)
↓
Administration — Training
↓ (Administration)
District TB Officer
↓
District TB Control Centre DTC
↓
Immunization — Treatment

Activities

- Case finding.
- Chemotherapy

Institutional Structure

• State TB control unit	:	1
• TB demonstration and training center	:	1 (Ajmer)
• District TB control clinics	:	32 (in all districts)
• Sub-district TB control clinics	:	2 (Churu and Pratapgarh)
• Chest and TB hospitals	:	7
• TB sanatorium	:	2
• TB units	:	Total 143
• General/Plain areas (at per 5 lakh pop.)	:	90
• Tribal areas (at per 2.5 lakh pop.)	:	29
• Desert areas (at per 2.5 lakh pop.)	:	19
• Microscopic centres	:	650 (in general/plain area, at per 1 lakh pop and in tribal/desert areas at per 50 thousand pop).
RNTCP treatment centres	:	1843 (at per 20-30 thousand pop.)
RNTCP sub-centres/treatment observation points	:	11296 (at per 3-5 thousand pop.)

Publication of quarterly news bulletin 'DOTS update' Active Participation in DOTS System

NGO	:	121
Private hospitals	:	231
Women groups	:	723
Health meetings organised	:	1803
Beneficiaries	:	27610

Recent Trends

- Strengthening of the state TB training center, Ajmer.
- Ideal DOTS centres are established at Bassi and Masooda.
- Persons under state employees insurance schemes are also being benefited.
- Involvement of medical colleges. Each medical college in an RNTCP area working collaboratively with the district TB officer of their area will establish a microscopy and treatment observation center.
- Medical college will be provided, as needed, with a medical officer, TB health visitor and laboratory technicians in order to establish effective RNTCP services at the medical college itself and to ensure effective coordination and referral with providers throughout the area.
- Efforts are also on to involve railway, private hospitals, armed forces, PSU, NGO and IMA in the implementation of the programme.

Intensification of IEC activities

For effective utilization of services, intensive IEC activities are being carried out:

- IEC material is being prepared in vernacular language.
- A training module for improved inter-personal communication (IPC) skills has been developed and incorporated in the existing modules.
- IEC strategy at different levels has been planned.

- Electronic connectivity: Information on RNTCP including updated RNTCP data, documents and training manuals published are accessible at the programmes website.
- Increased people participation through IEC.
- 2939 IEC homes are established. Planning to establish IEC homes at per 1000 population is in progress.
- Referral system establish to detect new patients of TB.

TABLE 5.7: Revised National TB Control Programme, Rajasthan: Achievements (2000-04)

Year	*Detection of New Patients of TB*			*Annual Detection Rate of New Patients of TB (135 Per Lakh pop. Per Annum)*		*Conversion Rate (%)*		*Cure Rate (%)*	
	Target ('000 No.)	*Achievement ('000 No.)*	*Achievement % of target*	*Target*	*Achievement*	*Target*	*Achievement*	*Target*	*Achievement*
2000	39.1	39.9	102	135	138	90	88	85	84
2001	76.1	84.4	110	135	152	90	90	85	85
2002	76.1	93.4	123	135	167	90	91	85	85
2003	80.2	98.1	122	135	165	90	91	85	87
2004	80.1	105.1	128	135	152	90	91	85	87

Source: 'Pragati Prativedan', 2004-05, Department of Medical and Health, GoR, Jaipur.

RAJASTHAN HEALTH SYSTEM DEVELOPMENT PROJECT (RHSDP)

Launched on : 24 August, 2004
Funding agency : World Bank
Period : 5 Years (Upto July 2009)
Project Size : Rs. 4.72 billion
Funding Share % : GoR : WB & GoI
16.02 83.98 → Loan 70%
→ GoI Grant 30%

Objectives

- To strengthen 238 secondary level hospitals so that in each block one hospital with 24 hours emergency facilities can be established.
- Quality improvement in health facilities provided by the hospitals.
- Imparting training to working staff for modernization.
- For timely availability of medicine and modern instruments / appliances to hospitals with adequate quantity.
- For effective disposal of hospital wastage.

Budget Provision for

- Free medicines to BPL families.
- Emergency facilities.
- Purchasing of new furniture.
- Repairing of furniture/instruments/appliances.

Functions

- Construction Work:
  - Renovation/upgradation/addition of work in hospitals

- Supply of medicines to 238 hospitals at the rate of
  - Rs. 5 per OPD
  - Rs. 1000 per bed per year
- Purchasing of furniture in hospitals
- Training and Workshop
  - Essential training of doctors and para-medical staff.
  - Preparation of training modules.
  - Organise workshops at division-level.
  - Implementation of IEC activities.

GUINEAWORM ERADICATION PROGRAMME (GWEP)

Started in	:	1983-84
Sponsored by	:	GoI
Sharing %	:	GoI: GoR 50 : 50
Nodal Agency and Technical Assistance by	:	NICD (National Institute of Communicable Diseases)
Objective	:	Total eradication of guineaworm by 1990

Administrative Set-Up

Director, M & HS
↓
Additional Director-Rural Health
(as state GWEP programme officer)
↓
Technical Officer
(planning, implementation and monitoring)
↓
District Health Officer
↓
Health Educator

Functions

- Searching of active GW cases, thrice a year (April, June and Dec.).
- Inter-search surveillance.
- Regular bandaging GW ulcers.
- Treatment of unsafe drinking water sources.
- Maintenance and supply of safe drinking water.
- Impart health education.
- To increase community participation in eradication of GW.

MOBILE SURGICAL UNIT (MSU)
Established in 1956

Objectives

- To provide free of cost medical facilities to rural masses in remote areas at their door-steps by organizing camps.

- To provide medical facility in local and homely environment.
- To benefit maximum number of rural patients.

MSU Capacity (at present)

500 beded modern hospital with 10 to 12 specialists and latest type of equipments comparable to an 'A' class hospital.

Functioning

- Organize camps on the request of local administrative agencies.
- The camp is usually of 10-15 days duration.
- In first three days of the camp out-door facilities are provided to the people by.different specialists.
- About 3-6 thousand patients are examined during this period.
- Around 500 to 800 patients are required for admission for operation or investigation.
- Both surgical operations and eye operations are undertaken.

Expenditure incurred during IX FYP : Rs. 22.82 million.
Provision for X FYP period : Rs. 19.6 million

TABLE 5.8: Progress of Mobile Surgical Units, Rajasthan (2004-05, Up to Dec. 04)

S. No.	*Particulars*	*Jaipur Unit*	*Udaipur Unit*	*Jodhpur Unit*
1.	No. of Beds	500	100	100
2.	No. of Camps			
	Target	24	12	12
	Achievement	18	20	10
3.	No. of Out-door Patients	38684	11643	2932
4.	Operations	4894	839	629
5.	No. of Sanctioned Posts	121	26	26
6.	No. of Working Persons	119	18	12

Source: *'Pragati Prativedan'*, 2004-05, Department of Medical and Health, GoR, Jaipur.

Achievement from 1956 to Dec. 2004

Camps Organised : 849
Operation Performed : 3.28 lakh
Outdoor Patients Treated : 2.39 million

CHIEF MINISTER JEEVAN RAKSHA KOSH/SAHAYATA KOSH (CMJRK/CMSK)

Launched on : 27th March 1999
Funding share : GoI: GoR
Functioning by : CMJRK committee, Jaipur

Objectives

- To provide financial assistance to BPL families who are suffering from chronic diseases e.g heart, cancer, kidney etc.
- Non-card holders of BPL families whose annual income is not more than Rs. 24 thousand are also entitled for financial assistance under this scheme.

Cases referred to AIIMS (If medical facility is not available in state govt. hospitals)

Financial assistance	: Generally 40 per cent of total treatment
Disease	: Max. Permissible Amount ('000 Rs.)
Change of One Heart Value	: 30
Change of Two Heart Valves or Bye-Pass Surgery	: 50
Kidney Transplant	: 50
Cancer Treatment	: 50

Revolving fund has been provided to the following hospitals under CMJRK

	Lakh Rs.
SMS Hospital, Jaipur	20
MBS Hospital, Udaipur	5
MBS Hospital, Kota	2
PBM Hospital, Bikaner	2
Samuhik Chikitsalaya Sangh, Ajmer	2
Samuhik Chikitsalaya Sangh, Jodhpur	2

TABLE 5.9 : CMJRK and CMSK: Achievements (1999-04)

Year	*Chief Minister Jeevan Raksha Kosh*		*Chief Minister Sahayata Kosh*	
	Beneficiaries	*Expenditure (Million Rs.)*	*Beneficiaries*	*Expenditure (Million Rs.)*
1999-2000	67	4.8	—	—
2000-2001	280	18.5	636	19.0
2001-2002	786	42.1	1405	37.8
2002-2003	1206	48.2	2151	62.1
2003-2004	1245	47.4	2571	79.1
2004-2005*	106	4.0	642**	21.1
Total	**3690**	**165.0**	**7405**	**219.1**

* up to Sep. 04 ** up to Nov. 04.
Source: 'Pragati Prativedan', 2003-04 & 2004-05, Department of Medical and Health, GoR, Jaipur.

SANJIVANI PROGRAMME/SCHEME

Launched on : Sep 2004

Revised in : Feb/March 2005

Objective : To organize health camps at selected CHCs and To provide specialists services.

District covered : Barmer, Jaisalmer, Baran, Udaipur, Banswara, Dungarpur, Sirohi, Chittaurgarh etc. (desert and tribal districts)

CHCs included

➢ *Tribal Areas*
- All CHCs of tribal districts of Dungarpur, Banswara and Udaipur districts
- Kelwar and Shahbad CHCs of Baran Distt.
- Pratapgarh and Arnod CHCs of Chittaurgarh Distt.
- Abu Road Block CHC of Sirohi Distt.

➢ *Desert Areas*
- All CHCs of Barmer Distt.
- All CHCs of Jaisalmer Distt.
- CHCs of other desert districts based on number of C-type villages

Duration of the camp : 3 days

Facilities provided	:	Specialist services
Functions performed	•	Inspection/Testing of patients,
	•	Provide knowledge about national programmes/schemes,
	•	Immunization,
	•	Provide knowledge about HIV/AIDS,
	•	Cancer counselling,
	•	Issue of certificates,
	•	Follow ups of referral cases and tracking
Action plan	•	CMHO & CMO will prepare action plan at district and block level
	•	Various committees are formed to ensure availability of specialists, medicines and instruments at CHC and for smooth conducting and after reporting
Role of CHC	➢	*Mass Communication* About the date of health camps and health services to be provided to all the health officers, para-medical staff, member of PRIs, other departments, NGOs and ensure their responsibility.
Role of PHC	•	Screening of patients at least 2 weeks before the health camp
	•	Supply list of patients to CHC
Role of SHC	:	ANM and MPW will provide informations of their respective areas about health facilities to be given, date of health camp, along with details of patients to PHC.
Financial management	•	By department of Medical and Health, GoR
	•	Rs. 1.5 lakh for medicines,
	•	Rs. 10 thousand for mass communication
	•	Provision of free medicines to BPL families

NATIONAL SURVEILLANCE PROGRAMME FOR COMMUNICABLE DISEASES (NSPCD)

Launched as a pilot programme in 1997-98

Selected Pilot Districts

1997-1998: Alwar, Udaipur and Jaipur
1998-1999: Ajmer
1999-2000: Kota, Sikar and Sirohi

Objectives

- To strengthen the disease surveillance system so that early warning signals of outbreaks are recognized and appropriate follow-up action is initiated.
- To build up additional capacities for effective communication and technology, upgradation of laboratories etc.
- Ensure involvement of public and private sector institutions, private practitioners and NGOs in the process of effective implementation of diseases surveillance programme.
- Develop proper urban surveillance system.
- Optimize the utilization of available resources and to bring about effective inter-sectoral cooperation among various agencies in the health and non-health sector.

Implemented Through

The existing health infrastructure and surveillance system involving training of medical and para-medical personnels, upgradation of laboratories and improvement in communication system.

Activities (The surveillance system strengthened through)

- Training of medical and para-medical personnels.
- Dissemination of technical information and guidelines.
- Upgradation of laboratories.
- Modernization of communication and data processing system.
- The programme includes IEC activities to promote community participation in the prevention and control of outbreaks.
- Multi-disciplinary Rapid Response Teams (RRTS) have been constituted as state and district levels under the programme. These teams have been provided training of surveillance, prevention and control of outbreaks.
- District laboratories have been strengthened through procurement of scientific equipment, reagents and rapid diagnostic kits etc. These district laboratories support in confirmation to diagnosis of common communicable diseases.
- Networking between districts, state, regional laboratories and other specialized institutes of repute in the country besides national level has been initiated. A NICD web-site has been established and this web-site connected all the 32 districts.
- *Capacity Building*: State nodal officers, district nodal officers have been trained at NICD. All the professional and para-professional of the districts have been trained. Laboratory staff has also been trained.
- *District Response*: The district response to surveillance, outbreak investigation and data analysis is improving. They have started sending reports on weekly basis regarding any outbreaks, any health events as reported in the newspapers and on monthly basis the reports of cases/deaths due to communicable diseases.
- Fund allotted by GoI : Rs. 10.55 million
- Expenditure incurred : Rs. 7.43 million

REVAMPING SCHEME

Launched in: 1984-85 in the slum areas of cities of the state having more than 1 lakh population.

Objectives

- To prevent diseases,
- Provide first aid facility,
- To provide information about personal hygiene, sanitation, food habit and about infectious diseases
- To popularize family planning measures (condom, pills, copper-T)
- Immunisation of children.
- T.T. injection to pregnant women.
- Iron Folic acid tablets to anemic women.
- To provide diagnostic services.

Activities

90 health posts are functioning in 11 urban areas (Ajmer, Bhilwara, Jaipur, Sikar, Alwar, Bharatpur, Bikaner, Ganganagar, Jodhpur, Kota and Udaipur).

Achievement (up to Dec. 04)

- Family Planning Operations held: 2964
- IUD Inserted: 1519
- Registration of pregnant women and immunization: 20394
- Total immunization of children: 20954

TABLE 5.10: Iodine Deficiency Control Programme, Rajasthan: Achievement 2000-04

Year	Sample Taken Under PFA	Sample Found Iodine Less & Challen Presented in Court	No. of Samples Taken Under Non PFA Act			Iodised Salt Used (%age)
			Iodine Less	< 15 PCM	> 15 PCM	
2000	42	4	4299	16663	34537	62
2001	66	7	12924	54486	80537	55
2002	25	—	2259	10756	22244	63
2003	25	3	11148	35413	63646	61
2004	44	—	10824	36983	79162	61

Source: *'Pragati Prativedan'*, 2004-05, Department of Medical and Health, GoR, Jaipur.

TABLE 5.11: Outbreak of Seasonal Diseases, Rajasthan (1999-04)

Year	Deaconry		Joundice		Hepatitis		Water Samples		Out Break		
	Patients	Deaths	Patients	Deaths	Patients	Deaths	Taken	Unsatisfied	Diacentry	Joundice	Food Poisining
1999	145491	59	5642	90	215	22	11491	2829	40	25	34
2000	169028	54	3055	27	67	3	11747	1935	74	15	32
2001	173631	44	4207	50	126	6	10568	1458	41	5	33
2002	186827	30	2497	24	109	5	11493	1980	24	5	46
2003	81515	37	2015	32	100	6	11885	1481	29	1	45
2004	83022	05	3051	22	62	3	20048	2353	17	9	33

Source: *'Pragati Prativedan'*, 2003-04 & 2004-05, Department of Medical and Health, GoR, Jaipur.

TABLE 5.12: Details of School Health Programme, Rajasthan (1999-2004)

Year	No. of Schools		No. of Students				Financial Provision (Million Rs.)
	Selected Under the Programme	Health Examined	Selected	Health Examined	Found Sick	Sent for Treatment	
1999-2000	38744	36705	4217605	3371305	473610	119335	15
2000-2001	42922	39540	4450567	3699745	441055	108427	10
2001-2002	46555	42336	4972515	4262978	530225	110514	8.5
2002-2003	49615	47523	6481746	5462366	607693	182174	5.5
2003-2004	53722	52749	9940746	5916508	691837	184768	6.4
2003-2004 (Up to Dec. 04)	36168	35046	6221548	3666030	351638	119656	6.4

Source: *'Pragati Prativedan'*, 2003-04 & 2004-05, Department Of Medical and Health, GoR, Jaipur.

REPRODUCTIVE AND CHILD HEALTH (RCH) PROGRAMME

Launched on : 15th Oct. 1997
Funding agency : World Bank

Stage I: **Project period** : Originally for 5 years, now it is extended up to April, 2005

Objectives

- To reduce MMR
- To reduce IMR
- Population stabilization
- Improvement in the quality and coverage in reproductive and child health services

BOX 5.6: Family Welfare and MCH Programmes: Rajasthan

Integrated FWP and MCH programmes are being launched in Rajasthan.

Objectives

- Population stabilization- to promote responsible parenthood with small family norm through independent choice of family planning method best suits to couple.
- To reduce IMR.
- To reduce MMR.

Changed strategy

Since 1976-77, Community Need Assessment Approach (CNAA) has been adopted in place of Target Free Approach (TFA). Under CNAA, the worker himself/herself determines target according to the demand of public.
Provision made during X FYP period (2002-07): Rs. 275 million

Progress 2004-05 (up to Dec. 04)

Sterlisation operation performed: 1.81 lakh
IUD inserted: 2.04 lakh
Oral Pills and Conventional Contraceptive Users:
- Routine users: 3.62 lakh
- New users: 3.97 lakh

Referral transport services
- Provided to 3415 pregnant women of BPL families.
- Amount spent: Rs. 1.6 million

Night deliveries held: 76693
Expenditure occurred made on round-the-clock delivery services: Rs. 23.27 million
National Maternity Benefit Scheme
- Women benefited: 4977
- Expenditure incurred: Rs. 2.49 million

Functioning

Vast institutional infrastructure along with special institutions in the form of ICDS scheme, universal immunization programme and post partum centres are being spread across the state.

Monitoring

Effective monitoring is done at each level-state, district and block level.

Districts covered	:	All districts covered under national component and Jaipur (slum) and Tonk districts under sub-project. (Sub-project ended on 31st Mar. 04).
Total project outlay	:	Rs. 2871.20 million
Total assistance received (up to Dec. 04)	:	Rs. 2164.14 million
• In cash		Rs. 470.53 million
• In materials		Rs. 1693.61 million
Total expenditure (up to Dec. 04)	:	2095.75 million Rs.
• In cash		Rs. 402.14 million
• In materials		Rs. 1693.61 million

Strategy adopted

- Provisional of capital investment in form of non-recurring grant for construction, repair and refurbishing health infrastructure.
- Provision of financial assistance to higher medical and para-medical personnel on contract basis.
- Supply of drugs, vaccines and equipment of delivering RCH including immunization services.
- Community based initiatives such as cash assistance for transport pregnant women to referral centres, community incentives for involving the PRIs, training and provision of training to TBAs in conducting safe deliveries, conducting of outreach camps in underserved areas etc.
- Computerisation and improved data management for family welfare.

Achievements of the I stage

Major civil construction works:
- Rs. 1 million allotted to each community health center and each district hospital for operation theatre, labour room, water and electricity works.

Minor civil construction works:
- At PHC & SHC in each districts.
- Rs. 1 million allotted to each district.
- Total expenditure incurred upto 31st Dec. 2004 is Rs. 30.8 million. Round-the-clock delivery services at maternity health centres

Referral transport services:
- Available in 25 per cent SHCs of remote and inaccessible area.
- District covered : 19
- Gram panchayats covered : 1441

Dais training programme

District covered: Initially 6 (Alwar, Barmer, Churu, Hanumangarh and Jalor). At present all the 32 districts.

RCH camps organised at 10 remote PHCs in each district

I stage

- 11 districts covered (Banswara, Baran, Bharatpur, Dhaulpur, Tonk, Jaisalmer, Jhalawar, Churu, Nagaur, Alwar, Jalor and Barmer)
- Rs. 5.5 million allotted by GoI.

II stage

- 5 districts covered (Sirohi, Udaipur, Bhilwara, Dausa and Pali)
- Rs. 9.6 million allotted by GoI.

III stage

- Remaining 16 districts covered
- Rs. 19.2 million allotted by GoI.

Appointment of Staff

Appointment of Sahayika at SHC level, PHN at PHC level and lab technicians at FRU level. (Sahayika scheme ended on Dec. 2002).

Appointment of additional ANM in 10 districts (7 desert + 3 tribal)

- *Desert districts*—Barmer, Jodhpur, Pali, Jalor, Jaisalmer, Bikaner and Nagaur
- *Tribal districts*—Udaipur, Dungarpur and Banswara
- *1321 additional posts of ANM are sanctioned*
- *1137 appointments made upto Dec. 04*
- *Rs. 59.5 million released by GoI*
- *Expenditured incurred (upto Dec. 04): Rs. 47.93 million*

Outreach services

- *Objective*: To generate awareness and to improve the quality of health services in the backward areas.
- *Districts covered*: 17 (Ajmer, Banswara, Dungarpur, Jaisalmer, Jaipur, Churu, Jodhpur, Ganganagar, Hanumangarh, Sikar, Jhunjhunun, Kota, Pali, Rajsamand, Bikaner, Nagaur and Sirohi.
- *Amount allotted*: Rs. 9.47 million
- *Expenditure incurred*: Rs. 9.03 million (upto 31st Dec. 04). At present this scheme is closed.

RCH material assistance

Up to Dec. 04, Rs. 1.7 billion has been granted by GoI as material assistance in the form of vaccine, cold storage equipments, drugs and instrument kits.

BOX 5.7: Medical Termination of Pregnancy (MTP)

- **Objective:** To prevent unrequired pregnancy.
- **Achievements up to Dec. 2004:**
  - 32,912 MTP services provided.
  - Imparted MTP training to 1200 doctors.
  - MTP training centers established in 8 districts.
  - 374 Private hospitals are also recognized for MTP.

SOCIAL SECURITY SCHEME

Launched in : 1992-93
Funded By : GoI
Objectives : To strengthen PHC
District Covered : 23, which are demographically poor/weak
PHC Covered
I Stage : 115
II Stage : 115
III Stage : 115
IV Stage : 56
Total : 401
Financial Assistance Received by GoI (At the rate of Rs. 1 million per PHC)
I Stage : Rs. 115 million
II Stage : Rs. 115 million
III Stage : Rs. 115 million
IV Stage : Rs. 56 million
Total : Rs. 401 million

TABLE 5.13: Construction Works Under Social Security Scheme: Rajasthan 2004-05

Particulars	*Stages*											
	*I**			*II**			*III*			*IV*		
	Sanc	*Const*	*Bal*	*Sanc*	*Const*	*Bal*	*Sanc*	*Const*	*Bal*	*Sanc*	*Const*	*Bal*
(A) Construction Work												
1. Operation Theatre	115	115	—	98	96	2	84	72	12	40	31	9
2. Observation Ward	61	61	—	70	69	1	58	51	7	33	27	6
3. Labour Room	90	90	—	92	90	2	73	65	8	43	32	11
4. Doctors Quarters	54	54	—	52	50	2	42	36	6	24	19	5
5. ANM Quarters	78	78	—	71	68	3	64	57	7	25	20	5
(B) Tube Well	61	46	15	62	36	26	321	281	40	165	129	36

Source: *'Pragati Prativedan'*, 2004-05, Deptt. of Medical and Health, GoR, Jaipur.
Sanc—sanctioned, Const—Construction, Bal—Balance. *Sanctions has also been granted for 150 Ambulances, 150 Generators, Operation Theater, instruments, Drug Bandages and for IEC Activities in each Phase.

UNFPA ASSISTED AREA PROJECT (UAAP) PHASE I (1980-85): RAJASTHAN

Objective

To implement 'Model Plan' for Rural Health Services to attain the goal 'Health for All' by the year 2000.

Districts covered

4 districts namely Kota, Sawai Madhopur, Bharatpur and Dhaulpur.

Total outlay: Rs. 130.2 million.

Achievements

- Provided training facilities to medical and para-medical personnels.
- Provided residential as well as functional accommodation for staff and
- Taken-up IEC services to achieve the goals of family welfare and MCH services.

INTEGRATED POPULATION AND DEVELOPMENT (IPD) PROJECT, PHASE II (2003-07): RAJASTHAN

Funding agency : UNFPA
Financial assistance : Rs. 150.8 million, through GoI, as 100% subsidy

Main objectives

Strengthening and expansion of family welfare and RCH services in the state.
Implementing agency: Health and Family Welfare.
Participating departments: Women and Child Welfare (WCD), Education, Women Reference Centre (WRC).

District covered

- 8 (Alwar, Bharatpur, Sawai Madhopur, Karauli, Bhilwara, Chittaurgarh, Udaipur and Rajsamand).
- In Tonk district, IEC activities will be strengthened.

Population covered: 14.75 million, 20 per cent of the state population.

Main activities

(A) State level

- Implementation of policies related to population and women empowerment.
- Advocacy to make public opinion on issues related to population and development.
- Expansion of managerial capacity for effective implementation of RCH programmes.
- Assisting activities related to women empowerment through women reference center (WRC).
- Provide information related to reproductive health, population and development, family life and sex education to youth through education department.

(B) District level

- To strengthen and improve quality of RCH programme and ensuring community participation.
- To strengthen emergency delivery services for reduction of MMR.
- To provide RCH information and services to youth.

Achievements (April to December 2004)

- Health camps organised in remote areas: 14,829
- Total No. of RTTI/STD institutions: 469

- No. of benefited patients through RTTI/STD: 30,889
- Services provided at BEOC/CEOC
  - ➢ Deliveries: 51,627
  - ➢ Scissors section: 1,437
  - ➢ OBST: 7,241
- Construction works sanctioned (upto Dec. 03): 31
- Jan Mangal couples selected (Jan-Dec., 04): 11,366
- Jan Mangal couples trained: 7,728
- Jan Mangal monthly meetings held: 1809
- OP beneficiaries: 108,956
- CC beneficiaries: 768,879

UNICEF ASSISTED BORDER DISTRICTS COMMUNITY STRATEGY PROJECT (BDCS)

- *Launched in*—Baran, Dhaulpur and Jhalawar district.

Objectives

- to reduce IMR.
- to MMR.
- to provide health for all.

Strategy adopted

Villages of each district are classified into three categories and then suitable strategy is being adopted accordingly:

Village Category	*Characteristics*	*Strategy Adopted*
A	Having SHC or PHC	Regular health services are being provided by medical officers or health workers at SHC/PHC.
B	Approachable within ½ an hour from the village having SHC	Twice in a month at AWC health day are being observed and health workers and AWW provide their services
C	Not approachable within ½ an hour from the village having SHC	Once in a month, health camp is being organised and health workers and observers provide their services

Activities

- To provide vehicles for organizing health camps in 'C' category villages.
- To provide required instruments namely, BP instruments, weighing machines, hemoglobinometer, pressure cooker etc. to all the SHCs of these three districts.
- Organised orientation training programmes.
- Health and Nutration Dal is organised at each SHC/PHC to provide health services.
- Budget allotted to each district for repairing of SHCs.
- Imparted training to health workers.

EUROPEAN COMMISSION ASSISTED HEALTH AND FWP (2000-05)

Stage I: launched as a pilot project in June 2001 in Barmer and Jalor districts.
Stage II: Rs. 500 million MOU (Memorendum of Understanding) signed between GoR and GoI: Oct. 2003. 8 new districts viz. (Pali, Jodhpur, Jaisalmer, Nagaur, Bikaner, Dungarpur, Banswara and Sirohi included in Oct. 2003.

Functioning

➢ State level
➢ District level
Subsidy received so for: Rs. 240 million
Expenditure incurred: Rs. 130 million

Objective

To strengthen health services by removing shortcomings of FW and RCH programmes.

Achievements

- Empowered committee is formed at state level.
- Formed of sector reform cell.
- Formed district health committees.
- Training of health personnels-training policy and programmes are prepared.
- Training at different levels has been imported by SIHFW (State Institute of Health & Family Welfare).
- Strengthening of material storage capacity.
- Protocol for the treatment of patients.
- Strengthening of PSM department.
- Strengthening of Rajasthan, Medical Relief Society.
- Formulation of 'Health Vision-2005'.

Stage-II Work plan

- Strengthening of health services at state, zonal and district level.
- Appointment has been made of specialists and project officers in all districts.
- Strengthening of selected 200 labour rooms, 150 BMOC, 97 model PHCs and 50 CMOC in progress.
- Strengthening of PSM departments of all the medical colleges.
- Strengthening of SHCs.
- All the district health and family welfare departments are linked with internet and website is going to be prepared.
- 17 NGOs have been selected for the effective implementation of RCH programme. Each NGO will boost this programme in 50 villages. Rs. 5 lakh is being paid to each NGO for the same.
- Training is being imparted to 32,925 Jan Mangal Couples.
- Orientation programmes are in progress.
- Internet and telephone facility is being provided to all district and sub-divisional offices.
- Strengthening of IEC activities.

RAJASTHAN HEALTH CARE PROJECT (EAP)

Started in the year 1998

Duration: 4 years

Objective: Improving health of the rural population particularly of women in tribal districts.

Agency: SANIPLAN and IIHMR have been entrusted with the job of preparing the project report in reference to "Comprehensive Health Service Improvement and school health education in selected tribal districts of Rajasthan".

District covered: 5 (Banswara, Dungarpur, Udaipur, Sirohi and Chittaurgarh).

Components: Infrastructure improvements and Strengthening health services through human resource development.

The proposed infrastructure improvements are:

- Renovate/extend and equip district hospital, sub-district hospitals and community health centres during the project duration.
- Improve training facilities through renovation of facilities/provision of equipment at the district level.
- Improve the infrastructure (building and equipment) of the district health managers officers.

Moreover, to improve service delivery and performance of the district health and hospital management units through technical support, training institutions have been identified which should be able to implement the proposed in-service training course through the following structure:

- Improve management through training courses for district managers.
- Improve service delivery through refresher training of nurses, physicians, midwives and technicians especially in reproductive and child health care.
- Improve training of health personnel through revised curricula development.
- Strengthen health financing aspects through training, planning and budgeting.

Phase-I

- Identification of architects.
- Finalisation of building assessment and drawings.
- Site development plans.
- Invitation of bid.
- Secure contractors-procurement of and goods and services.
- Initiate procurement procedures of equipment.
- Start renovation and construction work at hospitals/CHC.

Phase-II

- Development of methodology of decentralized planning.
- Curricula development training.
- Planning workshops at different level.
- Development and implementation of project activities by NGOs at community level.
- Further construction and renovation works.
- Distribution of equipment and vehicles.
- Start technical training for the use of new equipment.
- Implementation of supportive supervision.
- Development of additional measures based on Phase I experience.

Phase-III

The district health planning and management process and training activities would be continued as well as NGO project activities, construction and renovation would be finalized. Phase III would include implementation of equality standards.

INTEGRATED CHILD DEVELOPMENT SERVICES (ICDS) SCHEME

Launched in 1975. Since then the programme had been expanded in phased manner.

World Bank assisted ICDS III (Since April, 1999)

Districts covered: all the 32

Block covered

➤ Rural: 237 (all)
➤ Urban: 20 (towns having one lakh or more pop.)
➤ Total: 257
Anganwadi covered: all the 35,710
Implementing agency: DWCD (Department of Women and Child Development)

Objectives

- To improve the nutritional status of children in the age group of 0-6 years.
- To lay the foundation for proper psychological, physical and social development.
- To reduce the incidence of mortality, morbidity, malnutrition and school dropout.
- To achieve effective co-ordination amongst the various departments to promote women and child development.
- To enhance the capability of the mother to look after the normal health and nutritional needs of the child through nutrition and health education.

Strategy

- Supplementary nutrition
- Immunization
- Health check-ups
- Referral services
- Nutrition and health education
- Pre-school education

The strategy of the Tenth Five Year Plan is based on reach the unreached children and mothers through ICDS programme. Emphasis is laid on the strengthening of the on going scheme and also provision for additional inputs in the services. It is also proposed to open additional *anganwaries* keeping parity with the decadel growth rate. The proposed outlay for the Tenth plan is of the order of Rs. 612.8 million (2860 under state plan + 326.81 under PMGY).

Supplementary nutrition

Supplementary nutrition to the malnourished children of the age group of 6 months to 6 years and to the pregnant and lactating women is made available at the Anganwari Centers for 300 days in a year.

TABLE 5.14: ICDS : Achievements (1997-02)

Year	*Physical Progress (Million No.)*				*Financial Progress (Million Rs.)*		
	Supplementary Nutrition		*Pre-school Education*		*State Plan*		
	Target	*Achievement*	*Target*	*Achievement*	*Outlay*	*Revised Allocation*	*Expenditure*
1997-1998	18.74	14.82	7.50	6.41	181.01	101.01	99.29
1998-1999	18.90	14.42	7.57	5.99	181.00	141.00	128.19
1999-2000	16.35	11.71	6.54	5.62	120.00	120.00	78.26
2000-2001	16.90	12.82	10.88	6.65	130.00	112.30	96.28
2001-2002*	21.99	17.15	10.70	9.00	100.00	210.40	79.80

- up to Jan., 02.

Source: Draft Tenth Five Year Plan, 2002-07, Volume-I, GoR, Planning Department, Jaipur.

BOX 5.8: Women Health Group (WHG), Rajasthan

Funding agency : GoI
Total No. : 6783

Objective

- To make FWP more extensive.
- To reduce IMR and BR.
- To increase women participation in FWP, RCH programme and other health parogrammes.

Meeting held : Once in a month.
Members : 15 including AWW, teacher, pregnant women, *sathin, dai, gram sevika,* public representative, effective women of different castes, active women of particular community etc.

VIKALP SCHEME*

Launched in April 1995

- *Implemented in*: Tonk and Dausa
- *Vikalp*: An alternative framework for improved management of the family planning programme in the broader context of reproductive health.
- *Devised jointly by a research team at the IIHMR, Jaipur and GoR*: Vikalp aims at fulfilling the unmet reproductive health and family planning needs. It provides a mechanism for centering the family planning programme around reproductive health, turning the formerly target-driven system on its hand.

Framework

- ➢ Provision of client-based services,
- ➢ Inclusion of non-medical issues,
- ➢ Integration of Maternal and Child Health with family planning and
- ➢ Utilization of a focused approach.

Provision of client-based services

With a legacy of targets set at the top, the current Indian family planning programme is provider-oriented, rather than client-based. Similarly, services delivery is supply-driven, as the material available does not reflect the client's needs. Thus, the system has resulted in service delivery that is often unsuitable for the recipient. A striking feature of India's demographic scenario is the unmet need for family planning services.

Inclusion of non-medical issues

To view family planning as a non-medical problem. The key player in such preventive and promotive measures is health education and it must focus on improving the health behaviour of clients. A few areas such as RTIs, STIs, adolescent sexual health and nutrition have emerged recently where preventive and promotive measures would have considerable impact.

The Vikalp framework argues in favour of creating a programme not integrated with curative health services.

Integration of maternal and child health with family planning

The Vikalp framework integrates MCH and FP. Rationalization of the existing structure by integrating MCH and FP accomplishes three things: (1) It consolidates vertical programmes that are already overlapping;

* *Vikalp*: Managing the family planning programme in the post ICPD Era: An Experiment in Rajasthan, India: Kothari Devedra etc., Occasional paper No. 2, Sep. 1997, IIHMR, Jaipur.

(2) Provides focused attention on family planning and reproductive health at the field level; and (3) It increases the acceptance of family planning, thus raising contraceptive use.

Utilization of a focused approach

The basis for a focused approach boils down to four essential components: (1) An essential package of services comprising basic family planning and MCH services should be offered during the initial programme period and it can be built upon in the future; (2) The programme should focus on the 'unmet need' segment, and gradually expand to other segments; (3) Full-time managers should be posted at both state and district levels exclusively to look after the programme and (4) Restructure the organization to focus on these issues with a clear-cut line command.

Essential package of services

The Vikalp package of services can well become a means to make an initial breakthrough in population stabilization. It includes essential services for family planning and reproductive health, including ante-natal (ANC) and post-natal care (PNC), with the following components:

- Improving access to and choice of family planning methods;
- Prevention and management of unwanted pregnancies;
- Interventions to promote safe motherhood;
- Intervention to improve child survival;
- Prevention and management of Reproductive Tract Infections (RTIs), and
- Sexually Transmitted Infections (STIs) in a phased manner.

BOX 5.9: Static and FRU Centres, Rajasthan

Objectives: to ensure quality in family planning operations and FW services.

Functions
- ➢ Family planning operations,
- ➢ Insertion of copper-T and
- ➢ Other FW services.

Achievement (up to Dec. 04)
- ➢ Family planning operations held: 68361
- ➢ Copper T inserted: 35665
- ➢ Total No. of static centres established : 214
- ➢ Total No. of FRU centres established: 138

NATIONAL MATERNITY BENEFIT SCHEME (NMBS)

Nodal Department

- ➢ WCD (Women and Child Department) up to 31st March 02
- ➢ FWD (Family Welfare Department) since 1st April, 02

Financial assistance by

- ➢ GoI (under National Social Assistance Programme)

Scheme

- ➢ Rs.500 in cash given to pregnant women of BPL family in the first and the second delivery (each) as pre-natal and post-natal care.

Eligibility

- Pregnant woman should belongs to BPL family
- Minimum age 19 years.
- Original residence of Rajasthan.
- Registered at the nearest PHC for delivery

Achievement (up to Dec. 2004)

- Women Benefited: 6543
- Expenditure incured: Rs. 3.27 million

EMPLOYEES STATE INSURANCE SCHEME (ESIS)

- Launched in 1956
- It is a social security scheme, sponsored by GoI where the expenditure between the ESI Corporation and the state government is shared in the ratio of 7:1.
- *Objectives*: To provide ideal medical facilities to the insured labourers of various industries, factories etc. and their family members
- **Other Programmes Undertaken**
  - ➢ Measures for birth control
  - ➢ Child immunization.
  - ➢ Specialized services also provided to insured patients and their family members.
- **Provision under Tenth Five Year Plan**
  - ➢ A sum of Rs. 24.29 million has been made during X FYP period as state's share.
- **Present position**
  - ➢ ESI hospitals: 4 (Kota, Jodhpur, Bhilwara and Pali)
  - ➢ ESI dispensaries: 62
  - ➢ ESI homeopathic dispensary: 1 (Jaipur)
  - ➢ In-door beds available in the hospitals: >600
  - ➢ A revolving fund of Rs. 13.75 million has been created.
  - ➢ Rs. 11.57 million has been provided to insured persons up to Dec. 04.
  - ➢ Patient treated up to Dec. 2004
- Out-door: 1.6 million
- In-door: 8884

JAN MANGAL SCHEME

- Launched in 1992
- Funding Agency: UNICEF, UNFPA, WB.
- Implementing Agency: Family Welfare Department through the network of health institution
- ***District Covered***
  - ➢ Initially launched in 2 districts (Alwar and Udaipur).
  - ➢ 11 districts covered under WB- financial assistance
  - ➢ 4 districts covered under UNICEF financial assistance

Objectives

- To motivate the eligible couples to use family planning methods.
- To promote spacing method for the health of the mother and child.

- To make contraceptive available through community volunteers in all villages having more than 500 population.
- To overcome geographical, cultural and motivational barriers to use contraceptives.
- To increase contraceptive prevalence rate by 12 per cent in the project area in 3 years.

Functioning

Jan Mangal (JM) scheme is a strategy to extend the reach of contraceptive availability in the community. Through Jan Mangal, community contraceptive distribution has been attempted. Identification and training of a couple (called JM couple) at the village level has been done to communicate with the people on the need for spacing their children.

Selection of JM couple in each village has been done by concerning ANM taking into consideration the cultural sensitivity of the village. The husband discusses the concept of spacing and promote condoms to males. The wife promotes oral pills. Selected couples are trained for 3 days on need and benefits of using spacing methods and their likely side effects. Constant contact and retraining is envisaged.

State government decided to create on independent unit headed by non-government person. A JM coordination unit was established in Feb. 1997 as part of the State Health and Family Welfare Society for Voluntary Sector, Rajasthan. This was headed by a state coordinator in April 1997. He was assisted by two assistants and support staff. This unit was established at the state level. District coordinators, who are to work closely with the district health system are appointed in each district.

Provision made for Tenth Five Year Plan period: Rs. 56.5 million

TABLE 5.15: Jan Mangal Scheme Rajasthan : Achievements (2000-04)

(in '000)

Year	*No. of Selected JM Couples*	*No. of Trained JM Couples*	*No. of Beneficiaries (Based on Contraceptives)*	
			Oral Pills	*Condoms*
2000-2001	15.4	14.0	92.8	151.0
2001-2002	16.7	10.5	82.2	118.8
2002-2003	28.3	12.9	78.9	115.8
2003-2004	35.4	26.2	110.4	167.4
2004-2005*	38.5	32.9	271.5	335.7

* Up to Dec. 04

Source: *'Pragati Prativedan'*, 2004-05, Directorate of Medical, Health and Family Welfare GoR, Jaipur.

VILLAGE HEALTH GUIDE SCHEME (VHGS)

Started on : 2nd Oct. 1977

Jointly run by : Department of Medical, Health and Family Welfare, Panchayati Raj and Rural Development

Objectives

- To impart training to rural persons to provide first aid needed for basic health services.
- AWWs are being also imparting training for the same.

BOX 5.10: Traditional Birth Attendant (Village-DAIS) Training Programme

Started in	: 1976-77
Objective	: To provide better delivery services to the rural community by a trained person.
Norm	: One TBA per 1000 population
Training	: Imparting 30 day training to practicing dais at PHC/sub-centre
Stipend	: Rs. 300 per month
Instrument kit given	: Worth of Rs. 150
Achievements	: More than 25,000 local dais have been trained.

MINIMUM NEEDS PROGRAMME (MNP)

Initiated by GoI as a separate programme in the Fifth Five Year Plan.

Objective

To provide primary health care to rural population mainly to people living below poverty line and to unreached communities and sectors.

Rural health facility-Norms

- One SHC per 3* to 5 thousand population.
- One PHC per 20*to 30 thousand population.
- One CHC per 100 thousand population.

BOX 5.11: Information, Education and Communication (IEC) Bureau, Rajasthan

- 'Apex organization at the state level for health education and family welfare communication programme'.
- It is the first attempt of its kind in the country in providing the needed status for communication activities for generating demand for the health and family welfare programmes.

Established in : 1990
Funded by : UNFPA

Formation

By integration of the existing health education bureau, the mass education and media wing of the Directorate of Medical and Health and other publicity and education cells of the Directorate into unified, functionally independent set up and by upgrading their facilities.

Objectives

To achieve the targets of FWPs by converting awareness and knowledge into acceptance through mass media, inter-personal communication and motivation.

Activities and FW Campaigning

- Intensive IEC campaigning through songs and drama division, doordarshan (TV), All India Radio, Directorate of Field Publicity, Directorate of Advertisement and Visual Publicity etc.
- To plan, execute, monitor and evaluate IEC programmes and extension activities.
- It provides communication material, train workers and carry out research.
- 'Niramaya' a departmental newsletter is also produced.
- Communication campaign on universal immunization programme, malaria, RCH, dengue, pulse-polio, seasonal diseases, FWPs etc.
- Communication campaign on increasing the age of marriage.
- Communication campaign of dirrhoea.
- Intensive health education of primary schools children.
- Training/orientation of the workers of Medical & Health ICDS and Adult Education Department.
- Organizing Mahila Swasthya Sangh.
- Use of out-door media like hoardings, signboards, wall painting, fold media, exhibitions etc. for campaigning.
- Observe Population day on 11th July (every year)-calls for population stabilization through community participation.

Achievements (April-Dec. 2004)

Cultural programmes organised	1868	MSS Meetings	16511
Exhibitions	949	District Level Seminars	424
Film Shows	18	Seminars on Child Marriages	183
Wall Paintings	9197	District-Level Workshop	439
Mothers' Meetings	45477	Audio-Cassette Publicity	269
Group Discussions	5607	Cinema Slide Show	10

UNIVERSAL IMMUNIZATION PROGRAMME (UIP)

UIP became an important and a major component of Child Survival and Safe Motherhood (CSSM) Programme.
Launched on : 19th Nov. 1985

Funding agency

- **UNICEF**—Support for supply of vaccines, ongoing training programmes and maintenance of equipments.
- **GoI**—Financial and material support.

Objectives

- To control IMR.
- To protect children by immunization against vaccine preventable diseases namely diphtheria, tetanus, pertussis, measles, tuberculosis and poliomyelitis and immunization of pregnant women with tetanus toxoid. The basic objectives of UIP are as under:
  - ➢ 85 per cent coverage of infants (0-1 year) with three doses of DPT and OVP and 1 dose of measles and BCG vaccine.
  - ➢ 100 per cent coverage of pregnant women with tetanus toxoid.
  - ➢ Eradication of poliomyelitis by 2005.
  - ➢ Reduce incidence of pertussis, diphtheria and childhood tuberculosis.
  - ➢ Reduce the incidence of measles by 90 per cent.
  - ➢ Eradication of neo-natal tetanus.

Beneficiaries

- All pregnant women are covered with 2 doses of Tetanus Toxoide in first pregnancy and with one dose of TT in subsequent pregnancy.
- All infants below one year of age are covered with 3 doses of DPT and polio, 1 dose of BCG and Measles.

Phases

The programme was implemented in a phased manner. Kota and Bharatpur districts were covered in the first year (1985-86) while, remaining other districts were covered by the year 1990 as shown in Table 5.16:

TABLE 5.16: District Covered Under UIP

Year	*District Covered*	
	No.	*Name*
1985-86	2	Kota and Bharatpur
1986-87	4	Ajmer, Sikar, Dungarpur and Banswara
1987-88	7	Bundi, Tonk, Jhalawar, Dhaulpur, S. Madhopur, Udaipur and Bikaner
1988-89	5	Nagaur, Bhilwara, Jhunjhunun, Chittaurgarh and Barmer
1989-90	9	Jaipur, Churu, Alwar, Ganganagar, Jodhpur, Jaisalmer, Pali, Sirohi and Jalor

TABLE 5.17: Universal Immunisation Programme, Rajasthan : Achievements (2002-04)

Year	*TT (Pregnant Women)*	*BCG*	*DPT-3*	*OPV-3*	*Measles*
2002-03	88.20	98.90	99.66	99.56	95.93
2003-04	87.82	102.67	99.66	99.54	91.87
2004-05 (Jan.05)	70.40	77.49	77.49	81.12	78.22

Source: *'Pragati Prativedan'*, 2004-05, Directorate of Medical, Health and Family Welfare GoR, Jaipur.

Administrative Set-up:

Director, Medical & Health Services
↓
State Immunization Officer
↓
District Immunization Officer
↓
CHC Officer
↓
PHC Officer
↓
SHC Officer

SPECIAL PULSE-POLIO CAMPAIGN (SPPC)

Objective: To attend the national goal for complete eradication of the polio. OPV are given in different phases to children in the age group of 0-5 years.

TABLE 5.18: Pulse Polio Programme: Rajasthan (2004)

Date	*Target (Million No.)*	*Achievement*	
		Million No.	*%*
4/01/2004	11.23	11.34	101.03
22/02/2004	11.34	11.39	100.41
4/04/2004	11.39	11.16	97.97
23/05/2004	11.39	11.30	99.18
10/10/2005	11.27	11.18	99.18
21/11/2005	11.27	11.33	100.51

Source: *Economic Review*, 2004 –05 DES, Rajasthan, Jaipur.

TABLE 5.19: National Polio Survey Programme Report: Rajasthan

Year	*No. of AFP Patients*	*Positive cases of Wild Polio*
2000	537	0
2001	453	0
2002	466	41
2003	452	4
2004	732	0

Source: *'Pragati Prativedan'*, 2004-05, Directorate of Medical,Health and Family Welfare GoR, Jaipur.

PILOT PROJECT ON HEPATITIS –B VACCINE

Launched on : 11th April 2003 as a pilot project in UIP for children.
Covered area : Slums area of Jaipur city.

Activity

- 3 doses of Hepatitis-B vaccine is given with 3 primary doses of DPT to children.
- Medical officers and para-medical workers have been oriented specifically to utilize the new vaccine and syringes to be used under the project.

RAJLAXMI (RL) SCHEME (1992-2000)

- ***Objectives*:** To improve the status of the girl child in the state by providing financial assistance to parents for marriage of the girl at the right age.
- RL scheme was an innovative attempt to address the issue of social naglect of the girl child, taken up by state government, that too in collaboration with a financial institution.

TABLE 5.20: Rajlaxmi Scheme—1992

Age at Entry to the Scheme	*Deposit Amount ('000 Rs.)*		*Amount at Maturity('000 Rs.)*		*Lock in Period*
	For General	*For SC/ST*	*For General*	*For SC/ST*	
1	*2*	*3*	*4*	*5*	*6*
Upto and Including 1 Year	1.0	1.5	21.0	31.5	20
1-2 Years	1.0	1.5	13.3	27.0	19
2-3 Years	1.0	1.5	11.8	22.5	18
3-4 Years	1.0	1.5	10.5	19.5	17
4-5 Years	1.0	1.5	9.3	16.5	16

Source: GoR, Note on Rajlaxmi Scheme, 1992 & 2000.

TABLE 5.21: Rajlaxmi Scheme: Beneficiaries and Expenditure Incurred

S.No.	*Year*	*Beneficiaries*				*Total*	*Expenditure Incured (Million Rs.)*
		General		*SC/ST*			
		No.	*% share of total beneficiaries*	*No.*	*% share of total beneficiarie*		
1	1992-93	4917	(100.0)	—	—	4917	4.92
2	1993-94	11957	(95.5)	559	(4.5)	12516	12.80
3	1994-95	11926	(88.8)	1507	(11.2)	13433	20.90
4	1995-96	9859	(86.7)	1508	(13.3)	11367	17.80
5	1996-97	10803	(94.2)	663	(5.8)	11466	17.53
6	1997-98	11520	(98.8)	144	(1.2)	11664	17.57
7	1998-99	9374	(99.7)	26	(0.3)	9400	14.11
8	1999-2000	14574	(100.0)	—	—	14574	21.86
9	2000-2001	1750	(100.0)	—	—	1750	2.63
Total		**86680**	**(95.2)**	**4407**	**(4.8)**	**91087**	**130.12**

Source: GoR, Note on Rajlaxmi Scheme, 2000.

6

HEALTH ORGANISATION

In Rajasthan, a three-tier system has been adopted in Health, Medical and Family Welfare Services both at the state level and at the district level. Directorate of Medical and Health Services is the apex body in the state. It is branching out to different zones represented by Zonal Directorates. Each zone has a cluster of districts with Chief Medical & Health Officer (CMHO) as head of the office (Model 6.1).

Community Health Centre (CHC) is the apex body in each district for rural health services. It is also spanning out to PHCs (Primary Health Centres). Each PHC is further branching out into SHCs (Sub-Health Centres, Model 6.2).

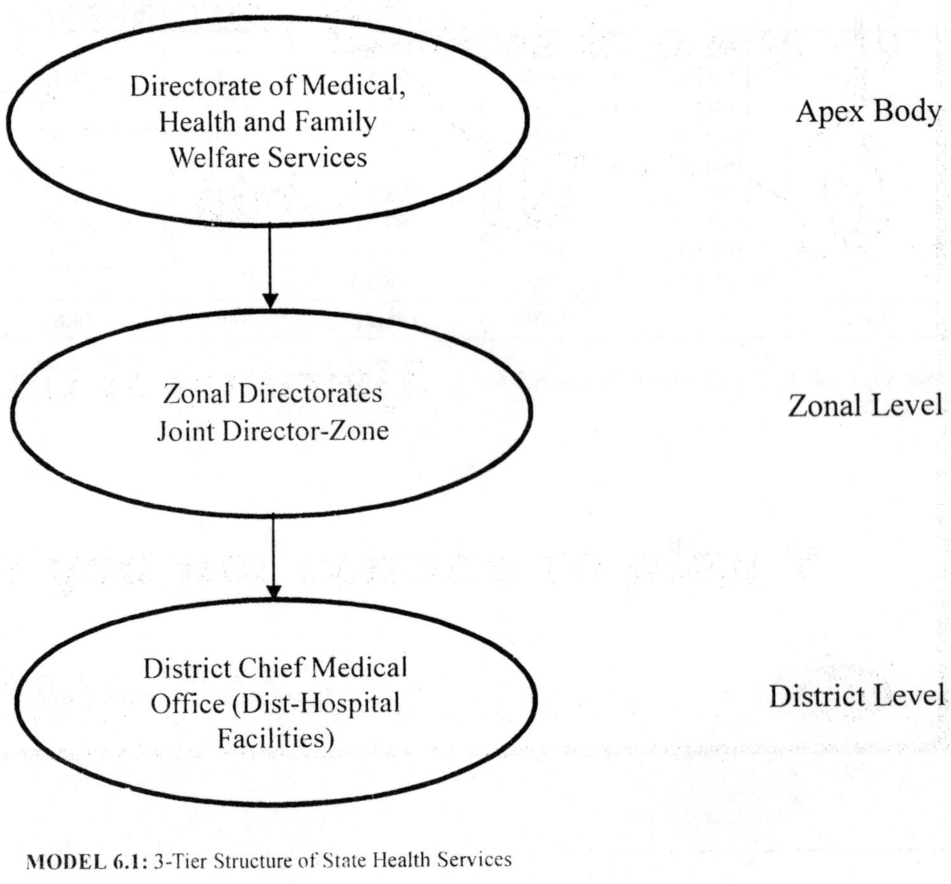

MODEL 6.1: 3-Tier Structure of State Health Services

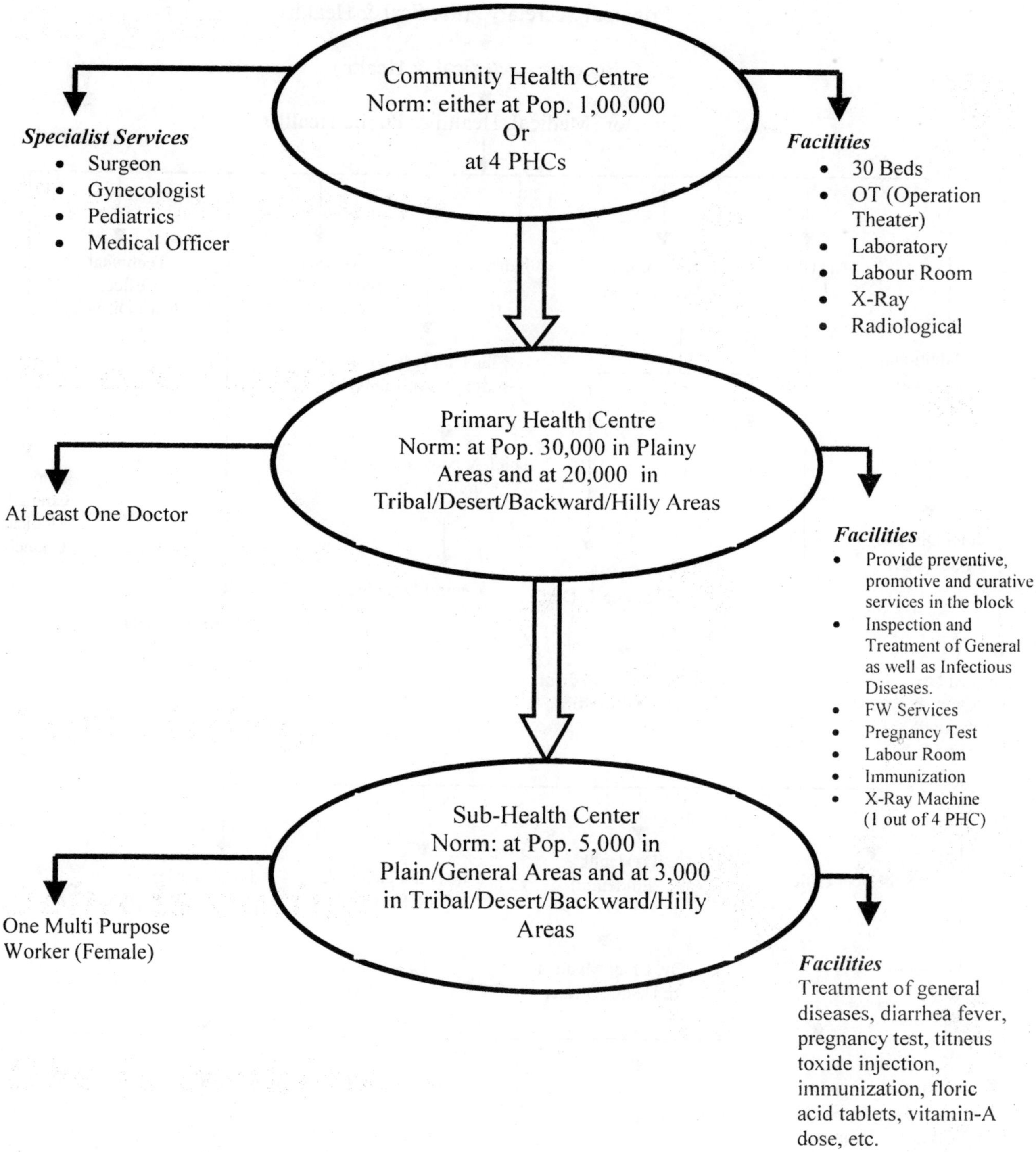

MODEL 6.2: 3-Tier Structure of Rural Health System

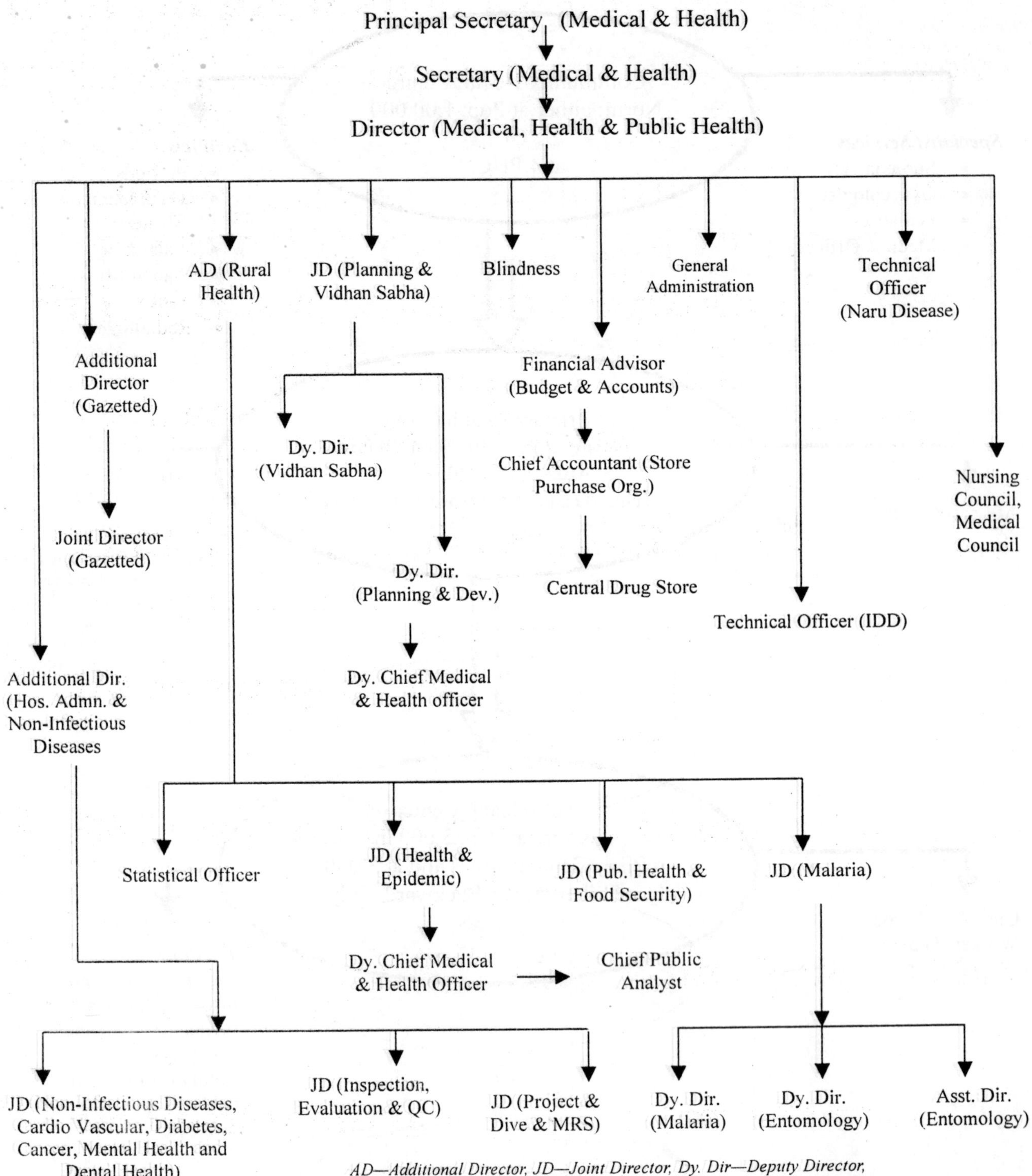

AD—Additional Director, JD—Joint Director, Dy. Dir—Deputy Director, QC—Quality Control, Hos—Hospital, Asst.—Assistant, Dev.—Development

CHART 6.1: Medical and Health Department: Administrative Structure

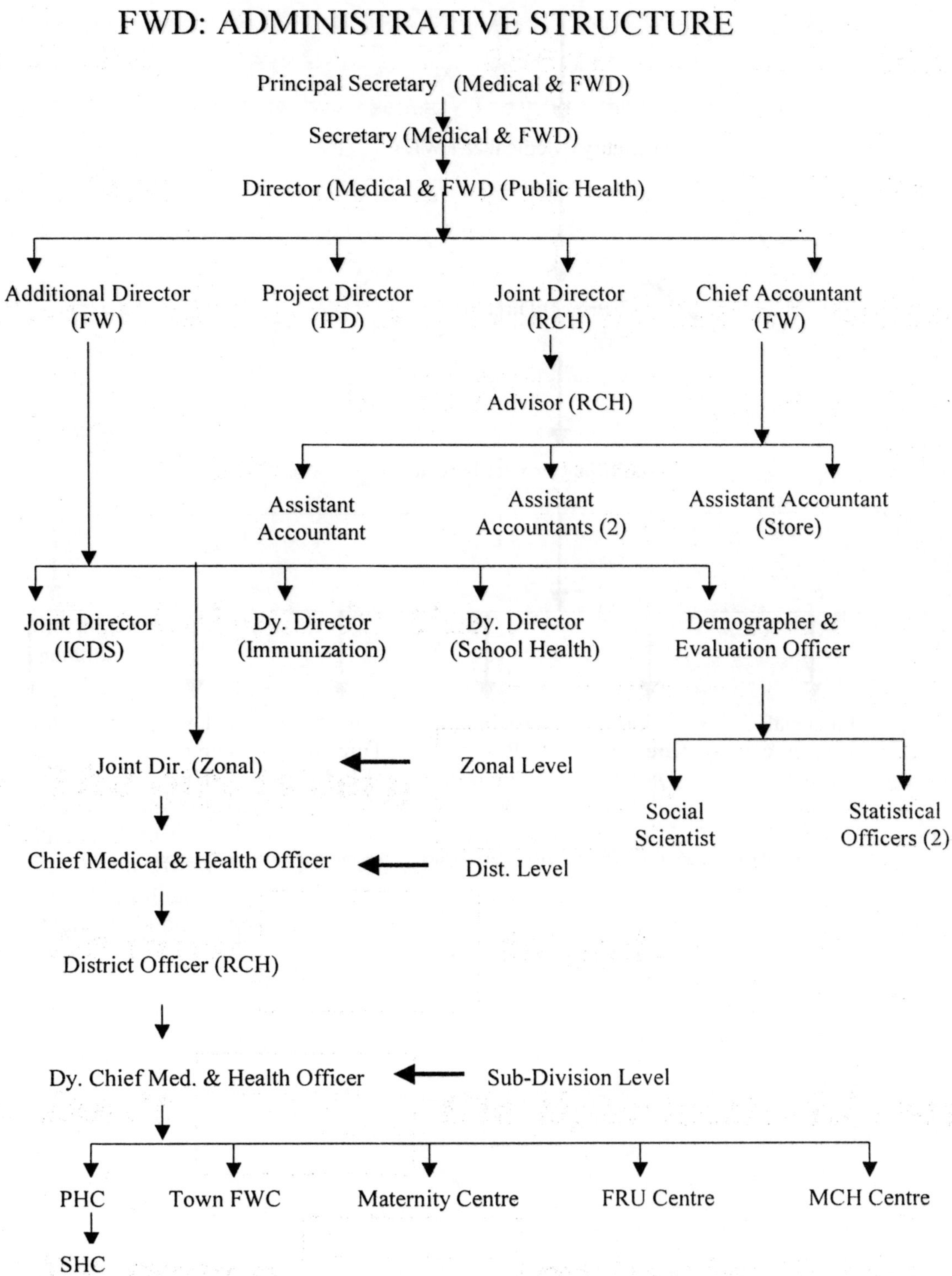

CHART 6.2: FWD: Administrative Structure

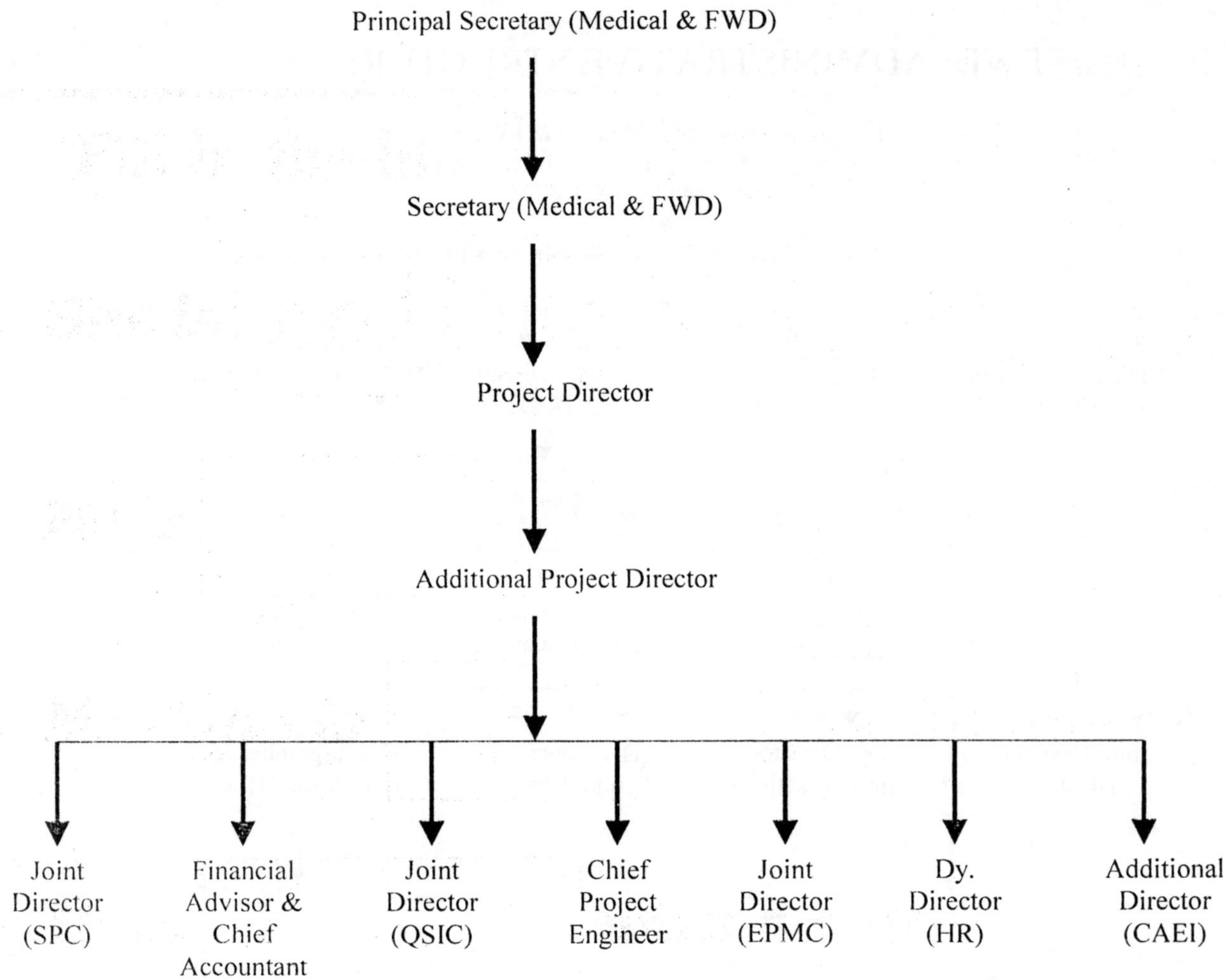

CHART 6.3: Rajasthan Health System Development Project: Administrative Structure

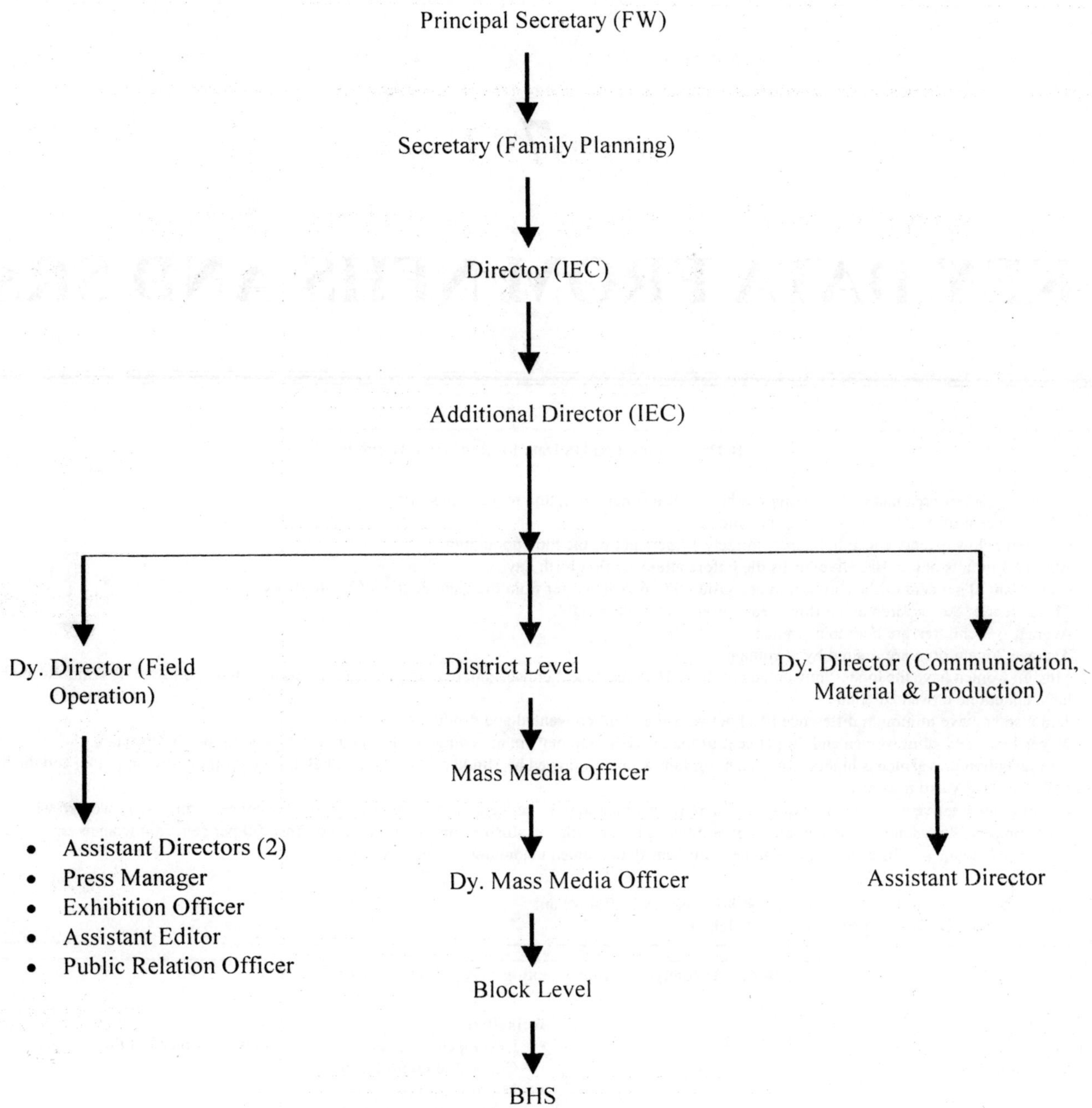

CHART 6.4: IEC Bureau: Administrative Structure

7

KEY DATA FROM NFHS AND SRS

BOX 7.1: Latest NFHS Data for Rajasthan: Highlights

- 51.55 per cent of pregnant and lactating mothers in Rajasthan are found to have anaemia.
- 48-49 per cent of working women are anaemic.
- Children below 6 years constitute approximately 17 per cent of the total population.
- About 83 infants out of 1000 live births die before attaining first birth day.
- More than 50 per cent of the children in age group 0 to 6 years suffer from different degree of malnutrition.
- 51 per cent of the children under three years of age are underweight.
- Average 3.8 children are born to a woman.
- Average 2.6 children are desired by a woman.
- Muslim women have the highest unwanted children. They produce 2 children more than they actually want to have followed by Hindu women who have about one unwanted child.
- Jain women have minimum difference (0.3) between the children wanted and produced.
- 75 per cent of Muslim women and 70 per cent of the SC & ST women are not using any FP method which is highest in the state.
- Contraception prevalence is highest (66%) among Jain women followed by Hindu (41%), women belonging to other religion (53%) and the lowest (25%) among Muslim women.
- Use of contraceptive methods increases with increasing education, 37 per cent among illiterate women to 59 per cent among women who have at least complete high school. Three quarters of Hindus and four-fifths of Muslims are illiterate. In contrast, 90 per cent Jain women are literate.
- The use of female sterilization is lower among Muslims than women belonging to other religions.

Source: 1. National Family Health Survey, 1998-99 (NFHS-2) Rajasthan.
2. *Hindustan Times*, 12th April, 2004, Jaipur.

BOX 7.2: Analysis of Implementing TFA in Rajasthan (1996-97)

Category	**Rajasthan**
Planning	• Developed a comprehensive strategy to implement the change.
Methodology	• Conducted eligible couple survey. • Microplanning. • Service delivery booklets. • Initiated several innovative schemes.
Training	• Training institute/centres were set-up and training policy made.
Monitoring and evaluation	• Developed their own monitoring and evaluation system. • The salient features of the system are concurrent evaluation and feedback mechanism.
Implementation	• Implemented as per plan.
Performance during the fiscal year 1996-97, as compared to 1995-96	• Overall performance for all methods improved.
Perception of the family welfare service providers about TFA	• Uniformity in understanding TFA. • Concept of unmet need, which is the basis for providing services, has percolated down to all levels.

Source: SRS.

TABLE 7.1: Crude Birth Rate and Total Fertility Rate: Rajasthan (NFHS 1 & 2)

	NFS-1 (1992-93)			*NFHS-2 (1998-99)*		
	Rural	*Urban*	*Total*	*Rural*	*Urban*	*Rural*
CBR	28.1	22.3	27.0	31.4	25.3	29.9
TFR	3.9	2.8	3.6	4.1	3.0	3.8

Source: *National Family Health Survey,* (NFHS-1 & 2) Rajasthan, Preliminary Report.

TABLE 7.2: Infant and Child Mortality Rates for Three Five-Year Periods Preceding the Survey: Rajasthan, (NFHS-1 & 2)

Years Preceding Survey	*Neonatal Mortality (NN)*		*Post-Neonatal Mortality (PNN)*		*Infant Mortality (1q0)*		*Child Mortality (4q1)*		*Under Five Mortality (5q0)*	
	NFHS-1	*NFHS-2*	*NFHS-1*	*NFHS-2*	*NFHS-1*	*NFHS-2*	*NFHS-1*	*NFHS-2*	*NFHS-1*	*NFHS-2*
0-4	37.2	49.5	35.4	30.9	72.6	80.4	32.3	37.6	10.2	114.9
5-9	—	58.4	—	36.9	—	95.4	—	43.2	—	134.5
10-14	—	58.3	—	39.0	—	97.3	—	53.0	—	145.1

Source: *Health Monitor,* 2004, Foundation for Research in Health Systems, Ahmedabad.

TABLE 7.3: Percentage of Live Births by Various Maternal Care Indicators: Rajasthan (NFHS-1 & 2)

	% Receiving Antenatal Care	*% Receiving Two Doses of TT Vaccine**	*% Receiving Iron/Folic Tablets*	*% of Births Delivered in Medical Institutions*	*% of Deliveries Assisted by Health Professionals***
NFHS-1	31.2	28.3	29.2	11.6	21.8
NFHS-2	47.5	52.1	39.3	21.5	35.8

* Includes women who received more than two doses.
** Aliopathic doctor or nurse/midwifes.
Source: *Health Monitor,* 2004, Foundation for Research in Health Systems, Ahmedabad.

TABLE 7.4: Achievements Under Some Selected Indicators of Health: Rajasthan (NFHS-1 & 2)

	IMR	*CMR*	*CBR*	*CPR*	*ANC*	*TT**	*BCG*	*DPT*	*OPV*	*Measels*	*Full Immunisation***
NFHS-1	72.6	32.3	27	31.8	31.2	28.3	45.7	29.7	32.8	31.2	21.1
NFHS-2	80.4	37.6	29.9	40.3	47.5	52.1	53.9	26.1	44.6	27.1	17.3

* Includes women who received more than two doses.
** BCG, Measles and three doses each of DPT and Polio Vaccine.
Source: *Health Monitor,* 2004, Foundation for Research in Health Systems, Ahmedabad.

TABLE 7.5: Age-Specific and Total Fertility Rates: Rajasthan (NFHS 1 & 2)

	Age-Specific Fertility Rates					
	Rural		*Urban*		*Total*	
	NFHS-1	*NFHS-2*	*NFHS-1*	*NFHS-2*	*NFHS-1*	*NFHS-2*
	1990-92	*1996-98*	*1990-92*	*1996-98*	*1990-92*	*1996-98*
15-19	124	139	63	91	112	126
20-24	264	280	184	219	247	264
25-29	181	189	181	157	181	181
30-34	113	113	87	76	107	103
35-39	61	53	31	36	55	48
40-44	17	27	0	13	14	23
45-49	11	11	7	4	10	9
TFR	387	406	277	298	363	378

Source: *National Family Health Survey,* 1998-99 (NFHS-2) Rajasthan, Preliminary Report.

TABLE 7.6: Percentage Distribution of Currently Married Women by Contraceptive Method Currently Used, According to Background Characteristics: Rajasthan, 1998-99

Contraceptive Methods	*Rural*	*Urban*	*Total 15-49*
Any Method	37.1	50.4	40.3
Modern Method	35.3	46.9	38.1
PILL	1.2	2.4	1.5
IUD	0.9	2.1	1.2
Condom	1.7	7.6	3.1
Female Sterilization	30.1	33.0	30.8
Male Sterilization	1.3	1.9	1.5
Traditional Method	1.6	2.9	1.9
Rhythm/Safe Period	1.2	1.9	1.3
Withdrawal	0.4	1.0	0.6
Other Method	0.2	0.5	0.3

Source: *National Family Health Survey*, 1998-99 (NFHS-2) Rajasthan, Preliminary Report.

TABLE 7.7: Percentage of Currently Married Women by Knowledge, Ever Use and Current Use of Family Planning Methods: Rajasthan, 1998-99

Contraceptive Methods	*Rural*			*Urban*			*Total*		
	% Who Know Method	*% Who Ever Used Method*	*% Currently Using Method*	*% Who Know Method*	*% Who Ever Used Method*	*% Currently Using Method*	*% Who Know Method*	*% Who Ever Used Method*	*% Currently Using Method*
Any Method	98.5	42.6	37.1	99.6	61.0	50.4	98.8	47.0	40.3
Modern Method	98.4	40.3	35.3	99.6	58.3	46.9	98.7	44.6	38.1
PILL	74.5	5.5	1.2	93.3	10.6	2.4	79.0	6.7	1.5
IUD	63.6	2.7	0.9	87.4	8.9	2.1	69.3	4.2	1.2
Condom	69.4	5.2	1.7	89.9	20.7	7.6	74.4	8.9	3.1
Female Sterilization	97.4	30.1	30.1	98.9	33.0	33.0	97.8	30.8	30.8
Male Sterilization	88.9	1.5	1.3	96.3	1.9	1.9	90.7	1.6	1.5
Tradiational Method	28.4	4.4	1.6	44.3	11.0	2.9	32.2	6.0	1.9
Rhythm/Safe Period	25.8	3.4	1.2	40.9	8.4	1.9	29.4	4.6	1.3
Withdrawal	13.9	1.7	0.4	28.0	7.2	1.0	17.3	3.0	0.6
Other Method	1.6	0.5	0.2	2.3	1.1	0.5	1.8	0.6	0.3

Source: *National Family Health Survey*, 1998-99 (NFHS-2) Rajasthan, Preliminary Report.

TABLE 7.8: Percentage of Currently Married Women Reporting Various Symptoms of Reproductive Tract Infections: Rajasthan (NFHS-2)

% with any abnormal vaginal discharge	36.8
% with symptoms of a urinary tract infection	19.1
% with any abnormal vaginal discharge or symptoms of a urinary tract infection	41.3
% with painful intercourse (often)	11.1
% with bleeding after intercourse (ever)	1.8
% with any reproductive health problem	43.2

Source: *Health Monitor*, 2004, Foundation for Research in Health Systems, Ahmedabad.

TABLE 7.9: Percentage Distribution of Women and Children by Degree of Iron-Deficiency Anemia, According to Background Characteristics: Rajasthan, 1998-89

Anemia	*Rural*	*Urban*	*Total*	*Rural*	*Urban*	*Rural*
	Percentage of Women With			*Percentage of Children (<3 Years of age) With*		
Mild Anemia	32.9	31.1	32.5	20.7	19.2	20.4
Moderate Anemia	14.2	13.9	14.1	48.2	47.2	48.0
Severe Anemia	2.3	1.7	2.1	8.1	7.7	8.0
Total	**49.3**	**46.7**	**48.7**	**77.0**	**74.1**	**76.4**

Source: *National Family Health Survey*, (NFHS-1 & 2) Rajasthan, Preliminary Report.

TABLE 7.10: Percentage of Children Age 12-23 Months with Vaccination Card Seen by the Interviewer, and the Percentage Who Have Received Each Vaccination (According to the Vaccination Card or Mother's Report), by Background Characteristics: Rajasthan, 1998-99.

Background Characteristic	*Rural*	*Urban*	*Total*	*Total From NFHS-1, 1992-93*
Percentae with a Card	11.2	27.2	14.7	16.3
	Percentage of Children Age 12-23 Months Who Received			
BCG	50.8	65.1	53.9	45.7
POLIO 0	4.0	9.5	5.2	11.4
DPT1	44.1	60.9	47.8	47.8
DPT2	36.3	53.9	40.2	38.6
DPT3	22.3	39.6	26.1	29.7
POLIO1	73.8	81.1	75.5	48.8
POLIO2	64.0	76.2	66.6	41.2
POLIO3	40.9	51.3	43.2	32.8
MEASLES	23.7	39.3	27.1	31.2
ALL	13.1	26.4	16.0	21.1
NONE	23.9	17.7	22.5	48.5

Source: *National Family Health Survey,* 1998-99 (NFHS-2) Rajasthan, Preliminary Report.

TABLE 7.11: Survey of Causes of Death Data for Rural Rajasthan (1985)

S.No.	**(A) Percentage Distribution of Deaths by Major Cause Groups** *Major Cause-Groups*	*Rajasthan*
1	Senility	17.2
2	Coughs (Disorders of Respiratory System)	27.7
3	Causes Peculiar to Infancy	8.9
4	Diseases of Circulatory System	8.8
5	Fevers	10.2
6	Other Clear Symptoms	6.9
7	Digestive Disorders	6.4
8	Accidents & Injuries	6.2
9	Others	7.7
S.No.	**(B) Percentage Distribution of Deaths by Sub Cause Groups** *Sub Cause-Groups*	*Rajasthan*
1	Prematurity	36.4
2	Birth Injury	1.9
3	Respiratory Infection	6.5
4	Cord Infection	18.7
5	Diarrhoea	10.3
6	Others	26.2
S.No.	**(C) Percentage Distribution of Deaths due to 10 Selected Important Diseases** *Important Causes of Death*	*Rajasthan*
1	Asthma & Bronchitis	7.0
2	T.B. of Lungs	3.5
3	Pneumonia	5.5
4	Heart Attack	8.4
5	Anaemia	2.1
6.	Cancer	4.1
7	Gasteroenterities	5.3
8	Typhoid	3.1
9	Malaria	0.6
10	Dysentery	1.4
S.No.	**(D) Proportion of Total Rural Deaths by Age Groups** *Age Group*	*Rajasthan*
1	< 1	22.3
2	1-04	11.0
3	5-14	4.5
4	15-24	4.2
5	25-34	5.5
6	35-44	6.3
7	45-54	8.0
8	55+	38.2

Source: *Survey of Causes of Death (Rural) Annual Report* 1985, Office of the Registrar General, India, Ministry of Home Affairs, New Delhi, 1987.

Table 7.12: SRS Data for Rajasthan

Item		*Rajasthan*
Life Expectancy at Birth (2001-06)	(i) Male	62.17
	(ii) Female	62.80
Infant Mortality Rate (per 1000 live births, 2002)	(i) Male	75
	(ii) Female	80
	(iii) Total	78
	(iv) Rural *	81
	(v) Urban *	55
	(vi) Total *	78
Crude Death Rate (per 1000), 2002 (P)	(i) Rural	8.0
	(ii) Urban	6.4
	(iii) Total	7.7
Crude Birth Rate (per 1000), 2002 (P)	(i) Rural	30.6
	(ii) Urban	31.9
	(iii) Total	24.2
Female Age at Effective Marriage, SRS, 2000	(i) Rural	19.1
	(ii) Urban	20.5
	(iii) Total	19.3
General Fertility Rate (GFR), SRS, 2000	(i) Rural	142.8
	(ii) Urban	97.8
	(iii) Total	134.2
Total Fertility Rate (TFR), SRS, 2000	(i) Rural	4.4
	(ii) Urban	2.9
	(iii) Total	4.1
Total Marital Fertility Rate (TMFR), SRS, 1998	(i) Rural	5.2
	(ii) Urban	4.1
	(iii) Total	5.0
Gross Reproduction Rate (GRR), SRS, 2000	(i) Rural	2.1
	(ii) Urban	1.4
	(iii) Total	2.0
Neo-natal Mortality Rates, SRS, 2000	(i) Rural	52
	(ii) Urban	32
	(iii) Total	49
Peri-natal Mortality Rates, SRS, 2000	(i) Rural	40
	(ii) Urban	30
	(iii) Total	39
Still- Birth Rates, SRS, 2000	(i) Rural	6
	(ii) Urban	9
	(iii) Total	6
Percentage of Neo-natal Deaths to Infant Deaths, 2000	(i) Rural	63.1
	(ii) Urban	54.4
	(iii) Total	62.2
ASFR/ASMFR, SRS, 2000	(i) 15-19	65.2
	(ii) 20-24	283.7
	(iii) 25-29	233.3
	(iv) 30-34	131.9
	(v) 35-39	68.9
	(vi) 40-44	31.4
	(vii) 45-49	10.8
ASMFR, SRS, 2000	(i) 15-19	165.9
	(ii) 20-24	342.7
	(iii) 25-29	241.9
	(iv) 30-34	135.3
	(v) 35-39	71.4
	(vi) 40-44	33.4
	(vii) 45-49	11.9
Percentage Share of Institutional Birth, SRS, 2002	(i) Rural	5.0
	(ii) Urban	29.3
	(iii) Total	8.4
Deliveries Attended by Doctor, Nurse or Trained Midwife	(i) Rural	24.1
	(ii) Urban	40.8
	(iii) Total	26.4

Source: 1. *'Statistical Report'*, 1998, SRS, RGI, New Delhi
2. *'SRS Bulletin'* Oct 2002, Vol. 36, No. 2, RGI, New Delhi

TABLE 7.13: Estimated Death Rate and IMR by Sex and Residence: Rajasthan, 1972-97

Year	Rural			Urban			Total		
	Total	Male	Female	Total	Male	Female	Total	Male	Female
1	2	3	4	5	6	7	8	9	10
	[I] Estimated Death Rate								
1972	18.3	18.1	18.5	10.1	9.8	10.3	16.8	16.7	16.9
1981	15.8	15.4	16.2	7.6	8.1	7.0	14.3	14.1	14.6
1991	10.6	10.6	10.6	7.7	7.8	7.5	10.1	10.1	10.1
1997	9.3	9.2	9.4	7.0	8.3	5.6	8.9	9.0	8.7
	[II] IMR								
1982	105	103	108	60	64	56	97	96	98
1991	84	83	85	50	47	54	79	77	80
1997	89	77	101	61	58	64	85	75	96

Source: Compendium of India's Fertility and Mortality Indicators, 1971-1997 Based on SRS-99.

TABLE 7.14: Infant Mortality Rate by Sex and Residence from 1970-75 and 1992-96

S.No.	At Age	Year	Rural			Urban			Total		
			Total	Male	Female	Total	Male	Female	Total	Male	Female
1	2	3	4	5	6	7	8	9	10	11	12
1	0	1970-75	48.4	49.2	49.2	46.6	47.5	45.6	59.6	59.8	59.3
		1992-96	59.5	58.6	59.6	57.5	57.6	57.5	63.9	64.4	64.8
2	1	1970-75	55.0	55.6	54.4	53.5	54.2	52.9	63.7	63.7	63.7
		1992-96	64.6	63.7	64.9	62.9	62.9	63.0	67.2	68.2	67.8
3	5	1970-75	58.4	57.8	59.2	57.5	56.9	58.3	63.6	62.8	64.4
		1992-96	63.1	61.6	63.9	61.4	60.9	62.1	64.7	65.7	66.0
4	50	1970-75	21.1	19.9	22.6	20.6	19.4	22.2	24.0	23.0	25.1
		1992-96	23.7	21.9	24.6	22.1	21.4	23.0	24.2	25.2	25.2
5	60	1970-75	14.6	13.6	15.7	14.3	13.2	15.4	16.9	16.3	17.4
		1992-96	16.0	14.7	16.3	14.3	14.2	14.6	17.0	17.8	16.6
6	70+	1970-75	10.0	9.3	10.7	9.7	9.0	10.4	11.8	11.4	12.3
		1992-96	9.8	8.8	9.5	7.9	8.3	7.7	11.2	12.1	9.4

Source: Compendium of India's Fertility and Mortality Indicators, 1971-1997 Based on SRS-99.

TABLE 7.15: Annual Estimates of Birth Rate, Death Rate, Natural Growth Rate, Infant Mortality Rate and Total Fertility Rate: Rajasthan, 1972-1997

S.No.	Year	Birth Rate			Death Rate			Natural Growth Rate			Infant Mortality Rate			Total Fertility Rate		
		Rural	Urban	Total	Rural	Urban	Total	Rural	Urban	Total	Rural	Urban	Total	Rural	Urban	Total
1	2	3	4	5	6	7	8	9	10	11	12	13	14	15	16	17
1	1972	43.5	37.2	42.4	18.3	10.1	16.8	25.2	27.1	25.6	132.0	76.0	123.0	6.4	5.4	6.3
2	1981	38.3	31.2	37.1	15.8	7.6	14.3	22.5	23.6	22.8	118.0	53.0	108.0	5.5	4.2	5.2
3	1991	36.0	30.3	35.0	10.6	7.7	10.1	25.4	22.6	24.9	84.0	50.0	79.0	4.9	3.7	4.6
4	1997	33.7	25.1	32.1	9.3	7.0	8.9	24.4	18.1	23.2	89.0	61.0	85.0	4.5	3.0	4.2

Source: *Compendium of India's Fertility and Mortality Indicators*, 1971-1997 Based on SRS-99.

TABLE 7.16: Infant Mortality Indicators by Residence from 1972-1997

S.No.	Year	Infant Mortality Rate			Neo-Natal Mortality Rate			Post-Natal Mortality Rate			Peri-Natal Mortality Rate			Still Birth Rate		
		Rural	Urban	Total	Rural	Urban	Total	Rural	Urban	Total	Rural	Urban	Total	Rural	Urban	Total
1	2	3	4	5	6	7	8	9	10	11	12	13	14	15	16	17
1	1972	132	76	123	75.8	39.5	70.4	59.2	36.5	52.6	66.6	39.7	62.6	14.8	11.6	14.3
2	1981	118	53	108	65.2	28.0	59.6	52.8	24.8	48.7	45.1	20.0	41.4	8.1	5.0	7.6
3	1991	84	50	79	52.0	28.7	48.4	31.7	21.5	30.2	42.2	24.2	39.5	6.5	2.7	5.9
4	1997	89	61	85	56.4	46.5	55.0	32.2	14.4	29.7	50.4	46.5	49.9	6.4	5.7	6.3

Source: *Compendium of India's Fertility and Mortality Indicators*, 1971-1997 Based on SRS-99.

TABLE 7.17: Fertility Indicators: Rajasthan, 1981, 1991 & 1997

S.No.	*Indicators*	*Age Group*	*1981*	*1991*	*1997*
1	*2*	*3*	*4*	*5*	*6*
		Rural			
1	Age Specific Fertility Rate	15-1	92.7	90.7	66.4
		20-24	280.3	294.2	296.4
		25-29	258.5	255.7	244.1
		30-34	211.9	167.2	149.5
		35-39	148.6	96.3	86.2
		40-44	74.6	46.7	39.1
		45-49	29.4	22.6	14.5
2	General Fertility Rate		166.6	154.8	145.6
3	Total Fertility Rate		5.5	4.9	4.5
4	Gross Reproduction Rate		2.6	2.3	2.1
		Urban			
1	Age Specific Fertility Rate	15-19	69.7	65.0	35.3
		20-24	235.0	239.7	206.8
		25-29	229.5	209.5	188.9
		30-34	134.1	115.7	86.8
		35-39	116.4	60.6	51.2
		40-44	36.4	26.5	18.2
		45-49	19.2	14.6	5.9
2	General Fertility Rate		134.4	122.2	100.2
3	Total Fertility Rate		4.2	3.7	3
4	Gross Reproduction Rate		2.0	1.7	1.3
		Total			
1	Age Specific Fertility Rate	15-19	88.6	86.3	60.5
		20-24	271.5	283.5	277.6
		25-29	253.2	246.7	233.6
		30-34	197.6	157.2	137.2
		35-39	143.2	89.7	79.7
		40-44	68.5	42.9	35
		45-49	27.7	21.2	13
2	General Fertility Rate		160.8	148.7	136.8
3	Total Fertility Rate		5.2	4.6	4.2
4	Gross Reproduction Rate		2.5	2.2	1.9

Source: *Compendium of India's Fertility and Mortality Indicators,* 1971-1997 Based on SRS-99.

TABLE 7.18: Maritial Fertility Indicators by Residence, 1997

S.No.	*Indicators*	*Age Group*	*Rural*	*Urban*	*Total*
1	*2*	*3*	*4*	*5*	*6*
1	Age Specific Maritial Fertility Rate	15-19	157.0	153.1	156.6
		20-24	323.3	282.9	316.3
		25-29	250.2	199.5	240.8
		30-34	153.7	88.9	141.0
		35-39	89.8	53.4	83.0
		40-44	41.9	19.5	37.6
		45-49	16.1	6.5	14.4
2	General Maritial Fertility Rate		172.7	130.5	165.1
3	Total Maritial Fertility Rate		5.2	4.0	4.9

Source: *Compendium of India's Fertility and Mortality Indicators,* 1971-1997 Based on SRS-99.

TABLE 7.19: Age Specefic Mortality Rate by Sex and Residence: Rajasthan, 1997

S.No.	*Age Group*	*Rural*	*Urban*	*Total*
1	*2*	*3*	*4*	*5*
		Total		
1	0-4	31.7	17.2	29.5
2	5-9	1.7	1.5	1.7
3	10-14	0.9	0.9	0.9
4	15-19	1.5	1.5	1.5
5	20-24	1.5	2	1.6
6	25-29	2.4	3.5	2.6
7	30-34	3	2.3	2.9
8	35-39	3.2	2.9	3.1
9	40-44	4.6	3	4.3
10	45-49	7	9.1	7.4
11	50-54	11.5	12.2	11.7
12	55-59	13.6	15.1	13.8
13	60-64	24.4	28	25
14	65-69	35.3	37.7	35.7
15	70+	83.1	69.8	80.8
16	All Ages	9.3	7	8.9
		Male		
1	0-4	27.8	17.5	26.1
2	5-9	1.2	1.2	1.2
3	10-14	0.8	1.5	0.9
4	15-19	1.3	1.8	1.4
5	20-24	1.5	1.4	1.5
6	25-29	2.1	4.1	2.5
7	30-34	3.1	2.5	3.0
8	35-39	4.4	5.3	4.6
9	40-44	6.2	2.1	5.4
10	45-49	9.1	13.0	9.8
11	50-54	16.4	18.5	165.8
12	55-59	17.8	19.5	18.1
13	60-64	26.0	36.4	27.7
14	65-69	46.4	55.2	47.8
15	70+	89.4	97.7	90.8
16	All Ages	9.2	8.3	9.0
		Female		
1	0-4	36.6	17.0	33.4
2	5-9	2.3	1.8	2.2
3	10-14	0.9	0.3	0.8
4	15-19	1.9	1.2	1.7
5	20-24	1.5	2.6	1.7
6	25-29	2.7	3.0	2.7
7	30-34	2.9	2.2	2.8
8	35-39	1.7	0.0	1.4
9	40-44	2.9	4.1	3.1
10	45-49	4.7	4.4	4.7
11	50-54	6.4	5.2	6.2
12	55-59	9.4	10.6	9.6
13	60-64	22.9	20.1	22.5
14	65-69	22.5	23.4	25.2
15	70+	77.5	47.1	72.1
16	All Ages	9.4	5.6	8.7

Source: *Compendium of India's Fertility and Mortality Indicators,* 1971-1997 Based on SRS-99.

8

MEDICAL AND OTHER RELATED AMENITIES (1991)

Percentage of Rural Population Served by Medical Amenities

- Only 46 per cent Rural Population of Rajasthan was served by Medical Amenities
- Percentage of Above Average PSs (AAPs) was 48.
- In 154 PSs, percentage of Rural Population served by Medical Amenities was below 50.
- Govindgarh PS had the highest 78.5 per cent Pop. served by Medical Amenities.
- Abu Road PS had the lowest 4.4 per cent Pop. served by Medical Amenities.

TABLE 8.1: Classification of PSs by Percentage of Rural Pop. Served by Medical Amenities (1991)

Group	*Included PSs*	
	No.	*%*
Very High (VH), (>=60)	36	15.2
High (H), (50-60)	47	19.8
Medium (M), (40-50)	74	31.2
Low (L), (30-40)	56	23.6
Very Low (VL), (<30)	24	10.1
Total	**237**	**100**

Source: Annex 8.1.

TABLE-8.2: District-wise First and Last PSs by Percentage of Rural Pop. Served by Medical Amenities (1991)

District	*First Rank*	*Last Rank*	*District*	*First Rank*	*Last Rank*
Ajmer	Kekri	Jawaja	Jaipur	Govindgarh	Jhotwara
Alwar	Thanagazi	Tijara	Jaisalmer	Jaisalmer	Sam
Banswara	Garhi	Kushalgarh	Jalor	Jalor	Raniwara
Baran	Atru	Chhabra	Jhalawar	Khanpur	Manoharthana
Barmer	Siwana	Baytoo	Jhunjhunun	Nawalgarh	Surajgarh
Bharatpur	Kumher	Nagar Pharai	Jodhpur	Bilara	Bap
Bhilwara	Banera	Kotri	Karauli	Nadoti	Karauli
Bikaner	Bikaner	Kolayat	Kota	Chechat	Sangod
Bundi	Nainwa	Hindoli	Nagaur	Merta	Didwana
Chittaurgarh	Rashmi	Chhoti Sadri	Pali	Bali	Rohat
Churu	Dungargarh	Sardarshahar	Rajsamand	Khamnor	Deogarh
Dausa	Sikrai	Lalsot	S. Madhopur	Gangapur	Bonli
Dhaulpur	Dhaulpur	Rajakhera	Sikar	Dhond	Lachhmangarh
Dungarpur	Sagwara	Dungarpur	Sirohi	Sheoganj	Abu Road
Ganganagar	Ganganagar	Anupgarh	Tonk	Deoli	Uniara
Hanumangarh	Hanumangarh	Nohar	Udaipur	Girwa	Kotra

Source: General Annex-III.

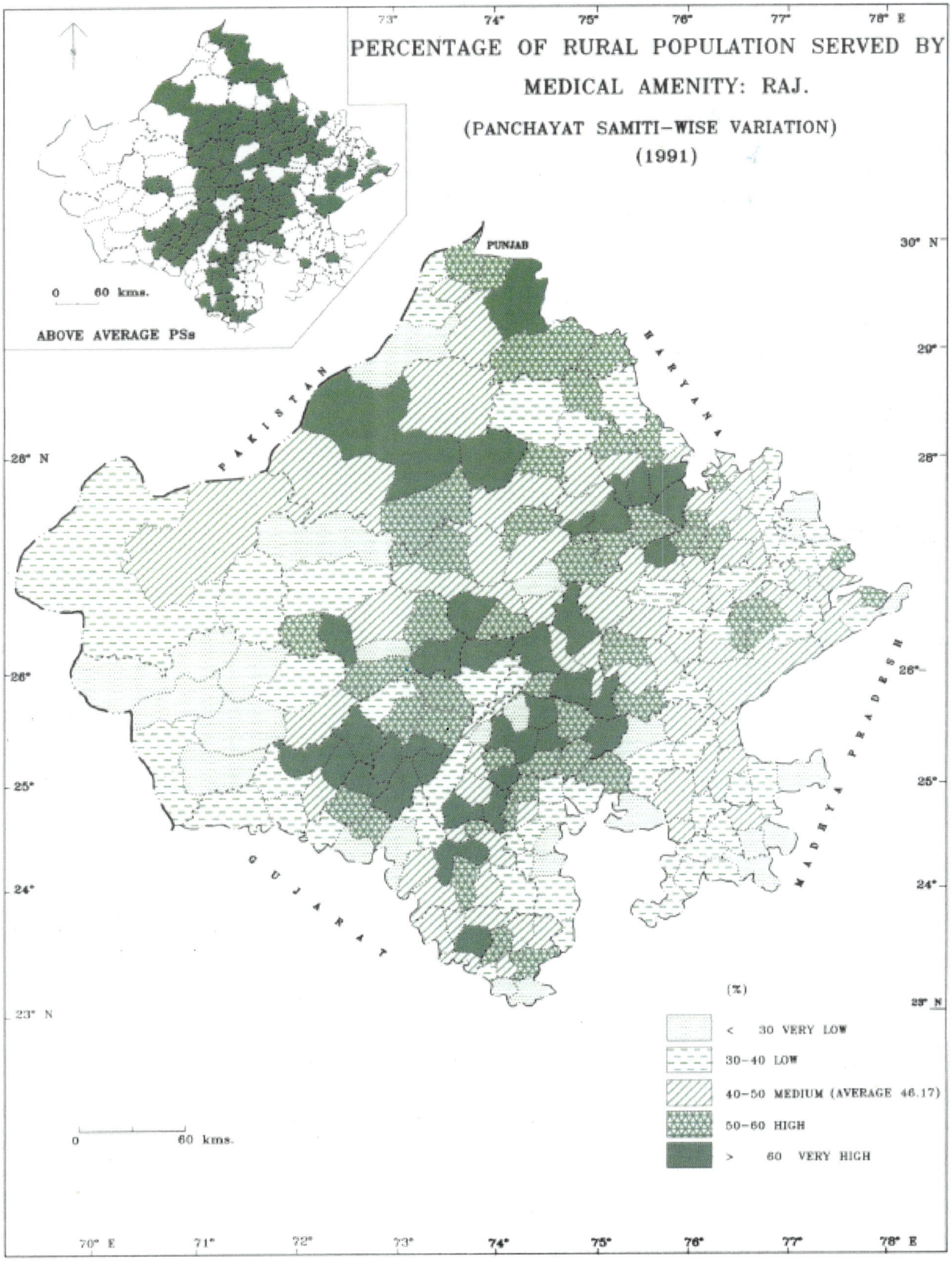
PERCENTAGE OF RURAL POPULATION SERVED BY MEDICAL AMENITY: RAJ.
(PANCHAYAT SAMITI-WISE VARIATION)
(1991)
ABOVE AVERAGE PSs
0 60 kms.
PUNJAB
HARYANA
PAKISTAN
GUJARAT
MADHYA PRADESH
(%)
< 30 VERY LOW
30-40 LOW
40-50 MEDIUM (AVERAGE 46.17)
50-60 HIGH
> 60 VERY HIGH
0 60 kms.
70° E
71°
72°
73°
74°
75°
76°
77°
78° E
30° N
29°
28° N
26°
25°
24°
23° N

FIG. 8.1

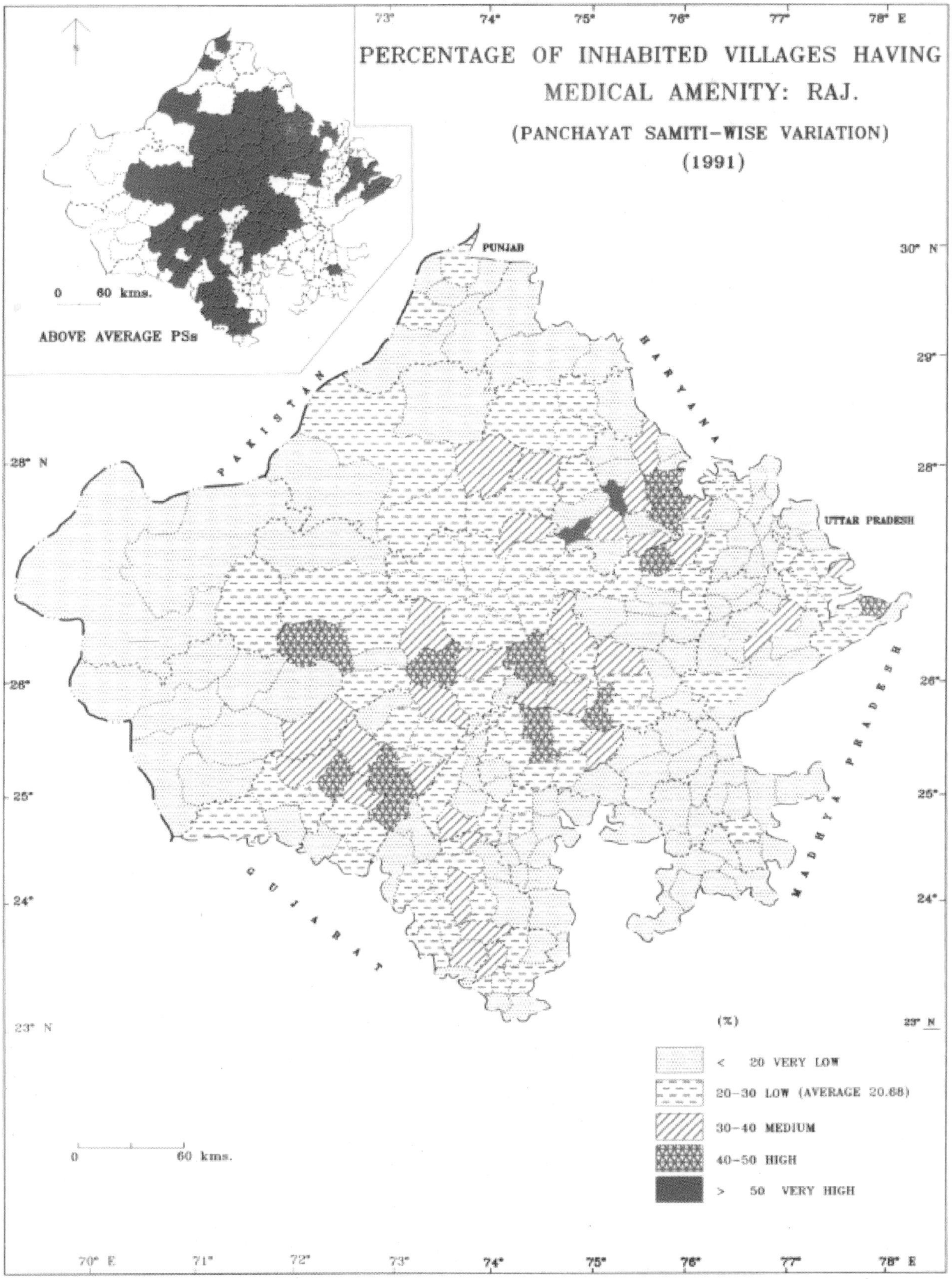
PERCENTAGE OF INHABITED VILLAGES HAVING MEDICAL AMENITY: RAJ.
(PANCHAYAT SAMITI-WISE VARIATION)
(1991)
ABOVE AVERAGE PSs
0 60 kms.
PUNJAB
HARYANA
UTTAR PRADESH
MADHYA PRADESH
GUJARAT
PAKISTAN
(%)
< 20 VERY LOW
20-30 LOW (AVERAGE 20.68)
30-40 MEDIUM
40-50 HIGH
> 50 VERY HIGH

FIG. 8.2

Percentage of Inhabited Villages Having Medical Amenities

- Only 20.7 per cent Villages of the State had Medical Amenities.
- Percentage of AAPs was 56.
- Nawalgarh PS (Jhunjhunun) had the highest 54.3 per cent villages having Medical Amenities.
- Chhoti Sadri PS (Chittaurgarh) had the lowest 6.4 per cent villages having Medical Amenities.

TABLE 8.3: Classification of PSs by Percentage of Inhabited Villages Having Medical Amenities (1991)

Group	*Included PSs*	
	No.	*%*
Very High (VH), (>=50)	2	0.8
High (H), (40-50)	14	5.9
Medium (M), (30-40)	35	14.8
Low (L), (20-30)	88	37.1
Very Low (VL), (<20)	98	41.4
Total	**237**	**100**

Source: Annex 8.2

TABLE 8.4: District-wise First and Last PSs by Percentage of Inhabited Villages Having Medical Amenities (1991)

District	*First Rank*	*Last Rank*	*District*	*First Rank*	*Last Rank*
Ajmer	Pisangan	Jawaja	Jaipur	Govindgarh	Sanganer
Alwar	Nimrana	Tijara	Jaisalmer	Sankra	Sam
Banswara	Garhi	Kushalgarh	Jalor	Jalor	Raniwara
Baran	Atru	Shahbad	Jhalawar	Pirawa	Bakani
Barmer	Siwana	Baytoo	Jhunjhunun	Nawalgarh	Alsisiar
Bharatpur	Kumher	Nagar Pahari	Jodhpur	Bilara	Mandor
Bhilwara	Banera	Mandalgarh	Karauli	Hindaun	Sapotra
Bikaner	Bikaner	Kolayat	Kota	Chechat	Sangod
Bundi	Talera	Hindoli	Nagaur	Ladnu	Makrana
Chittaurgarh	Rashmi	Chhoti Sadri	Pali	Sumerpur	Rohat
Churu	Dungargarh	Rajgarh	Rajsamand	Khamnor	Deogarh
Dausa	Sikrai	Lalsot	Sawai Madhopur	Gangapur	Bonli
Dhaulpur	Dhaulpur	Rajakhera	Sikar	Dhond	Lachhmangarh
Dungarpur	Sagwara	Simalwara	Sirohi	Sheoganj	Reodar
Ganganagar	Ganganagar	Anupgarh	Tonk	Malpura	Niwai
Hanumangarh	Bhadra	Hanumangarh	Udaipur	Mavli	Kotra

Source: General Annex-IV.

Total No. of Medical Institutions

- Total No. of Medical Institutions: 10050.
- Per PS Average No. of Medical Institutions: 42.4.
- Percentage of AAPs: 43.88.
- Garhi PS of Udaipur district had the highest 104 Medical Institutions.
- Karanpur PS of Ganganagar had the lowest 12 Medical Institutions.

TABLE 8.5: Classification of PSs by Total No. of Medical Institutions

Group	*Included PSs*	
	No.	*%*
Very High (VH), (>=80)	4	1.7
High (H), (60-80)	22	9.3
Medium (M), (40-60)	102	43.0
Low (L), (20-40)	99	41.8
Very Low (VL), (<20)	10	4.2
Total	**237**	**100**

Source: Annex 8.3.

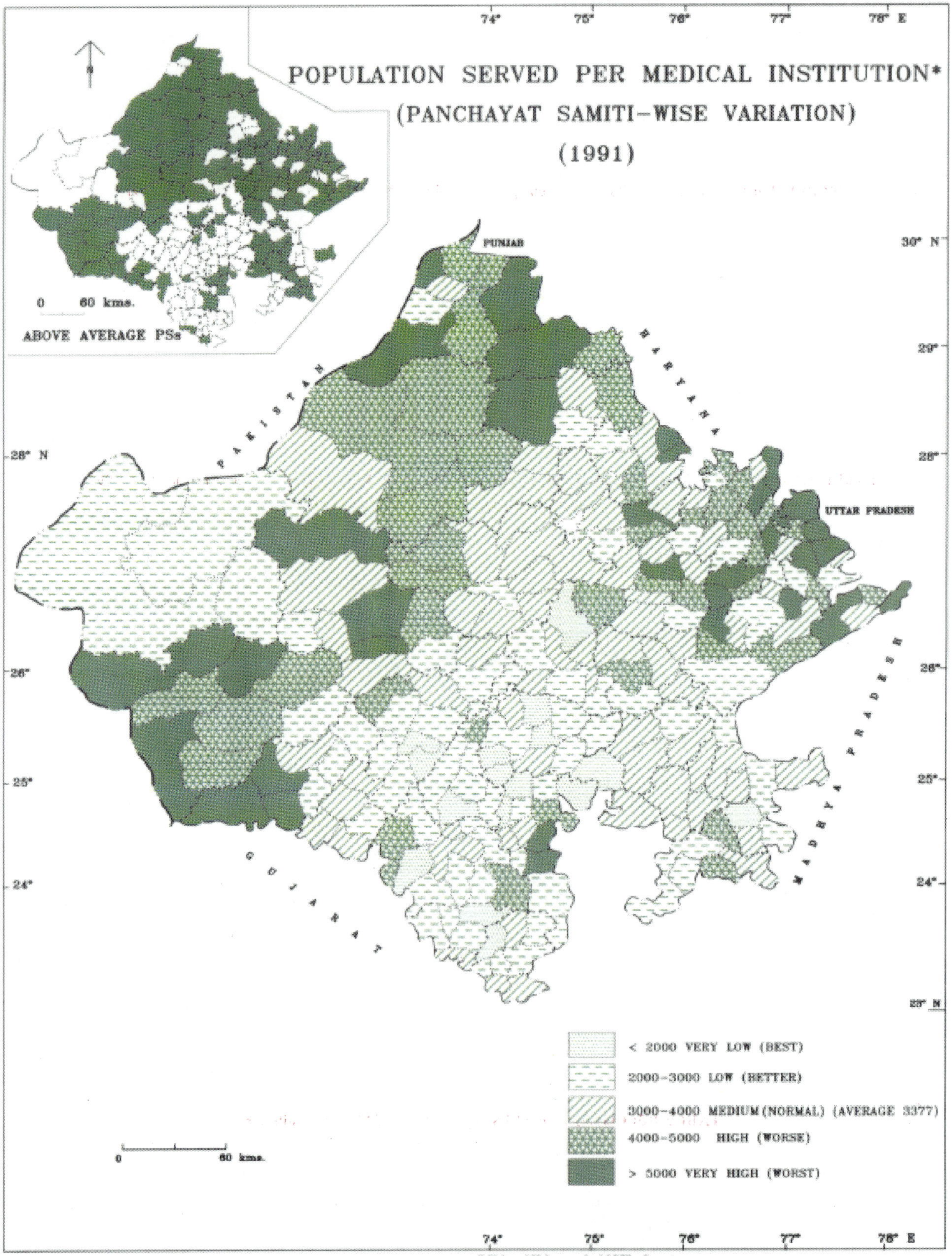

Note: * Medical Institution Includes Hospital. Dispensary, PHC, CHC and MCW Center.

FIG 8.3

TABLE 8.6: District-wise First and Last PSs by Total No. of Medical Institutions (1991)

District	*First Rank*	*Last Rank*	*District*	*First Rank*	*Last Rank*
Ajmer	Pisangan	Arian	Jaipur	Govindgarh	Jhotwara
Alwar	Kathumar	Kishangarh Bas	Jaisalmer	Sankara	Jaisalmer
Banswara	Garhi	Sajjangarh	Jalor	Ahore	Raniwara
Baran	Atru	Shahbad	Jhalawar	Dag	Khanpur
Barmer	Siwana	Sheo	Jhunjhunun	Jhunjhunun	Surajgarh
Bharatpur	Rupbas	Kaman	Jodhpur	Osian	Bap
Bhilwara	Mandalgarh	Raipur	Karauli	Karauli	Hindaun
Bikaner	Bikaner	Lunkaransar	Kota	Itawa	Ladpura
Bundi	Talera	Nainwa	Nagaur	Kuchaman	Mundwa
Chittaurgarh	Pratapgarh	Nimbahera	Pali	Bali & Kharchi	Rohat
Churu	Sujangarh	Sardarshahar	Rajsamand	Khamnor	Deogarh
Dausa	Mahwa	Lalsot	Sawai Madhopur	S. Madhopur	Bamanwas
Dhaulpur	Dhaulpur	Rajakhera	Sikar	Danta Ramgarh	Khandela
Dungarpur	Aspur	Simalwara	Sirohi	Pindwara	Abu Road
Ganganagar	Raisinghnagar	Karanpur	Tonk	Deoli & Tonk	Todaraisingh
Hanumangarh	Nohar	Bhadra	Udaipur	Jhadol & Kherwara	Kotra

Source: General Annex-II.

Total No. of Hospitals

- Total No. of Hospitals: 1433.
- Per PS Average No. of Hospital: 6.05.
- Percentage of AAPs: 39.7.
- Bagidora PS of Banswara district had the highest 20 Hospitals.
- Dhariawad, Todaraisingh, Niwai, Amet, Mandor, Chaksu, Bandikui, Baytoo, Tijara and Kishangar Bas PSs had no Hospital at all.

TABLE 8.7: Classification of PSs by No. of Hospitals (1991)

Group	*Included PSs*	
	No.	*%*
Very High (VH), (>=8)	72	30.4
High (H), (6-8)	45	19.0
Medium (M), (4-6)	57	24.1
Low (L), (2-4)	42	17.7
Very Low (VL), (<2)	11	4.6
Nil, (0)	10	4.2
Total	**237**	**100**

Source: Annex 8.4.

TABLE 8.8: District-wise First and Last PSs by No. of Hospitals (1991)

District	*First Rank*	*Last Rank*	*District*	*First Rank*	*Last Rank*
Ajmer	Pisangan	Masooda & Srinagar	Jaipur	Shahpura	Chaksu*
Alwar	Behror	Tijara & Kishangarh Bas*	Jaisalmer	Sankra	Jaisalmer & Sam
Banswara	Bagidora	Anandpuri & Kushalgarh	Jalor	Jaswantpura	Bhinmal
Baran	Atru	Chhabra	Jhalawar	Dag	Bakani
Barmer	Siwana	Baytoo*	Jhunjhunun	Khetri	Chirawa* &
Surajgarh*					
Bharatpur	Weir	Deeg	Jodhpur	Balesar	Mandor*
Bhilwara	Mandalgarh	Banera & Shahpura	Karauli	Karauli	Nadoti
Bikaner	Nokha	Bikaner	Kota	Itawa	Ladpura
Bundi	Keshoraipatan	Nainwa	Nagaur	Kuchaman	Mundwa
Chittaurgarh	Amod	Kapasan & Rashmi	Pali	Bali	Rohat
Churu	Rajgarh, Sujangarh & Churu	Sardarshahar & Dungargarh	Rajsamand	Bhim	Amet*
Dausa	Mahwa	Bandikui*	S. Madhopur	S. Madhopur	Khandar
Dhaulpur	Dhaulpur	Rajakhera	Sikar	Danta Ramgarh	Dhond
Dungarpur	Bichhiwara & Sagwara	Simalwara	Sirohi	Pindwara	Sirohi
Ganganagar	Sadulshahar	Anupgarh, Karanpur & Padampur	Tonk	Deoli	Niwai* and Todaraisingh*
Hanumangarh	Nohar	Hanumangarh	Udaipur	Binder	Dhariawad*

Source: General Annex-II. * PS/PSs having no facility at all.

Total No. of Dispensaries

- Total No. of Dispensaries: 3377.
- Per PS Average No. of Dispensaries: 14.25.
- Percentage of AAPs: 43.5.
- Nohar PS of Hanumangarh district had the highest 35 Dispensaries.
- Bhainsrorgarh PS of Chittaurgarh district had the lowest 1 Dispensary.

TABLE 8.9: Classification of PSs by No. of Dispensaries (1991)

Group	*Included PSs*	
	No.	*%*
Very High (VH), (>=20)	44	18.6
High (H), (15-20)	59	24.9
Medium (M), (10-15)	78	32.9
Low (L), (5-10)	44	18.6
Very Low (VL), (<5)	12	5.1
Total	**237**	**100**

Source: Annex 8.5.

TABLE 8.10: District-wise First and Last PSs by No. of Hospitals (1991)

District	*First Rank*	*Last Rank*	*District*	*First Rank*	*Last Rank*
Ajmer	Pisangan	Arian & Jawaja	Jaipur	Govindgarh	Jhotwara
Alwar	Bansure	Kishangarh Bas	Jaisalmer	Sankra	Jaisalmer
Banswara	Garhi & Ghatol	Anandpuri	Jalor	Ahore & Sayla	Bhinmal
Baran	Atru	Baran	Jhalawar	Dag & Jhalarapatan	Bakani
Barmer	Balotra, Chohtan, Sindhari & Siwana	Baytoo	Jhunjhunun	Jhunjhunun	Surajarh
Bharatpur	Weir	Kaman	Jodhpur	Osian	Bap
Bhilwara	Mandalgarh	Raipur	Karauli	Sapotra & Todabhim	Hindaun
Bikaner	Bikaner	Kolayat	Kota	Itawa	Ladpura & Chechat
Bundi	Talera	Hindoli	Nagaur	Kuchaman	Degana
Chittaurgarh	Pratapgarh	Bhainsrorgarh	Pali	Bali	Rohat
Churu	Sujangarh	Ratangarh & Dungargarh	Rajsamand	Rajsamand	Deogarh
Dausa	Dausa & Mahwa	Lalsot	Sawai Madhopur	Sawai Madhopur	Bamanwas
Dhaulpur	Dhaulpur	Rajakhera	Sikar	Danta Ramgarh	Khandela
Dungarpur	Sagwara	Dungarpur	Sirohi	Reodar	Sheoganj
Ganganagar	Suratgarh	Karanpur	Tonk	Deoli	Uniara
Hanumangarh	Nohar	Bhadra & Hanumangarh	Udaipur	Sarada	Kotra

Source: General Annex-II.

Primary Health Centres

- Total No. of PHCs in Rural Rajasthan: 1516.
- Per PS Average No. of PHCs: 6.4.
- Percentage of AAPs : 43.9.
- Garhi PS of Udaipur district had the highest 22 PHCs.
- Bayana, Bari Sadri and Ladpura PSs had no PHC at all.

TABLE 8.11: Classification of PSs by Pop. No. of PHC (1991)

Group	*Included PSs*	
	No.	*%*
Very High (VH), (>=8)	79	33.3
High (H), (6-8)	48	20.3
Medium (M), (4-6)	51	21.5
Low (L), (2-4)	43	18.1
Very Low (VL), (<2)	13	5.5
Nil (0)	3	1.3
Total	**237**	**100**

Source: Annex 8.6.

TABLE 8.12: District-wise First and Last PSs by No. of PHCs (1991)

District	*First Rank*	*Last Rank*	*District*	*First Rank*	*Last Rank*
Ajmer	Kishangarh	Masooda	Jaipur	Jamwa Ramgarh	Chaksu[8]
Alwar	Kathumar	Nimrana	Jaisalmer[5]	NA	NA
Banswara	Garhi	Sajjangarh[3]	Jalor	Jalor	Raniwara
Baran	Kishanganj	Shahbad	Jhalawar	Jhalrapatan[6]	Khanpur
Barmer	Siwana	Sheo	Jhunjhunun	Buhana[7]	Khetri
Bharatpur	Nagar Pahari[2]	Bayana	Jodhpur	Osian	Bap
Bhilwara	Kotri	Shahpura[4]	Karauli	Sapotra	Karauli
Bikaner	Kolayat	Lunkaransar	Kota	Chechat	Ladpura*
Bundi	Talera	Nainwa	Nagaur	Merta	Mundwa
Chittaurgarh	Pratapgarh	Bari Sadari*	Pali	Kharchi	Rohat
Churu	Sujangarh	Churu	Rajsamand	Railmagra	Deogarh
Dausa	Mahwa	Lalsot	Sawai Madhopur	Bamanwas	Khandar[9]
Dhaulpur	Rajakhera	Bari	Sikar	Danta Ramgarh	Khandela
Dungarpur	Bichhiwara	Simalwara	Sirohi	Reodar	Sirohi[10]
Ganganagar	Ganganagar	Karanpur	Tonk	Tonk	Todaraisingh
Hanumangarh	Hanumangarh	Bhadra	Udaipur	Jhadol	Dhariawad[11]

Note: * PS/PSs having no facility at all.
1. and Lachhmangarh & Ramgarh, 2. and Rupbas, 3. and Anandpuri, 4. and Banera & Sahara,
5. All the three Pss had equal rank, 6. and Pirawa, 7. and Udaipurwati, 8. and Bassi
9. and Gangapur, 10. and Abu Road, 11. and Bargaon.
Source: General Annex-II.

Sub-Health Centres

- Total No. of SHCs in Rural Rajasthan: 2942.
- Per PS Average No. of SHCs: 12.4.
- Percentage of AAPs : 46.
- Mandalgarh PS of Bhilwara district had the highest 31 SHCs.
- Reodar, Surajgarh and Sardarshahar PSs each had the lowest 2 SHCs.

TABLE 8.13: Classification of PSs by No. of SHCs (1991)

Group	*Included PSs*	
	No.	*%*
Very High (VH), (>=20)	33	13.9
High (H), (15-20)	43	18.1
Medium (M), (10-15)	76	32.1
Low (L), (5-10)	71	30.0
Very Low (VL), (<5)	14	5.9
Total	**237**	**100**

Source: Annex 8.7.

TABLE 8.14: District-wise First and Last PSs by No. of SHCs (1991)

District	*First Rank*	*Last Rank*	*District*	*First Rank*	*Last Rank*
Ajmer	Pisangan	Srinagar	Jaipur	Chaksu	Viratnagar
Alwar	Rajgarh	Bansure	Jaisalmer	Sam	Jaisalmer
Banswara	Garhi	Kushalgarh	Jalor	Sanchore	Raniwara
Baran	At[illegible]	Shahbad	Jhalawar	Dag	Khanpur
Barmer	Sin[illegible]ari	Sheo	Jhunjhunun	Khetri	Surajgarh
Bharatpur	Bayana	Weir	Jodhpur	Bilara	Bap
Bhilwara	Mandalgarh	Raipur	Karauli	Karauli	Hindaun
Bikaner	Bikaner	Kolayat	Kota	Ladpura	Itawa
Bundi	Nainwa	Keshoraipatan	Nagaur	Degana	Riyan & Parbatsar
Chittaurgarh	Pratapgarh	Nimbahera & Chhoti Sadri	Pali	Rani Station	Rohat
Churu	Churu	Sardarshahar	Rajsamand	Khamnor	Railmagra
Dausa	Lalsot & Mahwa	Dausa	Sawai Madhopur	S. Madhopur	Bonli & Bamanwas
Dhaulpur	Bari	Rajakhera	Sikar	Dhond	Sri Madhopur
Dungarpur	Dungarpur	Bichhiwara	Sirohi	Pindwara	Reodar
Ganganagar	Raisinghnagar	Padampur	Tonk	Tonk	Todaraisingh
Hanumangarh	Hanumangarh	Nohar	Udaipur	Jhadol	Dhariawad & Bargaon

Source : General Annex-II.

Mother and Child Workers Centres

- Total No. of MCWCs in Rural Rajasthan: 782.
- Per PS Average No. of MCWCs: 3.3.
- Percentage of AAPs : 32.
- Raisinghnagar PS of Ganganagar district had the highest 28 MCWCs.
- 53 PSs had no MCWCs at all.

TABLE 8.15: Classification of PSs by No. of MCWCs (1991)

Group	*Included PSs*	
	No.	*%*
Very High (VH), (>=8)	32	13.5
High (H), (6-8)	14	5.9
Medium (M), (4-6)	30	12.7
Low (L), (2-4)	65	27.4
Very Low (VL), (<2)	43	18.1
Nil, (0)	53	22.4
Total	**237**	**100**

Source: Annex 8.8.

TABLE 8.16: District-wise First and Last PSs by No. of MCWCs (1991)

District	*First Rank*	*Last Rank*	*District*	*First Rank*	*Last Rank*
Ajmer	Pisangan	Arain	Jaipur	Sanganer	Kotputli
Alwar	Kathumar	Nimrana & Kotkasim*	Jaisalmer	Sam	Sankra & Jaisalmer*
Banswara	Garhi	Peepalkhoont & Kushalgarh*	Jalor	Ahore	Sanchore & Jaswantpura*
Baran	Atru	Chhabra	Jhalawar	Jhalrapatan	Pirawa & Khanpur*
Barmer	Barmer	Chohtan & Baytoo*	Jhunjhunun	Surajgarh	Jhunjhunun & Buhana*
Bharatpur	Rupbas	Sewar & Kaman*	Jodhpur	Phalodi	Shergarh, Bilara & Bap*
Bhilwara	Mandalgarh	Asind, Hurda & Sahara	Karauli	Hindaun	Todabhim
Bikaner	Kolayat	Lunkaransar & Bikaner*	Kota	Chechat	Sangod
Bundi	All, Except Talera	Talera	Nagaur	Degana	Nagaur, Makrana, Ladnu & Kuchaman*
Chittaurgarh	Pratapgarh	Nimbahera, Dungla, Chittaurgarh, Bhopalsagar, Bhainsrorgarh & Bhadesar*	Pali	Raipur	Pali & Bali*
Churu	Rajgarh	Sardarshahar & Ratangarh*	Rajsamand	Kumbhalgarh	Deogarh & Amet*
Dausa	Mahwa	Lalsot & Bandikui	Sawai Madhopur	Gangapur	Sawai Madhopur
Dhaulpur	Dhaulpur	Rajakhera*	Sikar	Danta Ramgarh	Lachhmangarh, Khandela, Fatehpur & Dhond*
Dungarpur	Aspur	Simalwara & Sagwara	Sirohi	Pindwara	Sheoganj*
Ganganagar	Raisinghnagar	Suratgarh, Padampur, Karanpur & Anupgarh*	Tonk	Malpura	Uniara & Todaraisingh*
Hanumangarh	Bhadra	Nohar*	Udaipur	Gogunda	Kotra*

* PS/PSs having no facility at all.
Source : General Annex-II.

Family Planning Centres

- Total No. of FPCs in Rural Rajasthan: 350.
- Per PS Average No. of FPCs: 1.48.
- Percentage of AAPs : 38.4.
- Bhopalgarh PS of Jodhpur district and Kherwara of Udaipur each had the highest 7 FPCs.
- 52 PSs had no FPC at all.

TABLE 8.17: Classification of PSs by Pop. No. of FPCs (1991)

Group	*Included PSs*	
	No.	*%*
Very High (VH), (>=5)	9	3.8
High (H), (4)	12	5.1
Medium (M), (3)	18	7.6
Low (L), (2)	52	21.9
Very Low (VL), (<1)	94	39.7
Nil, (0)	52	21.9
Total	**237**	**100**

Source: Annex 8.9

TABLE 8.18: District-wise First and Last PSs by No. of FPCs (1991)

District	*First Rank*	*Last Rank*	*District*	*First Rank*	*Last Rank*
Ajmer	Kekri	Masooda, Kishangarh, Jawaja & Bhinay	Jaipur	Amber, Govindgarh & Kotputli	Bassi*
Alwar	Thanagazi	Tijara, Mandawar, Lachhmangarh & Kishangarh Bas*	Jaisalmer	Jaisalmer	Sankra & Sam*
Banswara	Talwara	Kushalgarh & Anandpuri*	Jalor	Ahore	Sayla, Raniwara & Bhinmal*
Baran	Atru & Kishanganj	Shahbad, Chhipabarod, Chhabra, Baran & Anta	Jhalawar	Bakani	Manoharthana*
Barmer	Siwana	Sindhari, Sheo, Baytoo, Dhorimanna and Barmer*	Jhunjhunun	Alsisar	Surajgarh & Chirawa
Bharatpur	Nagar Pahari	Weir, Sewar, Nadbai, Kaman & Deeg*	Jodhpur	Bhopalgarh	Mandor & Bap*
Bhilwara	Asind	Hurda*	Karauli	Sapotra	Karauli*
Bikaner	#	#	Kota	Sultanpur	Sangod & Chechat*
Bundi	Hindoli	Talera & Keshoraipatan	Nagaur	Riyan	Mundwa & Ladnu*
Chittaurgarh	Begun, Bhopalsagar & Rashmi	Nimbahera, Gangrar, Chhoti Sadri & Bhadesar*	Pali	Desauri	Raipur, Pali & Bali
Churu	All Except Churu	Churu*	Rajsamand	Amet, Bhim & Kumbhalgarh	Deogarh*
Dausa	Sikrai	Mahwa & Dausa*	S. Madhopur	Bonli	Gangapur*
Dhaulpur	Dhaulpur & Rajakhera	Baseri & Bari*	Sikar	Danta Ramgarh	Lachhmangarh*
Dungarpur	Bichhiwara	Dungarpur*	Sirohi	Reodar	Sirohi, Sheoganj & Abu Road*
Ganganagar	Padampur	Suratgarh & Karanpur*	Tonk	Tonk	Niwai*
Hanumangarh	Hanumangarh	Nohar*	Udaipur	Kherwara	Dhariawad*

Source : General Annex-II.
* PS/PSs having no facility at all.
\# All PSs had equal rank.

Drinking Water Amenities

- 99.7 per cent Rural Population of the State was Served by Drinking Water Amenities.
- Percentage of AAPs was 88.
- 180 PSs had almost Perfect Amenities of Drinking Water (had 100% of their Rural Population Served by Drinking Water Amenities.
- Phalodi PS (93%) of Jodhpur District was the Worst Deprived.

TABLE 8.19: Classification of PSs by Percentage of Rural Population Served by Drinking Water Amenities (1991)

Group	*Included PSs*	
	No.	*%*
Perfect, (100)	180	75.9
Very High (VH), (98-100)	51	21.5
High (H), (96-98)	3	1.3
Medium (M), (94-96)	2	0.8
Low (L), (<94)	1	0.4
Total	**237**	**100**

Source: Annex 8.10.

TABLE 8.20: District-wise First and Last Percentage of Rural Population Served by Drinking Aminites (1991)

District	*First Rank*	*Last Rank*	*District*	*First Rank*	*Last Rank*
Ajmer	7 PSs*	Jawaja	Jaipur	6 PSs*	Phagi
Alwar	All PSs*	—	Jaisalmer	Sankra*	Jaisalmer
Banswara	7 PSs*	Kushalgarh	Jalor	5 PSs*	Sanchore
Baran	5 PSs*	Shahbad	Jhalawar	All PSs*	—
Barmer	3 PSs*	Baytoo	Jhunjhunun	5 PSs*	Surajgarh
Bharatpur	6 PSs*	Kumher	Jodhpur	Bilara & Jodhpur	Phalodi
Bhilwara	All PSs*	—	Karauli	4 PSs*	Sapotra
Bikaner	Lunkaransar	Kolayat	Kota	4 PSs*	Chechat
Bundi	All PSs*	—	Nagaur	8 PSs*	Parbatsar
Chittaurgarh	13 PSs*	Nimbahera	Pali	All PSs*	—
Churu	Taranagar*	Rajgarh	Rajsamand	All PSs*	—
Dausa	All PSs*	—	Sawai Madhopur	4 PSs*	Bonli
Dhaulpur	All PSs*	—	Sikar	5 PSs*	Neem Ka Thana
Dungarpur	4 PSs*	Aspur	Sirohi	4 PSs*	Pindwara
Ganganagar	6 PSs*	Sadulshahar	Tonk	All PSs*	—
Hanumangarh	Bhadra & Hn	Nohar	Udaipur	All PSs*	—

Source: General Annex-III.
* PS/PSs Having Almost Perfect (100%) Amenity.

Education Amenities

- 94 per cent Rural Population of the state was served by Education Amenities.
- Percentage of AAPs was 64.
- Nawalgarh PS of Jhunjhunun district and Shergarh, of Jodhpur had almost Perfect Amenities of Education (had 100% of their Rural Pop. Served by Education Amenities.
- Anupgarh PS (56.5%) of Ganganagar District was at the Bottom.

TABLE 8.21: Classification of PSs by Percentage of Rural Pop. Served by Education Amenities (1991)

Group	*Included PSs*	
	No.	*%*
Perfect, (100)	2	0.8
Very High (VH), (95-100)	134	56.5
High (H), (90-95)	60	25.3
Medium (M), (85-90)	22	9.3
Low (L), (<85)	19	8.0
Total	**237**	**100**

Source: Annex 8.11.

TABLE 8.22: District-wise First and Last PSs by Percentage of Rural Pop. Served by Education Amenities (1991)

District	*First Rank*	*Last Rank*	*District*	*First Rank*	*Last Rank*
Ajmer	Srinagar	Jawaja	Jaipur	Shahpura	Chaksu
Alwar	Behror	Tijara	Jaisalmer	Sankra	Sam
Banswara	Garhi	Peepalkhoont	Jalor	Raniwara	Bhinmal
Baran	Baran	Kishanganj	Jhalawar	Pirawa	Manoharthana
Barmer	Siwana	Baytoo	Jhunjhunun	Nawalgarh*	Jhunjhunun
Bharatpur	Kumher	Kaman	Jodhpur	Shergarh*	Osian
Bhilwara	Hurda	Mandalgarh	Karauli	Hindaun	Karauli
Bikaner	Nokha	Kolayat	Kota	Ladpura	Sangod
Bundi	Hindoli	Talera	Nagaur	Degana	Merta
Chittaurgarh	Rashmi	Bhainsrorgarh	Pali	Bali	Raipur
Churu	Churu	Sardarshahar	Rajsamand	Rajsamand	Deogarh
Dausa	Sikrai	Bandikui	Sawai Madhopur	Gangapur	Khandar
Dhaulpur	Dhaulpur	Bari	Sikar	Sri Madhopur	Neem Ka Thana
Dungarpur	Sagwara	Aspur	Sirohi	Abu Road	Reodar
Ganganagar	Padampur	Anupgarh	Tonk	Malpura	Uniara
Hanumangarh	Bhadra	Hanumangarh	Udaipur	Mavli	Kotra

Source: General Annex-III.
* PS had almost perfect (100%) amenity.

Power Amenities

- 77 per cent Rural Pop. of the state was Served by Power Amenities.
- Percentage of AAPs was 62.9.
- In 34 PSs, percentage of Rural Pop. Served by Power Amenities was Below 50.
- 7 PSs had almost Perfect Amenities of Power (had 100% of Their Rural Population Served By Power Amenities. These were: Hurda (Bhilwara district), Govindgarh (Jaipur), Chirawa & Nawalgarh (Jhunjhunun), Sumerpur (Pali), Railmagra (Rajsamand) and Dhond (Jaisalmer) PSs.
- Sam PS (1.5%) of Jaisalmer District was the Worst Deprived.

TABLE 8.23: Classification of PSs by Percentage of Rural Pop. Served by Power Amenities (1991)

Group	*Included PSs*	
	No.	*%*
Perfect, (100)	7	3.0
Very High (VH), (75-100)	151	63.7
High (H), (50-75)	45	19.0
Medium (M), (25-50)	29	12.2
Low (L), (<25)	5	2.1
Total	**237**	**100**

Source: Annex 8.12.

TABLE 8.24: District-wise First and Last PSs by Percentage of Rural Population Served by Power Amenities (1991)

District	*First Rank*	*Last Rank*	*District*	*First Rank*	*Last Rank*
Ajmer	Pisangan	Jawaja	Jaipur	Govindgarh*	Dudu
Alwar	Nimrana	Lachhmangarh	Jaisalmer	Jaisalmer	Sam
Banswara	Grahi	Peepalkhoont	Jalor	Raniwara	Sanchore
Baran	Baran	Chhipabarod	Jhalawar	Jhalrapatan	Manoharthana
Barmer	Siwana	Barmer	Jhunjhunun	Chirawa *#	Alsisar
Bharatpur	Weir	Nagar Pahari	Jodhpur	Bilara	Bap
Bhilwara	Hurda	Kotri	Karauli	Hindaun	Karauli
Bikaner	Nokha	Kolayat	Kota	Chechat	Itawa
Bundi	Hindoli *	Keshoraipatan	Nagaur	Kuchaman	Jayal
Chittaurgarh	Kapasan	Pratapgarh	Pali	Sumerpur *	Raipur
Churu	Ratangarh	Rajgarh	Rajsamand	Railmagra *	Rajsamand
Dausa	Bandikui	Mahwa	Sawai Madhopur	Gangapur	Khandar
Dhaulpur	Rajakhera	Bari	Sikar	Dhond *	Piprali
Dungarpur	Aspur	Dungarpur	Sirohi	Sirohi	Sheoganj
Ganganagar	Karanpur	Anupgarh	Tonk	Niwai	Todraisingh
Hanumangarh	Hanumangarh	Nohar	Udaipur	Bargaon	Kotra

Source: General Annex-III.
* PS had almost perfect (100%) amenities. # and Nawalgarh*.

PUCCA ROAD AMENITIES

- 48 per cent Rural Population of the State was Served by Pucca Road Amenities.
- Percentage of AAPs was 49.
- In 133 PSs, percentage of Rural Population Served by Pucca Road Amenities was Below 50.
- Sheoganj PS (Pali), had the highest 98% Rural Pop. Served by Pucca Road Amenities.
- Didwana PS (Nagaur), had the lowest 4.8% Rural Pop. Served by Pucca Road Amenities.

TABLE 8.25: Classification of PSs by Percentage of Rural Pop. Served by Pucca Road Amenities (1991)

Group	*Included PSs*	
	No.	*%*
Very High (VH), (>80)	3	1.3
High (H), (60-80)	40	16.9
Medium (M), (40-60)	120	50.6
Low (L), (20-40)	69	29.1
Very Low (VL), (<20)	5	2.1
Total	**237**	**100**

Source: Annex 8.13.

TABLE 8.26: District-wise First and Last PSs by Percentage of Rural Population Served by Pucca Road Amenity (1991)

District	*First Rank*	*Last Rank*	*District*	*First Rank*	*Last Rank*
Ajmer	Pisangan	Arain	Jaipur	Jhotwara	Chaksu
Alwar	Thanagazi	Tijara	Jaisalmer	Jaisalmer	Sam
Banswara	Talwara	Kushalgarh	Jalor	Jalor	Sanchore
Baran	Baran	Chhabra	Jhalawar	Bakani	Pirawa
Barmer	Sheo	Baytoo	Jhunjhunun	Udaipurwati	Buhana
Bharatpur	Kumher	Kaman	Jodhpur	Bhopalgarh	Bap
Bhilwara	Hurda	Raipur	Karauli	Hindaun	Karauli
Bikaner	Bikaner	Nokha	Kota	Ladpura	Sultanpur
Bundi	Talera	Keshoraipata	Nagaur	Merta	Didwana
Chittaurgarh	Bhopalsagar	Pratapgarh	Pali	Sumerpur	Jaitaran
Churu	Dungargarh	Sujangarh	Rajsamand	Railmagra	Amet
Dausa	Sikrai	Bandikui	S.M.	Bamanwas	Sawai Madhopur
Dhaulpur	Baseri	Bari	Sikar	Piprali	Fatehpur
Dungarpur	Sagwara	Siamalwara	Sirohi	Sheoganj	Reodar
Ganganagar	Ganganagar	Padampur	Tonk	Malpura	Niwai
Hanumangarh	Hanumangarh	Nohar	Udaipur	Girwa	Kotra

Source: General Annex-III.

9

MEDICAL AND OTHER RELATED AMENITIES (2001)

Percentage of Rural Population Served by Medical Amenities

- Only 57 per cent Rural Population of Rajasthan was served by Medical Amenities.
- Percentage of Above Average PSs (AAPs) was 47.
- In 82 PSs, percentage of Rural Population served by Medical Amenities was below 50.
- Sirohi PS had the highest 88 per cent Pop. served by Medical Amenities.
- Chhabra PS had the lowest 14.8 per cent Pop. served by Medical Amenities.

TABLE 9.1: Classification of PSs by Percentage of Rural Pop. Served by Medical Amenities (2001)

Group	*Included PSs*	
	No.	*%*
Very High (VH), (>60)	91	38.4
High (H), (50-60)	65	27.4
Medium (M), (40-50)	54	22.8
Low (L), (30-40)	21	8.9
Very Low (VL), (<30)	6	2.5
Total	**237**	**100**

Source: Annex 9.1.

TABLE 9.2: District-wise First and Last Percentage of Rural Population Served by Drinking Aminites (1991)

District	*First Rank*	*Last Rank*	*District*	*First Rank*	*Last Rank*
Ajmer	Kekri	Jawaja	Jaipur	Govindgarh	Chaksu
Alwar	Nimrana	Kishanagarh Bas	Jaisalmer	Jaisalmer	Sam
Banswara	Garhi	Kushalgarh	Jalor	Ahore	Sanchore
Baran	Atru	Chhabra	Jhalawar	Khanpur	Manoharthana
Barmer	Siwana	Baytoo	Jhunjhunun	Udaipurwati	Surajgarh
Bharatpur	Bayana	Nagar Pahari	Jodhpur	Balesar	Bap
Bhilwara	Banera	Kotri	Karauli	Hindaun	Karauli
Bikaner	Nokha	Bikaner	Kota	Sultanpur	Sangod
Bundi	Hindoli	Keshoraipatan	Nagaur	Ladnu	Kuchaman
Chittaurgarh	Rashmi	Kapasan	Pali	Bali	Rohat
Churu	Ratangarh	Sardarshahar	Rajsamand	Railmagra	Deogarh
Dausa	Dausa	Lalsot	S. Madhopur	Gangapur	Bamanwas
Dhaulpur	Bari	Rajakhera	Sikar	Dhond	Lachhmangarh
Dungarpur	Sagwara	Simalwara	Sirohi	Sirohi	Abu Road
Ganganagar	Sadulshahar	Anupgarh	Tonk	Tonk	Niwai
Hanumangarh	Bhadra	Nohar	Udaipur	Mavli	Kotra

Source : General Annex-VI.

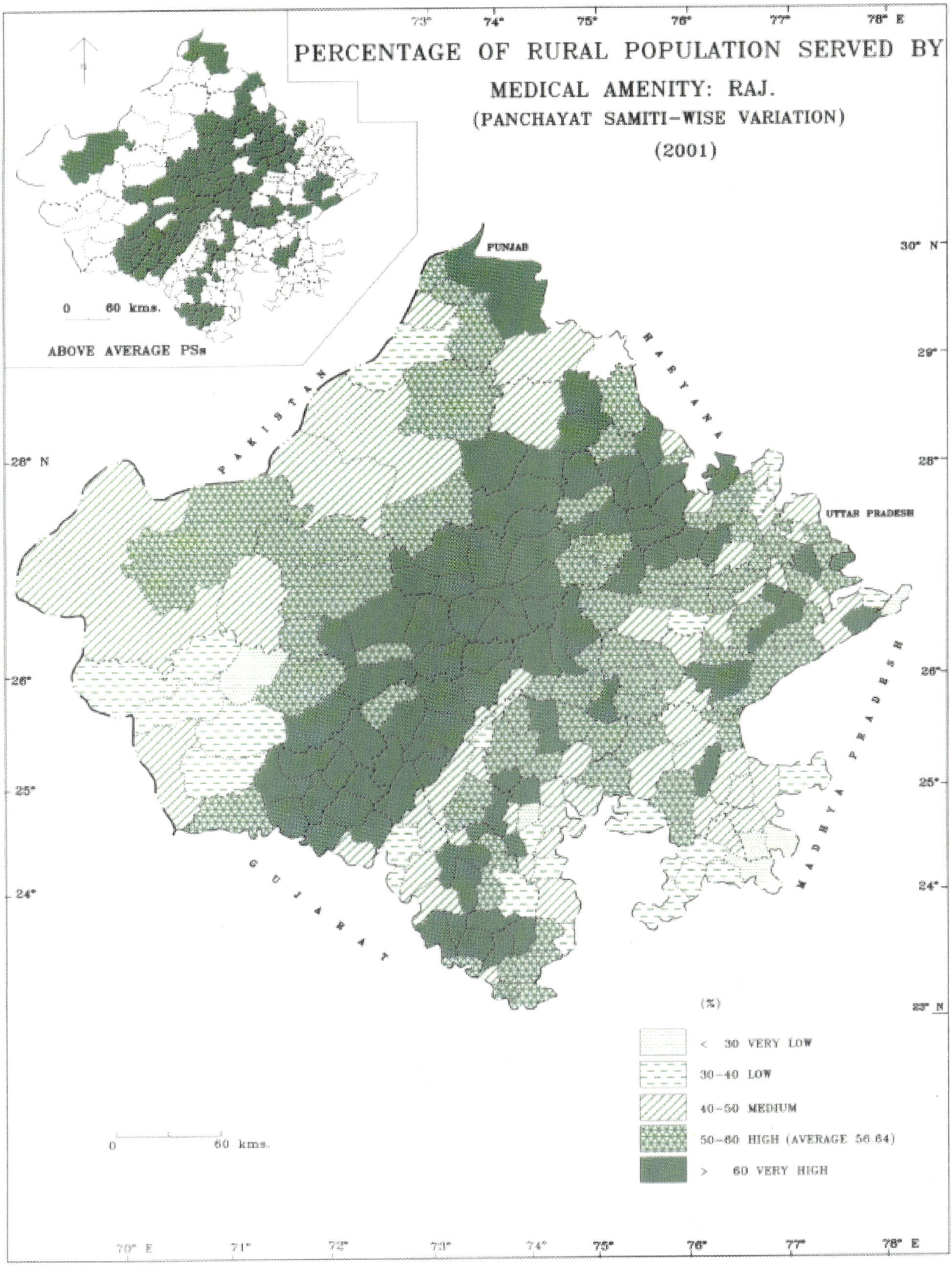

PERCENTAGE OF RURAL POPULATION SERVED BY
MEDICAL AMENITY: RAJ.
(PANCHAYAT SAMITI-WISE VARIATION)
(2001)
0 60 kms.
ABOVE AVERAGE PSs
PUNJAB
HARYANA
UTTAR PRADESH
MADHYA PRADESH
GUJARAT
PAKISTAN
(%)
< 30 VERY LOW
30-40 LOW
40-50 MEDIUM
50-60 HIGH (AVERAGE 56.64)
> 60 VERY HIGH
0 60 kms.

FIG. 9.1

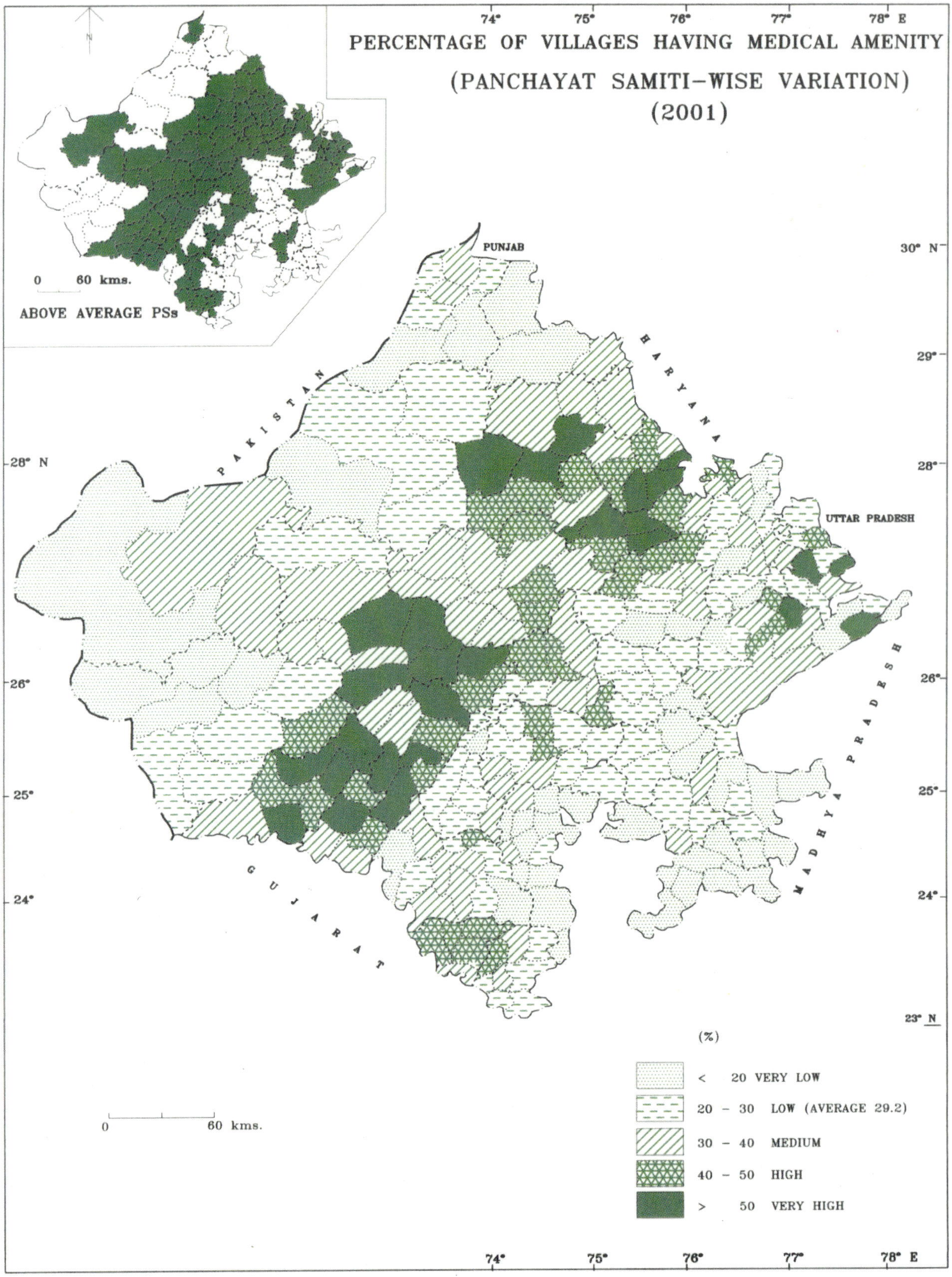
PERCENTAGE OF VILLAGES HAVING MEDICAL AMENITY
(PANCHAYAT SAMITI–WISE VARIATION)
(2001)
ABOVE AVERAGE PSs
0 60 kms.
PUNJAB
HARYANA
UTTAR PRADESH
MADHYA PRADESH
GUJARAT
PAKISTAN
74° 75° 76° 77° 78° E
30° N
29°
28° N
26°
25°
24°
23° N
(%)
< 20 VERY LOW
20 – 30 LOW (AVERAGE 29.2)
30 – 40 MEDIUM
40 – 50 HIGH
> 50 VERY HIGH
0 60 kms.

FIG. 9.2

Percentage of Inhabited Villages Having Medical Amenities

- Only 29.2 per cent Villages of the State had Medical Amenities.
- Percentage of AAPs was 58.
- In 90.3 per cent PSs, percentage of villages having Medical Amenities was below 50.
- Bilara PS (Jodhpur) had the highest 69.7 per cent villages having Medical Amenities.
- Chhabra PS (Jhalawar) had the lowest 7.5 per cent villages having Medical Amenities.

TABLE 9.3: Classification of PSs by Percentage of Inhabited Villages Having Medical Amenities (2001)

Group	*Included PSs*	
	No.	*%*
Very High (VH), (>50)	28	11.8
High (H), (40-50)	38	16.0
Medium (M), (30-40)	61	25.7
Low (L), (20-30)	64	27.0
Very Low (VL), (<20)	46	19.4
Total	**237**	**100**

Source: Annex 9.2.

TABLE 9.4: District-wise First and Last PSs by Percentage of Inhabited Villages Having Medical Amenity (2001)

District	*First Rank*	*Last Rank*	*District*	*First Rank*	*Last Rank*
Ajmer	Pisangan	Masooda	Jaipur	Govindgarh	Chaksu
Alwar	Nimrana	Kotkasim	Jaisalmer	Jaisalmer	Sam
Banswara	Garhi	Ghatol	Jalor	Jalor	Sanchore
Baran	Baran	Chhabra	Jhalawar	Khanpur	Manoharthana
Barmer	Siwana	Sheo	Jhunjhunun	Udaipurwati	Alsisar
Bharatpur	Nadbai	Nagar Pahari	Jodhpur	Bilara	Bap
Bhilwara	Banera	Mandal	Karauli	Hindaun	Sapotra
Bikaner	Nokha	Kolayat	Kota	Sultanpur	Itawa
Bundi	Hindoli	Nainwa	Nagaur	Parbatsar	Kuchamana
Chittaurgarh	Dungla	Kapasan	Pali	Sumerpur	Rohat
Churu	Ratangarh	Taranagar	Rajsamand	Railmagra	Deogarh
Dausa	Mahwa	Lalsot	S. Madhopur	Gangapur	Bonli
Dhaulpur	Bari	Rajakhera	Sikar	Dhond	Lachhmangarh
Dungarpur	Sagwara	Simalwara	Sirohi	Sirohi	Abu Road
Ganganagar	Padampura	Anupgarh	Tonk	Tonk	Uniara
Hanumangarh	Bhadra	Nohar	Udaipur	Mavli	Kotra

Source: General Annex-VII.

Total No. of Medical Institutions

- Total No. of Medical Institutions in Rural Rajasthan: 14231.
- Per PS Average No. of Medical Institutions: 60.05.
- Percentage of AAPs: 45.15.
- Aspur PS of Dungarpur district had the highest 137 Medical Institutions.
- Kapasan, Bari Sadri (both of Chittaurgarh district) and Chhabra (Baran) PSs each had the lowest 14 Medical Institutions.

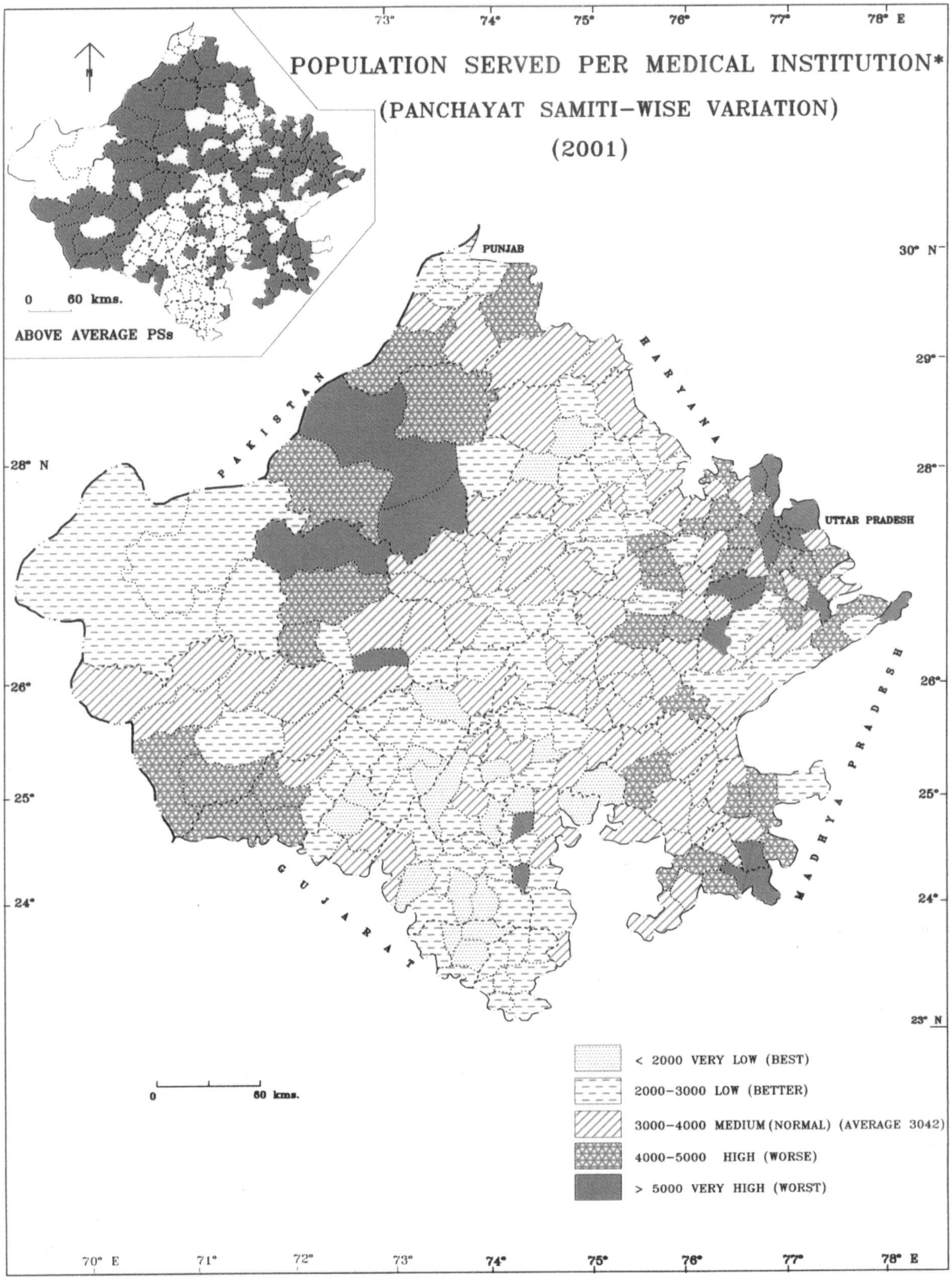

Note: * Medical Institution Includes Hospital. Dispensary, PHC, CHC and MCW Center.

FIG 9.3

TABLE 9.5: Classification of PSs by Total No. of Medical Institutions (2001)

Group	*Included PSs*	
	No.	*%*
Very High (VH), (>80)	50	21.1
High (H), (60-80)	62	26.2
Medium (M), (40-60)	77	32.5
Low (L), (20-40)	43	18.1
Very Low (VL), (<20)	5	2.1
Total	**237**	**100**

Source: Annex 9.3.

TABLE 9.6: District-wise First and Last PSs by Total no. of Medical Institutions (2001)

District	*First Rank*	*Last Rank*	*District*	*First Rank*	*Last Rank*
Ajmer	Pisangan	Arian & Srinagar	Jaipur	Dudu	Jhotwara
Alwar	Mandawar	Kotkasim	Jaisalmer	Sankra	Jaisalmer
Banswara	Garhi	Anandpuri	Jalor	Sanchore	Raniwara
Baran	Anta	Chhabra	Jhalawar	Khanpur	Manoharthana
Barmer	Sindhari	Sheo	Jhunjhunun	Buhana	Surajgarh
Bharatpur	Rupbas	Kaman	Jodhpur	Osian	Mandor
Bhilwara	Mandalgarh	Hurda	Karauli	Sapotra	Nadoti
Bikaner	Bikaner	Nokha	Kota	Sangod	Chechat
Bundi	Hindoli & Talera	Nainwa	Nagaur	Degana	Merta & Mundwa
Chittaurgarh	Pratapgarh	Badi Sadri & Kapasan	Pali	Sojat	Pali
Churu	Ratangarh	Sardarshahar	Rajsamand	Kumbhalgarh	Deogarh
Dausa	Dausa	Bandikui	S. Madhopur	S.Madhopur	Bamanwas
Dhaulpur	Dhaulpur	Rajakhera	Sikar	Danta Ramgarh	Sri Madhopur
Dungarpur	Aspur	Dungarpur	Sirohi	Sirohi	Abu Road
Ganganagar	Anupgarh	Padampur	Tonk	Tonk	Uniara
Hanumangarh	Hanumangarh	Bhadra	Udaipur	Sarada	Bargaon

Source: General Annex-VIII.

Primary Health Centres

- Total No. of PHCs in Rural Rajasthan: 2746.
- Per PS Average No. of PHCs: 11.6.
- Percentage of AAPs : 44.7.
- Sojat PS of Pali district had the highest 35 PHCs.
- Manoharthana PS of Jhalawar & Chhabra of Baran each had the lowest 1 PHC.

TABLE 9.7: Classification of PSs by No. of PHCs (2001)

Group	*Included PSs*	
	No.	*%*
Very High (VH), (>=5)	217	91.6
High (H), (4)	9	3.8
Medium (M), (3)	7	3.0
Low (L), (2)	2	0.8
Very Low (VL), (<1)	2	0.8
Total	**237**	**100**

Source: Annex 9.6.

TABLE 9.8: District-wise First and Last PSs by No. PHCs (2001)

District	*First Rank*	*Last Rank*	*District*	*First Rank*	*Last Rank*
Ajmer	Pisangan	Jawaja	Jaipur	Dudu & Jamwa Ramgarh	Jhotwara
Alwar	Lachhmangarh & Mandawar	Kotkasim	Jaisalmer	Jaisalmer	Sam
Banswara	Talwara	Anandpuri	Jalor	Sanchore	Ahore & Raniwara
Baran	Anta	Chhabra	Jhalawar	Jhalrapatan	Manoharthana
Barmer	Sindhari	Sheo	Jhunjhunun	Khetri	Alsisar & Jhunjhunun
Bharatpur	Kumher	Bayana	Jodhpur	Bilara	Mandor
Bhilwara	Mandalgarh	Banera	Karauli	Sapotra	Nadoti
Bikaner	Bikaner	Nokha	Kota	Sangod, Sultanpur & Ladpura	Chechat
Bundi	Hindoli	Nainwa	Nagaur	Parbatsar	Nagaur
Chittaurgarh	Begun	Bhainsrorgarh	Pali	Sojat	Rani Station
Churu	Rajgarh, Sujangarh & Churu	Sardarshahar	Rajsamand	Kumbhalgarh	Amet & Deogarh
Dausa	Dausa	Bandikui, Lalsot & Sikrai	S. Madhopur	S. Madhopur	Gangapur
Dhaulpur	Bari	Baseri	Sikar	Danta Ramgarh	Lachhmangarh & Sri Madhopur
Dungarpur	Aspur	Simalwara	Sirohi	Reodar, Sheoganj & Sirohi	Abu Road
Ganganagar	Anupgarh & Sadulshahr	Karanpur	Tonk	Tonk	Niwai
Hanumangarh	Hanumangarh	Bhadra	Udaipur	Sarada	Gogunda

Source: General Annex VIII.

Sub-Health Centres

- Total No. of SHCs in Rural Rajasthan: 6353.
- Per PS Average No. of SHCs: 26.8.
- Percentage of AAPs : 46.
- Osian PS of Jodhpur district had the highest 70 SHCs.
- Kotkasim PS of Alwar and Chhabra of Baran each had the lowest 4 SHCs.

TABLE 9.9: Classification of PSs by No. of SHCs (2001)

Group	*Included PSs*	
	No.	*%*
Very High (VH), (>20)	166	70.0
High (H), (15-20)	32	13.5
Medium (M), (10-15)	28	11.8
Low (L), (5-10)	10	4.2
Very Low (VL), (<5)	1	0.4
Total	**237**	**100**

Source: Annex 9.7.

Family Welfare Centres

- Total No. of FWCs in Rural Rajasthan: 675.
- Per PS Average No. of FWCs: 2.85.
- Percentage of AAPs : 48.5.
- Kumbhalgarh PS of Rajsamand district is at the Top Rank with 14 FWCs.
- 27 PSs in the state had No FWC.

TABLE 9.10: District-wise First and Last PSs by No. of SHCs (2001)

District	*First Rank*	*Last Rank*	*District*	*First Rank*	*Last Rank*
Ajmer	Jawaja	Srinagar & Masooda	Jaipur	Amber	Jhotwara
Alwar	Umren	Kotkasim	Jaisalmer	Sam	Sankra
Banswara	Garhi	Sajjangarh	Jalor	Ahore	Bhinmal
Baran	Atru	Chhabra	Jhalawar	Dag	Manoharthana
Barmer	Barmer	Chohtan & Siwana	Jhunjhunun	Jhunjhunun	Chirawa & Surajgarh
Bharatpur	Nadbai	Weir	Jodhpur	Osian	Mandor
Bhilwara	Mandalgarh	Kotri & Raipur	Karauli	Sapotra	Nadoti
Bikaner	Nokha	Lunkaransar	Kota	Sangod	Itawa
Bundi	Talera	Hindoli	Nagaur	Didwana	Parbatsar
Chittaurgarh	Pratapgarh	Bari Sadri & Kapasan	Pali	Sojat	Rohat
Churu	Ratangarh	Taranagar	Rajsamand	Kumbhalgarh	Deogarh
Dausa	Dausa	Mahwa	S. Madhopur	S.Madhopur	Gangapur
Dhaulpur	Bari	Rajakhera	Sikar	Neem Ka Thana	Sri Madhopur
Dungarpur	Sagwara	Aspur	Sirohi	Sirohi	Abu Road
Ganganagar	Anupgarh	Suratgarh	Tonk	Tonk	Malpura, Todaraisingh & Uniara
Hanumangarh	Hanumangarh	Bhadra	Udaipur	Kherwara	Bargaon

Source : General Annex-VIII.

TABLE 9.11: Classification of PSs by No. of FWCs (2001)

Group	*Included PSs*	
	No.	*%*
Very High (VH), (>=5)	47	19.8
High (H), (4)	27	11.4
Medium (M), (3)	41	17.3
Low (L), (2)	50	21.1
Very Low (VL), (1)	45	19.0
Nil (0)	27	11.4
Total	**237**	**100**

Source: Annex 9.9.

TABLE 9.12: District-wise First and Last PSs by No. of FWCs (2001)

District	*First Rank*	*Last Rank*	*District*	*First Rank*	*Last Rank*
Ajmer	Bhinay	Kishangarh & Srinagar	Jaipur	Amber	Sanganer
Alwar	Bansure	Kotkasim	Jaisalmer	Sankra	Jaisalmer
Banswara	Peepalkhoont & Talwara	Anandpuri	Jalor	Ahore, Jaswantpura, Raniwara & Sayla	Jalor, Sanchore & Bhinmal
Baran	Anta, Atru, Kishanganj & Shahbad	Baran, Chhabra & Chhipabarod	Jhalawar	Khanpur	Pirawa
Barmer	Sindhari	Sheo	Jhunjhunun	Buhana	Jhunjhunun
Bharatpur	Nagar Pahari	Kaman & Weir	Jodhpur	Bhopalgarh	Bap & Phalodi
Bhilwara	Mandalgarh	Banera, Hurda & Shahpura	Karauli	Sapotra & Todabhim	Hindaun
Bikaner	Bikaner	Nokha	Kota	Chechat	Sangod
Bundi	Nainwa	Talera	Nagaur	Kuchaman	Mundwa
Chittaurgarh	Pratapgarh	Bari Sadri, Chittaurgarh, Gangarar & Kapasan	Pali	Sojat	Rani Station
Churu	Rajgarh	Taranagar	Rajsamand	Kumbhalgarh	Amet
Dausa	Dausa, Mahwa & Sikrai	Bandikui & Lalsot	S. Madhopur	Gangapur	Bamanwas
Dhaulpur	Dhaulpur	Bari	Sikar	Dhond, Lachhmangarh & Piprali	Fatehpur & Sri Madhopur
Dungarpur	Dungarpur	Sagwara	Sirohi	Reodar	Abu Road
Ganganagar	Anupgarh	Karanpur	Tonk	Tonk	Todoraisingh & Uniara
Hanumangarh	Hanumangarh	Bhadra & Nohar	Udaipur	Girwa	Gogunda

Source: General Annex-VIII.

Improved Drinking Water Amenities

- 95.4 per cent Rural Population of the State was Served by Drinking Water Amenities,
- Percentage of AAPs was 77.
- 47 PSs had almost Perfect Amenities of Drinking Water (had 100% of their Rural Population Served by Drinking Water Amenities.
- Sardarshahar PS (52.5%) of Churu District was the most Deprived.

TABLE 9.13: Classification of PSs by Percentage of Rural Population Served by Improved Drinking Water Amenities (2001)

Group	*Included PSs*	
	No.	*%*
Perfect, 100	47	19.8
Very High (VH), (98-100)	105	44.3
High (H), (96-98)	24	10.1
Medium (M), (94-96)	18	7.6
Low (L), (<94)	43	18.1
Total	**237**	**100**

Source: Annex 9.10.

TABLE 9.14: District-wise First and Last PSs by Percentage of Rural Pop. Served by Improved Drinking Water Amenities (2001)

District	*First Rank*	*Last Rank*	*District*	*First Rank*	*Last Rank*
Ajmer	Jawaja*, Kekri*, Masooda*, Pisangan* & Srinagar*	Bhinay	Jaipur	Amber*, Govindgarh*, Kotputli* & Shahpura*	Jhotwara
Alwar	Kotkasim*, Lachhmangarh*, Mandawar* & Ramgarh*	Rajgarh	Jaisalmer	Sankra	Jaisalmer
Banswara	Garhi* & Sajjangarh*	Anandpuri	Jalor	Ahore & Jalor	Bhinmal
Baran	Anta*, Atru* & Baran*	Chhabra	Jhalawar	Pirawa	Bakani
Barmer	Siwana	Barmer	Jhunjhunun	Nawalgarh	Alsisar
Bharatpur	Deeg* & Nadbai*	Kaman	Jodhpur	Bilara	Bap
Bhilwara	Suwana*	Shahpura	Karauli	Hindaun*	Karauli
Bikaner	Nokha	Kolayat	Kota	Sangod* & Sultanpur*	Chechat
Bundi	Talera	Keshoraipatan	Nagaur	Ladnu	Jayal
Chittaurgarh	Begun*, Bhadesar*, Dungla*, Kapasan*, Nimbahera* & Rashmi*	Arnod	Pali	Bali*, Raipur* & Rani Station*	Pali
Churu	Ratangarh	Sardarshahar	Rajsamand	Amet*, Deogarh* & Rajsamand*	Bhim
Dausa	Sikrai*	Dausa	S. Madhopur	Sawai Madhopur*	Bamanwas
Dhaulpur	Dhaulpur	Bari	Sikar	Fatehpur* & Neem Ka Thana*	Danta Ramgarh
Dungarpur	Aspur* & Sagwara*	Dungarpur	Sirohi	Reodar	Sheoganj
Ganganagar	Ganganagar	Suratgarh	Tonk	Todaraisingh	Uniara
Hanumangarh	Bhadra	Nohar	Udaipur	Bhindar*, Mavli* & Sarada*	Kotra

Source: General Annex-VI. * PS/PSs having almost Perfect (100%) amenity.

Education Amenities

- 98 per cent Rural Population of the state was served by Education Amenities.
- Percentage of AAPs was 71.
- 21 PSs had almost Perfect Education Amenities (had 100% of their Rural Pop. Served by Education Amenities).
- Anupgarh PS (78%) of Ganganagar District was at the Bottom.

TABLE 9.15: Classification of PSs by Percentage of Rural Population Served by Education Amenities (2001)

Group	*Included PSs*	
	No.	*%*
Perfect, (100)	21	8.9
Very High (VH), (95-100)	189	79.7
High (H), (90-95)	21	8.9
Medium (M), (85-90)	4	1.7
Low (L), (<85)	2	0.8
Total	**237**	**100**

Source: Annex 9.11.

TABLE 9.16: District-wise First and Last PSs by Percentage of Rural Pop. Served by Education Amenity (2001)

District	*First Rank*	*Last Rank*	*District*	*First Rank*	*Last Rank*
Ajmer	Bhinay* & Pisangan*	Jawaja	Jaipur	Kotputli* & Shahpura*	Chaksu
Alwar	Kathumar* & Nimrana*	Rajgarh	Jaisalmer	Sankra	Sam
Banswara	Garhi	Peepalkhoont	Jalor	Bhinmal*, Jalor* & Raniwara*	Sanchore
Baran	Baran	Chhabra	Jhalawar	Pirawa	Bakani
Barmer	Sindhari	Barmer	Jhunjhunun	Chirawa*, Khetri*, Nawalgarh*, Surajgarh* & Udaipurwati	Alsisar
Bharatpur	Deeg*	Sewar	Jodhpur	Bhopalsagar*	Bap
Bhilwara	Banera	Jahazpur & Mandalgarh	Karauli	Todabhim	Sapotra
Bikaner	Kolayat	Lunkaransar	Kota	Chechat & Sultanpur	Itawa
Bundi	Talera	Hindoli	Nagaur	Degana	Merta, Mundwa & Riyan
Chittaurgarh	Bhopalsagar	Bhainsrorgarh	Pali	Sojat*	Pali
Churu	Dungargarh	Sardarshahar	Rajsamand	Bhim	Deogarh
Dausa	Sikrai	Mahwa	S. Madhopur	Gangapur	Khandar
Dhaulpur	Dhaulpur	Bari	Sikar	Dhond & Sri Madhopur*	Neem Ka Thana
Dungarpur	Dungarpur*	Aspur	Sirohi	Abu Road*	Reodar
Ganganagar	Karanpur	Anupgarh	Tonk	Malpura	Uniara
Hanumangarh	Bhadra	Hanumangarh	Udaipur	Gogunda	Kotra

*PS/PSs having almost perfect (100%) amenity
Source: General Annex-VI.

Power Amenities

- 92 per cent Rural Pop. of the state was Served by Power Amenities.
- Percentage of AAPs was 73.
- In 4 PSs viz. Kotra (Udaipur), Baytoo (Barmer), Sam (Jaisalmer) and Peepalkhoont (Banswara), the percentage of Rural Pop. Served by Power Amenities was below 50.
- 29 PSs had almost Perfect Power Amenities (had 100% of their Rural Population Served By Power Amenities.
- Kotra PS (33.3%) of Udaipur District as well as Division was the most Deprived.

TABLE 9.17: Classification of PSs by Percentage of Rural Population Served by Power Amenities (2001)

Group	*Included PSs*	
	No.	*%*
Perfect (100)	29	12.2
Very High (VH), (75-100)	185	78.1
High (H), (50-75)	19	8.0
Medium (M), (25-50)	4	1.7
Total	**237**	**100**

Source: Annex 9.12.

TABLE 9.18: District-wise First and Last PSs by Percentage of Rural Pop. Served by Power Amenity (2001)

District	*First Rank*	*Last Rank*	*District*	*First Rank*	*Last Rank*
Ajmer	Masooda	Jawaja	Jaipur	Jamwa Ramgarh, Sanganer & Viratnagar	Chaksu
Alwar	Bansure*, Nimrana* & Reni*	Rajgarh	Jaisalmer	Jaisalmer	Sam
Banswara	Garhi	Peepalkhoont	Jalor	Jaswantpura*	Sanchore
Baran	Baran*	Shahbad	Jhalawar	Pirawa	Manoharthana
Barmer	Siwana	Baytoo	Jhunjhunun	Chirawa*, Nawalgarh* & Surajgarh*	Alsisar
Bharatpur	Sewar	Kaman	Jodhpur	Bilara*	Shergarh
Bhilwara	Banera* & Sahara*	Kotri	Karauli	Hindaun	Sapotra
Bikaner	Nokha	Bikaner	Kota	Chechat	Itawa
Bundi	Nainwa	Keshoraipatan	Nagaur	Kuchaman*, Merta* & Parbatsar*	Nagaur
Chittaurgarh	Bhadesar*	Pratapgarh	Pali	Sumerpur	Raipur
Churu	Churu*	Rajgarh	Rajsamand	Amet*, Railmagra* & Rajsamand*	Bhim
Dausa	Bandikui*	Lalsot	S. Madhopur	Gangapur	Khandar
Dhaulpur	Rajakhera	Bari	Sikar	Danta Ramgarh*, Dhond*, Fatehpur* & Sri Madhopur*	Neem Ka Thana
Dungarpur	Bichhiwara	Simalwara	Sirohi	Reodar	Abu Road
Ganganagar	Ganganagar	Suratgarh	Tonk	Todaraisingh	Deoli
Hanumangarh	Bhadra	Nohar	Udaipur	Mavli*	Kotra

* PS/PSs having almost Perfect (100%) amenity.
Source : General Annex-VI.

Pucca Road Amenities

- 73 per cent Rural Population of the State was Served by Pucca Road Amenities.
- Percentage of AAPs was 54.
- In 9 PSs namely, Manoharthana, Bakani, Dag and Pirawa (all of Jhalawar district), Chhabra (Baran), Baytoo (Barmer), Kushalgarh, Peepalkhoont (both of Banswara) and Kotra (Udaipur) the percentage of Rural Population Served by Pucca Road Amenities was Below 50.
- Sumerpur PS had the highest 99.8 per cent Rural Pop. Served by Pucca Road Amenities.
- Monaharthana PS had the lowest 31 per cent Rural Pop. Served by Pucca Road Amenities.

TABLE 9.19: Classification of PSs by Percentage of Rural Population Served by Pucca Road Amenities (2001)

Group	*Included PSs*	
	No.	*%*
Very High (VH), (>80)	69	29.1
High (H), (60-80)	125	52.7
Medium (M), (40-60)	41	17.3
Low (L), (<40)	2	0.8
Total	**237**	**100**

Source: Annex 9.13.

TABLE 9.20: District-wise First and Last PSs by Percentage of Rural Pop. Served by Pucca Road Amenity (2001)

District	*First Rank*	*Last Rank*	*District*	*First Rank*	*Last Rank*
Ajmer	Srinagar	Arian	Jaipur	Govindgarh	Chaksu
Alwar	Nimrana	Kotkasim	Jaisalmer	Jaisalmer	Sankra
Banswara	Garhi	Kushalgarh	Jalor	Jalor	Sanchore
Baran	Baran	Chhabra	Jhalawar	Khanpur	Manoharthana
Barmer	Siwana	Baytoo	Jhunjhunun	Chirawa	Surajgarh
Bharatpur	Sewar	Weir	Jodhpur	Bhopalgarh	Shergarh
Bhilwara	Hurda	Raipur	Karauli	Hindaun	Sapotra
Bikaner	Bikaner	Kolayat	Kota	Ladpura	Sangod
Bundi	Talera	Keshoraipatan	Nagaur	Merta	Kuchahman
Chittaurgarh	Rashmi	Kapasan	Pali	Sumerpur	Rohat
Churu	Ratangarh	Sardarshahar	Rajsamand	Railmagra	Deogarh
Dausa	Sikrai	Lalsot	S. Madhopur	Gangapur	Sawai Madhopur
Dhaulpur	Dhaulpur	Bari	Sikar	Sri Madhopur	Fatehpur
Dungarpur	Aspur & Sagwara	Dungarpur	Sirohi	Sirohi	Reodar
Ganganagar	Ganganagar	Raisinghnagar	Tonk	Malpura	Uniara
Hanumangarh	Hanumangarh	Nohar	Udaipur	Girwa	Kotra

Source : General Annex-VI.

10

HEALTH STATUS INDEX (1991)

Highlights

- Rural Health Status Index—Rajasthan : 0.559
- Percentage of AAPS: 52.74
- 39 PSs had HSI below 0.5 • No PS crossed 0.75 HSI

• *First Rank*

Panchayat Samiti	*District*	*Division*
Sumerpur (HSI 0.729)	Pali	Jodhpur

• *Last Rank*

Sam (HSI 0.346)	Jaisalmer	Jodhpur

The Health Status Index (HSI) of rural Rajasthan in the year 1991 was 0.559. There were 125 PSs having HSI above the state average. A great deal of regional disparity is observed in HSI across the state. Whereas, 50 per cent PSs of Jodhpur division, 44 per cent of Ajmer and 39 per cent PSs of Jaipur division had Medium to High level of HSI (>0.6), 100 per cent PSs of Kota division, 86 per cent of Bikaner and more than 70 per cent PSs of Udaipur division had Low to Very low of HSI (Fig. 10.1 & Annex 10.1). The HSI level in the state increases mainly from the South-East and South to the South-West, Central and North-East direction.

TABLE 10.1: Distribution of First & Last Ten Panchayat Samities by HSI, 1991 : Rajasthan

S. No.	*First Ten PSs (Descending Order)*						*Last Ten PSs (Ascending Order)*						
	Districts/ PSs						*Districts/ PSs*						
	Pali	*Jhunjhunun*	*Jodhpur*	*Jaipur*	*Ajmer*	*Sikar*	*Barmer*	*Jhalawar*	*Jodhpur*	*Udaipur*	*Ganga-nagar*	*Dhaulpur*	*Jaisalmer*
	(4)	*(2)*	*(1)*	*(1)*	*(1)*	*(1)*	*(4)*	*(1)*	*(1)*	*(1)*	*(1)*	*(1)*	*(1)*
1	Sumerpur	Nawal-garh	Bilara	Govind-garh	Pisangan	Dhond	Baytoo	Manohar-thana	Bap	Kotra	Anupgarh	Bari	Sam
2	Bali	Udaipur-wati	—	—	—	—	Barmer	—	—	—	—	—	—
3	Rani Station	—	—	—	—	—	Sheo	—	—	—	—	—	—
4	Desuri	—	—	—	—	—	Sindhari	—	—	—	—	—	—

Source: Annex 10.2.

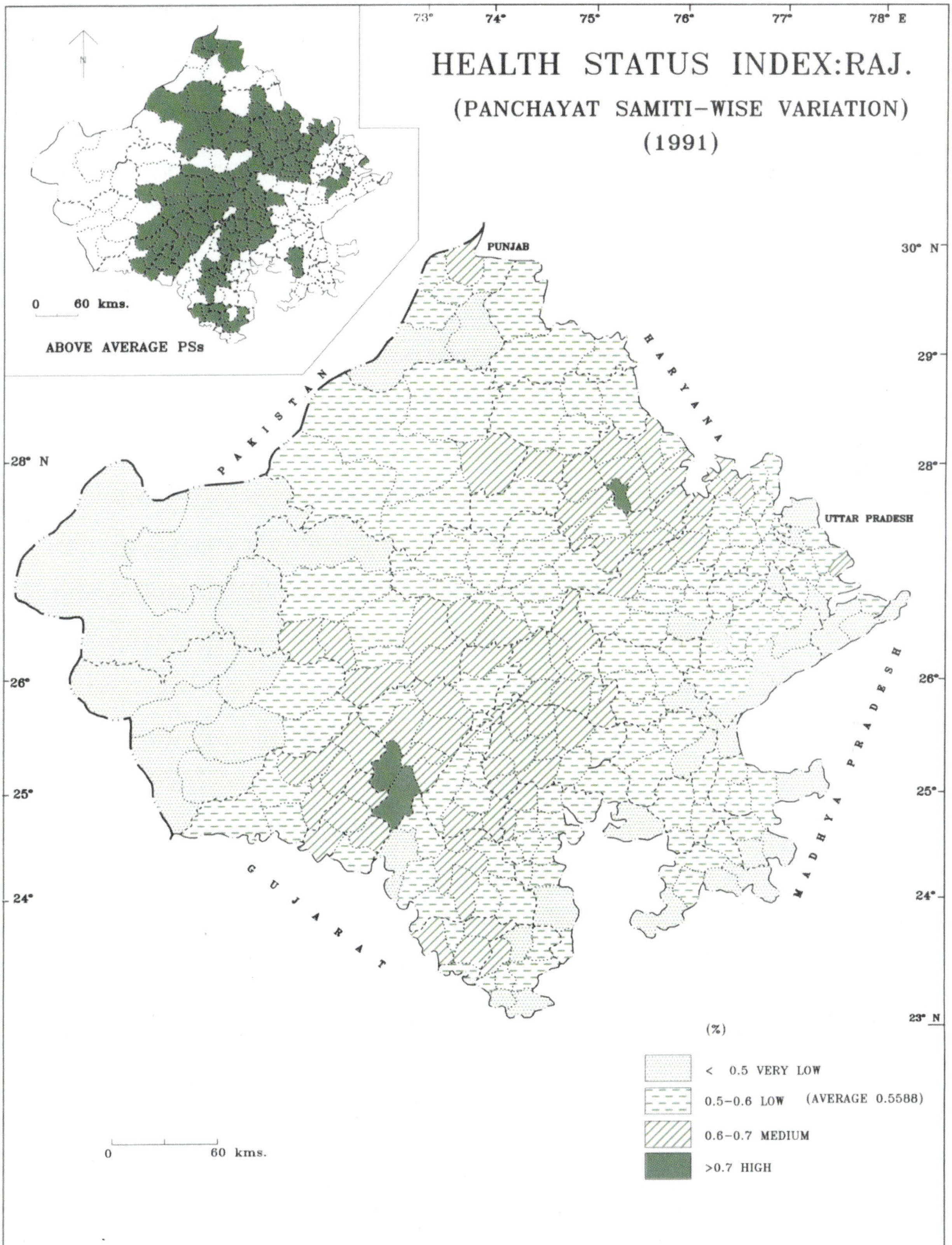
HEALTH STATUS INDEX:RAJ.
(PANCHAYAT SAMITI–WISE VARIATION)
(1991)
ABOVE AVERAGE PSs
0 60 kms.
N
PUNJAB
HARYANA
UTTAR PRADESH
MADHYA PRADESH
GUJARAT
PAKISTAN
(%)
< 0.5 VERY LOW
0.5–0.6 LOW (AVERAGE 0.5588)
0.6–0.7 MEDIUM
>0.7 HIGH
0 60 kms.
70° E
71°
72°
73°
74°
75°
76°
77°
78° E
30° N
29°
28° N
28°
26°
25°
24°
23° N

FIG. 10.1

Sumerpur PS of Pali district had the maximum HSI (0.7291) followed by Nawalgarh, Bali, Bilara, Udaipurwati, Govindgarh, Pisangan, Rani Station, Dhond and Desuri PSs (in descending order, Annex 10.2). These top ten PSs were spread over six districts. Pali led with four PSs followed by Jhunjhunun (2) and Jodhpur, Jaipur, Ajmer and Sikar (one each) districts (Table 10.1).

Sam PS of Jaisalmer district, on the other hand, had the minimum (0.346) HSI. It was preceded by Baytoo, Barmer, Bari, Anupgarh, Kotra, Bap, Sheo, Manoharthana, and Sindhari PSs (in ascending order). These last ten PSs were concentrated in seven districts. Barmer dominated with 4 PSs while Jhalawar, Jodhpur, Udaipur, Ganganagar, Dhaulpur and Jaisalmer districts had one PS each, Similarly, district-wise first and the last PSs by HSI is shown in Table 10.2.

TABLE 10.2: HSI (1991) : District-wise First and Last PSs

District	*First Rank*	*Last Rank*
Ajmer	Pisangan	Jawaja
Alwar	Nimrana	Lachhmangarh
Banswara	Garhi	Kushalgarh
Baran	Atru	Chhipabarod
Barmer	Siwana	Bayatoo
Bharatpur	Kumher	Nagar Pahari
Bhilwara	Hurda	Mandalgarh
Bikaner	Nokha	Kolayat
Bundi	Nainwa	Keshoraipatan
Chittaurgarh	Bhopalsagar	Bhainsrorgarh
Churu	Ratangarh	Rajgarh
Dausa	Dausa	Lalsot
Dhaulpur	Dhaulpur	Bari
Dungarpur	Sagwara	Simalwara
Ganganagar	Ganganagar	Anupgarh
Hanumangarh	Hanumangarh	Nohar
Jaipur	Govindgarh	Chaksu
Jaisalmer	Jaisalmer	Sam
Jalor	Jalor	Sanchore
Jhalawar	Jhalrapatan	Manoharthana
Jhunjhunun	Nawalgarh	Surajgarh
Jodhpur	Bilara	Bap
Karauli	Hindaun	Karauli
Kota	Ladpura	Itawa
Nagaur	Merta	Didwana
Pali	Sumerpur	Rohat
Rajsamand	Railmagra	Kumbhalgarh
Sawai Madhopur	Gangapur	Khandar
Sikar	Dhond	Piprali
Sirohi	Sirohi	Abu Road
Tonk	Malpura	Uniara
Udaipur	Mavli	Kotra
Rajasthan	**Sumerpur (Pali)**	**Sam (Jaisalmer)**

Source: Annex 10.1.

Classification of PSs By HSI

Table 10.3 presents classification of PSs by HSI. The state had dominance of Low Level PSs (51.1%) followed by Medium (30.8%), Very Low (16.5%), and High (1.3%) level PSs.

TABLE 10.3: Classification of PSs on the Basis of HSI (1991) : Rajasthan

Group	*Included PSs*			
	No.	*%*	*Distributed in*	
			Districts	*Divisions*
High (H), (0.7-0.8)	3	1.3	2	2
Medium (M), (0.6-0.7)	73	30.8	19	6
Low (L), (0.5-0.6)	122	51.5	31	6
Very Low (VL), (<0.5)	39	16.5	18	6
Total	237	100		

Source: Annex 10.2.

If we look at division-wise classification and distribution of PSs by HSI (Table 10.4) following interpretations can be made:

- Both Jaipur and Jodhpur divisions had PSs of all the four levels, while Ajmer, Bikaner and Udaipur divisions had PSs of 3 levels. Kota was the only division having PSs of 2 levels.
- Jodhpur division secured the top position in the state with 67 per cent share of High level PSs.
- Kota division was the most deprived led in PSs having VL (28.2%) HSI level while, Jaipur division led in M (30%) as well as L (23.8%) level PSs.
- Except Jodhpur, all the divisions have dominance of L level PSs. Jodhpur division had dominance of M level PSs.
- The percentage of H level PSs in Jodhpur and Jaipur divisions; M level in Jodhpur, Ajmer and Jaipur divisions; L level in Bikaner, Udaipur, Kota and Ajmer, divisions and VL level in Kota and Jodhpur divisions was higher than the state average.

TABLE 10.4: Division-wise Classification and Distribution of PSs on the Basis of HSI Level (1991)

Divisions	*Classification*					*Distribution (% Share)*			
	HSI Level					*HSI Level*			
	High	*Medium*	*Low*	*Very Low*	*Total*	*High*	*Medium*	*Low*	*Very Low*
Jaipur	1	22	29	9	61	33.3	30.1	23.8	23.1
(%)	(1.6)	(36.1)	(47.5)	(14.8)	(100.0)				
Bikaner	—	3	16	2	21	—	4.1	13.1	5.1
(%)	—	(14.3)	(76.2)	(9.5)	(100.0)				
Ajmer	—	16	19	1	36	—	21.9	15.6	2.6
(%)	—	(44.4)	(52.8)	(2.8)	(100.0)				
Kota	—	—	21	11	32	—	—	17.2	28.2
(%)	—	—	(65.6)	(34.4)	(100.0)				
Jodhpur	2	19	11	10	42	66.7	26.0	9.0	25.6
(%)	(4.8)	(45.2)	(26.2)	(23.8)	(100.0)				
Udaipur	—	13	26	6	45	—	17.8	21.3	15.4
(%)	—	(28.9)	(57.8)	(13.3)	(100.0)				
Total	**3**	**73**	**122**	**39**	**237**	**100**	**100**	**100**	**100**
(%)	**(1.3)**	**(30.8)**	**(51.5)**	**(16.5)**	**(100.0)**				

Figure in brackets shows % share of total Panchayat Samities
Note: HSI Level H: (0.7-0.8), M : (0.6-0.7), L : (0.5-0.6), VL : (<0.5)
Source: Annex 10.2.

Different HSI Regions

High HSI Region

There were only 3 PSs viz. Sumerpur and Bali of Pali District and Nawalgarh of Jhunjhunun having High HIS. Both these districts had greater percentage of H level PSs in comparison to the state average (1.3). The percentage ranged from 20 in Pali district to 12.5 in Jhunjhunun (Table 10.5 and 10.6).

TABLE 10.5: District-wise Classification of PSs on the Basis of HSI Level, 1991

District	*H*	*M*	*L*	*VL*	*TOTAL*
Ajmer	—	6	2	—	8
(%)	—	(75.0)	(25.0)	—	(100.0)
Alwar	—	3	11	—	14
(%)	—	(21.4)	(78.6)	—	(100.0)
Banswara	—	1	4	3	8
(%)	—	(12.5)	(50.0)	(37.5)	(100.0)
Baran	—	—	4	3	7
(%)	—	—	(57.1)	(42.9)	(100.0)
Barmer	—	—	2	6	8
(%)	—	—	(25.0)	(75.0)	(100.0)
Bharatpur	—	1	5	3	9
(%)	—	(11.1)	(55.6)	(33.3)	(100.0)
Bhilwara	—	8	3	—	11
(%)	—	(72.7)	(27.3)	—	(100.0)
Bikaner	—	—	4	—	4
(%)	—	—	(100.0)	—	(100.0)
Bundi	—	—	3	1	4
(%)	—	—	(75.0)	(25.0)	(100.0)
Chittaurgarh	—	2	10	2	14
(%)	—	(14.3)	(71.4)	(14.3)	(100.0)
Churu	—	2	5	—	7
(%)	—	(28.6)	(71.4)	—	(100.0)
Dausa	—	—	3	2	5
(%)	—	—	(60.0)	(40.0)	(100.0)
Dhaulpur	—	—	1	3	4
(%)	—	—	(25.0)	(75.0)	(100.0)
Dungarpur	—	3	2	—	5
(%)	—	(60.0)	(40.0)	—	(100.0)
Ganganagar	—	1	4	2	7
(%)	—	(14.3)	(57.1)	(28.6)	(100.0)
Hanumangarh	—	—	3	—	3
(%)	—	—	(100.0)	—	(100.0)
Jaipur	—	5	7	1	13
(%)	—	(38.5)	(53.8)	(7.7)	(100.0)
Jaisalmer	—	—	—	3	3
(%)	—	—	—	(100.0)	(100.0)
Jalor	—	4	3	—	7
(%)	—	(57.1)	(42.9)	—	(100.0)
Jhalawar	—	—	3	3	6
(%)	—	—	(50.0)	(50.0)	(100.0)
Jhunjhunun	1	6	1	—	8
(%)	(12.5)	(75.0)	(12.5)	—	(100.0)
Jodhpur	—	5	3	1	9
(%)	—	(55.6)	(33.3)	(11.1)	(100.0)
Karauli	—	—	3	2	5
(%)	—	—	(60.0)	(40.0)	(100.0)
Kota	—	—	4	1	5
(%)	—	—	(80.0)	(20.0)	(100.0)
Nagaur	—	2	9	—	11
(%)	—	(18.2)	(81.8)	—	(100.0)
Pali	2	6	2	—	10
(%)	(20.0)	(60.0)	(20.0)	—	(100.0)
Rajsamand	—	3	4	—	7
(%)	—	(42.9)	(57.1)	—	(100.0)
Sawai Madhopur	—	—	4	1	5
(%)	—	—	(80.0)	(20.0)	(100.0)
Sikar	—	7	1	—	8
(%)	—	(87.5)	(12.5)	—	(100.0)
Sirohi	—	4	1	—	5
(%)	—	(80.0)	(20.0)	—	(100.0)
Tonk	—	—	5	1	6
(%)	—	—	(83.3)	(16.7)	(100.0)
Udaipur	—	4	6	1	11
(%)	—	(36.4)	(54.5)	(9.1)	(100.0)
Rajasthan	**3**	**73**	**122**	**39**	**237**
(%)	**(1.3)**	**(30.8)**	**(51.5)**	**(16.5)**	**(100.0)**

Note: HSI Level H: (0.7-0.8), M : (0.6-0.7), L : (0.5-0.6), VL : (<0.5)
Figure in brackets shows per cent share of total Panchayat Samities.
Source: Annex 10.2.

TABLE 10.6: Distribution of PSs Having High to Very Low HSI Level, 1991

S.No.	*District*	*Name of PS*	*Descending Order*
		[I] High Level (3)	
1	Pali	Sumerpur and Bali	(2)
2	Jhunjhunun	Nawalgarh	(1)
		[II] Medium Level (73)	
1	Bhilwara	Hurda, Sahara, Banera, Mandal, Raipur, Suwana, Shahpura and Asind	(8)
2	Sikar	Dhond, Danta Ramgarh, Sri Madhopur, Khandela, Neem ka Thana, Lachhmangarh and Fatehpur	(7)
3	Ajmer	Pisangan, Kekri, Srinagar, Bhinay, Kishangarh and Masooda	(6)
4	Jhunjhunun	Udaipurwati, Chirawa, Jhunjhunun, Khetri, Alsisar and Buhana	(6)
5	Pali	Rani Station, Desuri, Sojat, Kharchi, Pali and Jaitaran	(6)
6	Jaipur	Govindgarh, Shahpura, Viratnagar, Sambhar and Kotputli	(5)
7	Jodhpur	Bilara, Bhopalgarh, Baleasr, Luni and Shergarh	(5)
8	Jalor	Jalor, Sayal, Ahore and Jaswantpura	(4)
9	Sirohi	Sirohi, Sheoganj, Pindwara and Reodar	(4)
10	Udaipur	Mavli, Sarada, Girwa and Bargaon	(4)
11	Alwar	Nimrana, Behror and Mandawar	(3)
12	Dungarpur	Sagwara, Aspur and Bichhiwara	(3)
13	Rajsamand	Railmagra, Khamnor and Bhim	(3)
14	Chittaurgarh	Bhopalsagar and Rashmi	(2)
15	Churu	Dungargarh and Ratangarh	(2)
16	Nagaur	Merta and Riyan	(2)
17	Banswara	Garhi	(1)
18	Bharatpur	Kumher	(1)
19	Bikaner	Dungarpur	(1)
20	Ganganagar	Ganganagar	(1)
		[III] Low Level (122)	
1	Alwar	Kishangarh Bas, Bansur, Thanagazi, Kotkasim, Rajgarh, Ramgarh, Umren, Reni, Khathumer, Tijara and Lachhmangarh	(11)
2	Chittaurgarh	Kapasan, Chittaurgarh, Nimbahera, Dungla, Bari Sadri, Begun, Gangrar, Arnod, Chhoti Sadri and Bhadesar	(10)
3	Nagaur	Kuchaman, Degana, Ladnu, Parbatsar, Mundwa, Makrana, Nagaur, Jayal and Didwana	(9)
4	Jaipur	Jhotwara, Amber, Jamwa Ramgarh, Bassi, Sanganer, Phagi and Dudu	(7)
5	Udaipur	Bhindar, Salumber, Gogunda, Kherwara, Jhadol and Dhariawad	(6)
6	Tonk	Malpura, Deoli, Niwai, Todaraisingh and Tonk	(5)
7	Churu	Taranagar, Churu, Sujangarh, Sardarshahar and Rajgarh	(5)
8	Bharatpur	Weir, Sewar, Nadbai, Rupbas and Deeg	(5)
9	Sawai Madhopur	Gangapur, Bamanwas, Bonli and Sawai Madhopur	(4)
10	Rajsamand	Amet, Rajsamand, Deogarh and Khumbalgarh	(4)
11	Kota	Ladpura, Chechat, Sultanpur and Sangod	(4)
12	Ganganagar	Karanpur, Sadulshahar, Padampur and Raisinghnagar	(4)
13	Bikaner	Nokha, Bikaner, Lunkaransar and Kolayat	(4)
14	Baran	Atru, Baran, Anta and Kishanganj	(4)
15	Banswara	Talwara, Bagidora, Ghatol and Anandpuri	(4)
16	Karauli	Hindaun, Nadoti and Todabhim	(3)
17	Jodhpur	Osian, Mandor and Phalodi	(3)
18	Jhalawar	Jhalrapatan, Khanpur and Piprali	(3)
19	Jalor	Raniwara, Bhinmal and Sanchore	(3)
20	Hanumangarh	Hanumangarh, Bhadra and Nohar	(3)
21	Dausa	Dausa, Sikrai and Bandikui	(3)
22	Bundi	Nainwa, Talera and Hindoli	(3)
23	Bhilwara	Jahazpur, Kotri and Mandalgarh	(3)
24	Pali	Raipur and Rohat	(2)
25	Dungarpur	Dungarpur and Simalwara	(2)
26	Barmer	Siwana and Balotra	(2)
27	Ajmer	Arian and Jawaja	(2)
28	Sirohi	Abu Road	(1)
29	Sikar	Piprali	(1)
30	Jhunjhunun	Surajgarh	(1)
31	Dhaulpur	Dhaulpur	(1)

(Contd.)

Table 10.6 (contd.)

S.No.	*District*	*Name of PS*	*Descending Order*
		[IV] Very Low Level (39)	
1	Barmer	Chohtan, Dhorimanna, Sindhari, Sheo, Barmer and Baytoo	(6)
2	Jhalawar	Bakani, Dag and Manoharthana	(3)
3	Jaisalmer	Jaisalmer, Sankra and Sam	(3)
4	Dhaulpur	Baseri, Rajakhera and Bari	(3)
5	Dausa	Mahwa and Lalsot	(3)
6	Bharatpur	Bayana, Kaman and Nagar Pharai	(3)
7	Baran	Shahbad, Chhabra and Chhipabarod	(3)
8	Banswara	Peepalknoont, Sajjangarh and Kushalgarh	(3)
9	Karauli	Sapotra and Karauli	(2)
10	Ganganagar	Suratgarh and Anupgarh	(2)
11	Chittaurgarh	Pratapgarh and Bhainsrorgarh	(2)
12	Udaipur	Kotra	(1)
13	Tonk	Uniara	(1)
14	Sawai Madhopur	Khandar	(1)
15	Kota	Itawa	(1)
16	Jodhpur	Bap	(1)
17	Jaipur	Chaksu	(1)
18	Bundi	Keshoraipatan	(1)

Source: Annex- 10.2.

Medium HSI Region

Medium HSI area was widely distributed in 5 divisions (Except Kota) and 19 districts. There were total 73 M level PSs. Jaipur division with 30.1 per cent share had the maximum concentration of these PSs follwed by Jodhpur (26%), Ajmer (21.9%), Udaipur (17.8%), and Bikaner (4.1%) divisions. The percentage share of M level PSs to total PSs was the highest in Jodhpur with 45.2 per cent, 44.4 in Ajmer, 36.1 in Jaipur, 28.9 in Udaipur, and the lowest 14.3 in Bikaner division.

District-wise distribution of these PSs makes it clear that both Bhilwara and Jhunjhunun secured the top rank with 8 PSs each followed by Sikar (7); Ajmer and Pali (6 each); Jaipur and Jodhpur (5 each); Jalor, Sirohi and Udaipur (4 each); Alwar Dungarpur and Rajsamand (3 each); Chittaurgarh, Churu and Nagaur (2 each); and Banswara, Bharatpur and Ganganagar (1each) respectively. All the above districts, except Alwar, Banswara, Bharatpur, Chittaurgarh, Churu, Ganganagar, and Nagaur had higher percentage of Medium level PSs in comparison to the state average (30.8). Sikar district had the highest percentage (87.5) of M level PSs while, Bharatpur had the lowest (11.1).

Low HSI Region

Low HSI area was widely spread over all the 6 divisions and 31 districts (except Jailsalmer). There were total 122 PSs in this category. Jaipur division led with 23.8 per cent share followed by Udaipur (21.3 %), Kota (17.2 %), Ajmer (15.6%), Bikaner (13.6%) and Jodhpur (9.0%) divisions.

Among the districts, Alwar dominated with 11 PSs followed by Chittarugarh (10); Nagaur (9); Jaipur (7), Udaipur (6), Bharatpur, Chittaurgarh, Tonk (5 each); Banswara, Baran, Bikaner, Ganganagar, Kota, Rajsamand and Sawai Madhopur (4 each); Bhilwara, Bundi, Dausa, Hanumangarh, Jalor, Jhalawar, Jodhpur and Karauli (3 each); Ajmer Barmer, Dungarpur and Pali (2 each) and Dhaulpur, Jhunjhunun, Sikar and Sirohi (1 each) districts respectively. All the above districts, except Banswara, Barmer, Bhilwara, Dhaulpur, Dungarpur, Jhunjhunun, Jodhpur, Pali Sikar and Sirohi had greater percentage of L level PSs in comparison to the state average (51.5). Tonk district had the highest percentage (83.3) of Low level PSs while, Jhunjhunun had the lowest (12.5%).

Very Low HSI Area

Very low HSI area was also widely distributed in all the 6 divisions and 18 districts. There were 39 PSs in this category. Kota division was the most deprived having 28.2 share preceded by Jodhpur (25.6%), Jaipur (23.14), Udaipur (15.4), Bikaner (5.1%) and Ajmer (2.6%) divisions. If we look at district-wise distribution of these PSs, it is clear that, Barmer led with 6 PSs followed by Banswara, Baran, Bharatpur, Dhaulpur, Jaisalmer, Jodhpur (3 each); Churu, Dausa, Ganganager, Karauli (2 each) and Bundi, Jaipur, Jodhpur, Kota, Sawai Madhopur, Tonk and Udaipur (one each) respectively. All the above districts except Chittaurgarh, Jaipur, Jodhpur and Udaipur had higher percentage of VL level PSs than the state average (16.5). Jaisalmer district had the maximum percentage (100%) of these PSs, while Jaipur had the minimum (7.7%).

11

HEALTH STATUS INDEX (2001)

Highlights

- Rural Health Status Index (HSI): Rajasthan : 0.6684
- Percentage of AAPS: 56
- 14% PSs had HSI above 0.75

• ***First Rank***

Panchayat Samiti	District	Division
Udaipurwati (0.8307)	Jhunjhunun	Jodhpur

• ***Last Rank***

Panchayat Samiti	District	Division
Sam (0.4749)	Jaisalmer	Jodhpur

Health Status Index of rural Rajasthan rose to 0.6684 in the year 2001. There were 132 PSs having HSI above the state average. Whereas, Jodhpur division led not only in PSs having very high HSI (66.7%) but also in PSs having very low HSI (80%). Jaipur division dominated in PSs having high (30.4%) as well as Medium (25.6%) HSI while Kota division led in low HSI level PSs.

Figure 11.1 depicts spatial distribution pattern of HSI at PS level. It is interesting to note that the PS having High and Very High HSI are mainly concentrated in a belt along with Aravalli hills area from South-West (Sirohi dist.) to North-East (Jhun/Alwar dists.) direction. The HSI level decreases towards both sides mainly towards Western arid and semi-arid areas.

TABLE 11.1: Distribution of First and Last Ten Panchayat Samities by HSI : Rajasthan (2001)

S. No.	*First Ten PSs (Descending Order)*							*Last Ten PSs (Ascending Order)*					
	Districts / PSs							*Districts / PSs*					
	Pali	*Sikar*	*Sirohi*	*Jodhpur*	*Jalor*	*Jhunjhunun*	*Churu*	*Barmer*	*Jaisalmer*	*Jhalawar*	*Udaipur*	*Ganganagar*	*Baran*
	(3)	*(2)*	*(1)*	*(1)*	*(1)*	*(1)*	*(1)*	*(3)*	*(2)*	*(2)*	*(1)*	*(1)*	*(1)*
1	Rani Station	Dhond	Sirohi	Bilara	Ahore	Udaipurwati	Ratangarh	Barmer	Sam	Manoharthana	Kotra	Suratgarh	Chhabra
2	Sumerpur pur	Piprali	—	—		—	—	Sheo	Sankra	Bakani	—	—	—
3	Bali	—	—			—	—	Baytoo	—	—	—	—	—

Source: Annex 11.2.

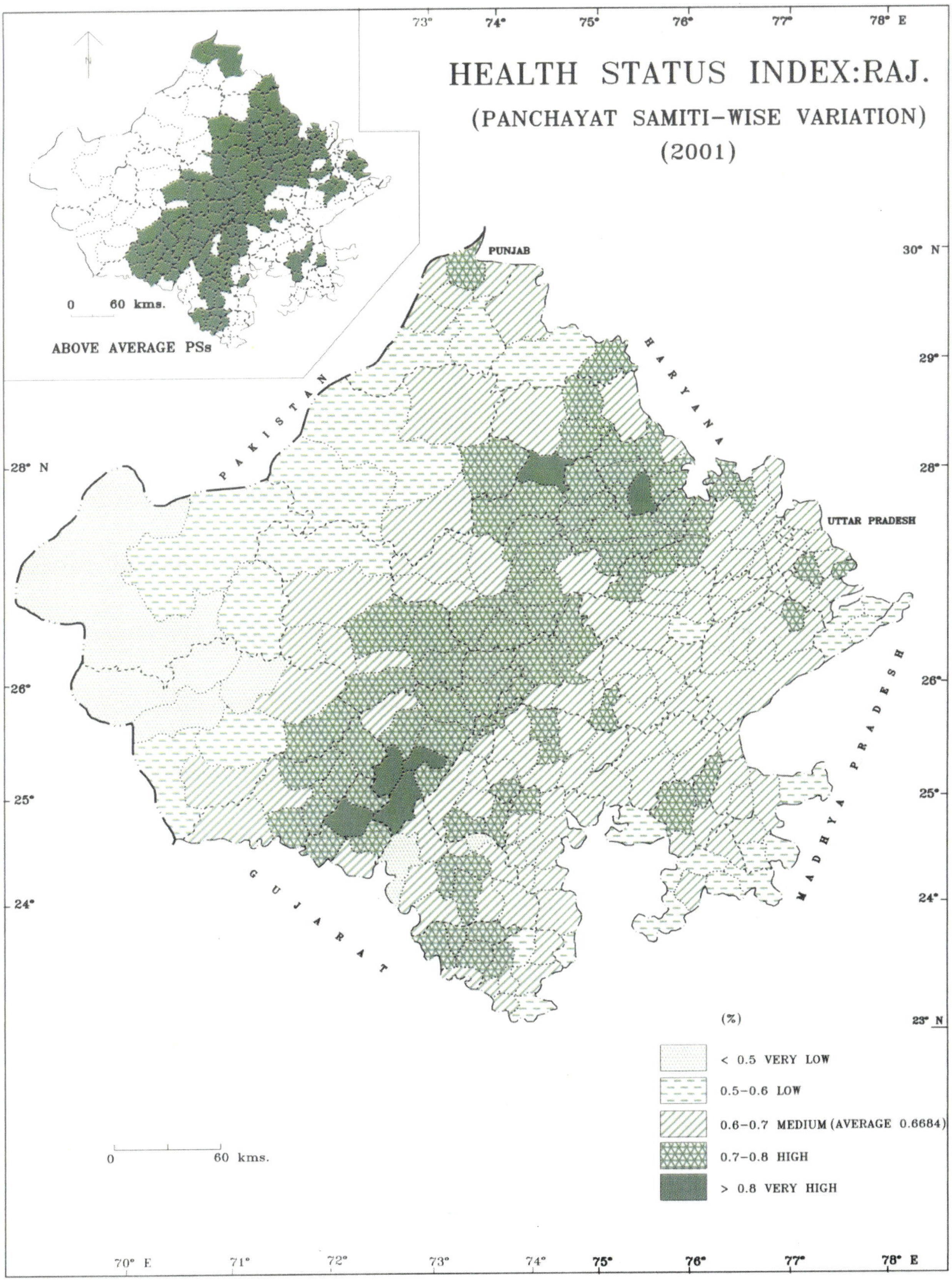
HEALTH STATUS INDEX:RAJ.
(PANCHAYAT SAMITI–WISE VARIATION)
(2001)
ABOVE AVERAGE PSs
0 60 kms.
PUNJAB
HARYANA
UTTAR PRADESH
MADHYA PRADESH
GUJARAT
PAKISTAN
(%)
< 0.5 VERY LOW
0.5–0.6 LOW
0.6–0.7 MEDIUM (AVERAGE 0.6684)
0.7–0.8 HIGH
> 0.8 VERY HIGH
0 60 kms.
70° E 71° 72° 73° 74° 75° 76° 77° 78° E
30° N 29° 28° N 26° 25° 24° 23° N

FIG. 11.1

Udaipurwati PS of Jhunjhunun district had the maximum 0.8307 HSI followed by Ratangarh, Rani Station, Sumerpur, Sirohi, Bali, Dhond, Ahore, Piprali and Bilara PSs (Descending order, Annex 11.2). These top ten PSs are distributed in seven districts. Pali district led with three PSs followed by Sikar (2), Sirohi, Jodhpur, Jalor, Juunjunun and Churu (one each) respectively (Table 11.1).

Sam PS of Jaisalmer district, on the other hand, was at the bottom with 0.4749 HSI. It was followed by Barmer, Sheo, Baytoo, Kotra, Manoharthana, Suratgarh, Chhabra, Sankra and Bakani PSs (Ascending order). These last ten PSs were concentrated in six districts viz. Barmer (3); Jaisalmer and Jhalawar (2 each); Udaipur, Ganganagar and Baran (one each) respectively. District-wise PSs with highest and lowest HSI is shown in Table 11.2.

TABLE 11.2: HSI (2001) : District-wise First and Last PSs

District	*First Rank*	*Last Rank*
Ajmer	Pisangan	Arain
Alwar	Behror	Tijara
Banswara	Garhi	Kushalgarh
Baran	Baran	Chhabra
Barmer	Siwana	Barmer
Bharatpur	Kumher	Bayana
Bhilwara	Banera	Kotri
Bikaner	Nokha	Kolayat
Bundi	Hindoli	Nainwa
Chittaurgarh	Rashmi	Bhainsrorgarh
Churu	Ratangarh	Sardarshahar
Dausa	Bandikui	Lalsot
Dhaulpur	Dhaulpur	Baseri
Dungarpur	Sagwara	Simalwara
Ganganagar	Ganganagar	Suratgarh
Hanumangarh	Bhadra	Nohar
Jaipur	Govindgarh	Chaksu
Jaisalmer	Jaisalmer	Sam
Jalor	Ahore	Sanchore
Jhalawar	Khanpur	Manoharthana
Jhunjhunun	Udaipurwati	Surajgarh
Jodhpur	Bilara	Bap
Karauli	Hindaun	Sapotra
Kota	Sultanpur	Itawa
Nagaur	Ladnu	Nagaur
Pali	Rani Station	Rohat
Rajsamand	Railmagra	Deogarh
Sawai Madhopur	Gangapur	Khandar
Sikar	Dhond	Lachhmangarh
Sirohi	Sirohi	Abu Road
Tonk	Todaraisingh	Uniara
Udaipur	Mavli	Kotra
RAJASTHAN	**Udaipurwati (Jhun.)**	**Sam (Jaisalmer)**

Source: Annex 11.1.

Classification of PSs By HSI

Table 11.3 presents classification of PSs by HSI. There is a clearcut dominance of Medium level PSs (51.1%) followed by High (33.3%), Low (11%), Very High (2.5%) and Very Low (2.1%) level PSs.

TABLE 11.3: Classification of PSs on the Basis of HSI (2001) : Rajasthan

Group	*Included PSs*			
	No.	*%*	*Distributed in*	
			Districts	*Divisions*
Very High (VH), (>=0.8)	6	2.5	4	3
High (H), (0.7-0.8)	79	33.3	23	6
Medium (M), (0.6-0.7)	121	51.1	29	6
Low (L), (0.5-0.6)	26	11.0	12	5
Very Low (VL), (<0.5)	5	2.1	3	2
Total	**237**	**100**		

Source: Annex 11.2.

If we look at division-wise classification and distribution of PSs by HSI (Table 11.4) following interpretations can be made:

- Jodhpur is the only division having PSs with all the five levels of HSI while, Ajmer had PSs with only two levels. PSs in Jaipur, Bikaner and Udaipur divisions had four levels while Kota had three.
- Jodhpur division led in PSs having Very High as well as Very Low HSI level while Jaipur in High and Medium and Kota led in PSs having Low HSI level.
- Medium level PSs were dominating in all the divisions except Jodhpur.
- The percentage share of VH level PSs in Jodhpur and Bikaner divisions; H level in Jaipur, Ajmer and Jodhpur divisions; M level in Ajmer, Kota and Udaipur divisions; L level in Bikaner, Kota and Jodhpur divisions and VL level in Jodhpur and Udaipur divisions was higher than the state average.

TABLE 11.4: Division-wise Classification and Distribution of PSs on the Basis of HSI Level (2001)

Divisions	*Classification*						*Distribution (% Share)*				
	HSI Level						*HSI Level*				
	Very High	*High*	*Medium*	*Low*	*Very Low*	*Total*	*Very High*	*High*	*Medium*	*Low*	*Very Low*
Jaipur	1	24	31	5	—	61	16.7	30.4	25.6	19.2	—
(%)	(1.6)	(39.3)	(50.8)	(8.2)	—	(100.0)					
Bikaner	1	6	9	5	—	21	16.7	7.6	7.4	19.2	—
(%)	(4.8)	(28.6)	(42.9)	(23.8)	—	(100.0)					
Ajmer	—	15	21	—	—	36	—	19.0	17.4	—	—
(%)	—	(41.7)	(58.3)	—	—	(100.0)					
Kota	—	3	22	7	—	32	—	3.8	18.2	26.9	—
(%)	—	(9.4)	(68.8)	(21.9)	—	(100.0)					
Jodhpur	4	19	10	5	4	42	66.7	24.1	8.3	19.2	80.0
(%)	(9.5)	(45.2)	(23.8)	(11.9)	(9.5)	(100.0)					
Udaipur	—	12	28	4	1	45	—	15.2	23.1	15.4	20.0
(%)	—	(26.7)	(62.2)	(8.9)	(2.2)	(100.0)					
Total	**6**	**79**	**121**	**26**	**5**	**237**					
(%)	**(2.5)**	**(33.3)**	**(51.1)**	**(11.0)**	**(2.1)**	**(100.0)**	**100**	**100**	**100**	**100**	**100**

Note: HSI Level VH : (>=0.8), H: (0.7-0.8), M : (0.6-0.7), L : (0.5-0.6), VL : (<0.5)
Source: Annex 11.2.

Different HSI Regions

Very High HSI Region

There were only 6 VH level PSs which were concentrated in four districts (Pali, Sirohi, Jhunjhunun and Churu) and three divisions (Jodhpur, Jaipur and Bikaner). Jodhpur division had 4 PSs while Jaipur and Bikaner divisions each had one PS. It is unfortunate that, no PS of Ajmer, Kota and Udaipur divisions found mention in this category. The percentage share of VH level PSs to total PSs ranged from a maximum of 9.5 in Jodhpur to a minimum of 1.6 in Jaipur division. Among the districts, Pali had 3 PSs while Churu, Jhunjhunun and Sirohi each had one PS. All the above four districts had higher percentage of VH level PSs than the state average (2.5%). The percentage varied from a maximum of 30 in Pali to a minimum of 12.5 in Jhunjhunun district (Table 11.4 to 11.6).

High HSI Region

High HSI region was spread over 23 districts and all the six divisions. There were 79 High level PSs in all. Jaipur division topped with 30.4 per cent PSs followed by Jodhpur (24.1%), Ajmer (19%), Udaipur (15.2%), Bikaner (7.6%) and Kota (3.8%) divisions. The highest percentage of H level PSs is 45.2 which is in Jodhpur, 41.7 in Ajmer, 39.3 in Jaipur, 28.6 in Bikaner, 26.7 in Udaipur and the lowest 9.4 in Kota division. Jodhpur, Ajmer and Jaipur divisions had higher percentage of M level PSs in comparison to the state average (33.3%). Among the districts, Sikar led with 8 PSs followed by Nagaur (7); Jhunjhunun, Pali (6 each); Ajmer, jaipur, Jalor (5 each); Churu, Dungarpur, Jodhpur (4 each); Alwar, Bhilwara, Rajsamand, Sirohi, Udaipur (3 each); Bharatpur, Kota (2 each) and Banswara, Barmer, Bikaner, Chittaurgarh, Ganganagar, Hanumangarh and Karauli (one each) districts respectively. Except, Alwar, Banswara, Barmer, Bharatpur, Bhilwara, Chittaurgarh, Ganganagar, Karauli and Udaipur all the above districts had greater percentage of H level PSs in comparison to the state average.

Medium HSI Region

Medium HSI region was widely distributed in 29 districts and all the six divisions. There were 121 PSs in this category. As explained earlier, Jaipur division had the maximum concentration of these PSs (25.6% share) in the state. It was followed by Udaipur (23.1%), Kota (18.2%), Ajmer (17.4%), Jodhpur (8.3%) and Bikaner (7.4%) divisions. The highest percentage share of M level PSs to total PSs was 68.8 in Kota division followed by 62.2 in Udaipur, 58.3 in Ajmer, 50.8 in Jaipur, 42.9 in Bikaner and the lowest 23.8 in Jodhpur division. Kota, Udaipur and Ajmer divisions had greater percentage of M level PSs than the state average (51.1). If we see district-wise distribution of these PSs, it is clear that Alwar and Chittaurgarh secured the top position with 11 PSs each followed by Bhilwara (8); Bharatpur, Jaipur and Udaipur (7 each); Tonk (6); Banswara, Dausa, Sawai Madhopur (5 each); Baran, Bundi, Gangngagar, Jodhpur, Karauli, Nagaur, Rajsamand (4 each); Ajmer, Kota (3 each); Barmer, Bikaner, Churu, Jalor, Jhalawar (2 each); Dungarpur, Hanumangarh, Jhunjhunun, Pali and Sirohi (1 each) districts respectively. Alwar, Banswara, Baran, Bharatpur, Bhilwara, Bundi, Chittaurgarh, Dausa, Ganganagar, Karauli, Kota, Rajsamand, Sawai Madhopur, Tonk and Udaipur districts had higher percentage of Medium level PSs than the state average. Moreover four districts, namely, Bundi, Dausa, Sawai Madhopur and Tonk had 100 per cent of their PSs in Medium category while Pali had the minimum (10) percentage of these PSs.

Low HSI Region

This region was spread over 12 districts and 5 divisions. There were 26 PSs having Low HSI. Kota division led with 26.9 per cent share followed by Jaipur, Bikaner, Jodhpur (19.2% each) and Udaipur (15.4%) divisions. Bikaner, Kota and Jodhpur divisions had higher percentage of these PSs in comparison to the state average (11%). Among the districts, Dhaulpur and Jhalawar led with 4 PSs each followed by Baran (3); Banswara, Barmer, Bikaner, Chittaurgarh, Gangannagar, Jaisalmer (2 each), Hanumangarh, Jaipur and Jodhpur (1 each) respectively. All the above districts, except Jaipur had higher percentage of these PSs in comparison to state average. Moreover, Dhaulpur district had 100 per cent of its PSs in this category.

Very Low HSI Region

Sam PS of Jaisalmer, Kotra of Udaipur and Baytoo, Sheo and Barmer PSs of Barmer district were the only PSs of the state in this category.

TABLE 11.5: District-wise Classification of PSs on the Basis of HSI Level, 2001

District	*VH*	*H*	*M*	*L*	*VL*	*Total*
Ajmer	—	5	3	—	—	8
(%)	—	(62.5)	(37.5)	—	—	(100.0)
Alwar	—	3	11	—	—	14
(%)	—	(21.4)	(78.6)	—	—	(100.0)
Banswara	—	1	5	2	—	8
(%)	—	(12.5)	(62.5)	(25.0)	—	(100.0)
Baran	—	—	4	3	—	7
(%)	—	—	(57.1)	(42.9)	—	(100.0)
Barmer	—	1	2	2	3	8
(%)	—	(12.5)	(25.0)	(25.0)	(37.5)	(100.0)
Bharatpur	—	2	7	—	—	9
(%)	—	(22.2)	(77.8)	—	—	(100.0)
Bhilwara	—	3	8	—	—	11
(%)	—	(27.3)	(72.7)	—	—	(100.0)
Bikaner	—	—	2	2	—	4
(%)	—	—	(50.0)	(50.0)	—	(100.0)
Bundi	—	—	4	—	—	4
(%)	—	—	(100.0)	—	—	(100.0)
Chittaurgarh	—	1	11	2	—	14
(%)	—	(7.1)	(78.6)	(14.3)	—	(100.0)
Churu	1	4	2	—	—	7
(%)	(14.3)	(57.1)	(28.6)	—	—	(100.0)
Dausa	—	—	5	—	—	5
(%)	—	—	(100.0)	—	—	(100.0)
Dhaulpur	—	—	—	4	—	4
(%)	—	—	—	(100.0)	—	(100.0)
Dungarpur	—	4	1	—	—	5
(%)	—	(80.0)	(20.0)	—	—	(100.0)
Ganganagar	—	1	4	2	—	7
(%)	—	(14.3)	(57.1)	(28.6)	—	(100.0)
Hanumangarh	—	1	1	1	—	3
(%)	—	(33.3)	(33.3)	(33.3)	—	(100.0)
Jaipur	—	5	7	1	—	13
(%)	—	(38.5)	(53.8)	(7.7)	—	(100.0)
Jaisalmer	—	—	—	2	1	3
(%)	—	—	—	(66.7)	(33.3)	(100.0)
Jalor	—	5	2	—	—	7
(%)	—	(71.4)	(28.6)	—	—	(100.0)
Jhalawar	—	—	2	4	—	6
(%)	—	—	(33.3)	(66.7)	—	(100.0)
Jhunjhunun	1	6	1	—	—	8
(%)	(12.5)	(75.0)	(12.5)	—	—	(100.0)
Jodhpur	—	4	4	1	—	9
(%)	—	(44.4)	(44.4)	(11.1)	—	(100.0)
Karauli	—	1	4	—	—	5
(%)	—	(20.0)	(80.0)	—	—	(100.0)
Kota	—	2	3	—	—	5
(%)	—	(40.0)	(60.0)	—	—	(100.0)
Nagaur	—	7	4	—	—	11
(%)	—	(63.6)	(36.4)	—	—	(100.0)
Pali	3	6	1	—	—	10
(%)	(30.0)	(60.0)	(10.0)	—	—	(100.0)
Rajsamand	—	3	4	—	—	7
(%)	—	(42.9)	(57.1)	—	—	(100.0)
Sawai Madhopur	—	—	5	—	—	5
(%)	—	—	(100.0)	—	—	(100.0)
Sikar	—	8	—	—	—	8
(%)	—	(100.0)	—	—	—	(100.0)
Sirohi	1	3	1	—	—	5
(%)	(20.0)	(60.0)	(20.0)	—	—	(100.0)
Tonk	—	—	6	—	—	6
(%)	—	—	(100.0)	—	—	(100.0)
Udaipur	—	3	7	—	1	11
(%)	—	(27.3)	(63.6)	—	(9.1)	(100.0)
Rajasthan	**6**	**79**	**121**	**26**	**5**	**237**
(%)	**(2.5)**	**(33.3)**	**(51.1)**	**(11.0)**	**(2.1)**	**(100.0)**

Note: HSI Level VH : (>=0.8), H: (0.7-0.8), M : (0.6-0.7), L : (0.5-0.6), VL : (<0.5)
Source: Annex 11.2.

TABLE 11.6: Distribution of PSs Having High to Very Low HSI Level, 2001

S.No.	*District*	*Name of PS*	*Descending Order*
		[I] High Level (6)	
1	Pali	Rani Station, Sumerpur and Bali	(3)
2	Churu	Ratangarh	(1)
3	Jhunjhunun	Udaipurwati	(1)
4	Sirohi	Sirohi	(1)
		[II] High (79)	
1	Sikar	Dhond, Piprali, Sri Madhopur, Khandela, Danta Ramgarh, Fatehpur, Neem Ka Thana and Lachhmangarh	(8)
2	Nagaur	Ladnu, Didwana, Parbatsar, Merta, Riyan, Degana and Makrana	(7)
3	Jhunjhunun	Khetri, Chirawa, Nawalgarh, Buhana, Jhunjhunun and Alsisar	(6)
4	Pali	Desuri, Sojat, Kharchi, Jaitaran, Raipur and Pali	(6)
5	Ajmer	Pisangan, Kekri, Jawaja, Kishangarh and Srinagar	(5)
6	Jaipur	Govindgarh, Shahpura, Sambhar, Viratnagar and Kotputli	(5)
7	Jalor	Ahore, Jalor, Sayala, Jaswantpura and Rasniwara	(5)
8	Churu	Churu, Dungargarh, Sujangarh and Taranagar	(4)
9	Dungarpur	Sagwara, Aspur, Bichhiwara and Dungarpur	(4)
12	Jodhpur	Bilara, Bhopalgarh, Luni and Osian	(4)
10	Alwar	Behror, Nimrana and Mandawar	(3)
11	Bhilwara	Banera, Sahara and Hurda	(3)
13	Rajsamand	Railmagra, Khamnor and Bhim	(3)
14	Sirohi	Sheoganj, Pindwara and Reodar	(3)
15	Udaipur	Mavli, Sarada and Girwa	(3)
16	Bharatpur	Kumher and Nadbai	(2)
17	Kota	Sultanpur and Ladpura	(2)
18	Banswara	Garhi	(1)
19	Barmer	Siwana	(1)
20	Chittaurgarh	Rashmi	(1)
21	Ganganagar	Ganganagar	(1)
22	Hanumangarh	Bhadra	(1)
23	Karauli	Hindaun	(1)
		[III] Medium (121)	
1	Alwar	Reni, Bansure, Umren, Thanagazi, Lachhmangarh, Kathumar, Kotkasim, Ramgarh, Rajgarh, Kishangarh Bas and Tijara	(11)
2	Chittaurgarh	Dungla, Nibahera, Bhopalsagar, Gangrar, Chhitaurgarh, Bari Sadri, Bhadesar, Begun, Pratapgarh, Chhoti Sadri and Kapasan	(11)
3	Bhilwara	Suwana, Raipur, Mandal, Asind, Shahapura, Jahazpur, Mandalgarh and Kotri	(8)
4	Bharatpur	Deeg, Sewar, Rupbas, Weir, Nagar Pahari, Kaman and Bayana	(7)
5	Jaipur	Jamwa Ramgarh, Amber, Bassi, Jhotwara, Dudu, Sanganer and Phagi	(7)
6	Udaipur	Bargaon, Bhinder, Salumber, Gogunda, Kherwara, Jhadol and Dhariawad	(7)
7	Tonk	Todaraisingh, Malpura, Tonk, Niwai, Deoli and Uniara	(6)
8	Banswara	Talwara, Ghatol, Bagidora, Anandpuri and Sajjangarh	(5)
9	Dausa	Bandikui, Dausa, Sikari, Mahwa and Lalsot	(5)
10	Sawai Madhopur	Gangapur, Sawai Madhopur, Bonli, Bamanwas and Khandar	(5)
11	Baran	Baran, Atru, Anta and Kishanganj	(4)
12	Bundi	Hindoli, Talera, Keshoraipatan and Nainwa	(4)
13	Ganganagar	Padampur, Karanpur, Sadulshahar and Raisinghnagar	(4)
14	Jodhpur	Mandor, Phalodi, Balesar and Shergarh	(4)
15	Karauli	Todabhim, Nadoti, Karauli and Sapotra	(4)
16	Nagaur	Mundwa, Jayal, Kuchaman and Nagaur	(4)
17	Rajsamand	Rajsamand, Kumbhalgarh, Amet and Deogarh	(4)
18	Ajmer	Masooda, Bhinay and Arian	(3)
19	Kota	Sultanpur, Ladpura and Chechat	(3)
20	Barmer	Balotra and Dhorimanna	(2)
21	Bikaner	Nokha and Lunkaransar	(2)
22	Churu	Rajgarh and Sardarshahar	(2)
23	Jalor	Bhinmal and Sanchore	(2)
24	Jhalawar	Khanpur and Pirawa	(2)
25	Dungarpur	Simalwara	(1)
26	Hanumangarh	Hanumangarh	(1)
27	Jhunjhunun	Surajgarh	(1)
28	Pali	Rohat	(1)
29	Sirohi	Abu Road	(1)

(Contd.)

Table 11.6 (contd.)

S.No.	*District*	*Name of PS*	*Descending Order*
		[IV] Low (26)	
1	Dhaulpur	Dhaulpur, Bari, Rajakhera and Baseri	(4)
2	Jhalawar	Jhalrapatan, Dag, Bakani and Manoharthana	(4)
3	Baran	Shahbad, Chhipabarod and Chhabra	(3)
4	Banswara	Peepalkhoont and Kushalgarh	(2)
5	Barmer	Chohtan and Sindhari	(2)
6	Bikaner	Bikaner and Kolayat	(2)
7	Chittaurgarh	Arnod and Bhainsrorgarh	(2)
8	Ganganagar	Anupgarh and Suratgarh	(2)
9	Jaisalmer	Jaisalmer and Sankra	(2)
10	Hanumangarh	Nohar	(1)
11	Jaipur	Chaksu	(1)
12	Jodhpur	Bap	(1)
		[IV] Very Low (5)	
1	Barmer	Baytoo, Sheo and Barmer	(3)
2	Jaisalmer	Sam	(1)
3	Udaipur	Kotra	(1)

Source: Annex-11.2.

12

MAIN FINDINGS AND ACTION PLAN

Growth Trends

Inspite of being a developing state with low socio-demographic indicators, Rajasthan registered multifold increase in Total Number of Medical Institutions, Doctors, Beds, Patients Treated, Health Infrastructural Facilities and Health Programmes/Schemes during the Five Year Plans Period (1951-2005). The state government has been continously endavoring to expand curative, preventive, promotive and rehabilatative services with special emphasis on rural population. Both qualitive and quantitative improvement is observed in Health Services. Special schemes have been also launched for the Arid/Semi-arid, Tribal, Backward and Remote Areas for making health services available to people at their door-steps. As a result, 'Life Expectancy at Birth' increased significantly while great decline is registered in 'Fertility, Mortality and Morbidity Indicators'.

The Health Status Index (HSI) of rural Rajasthan in the year 1991 was 0.559. A great deal of regional disparity is observed in HSI across the state. Whereas, 50 per cent PSs of Jodhpur division, 44 per cent of Ajmer and 39 per cent PSs of Jaipur division had Medium to High level of HSI (>0.6), 100 per cent PSs of Kota division, 86 per cent of Bikaner and more than 70 per cent PSs of Udaipur division had Low to Very Low level of HSI. The HSI level in the state increases mainly from the South-East and South to the South-West, Central and North-East direction. Sumerpur PS of Pali district had the maximum HSI (0.7291) while Sam PS of Jaisalmer district had the minimum (0.346).

In the year 2001, HSI rose to 0.6684. There were 132 PSs having HSI above the state average. Jodhpur division led not only in PSs having Very High HSI (66.7%) but also in PSs having Very Low HSI (80%). Jaipur division dominated in PSs having High (30.4%) as well as Medium (25.6%) HSI while Kota division led in PSs having Low HSI.

It is interesting to note that the PS having High and Very High HSI are mainly concentrated in a belt along with Aravalli hills area from South-West (Sirohi dist.) to North-East (Jhun/Alwar dists.) direction. The HSI level decreases towards both sides mainly towards Western arid and semi-arid areas. Udaipurwati PS of Jhunjhunun district had the highest 0.8307 HSI while Sam PS of Jaisalmer district had the lowest (0.4749).

ISOHSI maps (Fig 12 A & B) depict increased pattern of health status in Rajasthan during 1991-01 period. ISOHSI denotes the line on a map, which joins the places of equal health status index. In the year 1991, the state was covered by four ISOHSI lines viz. 0.7 (highest), 06, 0.5 and 0.4 (lowest). More than half portion of the state lied between 0.5 and 0.6 ISOHSI lines. The included PSs in this group were spread over whole Rajasthan except Jodhpur division where only 3 PSs namely Osian, Mandor and Pholodi entered in this group. The main districts covered between 0.5 and 0.6 ISOHSI lines are: Alwar, Bharatpur and Dausa in the NE; Ganganagar, Hanumangarh, Churu and Bikaner in the North; Nagaur in the Central; Kota, Bundi, Jhalawar,

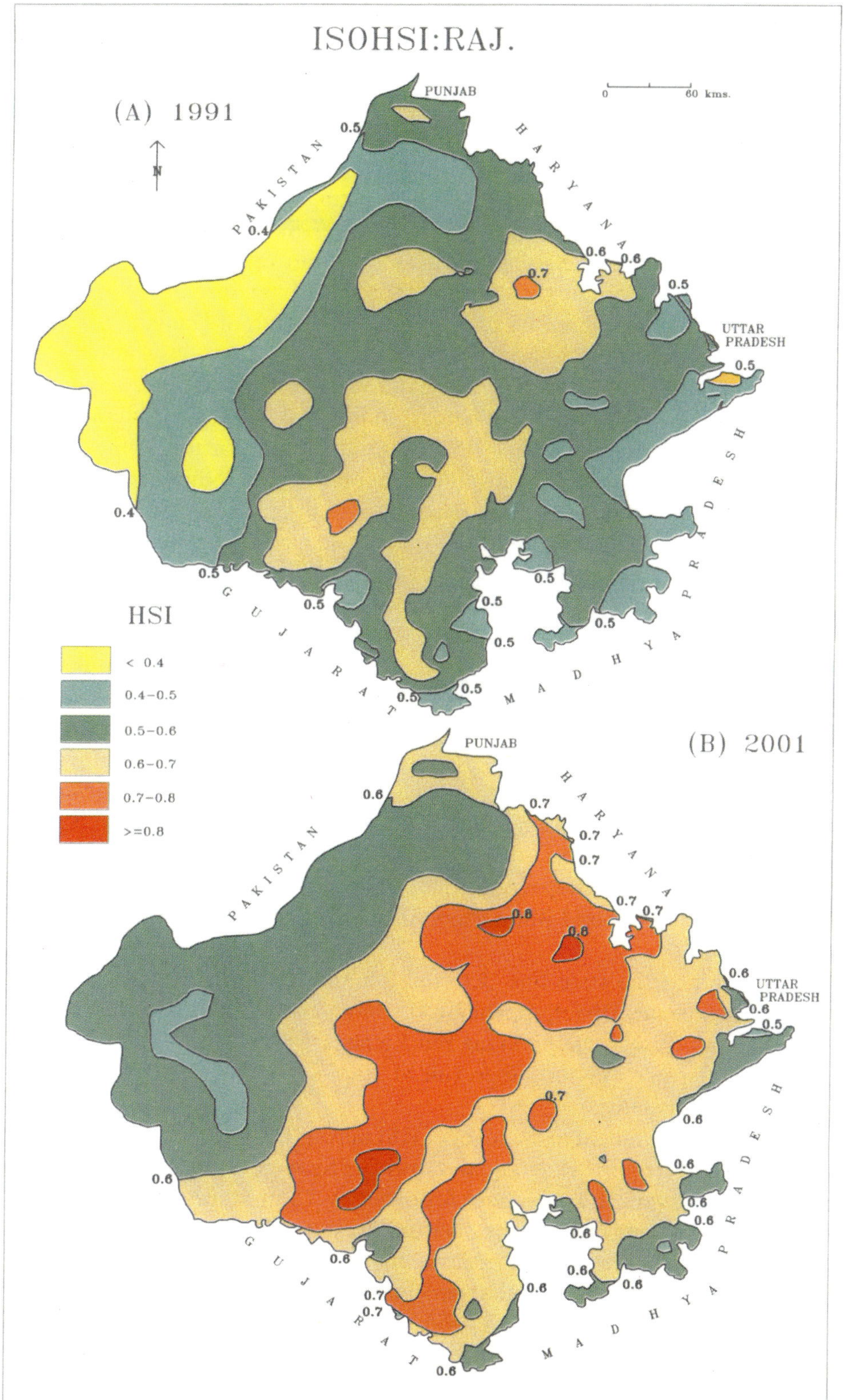

Note: 'ISOHSI': Line Joins Places Having Equal HSI.

FIG. 12.1

Baran, Sawai Madhopur, Karauli and Tonk in the South-East and Banswara, Udaipur, Rajsamand and Chittaurgarh in the Southern Rajasthan.

Nearly 1/3 portion of the state covering Sikar, Jhunjhunun, Jaipur, Ajmer, Bhilwara, Pali, Jodhpur, Jalor, Sirohi, Alwar (Nimrana, Behror and Mandawar PSs), Dungarpur, (Sagwara, Aspur and Bichhiwara PSs) and Rajsamand (Railmagra, Khamnor and Bhim PSs) districts lied between 0.6 and 0.7 ISOHSI lines. Similarly, a small portion of Pali (Sumerpur and Bali PSs) and Jhunjhunun (Nawalgarh PS) had above 0.7 HSI. Remaining area of the state mainly of Jaisalmer, Barmer, Bikaner, Dhaulpur, Jhalawar (Bakani, Dag and Manoharthana PSs), Bharatpur (Bayana, Kaman and Nagar Pahari PSs), Baran (Shahbad, Chhabra and Chhipabarod PSs), Banswara (Peepalkhoont, Sajjangarh and Kushalgarh PSs), Karauli (Sapotra and Karauli PSs), Ganganagar (Suratgarh and Anupgarh PSs) and Chittaurgarh (Pratapgarh and Bhainsrorgarh PSs) districts covered by 0.5 ISOHSI line and a small patch including Sam PS of Jaisalmer, Anupgarh of Ganganagar and Baytoo of Barmer district covered by 0.4 ISOHSI line were in the worst position

In the year 2001, with the increase in over all health status in the state, the value of ISOHSI lines also rose viz. 0.8 (highest), 0.7, 0.6 and 0.5 (lowest). Whereas, in the year 1991, more than half portion of the state lied between 0.5 an 0.6 ISOHSI lines, in the year 2001, more than half portion of the state jumped in 0.6 and 0.7 ISOHSI lines. The districts covered are; Alwar (all PSs, except Behror, Nimrana and Mundawar); Bharatpur (except Kumher and Nadbai PSs), Jaipur (Jamwa Ramgarh, Amber, Jhotwara, Sanganer, Bassi and Phagi PSs), Dausa, Ajmer (Masooda, Bhinay and Arian PSs), Ganganagar (Padampur, Karanpur, Sadulshahar and Raisinghnagar), Bikaner (Nokha and Lunkaransar), Churu (Rajgarh and Sardarshahar), Hanumangarh (Hanumangarh), Chittaurgarh (except Rashmi, Arnod and Bhainsorgarh PSs), Bhilwara (except Banera, Sahara and Hurda PSs), Udaipur (except Girwa, Mavli, Kotra and Sarada PSs), Banswara (except Garhi, Peepalkhoont and Kushalgarh), Rajsamand (Rajsamand, Kumbhalgarh, Amet and Deogarh PSs), Tonk, S. Madhopur, Bundi, Baran (Baran, Atru, Anta and Kishangarh PSs), Karauli (except Hindaun PS), Kota (Sultanpur, Ladpura and Chechat PSs), Jhalawar (Khanpur and Pirawa PSs), Barmer (Balotra and Dhorimanna PSs) and Jalor (Bhinmal and Sanchore PSs) districts.

Similarly, more than 1/3 portion of the state jumped in 0.7 and 0.8 ISOHSI lines covering Jhunjhunun, Jaipur (Govindgarh, Shahpura, Sambhar, Viratnagar and Kotputli PSs), Alwar (Behror, Nimrana and Mandawar PSs), Bharatpur (Kumher and Nadbai PSs), Churu (Churu, Dungargarh, Sujangarh and Taranagar PSs), Dungarpur, Pali, Jalor, Jodhpur (Bilara, Bhopalgarh, Luni and Osian PSs), Bhilwara (Hurda, Bunera and Sahara PSs), Rajsanand (Railmagra, Khamnor and Bhim PSs), Sirohi (Reodar, Pindwara, Sheoganj PSs) and Udaipur (Mavli and Girwa PSs) districts.

Like-wise, one-tenth part of the state line between 0.5 and 0.6 ISOHSI lines encompassing Jaisalmer, Barmer, Bikaner, South Ganganagar, Dhaulpur, Jhalawar, Baran and Chittaurgarh etc. districts. A small patch having Rani Station, Sumerpur, Sirohi, Jhunjhunun and Ratangarh PSs were covered by 0.8 ISOHSI were in the best health status while Barmer, Baytoo, Sheo (all of Barmer) and Kotra (Udaipur) PSs covered by 0.5 ISOHSI were in the worst health status.

Table 12.1 reveals upward movement in the level of HSI during 1991–2001. In the year 1991, unfortunately, there was no PS entered in Very High HSI group and only 3 PSs were found mention in High group. On the other hands, maximum 122 PSs were in Low group followed by 73 in Medium and 39 in Very Low group. In the year 2001, with the improvement in HSI level across the state, 6 PSs entered in Very High group, 79 in High and 121 PSs entered in Medium group. Therefore, the number of PSs in the Low and Very Low groups decreased sharply. It means, during the period, the percentage of PSs above 0.7 HSI level rose up from merely 1.3 to 35.8 and between 0.6 and 0.7 HSI level rose from 30.8 to 51.1. As a result, the percentage of PSs below 0.6 level sharply fell down from 68 to 13.

On the basis of HSI growth pattern, PSs of the state can be classified into four groups viz.: (A) PSs (46%) which registered improvement in both HSI value and rank, (B) PSs (50.6%) which registered improvement in HSI value but their ranks deteriorated, (C) PSs (3%) which registered improvement in HSI value but their ranks remained constant and (D) PSs (0.4%) which registered deterioration in both HSI value and rank (Table 12.2).

TABLE 12.1: Upward Movement in HSI Level (1991-01)

HSI Level	*Panchayat Samities*			
	1991		*2001*	
	No.	*%*	*No.*	*%*
Very High (VH), (>=0.8)	—	—	6	2.5
High (H), (0.7-0.8)	3	1.3	79	33.3
Medium (M), (0.6-0.7)	73	30.8	121	51.1
Low (L), (0.5-0.6)	122	51.5	26	11.0
Very Low (VL), (<0.5)	39	16.5	5	2.1
Total	**237**	**100**	**237**	**100**

Source: Tables 10.3 & 11.3.

TABLE 12.2: Classification of Panchayat Samities on the Basis of HSI Growth Trend

Growth Trend	*Panchayat Samities*	
	No.	*%*
(A) Improvement in Both HSI Value and Rank	109	46.0
(B) increase in HSI Value but Rank Deteriorated	120	50.6
(C) increase in HSI Value but Rank Remained Constant	7	3.0
(D) Deterioration in Both HSI Value and Rank	1	0.4
	237	**100.0**

Source: Compiled from Annex 12.1.

Bari PS of Dhaulpur district was at the top rank with 47 per cent increase in HSI (1991-01) followed by Nagar Pahari, Dhorimanna, Anupgarh, Karauli, Deeg, Nadbai, Sam, Chohtan, Rajgarh and Ratangarh PSs. On the other side, Shergarh PS of Jodhpur district was at the bottom (0%) preceded by Bikaner, Balesar, Kapasan, Shahpura, Bhopalsagar, Hurda, Nawalgarh, Kolayat, Pisangan and Bhinay PSs.

With respect to increased value of HSI, Ratangarh PS of Churu district secured the first rank (0.2164) followed by Nadbai, Churu, Piprali, Deeg, Nagar Phari, Bari, Didwana, Rajgarh and Sultanpur PSs. Shergarh PS, on the other hand, was at the last rank (-0.0008) preceded by Bikaner, Balesar, Kapasan, Shahpura, Kolayat, Hurda, Bhopalsagar, Kotri and Bhinay PSs.

If we look at the change in HSI rank, Nadbai PS of Bharatpur district registered maximum improvement in its rank (+113) followed by Deeg, Didwana, Rajgarh, Churu, Sultanpur, Kumbhalgarh, Bhadra, Raipur and Piprali PSs. On the other side, Shergarh PS registered maximum deterioration (-132) in its rank preceded by Bikaner, Balesar, Kapasan, Shahpura, Jahazpur, Bhopalsagar, Kotri, Kishangar Bas and Bagidora PSs.

Table 12.3 shows classification of districts in to 3 groups by per cent increase in HSI. It is unfortunate that, the state registered only 20 per cent growth in HSI and no district even achieved 30 per cent growth. Barmer, Bharatpur and Karauli districts registered highest 29 per cent increase while Bikaner registered the

TABLE 12.3: Classification of Districts on the Basis of % Increase in HSI (1991-01)

Group	*% Increase*	*District*		
		No.	*%*	*Name*
Medium (M)	20-30	20	62.5	Barmer, Bharatpur, Karauli, Alwar, Baran, Bundi, Churu, Dausa, Dhaulpur, Dungarpur, Ganganagar, Jaisalmer, Jalor, Jodhpur, Kota, Nagaur, Rajsamand, S. Madhopur, Sikar and Tonk
Low (L)	10-20	11	34.4	Ajmer, Banswara, Bhilwara, Chittaurgarh, Hanumangarh, Jaipur, Jhunjhunun, Jhalawar, Pali, Sirohi and Udaipur
Very Low (VL)	0-10	1	3.1	Bikaner
State Average	20	32	100.0	

Source: Compiled from Annex 12.1.

- GROWTH TRENDS ⇨
  - Declining Fertility, Mortality & Morbidity Indicators, 1985-03)
    - CBR 39.7 to 30.6
    - CDR 13.2 to 7.7
    - IMR 108 to 78
  - Increasing 'Life Expectancy at Birth', 32 to 62.1, 1951-02
  - Substantial Expansion of Health Infrastructural Facilities*
    - 140 times increase in No. of PHCs [a]
    - 15 times increase in No. of SHCs [b]
    - 4.2 times increase in No. of MCWCs [c]
    - 4.13 times increase in FWCs [a]
    - 1.34 times increase in No. of Disp. [a]
    - 30 times increase in Total No. of Medical Institutions [c]
    - 7.44 times increase in No. of Doctors [a]
    - 6.8 times increase in No. of Beds [c]
    - 48% Decreases in Pop. Served Per Bed [c]
    - 89% Decreases in Pop. Served Per Inst. [c]
    - 60% Decreases in Pop. Served Per Doctor [a]
  - Qualitative and Quantitative Improvement in Health Delivery Services
  - Increase in National/State Level Health Programmes/Schemes
  - Launching of Special Schemes for Arid, Semi-Arid, Tribal & Back Ward Areas
  - Laudable Achievements in FWP**
    - 390 times increase in OP Users [d]
    - 28.1 times increase in Nirodh Users [e]
    - 15.7 times increase in CT Insertion [e]
    - 8.9 times increase in Sterilisation [e]
  - 2.2 times increase in CPR (19.8 to 43) [f]
  - Intensity of Diseases/Deaths Decreased
  - 7825 times increase in No. of Patients Treated (4 thousand to 31.3 mln 1955-03)
  - 1022 Times Increase in Health Budget [c]
  - 317 Times Increase in Per Capita Health Budget [c]

Note a—During 1955-04, b—During 1965-04, c—During 1951-04, d—During 1981-03, e—During 1971-03, f—During 1985-04.

CHART 12.1

lowest 6 per cent increase. Maximum 20 districts entered in Medium group, 11 in Low group while Bikaner is the only district entered in Very low group. Classification of districts on the basis of HSI growth trends is presented in Table 12.4. Out of 32 districts, 100 per cent PSs of Dausa and Dungarpur districts and more than 50 per cent PSs of Baran, Barmer, Bharatpur, Bundi, Churu, Jaisalmer, Jalor, Kota, Karauli, Nagaur, Pali, Sawai Madhopur and Sikar districts registered improvement in both HSI value and their ranks. On the other hand, 100 per cent PSs of Bhilwara and Jhalawar districts and more than 50 per cent PSs of remaining 15 districts had although registered increase in HSI value but their ranks deteriorated.

TABLE 12.4: Classification of Districts on the Basis of HSI Growth Trends (1991-01)

Growth Trends	*Districts*		
	No.	*%*	*Name*
(A) All Panchayat Samities (100 %) registered improvement in both HSI value and rank	2	6.3	Dausa and Dungarpur
(B) All Panchayat Samities registered improvement in HSI value but rank deteriorated in :			
(a) 100 % Panchayat Samities	2	6.3	Bhilwara and Jhalawar
(b) >=50 % Panchayat Samities	15	46.9	Ajmer, Alwar, Banswara, Bikaner, Chittaurgarh, Dhaulpur, Ganganagar, Hanumangarh, Jaipur, Jhunjhunun, Jodhpur, Rajsamand, Sirohi, Tonk and Udaipur
(c) < 50 % Panchayat Samities	13	40.6	Baran, Barmer, Bharatpur, Bundi, Churu, Jaisalmer, Jalor, Kota, Karauli, Nagaur, Pali, S.Madhopur and Sikar
	32	**100.0**	

Source: Compiled from Annex 12.1.

Panchayat Samiti-wise Growth Trends 1991-01

- 20 per cent Increase in HSI (0.5588 to 0.6684) Still, a Long Way to Go
- Increasing HSI From South-East, South & West to North-East & Central Direction
- Udaipurwati PS (Jhun, 0.8307) Snatched the First Rank From Sumerpur (Pali, 0.729)
- Sam PS Maintained its Bottom Rank
- 18 PSs Maintained their First / Last Ranks in their Respective Districts
- Bari (Dhaul, 47%) and Ratangarh (Churu, 0.2164) PSs Registered highest growth.
- Shergarh PS of Jodhpur is the Only PS Registered Decrease in HSI
- 46% PSs Improved their Ranks
- Nadbai (Bharat, + 113) PS Registered Maximum Improvement in HSI Rank While Shergarh (Jodhpur, -132) Registered Maximum Deterioration
- 7 PSs Maintained their Ranks

CHART 12.2

TABLE 12.5: Classification of PSs by Different Health Indicators (2001)

Group	*Critaria/Panchayat Samities*							
	Pop. Served Per Medical Institution		*Area Served Per Medical Institution*		*Pop. Served Per Bed*		*Pop. Served Per Doctor*	
	No.	*%*	*No.*	*%*	*No.*	*%*	*No.*	*%*
Very High (Worst)	19	8.0	26	11.0	21	8.9	24	10.1
High (Worse)	39	16.5	17	7.2	32	13.5	27	11.4
Medium (Normal)	70	29.5	49	20.7	109	46.0	63	26.6
Low (Better)	89	37.6	109	46.0	72	30.4	89	37.6
Very Low (Best)	20	8.4	36	15.2	3	1.3	34	14.3
Total	**237**	**100**	**237**	**100**	**237**	**100**	**237**	**100**

Source: Annex 12.6, 12.8 & 12.9.

TABLE 12.6: Classification of PSs by Sex-Ratio and Female Literacy Rate (2001)

Group	*Critaria/Panchayat Samities*					
	Sex-Ratio (0-6) Pop.		*Sex-Ratio (Total Pop.)*		*Female Literacy*	
	No.	*%*	*No.*	*%*	*No.*	*%*
Very High (Best)	1	0.4	27	11.4	9	3.8
High (Better)	31	13.1	69	29.1	52	21.9
Medium (Normal)	138	58.2	92	38.8	104	43.9
Low (Worse)	56	23.6	33	13.9	70	29.5
Very Low (Worst)	11	4.6	16	6.8	2	0.8
Total	**237**	**100**	**237**	**100**	**237**	**100**

Source: Annex 12.11 to 12.13.

TABLE 12.7: Population Served Per Medical Institution: Distribution of the Best and the Worst PSs (1991 & 2001)

S.No.	*District*	*1991*		*2001*	
		No.	*Name of PSs*	*No.*	*Name of PSs*
			[A] Best PSs		
1	Ajmer	1	Kishangar Bas	—	—
2	Banswara	1	Garhi	—	—
3	Baran	1	Atru	—	—
4	Bhilwara	5	Banera*, Hurda, Mandalgarh*, Sahara and Raipur*	3	Banera, Mandalgarh and Raipur
5	Chittaurgarh	3	Begun*, Bhopalgarh and Rashmi*	2	Begun and Rashmi
6	Churu	—	—	2	Churu and Ratangarh
7	Dungarpur	2	Aspur*	3	Aspur, Dungapur and Sagwara
8	Pali	2	Desuri* and Rani Station*	3	Desuri, Rani Station and Sojat
9	Rajsamand	1	Khamnor	2	Kumbhalgarh and Railmagra
10	Sirohi	—	—	2	Sheoganj and Sirohi
11	Udaipur	1	Jhadol*	3	Jhadol, Salumber and Sarada
	Total	**16**		**20**	
			[B] Worst PSs		
1	Alwar	3	Kishangarh Bas, Lachhmangarh* and Tijara*	4	Lachhmangarh, Tijara, Kotkasim and Ramgarh
2	Baran	—	—	1	Chhabra
3	Barmer	3	Baytoo, Chohtan and Sheo	—	—
4	Bharatpur	4	Deeg, Kaman* Nadbai and Sewar	3	Kaman, Bayana and Nagar Pahari
5	Bikaner	—	—	2	Bikaner and Nokha
6	Chittaurgarh	1	Chittaurgah and Nimbhera	2	Bari Sadri and Kapasan
7	Churu	1	Sardarshahar	—	—
8	Dausa	3	Bandikui*, Dausa and Lalsot*	3	Bandikui, Lalsot and Sikrai
9	Dhaulpur	2	Baseri and Rajkhera*	1	Rajakhera
10	Ganganagar	2	Anupgarh and Karanpur	—	—
11	Hanumangarh	2	Hanumangarh and Nohar	—	—
12	Jaipur	1	Amber	—	—
13	Jalor	3	Bhinmal, Raniwara and Sanchore	—	—
14	Jhalawar	—	—	1	Manoharthana
15	Jhunjhunun	2	Buhana and Surajgarh	—	—
16	Jodhpur	3	Bap*, Mandor* and Osian	2	Bap and Mandor
17	Karauli	1	Hindaun	—	—
18	Sikar	1	Khandela	—	—
	Total	**33**		**19**	

Note: Best PS: Popluation Served Per Medical Institution is <2000.
Worst PS : Popluation Served Per Medical Institution is >=5000.
* Best/Worst PS in Both The Years.
Source: Annex-8.4 and 9.4.

TABLE 12.8: Area Served Per Medical Institution: Distribution of the Best and the Worst PSs, 2001

S.No.	*District*	*No.*	*PSs Name*
			[I] Best (36)
1	Banswara	(7)	Sajjangarh, Anandpuri, Bichhiwara, Bagidora, Talwara, Ghatol and Kushalgarh
2	Jhunjhunun	(5)	Buhana, Nawalgarh, Chirawa, Udaipurwati and Jhunjhunun
4	Udaipur	(5)	Garhi, Salumber, Sarada, Mavli and Ghatol
3	Sikar	(4)	Danta Ramgarh, Piprali, Dhond and Khandela
5	Alwar	(3)	Behrore, Reni and Mandawar
6	Dungarpur	(3)	Aspur, Sagwara and Dungarpur
7	Rajsamand	(3)	Khamnor, Railmagara and Kumbhalgarh
8	Bharatpur	(2)	Rupbas and Kumher
9	Jaipur	(2)	Shahpura and Bassi
10	Dhaulpur	(1)	Dhaulpur
11	Karauli	(1)	Todabhim
			[II] Worst (26)
1	Barmer	(6)	Sheo, Chohtan, Barmer, Balotra, Baytoo and Dhorimanna
2	Bikaner	(4)	Kolyat, Bikaner, Lunkaransar and Nokha
3	Jodhpur	(4)	Bap, Phalodi, Shergarh and Mandor
4	Jaisalmer	(3)	Sam, Jaisalmer and Sankra
5	Baran	(2)	Chhabra and Kishangarh
6	Churu	(2)	Sardarshahar and Dungargarh
7	Ganganagar	(2)	Suratgarh and Anupgarh
8	Chittaurgarh	(1)	Bhainsrorgarh
9	Hanumangarh	(1)	Nohar
10	Jhalawar	(1)	Manoharthana

Note: 1. Best PSs: Area served per medical institute is <10 sq. km.
2. Worst PSs: Area served per medical institute is >=40 sq. km.

Source: Annex-12.8.

TABLE 12.9: Populaton Served Per Bed: Distribution of the Best and the Worst Ten PSs, 2001

S.No.	*District*	*No.*	*PSs Name*
			[I] Best PSs
1	Bhilwara	(3)	Sahara, Hurda and Jahajpur
2	Kota	(1)	Ladpura
3	Rajsamand	(1)	Rajsamand
4	Alwar	(1)	Behror
5	Jodhpur	(1)	Bilara
6	Chittaurgarh	(1)	Bagun
7	Sirohi	(1)	Abu Road
8	Baran	(1)	Shahabad
			[II] Worst PSs
1	Ajmer	(2)	Srinagar and Kishangarh
2	Barmer	(2)	Barmer and Balotra
3	Bharatpur	(1)	Sewar
4	Jaisalmer	(1)	Jaisalmer
5	Jhalawar	(1)	Jhalarapatan
6	Jaipur	(1)	Jhotwara
7	Chittaurgarh	(1)	Chittaurgarh
8	Jodhpur	(1)	Phalodi

Source: Annex-12.9.

TABLE 12.10: Population Served Per Doctor: Distribution of the Best and the Worst Ten PSs, 2001

S.No.	*District*	*No.*	*PSs Name*
			[I] Best PSs
1	Rajsamand	(3)	Deogarh, Rajsamand and Khamnor
2	Alwar	(1)	Behror
3	Baran	(1)	Anta
4	Jhalawar	(1)	Dag
5	Jodhpur	(1)	Bilara
6	Kota	(1)	Ladpura
7	Pali	(1)	Desuri
8	Sikar	(1)	Fatehpur
			[II] Worst PSs
1	Jaipur	(3)	Chaksu, Shahpura and Jhotwara
2	Bharatpur	(2)	Sewar and Kaman
3	Ajmer	(1)	Srinagar
4	Jaisalmer	(1)	Sankra
5	Jodhpur	(1)	Phalodi
6	Sawai Madhopur	(1)	Sawai Madhopur
7	Udaipur	(1)	Kotra

Source: Annex-12.10.

BOX 12.1: National Rural Health Mission (NRHM)

Launched by Hon'ble PM	:	On 12th April, 2005
States covered	:	18, which had low human development indices such as Rajasthan, Madhya Pradesh and the north-eastern states.
Launched in Rajasthan	:	On 6th June, 2005
Period	:	2005-12
Outlay for the year 2005-06	:	Rs. 2.64 billion (Rs. 67.13 billion for India)

Objectives

- To take quality health care to the last man in the last village.
- To attempt a major shift in the governance of public health by giving leadership to the Panchayati Raj institutions in all matters related to health at the district and sub-district levels.
- To empower district-level institutions.
- To lower disease and death rates by 2012 by strengthening healthcare delivery in rural areas and integrating nutrition, sanitation, hygiene and safe drinking water into one plan.
- Setting up of Indian Public Health Standards that will specify personnel, management and equipment norms, including those for community control based on which these hospitals will need to be built up.
- To increase the outreach of the health system to village and even household levels through the provision of a voluntary trained female, called ASHA (Accredited Social Health Activist).
- To promote of alternative systems of medicine.

Highlights

- The mission will focus on both the preventive and treatment aspects of health care.
- The public health infrastructure will be strengthened under the Mission through the construction of sub-centre buildings and the upgrading of public health centers and community health centers.
- An untied fund of Rs. 10000 will be provided to every sub-centre to cater to the unmet needs reflected in the village health plan.
- ASHA will be responsible for promoting various healthcare initiatives such as universal immunization, safe delivery, newborn care and promotion of household toilets. She will be a daughter-in-law of the village selected by the people from the village. One ASHA worker will be selected for every population cluster of a thousand but concessions are likely to be made for remote and inaccessible areas.
- It will cover a wide gamut of issues, including improvement of literacy levels, better sanitation and provision of clean drinking water, apart from measures to ensure adequate availability of trained doctors and paramedical staff.

First Community Eye Bank at Jaipur

On 25th August, 2005, under the project 'Eye Banking Services in Rajasthan State' (in collaboration with 'Orbis International of USA'), the Eye Bank Society of Rajasthan established state's first community eye bank at Jaipur. The society will soon open community eye banks at Jodhpur and Udaipur also. Eye donation centres

TABLE 12.11: District-wise Best and The Worst PSs by Population Served Per Medical Institution/ Per Bed/ Per Doctor. Area Served Per Medical Institution and % Increase in HSI

Districts	*Critaria/Panchayat Samities*									
	2001								*1991-2001*	
	Pop. Served Per Medical Institution		*Area Served Per Medical Institution*		*Pop. Served Per Bed*		*Pop. Served Per Doctor*		*% Increase in HSI Value*	
	Best	*Worst*	*Best*	*Worst*	*Best*	*Worst*	*Best*	*Worst*	*Best*	*Worst*
Ajmer	Kekri	Srinagar	Jawaja	Arian	Kekri	Srinagar	Kekri	Srinagar	Jawaja	Pisangan
Alwar	Reni	Kotkasim	Behror	Rajgarh	Behror	Umren	Behror	Ramgarh	Lachhman-garh	Kishangarh Bas
Banswara	Kushalgarh	Bagidora	Garhi	Peepalkhoont	Garhi	Talwara	Garhi	Anandpuri	Sajjangarh	Bagidora
Baran	Shahbad	Chhabra	Anta	Chhabra	Shahbad	Baran	Anta	Baran	Chhipabarod	Chhabra
Barmer	Sindhari	Chohtan	Siwana	Sheo	Dhorimanna	Barmer	Siwana	Sindhari	Dhorimanna	Sheo
Bharatpur	Kumher	Kaman	Rupbas	Bayana	Weir	Sewar	Weir	Sewar	Nagar Pahari	Weir
Bhilwara	Mandalgarh	Mandal	Raipur	Mandal	Sahara	Shahpura	Jhazpur	Shahpura	Mandalgarh	Shahpura
Bikaner	Lunkaransar	Nokha	Nokha	Kolayat	Bikaner	Lunkaransar	Lunkaransar	Kolayat	Nokha	Bikaner
Bundi	Nainwa	Talera	Nainwa	Talera	Nainwa	Hindoli	Keshoraipatan	Talera	Hindoli	Nainwa
Chittaurgarh	Begun	Badi Sadri	Rashmi	Bhainsrorgarh	Begun	Chittaurgah	Begun	Pratapgarh	Dungla	Kapasan
Churu	Ratangarh	Sardars-shahar	Ratangarh	Sardarshahar	Churu	Sardarshahar	Ratangarh	Sardarshahar	Rajgarh	Sardar-shahar
Dausa	Dausa	Bandikui	Mahwa	Lalsot	Dausa	Sikrai	Mahwa	Lalsot	Bandikui	Dausa
Dhaulpur	Bari	Rajakhera	Dhaulpur	Rajakhera	Bari	Dhaulpur	Bari	Baseri	Bari	Dhaulpur
Dungarpur	Aspur	Bichhiwara	Aspur	Simalwara	Sagwara	Bichhiwara	Sagwara	Bichhiwara	Simalwara	Sagwara
Ganganagar	Sadulshahar	Anupgarh	Ganganagar	Suratgarh	Karanpur	Anupgarh	Karanpur	Sadulshahar	Anupgarh	Suratgarh
Hanumangarh	Bhadra	Hanumangarh	Hanumangarh	Nohar	Nohar	Hanumangarh	Nohar	Hanumangarh	Bhadra	Hanuman-garh
Jaipur	Sanganer	Amber	Shahpura	Phagi	Viratnagar	Jhotwara	Jamwa Ramgarh	Chaksu	Dudu	Govindgarh
Jaisalmer	Jaisalmer	Sankra	Sankra	Sam	Sankra	Jaisalmer	Jaisalmer	Sankra	Sam	Sankra
Jalor	Jalor	Bhinmal	Jalor	Sanchore	Bhinmal	Sayla	Jaswantpura	Sanchore	Bhinmal	Jalor
Jhalawar	Khanpur	Manoharthana	Khanpur	Manoharthana	Dag	Jhalrapatan	Dag	Jhalrapatan	Manohar-thana	Bakani
Jhunjhunun	Jhunjhunun	Surajgarh	Buhana	Surajgarh	Jhunjhunun	Khetri	Nawalgarh	Khetri	Buhana	Nawalgarh
Jodhpur	Bilara	Mandor	Bilara	Bap	Bilara	Phalodi	Bilara	Phalodi	Bap	Shergarh
Karauli	Nadoti	Hindaun	Todabhim	Sapotra	Nadoti	Karauli	Nadoti	Sapotra	Karauli	Nadoti
Kota	Sangod	Chechat	Sangod	Ladpura	Ladpura	Itawa	Ladpura	Sangod	Sultanpur	Ladpura
Nagaur	Degana	Didwana	Parbatsar	Mundwa	Merta	Nagaur	Makrana	Parbatsar	Didwana	Merta
Pali	Rani Station	Raipur	Rani Station	Pali	Desuri	Pali	Desuri	Pali	Raipur	Sumerpur
Rajsamand	Kumbhalgarh	Deogarh	Khamnor	Deogarh	Rajsamand	Khamnor	Deogarh	Amet	Kumbhalgarh	Khamnor
S. Madhopur	S.Madhopur	Gangapur	Gangapur	Khandar	Gangapur	Sawai Madhopur	Gangapur	S. Madhopur	Khandar	Bamanwas
Sikar	Dhond	Sri Madhopur	Danta Ramgarh	Lachhmangarh	Fatehpur	Lachhmangarh	Fatehpur	Dhond	Piprali	Dhond
Sirohi	Sirohi	Abu Road	Sirohi	Abu Road	Abu Road	Pindwara	Abu Road	Pindwara	Sirohi	Shergarh
Tonk	Tonk	Uniara	Tonk	Uniara	Tonk	Uniara	Todhabhim	Deoli	Todaraisingh	Malpura
Udaipur	Jhadol	Kotra	Salumber	Kotra	Bhinder	Gogunda	Bhinder	Kotra	Jhadol	Sarada

Source : 1. General Annex-VIII.
2. General Annex-IX
3. Annex-12.1

will also be established at Shahpura, Kotputli, Alwar, Dausa, Mahuwa and Chomu. The Eye Bank Society of Rajasthan is established in the year 2002. The achievements of the society is as under:

Year	*No. of Cornea Collected*
2002	76
2003	106
2004	204
2005*	123
Total	**509**

* up to August 2005.

BOX 12.2: State-of-the-Art Health Care Facilities in Rajasthan

Funding agency	:	WB
Amount funded	:	Rs. 4.72 billion
Period	:	5 years
Investment from GoR	:	Rs. 220 million

Objective

- To improve the health care scenario of the state by upgrading the infrastructure and creating latest facility for the benefit of the masses.

Highlights

- State-of-the-art health care facility will be developed in at least ten general and three referral hospitals in selected districts.
- Health care facility will be improved in various hospitals and primary health centers located in 25 districts across the state.
- Adequate infrastructure will also be created in five CHCs and seven PHCs.

'Apollo Health Clinics in Rajasthan'

➢ A chain of franchies health clinic are being set up by the Appollo group of hospitals in the state. These family clinics will provide complete solutions for day-to day health care needs of family and offer special consultation services and diagnostic facilities.

'Family Life Education' Subject Introduced by RSEB

➢ From the academic session 2003-04, Board of Secondary Education introduced new subject Family Life Education' in the syllabus of secondary education.

'New hospitals on 'AIIMS Pattern' in Rajasthan

➢ On the pattern of the All India Institute of Medical Science, Delhi one hospital is going to be set up in the state under (PMSSY) Pradhan Mantri Swasthya Suraksha Yojana.

'Free Medical Facility to Journalists'

In July 2005, GoR has launched a novel scheme for journalist which will entitle them to get the facility of treatment, diagnostic tests and medicines free of cost at the government hospitals. Medical diaries, in which entries will be made in the hospitals are given away to 15 senior journalists. Financial assistance was also given to the wives of two journalists who passed away recently.

BOX 12.3: 'Station Medical Teams on Long-Distance Trains'

In an striking judgement on 4th May, 2005, the Rajasthan High Court directed the Indian Railway Board to provide a team of medical officer, a male nurse and an attendant each to travel in all long distance trains running throughout the country.

Source: *Hindustan Times*, 4th May, 2005, Jaipur.

Anti Malaria Drive in Western and Tribal Areas

- Rs. 28 million expended for Malaria Project: GoR spent more than 28 million rupees under Intensive Malaria Project in the year 2003-04. The project was executed in 8 districts namly Udaipur, Banswara, Rajsamand, Dungarpur, Chittaurgarh, Sirohi, Jhalawar and Bundi. Free medicine distribution centres were also opened through out the state. Training was also imparted to 2350 *Anganbari* worker for this purpose.
- In western areas, there are four affected districts viz. Jaisalmer, Barmer, Bikaner and Jodhpur.
  - ➢ GoR has authorised the district collectors to fill the 80 posts of ANMs immediately.
  - ➢ Additional 5 lab technicians have been deputed.
  - ➢ 5000 rapid diagnostic tests have been made available to the medical teams.
  - ➢ 65 mobile teams have been constituted for distributing chloroquine tablets free to cost to the people suffering from malaria and testing the blood slides of the malaria affected people.
- In tribal areas the affected districts are Banswara, Dungarpur, Udaipur, Rajsamand, Chittaurgarh and Sirohi
  - ➢ Focus of the Enhanced Malaria Control Programme in the year 2005-06 is in tribal areas where Synthetic Pyrethroid spray will be used. This insecticide is used where mosquitoes have developed immunity against DDT.
  - ➢ Rapid diagnostic kits have been handed to the mobile teams to speed up the detection and treatment

BOX 12.4: HEALTH CAMPS BY DEVASTHAN DEPARTMENT

The Devasthan department of the GoR will conduct health camps in the entire state, with the help of the religious charitable trusts to benefit the poor and the needy. These trusts will adopt districts and conduct public welfare works and medical camps for which the department will prepare an action plan.

BOX 12.5: AIDS IN RAJASTHAN: HIGHLIGHTS

- First case of HIV positive reported in Pushkar (Ajmer Distt.) in 1986.
- Up to Dec 2004, the total cases reported are 1322.
- 50 per cent of the total AIDS cases are registered from five districts viz. Jaipur, Churu, Jhunjhunun, Nagaur and Sikar.
- 70 per cent cases are reported from rural areas.
- Fresh cases of AIDS registered in the year 2004-05 are 463.
- The first community care center for AIDS opened in Jaipur on the occasion of World Aids Day on 1st Dec. 2005 and the second one is expected soon in Sikar. The GOR is going to open such CCC for AIDS patients in each divisional headquarter.
- As per announcement made by state government, anti-retroviral (ARV) drugs will be included in the essential drug list and will be made available for free to the BPL patients. The kind of ARV drugs offered will depend on the severity of the patient's condition. Other poor patients, who do not fall in the BPL category, will also be offered assistance from the CM's Relief Fund.
- The state government is mooting the proposal of permitting people living with HIV/AIDS to travel free in buses together with an attendant. A pension policy for such persons is also on the cards.
- SOS fund will be created to route the funds donated for tackling Aids.
- Free primary education for boys of HIV/AIDS infected parents is also being planned, as the government already provides free education for all girls.
- Several awards are also being given to organizations and individuals who have made a significant contribution to fight against AIDS.
- *Women Join Fight Against AIDS*: Wives of migrant labourers in Churu, Jhunjhunun and Sikar districts have now emerged as quiet but fierce campaigners in the struggle against the AIDS. These women have begun stocking condoms at their homes for easy accessibility and teaching others in the area about the virtues of safe sex. Under 'Hamara' a project that covers nearly 24000 migrants wives in 133 villages more than 3 lakhs condoms were distributed during the year 2003-04. India-Canada Collaborative HIV and AIDS Project (ICHAP) communication programme which begin in 2001 and which promoted safe sex without disheveling cultural sensitivity.
- Thrust on Research-ICMR is keenly following the trials on herbal medicine to cure hepatitis B and C, which are on at several places including Jaipur to allowed varied patients profiles. It will enable to reach the poor as it will reduce the cost of vaccines by nearly 50 per cent. This herbal vaccine is derived from Mulethi (Glycyrrhiza Glabra) and helps control cirrhosis lung cancer.
- *Jaipur to be 'Epicenter of AIDS Research'**: It is a matter of great pleasure that Jaipur will soon get a research centre dedicated to work on various facets of AIDS. The centre excepted to come up in another six months, will focus on the extensive database of the SMS Medical College that has over 1250 registered AIDS patients with their treatment records dating back to as many as four years. One of the possible projects that could be carried out here includes the usage of microbicides, such as the Praneem cream made out of the Neem tree, to destroy the HIV virus. The cream is used as a suppository and applied around the genitals. The centre would consist of a multi-specialty team dedicated to patient care and research.

* *HIndustan Times*, 11th Oct. 2004, Jaipur.

Biotechnological parks

Three biotech parks at Sitapura (Jaipur), Boranada (Jodhpur) and Sotanala (Alwar) are giving to be developed by RIICO.

Cancer Hospital in Kota

Rajasthan's second cancer hospital is established in Kota with an investment of Rs. 30 million by Kota Cancer society. The hospital will have close collaboration with Tata Memorial Hospital-Mumbai and Mahaveer Cancer Hospital, Jaipur.

BOX 12.6: FAMILY PLANNING / FWP: TRENDS

- Family planning programme was launched in Rajasthan in the year 1952 and was renamed 'Family Welfare Programme (FWP)' in 1978 to offer family planning and mother & child health (MCH) services.
- FP programme was earlier started as clinic based but in late 1960s' and 1970s' the emphasis shifted to the expansion and strengthening of existing rural infrastructure.
- Tubectomy method of strelisation is more popular in rural areas than vasectomy.
- The Panchayati Raj Legislates debar anyone with more than 2 children from becoming a panchayat member in the state.

Prize Incentive Scheme for the Institutions Performing Best Results in Population Stablisation

S.No.	*Particulars of Prizes*	*Prize Amount *(lakh Rs.)*	*No. of Prizes*
1.	Best District in Rajasthan	50	01
2.	Best PS in each district	5	32
3.	Best gram panchayat in each PS	1	237
4.	Best NGO in each district	1	32
5	Best private hospital in each district	1	32
6.	Best govt. hospital in each district	1	32

Note: *The prize amount should be utilized within one year for construction, renovation work and for purchase of medical instruments/materials.
Source: *Pragati Prativeden*, 2004-05, Directorate of Medical, Health and Family Welfare Services Raj.

- In the year 2004-05, 1868 FP operations held (up to Jan 2005).
- NSV (Non-Scalped Vasectomy)
  - ➢ Constant efforts are been made to propagate the use of NSV for increasing participation of men in planned parenthood.
  - ➢ Special training campaign are being promoted in all district hospitals. 110 doctors trained so far as NSV service provider.
  - ➢ NSV camps are being organised on 5th of each month at all the district hospitals.
- For family planning operation, cash payment of Rs. 250 will be given to male and Rs. 200 to female. Similarly, the promoter will be given Rs. 50 for male Rs. 25 for female FP operation.
- Compensation amount for FP operation raised from Rs. 50,000 to Rs. 2,00,000, if a women died within 30 days of operation
- Compensation amount in case of failure of FP operation: Rs. 5000 in cash with free MTP facility.
- From 17th May 2004, Rs. 400 per FP operation and Rs. 75 per IUD insertion will be given to NGO and private hospitals with the condition that minimum 20% operations and IUD insertion should be of BPL families with free of cost.
- Increased availability of contraceptives in each village through:
  - ➢ AWC
  - ➢ SHC
  - ➢ PHC
  - ➢ CHC
  - ➢ FRU
  - ➢ Hospital
  - ➢ Dispensary
  - ➢ Ayurvedic Hospital
  - ➢ Jan Mangal Couple
  - ➢ Dairy
  - ➢ Cooperative Society
  - ➢ Fair Price Shop

'Condom Vending Machines Established in Jaipur'

- 100 vending machines established across the city in public places such as the sulabh complexes, railway stations and bus stations.
- The machine would dispense a packet containing five condoms once a person inserts an Rs 5 coin.
- Depending on the reaction to these machines, the government plans to install similar machines across the state.

'Parivar Kalyan Pension Scheme' (PKPS)

Rajasthan is the first state in India to implement this scheme. Pension of Rs. 150 per month will be given to men (after the age of 60 years) who had undergone family planning operation after two children. In case of his death, his widow will be given the pension (after the age of 55 years).
MCH special monitoring movement was held during 5th Feb. 2005 to 31st March 2005.
'MCH Day' : Since 4th Oct. 2004, mother and child day (once in a month) is observed across the state with the objective of strengthening MCH services.

TFA/CNNA

- ➢ The family welfare programme was being implemented under the 'Target Free Approach (TFA)' since 1st April 1996 all over India and under the system of decentralized participatory planning.
- ➢ TFA has been renamed as **Community Needs Assessment Approach (CNAA)** from 1997.
- ➢ The preparation of the annual action plans at district and state levels is based on the assessed needs of the people for FW services is one of the most essential and vital activities in the programme.
- ➢ This approach is expected to bring about improvements in the quality of services and client satisfaction.
- ➢ The decentralized participatory planning strategy adopted under this approach involves inter-alia, close association of the community and its leading lights and opinion leaders such as village pradhans, mahila swasthya sanghs, primary school teachers etc. in the formulation of the PHC based family welfare and health care plans.
- ➢ "Guidelines as a supplement to CNAA Manual", a supplementary booklet has also been got printed and circulated across the state.
- ➢ NIC has developed new software for transmission of data from district health officers to the state health office. This software is being download in the computer at district and state level.

Rs. 8 billion for Health Projects (Raj.)*

GoR plans to spend Rs. 8 billion in the three years to implement various health projects. This included the Rs. 4.72 billion World Bank-aided health system. A sum of Rs. 319.4 million were spent on the implementation of the reproductive and child health care programme. Construction of 74 operation theatres and 91 labour rooms was started at a cost Rs. 72.1 million. The construction of smaller structures with the provision of electricity and water supply was taken up at a cost of Rs. 30.8 million. Round-the-clock delivery facility has been made available at 1178 primary health centres and 194 community health centres across the state and an expenditure of Rs. 25.3 million was incurred. More than 3400 women from the backward and weaker sections were given the benefit of referral transport for delivery from the health sub-centres situated in the far-flung areas. The service was provided at a cost of Rs. 1.66 million. About 3345 special camps on reproductive and child health care were organised at the primary health centres in the remote areas at a cost of Rs. 34.2 million.

A target of recruiting 10,000 maids has been set for the year 2005-06. An additional 1,321 nurses were appointed on contract in the tribal dominated districts of Udaipur, Dungarpur and Banswara and the desert districts of Barmer, Jodhpur, Pali, Jalor, Jaisalmer, Bikaner and Nagaur. Similarly, the services of assistants, laboratory technicians and anaesthetists were obtained on contract at a cost of Rs. 20.3 million. Besides, the vaccine cold-storage and drugs and equipment kits were supplied to various health care organizations at a cost of Rs. 19.3 million under the programme.

Five Self-help Groups at Each Anganwadi Centre (AWCs)

According to the Ministry of Women & Child Development five women SHG will be set up at each anganwadi centre in Rajasthan by October 2003. These SHGs would be provided the capacity building training along with the efforts to associate them with the credit linking activities in the state. Over five lakhs women have been associated with SHGs. 7725 SHGs have been provided the loans of Rs. 116 million through different banks and financial institutions. Women members of 28000 SHGs are having the mutual transactions of 143 million.

BOX 12.7: Budget Highlights: Annual Plan 2005-06, Medical and Health, Rajasthan

Particulars	*Budget Provision (million Rs.) Descending Order*
For Directorate of Ayurved, Ajmer	116.4
For new medical science, university	50.0
For providing all type of medical facilities to school going children in 23 tribal blocks	26.84
For medical and health sector including ayurved	23.93
For ayurved university, Jodhpur	20.0
For providing micronutrients to 20000 Saharia tribal families	18.0
For setting-up 5 community health centers	8.57
For purchasing 14 ambulances for 10 CHC's and 4 district hospitals located on National Highways	5.25
For establishing 6 PHC's (Rural) and 2 PHC's (Urban)	5.15
For providing machinery and equipment etc. to rural and urban institutions respectively	3.1
For opening of 12 sub-centres in desert district, Jaisalmer and 20 sub-centres in Barmer	2.98
For upgrading CHC Jhalrapatan (Jhalawar) from 30 to 50 bedded	2.32
For opening of 2 sub-centres and for upgradation of 2 sub-centres in Saharia block of Baran district.	0.4

Source: *Budget at a Glance*, 2005-06, DES, Raj., Jaipur.

'World Bank Funding of $89 million, For Health'

Funding of $89 million for the expansion of the public health project in Rajasthan has been approved by the world bank.

* Monthly Review of Rajasthan Economy, Center for Monitoring Indian Economy Jaipur, June, 2005, p 111 & 112.

Objectives

To improve the quality and efficiency of state health services at the primary and secondary level. Increase the access of poor and tribal households of health care.

Benefits

Expansion of healthcare access to about three million out patients and about 34000 in-patients annually.

Implementation

By focusing resources in the areas with the lowest outcomes and by targeting communicable diseases and health problems related to maternal and child health.

COMPONENTS: 3

Components	*Outlay %age to total Funding*	*Focus*
I	20	For supporting the improvement of the state's institutional capacity for health policy planning and development and for implementing health sector programmes.
II	50	Enhancing the capacity of district hospitals and sub-divisional hospitals. Through this, 28 district hospitals, 23 sub-divisional hospitals, 185 community health centres and two-block community health centres will be upgraded.
III	30	For reduction in geographical and financial barriers to health care through refurbishing community health centres in Rajasthan.

- Under the project, upliftment of atleast one community hospital at every sub-division of the state will be undertaken. The plan is to provide new instruments starting 24-hour emergency services, make available services of gynecologists, physicians, surgery, anesthesia specialists in the selected hospitals.

Rs. 190 million for Development of Hospitals under ADB

The GoR is going to upgrade following hospitals with ADB loan assistance:

- Expansion and rehabilitation of hospital building and development of infrastructure at JLN hospital at Ajmer, PBM hospital at Bikaner, SMS hospital at Jaipur, MDM hospital in Jodhpur and MB hospital at Udaipur.
- Development and rehabilitation of infrastructure facilities and expension of exesting building of TB and Chest diseases hospitals in Jaipur.
- Upgradation of medical facilities in Medical College at Shirnathpuram at Kota.
- Construction of cardiothoracic surgery centre at MDM hospital at Jodhpur.
- Development and rehabilitation of infrastructure facilities at Ummeid hospital and MG hospital at Jodhpur.
- Construction of operation theatre, ward blood bank and other ancillary work at SDM sattelite hospital at Bikaner.
- Construction and extension of building at Navchokiya, Poata Satellite hospital and Govt. Husain (Mahila bagh) at Jodhpur.
- The development works include enhancement of infrastuructual facilities and extension of following hospitals:

S. No.	*Hospitals*	*Amount to be Spent (Million Rs.)*
1.	Kota Satellite Hospital	30
2.	Renovation of Mahila Chikstsalaya Sanganari Gate, Jaipur	30
3.	Construction of Super Speciality Hospital in Bikaner	30
4.	Mathuradas Mathur Hospital in Jodhpur	30
5.	Renovation of Zanana Hospital Chandpol Bazar in Jaipur	10

BOX 12.8: SMS Hospital, Jaipur

- The Sawai Man Sing hospital, Jaipur is the biggest government hospital of Rajasthan and is going to become as one of the best hospitals of India.
- The hospital will be developed soon as a leading centre for cancer care in Rajasthan*.
- Efforts are on to start 'DOTS Plus Scheme' for TB patients in SMS hospital.
- A new Cath Lab will soon be built at the hospital.
- The hospital will soon be 'Epicenter of AIDS Research'.

SMS Hospital to be developed as a "Center for Excellence"

Master plan worth Rs. 1.0 billion is going to be prepared by GoR to upgrade the health facilities at SMS Hospital to develop it into a 'Centre for Excellence'.

- An 8-storey building will be constructed in the main premises where 300 cottage wards will be set up for the convenience of the patients.
- Constructing a five-storeyed block to house the entire OPD and new operation theatres.
- A state-of-the-art machine costing Rs. 150 million will be procured for the treatment of patients suffering from cancer.
- Adding another 2000 beds with the aim of improving health care services.
- Provision of Rs. 200 million has been made for modernization of the hospital
- Building a paraplegic ward and trauma ward in the main block.
- A sub-way will also be constructed in order of link the new building with the existing hospital building.
- 50 shops will be constructed on the vacant land whereas the building would come up on top of the shops and will house the dental and ophthalmology department.
- A huge parking lot and a dharmshala will also come up nearby.
- Emergency Ward
  - ➢ Rs. 50 million is earmarked for expansion of five state of the art operation theatres which will be added to the existing emergency ward to separately handle cases in neurosurgery, opthalmology, medicine, accidents and trauma.
  - ➢ The present emergency ward will be converted into more spacious emergency complex with super specialty services. Patient capicity will be increased from the present 25 to 80 beds. Ten other observation cabins will be built to supplement the existing five. The new complex will considerably reduce pressure in emergency services, besides relieving other departments, especially neurosurgery.

* As per announcement made by Hon'ble Chief Minister on 12th Oct, 2004.

BOX 12.9: 'New Standards for CHC'

Announced by GoI on 12th April, 05, during launching of National Rural Health Mission.

Objectives

- Indian Public Health Standard (IPHS) for the community health centers to provide expert care and maintain an acceptable standard of quality of care.
- To make the services more responsive and sensitive to the needs of the community.
- Strengthening referral hospital care for every one lakh person as per the new standards.

Highlights

- The service assured in community health centres such as routine and emergency care in surgery, medicine, obstetrics, gynecology and pediatrics are to be made available under the IPHS.
- Two specialists anaesthetics and public health programme manager will be provided on a contractual basis in addition to the available specialists.
- The support manpower will include a public health nurse and an auxiliary nurse and midwife (ANM) in addition to the existing staff.
- An ophthalmic assistant will be provided at the centres where there is none at present.
- The routine and emergency services that the community health centres must provide include incision and drainage, hernia, appendicitis and fistula.
- They should be able to handle emergencies such as intestinal obstruction and haemorrhage. Besides, 24-hour delivery services including normal and assisted deliveries, the centers will have a full range of family planning services, safe abortion services and newborn care.
- All the National Health Programmes (NHP) will have to be delivered through these health centres.
- The centers will also have a blood storage facility, essential laboratory services and referral (transport) services.

'10 Districts Benefited under European Commission Health Assistance'

➢ Total 10 districts namely Jalore, Barmer, Pali, Jodhpur, Jaisalmer, Nagaur, Bikaner, Sirohi, Banswara and Dungargarh are being benefited under European Commission health assistance by providing aid to construct hospitals, purchase of equipments and training to medical staff.

WHO's-ORS Campaign Regenerated in Rajasthan

➢ The World Health Organisation (WHO) Oral Dehydration Salts (ORS) campaign has been regenerated in the alongwith of other northern states. With the use of television and print media, it specially targets mothers to teach them the correct usages of ORS as studies have show that mothers often mix the ORS solution incorrectly.

'Special Polio Correction Camps'

- The State Social Welfare Department has decided to organise special polio correction campaign in the state. These campaigns will be continued throughout the year. Last year, against a budget of Rs. 30 million only Rs. 1.5 million was utilised for the polio correction activities. The department has decided to benefit, as many people through polio correction surgeries and thus the leftover budget of last year will be utilised this year by conducting more polio correction activities. Organisations are given Rs. 3500 per patient by the department which includes food, transportation and calipers of the patients.

'UNFPA Project on Rajasthan Praised in `World Population Report, 2004'

- The United Nations Population Fund (UNPF) infrastructure development programme in Rajasthan to promote safe motherhood has come in for praise in its annual state of World Population report.
- As a result of the UNPF/Averting Maternal Death and Disability (AMDD) efforts, the number of women treated for obstetric complications in Rajasthan "has increased 50% in four years and India has introduced similar interventions in other states".
- Under this programme, 83 emergency obstetric care facilities were upgrade in the state and 59 teams of health professionals were trained to provide emergency obstetric care. The report adds that 12 teams were trained in infection prevention and management information systems "were introduced to improve monitoring and evaluation of services".

BOX 12.10: 'TOTAL SANITATION CAMPAIGN'

Sponsored by	:	GoI
Partnered by	:	UNICEF
Launched in	:	2000
Project Cost	:	Rs. 1.29 billion
Expenditure Ratio	:	GoI : GoR 1.85 : 1
District covered	:	Initially 5 at Present 11 (Rajsamand, Jaipur, Kota, Bundi, Jhalawar, Dhaulpur, Tonk, Sawai Madhopur, Sikar, Ajmer, Alwar)
Nodal agency	:	Panchayati Raj Department
Executed through	:	Village Panchayats

UNICEF is supporting the TSC programme by way of operating production centres and rural sanitary marts, conducting baseline surveys and carrying out awareness generation campaigns

IIHMR Redesignated as a 'WHO Collaborating Centre'

The Indian Institute of Health Management Research (IIHMR) is redesignated as a WHO collaborating centre for district health System based on primary health-care. First redesignated as a WHO collaborating centre in 1998, the institute has closely been associated with the activities of SEARO (South-east Asia Regional Office) of WHO in undertaking research, training fellowships, networking and consultation in primary health care. The redesignation would be in effect for the next four years. Thus, the institute would serve as a resource centre in the area of quality assurance in health care and organisation and management of health system based on primary health care with particular emphasis on district health system in urban and rural districts. Organising in country and inter-country training courses on organisation and management of district health system and health care, the institute will collaborate with WHO in monitoring and evaluation of the progress in the implementation of district health system approach and quality assurance.

BOX 12.11: DRINKING WATER PROJECTS: HIGHLIGHTS

- Rs. 1.51 billion has been earmarked by GoI for drinking water projects to be undertaken in Rajasthan during the year 2005-06.
- Rs. 753 million granted by GoI for drinking water under Twarit Gramin Payjal Yojana (TGPY) to provide potable drinking water in rural areas of the state.
- The public health engineering department launched a campaign to repair hand pumps from Ist of January 2005.

Survey to Assess Drinking Water Problem

Survey is going to be conducted by	:	GoR
Costing	:	Rs. 2.23 billion
Expenditure share (%)	:	Rural : Urban 76 : 24
Objectives	:	To prepare a contingency plan to solve water problem.

'Water Transportation'

Plan to transport water by road to 60 towns and 10,000 villages and dhanis. Water will also be transported through rail to eight towns and 27 villages and dhanis. In urban areas, 410 tube wells and 1700 hand pumps will be installed. In rural areas, the number of tube wells is 1000 tube wells and 7000 haird pumps will be installed.

'Water Project Under The Vision Document 2005'

Under the Vision Document 2005, priority has been given to complete all pending projects in rural and urban areas. Besides new projects have also been undertaken to improve the surface and underground water situation in the entire state.

'National Fluoride Mitigation Sub-Center'

NFMSC is being set-up at Jaipur with an investment of Rs. 650 million. The center will purify water and make it safe for drinking.

Rural Water Supply Scheme

Revenue Expenditure	million Rs.
Accounts, 2003-04	2629.85
Revised Estimates, 2004-05	2571.54
Budget Estimates, 2005-06	2286.24

Villages/Habitations Covered With Drinking Water Facility (As on Dec. 2004) (No.)

	Villages/Habitations	*Covered (fully/partially)*
Main Villages	37889	37680
Other Habitations	56057	53614
Total	**93946**	**91294**

'Rs. 80 million to Crub Fluoride Contamination in Drinking Water'

GoR earmarked Rs. 80 million to crub fluoride contamination in drinking water (2004-05) in 2642 villages having fluoride content more than 5 ppm (above the permissible limit) for testing of water sample of the villages, special cell has been set-up at Jaipur and special committies has been constituted in ratio of villages by the water works department. The cell in association with other departments would check the water samples and inform about the extent of fluoride contamination affecting the water.

The Central Ground Water Board (CGWB) has identified 11 blocks across Rajasthan to control and regulate the use of ground water in these areas, as situation in these blocks is not very good. CGWB is in the process of notifying these 11 blocks to start development work. These blocks are:

Identified Blocks	*District*
Pushkar Ghati and Ghor Pisangan	Ajmer
Behror	Alwar
Bhinmal, Raniwara and Jalor	Jalor
Buhana, Surajgarh and Chirawa	Jhunjhunun
Mundawa	Nagaur
Sri Madhopur	Sikar

'Rs. 26.41 billion spent on Drinking Water Supply Schemes'

- GoR has expended Rs. 26.41 billion during the first four and a half years for implementing drinking water supply schemes in the state. Details are as below:

Particulars	*Rs. Billion*
Amount Spent in Rural Areas	20.23
Amount Spent in Urban Areas	6.18
Benefited Villages and Towns	37643
Benefited Hamlets	51343

Rs. 7.33 billion World Bank 'Rajasthan Water Area Rehabilitation Project' Commenced

- Under the project, repair and reconstruction of 91 canals 16 dams will be taken up.

Problems

Inspite of 1022 times increase in health budget during the last fifty-four years (1951-04), the health status of Rajasthan is still poor in India. Fertility, Mortality and Morbidity indicators in the state are continue to be higher than the national average. The basic medical, family welfare and nutrition services are still meager and poorly received. A vicious cycle has been emerged between high population, poverty, poor health status and degraded environment in the state (Chart 12.3).

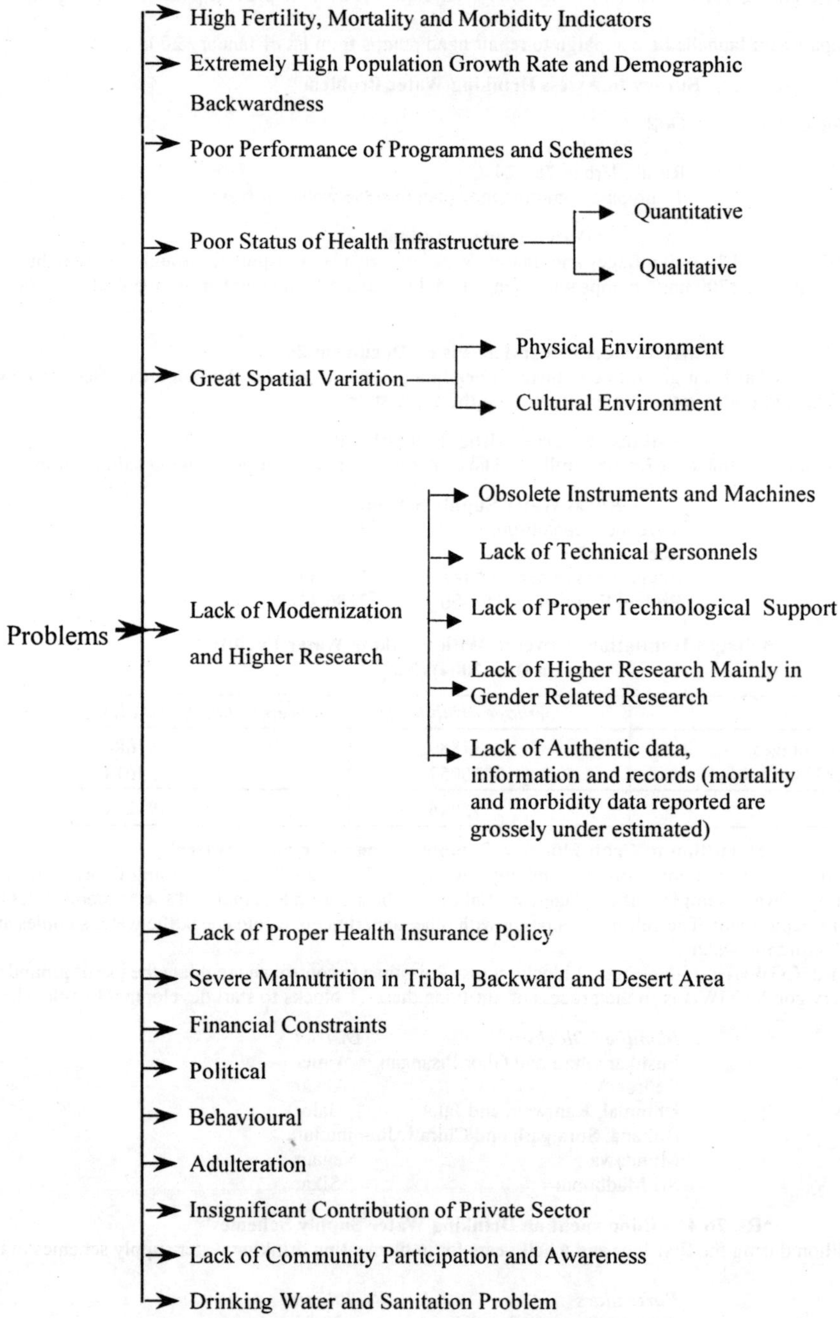

CHART 12.3

High Population Growth and Demographic Backwardness

- *Galloping population*: It is a matter of great concern that the state recorded unprecedented highest decadal (1991-01) population growth rate in the country. Major factors responsible for this include suitable climate, preference for sons, high IMR, illiteracy, poverty, religious, political etc. Preference for sons plays an important role in discrimination against daughters through sex-selective abortion, neglect of and high mortality among young girls and lack of parental motivation to educate girls.

- Low status of women-low female literacy and work participation rate, early marriage, frequent and prolonged child bearing associated with poverty means women often uneducated without power to control fertility.
- Tribal and backward areas have very high population growth rate and have critical demographic problems. Very low child sex-ratio speaks of poor status of girl child. Low density of population along with its unequal and sparsely distribution pose a serious obstacles in accessibility of health services.
- Lack of minimum security, which makes large families attractive.
- A very high degree of positive correlation is observed between low density of population and low health status in the arid, semi-arid and hilly areas.
- High infant mortality rate leads parents to have more children.

BOX 12.12: Causes of High IMR in Rajasthan

- Pre-maturity of birth.
- Low birth weight. 51 per cent of the children under three years of age are underweight. (NFHS – 2)
- Low peri-natal, neo-natal and post-natal care. About 83 infants out of 1000 live births die before attaining first birth day. (NFHS – 2)
- Diseases like-acute respiratory infection, diarrhoea, fever.
- Poor birth practices.
- Malnutrition. More than 50% of the children in age group 0 to 6 years suffer from different degree of malnutrition. (NFHS – 2)
- Early age at motherhood.
- Anaemic.
- Low status of women.
- Low level of immunization.
- Lack of awareness and access to the health facilities.

Poor Status of Health Infrastructure

Tables 12.12 to 12.17 highlight poor health instrastructural status of the State. The major factor responsible are as under:

- Geographical- Inaccessibility in arid, semi-arid and hilly areas.
- Inadequate number of medical institutions (hospitals, dispensaries, PHCs, SHC, CHCs, MCWCs, FWCs etc). A wide gap is seen between the required and the actual number of these institutions throughout the state.
- Poor quality of health infrastructure.
- Inadequate number of health personnels, mainly para-medical staff. Vacant posts further worsen the situation.
- Financial constraints.
- Socio-economic backwardness.
- Lack of awareness among people.
- Indifference attitude of doctors, staff, health workers etc.
- Lack of facilities and desire skills among care providers.
- No comprehensive geriatric care system for rising elderly peoples.
- Lack of access to health care facilities and contraceptives.
- Lack of basic equipments and resources. Many CHCs also lack ambulance facility.
- EmOc services are inadequate or absent at the level of CHC and PHC.

TABLE 12.12: Decline in Child Sex-Ratio: Rajasthan (1951-01)

S.No.	*Census Year*	*Sex Ratio*	
		0-6 Age Group	*All Ages*
1.	1951	976	921
2.	1961	964	908
3.	1971	968	911
4.	1981	954	919
5.	1991	916	910
6.	2001	909	922

Source: Compiled from Census of India, 2001, Rajasthan Provisional/Final Pop. Tables.

TABLE 12.13: Area-wise Shortage of SHCs, PHCs & CHCs: Rajasthan, 2003

S. No.	*Category of Area*	*SHCs*			*PHCs*			*CHCs*		
		Total Required (No.)	*In Position (No.)*	*Shortage as Percentage to Total Required*	*Total Required (No.)*	*In Position (No.)*	*Shortage as Percentage to Total Required*	*Total Required (No.)*	*In Position (No.)*	*Shortage as Percentage to Total Required*
1	*2*	*3*	*4*	*5*	*6*	*7*	*8*	*9*	*10*	*11*
1	Total in State	11298	9926	-12	1774	1674	-6	438	287	-34
2	In Plain Areas	4686	5107	9	784	838	7	241	159	-34
3	In Tribal Areas	1414	1119	-21	212	181	-15	40	30	-25
4	In Desert Areas	5195	3700	-29	778	655	-16	157	98	-38

Source: Deptt. of Medical, Health & Family Welfare, Raj.

TABLE 12.14: Poor Functional Status of Primary Health Infrastructure: Rajasthan, 2003

Particulars	
Primary Health Centres	
No.of PHCs functioning without a doctor	35
No. of PHCs functioning without lab. technician	101
No. of PHCs functioning without pharmacist	213
No. of PHCs functioning without lab. technician and pharmacist	95
No. of PHCs functioning without nurse midwife	17
Sub Health Centres	
No. of SHCs functioning without ANMs	350
No. of SHCs functioning without health worker (M)	596
No. of SHCs functioning without building in any.	2012
No. of SHCs functioning without health worker (M) and ANM 530	

Source: Department of Medical, Health and Family Welfare, Rajasthan

TABLE 12.15: Vacant Posts of Health Personnels in Rural and Tribal Areas: Rajasthan, 2003

Category	*Rural Areas*		*Tribal Areas*	
	No. of Vacant Posts	*No. of Vacant Posts as Percentage of Sanctioned Posts*	*No. of Vacant Posts*	*No. of Vacant Posts as Percentage of Sanctioned Posts*
1	*2*	*3*	*4*	*5*
1. Specialists at CHCs				
Surgeon	91	33	17	50
Obstetricians/Gyne	41	27	8	57
Physicians	50	19	17	53
Pediatricians	27	29	7	78
Anaesthatist	2	67	0	0
Lady Doctor	15	19	2	50
Total	226	26	51	54
2. Doctors/Medical Officers at PHCs				
Allopathic Doctor	47	3	—	—
Lady Doctor	19	11	—	—
Medical Officers	—	—	150	93
Total	66	4	150	93
3. Block Extension Educator	172	74	—	—
4. Health Worker (M)	1440	36	—	—
5. Lab. Tchnician	88	4	—	—

Source: Deptt. of Medical, Health & Family Welfare, Rajasthan.

TABLE 12.16: Vacant Posts in Rural Family Welfare Centres: Rajasthan (2004-05)

S.No.	*Category*	*No. of Vacant Posts*	*No. of Vacant Posts as Percentage of Sanctioned Posts*
1.	Assistant Accountant	1	33
2.	Enumerator	3	50
3.	Sector Supervisor	799	86
4.	Family Welfare Workers	148	89
5.	Asstt. Surgeon*	52	22
6.	B.E. Educator*	147	63
7.	Health Assistants	834	90
8.	Computer Operator*	100	45
9.	Driver*	63	28

* For the Year 2003.
Source: Department of Family Welfare, Jaipur.

TABLE 12.17: Vacant Posts in National Leproacy Eradication Programme: Rajasthan (2004-05)

S.No.	*Category*	*No. of Vacant Posts*	*Vacant Posts as Percentage of Sanctioned Posts*
1.	NMS	19	50
2.	NMA	95	95
3.	Senior NMS	4	100

Source: Compiled from *Pragati Prativedan,* Department of Medical and Health, 2004-05, pp. 13.

BOX 12.13: Worst Condition of PHCs, SHCs and FRUs in Remote/BACKWARD Areas: Rajasthan

Many PHCs and SHCs located in remote areas (tribal, hilly and desert areas) of the state are lacking in with basic infrastructural facilities like all weather motorable approach road, water supply, electricity, telephone facility and round the clock delivery facility. Similarly, many FRUs (First Referal Units) are without operation theatre, labour room, X-ray machine lab, anesthetist, gynecologist, pediatrician, round the clock delivery services, emergency services etc.

BOX 12.14: Poor Hospital Hygiene

Infection in hospitals even in ICU (intensive care unit) and OT (Operation Theatre) is very common. It is mainly due to lack of proper sterilisation procedure and effective monitoring. In hospitals, surgical instruments are generally spread out in the open, exposed to germs, dust and insects. Cotton pads are kept in unsterlised steel containers. Similarly, pus and blood infected guaze, linem, sheet etc. are carelessly disposed, often next to instruments.

Poor Performance of Health Programmes and Schemes

Factors

- Lack of technical as well as effective leadership.
- *Financial Paucity*: Rajasthan is a under developed state. Most of the health programmes are centrally funded. Therefore, their sustainability is dependent on continued financial support. Lack of timely release of fund with sufficient quantity is a serious hurdle.
- Lack of infrastructural facilities.
- Fixation of targets to functionarise without seeing the respective areas population.
- Less than optimal use of available resources.
- Political, social and cultural constraints.
- Role of communication to increase community participations is not successful. Exposure to FP message through mass media is about 20-25 per cent only. Existing channels of communications are not adequate to build a sound understanding of critical diseases and their respective programmes.
- Lack of inter-department cooperation.
- Lack of enthusiasm among the medical fraternity and health officers in supporting and monitoring the project activities. Similarly, high predisposition of the doctors towards curative care and less emphasis they place on the preventive aspects.

- These programmes are perceived *sarkari* programme and due to top-down approach, various programmes have not been able to reach the beneficiaries. Moreover, due to the centrally nature of most by the programmes, the staff and health workers are simply seen a dispenser of services.
- Shortage of staff (vacant posts).
- Absentism mainly in tribal hilly and arid areas.
- Increasing unwanted political pressure and interference.
- Lack of awareness and community participation.
- The technical knowledge of the health workers is below the desired level.
- In paucity of any systematic survey on the prevalence and incidence of different diseases in the state, it is difficult to make any assessment on the efforts put by medical institutions.
- *Misuses/Non-utilisation of Funds*: In many cases very little work has been done under the health projects. Most of the funds nave been eaten up by the powerful nexus of politicians, bureaucrats and NGO activities.

Dismal Performance of FWP

- Lack of technical leadership
- Apart from the population problem, quality of care and reproductive health are other issues which also pose a challenge to the states FWP.
- Lack of enthusiasm and indifference attitude of the family welfare service providers.
- The programme does not taken characteristics of the area in to account.
- It failed to provide need-based services.
- Existence of heterogeneous incentives strategies.
- Lack of accessibility of services and poor quality of services especially follow-up.
- Centralized nature of the programme.
- Overlaps due to multiplicity of allocations, staff and facilities exist for FW services, due to multipurpose programmes, overlaps occure.
- Poor management.
- Sterilisation services received a jolt during the emergency period.

BOX 12.15: Poor Acceptance of FP Methods Mainly by Muslims and SC/ST Women in Rajasthan

As per the latest NFHS data, 75 per cent Muslim women and 70 per cent of the SC/ST women are not using any family planning methods. They produce about two children more than they actually want to have followed by Hindu women, who have about one unwanted child. On an average, 3.8 children are born to a women here, contrary to her desire to have only 2.6 children. The use of female sterilisation is much lower among Musilms than women belonging to other religions.

Source: (1). NFHS – II, (2). *Hindustan Times,* 12 Oct., 2004, Jaipur.

- The acceptance of FP methods and more particularly of spacing methods is very low (7 to 8%). Coverage of spacing methods which is highly dependent on communication efforts by the health workers seems not to have been accomplished successfully. The poor status communications activities by the health system, could have contributed to the low coverage of spacing methods.
- The increased use of non-terminal methods, reflected in service statistics, suffer from inaccuracy and generally these statistics are inflated by the workers to achieve targets.
- The awareness of terminal methods is not universal.
- Lack of education means less awareness of family planning methods and benefits.
- Lack of confidence and hope in future which is the great enemy of FP.
- It is also alarming to note that 46 to 49 of the children in Rajasthan are not immunized for any dose of any vaccine. Rajasthan also compares very low with regard to complete immunization with other states and very high with regard to no immunization coverage provided to any child.
- Low density of population mainly in western arid and southern-tribal region hinders provision of FW services due to the increased operational cost of reaching services to inaccessible areas

Lack of Proper Health Insurance Policy

Health Insurance Scheme is skewed in favour of the non-poor. As a result, only few BPL families have been covered. Although the premiums are low, BPL families seem to avoid the scheme due to their inability to pay the premium.

Political

- Absence of long-term rational and pragmatic health policy.
- Absence of area specific and need-based policy.
- Lacuna in effective monitoring and implementation.
- Red tapism and corruption.

Behavioral Problem

- Indifference, arrogant and rude behaviour of medical and para-medical personnels mainly in rural areas.

Causes

- ➢ High work load due to great pressure of out-door as well as in-door patients.
- ➢ Inadequate staff and vacant posts.
- ➢ Poor health infrastuctural facilities.
- ➢ Resource constraints.
- ➢ Increasing commercial attitude of the health personnels.

BOX 12.16: Malnutrition in Rajasthan

Chronic nutrition deficiency in children, adolescent girls and pregnant women

Most Suffering Areas
- Arid/Semi-arid/hilly.
- Tribal.
- Backward.

Causes
- Inadequate food supply.
- Lack of knowledge regarding nutritious foods.
- Foods taboos.
- Gender biasness, inequitable distribution of food within the family.
- Inaccessibility to nutritional services.
- Poverty.
- Poor Performance of ICDS.
- Negligence of women.
- Lack of community consciousness.

Effects
- Stunt growth.
- Increases susceptibility to infections and diseases.
- Impedes physiological maturity.
- Due to Iodine deficiency, women have higher rates of foetal wastages, still-birth and low-birth-weight babies.
- Anemia causes fatigue, poor appetite, poor learning capacity, gastrointestinal and neurological problems.

Strengthening Health Infrastructure

- Establishing and upgrading adequate number of medical institutions at primary, secondary and tertiary level as per norms. Special thrust should be given in desert, hilly, tribal and backward areas.
- Infrastructure gaps should be removed in a time-bound manner.
- Strengthening health institutions at the block, community, district and state level.

- **Promoting 50 to 100 beded new hospitals in private sector across the state.**
- **The poor status of government hospitals can be improved through ensuring and by mobilizing support and involvement of the local community. Similarly, donors (rich persons) of concerning area can also be encouraged for the same.**
- **Establishing senior citizen centers/old age homes, Day care facilities can be attached to these centers providing physical rehabilitation and the opportunity to socialize.**
- **Promoting multi-approach/pronged clinics for holistic approach of treatment. At these clinics for example a rheumatoid patient can be examined by an orthopedic surgeon, a rheumatologist and a physiotherapist at the same time and also plan an extensive course of treatment.**

BOX 12.17: Drinking Water and Sanitation Problems in Rajasthan

[I] 'DRINKING WATER'

- Rajasthan accounts for 5.65 India's population but only 1.28 per cent of available water source.
- There are 74 over-exploited blocks, where annual extraction of ground water is more than annual recharge*.
- There are 20 dark blocks, where annual extraction is 85-100 per cent of the annual recharge*.

Decline in Ground Water*	Districts
Up to 2 metres	Bundi, Banswara, Dhaulpur, Udaipur, Bharatpur, Baran, Dungarpur, Karauli, Alwar and Jhalawar
2 to 4 metres	Sikar, Dausa, Dungarpur, Jhunjhunun and Alwar
More than 4 metres	Jalor, Sirohi, Bhilwara, Jaipur, Pali, Dausa and Tonk

- There are 11000 habitations (10% of India) in Rajasthan, where water level has gone down and water availability for drinking contains fluoride, iron and other impurities.
- 2642 villagers are severely affected by fluoride contamination (>5 ppm, above permissible limit).
- Out of the total 47000 sites identified for water harvesting structures, only 8 per cent structures have been completed so far.

Causes

- Non-availability of perrential sources of water in major portion of the state.
- Groundwater is also available at considerable depth.
- Groundwater in many places is not safe for drinking purpose.
- Frequent failure of rain further complicates the situation.
- Lack of public awareness. Wastage and misuse of water is common.

[II] SANITATION

- More than 75 per cent diseases in rural Rajasthan are related to inadequate sanitation which is also one of the major causes of high IMR.
- Poor performance of Total Sanitation Campaign:
  - ➢ Only one-fourth of released funds have been utilised during last four years.
  - ➢ Against the target of covering 320,000 households under the Individual Household Latrine (IHHL) project, the achievement was only 5 per cent (17,201) in the first two years.
  - ➢ Against the target of covering 14,730 schools in the first two years, the achievement was less than 15 per cent (2145).

* As per groundwater resources estimation made by groundwater board for Rajasthan.

BOX 12.18: Recommendations

- Strengthening Health Infrastructure
- Improving Quality of Health Services
- Improving Performance of Health and Family Welfare Programmes/Schemes
- Modernization
- Comprehensive and Integrated Training Programmes
- Health Insurance
- Effective Role of Public Representatives and PRIs
- Financial Support
- Focus on Govt-NGO ties
- Health Research
- Tackling Drinking Water Crises Effectively
- Effective Implementation of Sanitation Programme

Improving Quality of Health Services

- Improving of the Quality of Health Care Delivery through enhancing techno-managerial and communication competence of large number of health workers, supervisors, medical officers, programme managers and support staff working in the system.

- Improving physical infrastructure and facilities at all the health institutions at block, sub-district, community and district level.
- Covering the backlog and deficiencies in buildings, staff, equipments etc. All the vacant posts of important health care functionaries like ANMs, medical officers etc. should be filled-up on a priority basic. Adequate training should be given to all these functionaries immediately after there recruitments.
- Improve the performance to the health care system and utilization of services.
- Enhancing the coverage and access of health care particularly for women and for SC/ST/ OBC population.
- Improving efficiency in the allocation and utilization of health care resources through policy and institutional development.
- Making provision of adequate emoluments, amenities and facilities for the medical staff.
- Special thrust should be given on quality health services in remote and backward areas and for vulnerable section such as children, pregnant and lactating mothers.
- To check infections, all hospitals should be well equipped with a Central Sterile Supply Department (CSSD), which should be response for the sterilisation of surgical instruments etc.

Improving Performance of Health and Family Welfare Programmes/Schemes

- Comprehensive and focused implementation of various programmes through:
  - Effective leadership and management
  - Motivation (staff motivation by systematizing their work and improving supervision, training and close guidance)
  - Monitoring, and
  - Evaluation
- Effective co-ordination and support among different health functionaries.
- Special efforts should be made in remote and backward areas under "Area Projects".
- Expanded Programme of Immunization (EPI) should be continued and further strengthened.
- Strengthening MCH through integrated comprehensive MCH care and referred services.
- The state government should continue to get financial assistance from the center on 100 per cent basics.
- Special IEC campaign should be organised to raise awareness and to improve utilization of health care facilities. Efforts should be made to mobilize all the available media outlets, both government and private owned to launch an effective and sustained communication campaign to create mass awareness about different programmes.
- Develop a Strategy for Implementing safe motherhood initiatives, specially EmOc.
- Government should make all programmes gender sensitive and make women's empowerment central to their strategy.
- FP should be voluntary, informal and choice based. Make FP as peoples movement programme.
- FP targets should be achieved through special drives and camps. Various incentive schemes for FP should be continued.
- Focus should be laid on improving health infrastructure and meeting the need for contraception.
- More thrust on proper and timely implementation of FWPs.
- The performance of the programme should be linked with age and parity of the users. Monitoring should also be done through conducting periodical sample surveys to find out the level of acceptors, retention rate of IUD acceptors and CC users. The whole FWP should be monitored and evaluated regularly and for this basis information should be readily available and computer facilities can be utilized for this purpose. Need to have computer facilities at district headquarters which have to be used exclusively for FWP.
- Improving FW services at primary, secondary and tertiary levels.
- The existing district family welfare bureau (DFWBs) should be a nodal point to manage the FWP in specific districts. There should not have any multiplicity of programme units, hence everything related to FWP should come under the DFWBs.
- Strength in the new organization should be on promoters (motivators) rather than providers (doctors).
- The FWP should be run through out the whole year rather than concentrating on a few months.

Modernization

- Computerization
  - ➢ Latest Information Technology (IT) should be developed in the health sector. All the district CM & HO offices should be linked with internet through NIC. Similarly, all SHCs, PHCs and CHCs should be connected to the district hospitals and apex body at the state level. This will make monitoring easy by any level of functionaries and will improve accountability.
  - ➢ Information bank should be established in the state. All informations and data related to hospitals, health programmes/schemes, FWCs, government policy, insurance schemes should be kept in a format which should be user friendly and accessible to researchers and regulators.
- Establishing latest instruments and machines in hospitals.
- Developing appropriate aptitudes and skills of health personnel through training.

BOX 12.19: Tackling HIV/AIDS

- Bold and determined efforts need to be made to achieve zero-level growth of HIV/AIDS through:
  - ➢ Improved surveillance by setting up of more sentinel sites,
  - ➢ Use of primary health centres to monitor HIV/AIDS,
  - ➢ Public awareness campaigns,
  - ➢ Promotion of safe sex by using of condoms,
  - ➢ Prevention of drug abuse and
  - ➢ Distribution of disposable syringes.
- Priority should be given to cost-effective epidemic logical surveillance and vital registration system.
- Intensive efforts for high risk behaviour groups and extensive efforts for the community at large be taken up to create a good understanding of HIV/AIDS.
- NGO should be effectively engaged in supplementing government efforts, particularly for high risk groups.
- Behaviour surveillance (BH) programme should be effectively implemented by state AIDS Control Society (SACs) especially in high risk groups eg: commercial sex workers, intravenous drug users and transport workers.
- BH should include monitoring of 4 key indicators:
  - ➢ Sexual intercourse with multiple partners.
  - ➢ Use of condoms with non-regular sex partners.
  - ➢ Awareness of preventive methods of HIV.
  - ➢ Treatment of STDs.

BOX 12.20: Alleviation of Hunger and Malnutrition

- Strategy for alleviation of hunger and malnutrition to all sections of society through poverty alleviation measures eg. Integrated Child Development Scheme (ICDS), Special Nutrition Programme (SNP), Mid-day Meals Programme, Education, Research and Evaluation.
- Improving performance of ICDS programme through:
  - ➢ Full capacity utilization of Anganwari Centres (AWC) along with their proper training.
  - ➢ Ensuring timely and adequately supply of supplementary nutrients (SN) to AWCs.
  - ➢ More AWCs should be opened in Saharia area (Baran District) in view of Supreme Court Judgment treating all Saharaias as BPL
  - ➢ Alternative SN (Supplementary Nutrients) should be introduced.
  - ➢ Effectively monitoring by Panchayats.
  - ➢ Community participation and awareness should be effectively generated.
  - ➢ Health education to adolescent girls and school students.

Comprehensive and Integrated Training Programmes

- Comprehensive and integrated training programme design should be prepared striking a balance of clinical, managerial and communication skills.
- Development of revised and updated training material appropriate for the specific needs of the state. These materials should be need-based and trainee-specific.
- Government should provide adequate facilities and opportunities for all functionaries to develop their potentials in pursuing the organizational goals.
- Not only medical but para-medical staff are also to be adequately trained in institutions to suit to the needs of the community based health care services.
- Developing training policy and strategy for PRIs.

Health Insurance

- Redesign the Health Insurance Schemes
- Special health insurance scheme should be launched with very low premium without any reduction in benefits.
- Regulation of health insurance.
- Encouraging community based health insurance.

Effective Role of Public Representatives and PRIs

- MP, MLA and PRIs should put health high on their development agenda and ensure that the health delivery system become truly functional.
- Play active role in population stabilization.

Financial Support

- Central government should give top priority for timely release of funds and assistance for different health programmes with adequate quantity.
- Additional budget provision should be made for basic health care and drinking water facility.
- Medical Grant Commission (MGC) should be created to ensure the funding of the medical colleges besides creating the infrastructure.
- Generating additional funds through donors and other social and religious institutions.

Focus on Government-NGO Ties

- A cell dedicated for enhancing Government-NGO partnership in the state should be formed.
- The role of NGOs should be expanded to mobilise the community and even for take up the management of primary health centres in rural parts of the state.
- An attempt to widen the ambit for NGOs and involve them as collaborators right from the policy-framing process to executing them at the ground level to primary health care.
- To control misuse of funds, the state government should revamp the panel of NGOs.

Health Research—Thrust on

- Gender related health research.
- Reproductive health.
- Primary health care management.
- Health economics.
- Hospital waste management.
- With regard to FWP, greater emphasis would be given in optional behavioural research (OBR) with a view to popularizing the existing FW planning methods, increasing the acceptability and removing or reducing the complications or inconvenience associated with the various methods of FW.

Sanitation

- Thrust should be laid on effective implementation of Restructured Central Sponsored Rural Sanitation Programme ('RCRSP') and Total Sanitation Compagain (TSC).

Tackling Drinking Water Crises Effectively

- Stress on water conservation and augmentation.
  - ➢ Use of the technological option for cutting down transportation and distribution losses.
  - ➢ Public awareness to check wastage of water and to collect each drop of rain water.
  - ➢ New hand pumps should be installed in scarcity areas.

- Renovate traditional sources of water collection.
- Development of new water collection areas.

Additional water tankers to supply drinking water in scarcity areas.

Increase sanction limit for district collectors from existing Rs. 2.5 million to Rs. 5.0 million for tackling drinking water crises in the state.

Generating additional revenues to enable the state government to complete pending schemes and projects.

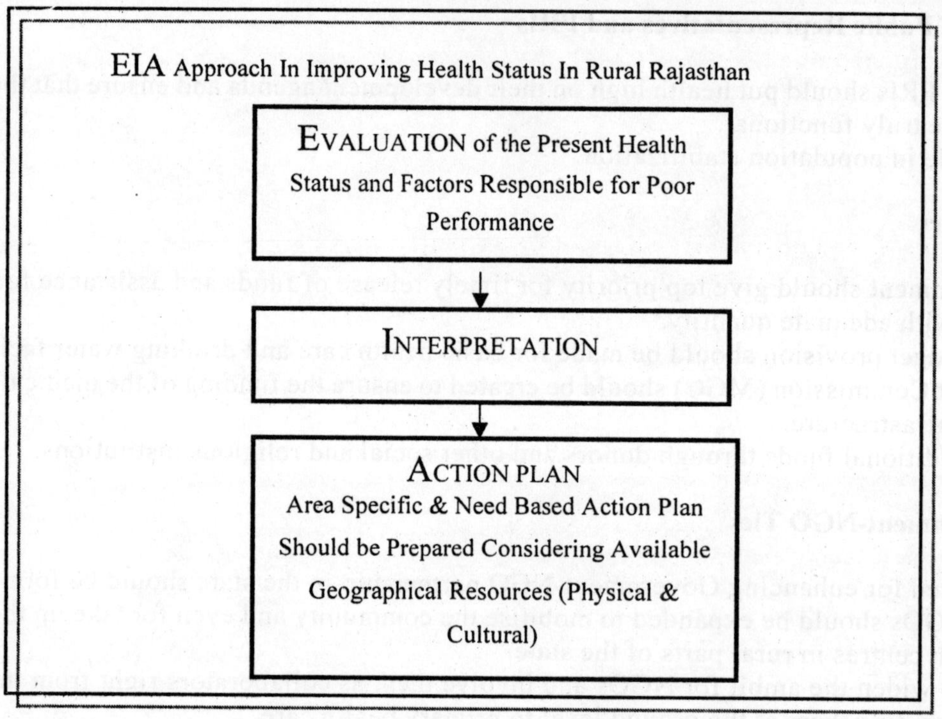

MODEL 12.1

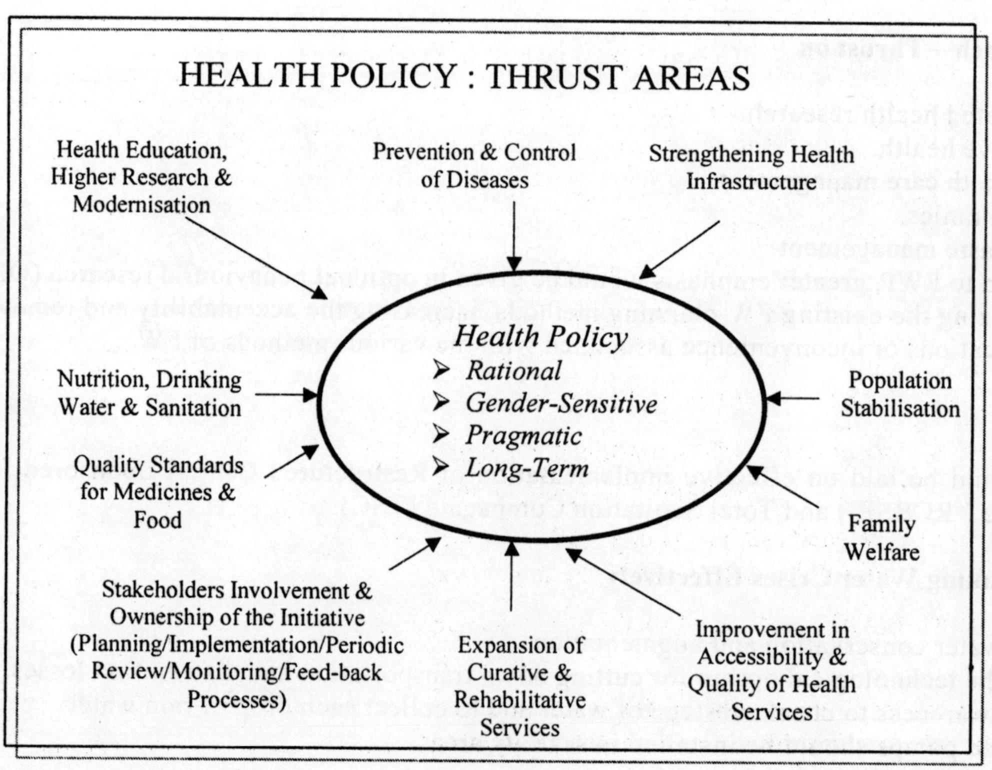

MODEL 12.2

BOX 12.21: Action Plan
Top Priority Should be given for the Improvement in Health Status of the following Bottom 50 PSs

(ascending order)

Bottom Rank	*Name of PSs, Criteria, 2001*						
	%Age of Rural Pop. Served by Medical Amenity	*%Age of Inhabited Villages Having Medical Amenity*	*Pop. Served Per Medical Institution*	*Area Served Per Medical Institution*	*Pop. Served Per Bed*	*Pop. Served Per Doctor*	*No. of PHCs*
1	Chhabra	Chhabra	Manoharthana	Sam	Sewar	Srinagar	Chhabra and
2	Manoharthana	Chaksu	Rajakhera	Jaisalmer	Srinagar	Sawai Madhopur	Manoharthana *
3	Kapasan	Kapasan	Kaman	Kolayat	Jaisalmer	Sewar	Bhainsrorgarh and
4	Baytoo	Manoharthana	Bandikui	Bap	Kishangarh	Sankra	Chechat *
5	Rajakhera	Chhipabarod	Chhabra	Sheo	Barmer	Phalodi	Bayana and
6	Chhipabarod	Chhoti Sadri	Kotkasim	Bikaner	Jhotwara	Chaksu	Chhipabarod *
7	Chhoti Sadri	Bhadesar	Nokha	Lunkaransar	Jhalrapatan	Kotra	Gangrar *
8	Sheo	Arnod	Bayana	Nokha	Phalodi	Kaman	Jhotwara *
9	Dhorimanna	Shahbad	Bari Sadri	Sankra	Chittaurgarh	Shahpura	Kapasan *
10	Chaksu	Pirawa	Nagar Pahari	Phalodi	Balotra	Jhotwara	Mandor *
11	Barmer	Kotra	Ramgarh	Chohtan	Nagaur	Sindhari	Nainwa *
12	Pirawa and	Lalsot	Kapasan	Sardarshahar	Shahpura	Nagar Pahari	Amet and
13	Jhalrapatan *	Bakani	Bikaner	Suratgarh	Sawai Madhopur	Sapotra	Bari Sadri *
14	Arnod	Jhalrapatan	Mandor	Barmer	Baran	Baseri	Chaksu *
15	Bhainsrorgarh and	Deogarh	Sikrai	Bhainsrorgarh	Bassi	Deoli	Deogarh*
16	Bakani *	Dag	Tijara	Chhabra	Mandor	Anandpuri	Karanpur *
17	Kushalgarh	Bhainsrorgarh and	Lachhmangarh	Balotra	Parbatsar	Parbatsar	Kotkasim *
18	Dag	Chittaurgarh *	Bap	Shergarh	Sardarshahar	Dhaulpur	Nadbai *
19	Deogarh	Nohar	Lalsot	Manoharthana	Umren	Bap	Sanganer *
20	Sindhari and	Uniara	Deeg	Kishanganj	Ramgarh	Amber	Shahpura *
21	Kishangarh Bas*	Begun	Bhinmal	Mandor	Anupgarh	Jhalrapatan	Abu Road and
22	Shahbad	Anupgarh	Anupgarh	Baytoo	Dhaulpur	Kishangarh	Atru *
23	Tijara	Rajakhera and	Kolayat	Dhorimanna	Khetri	Peepalkhoont	Baran *
24	Kotra	Sam *	Sewar	Dungargarh	Nagar Pahari	Hanumangarh	Bhadesar *
25	Bhadesar	Sheo	Kishangarh Bas	Anupgarh	Sikrai	Ramgarh	Dungla *
26	Dhaulpur and	Nainwa	Baran	Nohar	Bonli	Todabhim	Itawa *
27	Anupgarh *	Baytoo	Jhalrapatan	Mundwa	Pratapgarh	Asind	Nokha *
28	Kotkasim	Dhariawad	Bhadesar	Shahbad	Lalsot	Khetri	Rani Station *
29	Lalsot	Baseri	Raniwara	Sindhari	Kotputli	Barmer	Tijara *
30	Nagar Pahari	Sikrai and	Amber	Pali	Pali	Kotkasim	Bakani and
31	Keshoraipatan	Khanpur *	Hanumangarh	Osian	Karauli	Baytoo	Banera *
32	Sikrai	Pratapgarh	Bansure	Sanchore	Hanumangarh	Bonli	Bansure *
33	Begun	Kishanganj and	Kishanganj	Bhinmal	Rajakhera	Sam	Baseri *
34	Jawaja	Bari Sadri *	Sawai Madhopur	Sujangarh	Kaman	Nagaur	Chhoti Sadri *
35	Pratapgarh and	Suratgarh *	Baseri	Kapasan	Sapotra	Sardarshahar	Dag *
36	Baseri and*	Hanumangarh *	Umren	Bari Sadri	Dudu	Umren	Deeg *
37	Suratgarh	Phagi *	Chhipabarod	Nagaur	Pindwara	Mandor	Gangapur *
38	Nainwa and	Kotkasim	Chaksu	Rohat	Baseri	Talera	Jawaja *
39	Dhariawad *	Kishangarh Bas and	Nadbai	Talera	Nadbai	Bamanwas	Niwai *
40	Talera	Rajgarh *	Phalodi	Uniara	Sindhari	Rajakhera	Padampur *
41	Phagi	Keshoraipatan *	Talera	Jayal	Hindaun	Jaisalmer	Pali *
42	Chittaurgarh	Bhopalsagar *	Hindaun	Jhalrapatan	Todabhim	Dudu	Raisinghnagar *
43	Raisinghnagar	Kolayat	Shergarh	Siwana	Kathumar	Sambhar	Rajgarh *
44	Amet	Anta	Govindgarh	Deogarh	Rupbas	Sadulshahar	Rashmi *
45	Kishanganj	Gangrar	Dhaulpur	Rajgarh	Baytoo	Ghatol	Sheo *
46	Bap	Barmer	Bakani	Chhoti Sadri	Sambhar	Kotputli	Ahore
47	Baran	Talera and	Nimrana	Phagi	Thanagazi	Pindwara	Alsisar *
48	Bari Sadri	Itawa *	Chohtan	Balesar	Hindoli	Balotra	Bap *
49	Nohar and	Amet	Chhoti Sadri	Chhipabarod	Bandikui	Phagi	Hurda *
50	Bayana, Kaman* and Rajgarh *	Tijara	Mahwa	Ladpura	Talera	Nadbai	Jhunjhunun * and 14 PSs **

Note: * PS having same rank as the preceding PS.
** Kaman, Khandar, Khanpur, Kishanganj, Nadoti, Phagi, Rajakhera, Rajsamand, Ramgarh, Raniwara, Sardarshahar, Umren, Uniara and Viratnagar PSs.

BOX 12.21: Action Plan

Top Priority Should be given for the Improvement in Health Status of the following Bottom 50 PSs

(ascending order)

Bottom Rank	Name of PSs, Criteria, 2001					
	No. of SHCs	*Sex Ratio (0-6)*	*FLR*	*%Age of Rural Pop. Served by Drinking Water Amenity*	*%Age of Rural Pop. Served by Education Amenity*	*HSI*
1	Kotkasim	Sadulshahar	Kotra	Sardarshahar	Anupgarh	Sam
2	Bari Sadri and	Ganganagar	Peepalkhoont	Bap	Suratgarh	Barmer
3	Kapasan *	Karanpur	Kushalgarh	Jaisalmer	Hanumangarh	Sheo
4	Arnod and	Sam	Dhariawad	Jayal	Bakani	Baytoo
5	Chhabra *	Buhana	Shergarh	Kolayat	Nohar	Kotra
6	Weir *	Padampur	Bhinmal	Nohar	Bhainsrorgarh	Manoharthana
7	Chhoti Sadri	Behror	Balesar	Bikaner	Begun	Suratgarh
8	Jhotwara and	Todabhim and	Khandar	Churu	Bap	Chhabra
9	Nimrana *	Nimrana *	Jaswantpura	Lunkaransar	Barmer	Sankra
10	Anta and	Bari *	Sajjangarh	Barmer	Baytoo	Bakani
11	Sewar *	Surajgarh *	Bhinay	Makrana	Raisinghnagar	Jaisalmer
12	Behror and	Sheo	Ghatol	Nagaur	Khanpur	Bap
13	Bhadesar *	Raisinghnagar	Tonk	Suratgarh	Manoharthana	Anupgarh
14	Bhainsrorgarh *	Chirawa	Mandor	Sadulshahar	Kotra	Sindhari
15	Bhopalsagar *	Hindaun	Kotri	Sheo	Ganganagar and	Kushalgarh and
16	Chhipabarod *	Rupbas	Uniara	Balotra	Bhadra *	Chaksu *
17	Itawa *	Bayana	Asind	Taranagar	Chaksu	Baseri
18	Mahwa *	Mandawar and	Sayla	Sindhari	Chhabra and	Chhipabarod
19	Nadoti *	Jhunjhunun *	Bhopalgarh	Sam	Padampur *	Peepalkhoont
20	Rajakhera *	Kotkasim	Deoli	Anupgarh	Bari Sadri and	Dag
21	Bandikui and	Hanumangarh and	Bakani	Sankra	Sadulshahar *	Kolayat
22	Bansure *	Nawalgarh *	Sam	Rajgarh	Chhipabarod and	Nohar and
23	Baran *	Rajakhera and	Anandpuri	Chohtan	Uniara *	Rajakhera *
24	Deogarh *	Baseri *	Bagidora	Bhinmal	Kishanganj	Shahbad
25	Kathumar *	Dhond	Raipur	Bhadra	Arnod	Bhainsrorgarh
26	Rajgarh *	Kotputli	Mundwa	Sanchore	Pratapgarh and	Bari
27	Chaksu and	Lachhmangarh	Shahpura	Alsisar	Bhindar *	Chohtan
28	Kaman *	Mahwa and	Mandal	Degana	Balesar	Arnod
29	Malpura *	Dhaulpur *	Kolayat and	Dungargarh	Sam	Bikaner
30	Manoharthana *	Piprali	Rashmi *	Shergarh	Jahazpur and	Dhaulpur
31	Todaraisingh *	Nadoti and	Simalwara *	Surajgarh	Mandalgarh *	Jhalrapatan
32	Uniara *	Sirohi *	Bap	Sujangarh	Shergarh *	Dhorimanna
33	Bargaon and	Khetri *	Sawai Madhopur	Kuchaman	Chhoti Sadri	Uniara
34	Kishanganj *	Bhadra *	Bari Sadri	Dhorimanna	Bhadesar and	Kapasan
35	Mandor *	Fatehpur	Kapasan	Baytoo	Bari *	Sajjangarh
36	Ramgarh *	Alsisar and	Kekri	Kotra	Jhalrapatan	Shergarh
37	Shahbad *	Karauli *	Mandalgarh	Raisinghnagar	Rajgarh and	Lalsot
38	Sikrai *	Kumher and	Sanchore	Ratangarh and	Sheo *	Khandar
39	Tijara *	Weir *	Thanagazi and	Mandor *	Shahbad and	Bayana
40	Baseri and	Deeg	Kaman *	Bamanwas	Bikaner *	Nainwa
41	Dhaulpur *	Jaisalmer	Suwana and	Kaman and	Lunkaransar *	Chhoti Sadri
42	Jhalrapatan *	Rajgarh	Abu Road *	Buhana *	Sanganer *	Keshoraipatan
43	Kishangarh Bas *	Gangapur and	Sahara	Didwana	Tijara and	Kaman
44	Kotputli *	Nadbai *	Talwara	Pali	Mahwa *	Sapotra
45	Nagar Pahari *	Sikrai *	Malpura	Riyan	Karanpur *	Pirawa
46	Phagi *	Anupgarh *	Jaitaran	Padampur	Lalsot	Anandpuri
47	Abu Road and	Danta Ramgarh	Jalor	Sumerpur	Dag and	Sardarshahar
48	Bamanwas *	Khandar and	Osian and	Jhotwara	Itawa *	Pratapgarh
49	Bayana *	Sankra *	Phalodi *	Luni	Deogarh	Tijara
50	Chechat* and 8 PSs #	Nagar Pahari *	Dungarpur	Jhunjhunun and Karanpur	Kherwara, Deogarh and Chittaurgarh	Begun

Note: * PS having same rank as the preceding PS.

\# Gangapur, Gangrar, Hindaun, Mandawar, Nimbahera, Pirawa, Rashmi and Reni PSs

Source: 1. Annex- 9.1, 9.2, 9.6, 9.7, 9.10 and 9.11.

2. Annex 11.2.

3. Annex 112.6, 12.8 to 12.11 and 12.13.

ANNEXURES

GENERAL ANNEX-I

PANCHAYAT SAMITI-WISE AREA, INHABITED VILLAGES AND POPULATION CHARACTERISTICS: RAJASTHAN (1991)

P. Code	Panchayat Samiti (Concerning Tehsil)	Total Rural Area (in sq. km)	Total No. of Inhabited Villages	Total Rural population: Persons	Total Rural population: Male	Total Rural population: Female No.	Total Rural population: Female %	Density Per sq. km	Sex Ratio (per Thousand and Pop.)	Literacy Rate %: Persons	Literacy Rate %: Male	Literacy Rate %: Female
1	2	3	4	5	6	7	8	9	10	11	12	13
1	ARAIN (Sarwar)	1201.80	122	109697	56513	53184	48.5	91	941	29.11	45.52	11.69
2	BHINAY (Bhinay)	1216.10	120	125267	64675	60592	48.4	103	937	32.67	50.89	13.27
3	JAWAJA* (Beawar)	662.00	193	120052	60437	59615	49.7	181	986	39.37	66.95	12.26
4	KEKRI* (Kekri)	993.40	94	115023	59192	55831	48.5	116	943	40.52	59.94	19.92
5	KISHANGARH (Kishangarh)	1106.90	110	122109	63837	58272	47.7	110	913	30.83	47.35	12.73
6	MASOODA* (Masooda)	875.10	137	127381	66365	61016	47.9	146	919	35.22	56.50	12.08
7	PISANGAN (Pisangan)	1203.50	114	173720	90279	83441	48.0	144	924	38.38	59.00	16.22
8	SRINAGAR (Ajmer)	897.70	95	132383	68796	63587	48.0	147	924	33.41	52.53	12.78
	AJMER DISTRICT	**8156.50**	**985**	**1025632**	**530094**	**495538**	**48.3**	**126**	**935**	**35.10**	**54.97**	**13.96**
9	BANSURE* (Bansure)	664.40	131	163582	86949	76633	46.8	246	881	33.66	51.94	12.73
10	BEHROR (Behror)	336.60	90	115045	59515	55530	48.3	342	933	51.65	73.33	28.57
11	KATHUMAR (Kathumar)	565.00	158	169565	92297	77268	45.6	300	837	35.58	55.48	11.44
12	KISHANGARH BAS (Kishangarh Bas)	505.40	135	136088	71565	64523	47.4	269	902	38.22	55.47	18.94
13	KOTKASIM* (Kotkasim)	344.40	115	95361	50302	45059	47.3	277	896	49.01	69.28	26.32
14	LACHHMANGARH (Lachmangarh)	618.90	184	176309	93697	82612	46.9	285	882	33.82	52.71	12.17
15	MANDAWAR* (Mandawar)	577.30	142	162010	84527	77483	47.8	281	917	48.19	69.17	25.29
16	NIMRANA (Behror)	378.30	85	120331	61905	58426	48.6	318	944	53.72	74.52	31.95
17	RAJGARH (Rajgarh)	1009.20	136	112540	59807	52733	46.9	112	882	35.15	55.08	12.21
18	RAMGARH (Ramgarh)	617.00	171	161672	86058	75614	46.8	262	879	33.90	50.73	14.38
19	RENI (Rajgarh)	392.00	102	105755	56388	49367	46.7	270	875	34.19	54.05	11.20
20	THANAGAZI* (Thanagazi)	1060.30	148	144119	76286	67833	47.1	136	889	28.09	44.79	8.93
21	TIJARA* (Tijara)	643.50	199	151193	80149	71044	47.0	235	886	33.41	50.17	14.27
22	UMREN (Alwar)	848.30	150	162723	87156	75567	46.4	192	867	32.40	49.93	11.92
	ALWAR	**8560.60**	**1946**	**1976293**	**1046601**	**929692**	**47.0**	**231**	**888**	**38.02**	**56.76**	**16.73**
23	ANANDPURI (Bagidora)	341.80	123	84905	43249	41656	49.1	248	963	21.16	34.56	7.08
24	BAGIDORA (Bagidora)	515.60	137	137270	69642	67628	49.3	266	971	23.93	36.80	10.60
25	GARHI* (Garhi)	704.10	163	188399	95494	92905	49.3	268	973	31.92	47.38	16.14
26	GHATOL (Ghatol)	783.30	218	175991	88626	87365	49.6	225	986	21.47	34.73	8.10
27	KUSHALGARH (Kushalgarh)	640.90	208	101900	51818	50082	49.1	159	966	12.56	20.85	3.91
28	PEEPALKHOONT (Banswara)	912.80	186	110617	56255	54362	49.1	121	966	11.23	19.17	2.95
29	SAJJANGARH (Kushalgarh)	402.50	182	103172	52713	50459	48.9	256	957	17.44	27.77	6.61
30	TALWARA (Banswara)	750.40	214	164157	82571	81586	49.7	219	988	21.94	34.89	8.87
	BANSWARA	**5051.40**	**1431**	**1066411**	**540368**	**526043**	**49.3**	**211**	**973**	**21.46**	**33.70**	**8.87**
31	ANTA (Mangrol & Anta)	932.20	147	123431	64669	58762	47.6	132	909	39.47	60.03	16.80
32	ATRU* (Atru)	859.50	135	107431	56737	50694	47.2	125	893	38.37	58.33	15.78
33	BARAN* (Baran)	612.60	98	80869	42465	38404	47.5	132	904	39.04	60.17	15.68
34	CHHABRA* (Chhabra)	783.70	172	102555	43316	38276	46.9	131	884	24.62	40.62	6.36
35	CHHIPABAROD* (Chhipabarod)	824.40	183	81592	53842	48713	47.5	99	905	25.99	42.87	7.12
36	KISHANGANJ* (Kishanganj)	1450.60	176	108345	56975	51370	47.4	75	902	25.63	38.63	11.10
37	SHAHBAD* (Shahbad)	1468.20	159	83028	44244	38784	46.7	57	877	27.84	42.41	10.92
	BARAN #	**6931.20**	**1070**	**687251**	**362248**	**325003**	**47.3**	**99**	**897**	**31.93**	**49.45**	**12.25**
38	BALOTRA* (Panchpadra)	3885.10	189	192132	100111	92021	47.9	49	919	23.31	38.30	6.93
39	BARMER (Ramsar)	3813.30	265	171158	92170	78988	46.1	45	857	19.38	32.98	3.42
40	BAYTOO (Baytoo)	3228.00	248	151787	79062	72725	47.9	47	920	20.22	34.57	4.70
41	CHOHTAN (Chohtan)	3266.50	167	171105	91349	79756	46.6	52	873	12.38	21.16	2.23
42	DHORIMANNA (Gudha Malani)	2668.30	252	181025	94679	86346	47.7	68	912	16.76	29.18	3.04
43	SHEO* (Sheo)	6616.40	167	121551	66572	54979	45.2	18	826	19.34	32.56	3.32
44	SINDHARI (Gudha Malani)	3115.70	240	167810	87661	80149	47.8	54	914	17.07	30.05	2.89
45	SIWANA* (Siwana)	1982.20	97	134488	69393	65095	48.4	68	938	22.59	37.31	7.06
	BARMER	**28575.50**	**1625**	**1291056**	**680997**	**610059**	**47.3**	**45**	**896**	**18.79**	**31.83**	**4.20**

P. Code	Panchayat Samiti (Concerning Tehsil)	Total Rural Area (in sq. km)	Total No. of Inhabited Villages	Total Rural population				Density Per sq. km	Sex Ratio (per Thousand Pop.)	Literacy Rate %		
				Persons	Male	Female No.	Female %			Persons	Male	Female
1	2	3	4	5	6	7	8	9	10	11	12	13
46	BAYANA* (Bayana)	799.70	159	151810	84944	66866	44.0	190	787	34.98	54.48	9.71
47	DEEG* (Deeg)	490.40	120	125627	69105	56522	45.0	256	818	37.46	57.83	12.00
48	KAMAN (Kaman)	556.50	187	154287	82777	71510	46.3	277	864	24.27	39.80	6.06
49	KUMHER* (Kumher)	440.20	111	129059	70678	58381	45.2	293	826	45.21	68.60	16.38
50	NADBAI* (Nadbai)	431.80	114	127668	70162	57506	45.0	296	820	43.44	67.13	14.21
51	NAGAR PAHARI (Nagar)	621.80	217	181672	98229	83443	45.9	292	849	30.75	48.33	9.75
52	RUPBAS* (Rupbas)	539.00	141	166569	91623	74946	45.0	309	818	43.38	64.65	16.96
53	SEWAR* (Bharatpur)	458.10	154	133563	73266	60297	45.1	292	823	42.56	65.26	14.38
54	WEIR* (Weir)	576.10	142	160526	87988	72538	45.2	279	824	41.10	63.19	13.85
	BHARATPUR	**4913.60**	**1345**	**1330781**	**728772**	**602009**	**45.2**	**271**	**826**	**37.84**	**58.43**	**12.48**
55	ASIND* (Asind)	1110.20	203	156028	78451	77577	49.7	141	989	24.38	40.33	8.41
56	BANERA* (Banera)	676.50	82	88063	45076	42987	48.8	130	954	25.69	40.39	10.15
57	HURDA* (Hurda)	617.30	68	72959	37811	35148	48.2	118	930	34.28	48.87	18.51
58	JAHAZPUR* (Jahazpur)	1033.30	181	132876	69362	63514	47.8	129	916	25.83	41.25	8.83
59	KOTRI* (Kotri)	950.10	146	121812	63084	58728	48.2	128	931	23.60	33.19	13.21
60	MANDAL* (Mandal)	1155.20	158	146986	73635	73351	49.9	127	996	23.39	37.76	9.05
61	MANDALGARH (Mandalgarh)	1392.40	270	156392	82265	74127	47.4	112	901	22.12	33.80	8.99
62	RAIPUR* (Raipur)	515.40	86	71377	35377	36000	50.4	138	1018	24.89	40.45	9.79
63	SAHARA* (Sahara)	633.20	91	85124	41743	43381	51.0	134	1039	24.97	40.65	10.14
64	SHAHPURA* (Sahahpura)	1127.30	149	120640	62144	58496	48.5	107	941	21.15	33.74	7.73
65	SUWANA* (Bhilwara)	832.30	131	129727	66211	63516	49.0	156	959	24.22	38.54	9.30
	BHILWARA	**10043.20**	**1565**	**1281984**	**655159**	**626825**	**48.9**	**128**	**957**	**24.48**	**38.36**	**9.96**
66	BIKANER (Bikaner)	8944.70	155	232046	124026	108020	46.6	26	871	25.46	38.75	10.03
67	DUNGARGARH* (Dungargarh) #	3002.80	90	133598	69106	64492	48.3	44	933	22.90	36.82	8.03
68	KOLAYAT* (Kolayat)	7318.60	169	132657	70699	61958	46.7	18	876	22.80	35.05	8.66
69	LUNKARANSAR (Lunkaransar)	6214.00	130	156382	82141	74241	47.5	25	904	24.93	38.04	10.30
70	NOKHA* (Nokha)	3767.70	126	208913	108483	100430	48.1	55	926	22.69	37.60	6.59
	BIKANER ##	**29247.80**	**580**	**729998**	**385349**	**344649**	**47.2**	**25**	**894**	**24.07**	**37.59**	**8.84**
71	HINDOLI* (Hindoli)	1339.00	174	151669	80188	71481	47.1	113	891	22.16	34.77	7.86
72	KESHORAIPATAN (Indragarh)	1287.20	216	149166	78619	70547	47.3	116	897	30.93	48.76	10.94
73	NAINWA* (Nainwa)	1140.00	175	121652	64536	57116	47.0	107	885	23.57	37.55	7.67
74	TALERA* (Bundi)	1882.60	261	214017	113956	100061	46.8	114	878	26.74	40.95	10.40
	BUNDI	**5648.80**	**826**	**636504**	**337299**	**299205**	**47.0**	**113**	**887**	**26.02**	**40.65**	**9.39**
75	ARNOD* (Arnod)	701.50	171	91408	46438	44970	49.2	130	968	27.32	41.36	12.77
76	BARI SADRI* (Bari Sadri)	474.50	144	76910	38859	38051	49.5	162	979	26.99	44.32	9.48
77	BEGUN (Begun)	957.50	219	85822	44048	41774	48.7	90	948	27.05	44.40	8.63
78	BHADESAR* (Bhadesar)	540.50	161	89539	45817	43722	48.8	166	954	26.33	42.22	9.78
79	BHAINSRORGARH (Rawatbhata)	1369.80	150	63941	33825	30116	47.1	47	890	25.05	38.95	9.27
80	BHOPALSAGAR (Kapasan)	398.20	83	64086	32533	31553	49.2	161	970	29.43	46.66	11.83
81	CHHOTI SADRI * (Chhoti Sadri)	691.90	141	84902	43383	41519	48.9	123	957	31.63	50.39	12.03
82	CHITTAURGARH* (Chittaurgarh)	814.00	218	135718	69237	66481	49.0	167	960	28.09	44.43	11.15
83	DUNGLA* (Dungla)	493.60	102	77050	38964	38086	49.4	156	977	27.36	44.65	9.84
84	GANGRAR* (Gangrar)	555.60	127	75031	38738	36293	48.4	135	937	25.99	40.88	9.99
85	KAPASAN (Kapasan)	482.60	107	72870	36814	36056	49.5	151	979	23.17	38.96	7.06
86	NIMBAHERA* (Nimbahera)	812.70	150	110286	56298	53988	49.0	136	959	33.56	54.03	12.20
87	PRATAPGARH* (Pratapgarh)	1427.90	320	159206	81501	77705	48.8	111	953	27.25	42.82	10.90
88	RASHMI* (Rashmi)	449.70	79	65794	32854	32940	50.1	146	1003	27.40	44.08	10.98
	CHITTAURGARH	**10170.00**	**2172**	**1252563**	**639309**	**613254**	**49.0**	**123**	**959**	**27.80**	**44.37**	**10.55**
89	CHURU* (Churu)	1559.60	101	123292	62987	60305	48.9	79	957	30.01	48.98	10.63
90	RAJGARH* (Rajgarh)	2197.30	205	221371	113925	107446	48.5	101	943	34.23	53.66	13.74
91	RATANGARH* (Ratangarh)	1642.30	96	125447	64764	60683	48.4	76	937	26.54	43.37	8.85
92	SARDARSHAHAR* (Sardarshahar)	3814.40	170	174959	90422	84537	48.3	46	935	22.38	37.70	6.13
93	SUJANGARH* (Sujangarh)	2596.00	153	194402	100128	94274	48.5	75	942	23.38	38.42	7.52
94	TARANAGAR* (Taranagar)	1782.90	111	124103	63704	60399	48.7	70	948	26.96	44.05	9.04
	CHURU ###	**13592.50**	**926**	**1097172**	**565036**	**532136**	**48.5**	**81**	**942**	**26.89**	**43.60**	**9.31**
95	BANDIKUI* (Baswa)	600.80	207	186479	98697	87782	47.1	310	889	37.27	58.72	12.89
96	DAUSA* (Dausa)	907.90	221	207958	110174	97784	47.0	229	888	33.42	54.21	9.78
97	LALSOT* (Lalsot)	854.00	293	187439	98885	88554	47.2	219	896	29.82	47.84	9.42
98	MAHWA* (Mahwa)	473.50	150	146684	79109	67575	46.1	310	854	39.26	60.73	13.92
99	SIKRAI* (Sikrai)	502.70	138	160624	84813	75811	47.2	320	894	30.67	49.82	9.05
	DAUSA #	**3338.90**	**1009**	**889184**	**471678**	**417506**	**47.0**	**266**	**885**	**33.96**	**54.15**	**10.90**
100	BARI* (Bari)	794.00	126	117351	66556	50795	43.3	148	763	26.24	40.73	6.68
101	BASERI* (Baseri)	1001.40	122	151187	84489	66698	44.1	151	789	31.56	46.56	11.99
102	DHAULPUR (Sepau)	577.30	156	201089	111852	89237	44.4	348	798	33.84	51.18	11.53
103	RAJAKHERA (Rajakhera)	572.00	147	151027	84595	66432	44.0	264	785	30.46	47.47	8.02
	DHAULPUR	**2944.70**	**551**	**620654**	**347492**	**273162**	**44.0**	**211**	**786**	**31.01**	**47.13**	**9.89**

P. Code	Panchayat Samiti (Concerning Tehsil)	Total Rural Area (in sq. km)	Total No. of Inhabited Villages	Total Rural population				Density Per sq. km	Sex Ratio (per Thousand and Pop.)	Literacy Rate %		
				Persons	Male	Female No.	Female %			Persons	Male	Female
1	2	3	4	5	6	7	8	9	10	11	12	13
104	ASPUR* (Aspur)	691.70	142	146507	71377	75130	51.3	212	1053	27.27	42.65	12.88
105	BICHHIWARA (Dungarpur)	745.90	174	180805	91481	89324	49.4	242	976	25.05	40.11	9.65
106	DUNGARPUR (Dungarpur)	575.10	158	133212	65893	67319	50.5	232	1022	26.54	43.35	10.29
107	SAGWARA (Sagwara)	611.80	153	160585	79459	81126	50.5	262	1021	32.98	49.94	16.57
108	SIMALWARA (Simalwara)	913.60	219	189623	96478	93145	49.1	208	965	23.87	36.87	10.32
	DUNGARPUR	**3538.10**	**846**	**810732**	**404688**	**406044**	**50.1**	**229**	**1003**	**27.01**	**42.26**	**11.92**
109	ANUPGARH (Garsana)	3543.70	1065	294097	157267	136830	46.5	83	870	32.05	44.63	17.46
110	GANGANAGAR (Ganganagar)	854.90	241	162395	87416	74979	46.2	190	858	44.63	58.33	28.49
111	KARANPUR* (Karanpur)	810.50	200	92181	48390	43791	47.5	114	905	40.12	51.29	27.83
112	PADAMPUR* (Padampur)	842.50	236	105870	55562	50308	47.5	126	905	42.88	56.17	28.31
113	RAISINGHNAGAR* (Raisinghnagar)	1315.40	353	128836	67266	61570	47.8	98	915	38.12	51.74	23.31
114	SADULSHAHAR (Sadulshahar)	1484.50	377	208380	111888	96492	46.3	140	862	39.65	54.05	22.83
115	SURATGARH* (Suratgarh)	3791.50	680	274376	148174	126202	46.0	72	852	33.55	48.03	16.32
	GANGANAGAR	**12643.00**	**3152**	**1266135**	**675963**	**590172**	**46.6**	**100**	**873**	**37.40**	**50.89**	**21.86**
116	BHADRA* (Bhadra)	1713.10	190	180760	94908	85852	47.5	106	905	37.37	56.07	16.76
117	HANUMANGARH (Hanumangarh)	2035.00	621	333914	176677	157237	47.1	164	890	33.33	46.42	18.58
118	NOHAR (Rawatsar)	4304.90	475	289856	151940	137916	47.6	67	908	30.25	46.86	12.06
	HANUMANGARH ##	**8053.00**	**1286**	**804530**	**423525**	**381005**	**47.4**	**100**	**900**	**33.14**	**48.75**	**15.81**
119	AMBER* (Amber)	839.40	194	205355	107576	97779	47.6	245	909	35.39	57.15	11.14
120	BASSI* (Bassi)	630.90	209	159749	83949	75800	47.4	253	903	33.47	54.76	9.72
121	CHAKSU* (Chaksu)	766.80	258	125703	65878	59825	47.6	164	908	29.14	48.24	7.99
122	DUDU (Dudu)	1855.20	210	210655	110037	100618	47.8	114	914	32.67	50.90	12.58
123	GOVINDGARH* (Chomu)	666.00	95	210430	109896	100534	47.8	316	915	40.89	63.88	15.66
124	JAMWA RAMGARH* (Jamwa Ramgarh)	1011.50	231	190822	100252	90570	47.5	189	903	31.75	51.86	9.24
125	JHOTWARA* (Jaipur)	385.00	102	103076	54701	48375	46.9	268	884	39.23	59.78	15.60
126	KOTPUTLI (Kotputli)	663.30	119	177608	92951	84657	47.7	268	911	36.09	56.35	13.91
127	PHAGI* (Phagi)	1113.30	168	130453	68466	61987	47.5	117	905	29.46	46.06	10.94
128	SAMBHAR (Phulara)	832.40	143	162221	84051	78170	48.2	195	930	36.39	58.39	12.62
129	SANGANER* (Sanganer)	583.90	205	153893	81279	72614	47.2	264	893	38.46	59.44	14.63
130	SHAHPURA (Shahpura)	408.00	79	128177	67148	61029	47.6	314	909	37.92	59.56	13.89
131	VIRATNAGAR (Viratnagar)	649.10	118	155270	81683	73587	47.4	239	901	34.36	53.91	12.45
	JAIPUR	**10404.80**	**2131**	**2113412**	**1107867**	**1005545**	**47.6**	**203**	**908**	**35.05**	**55.52**	**12.32**
132	JAISALMER (Jaisalmer)	12849.50	137	80310	45121	35189	43.8	6	780	26.86	42.53	6.38
133	SAM (Jaisalmer)	21111.00	251	94930	52919	42011	44.3	4	794	21.21	35.15	3.48
134	SANKRA (Pokaran)	5486.60	130	115677	62258	53419	46.2	21	858	22.02	36.88	4.58
	JAISALMER	**39447.10**	**518**	**290917**	**160298**	**130619**	**44.9**	**7**	**815**	**23.10**	**37.92**	**4.71**
135	AHORE (Ahore)	1596.50	108	150191	75636	74555	49.6	94	986	28.44	46.36	10.89
136	BHINMAL (Bagora)	1337.70	79	146196	75699	70497	48.2	109	931	17.50	30.92	3.20
137	JALOR (Jalor)	1054.80	66	107936	54808	53128	49.2	102	969	26.03	42.43	9.38
138	JASWANTPURA (Bhinmal)	1068.80	72	106325	54181	52144	49.0	99	962	20.73	35.53	5.49
139	RANIWARA* (Raniwara)	984.00	83	123125	64108	59017	47.9	125	921	20.23	34.38	4.82
140	SANCHORE* (Sanchore)	3008.50	180	260312	135290	125022	48.0	87	924	19.17	34.17	2.99
141	SAYLA (Sayla)	1459.40	77	165270	84509	80761	48.9	113	956	19.79	32.72	6.36
	JALOR	**10509.70**	**665**	**1059355**	**544231**	**515124**	**48.6**	**101**	**947**	**21.36**	**36.20**	**5.85**
142	BAKANI (Jhalrapatan)	885.50	282	129817	67593	62224	47.9	147	921	23.37	36.64	8.79
143	DAG (Gangdhar)	1130.50	220	138701	71529	67172	48.4	123	939	21.07	32.82	8.43
144	JHALRAPATAN (Jhalrapatan)	1329.20	282	162994	84932	78062	47.9	123	919	29.35	46.88	10.25
145	KHANPUR* (Khanpur)	940.10	190	118513	62502	56011	47.3	126	896	38.97	60.50	14.91
146	MANOHARTHANA (Manoharthana)	922.70	274	126037	65774	60263	47.8	137	916	15.92	27.47	3.18
147	PIRAWA* (Pirwa)	1001.10	200	129946	67323	62623	48.2	130	930	29.63	47.51	10.29
	JHALAWAR	**6209.10**	**1448**	**806008**	**419653**	**386355**	**47.9**	**130**	**921**	**26.32**	**41.89**	**9.29**
148	ALSISAR (Jhunjhunun)	747.00	113	112705	56906	55799	49.5	151	981	43.12	64.58	21.57
149	BUHANA* (Buhana)	653.50	122	172845	89282	83563	48.3	264	936	48.66	70.82	25.30
150	CHIRAWA (Chirawa)	489.00	82	124621	63972	60649	48.7	255	948	45.37	66.63	23.33
151	JHUNJHUNUN (Jhunjhunun)	820.50	156	157320	80014	77306	49.1	192	966	48.20	70.89	25.25
152	KHETRI* (Khetri)	796.20	80	179811	94715	85096	47.3	226	898	42.00	62.62	18.90
153	NAWALGARH* (Nawalgarh)	665.20	70	181313	92535	88778	49.0	273	959	45.31	68.13	21.94
154	SURAJGARH (Chirawa)	781.40	120	141222	73678	67544	47.8	181	917	43.34	63.31	21.70
155	UDAIPURWATI* (Udaipurwati)	831.00	81	187540	96238	91302	48.7	226	949	41.25	62.73	18.91
	JHUNJHUNUN	**5783.80**	**824**	**1257377**	**647340**	**610037**	**48.5**	**217**	**942**	**44.65**	**66.23**	**22.04**
156	BALESAR (Shergarh)	1854.10	68	127529	66288	61241	43.6	69	924	24.98	39.76	4.92
157	BAP (Phalodi)	4431.20	93	103647	54995	48652	46 9	23	885	20.30	33.52	5.25
158	BHOPALGARH (Bhopalgarh)	1743.30	84	156516	81088	75428	48.2	90	930	28.40	48.61	6.97
159	BILARA* (Bilara)	1499.40	79	141630	73774	67856	47.9	94	920	30.93	51.44	8.77
160	LUNI (Luni)	1982.50	128	166729	86946	79783	47.9	84	918	30.34	49.53	9.37
161	MANDOR (Jodhpur)	1269.20	105	111928	58734	53194	47.5	88	906	29.99	50.30	7.52

P. Code	Panchayat Samiti (Concerning Tehsil)	Total Rural Area (in sq. km)	Total No. of Inhabited Villages	Total Rural population				Density Per sq. km	Sex Ratio (per Thousand and Pop.)	Literacy Rate %		
				Persons	Male	Female No.	Female %			Persons	Male	Female
1	2	3	4	5	6	7	8	9	10	11	12	13
162	OSIAN (Osian)	4184.50	167	306437	160069	146368	47.8	73	914	24.87	42.14	5.92
163	PHALODI (Phalodi)	3237.90	86	161438	84239	77199	47.8	50	916	23.61	39.79	5.78
164	SHERGARH (Shergarh)	1975.00	50	113079	59679	53400	47.2	57	895	21.74	37.30	4.28
	JODHPUR	**22177.10**	**860**	**1388933**	**725812**	**663121**	**47.4**	**63**	**914**	**26.24**	**43.82**	**6.62**
165	HINDAUN* (Hindaun)	631.50	119	196305	107094	89211	45.4	311	833	35.41	56.62	9.75
166	KARAULI* (Karauli)	1219.70	196	166459	91581	74878	45.0	136	818	25.36	40.08	6.99
167	NADOTI* (Nadoti)	646.00	84	101680	54560	47120	46.3	157	864	35.43	56.58	10.97
168	SAPOTRA (Sapotra)	1962.00	209	182378	99753	82625	45.3	93	828	27.47	41.78	9.74
169	TODABHIM* (Todabhim)	522.50	142	154373	83775	70598	45.7	295	843	35.31	57.58	8.86
	KARAULI ###	**4981.70**	**750**	**801195**	**436763**	**364432**	**45.5**	**161**	**834**	**31.51**	**49.92**	**9.17**
170	CHECHAT* (Ranganjmandi)	770.90	146	120614	64065	56549	46.9	156	883	37.45	56.01	16.30
171	ITAWA* (Pipalda)	887.10	161	127120	67286	59834	47.1	143	889	34.91	53.67	13.78
172	LADPURA* (Ladpura)	1307.50	146	109602	57801	51801	47.3	84	896	37.40	55.71	16.79
173	SANGOD* (Sangod)	1046.20	198	122585	64303	58282	47.5	117	906	40.50	61.41	17.18
174	SULTANPUR* (Digod)	911.80	160	123824	65430	58394	47.2	136	892	41.22	61.77	18.01
	KOTA	**4923.50**	**811**	**603745**	**318885**	**284860**	**47.2**	**123**	**893**	**38.30**	**57.74**	**16.39**
175	DEGANA (Degana)	1457.50	146	154314	78707	75607	49.0	106	961	27.84	45.77	9.40
176	DIDWANA* (Didwana)	1608.10	167	224202	113117	111085	49.5	139	982	30.89	50.91	10.87
177	JAYAL* (Jayal)	2088.20	132	176728	90450	86278	48.8	85	954	24.03	40.22	7.25
178	KUCHAMAN* (Nawa)	1436.10	146	205068	105502	99566	48.6	143	944	30.72	49.19	11.25
179	LADNU* (Ladnu)	1371.20	96	123172	62293	60879	49.4	90	977	32.01	51.52	12.41
180	MAKRANA* (Makrana)	1106.20	120	156267	79940	76327	48.8	141	955	30.79	48.92	11.96
181	MERTA (Merta)	1397.10	96	142563	74295	68268	47.9	102	919	31.24	49.66	11.16
182	MUNDWA (Nagaur)	2184.30	110	152729	79149	73580	48.2	70	930	23.41	39.46	6.30
183	NAGAUR (Nagaur)	2380.60	133	181365	93742	87623	48.3	76	935	24.93	41.73	7.07
184	PARBATSAR* (Parbatsar)	1070.90	108	142838	73565	69273	48.5	133	942	26.32	41.30	10.51
185	RIYAN (Merta)	1239.40	120	142928	73687	69241	48.4	115	940	27.25	44.00	9.50
	NAGAUR	**17339.60**	**1374**	**1802174**	**924447**	**877727**	**48.7**	**104**	**949**	**28.14**	**45.76**	**9.75**
186	BALI* (Bali)	1369.80	89	149232	75114	74118	49.7	109	987	30.57	45.91	15.35
187	DESURI (Desuri)	829.10	76	85369	42543	42826	50.2	103	1007	31.36	49.72	13.59
188	JAITARAN* (Jaitaran)	1289.80	92	134851	69221	65630	48.7	105	948	26.04	43.59	7.75
189	KHARCHI/MARWAR JUN.	1390.60	137	154855	78087	76768	49.6	111	983	31.01	50.90	11.18
190	PALI (Pali)	1296.60	80	84540	43740	40800	48.3	65	933	27.45	45.23	8.73
191	RAIPUR* (Raipur)	986.50	103	132128	67364	64764	49.0	134	961	28.62	47.96	8.87
192	RANI STATION (Desuri)	762.60	73	94105	46950	47155	50.1	123	1004	33.49	51.85	15.77
193	ROHAT* (Rohat)	1404.40	79	81290	41822	39468	48.6	58	944	27.00	45.67	7.50
194	SOJAT* (Sojat)	1627.00	112	131378	66535	64843	49.4	81	975	32.57	53.97	11.14
195	SUMERPUR* (Sumerpur)	911.90	63	115337	58478	56859	49.3	126	972	32.47	51.00	13.79
	PALI	**11868.30**	**904**	**1163085**	**589854**	**573231**	**49.3**	**98**	**972**	**30.13**	**48.63**	**11.47**
196	AMET* (Amet)	505.40	136	71557	36287	35270	49.3	142	972	22.93	37.72	7.80
197	BHIM* (Bhim)	677.70	109	104066	50892	53174	51.1	154	1045	32.02	56.46	9.56
198	DEOGARH* (Deogarh)	589.10	131	63804	31692	32112	50.3	108	1013	22.72	39.24	6.64
199	KHAMNOR* (Nathdwara)	594.80	132	112075	55637	56438	50.4	188	1014	30.74	48.31	13.66
200	KUMBHALGARH* (Kumbhalgarh)	776.00	161	113501	56953	56548	49.8	146	993	23.33	38.39	8.29
201	RAILMAGRA* (Railmagra)	544.20	90	100294	50490	49804	49.7	184	986	32.57	50.38	14.69
202	RAJSAMAND* (Rajsamand)	569.30	130	108526	54712	53814	49.6	191	984	31.70	49.84	13.34
	RAJSAMAND #	**4256.50**	**889**	**673823**	**336663**	**337160**	**50.0**	**158**	**1001**	**28.51**	**46.35**	**10.94**
203	BAMANWAS* (Bamanwas)	728.80	132	120238	64413	55825	46.4	165	867	32.66	52.32	9.85
204	BONLI (Bonli)	1009.50	157	164512	87397	77115	46.9	163	882	30.45	48.08	10.38
205	GANGAPUR* (Gangapur)	644.70	115	146685	78993	67692	46.1	228	857	35.34	55.97	11.06
206	KHANDAR (Khandar)	1352.30	156	119379	64245	55134	46.2	88	858	24.53	39.23	7.26
207	SAWAI MADHOPUR (S. Madhopur)	1232.40	154	173279	91800	81479	47.0	141	888	31.57	51.47	9.02
	S. MADHOPUR	**4967.70**	**714**	**724093**	**386848**	**337245**	**46.6**	**146**	**872**	**31.09**	**49.71**	**9.59**
208	DANTA RAMGARH (Danta Ramgarh)	1115.70	135	206470	105950	100520	48.7	185	949	38.04	59.84	15.19
209	DHOND (Sikar)	912.30	108	171290	87053	84237	49.2	188	968	38.65	62.18	14.71
210	FATEHPUR (Fatehpur)	1236.90	141	157370	78862	78508	49.9	127	996	37.57	60.75	15.18
211	KHANDELA (Sri Madhopur)	783.80	116	176571	90844	85727	48.6	225	944	39.32	63.08	14.45
212	LACHHMANGARH (Lachhmangarh)	1027.00	136	158995	80062	78933	49.6	155	986	38.50	61.74	15.49
213	NEEM KA THANA* (Neem Ka Thana)	1186.70	143	252849	132085	120764	47.8	213	914	39.02	60.39	15.71
214	PIPRALI (Sikar)	797.70	91	164117	84316	79801	48.6	206	946	39.83	62.88	15.89
215	SRI MADHOPUR (Sri Madhopur)	566.60	61	167731	86598	81133	48.4	296	937	41.43	64.57	16.77
	SIKAR	**7626.70**	**931**	**1455393**	**745770**	**709623**	**48.8**	**191**	**952**	**39.03**	**61.80**	**15.42**
216	ABU ROAD* (Abu Road)	858.10	78	80611	41533	39078	48.5	94	941	18.53	28.89	7.37
217	PINDWARA* (Pindwara)	1138.30	98	128032	65180	62852	49.1	112	964	22.76	34.67	10.60
218	REODAR* (Reodar)	1086.80	122	132122	67862	64260	48.6	122	947	21.26	33.71	8.23

P. Code	Panchayat Samiti (Concerning Tehsil)	Total Rural Area (in sq. km)	Total No. of Inhabited Villages	Total Rural population				Density Per sq. km	Sex Ratio (per Thousand and Pop.)	Literacy Rate %		
				Persons	Male	Female No.	Female %			Persons	Male	Female
1	2	3	4	5	6	7	8	9	10	11	12	13
219	SHEOGANJ* (Sheoganj)	892.30	66	79876	40724	39152	49.0	90	961	24.03	39.38	8.36
220	SIROHI* (Sirohi)	1090.40	82	105806	52639	53167	50.2	97	1010	28.22	46.49	10.74
	SIROHI	**5065.90**	**446**	**526447**	**267938**	**258509**	**49.1**	**104**	**965**	**23.05**	**36.57**	**9.23**
221	DEOLI* (Deoli)	1235.30	157	135553	70652	64901	47.9	110	919	30.96	49.15	11.12
222	MALPURA* (Malpura)	1439.10	123	148406	76818	71588	48.2	103	932	27.33	43.37	10.13
223	NIWAI* (Niwai)	1030.10	191	137463	70877	66586	48.4	133	939	29.94	46.34	12.46
224	TODARAISINGH* (Todaraisingh)	985.50	109	90790	46695	44095	48.6	92	944	28.51	47.38	8.71
225	TONK (Tonk)	1415.50	248	168956	88261	80695	47.8	119	914	26.51	44.54	6.70
226	UNIARA* (Uniara)	986.40	191	103418	54127	49291	47.7	105	911	26.65	43.90	7.58
	TONK	**7091.90**	**1019**	**784586**	**407430**	**377156**	**48.1**	**111**	**926**	**28.29**	**45.68**	**9.48**
227	BARGAON (Girwa)	648.00	143	123482	63797	59685	48.3	191	936	32.97	49.92	14.81
228	BHINDER* (Vallabhnagar)	985.10	264	169382	85830	83552	49.3	172	973	29.17	46.86	11.16
229	DHARIAWAD* (Dhariawad)	1177.40	246	156024	79516	76508	49.0	133	962	12.93	20.64	4.90
230	GIRWA (Girwa)	1349.10	159	177158	91243	85915	48.5	131	942	27.20	41.69	11.72
231	GOGUNDA* (Gogunda)	871.80	146	121703	61630	60073	49.4	140	975	23.01	36.84	8.85
232	JHADOL* (Jhadol)	1428.30	256	147044	75228	71816	48.8	103	955	19.81	31.83	7.18
233	KHERWARA* (Kherwara)	1076.70	241	199059	98413	100646	50.6	185	1023	32.11	51.77	13.06
234	KOTRA* (Kotra)	1191.50	302	130449	66743	63706	48.8	109	954	8.67	14.42	2.57
235	MAVLI* (Mavli)	798.90	148	164468	83914	80554	49.0	206	960	31.58	48.60	13.93
236	SALUMBAR* (Salumbar)	921.80	231	161630	80736	80894	50.0	175	1002	22.10	35.89	8.45
237	SARADA* (Sarada)	1078.20	154	171060	85065	85995	50.3	159	1011	26.95	42.62	11.59
	UDAIPUR	**11526.80**	**2290**	**1721459**	**872115**	**849344**	**49.3**	**149**	**974**	**24.74**	**39.04**	**10.08**
	RAJASTHAN	**335589**	**37889**	**33938882**	**17686463**	**16252414**	**47.9**	**101**	**919**	**30.39**	**47.64**	**11.61**

Note: * Dungargarh PS shifted from Churu to Bikaner district on 1st April 2001
** Excluding data of Dungargarh PS; *** Including data of Dungargarh PS.
# Came in force from April, 1991; ## Came in force from July 1994
Came in force from July 1997.

Source: 1. Computed from data given in Primary Census Abustract, Rajasthan, Series -21, Census of India, 1991.
2. District Census Handbooks (all districts), Rajasthan, 1991.

GENERAL ANNEX-II

PANCHAYAT SAMITI-WISE NO. OF MEDICAL INSTITUTIONS: RAJASTHAN, 1991

P. Code	Panchayat Samiti District	No. of Medical Institutions: Dispensary	Hospital	MCWC	PHC	FPC	SHC	Others	Total No. of Medical Institutions S	Community Health Workers	Pop. Served Per Medical Institution	Area Served Per Medical Institution (sq. km)
1	2	3	4	5	6	7	8	9	10	11	12	13
1	ARAIN	5	7	1	8	2	13	4	34	16	3226	35.35
2	BHINAY	20	6	3	9	1	21	10	59	29	2123	20.61
3	JAWAJA	5	7	5	9	1	15	1	41	17	2928	16.15
4	KEKRI	23	9	2	5	3	16	4	55	18	2091	18.06
5	KISHANGARH	19	10	4	14	1	15	14	62	8	1970	17.85
6	MASOODA	14	4	4	3	1	14	5	39	22	3266	22.44
7	PISANGAN	27	12	6	8	2	25	9	78	17	2227	15.43
8	SRINAGAR	9	4	5	6	2	11	7	35	12	3782	25.65
	AJMER DISTRICT	**122**	**59**	**30**	**62**	**13**	**130**	**54**	**403**	**139**	**2545**	**20.24**
9	BANSURE	21	1	6	4	1	4	17	36	8	4544	18.46
10	BEHROR	13	11	4	5	1	6	30	39	5	2950	8.63
11	KATHUMAR	15	6	8	8	3	7	9	44	6	3854	12.84
12	KISHANGARH BAS	8	0	1	2	0	7	37	18	14	7560	28.08
13	KOTKASIM	13	5	0	2	1	6	40	26	21	3668	13.25
14	LACHHMANGARH	12	6	2	8	0	5	27	33	10	5343	18.75
15	MANDAWAR	18	6	1	2	0	12	14	39	4	4154	14.80
16	NIMRANA	12	7	0	1	1	8	18	28	2	4298	13.51
17	RAJGARH	16	5	1	2	1	14	7	38	9	2962	26.56
18	RAMGARH	11	2	3	8	2	11	44	35	18	4619	17.63
19	RENI	10	3	1	4	2	6	15	24	2	4406	16.33
20	THANAGAZI	18	4	3	6	5	9	18	40	8	3603	26.51
21	TIJARA	16	0	1	5	0	6	23	28	4	5400	22.98
22	UMREN	12	8	1	3	2	9	22	33	5	4931	25.71
	ALWAR	**195**	**64**	**32**	**60**	**19**	**110**	**321**	**461**	**116**	**4287**	**18.57**
23	ANANDPURI	5	1	1	7	0	20	1	34	4	2497	10.05
24	BAGIDORA	10	20	6	11	2	15	8	62	8	2214	8.32
25	GARHI	25	6	26	22	1	25	1	104	7	1812	6.77
26	GHATOL	25	5	4	12	1	20	4	66	3	2667	11.87
27	KUSHALGARH	14	1	0	9	0	8	0	32	6	3184	20.03
28	PEEPALKHOONT	8	4	0	10	2	11	0	33	28	3352	27.66
29	SAJJANGARH	7	2	2	7	1	10	4	28	12	3685	14.38
30	TALWARA	16	6	10	17	4	23	3	72	5	2280	10.42
	BANSWARA	**110**	**45**	**49**	**95**	**11**	**132**	**21**	**431**	**73**	**2474**	**11.72**
31	ANTA	13	6	5	7	1	9	17	40	10	3086	23.31
32	ATRU	14	13	12	6	2	14	15	59	15	1821	14.57
33	BARAN	4	9	2	4	1	7	4	26	3	3110	23.56
34	CHHABRA	13	4	1	3	1	8	7	29	8	3536	27.02
35	CHHIPABAROD	7	5	2	7	1	8	8	29	6	2814	28.43
36	KISHANGANJ	11	6	3	11	2	8	13	39	6	2778	37.19
37	SHAHBAD	8	5	3	2	1	3	22	21	2	3954	69.91
	BARAN #	**70**	**48**	**28**	**40**	**9**	**57**	**86**	**243**	**50**	**2828**	**28.52**
38	BALOTRA	11	7	1	7	1	14	3	40	3	4803	97.13
39	BARMER	9	2	3	7	0	14	0	35	4	4890	108.95
40	BAYTOO	7	0	0	6	0	12	0	25	4	6071	129.12
41	CHOHTAN	11	4	0	5	1	10	0	30	11	5704	108.88
42	DHORIMANNA	9	4	3	10	0	16	2	42	6	4310	63.53
43	SHEO	10	1	1	3	0	5	0	20	9	6078	330.82
44	SINDHARI	11	3	1	7	0	17	5	39	0	4303	79.89
45	SIWANA	11	9	2	12	2	11	4	45	3	2989	44.05
	BARMER	**79**	**30**	**11**	**57**	**4**	**99**	**14**	**276**	**40**	**4678**	**103.53**

P. Code	Panchayat Samiti/District	No. of Medical Institutions Dispen-sary	Hos-pital	MCWC	PHC	FPC	SHC	Others	Total No. of Medical Institutions $	Community Health Workers	Pop. Served Per Medical Institution	Area Served Per Medical Institution (sq. km)
1	2	3	4	5	6	7	8	9	10	11	12	13
46	BAYANA	11	5	1	0	1	15	17	32	8	4744	24.99
47	DEEG	10	2	3	3	0	5	8	23	14	5462	21.32
48	KAMAN	6	6	0	1	0	4	10	17	25	9076	32.74
49	KUMHER	16	3	5	5	1	6	21	35	13	3687	12.58
50	NADBAI	14	4	1	1	0	4	9	24	3	5320	17.99
51	NAGAR PAHARI	13	5	11	8	4	8	29	45	16	4037	13.82
52	RUPBAS	20	12	12	8	2	9	47	61	9	2731	8.84
53	SEWAR	7	8	0	5	0	6	24	26	5	5137	17.62
54	WEIR	29	17	4	3	0	5	6	58	9	2768	9.93
	BHARATPUR	**126**	**62**	**37**	**34**	**8**	**62**	**171**	**321**	**102**	**4146**	**15.31**
55	ASIND	18	3	1	7	4	13	5	42	7	3715	26.43
56	BANERA	15	1	4	6	1	23	1	49	11	1797	13.81
57	HURDA	22	5	1	9	0	20	1	57	31	1280	10.83
58	JAHAZPUR	25	2	2	13	2	22	4	64	15	2076	16.15
59	KOTRI	15	11	4	18	1	11	0	59	6	2065	16.10
60	MANDAL	20	8	6	15	1	23	8	72	10	2041	16.04
61	MANDALGARH	34	12	8	15	2	31	2	100	11	1564	13.92
62	RAIPUR	7	8	4	10	3	9	2	38	0	1878	13.56
63	SAHARA	12	9	1	6	2	16	0	44	1	1935	14.39
64	SHAHPURA	24	1	2	6	1	23	2	56	2	2154	20.13
65	SUWANA	13	4	2	9	3	14	3	42	2	3089	19.82
	BHILWARA	**205**	**64**	**35**	**114**	**20**	**205**	**28**	**623**	**96**	**2058**	**16.12**
66	BIKANER	24	7	0	4	2	16	9	51	3	4550	175.39
67	DUNGARGARH *	14	2	1	2	1	9	0	28	2	4771	107.24
68	KOLAYAT	13	8	1	10	2	7	9	39	2	3401	187.66
69	LUNKARANSAR	19	9	0	1	2	8	33	37	15	4227	167.95
70	NOKHA	18	10	1	4	2	10	4	43	7	4858	87.62
	BIKANER **	**88**	**36**	**3**	**21**	**9**	**50**	**55**	**198**	**29**	**3687**	**147.72**
71	HINDOLI	9	11	3	9	2	12	13	44	4	3447	30.43
72	KESHORAIPATAN	15	13	3	4	1	8	20	43	13	3469	29.93
73	NAINWA	18	6	3	3	2	13	9	43	9	2829	26.51
74	TALERA	21	12	2	13	1	9	31	57	16	3755	33.03
	BUNDI	**63**	**42**	**11**	**29**	**6**	**42**	**73**	**187**	**42**	**3404**	**30.21**
75	ARNOD	11	10	5	9	1	8	4	43	3	2126	16.31
76	BARI SADRI	8	9	1	0	1	8	3	26	10	2958	18.25
77	BEGUN	12	7	6	4	2	14	4	43	11	1996	22.27
78	BHADESAR	8	5	0	6	0	7	1	26	1	3444	20.79
79	BHAINSRORGARH	1	4	0	3	1	8	1	16	1	3996	85.61
80	BHOPALSAGAR	10	9	0	7	2	11	2	37	2	1732	10.76
81	CHHOTI SADRI	4	3	6	2	0	3	1	18	5	4717	38.44
82	CHITTAURGARH	8	4	0	4	1	7	6	23	3	5901	35.39
83	DUNGLA	7	5	0	1	1	8	1	21	3	3669	23.50
84	GANGRAR	9	4	1	1	0	11	1	26	3	2886	21.37
85	KAPASAN	4	2	2	6	1	15	1	29	9	2513	16.64
86	NIMBAHERA	3	5	0	5	0	3	3	16	2	6893	50.79
87	PRATAPGARH	13	3	8	17	1	17	10	58	2	2745	24.62
88	RASHMI	10	2	2	10	2	13	0	37	4	1778	12.15
	CHITTAURGARH	**108**	**72**	**31**	**75**	**13**	**133**	**38**	**419**	**59**	**2989**	**24.27**
89	CHURU	19	7	1	1	0	21	3	49	2	2516	31.83
90	RAJGARH	20	7	2	7	1	16	15	52	10	4257	42.26
91	RATANGARH	14	3	0	5	1	14	4	36	8	3485	45.62
92	SARDARSHAHAR	18	2	0	3	1	2	3	25	17	6998	152.58
93	SUJANGARH	23	7	1	8	1	17	8	56	3	3471	46.36
94	TARANAGAR	15	5	1	5	1	7	6	33	20	3761	54.03
	CHURU ***	**109**	**31**	**5**	**29**	**5**	**77**	**39**	**251**	**60**	**4371**	**54.15**
95	BANDIKUI	19	0	2	3	1	7	6	31	8	6015	19.38
96	DAUSA	21	4	3	6	0	6	13	40	10	5199	22.70
97	LALSOT	15	1	2	1	1	11	4	30	12	6248	28.47
98	MAHWA	21	10	8	9	0	11	11	59	7	2486	8.03
99	SIKRAI	19	3	4	5	2	7	21	38	10	4227	13.23
	DAUSA #	**95**	**18**	**19**	**24**	**4**	**42**	**55**	**198**	**47**	**4491**	**16.86**
100	BARI	10	9	1	1	0	13	3	34	5	3452	23.35
101	BASERI	9	5	3	5	0	8	14	30	11	5040	33.38
102	DHAULPUR	18	10	8	3	1	9	47	48	34	4189	12.03
103	RAJAKHERA	7	2	0	8	1	6	9	23	10	6566	24.87
	DHAULPUR	**44**	**26**	**12**	**17**	**2**	**36**	**73**	**135**	**60**	**4597**	**21.81**

P. Code	Panchayat Samiti/District	No. of Medical Institutions							Total No. of Medical Institutions $	Community Health Workers	Pop. Served Per Medical Institution	Area Served Per Medical Institution (sq. km)
		Dispensary	Hospital	MCWC	PHC	FPC	SHC	Others				
1	2	3	4	5	6	7	8	9	10	11	12	13
104	ASPUR	22	8	27	14	1	17	0	88	4	1665	7.86
105	BICHHIWARA	17	12	11	15	2	13	1	68	8	2659	10.97
106	DUNGARPUR	12	8	8	9	0	25	1	62	6	2149	9.28
107	SAGWARA	28	12	3	8	1	23	4	74	4	2170	8.27
108	SIMALWARA	22	4	3	6	1	16	7	51	5	3718	17.91
	DUNGARPUR	**101**	**44**	**52**	**52**	**5**	**94**	**13**	**343**	**27**	**2364**	**10.32**
109	ANUPGARH	12	2	0	8	1	6	110	28	15	10503	126.56
110	GANGANAGAR	10	4	2	11	2	9	116	36	21	4511	23.75
111	KARANPUR	3	2	0	2	0	5	30	12	6	7682	67.54
112	PADAMPUR	19	2	0	8	3	3	47	32	11	3308	26.33
113	RAISINGHNAGAR	12	4	28	3	1	13.	59	60	52	2147	21.92
114	SADULSHAHAR	15	7	2	7	2	11	112	42	25	4961	35.35
115	SURATGARH	33	6	0	9	0	11	129	59	12	4650	64.26
	GANGANAGAR	**104**	**27**	**32**	**48**	**9**	**58**	**603**	**269**	**142**	**4707**	**47.00**
116	BHADRA	25	7	2	1	1	5	38	40	13	4519	42.83
117	HANUMANGARH	25	5	1	8	2	15	170	54	46	6184	37.69
118	NOHAR	35	15	0	2	0	3	100	55	5	5270	78.27
	HANUMANGARH ##	**85**	**27**	**3**	**11**	**3**	**23**	**308**	**149**	**64**	**5400**	**54.05**
119	AMBER	12	1	2	8	[illegible]	10	14	33	19	6223	25.44 [illegible]
120	BASSI	13	5	4	2	0	[illegible]	23	39	38	4096	16.18
121	CHAKSU	15	0	5	2	1	22	15	44	21	2857	17.43
122	DUDU	24	4	5	4	1	13	[illegible]	50	16	4213	37.10
123	GOVINDGARH	34	5	5	3	3	14	22	61	29	3450	10.92
124	JAMWA RAMGARH	30	2	1	11	1	7	16	51	19	3742	19.83
125	JHOTWARA	10	1	1	3	1	7	8	22	5	4685	17.50
126	KOTPUTLI	27	6	0	6	3	11	22	50	6	3552	13.27
127	PHAGI	15	2	3	3	1	12	5	35	15	3727	31.81
128	SAMBHAR	28	1	3	5	1	15	6	52	12	3120	16.01
129	SANGANER	17	3	8	3	2	10	26	41	8	3753	14.24
130	SHAHPURA	25	7	1	4	2	8	1	45	3	2848	9.07
131	VIRATNAGAR	19	4	2	6	1	5	15	36	25	4313	18.03
	JAIPUR	**269**	**41**	**40**	**60**	**20**	**149**	**207**	**559**	**21[illegible]**	**3781**	**18.61**
132	JAISALMER	8	2	0	9	2	11	0	30	6	2677	428.32
133	SAM	9	2	2	9	0	14	2	36	0	2637	586.42
134	SANKRA	15	9	0	9	0	12	0	45	8	2571	121.92
	JAISALMER	**32**	**13**	**2**	**27**	**2**	**37**	**2**	111	**14**	**2621**	**355.38**
135	AHORE	12	9	4	7	3	22	9	54	15	2781	29.56
136	BHINMAL	4	2	1	5	0	11	0	23	6	6356	58.16
137	JALOR	11	7	1	11	1	17	7	47	1	2297	22.44
138	JASWANTPURA	9	10	0	4	1	14	4	37	4	2874	28.89
139	RANIWARA	6	3	1	3	0	3	3	16	10	7695	61.50
140	SANCHORE	7	5	0	10	1	25	3	47	9	5539	64.01
141	SAYLA	12	5	2	8	0	22	1	49	4	3373	29.78
	JALOR	**61**	**41**	**9**	**48**	**6**	**114**	**27**	**273**	**49**	**3880**	**38.50**
142	BAKANI	7	6	2	5	4	11	8	31	35	4188	28.56
143	DAG	17	16	4	7	1	20	9	64	10	2167	17.66
144	JHALRAPATAN	17	11	6	8	1	15	14	57	14	2860	23.32
145	KHANPUR	10	7	0	3	1	9	7	29	11	4087	32.42
146	MANOHARTHANA	8	7	4	4	0	12	30	35	28	3601	26.36
147	PIRAWA	13	15	0	8	2	14	7	50	4	2599	20.02
	JHALAWAR	**72**	**62**	**16**	**35**	**9**	**81**	**75**	**266**	**102**	**3030**	**23.34**
148	ALSISAR	14	9	4	5	4	6	5	38	2	2966	19.66
149	BUHANA	18	4	0	7	2	5	12	34	3	5084	19.22
150	CHIRAWA	20	3	2	5	1	4	6	34	9	3665	14.38
151	JHUNJHUNUN	27	10	0	4	3	9	10	50	10	3146	16.41
152	KHETRI	17	13	1	3	2	14	23	48	9	3746	16.59
153	NAWALGARH	19	6	7	6	3	10	15	48	25	3777	13.86
154	SURAJGARH	9	3	8	6	1	2	7	28	5	5044	27.91
155	UDAIPURWATI	19	9	3	7	2	3	19	41	14	4574	20.27
	JHUNJHUNUN	**143**	**57**	**25**	**43**	**18**	**53**	**97**	**321**	**77**	**3917**	**18.02**
156	BALESAR	9	10	3	9	2	10	1	41	10	3110	45.22
157	BAP	2	3	0	3	0	5	0	13	5	7973	340.86
158	BHOPALGARH	9	5	1	7	7	14	0	36	5	4348	48.43
159	BILARA	13	7	0	7	2	24	2	51	9	2777	29.40

P. Code	Panchayat Samiti/District	*No. of Medical Institutions* Dispensary	Hospital	MCWC	PHC	FPC	SHC	Others	Total No. of Medical Institutions $	Community Health Workers	Pop. Served Per Medical Institution	Area Served Per Medical Institution (sq. km)
1	2	3	4	5	6	7	8	9	10	11	12	13
160	LUNI	7	7	6	10	5	15	3	45	7	3705	44.06
161	MANDOR	3	0	1	6	0	8	3	18	1	6218	70.51
162	OSIAN	21	9	3	12	4	13	8	58	7	5283	72.15
163	PHALODI	13	7	8	8	5	11	6	47	3	3435	68.89
164	SHERGARH	20	4	0	7	1	9	6	40	0	2827	49.38
	JODHPUR	**97**	**52**	**22**	**69**	**26**	**109**	**29**	**349**	**47**	**3980**	**63.54**
165	HINDAUN	11	5	8	4	1	6	16	34	24	5774	18.57
166	KARAULI	13	7	3	3	0	18	10	44	14	3783	27.72
167	NADOTI	14	4	6	4	1	8	5	36	4	2824	17.94
168	SAPOTRA	15	6	3	8	3	11	12	43	25	4241	45.63
169	TODABHIM	15	5	2	4	2	16	16	42	10	3676	12.44
	KARAULI ###	**68**	**27**	**22**	**23**	**7**	**59**	**59**	**199**	**77**	**4026**	**25.03**
170	CHECHAT	8	9	4	8	0	10	21	39	13	3093	19.77
171	ITAWA	16	13	3	6	1	9	11	47	13	2705	18.87
172	LADPURA	8	4	2	0	1	17	10	31	5	3536	42.18
173	SANGOD	14	8	0	2	0	10	20	34	4	3605	30.77
174	SULTANPUR	10	7	2	7	3	10	28	36	15	3440	25.33
	KOTA	**56**	**41**	**11**	**23**	**5**	**56**	**90**	**187**	**50**	**3229**	**26.33**
175	DEGANA	8	5	9	8	1	26	2	56	2	2756	26.03
176	DIDWANA	15	13	4	6	4	19	7	57	5	3933	28.21
177	JAYAL	14	8	1	5	5	25	2	53	4	3334	39.40
178	KUCHAMAN	16	18	0	5	1	21	11	60	8	3418	23.94
179	LADNU	10	6	0	9	0	15	6	40	3	3079	34.28
180	MAKRANA	11	5	0	9	1	15	2	40	3	3907	27.66
181	MERTA	12	6	1	10	1	14	0	43	3	3315	32.49
182	MUNDWA	10	2	2	1	0	19	4	34	4	4492	64.24
183	NAGAUR	13	5	0	5	2	18	6	41	19	4424	58.06
184	PARBATSAR	14	8	1	9	1	11	5	43	6	3322	24.90
185	RIYAN	14	5	3	4	6	11	6	37	15	3863	33.50
	NAGAUR	**137**	**81**	**21**	**71**	**22**	**194**	**51**	**504**	**72**	**3576**	**34.40**
186	BALI	24	17	0	3	1	15	8	59	0	2529	23.22
187	DESURI	17	15	2	2	4	18	5	54	2	1581	15.35
188	JAITARAN	10	9	3	7	3	14	8	43	3	3136	30.00
189	KHARCHI/MARWAR JUN.	12	15	2	12	2	18	9	59	3	2625	23.57
190	PALI	6	5	0	4	1	14	0	29	4	2915	44.71
191	RAIPUR	13	8	10	6	1	16	0	53	15	2493	18.61
192	RANI STATION	15	5	6	4	2	22	8	52	12	1810	14.67
193	ROHAT	4	3	3	1	2	9	1	20	1	4065	70.22
194	SOJAT	7	11	4	5	3	16	1	43	1	3055	37.84
195	SUMERPUR	10	9	4	7	2	13	6	43	6	2682	21.21
	PALI	**118**	**97**	**34**	**51**	**21**	**155**	**46**	**455**	**47**	**2556**	**26.08**
196	AMET	7	0	0	4	2	20	1	31	8	2308	16.30
197	BHIM	11	6	7	6	2	10	6	40	4	2602	16.94
198	DEOGARH	3	2	0	1	0	7	0	13	3	4908	45.32
199	KHAMNOR	12	4	9	7	1	27	0	59	19	1900	10.08
200	KUMBHALGARH	13	1	14	7	2	11	6	46	4	2467	16.87
201	RAILMAGRA	15	4	2	8	1	6	2	35	1	2866	15.55
202	RAJSAMAND	19	2	5	2	1	16	0	44	3	2467	12.94
	RAJSAMAND #	**80**	**19**	**37**	**35**	**9**	**97**	**15**	**268**	**42**	**2514**	**15.88**
203	BAMANWAS	12	6	2	6	1	7	13	33	11	3644	22.08
204	BONLI	15	10	2	6	5	7	8	40	2	4113	25.24
205	GANGAPUR	23	9	10	2	0	10	14	54	13	2716	11.94
206	KHANDAR	19	4	8	2	2	9	7	42	12	2842	32.20
207	SAWAI MADHOPUR	25	12	1	5	4	16	11	59	2	2937	20.89
	SAWAI MADHOPUR	**94**	**41**	**23**	**21**	**12**	**49**	**53**	**228**	**40**	**3176**	**21.79**
208	DANTA RAMGARH	26	13	5	18	4	19	22	81	10	2549	13.77
209	DHOND	23	2	0	16	3	24	12	65	5	2635	14.04
210	FATEHPUR	13	9	0	6	1	12	12	40	7	3934	30.92
211	KHANDELA	8	7	0	3	2	14	14	32	18	5518	24.49
212	LACHHMANGARH	16	4	0	4	0	21	7	45	8	3533	22.82
213	NEEM KA THANA	19	12	3	10	3	21	31	65	26	3890	18.26
214	PIPRALI	13	3	2	5	1	19	3	42	6	3908	18.99
215	SRI MADHOPUR	15	7	3	4	2	8	9	37	7	4533	15.31
	SIKAR	**133**	**57**	**13**	**66**	**16**	**138**	**110**	**407**	**87**	**3576**	**18.74**

P. Code	Panchayat Samiti District	No. of Medical Institutions							Total No. of Medical Institutions $	Community Health Workers	Pop. Served Per Medical Institution	Area Served Per Medical Institution (sq. km)
		Dispensary	Hospital	MCWC	PHC	FPC	SHC	Others				
1	2	3	4	5	6	7	8	9	10	11	12	13
216	ABU ROAD	7	6	2	2	0	6	4	23	3	3505	37.31
217	PINDWARA	5	8	10	4	1	19	3	46	1	2783	24.75
218	REODAR	12	4	3	17	4	2	5	38	2	3477	28.60
219	SHEOGANJ	2	6	0	4	0	14	6	26	2	3072	34.32
220	SIROHI	11	3	2	2	0	12	4	30	11	3527	36.35
	SIROHI	**37**	**27**	**17**	**29**	**5**	**53**	**22**	**163**	**19**	**3230**	**31.08**
221	DEOLI	19	10	1	9	1	13	4	52	47	2607	23.76
222	MALPURA	18	2	6	5	1	11	3	42	28	3533	34.26
223	NIWAI	17	0	1	4	0	13	9	35	12	3928	29.43
224	TODARAISINGH	10	0	0	2	2	9	0	21	25	4323	46.93
225	TONK	16	4	1	13	4	18	9	52	17	3249	27.22
226	UNIARA	8	2	0	3	1	15	10	28	22	3694	35.23
	TONK	**88**	**18**	**9**	**36**	**9**	**79**	**35**	**230**	**151**	**3411**	**30.83**
227	BARGAON	15	2	5	4	1	9	8	35	4	3528	18.51
228	BHINDER	20	11	9	11	5	13	0	64	3	2647	15.39
229	DHARIAWAD	14	0	12	4	0	9	3	39	3	4001	30.19
230	GIRWA	18	5	7	7	2	18	7	55	15	3221	24.53
231	GOGUNDA	11	8	13	7	1	10	4	49	3	2484	17.79
232	JHADOL	23	6	4	21	1	25	7	79	14	1861	18.08
233	KHERWARA	15	10	11	19	7	24	12	79	11	2520	13.63
234	KOTRA	10	4	0	5	1	13	1	32	1	4077	37.23
235	MAVLI	19	6	9	8	3	22	2	64	10	2570	12.48
236	SALUMBAR	17	3	10	10	1	16	10	56	23	2886	16.46
237	SARADA	26	9	11	15	1	10	4	71	16	2409	15.19
	UDAIPUR	**188**	**64**	**91**	**111**	**23**	**169**	**58**	**623**	**103**	**2763**	**18.50**
	RAJASTHAN	**3377**	**1433**	**782**	**1516**	**350**	**2942**	**2928**	**10050**	**2339**	**3377**	**33.39**

Note: $ Include dispensary, hospital, MCWC, PHC and SHC, * Dungargarh PS shifted from Churu to Bikaner district on 1st April 2001,
** Excluding data of Dungargarh PS; *** Including data of Dungargarh PS.
# Came in force from April, 1991; ## Came in force from July 1994
Came in force from July 1997.

Source: 1. Computed from data given in Primary Census Abustract, Rajasthan, Series -21, Census of India, 1991.
2. District Census Handbooks (all districts), Rajasthan, 1991.
3. General Annex-I, Col. 3 & 5.

GENERAL ANNEX-III

PANCHAYAT SAMITI-WISE PROPORTION OF RURAL POPULATION SERVED BY MEDICAL AND OTHER RELATED AMENITIES: RAJASTHAN (1991)

P. Code	Panchayat Samiti/District	Medical	Drinking Water	Education	Post & Telegraph	Market/ Hat	Commu- nications	Approach By Pucca Road	Power Supply
1	2	3	4	5	6	7	8	9	10
1	ARAIN	49.69	100.00	99.06	53.01	—	47.98	33.04	75.23
2	BHINAY	61.21	100.00	99.35	64.12	—	58.74	54.30	83.15
3	JAWAJA	33.60	99.08	93.02	40.24	—	41.93	56.92	61.43
4	KEKRI	66.66	100.00	99.60	72.09	—	29.04	56.23	94.58
5	KISHANGARH	61.56	100.00	96.24	70.48	—	59.56	56.80	92.28
6	MASOODA	53.89	100.00	95.36	57.57	—	54.18	59.51	88.78
7	PISANGAN	66.45	100.00	99.74	71.21	—	51.72	75.18	99.02
8	SRINAGAR	48.26	100.00	99.84	54.55	—	59.60	71.81	94.48
	AJMER DISTRICT	**55.71**	**99.89**	**97.87**	**60.94**	—	**50.74**	**59.29**	**86.98**
9	BANSURE	43.66	100.00	98.03	49.09	6.74	46.67	49.59	99.32
10	BEHROR	51.70	100.00	99.14	61.31	—	45.34	46.41	99.77
11	KATHUMAR	44.10	100.00	98.16	44.71	—	33.55	45.42	67.66
12	KISHANGARH BAS	39.46	100.00	94.84	48.70	5.00	36.76	53.29	99.82
13	KOTKASIM	40.96	100.00	95.15	45.28	—	38.80	44.12	84.95
14	LACHHMANGARH	33.66	100.00	95.38	41.57	—	33.99	47.48	63.11
15	MANDAWAR	44.44	100.00	98.94	48.70	—	46.83	48.61	97.08
16	NIMRANA	49.90	100.00	98.47	61.42	—	39.77	52.25	99.99
17	RAJGARH	47.48	100.00	94.10	52.99	—	34.23	55.58	79.08
18	RAMGARH	36.72	100.00	93.48	41.31	9.68	34.24	52.36	88.68
19	RENI	40.87	100.00	93.94	54.90	—	34.76	42.11	80.84
20	THANAGAZI	54.16	100.00	96.97	49.58	—	52.39	56.25	82.39
21	TIJARA	30.22	100.00	92.70	37.39	—	24.20	38.57	80.50
22	UMREN	40.52	100.00	93.88	49.07	4.90	43.74	43.41	95.59
	ALWAR	**42.28**	**100.00**	**95.97**	**48.27**	**2.10**	**38.97**	**48.23**	**86.60**
23	ANANDPURI	39.46	100.00	96.69	32.92	—	36.27	44.38	48.42
24	BAGIDORA	49.32	100.00	93.58	36.56	—	48.64	59.05	58.17
25	GARHI	57.70	100.00	97.85	47.91	—	58.44	59.48	90.16
26	GHATOL	42.31	100.00	95.51	44.71	8.63	39.34	48.55	68.35
27	KUSHALGARH	16.90	99.75	85.70	7.35	4.70	18.68	21.96	41.36
28	PEEPALKHOONT	44.79	100.00	85.08	27.46	16.13	25.91	36.75	28.32
29	SAJJANGARH	23.46	100.00	85.12	22.56	3.37	22.31	31.53	35.33
30	TALWARA	50.26	100.00	92.30	42.39	0.60	54.48	59.56	63.92
	BANSWARA	**42.93**	**99.98**	**92.25**	**35.42**	**3.97**	**40.98**	**47.78**	**58.70**
31	ANTA	45.34	100.00	95.29	50.07	25.62	37.92	37.02	78.99
32	ATRU	49.63	100.00	91.66	56.57	25.89	40.55	34.85	86.89
33	BARAN	31.62	100.00	99.06	42.22	8.70	27.23	38.47	92.87
34	CHHABRA	24.20	100.00	89.27	25.35	7.41	12.50	13.71	70.79
35	CHHIPABAROD	29.30	100.00	88.85	31.35	13.51	26.72	21.67	46.26
36	KISHANGANJ	37.27	99.90	83.73	35.20	24.98	42.28	33.70	83.90
37	SHAHBAD	29.04	99.45	85.51	36.42	13.58	28.16	34.95	65.45
	BARAN #	**36.10**	**99.92**	**90.50**	**40.26**	**17.96**	**31.46**	**30.78**	**75.89**
38	BALOTRA	34.77	99.68	91.72	61.05	—	79.52	48.60	61.52
39	BARMER	20.21	97.29	83.65	44.92	—	36.34	46.00	21.99
40	BAYTOO	15.49	96.39	74.35	37.35	3.94	38.04	19.60	25.00
41	CHOHTAN	36.45	100.00	90.54	59.00	—	44.91	34.84	28.30
42	DHORIMANNA	20.23	100.00	77.69	37.75	—	35.75	29.64	49.91
43	SHEO	21.26	99.24	91.67	38.22	—	51.52	52.70	33.15
44	SINDHARI	25.07	99.71	79.53	38.31	0.47	44.61	37.19	34.02
45	SIWANA	45.72	100.00	98.01	68.24	3.20	77.92	40.98	90.23
	BARMER	**27.37**	**99.06**	**85.55**	**48.23**	**0.86**	**50.86**	**38.47**	**42.70**
46	BAYANA	44.02	100.00	97.91	58.64	1.54	31.94	43.22	72.19
47	DEEG	33.08	100.00	97.64	45.10	9.30	10.81	53.77	72.50
48	KAMAN	29.99	99.86	92.16	41.58	—	16.43	30.99	54.12
49	KUMHER	58.39	99.43	99.42	58.56	—	31.15	63.22	94.74
50	NADBAI	34.37	100.00	98.55	54.45	4.41	43.18	46.51	87.60

P. Code	*Panchayat Samiti/District*	*Medical*	*Drinking Water*	*Education*	*Post & Telegraph*	*Market/ Hat*	*Commu- nications*	*Approach By Pucca Road*	*Power Supply*
1	*2*	*3*	*4*	*5*	*6*	*7*	*8*	*9*	*10*
51	NAGAR PAHARI	24.36	100.00	93.95	44.77	1.13	27.13	39.78	44.80
52	RUPBAS	42.28	100.00	98.35	47.87	10.62	46.01	53.20	61.63
53	SEWAR	33.86	99.89	98.18	40.48	—	29.20	60.67	85.68
54	WEIR	47.23	100.00	98.86	60.69	7.06	30.76	49.05	99.09
	BHARATPUR	**38.29**	**99.92**	**97.08**	**50.07**	**3.81**	**29.84**	**48.29**	**73.33**
55	ASIND	55.33	100.00	93.89	53.56	—	62.25	43.62	87.27
56	BANERA	74.52	100.00	97.32	58.04	—	58.35	53.29	97.74
57	HURDA	72.82	100.00	99.29	48.91	6.22	75.25	62.07	100.00
58	JAHAZPUR	60.42	100.00	95.72	49.81	1.51	40.85	44.23	87.71
59	KOTRI	51.05	100.00	96.26	49.69	—	53.22	42.57	85.41
60	MANDAL	60.90	100.00	96.74	51.25	—	70.56	46.93	92.72
61	MANDALGARH	51.48	100.00	87.08	45.23	—	43.47	46.04	88.47
62	RAIPUR	58.84	100.00	98.27	55.55	—	73.60	38.20	92.67
63	SAHARA	64.86	100.00	97.82	65.50	—	63.69	47.41	97.50
64	SHAHPURA	54.26	100.00	98.07	50.19	—	56.82	53.29	93.70
65	SUWANA	52.81	100.00	98.14	52.86	—	62.94	61.51	97.57
	BHILWARA	**58.41**	**100.00**	**95.67**	**52.08**	**0.51**	**58.58**	**48.64**	**91.98**
66	BIKANER	62.59	98.42	98.48	53.04	—	64.48	60.00	80.10
67	DUNGARGARH *	61.86	99.18	97.62	73.38	—	65.87	54.62	90.27
68	KOLAYAT	44.43	97.53	94.12	55.51	1.92	65.20	56.99	76.59
69	LUNKARANSAR	44.96	99.81	97.98	51.89	—	56.67	54.02	86.80
70	NOKHA	51.78	99.43	98.50	64.79	—	65.35	52.29	91.41
	BIKANER **	**52.42**	**98.85**	**97.54**	**56.60**	**0.35**	**63.19**	**55.97**	**84.14**
71	HINDOLI	26.47	100.00	96.24	39.42	2.32	37.56	32.55	86.26
72	KESHORAIPATAN	38.22	100.00	93.11	44.40	12.93	36.97	29.43	58.07
73	NAINWA	42.07	100.00	94.52	41.67	17.19	44.81	35.42	85.91
74	TALERA	34.98	100.00	90.99	40.08	18.07	34.60	45.82	79.43
	BUNDI	**35.07**	**100.00**	**93.41**	**41.24**	**12.94**	**37.81**	**36.82**	**68.00**
75	ARNOD	39.79	100.00	89.30	46.66	17.59	37.71	31.82	72.13
76	BARI SADRI	33.53	100.00	86.91	39.08	—	46.57	41.15	79.58
77	BEGUN	34.91	100.00	83.91	33.65	—	42.62	44.37	86.83
78	BHADESAR	36.66	100.00	86.85	42.57	—	49.21	43.04	68.60
79	BHAINSRORGARH	23.52	100.00	81.15	23.76	6.42	52.81	39.55	76.44
80	BHOPALSAGAR	52.38	100.00	94.01	50.34	—	64.52	65.40	98.43
81	CHHOTI SADRI	20.08	100.00	91.21	40.08	—	42.41	32.39	93.32
82	CHITTAURGARH	33.39	100.00	90.65	48.53	—	54.54	45.17	86.91
83	DUNGLA	36.47	100.00	94.79	45.17	—	45.90	33.99	80.62
84	GANGRAR	39.45	100.00	91.41	42.92	1.08	56.69	34.50	83.01
85	KAPASAN	40.30	100.00	93.20	41.34	—	50.33	36.67	98.59
86	NIMBAHERA	25.09	99.88	93.17	45.02	—	47.04	42.87	94.73
87	PRATAPGARH	33.18	100.00	84.47	34.14	0.83	40.11	27.99	57.96
88	RASHMI	57.13	100.00	98.29	56.04	3.45	74.66	54.92	81.47
	CHITTAURGARH	**35.21**	**99.99**	**89.60**	**41.92**	**1.96**	**49.14**	**39.93**	**81.86**
89	CHURU	37.04	98.21	99.24	43.21	—	70.79	41.65	89.99
90	RAJGARH	33.61	95.52	96.82	49.06	—	56.58	41.20	48.25
91	RATANGARH	54.03	99.94	97.66	71.34	—	71.97	33.55	96.21
92	SARDARSHAHAR	33.05	99.67	96.60	49.11	—	66.08	33.71	65.90
93	SUJANGARH	48.32	99.18	97.69	62.75	—	67.26	31.30	81.40
94	TARANAGAR	54.77	100.00	97.08	63.34	8.02	67.99	47.70	78.86
	CHURU ***	**44.68**	**99.40**	**97.43**	**57.85**	**0.91**	**65.77**	**39.80**	**75.68**
95	BANDIKUI	35.14	100.00	87.60	38.18	1.53	29.68	27.56	96.02
96	DAUSA	41.91	100.00	91.84	50.76	—	48.71	43.96	86.02
97	LALSOT	31.00	100.00	89.73	36.67	4.88	34.05	36.70	70.32
98	MAHWA	39.16	100.00	95.78	50.85	4.40	17.30	43.14	59.28
99	SIKRAI	42.43	100.00	95.87	48.70	5.18	42.06	44.26	70.09
	DAUSA #	**37.83**	**100.00**	**91.88**	**44.79**	**3.01**	**35.25**	**38.91**	**77.52**
100	BARI	36.22	100.00	92.99	41.80	1.90	19.90	35.05	22.36
101	BASERI	48.81	100.00	96.25	52.49	—	40.78	60.56	37.45
102	DHAULPUR	54.95	100.00	99.64	50.93	18.03	21.89	52.65	48.88
103	RAJAKHERA	28.16	100.00	96.21	46.81	5.06	11.05	38.87	72.47
	DHAULPUR	**43.40**	**100.00**	**96.72**	**48.58**	**7.43**	**23.47**	**47.89**	**46.82**
104	ASPUR	49.97	99.97	92.25	52.63	0.66	57.58	51.20	78.67
105	BICHHIWARA	48.60	100.00	97.03	62.22	—	54.76	58.76	78.26
106	DUNGARPUR	40.56	100.00	96.75	43.57	—	47.52	53.17	57.59
107	SAGWARA	64.03	100.00	98.99	56.66	—	68.22	60.25	68.11
108	SIMALWARA	41.42	100.00	93.24	46.63	—	48.10	45.52	61.29
	DUNGARPUR	**48.90**	**99.99**	**96.62**	**52.65**	**0.12**	**55.55**	**53.70**	**65.24**
109	ANUPGARH	23.07	100.00	56.53	27.35	—	54.75	55.68	23.09
110	GANGANAGAR	53.05	100.00	87.95	65.27	—	63.86	71.40	93.11
111	KARANPUR	34.03	100.00	92.46	59.98	—	53.36	56.84	97.91
112	PADAMPUR	40.47	100.00	92.63	47.18	1.34	56.19	51.18	75.74
113	RAISINGHNAGAR	39.53	100.00	82.59	34.69	—	59.22	51.38	62.02

P. Code	Panchayat Samiti/District	Medical	Drinking Water	Education	Post & Telegraph	Market Hat	Commu-nications	Approach By Pucca Road	Power Supply
1	2	3	4	5	6	7	8	9	10
114	SADULSHAHAR	51.17	99.73	85.51	56.76	—	70.23	70.57	86.71
115	SURATGARH	41.22	100.00	74.25	34.60	—	63.60	57.34	43.31
	GANGANAGAR	**39.40**	**99.96**	**77.46**	**43.41**	**0.11**	**60.86**	**59.78**	**60.73**
116	BHADRA	58.13	100.00	94.23	65.30	—	67.75	47.44	54.97
117	HANUMANGARH	61.81	100.00	76.20	52.89	—	70.17	75.79	82.33
118	NOHAR	53.42	99.73	88.34	50.06	4.27	57.25	37.22	48.94
	HANUMANGARH ##	**57.96**	**99.9**	**84.62**	**54.66**	**1.54**	**64.97**	**55.52**	**64.15**
119	AMBER	40.10	99.85	92.59	48.81	—	56.63	57.57	98.01
120	BASSI	45.36	100.00	93.16	42.11	—	61.74	61.51	85.38
121	CHAKSU	37.06	99.98	78.13	29.70	—	33.80	28.30	67.92
122	DUDU	45.57	99.73	94.97	54.51	—	47.38	50.46	40.58
123	GOVINDGARH	78.48	100.00	99.34	79.30	—	68.43	67.16	100.00
124	JAMWA RAMGARH	46.40	100.00	94.75	43.82	0.72	51.70	50.93	99.01
125	JHOTWARA	37.02	100.00	94.81	55.62	—	56.78	75.19	99.92
126	KOTPUTLI	47.34	100.00	97.87	62.23	—	46.70	53.49	93.58
127	PHAGI	46.57	99.70	93.40	50.27	—	48.89	46.47	73.50
128	SAMBHAR	46.52	99.86	97.29	49.34	—	56.07	54.29	98.71
129	SANGANER	39.08	100.00	89.88	43.54	4.81	51.91	61.05	99.94
130	SHAHPURA	57.66	99.96	99.96	56.36	—	39.76	69.72	99.54
131	VIRATNAGAR	55.76	99.75	92.62	46.85	—	38.00	58.97	99.18
	JAIPUR	**48.74**	**99.91**	**94.09**	**51.84**	**0.42**	**51.38**	**56.45**	**88.41**
132	JAISALMER	40.03	98.50	94.45	59.47	1.31	58.49	54.67	38.59
133	SAM	30.42	99.91	90.78	48.57	7.25	47.90	30.11	1.51
134	SANKRA	32.92	100.00	94.69	53.05	—	64.28	48.92	19.51
	JAISALMER	**34.07**	**99.56**	**93.35**	**53.36**	**2.73**	**57.34**	**44.37**	**18.90**
135	AHORE	61.62	100.00	98.94	67.49	—	85.53	44.36	98.30
136	BHINMAL	37.27	100.00	98.24	60.49	—	73.55	40.64	88.50
137	JALOR	63.83	100.00	99.66	63.27	—	87.47	64.94	98.77
138	JASWANTPURA	46.36	100.00	98.86	60.58	—	77.22	54.35	97.74
139	RANIWARA	35.35	100.00	99.98	56.69	—	74.22	58.53	99.74
140	SANCHORE	35.96	98.29	98.33	45.48	—	68.06	38.18	60.02
141	SAYLA	62.45	99.92	99.91	70.70	—	90.36	58.32	97.38
	JALOR	**47.69**	**99.57**	**99.04**	**59.24**	—	**78.39**	**49.21**	**87.57**
142	BAKANI	37.62	100.00	80.66	39.76	19.97	33.97	38.87	68.18
143	DAG	37.02	100.00	89.62	37.71	14.37	37.38	32.18	46.85
144	JHALRAPATAN	33.21	100.00	85.26	34.38	7.87	33.44	36.92	90.24
145	KHANPUR	39.25	100.00	89.75	34.86	17.06	30.23	33.22	83.13
146	MANOHARTHANA	28.21	100.00	74.31	24.65	8.38	20.80	23.14	40.79
147	PIRAWA	35.14	100.00	96.82	36.42	13.04	23.58	12.43	88.43
	JHALAWAR	**35.00**	**100.00**	**86.08**	**34.71**	**13.20**	**30.17**	**29.77**	**70.15**
148	ALSISAR	54.82	100.00	98.87	59.37	8.83	69.19	54.93	83.48
149	BUHANA	41.81	100.00	99.00	68.75	—	61.11	48.81	92.29
150	CHIRAWA	55.30	99.65	98.43	69.64	—	74.51	66.65	100.00
151	JHUNJHUNUN	46.68	99.68	98.06	52.43	7.85	71.94	70.30	97.59
152	KHETRI	64.87	100.00	98.21	65.33	—	76.23	62.31	94.15
153	NAWALGARH	73.61	100.00	100.00	81.64	13.51	82.12	69.44	100.00
154	SURAJGARH	35.21	98.87	99.67	54.23	—	60.27	49.19	95.91
155	UDAIPURWATI	62.41	100.00	99.38	77.88	—	74.18	83.25	99.11
	JHUNJHUNUN	**55.14**	**99.80**	**98.98**	**67.06**	**3.72**	**71.56**	**63.90**	**95.73**
156	BALESAR	65.93	99.52	99.43	65.29	5.56	76.73	50.89	93.05
157	BAP	26.40	99.79	90.26	49.95	0.49	57.50	20.79	33.77
158	BHOPALGARH	57.94	99.34	98.94	69.95	—	89.94	79.73	93.15
159	BILARA	75.35	100.00	99.73	75.33	—	93.18	77.71	99.59
160	LUNI	54.43	100.00	99.04	60.79	—	84.48	71.73	83.01
161	MANDOR	27.67	98.37	98.81	56.44	—	60.65	64.26	90.45
162	OSIAN	42.29	99.86	90.02	73.83	—	97.07	57.89	82.44
163	PHALODI	36.59	93.03	97.26	57.81	1.36	69.30	50.31	75.41
164	SHERGARH	56.34	95.15	100.00	72.50	35.33	84.37	62.89	77.72
	JODHPUR	**46.93**	**95.64**	**94.73**	**61.27**	**3.56**	**73.04**	**58.04**	**78.62**
165	HINDAUN	49.73	100.00	97.83	50.85	11.12	41.39	55.31	94.97
166	KARAULI	37.77	100.00	91.38	41.94	3.68	26.16	32.14	55.68
167	NADOTI	50.63	100.00	94.53	59.77	17.46	57.40	52.95	89.21
168	SAPOTRA	45.68	99.54	93.49	51.81	9.37	35.10	37.54	57.96
169	TODABHIM	44.80	100.00	96.24	50.48	6.91	25.80	49.57	69.77
	KARAULI ###	**45.49**	**99.90**	**94.78**	**50.28**	**9.17**	**35.82**	**45.05**	**72.80**
170	CHECHAT	48.55	99.89	92.39	46.61	20.61	39.88	49.46	97.92
171	ITAWA	45.23	100.00	91.19	50.02	37.48	43.33	37.61	44.90
172	LADPURA	44.19	100.00	95.43	37.45	8.70	25.09	74.97	86.66
173	SANGOD	38.03	100.00	83.71	42.48	22.16	37.01	38.99	85.45
174	SULTANPUR	42.97	100.00	92.60	48.58	30.13	39.37	36.39	81.21
	KOTA	**43.78**	**99.98**	**90.97**	**45.23**	**24.27**	**37.23**	**46.79**	**78.75**

P. Code	*Panchayat Samiti/District*	*Medical*	*Drinking Water*	*Education*	*Post & Telegraph*	*Market/ Hat*	*Commu- nications*	*Approach By Pucca Road*	*Power Supply*
1	*2*	*3*	*4*	*5*	*6*	*7*	*8*	*9*	*10*
175	DEGANA	47.79	100.00	99.32	49.97	—	74.88	46.16	83.96
176	DIDWANA	43.15	100.00	97.60	59.09	3.36	77.27	4.84	87.87
177	JAYAL	49.20	100.00	97.99	58.95	11.32	72.14	41.60	61.73
178	KUCHAMAN	50.62	99.83	98.26	65.16	—	73.52	28.74	99.58
179	LADNU	53.60	100.00	98.74	65.98	—	82.42	33.19	75.53
180	MAKRANA	47.23	100.00	98.30	71.56	1.99	70.89	19.99	90.66
181	MERTA	60.84	100.00	97.35	60.97	3.17	86.95	63.84	97.96
182	MUNDWA	46.95	100.00	98.76	61.68	—	75.83	47.85	80.57
183	NAGAUR	56.47	100.00	97.38	52.73	3.55	70.18	32.85	68.65
184	PARBATSAR	45.59	99.27	98.03	60.16	3.05	70.02	33.20	98.68
185	RIYAN	51.70	99.58	98.92	61.17	10.75	71.26	58.40	95.87
	NAGAUR	**49.99**	**99.89**	**98.19**	**60.52**	**3.40**	**74.81**	**35.58**	**85.44**
186	BALI	73.69	100.00	99.86	66.52	—	78.23	66.07	93.69
187	DESURI	69.91	100.00	98.10	59.39	14.70	63.88	57.32	96.47
188	JAITARAN	60.77	100.00	97.54	64.99	—	67.83	32.30	94.95
189	KHARCHI/MARWAR JUN.	56.45	100.00	95.37	67.14	7.63	78.51	54.49	91.71
190	PALI	52.13	100.00	99.15	55.72	—	78.93	62.32	97.32
191	RAIPUR	36.11	100.00	95.25	66.87	—	54.34	42.68	77.13
192	RANI STATION	72.90	100.00	99.39	78.51	6.86	81.60	44.43	99.59
193	ROHAT	34.73	100.00	99.17	38.53	—	65.36	36.26	94.98
194	SOJAT	52.75	100.00	99.51	66.37	3.76	75.74	53.56	90.21
195	SUMERPUR	71.11	100.00	98.36	82.52	—	89.47	87.74	100.00
	PALI	**60.65**	**100.00**	**98.05**	**60.05**	**2.00**	**73.89**	**53.95**	**92.96**
196	AMET	41.18	100.00	90.05	40.08	—	64.89	34.17	86.00
197	BHIM	47.94	100.00	95.03	55.52	—	57.60	60.06	80.18
198	DEOGARH	28.25	100.00	80.52	35.37	—	52.87	40.34	73.96
199	KHAMNOR	61.20	100.00	96.90	54.45	—	73.47	48.45	94.22
200	KUMBHALGARH	39.80	100.00	92.88	43.65	—	60.14	42.14	26.08
201	RAILMAGRA	60.35	100.00	97.04	55.84	—	70.88	60.30	100.00
202	RAJSAMAND	45.94	100.00	97.51	58.55	—	79.59	48.26	26.00
	RAJSAMAND #	**47.72**	**100.00**	**93.77**	**50.33**	**—**	**66.51**	**48.63**	**67.66**
203	BAMANWAS	50.75	100.00	97.30	51.68	10.76	38.19	50.14	77.86
204	BONLI	42.81	99.83	95.86	49.38	28.82	43.95	36.28	88.02
205	GANGAPUR	57.32	100.00	98.87	59.11	7.34	43.46	45.02	90.65
206	KHANDAR	46.80	100.00	89.45	43.45	17.09	55.00	40.69	43.50
207	SAWAI MADHOPUR	47.33	100.00	97.68	56.12	13.64	38.35	35.37	74.47
	SAWAI MADHOPUR	**48.81**	**99.96**	**96.09**	**52.37**	**15.90**	**43.38**	**40.86**	**76.28**
208	DANTA RAMGARH	64.52	100.00	98.34	71.13	0.75	79.79	57.35	94.24
209	DHOND	70.61	99.76	98.47	65.57	—	79.24	52.68	100.00
210	FATEHPUR	47.62	100.00	99.76	64.49	—	67.65	24.68	97.62
211	KHANDELA	57.41	100.00	98.76	68.66	—	61.45	53.51	99.59
212	LACHHMANGARH	47.16	99.73	99.15	57.96	—	66.81	37.38	99.30
213	NEEM KA THANA	61.28	99.34	97.70	64.40	—	53.35	47.73	93.39
214	PIPRALI	61.62	100.00	99.23	78.90	8.18	25.86	68.81	38.37
215	SRI MADHOPUR	52.56	100.00	99.93	76.68	—	71.13	58.77	99.76
	SIKAR	**58.38**	**99.82**	**98.82**	**68.36**	**1.02**	**62.68**	**48.97**	**90.67**
216	ABU ROAD	4.41	100.00	99.71	52.46	—	46.46	73.83	76.11
217	PINDWARA	54.31	99.42	99.13	80.37	—	64.47	68.95	83.82
218	REODAR	38.66	100.00	98.09	49.93	2.66	58.62	64.81	97.24
219	SHEOGANJ	62.27	100.00	98.80	67.83	6.51	68.78	98.01	65.25
220	SIROHI	51.63	100.00	98.84	78.48	—	66.36	66.05	99.68
	SIROHI	**43.40**	**99.86**	**98.85**	**61.31**	**1.66**	**61.28**	**72.48**	**86.38**
221	DEOLI	59.57	100.00	95.39	55.41	—	42.69	37.15	61.79
222	MALPURA	57.64	100.00	97.62	58.59	—	34.12	45.15	82.89
223	NIWAI	40.04	100.00	93.73	43.57	10.31	34.33	29.38	88.31
224	TODARAISINGH	48.57	100.00	91.58	0.44	—	52.54	34.54	49.23
225	TONK	43.08	100.00	91.48	42.64	—	26.38	30.92	62.37
226	UNIARA	38.55	100.00	87.49	45.03	10.70	41.75	33.35	70.80
	TONK	**48.19**	**100.00**	**93.20**	**49.90**	**3.22**	**35.52**	**35.16**	**70.29**
227	BARGAON	44.27	100.00	96.55	58.16	—	56.11	54.57	93.85
228	BHINDER	46.70	100.00	91.20	43.15	—	56.36	54.96	89.10
229	DHARIAWAD	34.79	100.00	86.99	39.40	—	49.07	37.89	65.53
230	GIRWA	61.35	100.00	95.96	64.67	0.59	62.26	61.28	81.16
231	GOGUNDA	36.94	100.00	97.17	47.45	—	54.38	40.13	76.94
232	JHADOL	45.76	100.00	90.58	32.84	—	42.14	33.00	46.34
233	KHERWARA	41.44	100.00	94.95	46.25	—	51.19	36.09	50.08
234	KOTRA	23.73	100.00	72.73	30.62	—	37.04	30.72	29.21
235	MAVLI	58.29	100.00	98.60	55.93	—	67.80	59.18	89.54
236	SALUMBAR	46.31	100.00	84.64	39.58	0.71	48.94	43.91	63.88
237	SARADA	59.24	100.00	95.70	65.45	—	65.67	51.71	75.39
	UDAIPUR	**46.15**	**100.00**	**91.63**	**48.04**	**0.13**	**54.19**	**46.13**	**69.24**
	RAJASTHAN	**46.17**	**99.68**	**93.90**	**52.19**	**3.40**	**53.43**	**48.21**	**77.09**

Note: * Dungargarh PS shifted from Churu to Bikaner district on 1st April 2001 ** Excluding data of Dungargarh PS; *** Including data of Dungargarh PS.
Came in force from April, 1991; ## Came in force from July 1994 ### Came in force from July 1997.

Source: 1. Computed from data given in Primary Census Abustract, Rajasthan, Series-21, Census of India, 1991.
2. District Census Handbooks (all districts), Rajasthan, 1991.

GENERAL ANNEX-IV

PANCHAYAT SAMITI-WISE PERCENTAGE OF INHABITED VILLAGES HAVING MEDICAL AND OTHER RELATED AMENITIES: RAJASTHAN (1991)

P. Code	Panchayat Samiti/District	Medical	Drinking Water	Education	Post & Telegraph	Market/ Hat	Commu- nications	Approach By Pucca Road	Power Supply
1	2	3	4	5	6	7	8	9	10
1	ARAIN	23.77	100.00	94.26	26.23	—	27.05	18.85	59.02
2	BHINAY	39.17	100.00	95.82	39.17	—	38.33	36.67	68.33
3	JAWAJA	19.69	98.45	76.68	21.24	—	29.53	44.56	47.67
4	KEKRI	37.23	100.00	96.81	42.55	—	16.17	39.36	84.04
5	KISHANGARH	32.73	100.00	90.00	38.18	—	43.64	40.91	83.64
6	MASOODA	27.01	100.00	79.56	23.36	—	31.39	37.96	73.72
7	PISANGAN	44.74	100.00	95.61	51.75	—	51.75	58.77	92.11
8	SRINAGAR	32.63	100.00	97.89	34.74	—	46.32	55.79	88.42
	AJMER DISTRICT	**30.86**	**99.70**	**89.24**	**33.10**	**—**	**36.95**	**41.32**	**71.78**
9	BANSURE	19.85	100.00	90.84	33.66	0.76	24.43	25.19	97.71
10	BEHROR	28.89	100.00	90.00	32.22	—	32.22	33.33	96.67
11	KATHUMAR	20.89	100.00	93.04	21.52	—	18.99	31.65	49.37
12	KISHANGARH BAS	20.00	100.00	82.96	25.19	0.74	22.96	40.00	98.52
13	KOTKASIM	20.00	100.00	84.35	20.00	—	22.61	27.83	77.39
14	LACHHMANGARH	13.69	100.00	86.96	19.57	—	19.57	33.15	46.20
15	MANDAWAR	26.06	100.00	95.77	27.46	—	33.80	35.21	94.37
16	NIMRANA	29.41	100.00	94.12	38.82	—	29.41	38.82	98.82
17	RAJGARH	16.18	100.00	76.47	22.06	—	19.85	29.41	62.50
18	RAMGARH	18.13	100.00	81.87	19.30	1.17	17.54	33.92	77.78
19	RENI	15.69	100.00	84.31	25.49	—	15.69	20.59	66.67
20	THANAGAZI	21.62	100.00	77.70	20.95	—	30.41	37.16	49.32
21	TIJARA	13.07	100.00	78.39	17.59	—	17.59	26.63	64.32
22	UMREN	20.00	100.00	77.33	24.00	0.67	26.00	44.00	86.67
	ALWAR	**19.48**	**100.00**	**84.74**	**23.12**	**0.26**	**23.07**	**32.68**	**73.74**
23	ANANDPURI	21.14	100.00	86.18	14.63	—	24.39	28.46	32.52
24	BAGIDORA	26.28	100.00	78.10	14.60	—	27.01	39.42	32.12
25	GARHI	38.04	100.00	87.73	22.70	—	37.42	40.49	74.23
26	GHATOL	16.06	100.00	77.98	16.51	1.38	22.48	30.28	41.74
27	KUSHALGARH	9.62	99.04	67.79	5.29	2.88	13.46	19.23	31.25
28	PEEPALKHOONT	22.58	100.00	55.91	9.68	3.76	14.52	21.51	13.44
29	SAJJANGARH	13.74	100.00	63.74	7.14	1.10	15.93	24.73	23.08
30	TALWARA	24.30	100.00	72.43	19.63	0.47	35.51	39.25	37.85
	BANSWARA	**20.82**	**99.86**	**72.82**	**13.63**	**1.33**	**23.55**	**30.55**	**35.57**
31	ANTA	17.69	100.00	81.63	19.73	4.76	17.01	18.37	59.86
32	ATRU	22.22	100.00	77.04	27.41	6.67	22.96	18.52	72.59
33	BARAN	15.31	100.00	93.88	21.43	2.04	18.37	22.45	86.73
34	CHHABRA	11.05	100.00	68.60	11.05	2.91	12.79	12.21	27.91
35	CHHIPABAROD	12.02	100.00	73.22	11.48	3.83	11.48	12.57	60.66
36	KISHANGANJ	11.93	99.43	56.82	11.36	5.11	18.18	14.20	65.34
37	SHAHBAD	8.80	96.86	58.49	12.58	3.14	9.43	13.84	35.85
	BARAN #	**13.74**	**99.44**	**71.12**	**15.61**	**4.11**	**15.33**	**15.42**	**56.26**
38	BALOTRA	14.81	99.47	73.54	32.80	—	62.43	33.33	41.27
39	BARMER	11.32	95.09	67.17	26.04	—	26.04	32.83	10.57
40	BAYTOO	6.85	94.35	60.08	21.77	1.21	25.00	11.69	15.32
41	CHOHTAN	18.56	100.00	79.64	34.73	—	28.14	23.35	16.17
42	DHORIMANNA	13.10	100.00	68.65	24.21	—	27.38	26.59	41.27
43	SHEO	10.78	98.20	80.84	23.35	—	37.72	38.92	20.36
44	SINDHARI	12.50	99.58	65.83	22.08	0.42	30.00	22.50	20.00
45	SIWANA	30.93	100.00	95.88	44.33	2.06	59.79	24.74	84.54
	BARMER	**13.35**	**98.03**	**71.26**	**27.02**	**0.37**	**34.34**	**26.34**	**27.02**
46	BAYANA	23.90	100.00	86.16	32.70	0.63	23.90	31.45	59.12
47	DEEG	15.00	100.00	85.83	22.50	2.50	6.67	30.00	55.83
48	KAMAN	18.72	99.47	76.47	18.18	—	9.63	19.25	31.55

P. Code	*Panchayat Samiti/District*	*Medical*	*Drinking Water*	*Education*	*Post & Telegraph*	*Market/ Hat*	*Commu- nications*	*Approach By Pucca Road*	*Power Supply*
1	*2*	*3*	*4*	*5*	*6*	*7*	*8*	*9*	*10*
49	KUMHER	32.43	98.20	95.50	27.93	—	18.02	44.14	87.39
50	NADBAI	21.05	100.00	88.60	29.82	2.62	29.82	34.21	79.82
51	NAGAR PAHARI	11.98	100.00	81.57	20.74	0.92	15.67	26.27	28.57
52	RUPBAS	23.40	100.00	95.04	25.53	2.84	34.04	40.43	48.23
53	SEWAR	20.13	98.70	84.42	16.23	—	17.53	40.91	72.73
54	WEIR	26.76	100.00	93.66	35.92	2.82	18.31	33.10	95.77
	BHARATPUR	**20.74**	**99.63**	**86.54**	**24.91**	**1.26**	**18.81**	**32.27**	**58.44**
55	ASIND	26.60	100.00	75.37	23.15	—	39.41	24.63	69.95
56	BANERA	42.68	100.00	90.24	26.83	—	30.49	29.27	90.24
57	HURDA	41.18	100.00	94.12	26.47	7.35	55.88	36.76	100.00
58	JAHAZPUR	30.94	100.00	78.45	19.34	0.55	23.20	23.20	68.51
59	KOTRI	24.66	100.00	87.61	21.92	—	34.25	20.55	80.82
60	MANDAL	27.85	100.00	85.44	22.15	—	50.00	27.22	81.01
61	MANDALGARH	19.63	100.00	59.63	14.44	—	21.48	22.59	72.59
62	RAIPUR	29.07	100.00	90.70	25.58	—	50.00	19.77	77.91
63	SAHARA	31.87	100.00	91.21	34.07	—	39.56	30.77	96.70
64	SHAHPURA	28.19	100.00	93.29	24.83	—	38.93	28.19	83.89
65	SUWANA	24.43	100.00	88.55	23.66	—	45.04	38.93	92.37
	BHILWARA	**27.73**	**100.00**	**81.34**	**22.30**	**0.38**	**36.29**	**26.39**	**79.94**
66	BIKANER	28.39	96.13	87.10	24.52	—	43.23	45.16	71.61
67	DUNGARGARH *	40.00	97.78	97.78	53.33	—	53.33	40.00	77.78
68	KOLAYAT	17.16	96.45	69.82	21.89	0.59	39.64	30.77	46.75
69	LUNKARANSAR	19.23	99.23	89.23	24.62	—	37.69	33.08	76.15
70	NOKHA	27.78	98.41	88.89	38.10	—	46.83	35.71	81.75
	BIKANER **	**22.93**	**97.41**	**82.93**	**26.72**	**0.17**	**41.72**	**36.21**	**67.59**
71	HINDOLI	11.49	100.00	82.76	15.52	0.57	18.39	20.11	73.56
72	KESHORAIPATAN	15.74	100.00	78.70	18.52	3.70	23.61	20.83	43.98
73	NAINWA	14.86	100.00	85.14	16.57	3.43	22.29	17.14	73.14
74	TALERA	16.86	100.00	79.69	17.62	5.36	22.22	29.89	63.60
	BUNDI	**15.01**	**100.00**	**81.23**	**17.19**	**3.51**	**21.79**	**22.76**	**62.59**
75	ARNOD	12.87	100.00	59.06	15.79	4.09	19.88	13.45	43.86
76	BARI SADRI	10.42	100.00	61.11	13.19	—	21.53	18.75	56.94
77	BEGUN	11.87	100.00	54.34	10.05	—	25.11	27.40	67.12
78	BHADESAR	10.56	100.00	63.35	15.53	—	29.19	24.22	57.14
79	BHAINSRORGARH	7.33	100.00	51.33	8.00	2.00	28.67	23.33	64.00
80	BHOPALSAGAR	18.07	100.00	79.52	16.87	—	39.76	40.96	92.77
81	CHHOTI SADRI	6.38	100.00	68.79	15.60	—	30.50	24.11	82.98
82	CHITTAURGARH	7.80	100.00	66.06	16.06	—	26.15	22.48	62.84
83	DUNGLA	12.75	100.00	81.37	18.63	—	28.43	20.59	62.75
84	GANGRAR	12.60	100.00	68.50	14.96	0.79	31.50	14.17	69.29
85	KAPASAN	21.50	100.00	79.44	16.82	—	31.78	22.43	97.20
86	NIMBAHERA	7.33	98.67	73.33	16.00	—	27.33	20.67	80.67
87	PRATAPGARH	13.44	100.00	57.50	12.81	0.63	25.31	16.25	40.63
88	RASHMI	25.32	100.00	89.87	24.05	1.27	48.10	34.18	63.29
	CHITTAURGARH	**11.88**	**99.91**	**65.10**	**14.55**	**0.64**	**27.90**	**21.96**	**63.54**
89	CHURU	24.75	96.04	96.04	27.72	—	60.40	38.61	80.20
90	RAJGARH	19.51	99.02	94.63	30.73	—	47.32	34.63	40.00
91	RATANGARH	34.37	97.92	90.63	48.96	—	57.29	22.92	88.54
92	SARDARSHAHAR	21.18	99.41	90.59	31.76	—	55.88	30.59	59.41
93	SUJANGARH	27.45	93.46	85.62	37.25	—	49.67	22.88	68.63
94	TARANAGAR	23.42	98.20	85.59	32.43	0.90	43.24	26.13	55.86
	CHURU ***	**25.70**	**97.52**	**91.36**	**35.96**	**0.11**	**51.84**	**30.67**	**63.28**
95	BANDIKUI	14.49	100.00	69.08	15.94	0.48	13.53	14.98	90.34
96	DAUSA	15.84	100.00	69.68	19.91	—	25.34	24.43	69.23
97	LALSOT	9.90	100.00	63.14	12.29	0.68	16.72	20.14	50.85
98	MAHWA	15.33	100.00	84.00	22.67	2.00	7.33	25.33	44.00
99	SIKRAI	18.84	100.00	83.33	23.91	0.72	24.64	30.43	53.62
	DAUSA #	**14.17**	**100.00**	**71.66**	**17.84**	**0.59**	**17.64**	**22.20**	**62.34**
100	BARI	23.02	100.00	83.33	25.40	0.79	14.29	33.33	16.67
101	BASERI	22.95	100.00	81.15	22.95	—	22.95	36.07	20.49
102	DHAULPUR	40.38	100.00	96.15	26.92	5.77	10.26	42.95	33.97
103	RAJAKHERA	15.65	100.00	89.80	29.93	1.36	7.48	33.33	65.31
	DHAULPUR	**25.95**	**100.00**	**88.20**	**26.50**	**2.18**	**13.25**	**36.66**	**35.39**
104	ASPUR	30.28	99.30	88.03	30.28	0.70	35.92	30.28	59.15
105	BICHHIWARA	24.71	100.00	86.78	28.16	0.00	35.06	40.80	66.09
106	DUNGARPUR	27.85	100.00	87.34	27.22	0.00	36.71	46.20	45.57
107	SAGWARA	32.68	100.00	92.16	25.49	0.00	41.83	36.60	63.40
108	SIMALWARA	17.35	100.00	77.17	21.92	0.00	26.03	29.22	51.60
	DUNGARPUR	**25.77**	**99.88**	**85.58**	**26.24**	**0.12**	**34.40**	**36.29**	**56.86**

P. Code	Panchayat Samiti/District	Medical	Drinking Water	Education	Post & Telegraph	Market/ Hat	Commu- nications	Approach By Pucca Road	Power Supply
1	2	3	4	5	6	7	8	9	10
109	ANUPGARH	7.61	100.00	27.89	8.45	—	36.15	11.64	11.64
110	GANGANAGAR	26.97	100.00	60.17	39.42	—	42.74	54.36	87.55
111	KARANPUR	14.50	100.00	74.00	39.00	—	37.00	40.00	87.00
112	PADAMPUR	18.64	100.00	71.19	22.46	0.42	41.95	36.86	62.29
113	RAISINGHNAGAR	21.81	100.00	56.94	17.85	—	45.33	41.08	47.03
114	SADULSHAHAR	14.85	99.47	34.22	15.38	—	35.54	39.79	43.24
115	SURATGARH	13.68	100.00	30.44	9.41	—	33.09	36.18	20.00
	GANGANAGAR	**14.12**	**99.94**	**41.09**	**15.89**	**0.03**	**37.44**	**30.55**	**35.56**
116	BHADRA	19.47	100.00	52.63	21.05	—	35.79	28.42	28.42
117	HANUMANGARH	15.30	100.00	25.76	14.01	—	31.24	47.34	57.00
118	NOHAR	17.68	99.37	42.53	13.68	0.84	28.63	22.53	17.05
	HANUMANGARH ##	**16.80**	**99.77**	**35.93**	**14.93**	**0.31**	**30.95**	**35.46**	**38.02**
119	AMBER	21.13	99.48	75.26	21.65	—	35.57	35.05	97.42
120	BASSI	24.40	100.00	78.95	17.22	—	38.76	44.50	72.73
121	CHAKSU	17.83	99.61	53.10	9.30	—	14.73	13.57	56.59
122	DUDU	18.10	99.52	81.43	22.86	—	25.24	27.14	66.67
123	GOVINDGARH	47.37	100.00	92.63	46.32	—	40.00	41.05	100.00
124	JAMWA RAMGARH	21.65	100.00	84.42	17.75	0.43	31.17	31.60	95.67
125	JHOTWARA	16.67	100.00	76.47	28.43	—	41.18	50.98	99.02
126	KOTPUTLI	31.09	100.00	94.96	37.82	—	35.29	44.45	87.39
127	PHAGI	18.45	98.81	80.36	20.24	—	23.21	22.62	55.95
128	SAMBHAR	23.08	98.60	87.21	24.48	—	37.76	36.36	97.20
129	SANGANER	16.10	100.00	65.37	20.00	0.98	30.73	36.10	98.05
130	SHAHPURA	39.24	98.73	98.73	31.65	—	22.78	49.37	98.73
131	VIRATNAGAR	26.27	99.15	89.83	21.19	—	24.58	45.76	95.76
	JAIPUR	**22.71**	**99.58**	**78.40**	**22.01**	**0.14**	**29.94**	**34.11**	**83.20**
132	JAISALMER	16.06	95.62	78.83	31.39	1.46	38.69	35.04	22.63
133	SAM	9.96	99.60	58.17	19.92	3.19	24.70	15.94	0.40
134	SANKRA	21.54	100.00	88.46	36.15	—	51.54	34.62	10.00
	JAISALMER	**14.48**	**98.65**	**71.24**	**27.03**	**1.93**	**35.14**	**25.68**	**8.69**
135	AHORE	32.41	100.00	92.59	36.11	—	65.74	25.00	91.67
136	BHINMAL	21.52	100.00	93.67	41.77	—	65.82	31.65	81.01
137	JALOR	45.45	100.00	96.97	39.39	—	72.73	48.48	95.45
138	JASWANTPURA	27.78	100.00	94.44	34.72	—	63.89	41.67	94.44
139	RANIWARA	19.28	100.00	98.80	34.94	—	60.24	42.17	97.59
140	SANCHORE	22.78	97.78	92.22	26.11	—	54.44	28.89	50.56
141	SAYLA	38.96	98.70	98.70	42.86	—	77.92	44.16	93.51
	JALOR	**28.42**	**99.25**	**94.74**	**34.89**	**—**	**63.91**	**35.34**	**80.90**
142	BAKANI	13.48	100.00	50.35	12.06	3.19	14.54	20.57	46.45
143	DAG	15.45	100.00	74.55	13.64	3.64	20.91	15.45	33.18
144	JHALRAPATAN	14.54	100.00	63.12	13.83	2.13	18.09	25.18	76.60
145	KHANPUR	14.21	100.00	69.47	12.11	3.16	12.63	17.37	63.68
146	MANOHARTHANA	14.60	100.00	50.36	10.22	2.92	12.77	15.69	26.64
147	PIRAWA	17.00	100.00	87.50	17.50	4.00	13.00	8.50	79.00
	JHALAWAR	**14.78**	**100.00**	**64.16**	**13.05**	**3.11**	**15.40**	**17.68**	**53.31**
148	ALSISAR	23.01	100.00	96.46	28.32	0.88	51.33	31.86	70.80
149	BUHANA	24.59	100.00	96.72	42.62	—	45.90	34.43	90.98
150	CHIRAWA	30.49	98.78	95.12	41.46	—	53.66	43.90	100.00
151	JHUNJHUNUN	24.36	99.36	91.67	31.41	5.13	58.97	56.41	94.87
152	KHETRI	41.25	100.00	95.00	42.50	—	55.00	42.50	88.75
153	NAWALGARH	54.29	100.00	100.00	55.71	2.86	70.00	48.57	100.00
154	SURAJGARH	23.33	97.50	98.33	34.17	—	45.83	39.17	96.67
155	UDAIPURWATI	37.04	100.00	97.53	55.56	—	58.02	60.49	96.30
	JHUNJHUNUN	**30.10**	**99.39**	**96.00**	**39.56**	**1.33**	**54.00**	**44.42**	**91.75**
156	BALESAR	42.65	100.00	97.06	45.59	1.47	57.35	35.29	85.29
157	BAP	16.13	98.92	80.65	27.96	1.08	45.16	25.81	29.03
158	BHOPALGARH	32.14	100.00	97.62	41.67	—	79.76	63.10	90.48
159	BILARA	48.10	100.00	97.47	49.37	—	60.76	59.49	98.73
160	LUNI	26.56	100.00	94.58	30.47	—	64.84	48.44	64.06
161	MANDOR	15.24	99.05	97.14	34.29	—	49.52	46.67	79.05
162	OSIAN	25.75	98.80	92.81	42.51	—	65.27	45.51	73.05
163	PHALODI	25.58	97.67	91.86	39.53	1.16	56.98	41.86	66.28
164	SHERGARH	46.00	96.00	100.00	56.00	28.00	72.00	48.00	70.00
	JODHPUR	**28.72**	**99.07**	**93.84**	**39.42**	**1.98**	**61.05**	**45.93**	**71.86**
165	HINDAUN	31.93	100.00	97.48	30.25	4.20	28.57	42.02	92.44
166	KARAULI	19.39	100.00	76.53	22.45	1.02	16.33	20.92	41.84
167	NADOTI	27.38	100.00	83.33	34.52	4.76	39.29	38.10	76.19
168	SAPOTRA	18.66	99.04	71.29	23.92	1.91	17.70	21.53	42.11

P. Code	Panchayat Samiti/District	Medical	Drinking Water	Education	Post & Telegraph	Market/ Hat	Commu-nications	Approach By Pucca Road	Power Supply
1	2	3	4	5	6	7	8	9	10
169	TODABHIM	26.76	100.00	86.62	28.87	2.82	19.01	36.62	57.75
	KARAULI ###	**23.47**	**99.73**	**81.07**	**26.67**	**2.53**	**21.73**	**29.33**	**56.80**
170	CHECHAT	19.86	99.31	73.97	17.12	3.42	21.92	30.82	93.15
171	ITAWA	16.15	100.00	70.19	17.39	9.32	20.50	16.77	21.12
172	LADPURA	18.49	100.00	78.08	13.70	2.05	17.12	60.96	73.29
173	SANGOD	13.64	100.00	62.12	16.16	5.05	19.70	22.22	74.75
174	SULTANPUR	16.87	100.00	75.63	20.62	6.87	17.50	18.12	63.12
	KOTA	**16.77**	**99.88**	**70.16**	**17.02**	**5.43**	**19.36**	**28.85**	**64.86**
175	DEGANA	24.66	100.00	95.21	26.03	—	59.59	31.51	73.29
176	DIDWANA	22.75	100.00	95.21	34.73	0.60	62.87	32.34	77.84
177	JAYAL	23.48	100.00	92.42	28.79	3.03	45.45	17.42	43.18
178	KUCHAMAN	29.45	98.63	93.15	39.04	—	57.53	21.23	97.26
179	LADNU	30.21	100.00	90.63	39.58	—	68.75	30.21	62.50
180	MAKRANA	20.83	100.00	90.83	41.67	0.83	57.50	8.33	85.00
181	MERTA	26.04	100.00	85.42	30.21	2.08	60.42	33.33	90.63
182	MUNDWA	24.55	100.00	91.82	32.73	—	58.18	32.73	70.00
183	NAGAUR	28.57	100.00	91.73	24.81	0.75	55.64	30.83	50.38
184	PARBATSAR	27.78	99.07	95.37	34.26	1.85	51.85	21.30	97.22
185	RIYAN	25.83	99.17	91.67	32.50	4.17	46.67	35.83	89.17
	NAGAUR	**25.69**	**99.71**	**92.43**	**32.97**	**1.16**	**56.70**	**26.78**	**75.76**
186	BALI	41.57	100.00	97.75	39.33	2.25	58.43	47.19	86.52
187	DESURI	39.47	100.00	86.84	30.26	6.58	43.42	34.21	88.16
188	JAITARAN	33.70	100.00	90.22	36.96	—	48.91	17.39	86.96
189	KHARCHI/MARWAR JUN.	26.28	100.00	89.05	36.50	2.19	54.01	32.85	78.83
190	PALI	26.25	100.00	95.00	32.50	—	67.50	42.50	90.00
191	RAIPUR	27.18	100.00	82.52	34.95	—	32.04	24.27	60.19
192	RANI STATION	43.84	100.00	93.15	52.05	2.74	65.75	26.03	94.52
193	ROHAT	18.99	100.00	97.47	22.78	—	55.70	26.58	88.61
194	SOJAT	31.25	100.00	96.43	39.29	0.89	58.04	33.04	82.14
195	SUMERPUR	46.03	100.00	95.24	60.32	—	79.37	74.60	100.00
	PALI	**32.52**	**100.00**	**92.04**	**37.83**	**1.22**	**55.09**	**34.51**	**84.07**
196	AMET	19.12	100.00	68.38	17.65	—	53.68	25.00	70.59
197	BHIM	22.02	100.00	82.57	27.52	—	45.87	45.87	58.72
198	DEOGARH	11.45	100.00	59.54	17.56	—	36.64	24.43	55.73
199	KHAMNOR	33.33	100.00	78.03	26.52	—	50.00	30.30	89.39
200	KUMBHALGARH	21.12	100.00	84.47	24.22	—	43.48	29.81	62.11
201	RAILMAGRA	28.89	100.00	92.22	26.67	—	53.33	41.11	100.00
202	RAJSAMAND	20.00	100.00	90.00	32.31	—	50.77	30.00	78.46
	RAJSAMAND #	**21.93**	**100.00**	**78.74**	**24.41**	**—**	**47.36**	**31.50**	**72.33**
203	BAMANWAS	19.70	100.00	80.30	25.76	2.27	20.45	27.27	56.09
204	BONLI	17.83	99.36	84.07	21.02	8.28	21.66	15.92	77.07
205	GANGAPUR	31.30	100.00	91.30	31.30	1.74	26.96	33.91	81.74
206	KHANDAR	17.95	100.00	66.67	18.59	3.85	28.85	21.79	33.97
207	SAWAI MADHOPUR	20.13	100.00	88.96	32.47	2.60	17.53	15.58	55.19
	SAWAI MADHOPUR	**20.87**	**99.86**	**81.79**	**25.49**	**3.92**	**22.97**	**22.13**	**60.36**
208	DANTA RAMGARH	37.04	100.00	88.89	43.70	0.74	60.74	35.56	92.59
209	DHOND	50.93	99.07	97.22	43.52	—	69.44	38.89	100.00
210	FATEHPUR	29.79	100.00	99.29	46.10	—	58.16	22.70	95.74
211	KHANDELA	31.90	100.00	88.79	43.97	—	43.97	38.79	94.83
212	LACHHMANGARH	26.47	99.26	97.79	38.24	—	58.82	27.21	98.53
213	NEEM KA THANA	41.26	99.30	89.51	40.56	—	36.36	34.27	86.01
214	PIPRALI	31.87	100.00	90.11	51.65	4.40	49.45	45.05	82.42
215	SRI MADHOPUR	39.34	100.00	98.36	52.46	—	47.54	39.34	98.36
	SIKAR	**35.66**	**99.68**	**93.56**	**44.15**	**0.54**	**53.28**	**34.16**	**93.45**
216	ABU ROAD	23.08	100.00	96.15	28.21	—	32.05	56.41	61.54
217	PINDWARA	29.59	98.98	88.78	26.53	—	43.88	47.96	65.31
218	REODAR	17.21	100.00	90.16	22.95	0.82	37.70	39.34	90.98
219	SHEOGANJ	30.30	100.00	92.42	34.85	3.03	45.45	42.42	89.39
220	SIROHI	25.61	100.00	86.59	48.78	—	46.34	41.46	97.56
	SIROHI	**24.44**	**99.78**	**90.58**	**31.17**	**0.67**	**40.81**	**45.07**	**81.17**
221	DEOLI	28.66	100.00	76.43	21.02	—	20.38	18.47	32.48
222	MALPURA	30.89	100.00	85.37	24.39	—	27.64	20.33	68.29
223	NIWAI	12.57	100.00	74.87	15.18	2.09	15.18	12.57	69.63
224	TODARAISINGH	23.85	100.00	73.39	22.02	—	18.35	15.60	33.03
225	TONK	18.15	100.00	69.76	16.94	—	10.89	21.37	39.92
226	UNIARA	13.09	100.00	59.69	14.14	1.57	18.32	17.80	40.84
	TONK	**19.92**	**100.00**	**72.13**	**18.16**	**0.69**	**17.37**	**17.86**	**47.20**

P. Code	Panchayat Samiti/District	Medical	Drinking Water	Education	Post & Telegraph	Market/ Hat	Commu-nications	Approach By Pucca Road	Power Supply
1	2	3	4	5	6	7	8	9	10
227	BARGAON	20.98	100.00	77.62	23.78	—	38.46	32.17	83.92
228	BHINDER	14.77	100.00	64.02	14.77	—	31.82	29.92	32.58
229	DHARIAWAD	10.98	100.00	58.94	13.41	—	30.08	28.05	43.09
230	GIRWA	27.67	100.00	78.62	29.56	0.63	33.96	35.85	62.26
231	GOGUNDA	18.49	100.00	89.73	25.34	—	40.41	30.14	68.49
232	JHADOL	23.83	100.00	69.53	11.72	—	27.73	16.41	31.25
233	KHERWARA	21.99	100.00	81.33	25.73	—	38.59	24.90	36.51
234	KOTRA	7.62	100.00	44.04	12.25	—	22.19	17.55	18.87
235	MAVLI	33.11	100.00	91.89	28.38	—	47.97	39.19	77.03
236	SALUMBAR	23.38	100.00	66.67	15.58	0.43	30.74	23.81	47.62
237	SARADA	31.12	100.00	83.12	32.52	—	49.35	37.01	59.09
	UDAIPUR	**19.87**	**100.00**	**70.13**	**19.39**	**0.09**	**34.19**	**27.47**	**47.55**
	RAJASTHAN	**20.68**	**99.63**	**74.97**	**23.37**	**1.02**	**33.20**	**29.66**	**59.78**

Note: * Dungargarh PS shifted from Churu to Bikaner district on 1st April 2001
** Excluding data of Dungargarh PS.
*** Including data of Dungargarh PS.
# Came in force from April, 1991;
Came in force from July 1994
Came in force from July 1997.

Source: 1. Computed from data given in Primary Census Abustract, Rajasthan, Series -21, Census of India, 1991.
2. District Census Handbooks (all districts), Rajasthan, 1991.

PANCHAYAT SAMITI-WISE PANCHAYATS AND POPULATION

P. Code	Panchayat Samiti (Concerning Tehsil)	Total No. of Villages	Total No. of Gram Panchayats	Total Population					% share of District Rural Pop.
				Person	Male		Female		
					No.	%	No.	%	
1	2	3	4	5	6	7	8	9	10
1	ARAIN (Sarwar)	129	30	133386	68020	(51.0)	65366	(49.0)	(10.2)
2	BHINAY (Bhinay)	128	35	155111	79164	(51.0)	75947	(49.0)	(10.2)
3	JAWAJA* (Beawar)	200	35	157901	79620	(50.4)	78281	(49.6)	(12.1)
4	KEKRI* (Kekri)	100	31	140921	72021	(51.1)	68900	(48.9)	(10.8)
5	KISHANGARH (Kishangarh)	114	31	153474	79324	(51.7)	74150	(48.3)	(11.7)
6	MASOODA* (Masooda)	143	32	159600	81668	(51.2)	77932	(48.8)	(12.2)
7	PISANGAN (Pisangan)	128	45	236459	121687	(51.5)	114772	(48.5)	(18.1)
8	SRINAGAR (Ajmer)	96	37	170142	88399	(52.0)	81743	(48.0)	(13.0)
	AJMER DISTRICT	**1038**	**276**	**1306994**	**669903**	**(51.3)**	**637091**	**(48.7)**	**(100.0)**
9	BANSURE* (Bansure)	132	36	214351	112580	(52.5)	101771	(47.5)	(8.4)
10	BEHROR (Behror)	90	29	139503	72777	(52.2)	66726	(47.8)	(5.5)
11	KATHUMAR (Kathumar)	160	41	211689	113325	(53.5)	98364	(46.5)	(8.3)
12	KISHANGARH BAS (Kishangarh Bas)	140	29	167495	87756	(52.4)	79739	(47.6)	(6.5)
13	KOTKASIM* (Kotkasim)	116	24	117687	61712	(52.4)	55975	(47.6)	(4.6)
14	LACHHMANGARH (Lachmangarh)	186	44	225836	119382	(52.9)	106454	(47.1)	(8.8)
15	MANDAWAR* (Mandawar)	142	40	197582	103015	(52.1)	94567	(47.9)	(7.7)
16	NIMRANA (Behror)	87	33	143329	74428	(51.9)	68901	(48.1)	(5.6)
17	RAJGARH (Rajgarh)	147	30	144726	76591	(52.9)	68135	(47.1)	(5.7)
18	RAMGARH (Ramgarh)	173	37	220219	116180	(52.8)	104039	(47.2)	(8.6)
19	RENI (Rajgarh)	102	26	136491	72533	(53.1)	63958	(46.9)	(5.3)
20	THANAGAZI* (Thanagazi)	159	35	189977	99870	(52.6)	90107	(47.4)	(7.4)
21	TIJARA* (Tijara)	205	38	226974	121997	(53.7)	104977	(46.3)	(8.9)
22	UMREN (Alwar)	155	36	221794	117622	(53.0)	104172	(47.0)	(8.7)
	ALWAR	**1994**	**478**	**2557653**	**1349768**	**(52.8)**	**1207885**	**(47.2)**	**(100.0)**
23	ANANDPURI (Bagidora)	129	26	111206	56613	(50.9)	54593	(49.1)	(8.0)
24	BAGIDORA (Bagidora)	165	41	176729	89141	(50.4)	87588	(49.6)	(12.7)
25	GARHI* (Garhi)	170	55	237521	120212	(50.6)	117309	(49.4)	(17.0)
26	GHATOL (Ghatol)	223	53	230344	115822	(50.3)	114522	(49.7)	(16.5)
27	KUSHALGARH (Kushalgarh)	210	29	138970	69946	(50.3)	69024	(49.7)	(10.0)
28	PEEPALKHOONT (Banswara)	197	36	151273	76900	(50.8)	74373	(49.2)	(10.8)
29	SAJJANGARH (Kushalgarh)	187	30	134456	68165	(50.7)	66291	(49.3)	(9.6)
30	TALWARA (Banswara)	223	55	213727	108311	(50.7)	105416	(49.3)	(15.3)
	BANSWARA	**1504**	**325**	**1394226**	**705110**	**(50.6)**	**689116**	**(49.4)**	**(100.0)**
31	ANTA (Mangrol & Anta)	156	38	148759	77618	(52.2)	71141	(47.8)	(17.5)
32	ATRU* (Atru)	138	34	127043	66673	(52.5)	60370	(47.5)	(15.0)
33	BARAN* (Baran)	102	27	103142	54173	(52.5)	48969	(47.5)	(12.1)
34	CHHABRA* (Chhabra)	192	27	99472	52510	(52.8)	46962	(47.2)	(11.7)
35	CHHIPABAROD* (Chhipabarod)	180	30	127858	66733	(52.2)	61125	(47.8)	(15.0)
36	KISHANGANJ* (Kishanganj)	203	32	135218	70458	(52.1)	64760	(47.9)	(15.9)
37	SHAHBAD* (Shahbad)	236	27	108146	57040	(52.7)	51106	(47.3)	(12.7)
	BARAN #	**1207**	**215**	**849638**	**445205**	**(52.4)**	**404433**	**(47.6)**	**(100.0)**
38	BALOTRA* (Panchpadra)	233	54	265596	138016	(52.0)	127580	(48.0)	(14.6)
39	BARMER (Ramsar)	309	50	238075	128483	(54.0)	109592	(46.0)	(13.1)
40	BAYTOO (Baytoo)	323	47	210345	110447	(52.5)	99898	(47.5)	(11.6)
41	CHOHTAN (Chohtan)	189	51	225754	120580	(53.4)	105174	(46.6)	(12.4)
42	DHORIMANNA (Gudha Malani)	261	47	250929	131262	(52.3)	119667	(47.7)	(13.8)
43	SHEO* (Sheo)	251	45	178539	96930	(54.3)	81609	(45.7)	(9.8)
44	SINDHARI (Gudha Malani)	259	46	236545	122971	(52.0)	113574	(48.0)	(13.0)
45	SIWANA* (Siwana)	116	40	213648	111155	(52.0)	102493	(48.0)	(11.7)
	BARMER	**1941**	**380**	**1819431**	**959844**	**(52.8)**	**859587**	**(47.2)**	**(100.0)**
46	BAYANA* (Bayana)	177	45	191632	106038	(55.3)	85594	(44.7)	(11.3)
47	DEEG* (Deeg)	132	36	154862	83742	(54.1)	71120	(45.9)	(9.2)
48	KAMAN (Kaman)	209	44	212139	112682	(53.1)	99457	(46.9)	(12.5)
49	KUMHER* (Kumher)	124	36	155122	83545	(53.9)	71577	(46.1)	(9.2)
50	NADBAI* (Nadbai)	117	37	161111	87568	(54.4)	73543	(45.6)	(9.5)
51	NAGAR PAHARI (Nagar)	227	49	236329	126007	(53.3)	110322	(46.7)	(14.0)
52	RUPBAS* (Rupbas)	158	45	211147	114581	(54.3)	96566	(45.7)	(12.5)

ANNEX-V

NO. OF VILLAGES, GRAM CHARACTERISTICS: RAJASTHAN (2001)

Person	Population 0-6				% of 0-6 Pop. To Total Pop.	Sex-Ratio		Literacy Rate (%)		
	Male		Female			Total Population	0-6 Population	Persons	Male	Female
	No.	%	No.	%						
11	12	13	14	15	16	17	18	19	20	21
24479	12553	(51.3)	11926	(48.7)	18.4	961	950	46.52	64.11	28.30
29934	15380	(51.4)	14554	(48.6)	19.3	959	946	42.66	63.33	21.23
33339	17449	(52.3)	15890	(47.7)	21.1	983	911	74.41	90.89	58.02
25678	13279	(51.7)	12399	(48.3)	18.2	957	934	47.14	67.95	25.57
29018	15060	(51.9)	13958	(48.1)	18.9	935	927	53.12	71.19	33.86
32896	16868	(51.3)	16028	(48.7)	20.6	954	950	54.63	76.35	31.93
46195	24025	(52.0)	22170	(48.0)	19.5	943	923	52.88	73.05	31.64
33894	17765	(52.4)	16129	(47.6)	19.9	925	908	52.25	72.58	30.31
255433	**132379**	**(51.8)**	**123054**	**(48.2)**	**19.5**	**951**	**930**	**53.09**	**72.60**	**32.72**
42987	22638	(52.7)	20349	(47.3)	20.1	904	899	58.15	75.04	39.51
23586	12806	(54.3)	10780	(45.7)	16.9	917	842	93.19	89.75	72.18
42290	22360	(52.9)	19930	(47.1)	20.0	868	891	57.35	75.12	36.76
36092	18844	(52.2)	17248	(47.8)	21.5	909	915	55.90	73.76	36.23
21563	11593	(53.8)	9970	(46.2)	18.3	907	860	69.69	85.26	52.73
47777	25133	(52.6)	22644	(47.4)	21.2	892	901	56.40	75.92	34.48
35992	19366	(53.8)	16626	(46.2)	18.2	918	859	69.29	85.07	52.37
24332	13158	(54.1)	11174	(45.9)	17.0	926	849	56.84	67.56	45.39
28264	14883	(52.7)	13381	(47.3)	19.5	890	899	54.94	74.69	32.72
48269	25284	(52.4)	22985	(47.6)	21.9	895	909	53.82	72.75	32.60
27459	14479	(52.7)	12980	(47.3)	20.1	882	896	57.24	76.55	35.18
40560	21167	(52.2)	19393	(47.8)	21.3	902	916	48.07	67.80	26.20
52773	27732	(52.5)	25041	(47.5)	23.3	860	903	53.14	70.37	32.81
45668	23918	(52.4)	21750	(47.6)	20.6	886	909	53.52	72.10	32.40
517612	**273361**	**(52.8)**	**244251**	**(47.2)**	**20.2**	**895**	**894**	**58.88**	**76.54**	**39.16**
23993	12058	(50.3)	11935	(49.7)	21.6	964	990	40.52	56.38	24.02
38799	19715	(50.8)	19084	(49.2)	22.0	983	968	41.04	57.82	24.03
45631	23510	(51.5)	22121	(48.5)	19.2	976	941	51.98	69.25	34.71
48828	24996	(51.2)	23832	(48.8)	21.2	989	953	39.95	58.32	21.70
32889	16384	(49.8)	16505	(50.2)	23.7	987	1007	33.61	48.80	18.10
34649	17441	(50.3)	17208	(49.7)	22.9	967	987	25.77	39.20	11.87
31212	15742	(50.4)	15470	(49.6)	23.2	973	983	37.51	53.39	21.12
44433	22726	(51.1)	21707	(48.9)	20.8	973	955	45.59	64.20	26.47
300434	**152572**	**(50.8)**	**147862**	**(49.2)**	**21.5**	**977**	**969**	**40.78**	**57.49**	**23.78**
26177	13730	(52.5)	12447	(47.5)	17.6	917	907	63.46	80.37	45.01
21897	11434	(52.2)	10463	(47.8)	17.2	905	915	63.42	81.14	43.82
17668	9249	(52.3)	8419	(47.7)	17.1	904	910	65.52	82.67	46.45
19789	10313	(52.1)	9476	(47.9)	19.9	894	919	53.62	72.10	32.77
25028	13069	(52.2)	11959	(47.8)	19.6	916	915	48.83	68.27	27.71
26838	13734	(51.2)	13104	(48.8)	19.8	919	954	52.88	68.36	35.83
22416	11680	(52.1)	10736	(47.9)	20.7	896	919	52.99	69.80	34.03
159813	**83209**	**(52.1)**	**76604**	**(47.9)**	**18.8**	**908**	**921**	**57.43**	**74.81**	**38.21**
60026	31002	(51.6)	29024	(48.4)	22.6	924	936	55.13	71.90	36.97
53302	27757	(52.1)	25545	(47.9)	22.4	853	920	54.85	70.15	36.53
47344	24726	(52.2)	22618	(47.8)	22.5	904	915	58.26	72.32	42.93
51713	26750	(51.7)	24963	(48.3)	22.9	872	933	50.66	63.92	35.17
58600	30150	(51.5)	28450	(48.5)	23.4	912	944	67.75	77.73	56.72
42110	22756	(54.0)	19354	(46.0)	23.6	842	851	57.63	72.64	39.80
53974	28060	(52.0)	25914	(48.0)	22.8	924	924	60.88	74.24	46.42
44554	23171	(52.0)	21383	(48.0)	20.9	922	923	59.54	74.35	43.56
411623	**214372**	**(52.1)**	**197251**	**(47.9)**	**22.6**	**896**	**920**	**58.14**	**72.15**	**42.43**
39961	21502	(53.8)	18459	(46.2)	20.9	807	858	57.27	76.01	33.74
31674	16856	(53.2)	14818	(46.8)	20.5	849	879	58.54	77.36	36.34
53276	27910	(52.4)	25366	(47.6)	25.1	883	909	47.68	66.52	26.20
30113	16037	(53.3)	14076	(46.7)	19.4	857	878	67.52	85.82	46.09
30836	16352	(53.0)	14484	(47.0)	19.1	840	886	68.76	87.36	46.83
52408	27722	(52.9)	24686	(47.1)	22.2	876	890	58.96	77.22	38.12
45376	24417	(53.8)	20959	(46.2)	21.5	843	858	67.72	84.97	47.27

P. Code	Panchayat Samiti (Concerning Tehsil)	Total No. of Villages	Total No. of Gram Panchayats	Total Population					% share of District Rural Pop.
				Person	Male		Female		
					No.	%	No.	%	
1	2	3	4	5	6	7	8	9	10
53	SEWAR* (Bharatpur)	177	33	167641	90380	(53.9)	77261	(46.1)	(9.9)
54	WEIR* (Weir)	151	46	202199	109491	(54.2)	92708	(45.8)	(11.9)
	BHARATPUR	**1472**	**371**	**1692182**	**914034**	**(54.0)**	**778148**	**(46.0)**	**(100.0)**
55	ASIND* (Asind)	204	44	192346	95304	(49.5)	97042	(50.5)	(12.0)
56	BANERA* (Banera)	85	26	106222	53578	(50.4)	52644	(49.6)	(6.6)
57	HURDA* (Hurda)	72	20	91088	46735	(51.3)	44353	(48.7)	(5.7)
58	JAHAZPUR* (Jahazpur)	230	37	167782	86965	(51.8)	80817	(48.2)	(10.5)
59	KOTRI* (Kotri)	175	33	148702	76073	(51.2)	72629	(48.8)	(9.3)
60	MANDAL* (Mandal)	191	46	197500	97168	(49.2)	100332	(50.8)	(12.4)
61	MANDALGARH (Mandalgarh)	299	50	199935	103648	(51.8)	96287	(48.2)	(12.5)
62	RAIPUR* (Raipur)	92	22	84354	41301	(49.0)	43053	(51.0)	(5.3)
63	SAHARA* (Sahara)	104	28	98050	47375	(48.3)	50675	(51.7)	(6.1)
64	SHAHPURA* (Sahahpura)	155	38	148955	76354	(51.3)	72601	(48.7)	(9.3)
65	SUWANA* (Bhilwara)	138	34	164004	83478	(50.9)	80526	(49.1)	(10.3)
	BHILWARA	**1745**	**378**	**1598938**	**807979**	**(50.5)**	**790959**	**(49.5)**	**(100.0)**
66	BIKANER (Bikaner)	244	63	374802	198540	(53.0)	176262	(47.0)	(34.7)
67	DUNGARGARH* (Dungargarh) #	97	30	182819	93917	(51.4)	88902	(48.6)	(16.9)
68	KOLAYAT* (Kolayat)	221	37	207749	110666	(53.3)	97083	(46.7)	(19.2)
69	LUNKARANSAR (Lunkaransar)	176	36	217341	113669	(52.3)	103672	(47.7)	(20.1)
70	NOKHA* (Nokha)	137	53	279343	146029	(52.3)	133314	(47.7)	(25.9)
	BIKANER ##	**778**	**189**	**1079235**	**568904**	**(52.7)**	**510331**	**(47.3)**	**(100.0)**
71	HINDOLI* (Hindoli)	174	41	189290	99580	(52.6)	89710	(47.4)	(24.2)
72	KESHORAIPATAN (Indragarh)	227	46	178625	93289	(52.2)	85336	(47.8)	(22.8)
73	NAINWA* (Nainwa)	181	33	156227	81783	(52.3)	74444	(47.7)	(20.0)
74	TALERA* (Bundi)	267	61	258916	135831	(52.5)	123085	(47.5)	(33.1)
	BUNDI	**849**	**181**	**783058**	**410483**	**(52.4)**	**372575**	**(47.6)**	**(100.0)**
75	ARNOD* (Arnod)	179	30	119837	60826	(50.8)	59011	(49.2)	(7.9)
76	BARI SADRI* (Bari Sadri)	153	23	88841	44432	(50.0)	44409	(50.0)	(5.9)
77	BEGUN (Begun)	254	31	102011	51917	(50.9)	50094	(49.1)	(6.7)
78	BHADESAR* (Bhadesar)	168	25	107393	54257	(50.5)	53136	(49.5)	(7.1)
79	BHAINSRORGARH (Rawatbhata)	212	23	80379	42227	(52.5)	38152	(47.5)	(5.3)
80	BHOPALSAGAR (Kapasan)	85	19	72675	36291	(49.9)	36384	(50.1)	(4.8)
81	CHHOTI SADRI * (Chhoti Sadri)	151	24	100067	50890	(50.9)	49177	(49.1)	(6.6)
82	CHITTAURGARH* (Chittaurgarh)	229	39	167960	85545	(50.9)	82415	(49.1)	(11.1)
83	DUNGLA* (Dungla)	108	26	89975	44919	(49.9)	45056	(50.1)	(5.9)
84	GANGRAR* (Gangrar)	128	21	88640	44978	(50.7)	43662	(49.3)	(5.9)
85	KAPASAN (Kapasan)	111	23	84531	42429	(50.2)	42102	(49.8)	(5.6)
86	NIMBAHERA* (Nimbahera)	170	35	135391	68774	(50.8)	66617	(49.2)	(8.9)
87	PRATAPGARH* (Pratapgarh)	358	49	201229	102788	(51.1)	98441	(48.9)	(13.3)
88	RASHMI* (Rashmi)	89	23	75326	37282	(49.5)	38044	(50.5)	(5.0)
	CHITTAURGARH	**2395**	**391**	**1514255**	**767555**	**(50.7)**	**746700**	**(49.3)**	**(100.0)**
89	CHURU* (Churu)	106	35	152178	77677	(51.0)	74501	(49.0)	(11.0)
90	RAJGARH* (Rajgarh)	215	55	267403	138313	(51.7)	129090	(48.3)	(19.3)
91	RATANGARH* (Ratangarh)	101	32	158090	80065	(50.6)	78025	(49.4)	(11.4)
92	SARDARSHAHAR* (Sardarshahar)	184	48	222979	114186	(51.2)	108793	(48.8)	(16.1)
93	SUJANGARH* (Sujangarh)	155	51	253207	128683	(50.8)	124524	(49.2)	(18.2)
94	TARANAGAR* (Taranagar)	121	28	151006	77840	(51.5)	73166	(48.5)	(10.9)
	CHURU ###	**979**	**279**	**1387682**	**710681**	**(51.2)**	**677001**	**(48.8)**	**(100.0)**
95	BANDIKUI* (Baswa)	213	44	267016	140609	(52.7)	126407	(47.3)	(22.6)
96	DAUSA* (Dausa)	233	52	271907	142567	(52.4)	129340	(47.6)	(23.0)
97	LALSOT* (Lalsot)	321	47	251370	131209	(52.2)	120161	(47.8)	(21.3)
98	MAHWA* (Mahwa)	152	41	179173	95701	(53.4)	83472	(46.6)	(15.2)
99	SIKRAI* (Sikrai)	139	41	211779	111505	(52.7)	100274	(47.3)	(17.9)
	DAUSA #	**1058**	**225**	**1181245**	**621591**	**(52.6)**	**559654**	**(47.4)**	**(100.0)**
100	BARI* (Bari)	171	31	150595	83853	(55.7)	66742	(44.3)	(18.7)
101	BASERI* (Baseri)	196	35	201777	110589	(54.8)	91188	(45.2)	(25.0)
102	DHAULPUR (Sepau)	232	48	262456	142925	(54.5)	119531	(45.5)	(32.5)
103	RAJAKHERA (Rajakhera)	203	39	191812	105639	(55.1)	86173	(44.9)	(23.8)
	DHAULPUR	**802**	**153**	**806640**	**443006**	**(54.9)**	**363634**	**(45.1)**	**(100.0)**
104	ASPUR* (Aspur)	146	49	184508	89104	(48.3)	95404	(51.7)	(18.0)
105	BICHHIWARA (Dungarpur)	175	48	236114	118009	(50.0)	118105	(50.0)	(23.0)
106	DUNGARPUR (Dungarpur)	159	36	172385	84844	(49.2)	87541	(50.8)	(16.8)
107	SAGWARA (Sagwara)	158	46	192681	92915	(48.2)	99766	(51.8)	(18.8)
108	SIMALWARA (Simalwara)	220	58	241099	120792	(50.1)	120307	(49.9)	(23.5)
	DUNGARPUR	**858**	**237**	**1026787**	**505664**	**(49.2)**	**521123**	**(50.8)**	**(100.0)**
109	ANUPGARH (Garsana)	1131	88	417746	220600	(52.8)	197146	(47.2)	(31.3)
110	GANGANAGAR (Ganganagar)	273	44	176517	93595	(53.0)	82922	(47.0)	(13.2)
111	KARANPUR* (Karanpur)	237	35	103094	54341	(52.7)	48753	(47.3)	(7.7)
112	PADAMPUR* (Padampur)	247	36	121362	63657	(52.5)	57705	(47.5)	(9.1)
113	RAISINGHNAGAR* (Raisinghnagar)	407	47	157334	82247	(52.3)	75087	(47.7)	(11.8)
114	SADULSHAHAR (Sadulshahar)	252	32	146629	79236	(54.0)	67393	(46.0)	(11.0)

Person	Population 0-6				% of 0-6 Pop. To Total Pop.	Sex-Ratio		Literacy Rate (%)		
	Male		Female			Total Population	0-6 Population	Persons	Male	Female
	No.	%	No.	%						
11	12	13	14	15	16	17	18	19	20	21
34807	18408	(52.9)	16399	(47.1)	20.8	855	891	67.89	85.91	46.66
40695	21666	(53.2)	19029	(46.8)	20.1	847	878	61.68	81.32	38.31
359146	**190870**	**(53.1)**	**168276**	**(46.9)**	**21.2**	**851**	**882**	**61.44**	**79.95**	**39.62**
38828	19773	(50.9)	19055	(49.1)	20.2	1018	964	41.93	61.57	22.93
19163	9602	(50.1)	9561	(49.9)	18.0	983	996	50.12	68.03	31.87
17024	8822	(51.8)	8202	(48.2)	18.7	949	930	51.88	70.79	32.11
30576	15884	(51.9)	14692	(48.1)	18.2	929	925	49.11	67.31	29.67
26205	13371	(51.0)	12834	(49.0)	17.6	955	960	39.48	55.71	22.53
36170	18368	(50.8)	17802	(49.2)	18.3	1033	969	43.19	62.75	24.62
37172	18866	(50.8)	18306	(49.2)	18.6	929	970	43.50	59.68	25.94
14690	7476	(50.9)	7214	(49.1)	17.4	1042	965	42.58	62.19	24.21
16559	8412	(50.8)	8147	(49.2)	16.9	1070	968	44.13	63.56	26.44
28732	14652	(51.0)	14080	(49.0)	19.3	951	961	42.82	60.13	24.59
29578	15221	(51.5)	14357	(48.5)	18.0	965	943	45.87	64.76	26.41
294697	**150447**	**(51.1)**	**144250**	**(48.9)**	**18.4**	**979**	**959**	**44.59**	**62.85**	**26.09**
79253	41309	(52.1)	37944	(47.9)	21.1	888	919	47.02	61.80	30.23
43153	22330	(51.7)	20823	(48.3)	23.6	947	933	58.36	74.16	41.71
47328	24860	(52.5)	22468	(47.5)	22.8	877	904	41.34	55.85	24.64
45981	23935	(52.1)	22046	(47.9)	21.2	912	921	46.62	61.41	30.34
65246	33836	(51.9)	31410	(48.1)	23.4	913	928	48.90	67.14	28.78
237808	**123940**	**(52.1)**	**113868**	**(47.9)**	**22.0**	**897**	**919**	**46.33**	**61.92**	**28.83**
36915	19315	(52.3)	17600	(47.7)	19.5	901	911	46.91	64.29	27.60
32106	16650	(51.9)	15456	(48.1)	18.0	915	928	56.21	73.90	36.89
29494	15476	(52.5)	14018	(47.5)	18.9	910	906	51.00	70.39	29.68
48941	25502	(52.1)	23439	(47.9)	18.9	906	919	52.11	68.15	34.39
147456	**76943**	**(52.2)**	**70513**	**(47.8)**	**18.8**	**908**	**916**	**51.59**	**68.99**	**32.41**
25560	13043	(51.0)	12517	(49.0)	21.3	970	960	47.08	63.98	29.72
15112	7767	(51.4)	7345	(48.6)	17.0	999	946	45.01	65.16	25.13
17548	8994	(51.3)	8554	(48.7)	17.2	965	951	48.87	68.32	28.76
18203	9376	(51.5)	8827	(48.5)	16.9	979	941	47.53	66.53	28.33
15574	8146	(52.3)	7428	(47.7)	19.4	903	912	46.37	63.07	27.93
11283	5855	(51.9)	5428	(48.1)	15.5	1003	927	51.10	70.20	32.38
17630	9107	(51.7)	8523	(48.3)	17.6	966	936	51.83	71.27	31.89
28749	14884	(51.8)	13865	(48.2)	17.1	963	932	50.36	68.66	31.58
14923	7782	(52.1)	7141	(47.9)	16.6	1003	918	47.93	67.60	28.62
15113	7884	(52.2)	7229	(47.8)	17.0	971	917	47.18	65.83	28.23
12882	6610	(51.3)	6272	(48.7)	15.2	992	949	45.25	65.23	25.30
23140	12154	(52.5)	10986	(47.5)	17.1	969	904	54.36	75.94	32.44
39889	20547	(51.5)	19342	(48.5)	19.8	958	941	52.53	68.97	35.45
12246	6295	(51.4)	5951	(48.6)	16.3	1020	945	43.97	64.01	24.64
267852	**138444**	**(51.7)**	**129408**	**(48.3)**	**17.7**	**973**	**935**	**49.11**	**67.91**	**29.98**
30213	15969	(52.9)	14244	(47.1)	19.9	959	892	66.67	80.19	52.87
48536	25780	(53.1)	22756	(46.9)	18.2	933	883	71.99	83.55	59.75
33556	17672	(52.7)	15884	(47.3)	21.2	975	899	65.28	78.74	51.80
49073	25335	(51.6)	23738	(48.4)	22.0	953	937	59.70	75.12	43.60
54856	28528	(52.0)	26328	(48.0)	21.7	968	923	62.65	76.27	48.74
28989	15132	(52.2)	13857	(47.8)	19.2	940	916	72.11	82.01	61.68
288376	**150746**	**(52.3)**	**137630**	**(47.7)**	**20.8**	**953**	**913**	**65.29**	**78.63**	**51.45**
52574	27671	(52.6)	24903	(47.4)	19.7	899	900	66.22	82.23	48.43
56352	29052	(51.6)	27300	(48.4)	20.7	907	940	58.37	78.31	36.15
53956	27977	(51.9)	25979	(48.1)	21.5	916	929	54.24	74.39	32.30
35823	19151	(53.5)	16672	(46.5)	20.0	872	871	65.00	82.35	45.15
43293	22954	(53.0)	20339	(47.0)	20.4	899	886	62.37	79.28	43.63
241998	**126805**	**(52.4)**	**115193**	**(47.6)**	**20.5**	**900**	**908**	**61.02**	**79.19**	**40.83**
35668	19288	(54.1)	16380	(45.9)	23.7	796	849	56.87	72.55	36.84
46117	24739	(53.6)	21378	(46.4)	22.9	825	864	61.87	77.41	42.82
61229	32728	(53.5)	28501	(46.5)	23.3	836	871	59.46	76.28	39.12
43679	23432	(53.6)	20247	(46.4)	22.8	816	864	57.95	73.92	38.01
186693	**100187**	**(53.7)**	**86506**	**(46.3)**	**23.1**	**821**	**863**	**59.22**	**75.29**	**39.37**
37060	19225	(51.9)	17835	(48.1)	20.1	1071	928	44.21	62.74	27.61
53041	26816	(50.6)	26225	(49.4)	22.5	1001	978	45.94	64.15	27.92
38452	19680	(51.2)	18772	(48.8)	22.3	1032	954	46.67	66.79	27.56
37047	19061	(51.5)	17986	(48.5)	19.2	1074	944	50.91	70.13	33.61
54560	27590	(50.6)	26970	(49.4)	22.6	996	978	41.52	58.49	24.64
220160	**112372**	**(51.0)**	**107788**	**(49.0)**	**21.4**	**1031**	**959**	**45.69**	**64.12**	**28.19**
77613	41149	(53.0)	36464	(47.0)	18.6	894	886	58.42	70.77	44.63
27938	15326	(54.9)	12612	(45.1)	15.8	886	823	64.42	75.93	51.58
16453	8986	(54.6)	7467	(45.4)	16.0	897	831	61.49	71.96	49.94
19848	10783	(54.3)	9065	(45.7)	16.4	906	841	63.03	74.49	50.58
26965	14551	(54.0)	12414	(46.0)	17.1	913	853	65.34	76.66	53.13
22830	12585	(55.1)	10245	(44.9)	15.6	851	814	62.41	74.60	48.16

P. Code	Panchayat Samiti (Concerning Tehsil)	Total No. of Villages	Total No. of Gram Panchayats	Total Population					% share of District Rural Pop.
				Person	Male		Female		
					No.	%	No.	%	
1	2	3	4	5	6	7	8	9	10
115	SURATGARH* (Suratgarh)	467	38	213384	116034	(54.4)	97350	(45.6)	(16.0)
	GANGANAGAR	**3014**	**320**	**1336066**	**709710**	**(53.1)**	**626356**	**(46.9)**	**(100.0)**
116	BHADRA* (Bhadra)	215	49	220582	116205	(52.7)	104377	(47.3)	(18.2)
117	HANUMANGARH (Hanumangarh)	1152	121	628123	331517	(52.8)	296606	(47.2)	(51.7)
118	NOHAR (Rawatsar)	538	81	365762	192199	(52.5)	173563	(47.5)	(30.1)
	HANUMANGARH ##	**1905**	**251**	**1214467**	**639921**	**(52.7)**	**574546**	**(47.3)**	**(100.0)**
119	AMBER* (Amber)	196	48	262029	137463	(52.5)	124566	(47.5)	(9.9)
120	BASSI* (Bassi)	215	39	229639	120214	(52.3)	109425	(47.7)	(8.6)
121	CHAKSU* (Chaksu)	287	35	161140	84148	(52.2)	76992	(47.8)	(6.1)
122	DUDU (Dudu)	229	56	272517	141434	(51.9)	131083	(48.1)	(10.2)
123	GOVINDGARH* (Chomu)	100	42	275780	143709	(52.1)	132071	(47.9)	(10.4)
124	JAMWA RAMGARH* (Jamwa Ramgarh)	241	43	250132	131112	(52.4)	119020	(47.6)	(9.4)
125	JHOTWARA* (Jaipur)	73	16	88946	46444	(52.2)	42502	(47.8)	(3.3)
126	KOTPUTLI (Kotputli)	121	42	228470	119860	(52.5)	108610	(47.5)	(8.6)
127	PHAGI* (Phagi)	171	31	161610	84238	(52.1)	77372	(47.9)	(6.1)
128	SAMBHAR (Phulara)	144	44	209528	108372	(51.7)	101156	(48.3)	(7.9)
129	SANGANER* (Sanganer)	147	25	131301	68604	(52.2)	62697	(47.8)	(4.9)
130	SHAHPURA (Shahpura)	86	30	181498	95431	(52.6)	86067	(47.4)	(6.8)
131	VIRATNAGAR (Viratnagar)	121	37	206414	108138	(52.4)	98276	(47.6)	(7.8)
	JAIPUR	**2131**	**488**	**2659004**	**1389167**	**(52.2)**	**1269837**	**(47.8)**	**(100.0)**
132	JAISALMER (Jaisalmer)	155	40	127798	70574	(55.2)	57224	(44.8)	(29.6)
133	SAM (Jaisalmer)	303	49	138679	77603	(56.0)	61076	(44.0)	(32.1)
134	SANKRA (Pokaran)	179	39	165376	88132	(53.3)	77244	(46.7)	(38.3)
	JAISALMER	**637**	**128**	**431853**	**236309**	**(54.7)**	**195544**	**(45.3)**	**(100.0)**
135	AHORE (Ahore)	113	41	177342	87839	(49.5)	89503	(50.5)	(13.2)
136	BHINMAL (Bagora)	81	35	184751	93570	(50.6)	91181	(49.4)	(13.8)
137	JALOR (Jalor)	69	28	131827	66029	(50.1)	65798	(49.9)	(9.8)
138	JASWANTPURA (Bhinmal)	75	29	128410	64363	(50.1)	64047	(49.9)	(9.6)
139	RANIWARA* (Raniwara)	85	30	163349	84512	(51.7)	78837	(48.3)	(12.2)
140	SANCHORE* (Sanchore)	206	63	342120	176546	(51.6)	165574	(48.4)	(25.6)
141	SAYLA (Sayla)	77	38	211147	106778	(50.6)	104369	(49.4)	(15.8)
	JALOR	**706**	**264**	**1338946**	**679637**	**(50.8)**	**659309**	**(49.2)**	**(100.0)**
142	BAKANI (Jhalrapatan)	326	42	152329	79045	(51.9)	73284	(48.1)	(15.1)
143	DAG (Gangdhar)	231	40	167192	85787	(51.3)	81405	(48.7)	(16.5)
144	JHALRAPATAN (Jhalrapatan)	316	48	205868	106879	(51.9)	98989	(48.1)	(20.3)
145	KHANPUR* (Khanpur)	207	39	153370	80141	(52.3)	73229	(47.7)	(15.2)
146	MANOHARTHANA (Manoharthana)	302	40	161425	83901	(52.0)	77524	(48.0)	(15.9)
147	PIRAWA* (Pirwa)	218	44	171897	88672	(51.6)	83225	(48.4)	(17.0)
	JHALAWAR	**1600**	**253**	**1012081**	**524425**	**(51.8)**	**487656**	**(48.2)**	**(100.0)**
148	ALSISAR (Jhunjhunun)	125	34	141416	71082	(50.3)	70334	(49.7)	(9.3)
149	BUHANA* (Buhana)	126	42	204411	105164	(51.4)	99247	(48.6)	(13.5)
150	CHIRAWA (Chirawa)	84	29	152843	78052	(51.1)	74791	(48.9)	(10.1)
151	JHUNJHUNUN (Jhunjhunun)	145	36	176693	89388	(50.6)	87305	(49.4)	(11.6)
152	KHETRI* (Khetri)	86	38	214474	110570	(51.6)	103904	(48.4)	(14.1)
153	NAWALGARH* (Nawalgarh)	90	35	217636	110563	(50.8)	107073	(49.2)	(14.3)
154	SURAJGARH (Chirawa)	122	37	175820	91102	(51.8)	84718	(48.2)	(11.6)
155	UDAIPURWATI* (Udaipurwati)	81	37	235280	119855	(50.9)	115425	(49.1)	(15.5)
	JHUNJHUNUN	**859**	**288**	**1518573**	**775776**	**(51.1)**	**742797**	**(48.9)**	**(100.0)**
156	BALESAR (Shergarh)	125	33	174179	90994	(52.2)	83185	(47.8)	(9.1)
157	BAP (Phalodi)	125	32	157290	82819	(52.7)	74471	(47.3)	(8.2)
158	BHOPALGARH (Bhopalgarh)	86	36	202321	104132	(51.5)	98189	(48.5)	(10.6)
159	BILARA* (Bilara)	90	38	180550	93477	(51.8)	87073	(48.2)	(9.5)
160	LUNI (Luni)	137	39	229097	118808	(51.9)	110289	(48.1)	(12.0)
161	MANDOR (Jodhpur)	107	25	151257	79220	(52.4)	72037	(47.6)	(7.9)
162	OSIAN (Osian)	175	67	422181	219499	(52.0)	202682	(48.0)	(22.1)
163	PHALODI (Phalodi)	111	37	229892	120126	(52.3)	109766	(47.7)	(12.0)
164	SHERGARH (Shergarh)	107	32	162656	85097	(52.3)	77559	(47.7)	(8.5)
	JODHPUR	**1063**	**339**	**1909423**	**994172**	**(52.1)**	**915251**	**(47.9)**	**(100.0)**
165	HINDAUN* (Hindaun)	127	51	262403	142377	(54.3)	120026	(45.7)	(25.3)
166	KARAULI* (Karauli)	203	45	222621	121045	(54.4)	101576	(45.6)	(21.5)
167	NADOTI* (Nadoti)	95	29	126089	66752	(52.9)	59337	(47.1)	(12.2)
168	SAPOTRA (Sapotra)	224	55	232513	125743	(54.1)	106770	(45.9)	(22.4)
169	TODABHIM* (Todabhim)	149	44	194094	104458	(53.8)	89636	(46.2)	(18.7)
	KARAULI ###	**798**	**224**	**1037720**	**560375**	**(54.0)**	**477345**	**(46.0)**	**(100.0)**
170	CHECHAT* (Ranganjmandi)	159	36	132073	69342	(52.5)	62731	(47.5)	(18.1)
171	ITAWA* (Pipalda)	169	30	155646	81675	(52.5)	73971	(47.5)	(21.3)
172	LADPURA* (Ladpura)	182	27	144691	76045	(52.6)	68646	(47.4)	(19.8)
173	SANGOD* (Sangod)	211	36	146951	76707	(52.2)	70244	(47.8)	(20.1)
174	SULTANPUR* (Digod)	171	33	150587	78726	(52.3)	71861	(47.7)	(20.6)
	KOTA	**892**	**162**	**729948**	**382495**	**(52.4)**	**347453**	**(47.6)**	**(100.0)**

Person	Population 0-6				% of 0-6 Pop. To Total Pop.	Sex-Ratio		Literacy Rate (%)		
	Male		Female			Total Population	0-6 Population	Persons	Male	Female
	No.	%	No.	%						
11	12	13	14	15	16	17	18	19	20	21
39489	20842	(52.8)	18647	(47.2)	18.5	839	895	53.58	64.65	40.06
231136	**124222**	**(53.7)**	**106914**	**(46.3)**	**17.3**	**883**	**861**	**60.39**	**72.00**	**47.27**
37137	19813	(53.4)	17324	(46.6)	16.8	898	874	67.65	81.01	52.87
106323	57123	(53.7)	49200	(46.3)	16.9	895	861	61.65	73.36	48.67
65983	34726	(52.6)	31257	(47.4)	18.0	903	900	64.67	77.41	50.61
209443	**111662**	**(53.3)**	**97781**	**(46.7)**	**17.2**	**898**	**876**	**63.65**	**75.97**	**50.01**
51383	26817	(52.2)	24566	(47.8)	19.6	906	916	59.82	79.52	38.11
46413	24254	(52.3)	22159	(47.7)	20.2	910	914	59.07	79.19	36.96
32849	17238	(52.5)	15611	(47.5)	20.4	915	906	51.93	72.40	29.66
51059	26708	(52.3)	24351	(47.7)	18.7	927	912	56.31	74.53	36.78
54182	28445	(52.5)	25737	(47.5)	19.6	919	905	66.24	83.67	47.39
50781	26434	(52.1)	24347	(47.9)	20.3	908	921	62.87	80.05	43.93
16783	8659	(51.6)	8124	(48.4)	18.9	915	938	66.68	82.09	49.73
45568	24418	(53.6)	21150	(46.4)	19.9	906	866	72.22	83.73	59.70
30415	15830	(52.0)	14585	(48.0)	18.8	918	921	60.92	76.65	43.83
38992	20236	(51.9)	18756	(48.1)	18.6	933	927	66.88	82.36	50.35
24558	12887	(52.5)	11671	(47.5)	18.7	914	906	62.86	80.70	43.38
34932	18350	(52.5)	16582	(47.5)	19.2	902	904	65.03	81.56	46.69
42440	22068	(52.0)	20372	(48.0)	20.6	909	923	68.38	82.53	52.78
520355	**272344**	**(52.3)**	**248011**	**(47.7)**	**19.6**	**914**	**911**	**62.96**	**79.96**	**44.42**
28527	15174	(53.2)	13353	(46.8)	22.3	811	880	47.32	63.21	27.72
31344	17067	(54.5)	14277	(45.5)	22.6	787	837	44.96	61.20	23.98
39043	20661	(52.9)	18382	(47.1)	23.6	876	890	48.55	64.68	30.03
98914	**52902**	**(53.5)**	**46012**	**(46.5)**	**22.9**	**827**	**870**	**47.02**	**63.09**	**27.45**
35199	18348	(52.1)	16851	(47.9)	19.8	1019	918	51.84	69.25	35.28
41857	21706	(51.9)	20151	(48.1)	22.7	974	928	40.07	60.49	19.50
26638	13794	(51.8)	12844	(48.2)	20.2	997	931	44.38	62.01	27.19
26847	14049	(52.3)	12798	(47.7)	20.9	995	911	39.16	58.16	20.68
36158	18975	(52.5)	17183	(47.5)	22.1	933	906	47.43	65.32	28.45
77502	40252	(51.9)	37250	(48.1)	22.7	938	925	46.00	64.81	26.09
46473	24101	(51.9)	22372	(48.1)	22.0	977	928	42.62	62.00	23.10
290674	**151225**	**(52.0)**	**139449**	**(48.0)**	**21.7**	**970**	**922**	**44.81**	**63.52**	**25.88**
28869	14934	(51.7)	13935	(48.3)	19.0	927	933	42.47	59.79	23.85
28177	14393	(51.1)	13784	(48.9)	16.9	949	958	46.08	63.62	27.58
36960	19169	(51.9)	17791	(48.1)	18.0	926	928	57.17	75.26	37.66
26359	13625	(51.7)	12734	(48.3)	17.2	914	935	66.17	83.50	47.17
33437	17148	(51.3)	16289	(48.7)	20.7	924	950	47.47	65.25	28.18
29352	15081	(51.4)	14271	(48.6)	17.1	939	946	65.33	80.68	49.01
183154	**94350**	**(51.5)**	**88804**	**(48.5)**	**18.1**	**930**	**941**	**54.13**	**71.46**	**35.51**
25485	13578	(53.3)	11907	(46.7)	18.0	989	877	73.89	86.24	61.72
33862	18406	(54.4)	15456	(45.6)	16.6	944	840	77.41	89.92	64.48
27065	14602	(54.0)	12463	(46.0)	17.7	958	854	74.51	87.45	61.32
29638	15939	(53.8)	13699	(46.2)	16.8	977	859	76.66	90.33	63.03
40381	21547	(53.4)	18834	(46.6)	18.8	940	874	65.85	80.46	50.40
37720	20265	(53.7)	17455	(46.3)	17.3	968	861	69.68	85.44	53.78
30828	16670	(54.1)	14158	(45.9)	17.5	930	849	70.67	84.62	55.94
44407	23410	(52.7)	20997	(47.3)	18.9	963	897	77.66	87.17	67.95
269386	**144417**	**(53.6)**	**124969**	**(46.4)**	**17.7**	**957**	**865**	**73.24**	**86.36**	**59.80**
39269	20445	(52.1)	18824	(47.9)	22.5	914	921	43.04	64.29	19.80
37045	19337	(52.2)	17708	(47.8)	23.6	899	916	43.36	60.38	24.67
38908	20287	(52.1)	18621	(47.9)	19.2	943	918	46.27	68.00	23.41
33862	17620	(52.0)	16242	(48.0)	18.8	931	922	50.45	71.35	28.18
47331	24493	(51.7)	22838	(48.3)	20.7	928	932	54.82	74.05	34.07
30591	16051	(52.5)	14540	(47.5)	20.2	909	906	44.30	64.87	22.08
92610	48055	(51.9)	44555	(48.1)	21.9	923	927	47.50	65.60	27.45
53415	27750	(52.0)	25665	(48.0)	23.2	914	925	47.50	65.60	27.45
37650	19148	(50.9)	18502	(49.1)	23.1	911	966	41.70	61.61	19.48
410681	**213186**	**(51.9)**	**197495**	**(48.1)**	**21.5**	**921**	**926**	**46.88**	**66.94**	**25.10**
56362	30366	(53.9)	25996	(46.1)	21.5	843	856	73.89	87.51	57.83
49330	26279	(53.3)	23051	(46.7)	22.2	839	877	57.54	75.48	35.89
24708	13187	(53.4)	11521	(46.6)	19.6	889	874	65.04	81.93	46.14
47756	25157	(52.7)	22599	(47.3)	20.5	849	898	58.30	75.34	37.87
38981	21080	(54.1)	17901	(45.9)	20.1	858	849	62.29	81.97	39.72
217137	**116069**	**(53.5)**	**101068**	**(46.5)**	**20.9**	**852**	**871**	**63.62**	**80.45**	**43.84**
25827	13363	(51.7)	12464	(48.3)	19.6	905	933	68.60	83.19	52.35
26315	13550	(51.5)	12765	(48.5)	16.9	906	942	62.48	78.59	44.58
25715	13394	(52.1)	12321	(47.9)	17.8	903	920	66.01	81.53	49.08
26270	13786	(52.5)	12484	(47.5)	17.9	916	906	69.82	85.11	53.14
25682	13458	(52.4)	12224	(47.6)	17.1	913	908	70.14	84.67	54.27
129809	**67551**	**(52.0)**	**62258**	**(48.0)**	**17.8**	**908**	**922**	**67.34**	**82.56**	**50.60**

P. Code	Panchayat Samiti (Concerning Tehsil)	Total No. of Villages	Total No. of Gram Panchayats	Total Population					% share of District Rural Pop.
				Person	Male		Female		
					No.	%	No.	%	
1	2	3	4	5	6	7	8	9	10
175	DEGANA (Degana)	152	43	190085	96026	(50.5)	94059	(49.5)	(8.3)
176	DIDWANA* (Didwana)	172	57	285031	143568	(50.4)	141463	(49.6)	(12.4)
177	JAYAL* (Jayal)	137	45	224944	114881	(51.1)	110063	(48.9)	(9.8)
178	KUCHAMAN* (Nawa)	193	55	268146	138687	(51.7)	129459	(48.3)	(11.7)
179	LADNU* (Ladnu)	98	32	158026	79851	(50.5)	78175	(49.5)	(6.9)
180	MAKRANA* (Makrana)	119	36	199671	102034	(51.1)	97637	(48.9)	(8.7)
181	MERTA (Merta)	115	34	183429	95317	(52.0)	88112	(48.0)	(8.0)
182	MUNDWA (Nagaur)	122	39	197532	101466	(51.4)	96066	(48.6)	(8.6)
183	NAGAUR (Nagaur)	154	47	224815	115606	(51.4)	109209	(48.6)	(9.8)
184	PARBATSAR* (Parbatsar)	110	35	186413	96084	(51.5)	90329	(48.5)	(8.1)
185	RIYAN (Merta)	128	38	179629	92456	(51.5)	87173	(48.5)	(7.8)
	NAGAUR	**1500**	**461**	**2297721**	**1175976**	**(51.2)**	**1121745**	**(48.8)**	**(100.0)**
186	BALI* (Bali)	91	39	183802	91349	(49.7)	92453	(50.3)	(12.9)
187	DESURI (Desuri)	78	24	102245	49781	(48.7)	52464	(51.3)	(7.2)
188	JAITARAN* (Jaitaran)	108	33	186938	94992	(50.8)	91946	(49.2)	(13.1)
189	KHARCHI/MARWAR JUN.	142	47	181445	90229	(49.7)	91216	(50.3)	(12.7)
190	PALI (Pali)	82	23	89939	45446	(50.5)	44493	(49.5)	(6.3)
191	RAIPUR* (Raipur)	113	35	182004	91683	(50.4)	90321	(49.6)	(12.7)
192	RANI STATION (Desuri)	76	29	106504	52220	(49.0)	54284	(51.0)	(7.5)
193	ROHAT* (Rohat)	79	23	102599	52215	(50.9)	50384	(49.1)	(7.2)
194	SOJAT* (Sojat)	115	38	155889	77614	(49.8)	78275	(50.2)	(10.9)
195	SUMERPUR* (Sumerpur)	65	29	137999	69169	(50.1)	68830	(49.9)	(9.7)
	PALI	**949**	**320**	**1429364**	**714698**	**(50.0)**	**714666**	**(50.0)**	**(100.0)**
196	AMET* (Amet)	137	20	88162	44077	(50.0)	44085	(50.0)	(10.3)
197	BHIM* (Bhim)	133	30	137578	67968	(49.4)	69610	(50.6)	(16.0)
198	DEOGARH* (Deogarh)	134	19	77865	38126	(49.0)	39739	(51.0)	(9.1)
199	KHAMNOR* (Nathdwara)	190	41	172395	85988	(49.9)	86407	(50.1)	(20.1)
200	KUMBHALGARH* (Kumbhalgarh)	164	37	131346	64616	(49.2)	66730	(50.8)	(15.3)
201	RAILMAGRA* (Railmagra)	94	29	110435	54685	(49.5)	55750	(50.5)	(12.9)
202	RAJSAMAND* (Rajsamand)	135	29	140520	71170	(50.6)	69350	(49.4)	(16.4)
	RAJSAMAND #	**987**	**205**	**858301**	**426630**	**(49.7)**	**431671**	**(50.3)**	**(100.0)**
203	BAMANWAS* (Bamanwas)	150	36	149429	79388	(53.1)	70041	(46.9)	(16.5)
204	BONLI (Bonli)	180	41	209833	110159	(52.5)	99674	(47.5)	(23.2)
205	GANGAPUR* (Gangapur)	122	38	179209	95561	(53.3)	83648	(46.7)	(19.8)
206	KHANDAR (Khandar)	180	35	150136	80241	(53.4)	69895	(46.6)	(16.6)
207	SAWAI MADHOPUR (S. Madhopur)	162	47	215810	113367	(52.5)	102443	(47.5)	(23.9)
	S. MADHOPUR	**794**	**197**	**904417**	**478716**	**(52.9)**	**425701**	**(47.1)**	**(100.0)**
208	DANTA RAMGARH (Danta Ramgarh)	157	45	262183	133320	(50.8)	128863	(49.2)	(14.4)
209	DHOND (Sikar)	109	43	209919	107068	(51.0)	102851	(49.0)	(11.6)
210	FATEHPUR (Fatehpur)	143	35	193473	97033	(50.2)	96440	(49.8)	(10.7)
211	KHANDELA (Sri Madhopur)	131	40	218560	111201	(50.9)	107359	(49.1)	(12.0)
212	LACHHMANGARH (Lachhmangarh)	140	37	197022	99917	(50.7)	97105	(49.3)	(10.9)
213	NEEM KA THANA* (Neem Ka Thana)	151	59	317049	164771	(52.0)	152278	(48.0)	(17.5)
214	PIPRALI (Sikar)	95	36	206064	105679	(51.3)	100385	(48.7)	(11.4)
215	SRI MADHOPUR (Sri Madhopur)	66	34	210980	108206	(51.3)	102774	(48.7)	(11.6)
	SIKAR	**992**	**329**	**1815250**	**927195**	**(51.1)**	**888055**	**(48.9)**	**(100.0)**
216	ABU ROAD* (Abu Road)	81	25	114818	59326	(51.7)	55492	(48.3)	(16.4)
217	PINDWARA* (Pindwara)	100	34	184803	94576	(51.2)	90227	(48.8)	(26.4)
218	REODAR* (Reodar)	126	37	175344	90145	(51.4)	85199	(48.6)	(25.0)
219	SHEOGANJ* (Sheoganj)	70	24	99663	50744	(50.9)	48919	(49.1)	(14.2)
220	SIROHI* (Sirohi)	85	31	125589	62387	(49.7)	63202	(50.3)	(17.9)
	SIROHI	**462**	**151**	**700217**	**357178**	**(51.0)**	**343039**	**(49.0)**	**(100.0)**
221	DEOLI* (Deoli)	171	40	169271	87592	(51.7)	81679	(48.3)	(17.7)
222	MALPURA* (Malpura)	138	36	176932	91000	(51.4)	85932	(48.6)	(18.5)
223	NIWAI* (Niwai)	201	41	165298	86153	(52.1)	79145	(47.9)	(17.2)
224	TODARAISINGH* (Todaraisingh)	118	31	110131	56442	(51.2)	53689	(48.8)	(11.5)
225	TONK (Tonk)	253	50	204362	105759	(51.8)	98603	(48.2)	(21.3)
226	UNIARA* (Uniara)	212	33	132509	69146	(52.2)	63363	(47.8)	(13.8)
	TONK	**1093**	**231**	**958503**	**496092**	**(51.8)**	**462411**	**(48.2)**	**(100.0)**
227	BARGAON (Girwa)	107	25	123802	63731	(51.5)	60071	(48.5)	(5.8)
228	BHINDER* (Vallabhnagar)	284	52	201832	101768	(50.4)	100064	(49.6)	(9.4)
229	DHARIAWAD* (Dhariawad)	250	49	203605	102067	(50.1)	101538	(49.9)	(9.5)
230	GIRWA (Girwa)	180	48	227623	116133	(51.0)	111490	(49.0)	(10.6)
231	GOGUNDA* (Gogunda)	148	40	151575	76505	(50.5)	75070	(49.5)	(7.1)
232	JHADOL* (Jhadol)	258	45	193810	97984	(50.6)	95826	(49.4)	(9.0)
233	KHERWARA* (Kherwara)	252	62	254301	126949	(49.9)	127352	(50.1)	(11.9)
234	KOTRA* (Kotra)	304	36	183504	92736	(50.5)	90768	(49.5)	(8.6)
235	MAVLI* (Mavli)	149	47	194148	98325	(50.6)	95823	(49.4)	(9.1)
236	SALUMBAR* (Salumbar)	234	48	196614	97075	(49.4)	99539	(50.6)	(9.2)
237	SARADA* (Sarada)	185	46	212181	105168	(49.6)	107013	(50.4)	(9.9)
	UDAIPUR	**2351**	**498**	**2142995**	**1078441**	**(50.3)**	**1064554**	**(49.7)**	**(100.0)**
	RAJASTHAN	**41353**	**9187**	**43292813**	**22426640**	**(51.8)**	**20866173**	**(48.2)**	

Note: Dungargarh PS shifted from Churu to Bikaner district on 1st April 2001. * Co-terminus Panchayat Samiti; ** Excluding data of Dungargarh PS; *** Including data of Dungargarh PS. # Came in force from April, 1991; ## Came in force from July 1994; ### Came in force from July 1997.

Source: Computed from data received from Directorate of Census Operations, Jaipur.

Person	Population 0-6				% of 0-6 Pop. To Total Pop.	Sex Ratio		Literacy Rate (%)		
	Male		Female			Total Population	0-6 Population	Persons	Male	Female
	No.	%	No.	%						
11	12	13	14	15	16	17	18	19	20	21
34928	18220	(52.2)	16708	(47.8)	18.4	980	917	53.58	71.80	35.32
55958	29147	(52.1)	26811	(47.9)	19.6	985	920	63.62	80.84	46.46
44400	23050	(51.9)	21350	(48.1)	19.7	958	926	51.12	69.46	32.19
49720	26143	(52.6)	23577	(47.4)	18.5	933	902	62.54	78.68	45.52
29895	15355	(51.4)	14540	(48.6)	18.9	979	947	60.68	78.72	42.38
37280	19482	(52.3)	17798	(47.7)	18.7	957	914	61.81	78.17	44.92
33003	17432	(52.8)	15571	(47.2)	18.0	924	893	54.85	73.90	34.44
39345	20463	(52.0)	18882	(48.0)	19.9	947	923	45.01	64.73	24.44
49544	25728	(51.9)	23816	(48.1)	22.0	945	926	49.84	68.04	30.80
34565	18165	(52.6)	16400	(47.4)	18.5	940	903	55.92	72.16	39.08
31763	16729	(52.7)	15034	(47.3)	17.7	943	899	51.92	70.66	32.30
440401	**229914**	**(52.2)**	**210487**	**(47.8)**	**19.2**	**954**	**916**	**55.92**	**73.66**	**37.58**
35840	18426	(51.4)	17414	(48.6)	19.5	1012	945	50.34	66.60	34.53
19174	10014	(52.2)	9160	(47.8)	18.8	1054	915	50.35	67.75	34.37
34714	18064	(52.0)	16650	(48.0)	18.6	968	922	46.77	66.52	26.68
33182	17140	(51.7)	16042	(48.3)	18.3	1011	936	49.99	69.86	30.73
17063	8867	(52.0)	8196	(48.0)	19.0	979	924	48.79	68.19	29.38
37212	19163	(51.5)	18049	(48.5)	20.4	985	942	50.37	71.03	29.66
18788	9786	(52.1)	9002	(47.9)	17.6	1040	920	52.73	70.23	36.43
21217	11087	(52.3)	10130	(47.7)	20.7	965	914	51.24	71.31	30.91
28933	14985	(51.8)	13948	(48.2)	18.6	1009	931	52.02	72.78	31.78
25646	13477	(52.6)	12169	(47.4)	18.6	995	903	52.69	70.41	35.36
271769	**141009**	**(51.9)**	**130760**	**(48.1)**	**19.0**	**1000**	**927**	**50.39**	**69.39**	**31.76**
16073	8191	(51.0)	7882	(49.0)	18.2	1000	962	49.11	67.53	30.90
29947	15382	(51.4)	14565	(48.6)	21.8	1024	947	56.50	80.98	33.15
15965	8274	(51.8)	7691	(48.2)	20.5	1042	930	49.46	68.85	31.44
30587	15994	(52.3)	14593	(47.7)	17.7	1005	912	50.41	67.01	34.30
25195	12960	(51.4)	12235	(48.6)	19.2	1033	944	46.45	65.71	28.21
17427	8963	(51.4)	8464	(48.6)	15.8	1019	944	54.97	73.83	36.75
25754	13230	(51.4)	12524	(48.6)	18.3	974	947	55.23	73.85	36.25
160948	**82994**	**(51.6)**	**77954**	**(48.4)**	**18.8**	**1012**	**939**	**51.93**	**71.23**	**33.22**
26550	13837	(52.1)	12713	(47.9)	17.8	882	919	60.11	78.76	38.71
40703	21300	(52.3)	19403	(47.7)	19.4	905	911	53.18	73.47	30.75
36353	19278	(53.0)	17075	(47.0)	20.3	875	886	58.27	79.12	34.37
28601	15136	(52.9)	13465	(47.1)	19.1	871	890	43.38	63.15	20.53
39675	20864	(52.6)	18811	(47.4)	18.4	904	902	50.83	74.54	24.74
171882	**90415**	**(52.6)**	**81467**	**(47.4)**	**19.0**	**889**	**901**	**53.24**	**74.13**	**29.69**
48280	25569	(53.0)	22711	(47.0)	18.4	967	888	70.18	84.44	55.74
37786	20259	(53.6)	17527	(46.4)	18.0	961	865	68.64	84.56	52.47
35401	18878	(53.3)	16523	(46.7)	18.3	994	875	74.52	87.10	62.22
42565	22496	(52.9)	20069	(47.1)	19.5	965	892	72.93	86.00	59.38
35575	19053	(53.6)	16522	(46.4)	18.1	972	867	74.49	87.39	61.57
60644	32007	(52.8)	28637	(47.2)	19.1	924	895	67.60	82.66	51.47
37506	20028	(53.4)	17478	(46.6)	18.2	950	873	70.10	85.53	54.18
39581	20927	(52.9)	18654	(47.1)	18.8	950	891	66.77	81.98	51.28
337338	**179217**	**(53.1)**	**158121**	**(46.9)**	**18.6**	**958**	**882**	**70.39**	**84.74**	**55.70**
27161	13788	(50.8)	13373	(49.2)	23.7	935	970	43.55	59.43	26.41
39139	20115	(51.4)	19024	(48.6)	21.2	954	946	52.73	69.02	35.65
36282	18689	(51.5)	17593	(48.5)	20.7	945	941	48.32	65.46	30.24
18871	9939	(52.7)	8932	(47.3)	18.9	964	899	49.51	66.05	32.75
23998	12807	(53.4)	11191	(46.6)	19.1	1013	874	48.75	67.91	30.51
145451	**75338**	**(51.8)**	**70113**	**(48.2)**	**20.8**	**960**	**931**	**48.97**	**65.94**	**31.47**
31077	16087	(51.8)	14990	(48.2)	18.4	932	932	45.81	66.75	23.45
32579	16724	(51.3)	15855	(48.7)	18.4	944	948	46.92	66.24	26.49
32660	17010	(52.1)	15650	(47.9)	19.8	919	920	50.97	71.02	29.16
19888	10273	(51.7)	9615	(48.3)	18.1	951	936	52.88	72.17	32.67
38964	20157	(51.7)	18807	(48.3)	19.1	932	933	45.48	67.42	21.93
25255	13288	(52.6)	11967	(47.4)	19.1	916	901	46.71	69.09	22.56
180423	**93539**	**(51.8)**	**86884**	**(48.2)**	**18.8**	**932**	**929**	**47.77**	**68.48**	**25.62**
22329	11584	(51.9)	10745	(48.1)	18.0	943	928	66.51	81.50	50.66
33962	17606	(51.8)	16356	(48.2)	16.8	983	929	60.82	77.09	44.49
45558	23098	(50.7)	22460	(49.3)	22.4	995	972	35.22	52.30	18.21
44331	22683	(51.2)	21648	(48.8)	19.5	960	954	57.93	74.74	40.48
30258	15394	(50.9)	14864	(49.1)	20.0	981	966	50.12	67.74	32.32
41804	21003	(50.2)	20801	(49.8)	21.6	978	990	59.26	74.73	43.43
54205	27615	(50.9)	26590	(49.1)	21.3	1003	963	55.78	75.68	36.17
44344	22215	(50.1)	22129	(49.9)	24.2	979	996	24.52	37.55	11.14
31824	16562	(52.0)	15262	(48.0)	16.4	975	922	53.72	71.80	35.43
38474	19818	(51.5)	18656	(48.5)	19.6	1025	941	57.38	74.16	41.44
42298	21698	(51.3)	20600	(48.7)	19.9	1018	949	55.34	74.55	36.82
429387	**219276**	**(51.1)**	**210111**	**(48.9)**	**20.0**	**987**	**958**	**52.52**	**69.52**	**35.46**
8587389	**4486277**	**(52.2)**	**4101112**	**(47.8)**	**19.8**	**930**	**914**	**55.92**	**72.96**	**37.74**

GENERAL ANNEX-VI

PANCHAYAT SAMITI-WISE PERCENTAGE OF RURAL POPULATION SERVED BY MEDICAL AND OTHER RELATED AMENITIES: RAJASTHAN (2001)

P. Code	Panchayat Samiti	Total Population	Type of Amenity Available									
			Medical	Improved Drinking Water#	Edu-cation	Power Supply	Approach by Pucca Road	Post Office##	Tele-phone	Transport Communi-cations###	Banks	Ag. Credit Societies
1	2	3	4	5	6	7	8	9	10	11	12	13
1	ARAIN	133386	57	99.6	99.8	96.9	64.1	57.9	94.8	53	26.3	25.3
2	BHINAY	155111	57.9	99.2	100	97.3	71.9	61	75.5	62.7	27.4	35.3
3	JAWAJA	157901	41.9	100	97.1	96.1	86.9	36.2	67.9	40.7	12.5	8.7
4	KEKRI	140921	73.1	100	99.8	97.8	82.5	68.4	89.2	63.2	24.8	32.6
5	KISHANGARH	153474	68.4	99.6	99.9	99.3	80.2	61.3	87.1	73.3	29	28.5
6	MASOODA	159600	52.5	100	98.3	99.4	80.2	63.3	78.4	63.7	17.2	35.3
7	PISANGAN	236459	72.4	100	100	98.2	86.3	58.7	87.3	77.9	21.8	31.3
8	SRINAGAR	170142	61.9	100	99.9	97.6	89.6	53.4	88.3	72.7	21.4	19.2
	AJMER DISTRICT	**1306994**	**61.2**	**99.8**	**99.4**	**97.9**	**81**	**57.4**	**83.5**	**64.5**	**22.4**	**27.2**
9	BANSURE	214351	50.9	99.9	99.9	100	76.5	50.1	63.6	68.3	19.4	17.3
10	BEHROR	139503	67.3	99.9	99.3	99.9	81.5	56.7	78.4	70.3	24.1	24.1
11	KATHUMAR	211689	51.4	98.1	100	98.6	82.6	53.7	72.4	40.7	20.9	29.3
12	KISHANGARH BAS	167495	36.2	99.6	98.5	98.2	73.3	42	78.3	35.1	12.6	17.1
13	KOTKASIM	117687	40.3	100	99.6	98.9	72.6	39.2	58.6	42.9	24.4	32.4
14	LACHHMANGARH	225836	54.2	100	99.5	98.3	75	44	70.2	48.9	15.6	43.1
15	MANDAWAR	197582	52.1	100	99.5	98.1	76.3	50.4	72.6	53.9	16	30.3
16	NIMRANA	143329	68	99.8	100	100	88.3	60	57	65.9	22.8	12.3
17	RAJGARH	144726	46.1	95.9	95.9	95	86.8	52.6	53.6	38.3	13.7	14.3
18	RAMGARH	220219	46.4	100	98.4	99.7	81.3	34.1	68.7	40.3	17.9	30.9
19	RENI	136491	58.6	98.6	98.8	100	82.1	54.6	64.7	36.7	26.3	31.6
20	THANAGAZI	189977	61	99.7	98.3	95.5	83.9	55.1	77.5	63.4	22.4	29.7
21	TIJARA	226974	36.6	99.9	96.2	97.9	79.5	28.2	56.3	31.5	15.7	17.8
22	UMREN	221794	54.7	99	97.3	98.4	87.4	46.8	78.4	34.6	16.4	38.1
	ALWAR	**2557653**	**51.3**	**99.4**	**98.6**	**98.5**	**80.5**	**46.9**	**68.4**	**47.5**	**18.7**	**26.9**
23	ANANDPURI	111206	48.1	97.7	98.2	75.4	59.1	34.5	13	39.3	7.1	10.9
24	BAGIDORA	176729	51.5	97.9	99.2	64.6	62.9	36.7	43.9	51.2	20.4	18.9
25	GARHI	237521	68.9	100	99.9	97	80.4	55.3	59.6	69.1	26.3	28.2
26	GHATOL	230344	54	99.9	99.4	84.4	68.4	45.4	40.9	54.9	18.1	18.4
27	KUSHALGARH	138970	34.7	98.2	99	57.8	46.5	11.4	21.1	26.2	3.8	4.6
28	PEEPALKHOONT	151273	61.5	98.9	97	41	47.2	32.5	23.5	38.1	12.9	12.2
29	SAJJANGARH	134456	46.6	100	98.9	66.9	53	17.1	22.6	43.9	8.1	11.5
30	TALWARA	213727	55.9	98.3	98.6	85.8	72.5	31.1	49.4	67.1	17.7	22.2
	BANSWARA	**1394226**	**54.2**	**99**	**98.9**	**74.5**	**63.7**	**35.4**	**37.9**	**51.7**	**15.9**	**17.4**
31	ANTA	148759	48.9	100	99	97.3	69.4	52.1	57.7	53.2	31.4	41.1
32	ATRU	127043	49.1	100	99.1	99.6	66.9	56.3	71.4	48.5	25.2	33.6
33	BARAN	103142	45.4	100	99.7	100	77.3	45.4	60.7	38	11.1	42
34	CHHABRA	99472	14.8	96.4	93.7	93.8	36.4	20.9	36.9	13.1	3.8	21.2
35	CHHIPABAROD	127858	28.8	98.1	94.3	91.8	53.5	35.2	46.7	35.3	12.4	28.9
36	KISHANGANJ	135218	44.9	99.7	94.6	94.3	62	28.1	52.8	42.9	23	25.4
37	SHAHBAD	108146	36.3	99.4	96.1	86.4	57.4	33	37.9	36	14.7	18.9
	BARAN	**849638**	**39.3**	**99.2**	**96.7**	**94.9**	**61**	**39.5**	**52.7**	**39.4**	**18.5**	**30.6**
38	BALOTRA	265596	54.1	82	97.1	77.7	69.6	60	76	85	22.2	26.3
39	BARMER	238075	31.4	77	92.1	51.5	56.9	37.7	41.6	64.5	4.7	16.1
40	BAYTOO	210345	27.4	91.2	92.3	35	44.2	25.4	49.3	52.6	8.6	14.3
41	CHOHTAN	225754	47.1	85.3	99.1	73.1	68.3	55.4	54.1	76.1	10.2	29.8
42	DHORIMANNA	250929	30.8	90.9	97.8	77.7	57.6	41.1	58.8	60.6	8.9	21
43	SHEO	178539	30.3	81	95.9	54.3	50.9	39.6	48.1	60.1	9.6	19.1
44	SINDHARI	236545	36.2	83.4	99.6	56.9	53.9	37.8	57.9	68.5	7.6	19.6
45	SIWANA	213648	70.3	97.7	99.4	98	75.2	71.8	82.5	84.5	27.7	47
	BARMER	**1819431**	**41.2**	**86**	**96.7**	**66.1**	**59.9**	**46.4**	**59**	**69.5**	**12.5**	**24.1**
46	BAYANA	191632	46.1	98.9	99.2	91	76.2	42	27.8	42.3	13.8	11.9
47	DEEG	154862	67	100	100	97.4	81.2	61.6	72.7	35.6	15.3	66.8
48	KAMAN	212139	46.1	93.4	99.4	88.4	71.7	40.4	29.9	22.8	10.5	8.2
49	KUMHER	155122	75.5	99.9	99.9	98.9	85.9	55.2	79.4	33.5	31	59.9
50	NADBAI	161111	76.2	100	99.7	99.1	79.1	62.3	82.3	49	21.3	14

P. Code	Panchayat Samiti	Total Population	Type of Amenity Available									
			Medical	Improved Drinking Water#	Education	Power Supply	Approach by Pucca Road	Post Office##	Telephone	Transport Communications###	Banks	Ag. Credit Societies
1	2	3	4	5	6	7	8	9	10	11	12	13
51	NAGAR PAHARI	236329	41.2	98.8	99.7	93.9	71.6	44.8	55.4	27.9	19.2	25.1
52	RUPBAS	211147	55.6	99.8	99.8	92.8	76	48	60.5	52.3	16.7	35.8
53	SEWAR	167641	54.1	98.9	99.1	99.8	94	48.6	72.2	30.5	20.5	46.3
54	WEIR	202199	52.8	99.6	99.6	99.1	63.8	58.2	62.6	38.2	18.5	9.6
	BHARATPUR	**1692182**	**55.7**	**98.7**	**99.6**	**95.2**	**76.9**	**50.5**	**58.6**	**36.6**	**18.1**	**29**
55	ASIND	192346	52.8	99.3	98.7	97.3	64.5	50	71.9	66	20	33.8
56	BANERA	106222	76.7	99.8	99.9	100	72.1	60.2	89.5	65	24.2	39.1
57	HURDA	91088	70.7	98.9	98.7	98.9	79.7	61.6	92	78.3	35.1	51.4
58	JAHAZPUR	167782	56.1	98.7	95.3	95.1	57	42.7	57.7	42.7	12.4	29.9
59	KOTRI	148702	49	99	98	93.4	56.7	45.1	54.4	55.8	14.3	32.2
60	MANDAL	197500	52.7	99.8	99	95	72.4	50.1	67.6	69.7	20.7	37.8
61	MANDALGARH	199935	50.5	99.6	95.3	96	66	45.7	63.4	53.9	24.8	35.3
62	RAIPUR	84354	57	98.4	99.5	99.9	56.1	50.9	82.2	76.8	20.6	37.7
63	SAHARA	98050	63.9	99.2	99.7	100	74.3	61.4	91.8	72	20.6	39.8
64	SHAHPURA	148955	55.1	97	99.4	95.2	56.3	46.1	62.1	54.2	14.2	32.3
65	SUWANA	164004	59.1	100	99.7	99.6	78.8	48.4	76.8	67.2	27.1	38.3
	BHILWARA	**1598938**	**56.9**	**99.1**	**98.2**	**96.9**	**66.4**	**49.8**	**70.8**	**62.1**	**20.8**	**36.2**
66	BIKANER	374802	47.7	74.3	96.1	71.9	90	40	47.1	76.9	31.3	31
67	DUNGARGARH *	182819	80.7	88.3	99.9	99.7	79.3	77.3	82.5	83.9	29.5	32.8
68	KOLAYAT	207749	49.2	73.2	98.1	80.1	79	51	37.6	80.7	25.4	29.9
69	LUNKARANSAR	217341	53.7	76.2	96.1	89.6	81.2	47.1	51.3	70.2	29	27.5
70	NOKHA	279343	53.9	95.7	98	97.9	79.5	71.4	57.3	87.2	30.8	39.7
	BIKANER **	**1079235**	**50.8**	**80**	**97**	**83.8**	**83.4**	**51.7**	**48.8**	**79**	**29.6**	**32.3**
71	HINDOLI	189290	52.7	98.7	97.5	94.7	66	45.6	48.6	42.3	16	21.8
72	KESHORAIPATAN	178625	41.3	97.4	98.2	91.4	57.9	43.4	30.4	45.9	14.1	37.1
73	NAINWA	156227	43.3	97.5	98.8	97	58.8	44.9	44.8	48.5	20.1	41.5
74	TALERA	258916	43.4	99.6	99.1	93.4	69.7	34.7	43.3	39.6	22.1	19.5
	BUNDI	**783058**	**45.1**	**98.5**	**98.4**	**94**	**63.9**	**41.4**	**41.9**	**43.5**	**18.4**	**28.5**
75	ARNOD	119837	33.8	97.8	94.7	81.6	56.6	50	23.8	45.8	15.4	19.2
76	BARI SADRI	88841	45.7	99.9	94.1	99.2	56.6	41.3	41.8	57.7	22.6	34.8
77	BEGUN	102011	41.6	100	91.4	97.1	55.4	34.9	50.2	52	15.3	23.3
78	BHADESAR	107393	37.3	100	95.5	100	60.3	33	44.5	48.8	21.9	26
79	BHAINSRORGARH	80379	34.1	99.6	88.8	92.3	62.5	24.1	12.1	61.9	8.8	20.4
80	BHOPALSAGAR	72675	50	99.7	99.5	99.2	62.4	47.2	70.8	76.2	36.9	45.9
81	CHHOTI SADRI	100067	30.2	99.8	95.4	99.9	57	38.8	60.8	43	12.1	35.4
82	CHITTAURGARH	167960	43.6	99.5	96.6	98.6	66.5	48.2	73.8	66.4	20.8	38.6
83	DUNGLA	89975	61.9	100	98.9	99.8	58.3	51	69.8	58.4	18	36.1
84	GANGRAR	88640	46.9	100	97.1	99.7	58.8	45.6	72.5	60.1	20.7	28.4
85	KAPASAN	84531	24.3	100	97.3	98.8	52.8	38.6	51.1	63.3	11.6	26.7
86	NIMBAHERA	135391	48.4	100	99.1	99.9	75.8	50.4	47.1	61.4	13.8	44.7
87	PRATAPGARH	201229	42.2	99.2	94.8	82.6	59.8	40.5	24.2	54	9.5	12.5
88	RASHMI	75326	65.2	100	98.1	99.8	78.2	62.9	77.3	80.6	7	48.6
	CHITTAURGARH	**1514255**	**42.8**	**99.6**	**95.8**	**95.3**	**61.7**	**43.4**	**49.6**	**58.3**	**16.2**	**30.3**
89	CHURU	152178	76.4	75.9	98.5	100	89.5	61.4	71.8	69.1	20.5	35.6
90	RAJGARH	267403	55	85.2	99.7	90	74	49.7	63.3	71.3	14.7	27.5
91	RATANGARH	158090	85.9	93	99.1	99.9	90.9	59.4	98	80.6	28.2	36.9
92	SARDARSHAHAR	222979	47.6	52.5	98.3	94.4	62.6	49	54.2	80.9	10.8	25.8
93	SUJANGARH	253207	66.9	89.6	98.5	99.8	69.4	59.3	55.4	82.3	19.4	23.1
94	TARANAGAR	151006	68	82.4	99.8	97.1	73.5	60.3	71.8	73.5	32.6	50.1
	CHURU ***	**1387682**	**66.6**	**80.7**	**99.1**	**96.8**	**75.6**	**58.5**	**68.7**	**77.6**	**21**	**31.5**
95	BANDIKUI	267016	51	98.9	98.9	100	75.9	41.3	50.3	38.8	21.3	20.6
96	DAUSA	271907	52.7	98.6	97.1	96.8	75.2	51.3	66.3	52.8	24.7	25.8
97	LALSOT	251370	40.5	99.7	96.3	90.2	65	38	44.1	38.9	20.4	21.5
98	MAHWA	179173	47.8	99.9	96.2	94.7	70.4	46.6	63.3	20.5	9.4	22.2
99	SIKRAI	211779	41.4	100	99	95.2	83.2	47.2	43.4	38.5	24.8	27.3
	DAUSA	**1181245**	**47**	**99.3**	**97.5**	**95.5**	**73.9**	**44.8**	**53.4**	**39.2**	**20.7**	**23.4**
100	BARI	150595	61.1	96.5	95.5	57.2	57.4	38.1	30.6	30.2	6	6.7
101	BASERI	201777	42.2	98.1	97.4	63.6	70.2	33.3	45.4	43.1	12.8	18.2
102	DHAULPUR	262456	37.9	99	97.8	82.3	73.6	39.4	41.6	32.9	14.8	21.1
103	RAJAKHERA	191812	28.1	98.3	97.6	94.1	72.1	38.9	41.6	19.8	3.3	7.3
	DHAULPUR	**806640**	**41**	**98.1**	**97.2**	**75.7**	**69.4**	**37.5**	**40.5**	**31.8**	**9.9**	**14.4**
104	ASPUR	184508	67.5	100	99.2	92.6	78.2	53.8	57.4	71	22.4	16.4
105	BICHHIWARA	236114	68.4	99.4	99.8	98.7	67.8	61.1	47.1	61	11.6	14.4
106	DUNGARPUR	172385	60.5	97.1	100	93.6	66.8	47.3	53.2	54.5	10.2	2.1
107	SAGWARA	192681	72.9	100	99.8	92.5	78.2	62.7	67	76.3	28	21.6
108	SIMALWARA	241099	58.5	99.7	99.6	87.8	72.4	49.1	47.4	55.8	17	16.1
	DUNGARPUR	**1026787**	**65.4**	**99.3**	**99.7**	**93**	**72.5**	**55**	**53.8**	**63.4**	**17.6**	**14.4**
109	ANUPGARH	417746	37.9	83.9	78.1	69	76.6	22.8	54.3	63.5	8.9	32.1
110	GANGANAGAR	176517	63.9	98.6	93.2	99.5	94.8	57.7	91.9	83	33.9	47.8
111	KARANPUR	103094	54.3	94.8	96.2	98.5	91.1	44.9	86.4	81.3	7.2	24.3
112	PADAMPUR	121362	59.6	94.2	93.7	97.8	77	37.6	81.9	65.6	17.6	33.4

P. Code	Panchayat Samiti	Total Population	Type of Amenity Available									
			Medical	Improved Drinking Water#	Edu-cation	Power Supply	Approach by Pucca Road	Post Office##	Tele-phone	Transport Communi-cations###	Banks	Ag. Credit Societies
1	2	3	4	5	6	7	8	9	10	11	12	13
113	RAISINGHNAGAR	157334	44.7	92.8	92.3	86.3	70.1	33.2	74.1	73.7	5.4	32.4
114	SADULSHAHAR	146629	77.2	79.5	94.1	98.7	92.2	51.0	92.2	82.1	25.8	48.4
115	SURATGARH	213384	42.4	78.7	78.9	56.5	71.8	29.0	57.3	72.1	8.0	33.1
	GANGANAGAR	**1336066**	**50.4**	**87.4**	**86.5**	**81.2**	**80.3**	**35.8**	**71.2**	**72.3**	**14.2**	**35.7**
116	BHADRA	220582	76.3	85.6	93.2	97.3	89.5	66.9	76.6	87.6	25.6	63.0
117	HANUMANGARH	628123	61.8	94.9	85.5	95.1	91.0	53.5	74.3	79.2	23.4	43.8
118	NOHAR	365762	45.8	73.5	87.9	72.0	72.1	47.7	64.1	74.8	18.6	35.1
	HANUMANGARH	**1214467**	**59.6**	**86.8**	**87.6**	**88.6**	**85.1**	**54.2**	**71.7**	**79.4**	**22.4**	**44.7**
119	AMBER	262029	59.0	100.0	98.5	99.6	74.5	43.2	58.8	63.8	20.9	21.9
120	BASSI	229639	56.3	99.9	98.3	99.7	82.4	44.5	55.7	68.4	19.5	31.8
121	CHAKSU	161140	31.4	99.0	93.5	88.4	50.1	31.1	30.0	37.5	16.2	22.7
122	DUDU	272517	58.0	97.1	98.5	94.9	78.2	58.3	68.6	65.2	21.5	35.0
123	GOVINDGARH	275780	79.4	100.0	99.5	99.5	90.1	72.8	79.9	79.5	33.0	59.1
124	JAMWA RAMGARH	250132	56.2	99.7	96.9	100.0	79.7	41.3	37.0	72.8	18.2	20.1
125	JHOTWARA	88946	51.7	94.4	98.1	99.4	83.2	37.8	81.7	69.6	12.3	26.3
126	KOTPUTLI	228470	46.9	100.0	100.0	96.2	85.2	52.6	74.4	54.8	12.8	17.0
127	PHAGI	161610	43.5	99.7	99.1	96.6	64.3	40.6	50.0	55.4	17.9	39.2
128	SAMBHAR	209528	63.6	95.6	99.7	99.9	75.1	52.9	77.4	69.0	16.9	31.2
129	SANGANER	131301	53.0	99.5	96.1	100.0	75.3	42.6	75.8	74.7	15.7	26.3
130	SHAHPURA	181498	72.6	100.0	100.0	99.5	88.1	64.3	71.3	58.1	22.2	37.2
131	VIRATNAGAR	206414	56.7	99.7	99.5	100.0	86.0	57.5	53.9	58.3	22.6	23.0
	JAIPUR	**2659004**	**57.4**	**99.0**	**98.4**	**98.1**	**78.7**	**50.8**	**62.3**	**64.3**	**20.0**	**30.7**
132	JAISALMER	127798	57.8	70.8	97.7	62.9	80.3	57.4	64.9	79.2	20.5	32
133	SAM	138679	47.3	83.5	95.1	39.5	65.0	48.5	66.1	75.5	14.2	13.8
134	SANKRA	165376	49.5	84.1	97.9	55.2	55.9	43.4	70.8	74.6	11.8	26.3
	JAISALMER	**431853**	**51.3**	**80.0**	**97.0**	**52.4**	**66.0**	**49.2**	**67.5**	**76.2**	**15.1**	**24.0**
135	AHORE	177342	83.2	98.8	99.6	99.5	80.6	71.9	84.3	90.9	28.5	56.6
136	BHINMAL	184751	63.8	85.4	100.0	93.7	79.5	62.9	82.6	90.1	17.6	32.3
137	JALOR	131827	73.2	99.8	100.0	99.7	91.8	66.7	81.3	82.8	26.1	43.7
138	JASWANTPURA	128410	70.1	98.5	99.9	100.0	84.0	61.8	81.7	85.6	20.9	25.8
139	RANIWARA	163349	71.0	95.3	100.0	99.7	78.6	61.7	63.5	78.4	17.9	25.0
140	SANCHORE	342120	48.4	85.9	99.3	86.0	72.0	45.0	53.8	73.6	14.2	32.5
141	SAYLA	211147	77.8	99.2	99.8	98.3	87.9	61.9	92.7	95.0	22.5	62.9
	JALOR	**1338946**	**67.1**	**93.4**	**99.7**	**95.1**	**80.6**	**59.5**	**74.5**	**84.2**	**20.2**	**40.0**
142	BAKANI	152329	34.1	97.8	87.0	86.0	46.1	30.7	33.2	29.8	16.3	11.2
143	DAG	167192	34.9	98.6	96.3	85.1	40.9	40.1	43.3	38.3	17.0	23.5
144	JHALRAPATAN	205868	33.2	97.9	95.6	96.7	50.7	30.5	58.0	33.2	14.8	26.2
145	KHANPUR	153370	46.9	99.4	92.6	97.6	54.2	44.4	60.7	42.6	19.1	24.7
146	MANOHARTHANA	161425	21.1	98.1	92.8	74.3	31.1	26.1	29.5	24.1	4.7	12.9
147	PIRAWA	171897	33.2	99.7	97.3	99.9	44.0	49.6	51.4	36.7	18.8	29.6
	JHALAWAR	**1012081**	**33.8**	**98.6**	**93.8**	**90.3**	**44.7**	**36.8**	**46.6**	**34.1**	**15.1**	**21.7**
148	ALSISAR	141416	58.6	86.2	98.7	98.7	77.5	62.0	77.3	77.8	27.2	44.5
149	BUHANA	204411	69.4	93.4	99.8	98.8	80.1	62.9	63.1	71.0	7.9	25.3
150	CHIRAWA	152843	66.8	98.6	100.0	100.0	90.1	69.3	93.4	87.0	23.4	51.8
151	JHUNJHUNUN	176693	62.1	94.8	99.9	99.9	79.5	56.8	92.1	79.6	6.1	25.3
152	KHETRI	214474	78.8	99.2	100.0	99.7	85.3	71.8	69.6	75.1	13.0	29.5
153	NAWALGARH	217636	66.1	100.0	100.0	100.0	88.9	72.4	96.3	87.5	15.5	52.9
154	SURAJGARH	175820	47.8	88.8	100.0	100.0	75.8	59.2	83.6	71.5	9.3	28.8
155	UDAIPURWATI	235280	80.1	99.8	100.0	99.1	89.9	77.0	84.1	88.3	17.6	25.6
	JHUNJHUNUN	**1518573**	**67.3**	**95.6**	**99.8**	**99.5**	**83.8**	**67.1**	**82.2**	**79.9**	**14.5**	**34.8**
156	BALESAR	174179	62.9	97.5	95.0	90.8	69.9	47.7	54.6	69.7	11.3	15.3
157	BAP	157290	45.0	66.4	91.7	81.4	69.6	45.3	42.5	74.7	17.2	33.0
158	BHOPALGARH	202321	77.1	95.7	100.0	99.4	93.2	72.0	84.2	98.4	29.5	37.2
159	BILARA	180550	86.1	99.4	99.5	100.0	89.9	62.4	87.8	84.7	28.9	51.2
160	LUNI	229097	78.7	94.5	99.7	95.1	84.7	57.0	86.8	83.7	18.5	37.7
161	MANDOR	151257	55.9	93.0	99.2	98.3	77.7	52.2	82.7	79.3	22.5	35.0
162	OSIAN	422181	71.6	99.1	99.7	99.1	84.5	64.4	73.1	89.7	20.2	38.7
163	PHALODI	229892	54.8	95.6	98.4	90.1	76.2	55.0	56.6	74.9	20.9	39.0
164	SHERGARH	162656	58.0	88.7	95.3	79.5	61.2	51.5	49.1	57.0	12.9	23.9
	JODHPUR	**1909423**	**67.0**	**93.6**	**98.0**	**93.7**	**79.9**	**57.8**	**69.8**	**81.0**	**20.4**	**35.5**
165	HINDAUN	262403	64.8	100.0	99.0	99.7	88.4	56.4	79.1	53.5	12.0	29.6
166	KARAULI	222621	55.1	95.8	98.7	84.6	71.0	56.1	28.9	53.6	12.4	10.0
167	NADOTI	126089	59.6	97.7	99.2	91.0	75.1	53.9	36.1	61.8	26.8	49.6
168	SAPOTRA	232513	57.8	96.9	98.0	72.1	69.7	52.1	29.4	49.7	18.4	20.8
169	TODABHIM	194094	63.3	98.2	99.3	91.8	82.8	60.2	57.4	47.0	10.0	33.0
	KARAULI	**1037720**	**60.2**	**97.8**	**98.8**	**87.8**	**77.8**	**55.8**	**47.9**	**52.5**	**14.9**	**26.5**
170	CHECHAT	132073	56.3	99.3	98.4	99.9	74.7	32.2	69.4	46.4	19.2	16.9
171	ITAWA	155646	53.4	99.8	96.3	90.3	64.7	52.8	55.6	51.6	29.5	46.9
172	LADPURA	144691	58.1	99.5	97.9	98.5	91.6	34.7	78.5	30.0	16.7	19.1
173	SANGOD	146951	46.3	100.0	97.6	99.3	60.6	44.5	57.1	44.5	20.4	33.3
174	SULTANPUR	150587	64.8	100.0	98.4	97.6	73.0	48.8	54.2	40.7	32.2	48.1
	KOTA	**729948**	**55.8**	**99.7**	**97.7**	**97.0**	**72.8**	**43.0**	**62.7**	**42.7**	**23.8**	**33.5**
175	DEGANA	190085	65.0	86.7	99.9	99.9	70.3	56.9	76.8	88.3	17.3	33.3

P. Code	Panchayat Samiti	Total Population	*Type of Amenity Available*									
			Medical	Improved Drinking Water#	Edu-cation	Power Supply	Approach by Pucca Road	Post Office##	Tele-phone	Transport Communi-cations###	Banks	Ag. Credit Societies
1	2	3	4	5	6	7	8	9	10	11	12	13
176	DIDWANA	285031	61.0	93.7	99.6	99.4	77.3	64.2	65.8	80.0	20.3	26.3
177	JAYAL	224944	68.6	73.0	99.5	97.4	72.7	63.8	85.5	85.9	17.3	53.1
178	KUCHAMAN	268146	54.5	89.9	98.9	100.0	66.0	56.3	59.9	69.8	18.7	27.0
179	LADNU	158026	73.4	99.7	99.0	98.1	77.0	65.1	61.8	93.9	23.4	51.3
180	MAKRANA	199671	66.1	77.5	99.8	99.3	67.0	64.8	82.0	84.1	24.9	34.4
181	MERTA	183429	72.4	95.1	98.7	100.0	89.8	71.5	79.4	90.5	36.7	53.0
182	MUNDWA	197532	66.5	96.3	98.7	96.4	73.6	56.1	44.3	85.2	19.4	39.2
183	NAGAUR	224815	62.1	78.3	99.0	91.9	71.3	50.9	64.0	76.3	11.8	22.0
184	PARBATSAR	186413	65.6	96.7	99.8	100.0	77.4	67.7	73.5	83.5	22.2	32.2
185	RIYAN	179629	68.6	94.1	98.7	99.2	84.3	64.7	61.4	81.4	27.4	41.8
	NAGAUR	**2297721**	**65.1**	**88.8**	**99.2**	**98.3**	**74.7**	**61.7**	**68.4**	**82.7**	**21.3**	**36.5**
186	BALI	183802	82.7	100.0	99.9	96.5	95.1	71.5	95.9	90.6	34.1	49.3
187	DESURI	102245	72.1	98.3	99.3	99.2	80.8	65.9	89.9	86.3	39.6	39.4
188	JAITARAN	186938	77.7	97.7	99.9	97.8	80.1	69.4	80.1	69.8	38.5	49.2
189	KHARCHI/MARWAR JUN.	181445	71.0	97.9	99.2	97.6	81.7	64.5	94.1	82.4	32.6	47.6
190	PALI	89939	66.0	94.0	98.9	99.6	83.3	55.9	93.7	88.5	41.2	47.5
191	RAIPUR	182004	72.8	100.0	99.3	94.7	80.5	71.4	83.9	73.1	34.6	46.8
192	RANI STATION	106504	82.1	100.0	99.9	99.9	86.8	77.9	96.6	94.5	39.9	42.9
193	ROHAT	102599	53.1	96.1	99.9	99.8	73.6	42.1	78.1	83.1	22.7	35.6
194	SOJAT	155889	72.6	95.5	100.0	98.8	81.3	61.8	94.0	88.7	29.2	51.1
195	SUMERPUR	137999	82.1	94.3	99.1	100.0	99.8	74.8	97.7	91.4	29.7	50.6
	PALI	**1429364**	**74.2**	**97.6**	**99.6**	**98.0**	**84.6**	**66.6**	**90.2**	**83.8**	**34.0**	**46.8**
196	AMET	88162	44.8	100.0	97.4	100.0	56.3	37.5	69.7	77.8	11.4	14.4
197	BHIM	137578	48.3	99.0	99.7	95.0	76.0	46.8	58.7	66.0	14.1	14.0
198	DEOGARH	77865	35.2	100.0	96.6	99.1	52.3	27.1	69.3	60.7	13.8	18.4
199	KHAMNOR	172395	56.2	99.7	98.3	98.8	78.6	44.2	74.0	75.1	13.3	27.0
200	KUMBHALGARH	131346	47.8	99.2	98.5	99.1	59.9	39.2	49.1	66.9	12.3	13.8
201	RAILMAGRA	110435	71.0	99.8	99.6	100.0	84.3	53.6	74.3	78.3	23.5	34.1
202	RAJSAMAND	140520	51.3	100.0	98.9	100.0	73.6	52.6	92.4	70.4	20.5	28.0
	RAJSAMAND	**858301**	**51.7**	**99.6**	**98.6**	**98.7**	**70.6**	**44.2**	**69.9**	**71.0**	**15.6**	**21.9**
203	BAMANWAS	149429	57.3	93.2	98.9	85.9	63.7	60.7	49.0	51.0	17.0	39.6
204	BONLI	209833	54.0	98.5	98.7	93.8	61.9	53.4	73.3	48.5	27.6	42.2
205	GANGAPUR	179209	71.1	98.3	99.5	98.1	75.1	55.3	55.5	56.1	24.1	38.5
206	KHANDAR	150136	55.5	99.3	97.7	79.8	69.3	46.1	52.9	56.7	11.0	30.1
207	SAWAI MADHOPUR	215810	64.5	100.0	99.4	88.2	58.3	58.0	80.7	47.2	29.7	44.9
	SAWAI MADHOPUR	**904417**	**60.7**	**98.1**	**98.9**	**89.7**	**65.2**	**54.9**	**64.1**	**51.5**	**22.9**	**39.7**
208	DANTA RAMGARH	262183	72.0	98.9	99.7	100.0	76.5	67.5	87.9	82.0	27.6	41.1
209	DHOND	209919	78.2	99.3	100.0	100.0	84.0	73.4	91.5	93.4	20.7	22.6
210	FATEHPUR	193473	63.4	100.0	99.6	100.0	60.3	63.9	91.7	81.4	9.4	22.5
211	KHANDELA	218560	74.5	99.3	99.4	99.9	71.5	69.4	73.3	76.3	19.6	33.7
212	LACHHMANGARH	197022	56.5	99.1	99.7	99.8	62.1	62.5	85.2	87.4	16.9	14.2
213	NEEM KA THANA	317049	71.6	100.0	99.0	98.2	75.0	61.0	81.4	56.6	23.4	32.9
214	PIPRALI	206064	76.6	99.4	99.9	99.8	88.0	72.3	89.9	82.6	33.3	36.4
215	SRI MADHOPUR	210980	70.9	99.5	100.0	100.0	90.4	75.7	89.3	77.6	26.3	45.4
	SIKAR	**1815250**	**70.7**	**99.4**	**99.6**	**99.6**	**76.1**	**67.9**	**85.9**	**78.3**	**22.5**	**31.7**
216	ABU ROAD	114818	49.7	98.6	100.0	84.5	80.9	64.0	64.2	58.0	16.1	26.7
217	PINDWARA	184803	76.1	99.0	99.4	89.0	85.0	66.5	75.2	59.1	23.2	26.0
218	REODAR	175344	66.2	99.9	99.0	99.8	77.7	61.3	80.2	66.0	22.0	37.4
219	SHEOGANJ	99663	74.5	96.9	99.8	98.6	87.5	73.8	86.5	73.5	30.4	36.6
220	SIROHI	125589	88.1	99.6	99.4	99.7	88.1	78.3	94.0	93.6	37.1	33.6
	SIROHI	**700217**	**71.2**	**99.0**	**99.5**	**94.3**	**83.4**	**68.0**	**79.8**	**68.9**	**25.2**	**31.8**
221	DEOLI	169271	58.2	99.7	97.3	84.4	60.1	55.3	66.3	44.7	23.8	37.2
222	MALPURA	176932	51.9	99.5	99.8	95.1	76.3	54.8	63.1	56.6	32.4	31.8
223	NIWAI	165298	47.3	98.6	97.0	95.9	66.1	47.7	69.9	44.0	20.0	30.5
224	TODARAISINGH	110131	56.7	99.8	98.5	97.0	65.9	54.0	57.1	44.8	12.6	43.1
225	TONK	204362	59.2	98.8	97.8	87.6	71.2	44.4	54.3	32.8	16.7	33.2
226	UNIARA	132509	48.1	98.2	94.3	94.5	57.8	48.3	54.7	43.7	21.6	41.3
	TONK	**958503**	**53.8**	**99.1**	**97.5**	**91.9**	**66.8**	**50.5**	**61.1**	**44.1**	**21.7**	**35.4**
227	BARGAON	123802	46.9	99.3	97.7	97.2	74.7	54.0	61.6	66.2	27.1	9.7
228	BHINDER	201832	54.1	100.0	94.8	98.5	63.5	42.1	60.0	57.2	19.3	13.2
229	DHARIAWAD	203605	43.3	97.8	97.1	86.9	61.6	37.5	47.1	56.7	8.1	10.2
230	GIRWA	227623	64.0	98.0	98.9	91.9	76.3	46.5	62.2	69.4	20.2	21.7
231	GOGUNDA	151575	49.7	97.6	99.5	89.2	64.1	47.1	58.5	63.2	10.4	6.1
232	JHADOL	193810	48.2	98.4	97.2	72.3	51.5	33.5	32.1	56.4	8.9	12.4
233	KHERWARA	254301	48.8	98.7	96.6	68.9	67.3	31.2	48.1	46.9	5.5	7.4
234	KOTRA	183504	36.7	92.4	93.1	33.3	46.8	26.7	11.2	43.1	8.4	9.5
235	MAVLI	194148	69.8	100.0	98.7	100.0	75.1	47.6	91.0	69.3	21.7	21.1
236	SALUMBAR	196614	50.9	99.6	97.7	82.6	58.5	39.0	41.0	61.7	11.2	11.1
237	SARADA	212181	60.6	100.0	98.9	83.1	75.7	53.3	52.7	66.7	18.5	15.6
	UDAIPUR	**2142995**	**52.5**	**98.4**	**97.3**	**81.7**	**65.1**	**41.1**	**51.2**	**59.3**	**14**	**12.8**
	RAJASTHAN	**43292813**	**56.64**	**95.39**	**97.65**	**91.57**	**73.48**	**51.32**	**63.99**	**63.15**	**19.30**	**29.90**

Note: * Dungargarh PS shifted from Churu to Bikaner district on 1st April 2001 ** Excluding data of Dungargarh PS; *** Including data of Dungargarh PS.
Improved Drinking Water (See Terminology), ## Post office includes post office, telegraph office and post and telegraph office.
Transport Communication includes bus service, rail facility and navigable waterways.
Source: Directorate of Census Operation, Jaipur.

GENERAL ANNEX-VII

PANCHAYAT SAMITI-WISE PERCENTAGE OF INHABITED VILLAGES HAVING MEDICAL AND OTEHR RELATED AMENITIES: RAJASTHAN (2001)

P. Code	Panchayat Samiti	Total Inhabited Villages	Percentage of Villages Having Amenity of									
			Medical	Improved Drinking Water#	Edu-cation	Power Supply	Approach by Pucca Road	Post Office##	Tele-phone	Transport Communi-cations###	Banks	Ag. Credit Societies
1	2	3	4	5	6	7	8	9	10	11	12	13
1	ARAIN	125	30.4	98.4	96.0	92.8	40.8	30.4	89.6	30.4	10.4	11.2
2	BHINAY	128	32.0	99.2	100.0	93.0	53.9	34.4	71.9	43.8	8.6	14.1
3	JAWAJA	199	25.6	100.0	86.9	93.0	68.8	19.1	57.8	31.7	4.0	4.0
4	KEKRI	99	47.5	100.0	98.0	91.9	65.7	39.4	85.9	39.4	7.1	15.2
5	KISHANGARH	111	37.8	99.1	98.2	96.4	63.1	32.4	72.1	54.1	9.9	12.6
6	MASOODA	139	23.0	100.0	90.6	97.8	56.1	26.6	63.3	43.2	4.3	10.8
7	PISANGAN	128	47.7	100.0	97.7	93.0	69.5	39.1	79.7	60.9	8.6	15.6
8	SRINAGAR	96	41.7	100.0	97.9	96.9	76.0	36.5	74.0	59.4	9.4	10.4
	AJMER DISTRICT	**1025**	**34.3**	**99.6**	**94.8**	**94.2**	**61.7**	**30.9**	**72.7**	**44.0**	**7.4**	**11.1**
9	BANSURE	131	29.8	98.5	99.2	100.0	57.3	26.0	45.0	46.6	5.3	6.1
10	BEHROR	90	40.0	97.8	91.1	98.9	67.8	28.9	60.0	53.3	7.8	10.0
11	KATHUMAR	158	30.4	95.6	98.7	95.6	69.6	28.5	58.2	29.7	7.6	14.6
12	KISHANGARH BAS	135	19.3	97.0	91.9	97.0	57.0	23.0	65.9	23.7	4.4	9.6
13	KOTKASIM	115	19.1	100.0	97.4	99.1	53.9	18.3	40.0	26.1	7.0	15.7
14	LACHHMANGARH	184	31.0	100.0	97.8	95.7	56.0	20.7	51.6	32.1	3.3	25.0
15	MANDAWAR	142	35.2	100.0	97.9	97.2	60.6	30.3	59.2	41.5	7.0	19.0
16	NIMRANA	85	48.2	97.6	98.8	98.8	72.9	41.2	41.2	51.8	11.8	10.6
17	RAJGARH	140	19.3	90.7	82.9	85.0	68.6	21.4	28.6	24.3	4.3	4.3
18	RAMGARH	173	24.9	98.8	93.6	97.7	64.7	13.9	45.1	22.0	4.6	13.3
19	RENI	102	31.4	97.1	95.1	100.0	64.7	28.4	41.2	18.6	7.8	16.7
20	THANAGAZI	148	29.1	96.6	82.4	75.7	62.2	23.0	50.7	38.5	4.7	6.8
21	TIJARA	202	20.8	98.5	90.1	94.6	67.3	13.9	36.6	21.8	5.4	6.9
22	UMREN	149	31.5	96.0	86.6	91.3	71.1	22.1	59.1	21.5	5.4	20.1
	ALWAR	**1954**	**28.3**	**97.5**	**92.9**	**94.3**	**63.7**	**23.1**	**48.7**	**30.9**	**5.8**	**12.9**
23	ANANDPURI	129	27.1	96.9	90.7	62.8	45.0	16.3	10.1	27.9	3.1	4.7
24	BAGIDORA	165	30.3	97.6	96.4	50.9	47.9	17.0	22.4	33.9	7.9	7.9
25	GARHI	168	48.8	99.4	97.6	91.1	61.3	28.0	41.1	48.8	10.1	11.3
26	GHATOL	220	25.0	99.5	91.4	68.6	45.9	19.1	25.5	36.4	5.5	5.9
27	KUSHALGARH	209	25.4	98.1	94.3	50.7	41.6	9.6	19.6	22.0	3.3	2.9
28	PEEPALKHOONT	187	32.6	95.7	85.0	24.1	26.2	10.7	12.3	21.4	3.7	3.2
29	SAJJANGARH	185	28.6	100.0	93.0	52.4	44.9	7.6	13.0	35.1	3.8	5.9
30	TALWARA	213	28.6	97.7	90.1	68.5	55.9	13.1	31.0	45.5	5.2	8.5
	BANSWARA	**1476**	**30.5**	**98.2**	**92.2**	**58.5**	**46.0**	**14.9**	**22.3**	**34.0**	**5.3**	**6.2**
31	ANTA	148	19.6	99.3	92.6	92.6	44.6	20.9	41.2	33.8	10.1	16.2
32	ATRU	136	25.7	100.0	94.1	98.5	42.6	27.9	59.6	28.7	5.1	16.9
33	BARAN	99	26.3	99.0	97.0	99.0	56.6	25.3	50.5	25.3	3.0	25.3
34	CHHABRA	186	7.5	94.6	80.1	87.6	25.8	10.8	24.7	9.7	1.6	8.6
35	CHHIPABAROD	173	11.0	96.0	78.6	83.8	34.1	15.6	27.2	18.5	2.9	10.4
36	KISHANGANJ	180	18.9	98.3	81.7	84.4	38.3	8.9	30.0	18.3	3.9	8.9
37	SHAHBAD	167	12.6	93.4	82.0	63.5	29.3	13.2	21.6	14.4	4.8	4.2
	BARAN	**1089**	**16.3**	**97.0**	**85.4**	**85.9**	**37.2**	**16.4**	**34.4**	**20.3**	**4.4**	**11.8**
38	BALOTRA	231	26.8	72.7	88.7	62.8	46.8	32.0	62.3	66.7	6.1	8.7
39	BARMER	307	19.9	70.4	90.2	35.8	47.9	23.1	28.3	51.8	2.0	11.4
40	BAYTOO	323	18.0	87.3	87.0	26.9	36.2	16.1	40.9	43.3	2.8	8.7
41	CHOHTAN	187	27.3	74.3	96.3	55.1	53.5	32.1	36.4	61.5	3.2	14.4
42	DHORIMANNA	261	21.5	89.3	95.8	69.7	47.1	28.0	50.2	49.4	3.8	12.3
43	SHEO	250	17.2	74.4	91.2	42.0	36.8	24.0	35.2	48.8	2.4	8.8
44	SINDHARI	259	21.2	79.5	98.5	41.7	40.5	22.0	48.3	55.6	3.5	9.7
45	SIWANA	115	40.9	95.7	97.4	93.9	51.3	40.0	62.6	65.2	7.8	20.0
	BARMER	**1933**	**22.4**	**79.7**	**92.5**	**49.0**	**44.0**	**25.5**	**43.8**	**53.7**	**3.6**	**11.0**
46	BAYANA	161	29.8	96.3	91.9	84.5	61.5	21.7	21.7	28.0	5.6	6.2
47	DEEG	119	45.4	99.2	97.5	90.8	60.5	31.1	61.3	21.0	4.2	53.8
48	KAMAN	194	27.3	90.2	95.9	78.9	54.6	19.1	18.0	12.9	2.6	5.2
49	KUMHER	117	54.7	99.1	98.3	97.4	74.4	28.2	61.5	17.9	14.5	37.6
50	NADBAI	114	57.0	100.0	94.7	97.4	57.9	37.7	76.3	33.3	11.4	7.0
51	NAGAR PAHARI	216	24.5	97.7	97.2	90.7	52.3	24.1	39.8	16.2	5.1	10.6
52	RUPBAS	142	38.7	98.6	97.9	87.3	60.6	26.1	47.9	39.4	3.5	21.1

P. Code	Panchayat Samiti	Total Inhabited Villages	Percentage of Villages Having Amenity of									
			Medical	Improved Drinking Water#	Edu-cation	Power Supply	Approach by Pucca Road	Post Office##	Tele-phone	Transport Communi-cations###	Banks	Ag. Credit Societies
1	2	3	4	5	6	7	8	9	10	11	12	13
53	SEWAR	157	29.3	96.2	89.2	98.1	80.3	22.3	61.1	24.8	7.6	28.7
54	WEIR	146	29.5	98.6	94.5	97.9	47.3	34.2	47.9	24.7	5.5	5.5
	BHARATPUR	**1366**	**35.2**	**96.9**	**95.2**	**90.7**	**60.3**	**26.3**	**45.5**	**23.4**	**6.2**	**17.7**
55	ASIND	204	25.0	98.5	91.7	92.6	39.7	22.1	53.4	45.1	4.9	11.3
56	BANERA	83	47.0	97.6	94.0	100.0	45.8	28.9	74.7	42.2	4.8	15.7
57	HURDA	70	41.4	98.6	95.7	98.6	58.6	30.0	84.3	58.6	11.4	24.3
58	JAHAZPUR	217	27.6	97.2	84.8	88.0	35.5	15.7	40.1	24.4	3.2	10.1
59	KOTRI	175	22.9	98.9	93.7	85.1	32.0	17.1	35.4	29.7	2.3	12.0
60	MANDAL	188	22.9	98.9	93.1	88.8	46.8	18.6	44.7	44.7	5.9	11.2
61	MANDALGARH	281	23.8	97.5	76.9	88.6	37.7	14.9	36.3	28.5	6.0	11.4
62	RAIPUR	89	30.3	97.8	97.8	98.9	28.1	25.8	60.7	55.1	5.6	14.6
63	SAHARA	99	31.3	99.0	96.0	100.0	51.5	27.3	75.8	50.5	4.0	14.1
64	SHAHPURA	151	29.8	96.0	94.7	90.7	36.4	24.5	45.0	36.4	3.3	13.2
65	SUWANA	136	30.1	100.0	97.1	98.5	57.4	22.1	58.8	51.5	8.1	15.4
	BHILWARA	**1693**	**27.9**	**98.1**	**90.3**	**91.8**	**41.1**	**20.6**	**49.7**	**39.0**	**5.1**	**12.8**
66	BIKANER	219	22.8	70.3	86.8	61.2	74.9	18.7	32.0	61.6	11.9	16.9
67	DUNGARGARH *	92	60.9	83.7	97.8	98.9	60.9	54.3	77.2	71.7	13.0	16.3
68	KOLAYAT	196	19.4	52.0	77.0	54.1	50.5	18.4	20.4	53.1	8.2	10.7
69	LUNKARANSAR	160	28.1	66.3	91.3	75.0	62.5	21.9	35.6	56.3	9.4	8.1
70	NOKHA	137	29.2	89.8	91.2	91.2	60.6	43.1	43.1	72.3	13.1	19.0
	BIKANER **	**712**	**24.3**	**68.1**	**86.0**	**68.1**	**62.6**	**24.0**	**31.7**	**60.1**	**10.5**	**13.6**
71	HINDOLI	174	28.7	98.9	93.7	90.2	51.1	23.0	31.0	24.1	4.0	7.5
72	KESHORAIPATAN	223	19.3	95.1	90.1	81.6	39.0	18.8	17.0	29.6	4.0	15.7
73	NAINWA	180	17.8	95.0	93.9	93.3	33.9	18.3	26.7	26.1	4.4	16.1
74	TALERA	262	20.2	99.6	94.7	86.6	50.8	15.6	29.0	24.8	6.5	8.4
	BUNDI	**839**	**21.2**	**97.3**	**93.1**	**87.5**	**44.1**	**18.6**	**25.7**	**26.2**	**4.9**	**11.8**
75	ARNOD	178	12.4	97.2	75.8	64.0	33.1	19.7	9.0	27.0	3.4	5.1
76	BARI SADRI	143	18.9	99.3	76.2	97.9	37.1	14.0	15.4	37.1	3.5	9.8
77	BEGUN	222	16.7	98.6	69.8	87.8	37.8	14.0	29.3	34.2	3.2	7.2
78	BHADESAR	163	11.7	100.0	81.6	100.0	37.4	9.2	19.0	28.8	3.7	11.7
79	BHAINSRORGARH	154	15.6	97.4	70.1	85.1	38.3	9.1	1.9	39.0	1.9	6.5
80	BHOPALSAGAR	83	19.3	98.8	92.8	97.6	43.4	16.9	45.8	53.0	8.4	20.5
81	CHHOTI SADRI	141	11.3	97.2	83.7	97.2	36.2	15.6	36.2	31.2	3.5	13.5
82	CHITTAURGARH	218	15.6	99.1	80.3	91.7	39.0	15.1	45.9	39.0	2.8	11.0
83	DUNGLA	102	33.3	100.0	93.1	99.0	32.4	20.6	50.0	35.3	4.9	13.7
84	GANGRAR	127	19.7	100.0	83.5	96.9	36.2	17.3	49.6	33.9	3.1	7.1
85	KAPASAN	107	10.3	100.0	90.7	97.2	39.3	17.8	29.0	47.7	2.8	10.3
86	NIMBAHERA	152	21.1	99.3	89.5	98.0	53.9	19.1	26.3	38.8	2.6	16.4
87	PRATAPGARH	330	18.8	97.6	80.3	70.0	40.3	17.0	12.4	33.9	3.9	4.8
88	RASHMI	81	30.9	98.8	86.4	97.5	46.9	27.2	49.4	53.1	2.5	18.5
	CHITTAURGARH	**2201**	**17.4**	**98.6**	**80.8**	**88.5**	**39.2**	**16.0**	**26.9**	**36.4**	**3.5**	**9.9**
89	CHURU	105	61.9	70.5	98.1	100.0	80.0	42.9	61.0	60.0	9.5	24.8
90	RAJGARH	213	35.7	80.8	98.1	84.0	59.2	29.6	54.5	59.2	5.2	16.9
91	RATANGARH	101	65.3	87.1	95.0	97.0	77.2	39.6	93.1	69.3	11.9	21.8
92	SARDARSHAHAR	170	34.7	47.1	97.1	91.2	51.2	32.4	42.4	70.6	5.3	17.1
93	SUJANGARH	155	41.3	86.5	92.9	98.7	56.8	37.4	44.5	69.0	7.7	12.9
94	TARANAGAR	110	33.6	67.3	92.7	88.2	49.1	36.4	44.5	46.4	9.1	23.6
	CHURU ***	**946**	**44.7**	**73.9**	**96.1**	**92.8**	**60.6**	**37.1**	**56.6**	**63.7**	**8.0**	**18.4**
95	BANDIKUI	211	25.1	98.6	92.4	99.5	57.8	19.4	30.8	22.7	5.7	8.5
96	DAUSA	223	22.4	97.8	84.3	91.9	51.6	21.5	39.0	26.9	5.8	7.2
97	LALSOT	300	14.3	97.3	77.0	80.7	39.7	15.0	19.3	17.3	4.0	5.7
98	MAHWA	152	29.6	98.7	88.2	88.8	46.7	21.7	45.4	9.9	3.3	11.2
99	SIKRAI	139	18.7	99.3	92.8	91.4	64.7	24.5	24.5	21.6	6.5	12.2
	DAUSA	**1025**	**21.2**	**98.1**	**85.6**	**89.7**	**50.4**	**19.6**	**30.5**	**20.0**	**5.0**	**8.3**
100	BARI	168	51.8	92.3	89.3	46.4	49.4	24.4	19.0	23.8	3.0	4.2
101	BASERI	190	18.4	95.8	91.1	48.9	51.6	14.7	25.3	26.3	4.7	8.4
102	DHAULPUR	229	22.3	97.8	95.2	75.1	59.4	21.8	29.3	19.7	3.9	10.0
103	RAJAKHERA	199	17.1	98.5	94.0	89.4	63.3	24.6	33.2	17.1	2.0	3.5
	DHAULPUR	**786**	**26.3**	**96.3**	**92.6**	**66.3**	**56.4**	**21.4**	**27.1**	**21.5**	**3.4**	**6.7**
104	ASPUR	143	48.3	100.0	95.8	82.5	62.2	33.6	40.6	54.5	8.4	6.3
105	BICHHIWARA	175	44.0	98.9	97.7	96.6	50.9	32.6	27.4	41.7	5.7	5.7
106	DUNGARPUR	159	46.5	95.6	99.4	91.2	59.7	28.9	40.9	45.9	5.0	2.5
107	SAGWARA	157	49.0	99.4	97.5	82.2	57.3	33.8	42.7	52.9	8.9	8.3
108	SIMALWARA	220	32.3	99.5	96.8	75.5	49.1	23.6	29.1	40.5	4.5	4.1
	DUNGARPUR	**854**	**43.1**	**98.7**	**97.4**	**85.1**	**55.2**	**30.0**	**35.4**	**46.4**	**6.3**	**5.3**
109	ANUPGARH	1090	16.8	72.7	49.4	48.5	59.7	7.3	29.9	49.4	1.2	15.5
110	GANGANAGAR	257	31.1	90.7	69.3	94.2	82.1	23.7	73.5	59.1	8.6	19.8
111	KARANPUR	207	26.6	88.4	82.6	92.8	83.1	22.7	74.9	69.1	2.4	14.5
112	PADAMPUR	239	38.9	90.0	79.5	92.9	64.9	15.9	70.3	54.0	5.4	16.3
113	RAISINGHNAGAR	367	26.4	88.3	72.2	73.0	56.9	16.3	55.6	58.3	1.6	18.0
114	SADULSHAHAR	237	27.0	53.6	49.4	86.5	69.6	12.7	51.9	54.9	3.8	16.5
115	SURATGARH	433	18.9	69.5	49.0	38.1	57.5	9.7	30.3	51.7	3.2	14.5
	GANGANAGAR	**2830**	**23.1**	**76.9**	**59.1**	**64.4**	**64.0**	**12.7**	**45.8**	**54.1**	**2.9**	**16.1**

P. Code	Panchayat Samiti	Total Inhabited Villages	Percentage of Villages Having Amenity of									
			Medical	Improved Drinking Water#	Edu-cation	Power Supply	Approach by Pucca Road	Post Office##	Tele-phone	Transport Communi-cations###	Banks	Ag. Credit Societies
1	2	3	4	5	6	7	8	9	10	11	12	13
116	BHADRA	198	35.9	87.9	58.1	71.7	63.1	23.7	39.4	53.5	7.6	27.8
117	HANUMANGARH	1074	18.9	84.6	36.6	80.0	64.5	11.0	35.8	39.9	3.6	8.2
118	NOHAR	501	16.2	67.9	50.5	43.9	50.3	15.6	37.1	49.3	3.8	11.0
	HANUMANGARH	**1773**	**20.0**	**80.3**	**42.9**	**68.9**	**60.3**	**13.7**	**36.6**	**44.0**	**4.1**	**11.2**
119	AMBER	192	37.5	100.0	91.7	99.5	53.6	21.4	44.3	45.8	6.8	7.8
120	BASSI	210	31.9	99.5	91.9	98.6	68.1	17.6	31.4	44.3	4.3	8.6
121	CHAKSU	267	10.1	96.3	74.2	78.3	30.3	10.9	15.4	18.4	3.4	5.6
122	DUDU	219	25.6	92.7	90.4	89.0	52.5	23.7	47.5	36.1	5.0	15.5
123	GOVINDGARH	100	49.0	100.0	93.0	99.0	72.0	44.0	62.0	58.0	11.0	30.0
124	JAMWA RAMGARH	233	35.6	98.3	88.0	99.1	62.7	17.6	21.0	53.6	7.3	8.6
125	JHOTWARA	73	26.0	90.4	90.4	98.6	68.5	15.1	63.0	52.1	2.7	9.6
126	KOTPUTLI	121	32.2	100.0	100.0	92.6	77.7	33.9	66.1	47.1	5.0	11.6
127	PHAGI	169	18.9	97.6	94.1	92.3	40.8	14.8	29.6	30.2	3.6	16.6
128	SAMBHAR	144	41.0	91.0	96.5	99.3	53.5	29.2	62.5	49.3	4.9	16.0
129	SANGANER	143	23.8	96.5	83.2	100.0	54.5	16.8	53.8	50.3	4.2	7.7
130	SHAHPURA	86	47.7	100.0	98.8	98.8	73.3	37.2	55.8	40.7	9.3	17.4
131	VIRATNAGAR	120	36.7	95.8	93.3	99.2	67.5	27.5	28.3	35.0	5.0	7.5
	JAIPUR	**2077**	**29.9**	**96.9**	**89.7**	**94.5**	**56.4**	**21.8**	**40.1**	**41.3**	**5.3**	**11.5**
132	JAISALMER	143	30.1	61.5	88.1	49.7	60.8	28.0	44.8	56.6	7.0	14.0
133	SAM	281	17.1	64.4	66.2	14.6	46.3	18.5	39.1	44.5	2.8	4.3
134	SANKRA	176	30.1	79.5	94.9	40.3	40.9	25.6	60.8	60.2	5.7	14.2
	JAISALMER	**600**	**24.0**	**68.2**	**79.8**	**30.5**	**48.2**	**22.8**	**46.8**	**52.0**	**4.7**	**9.5**
135	AHORE	110	57.3	95.5	95.5	96.4	58.2	42.7	68.2	75.5	10.0	31.8
136	BHINMAL	80	47.5	82.5	100.0	87.5	68.8	45.0	73.8	80.0	10.0	25.0
137	JALOR	68	60.3	98.5	100.0	98.5	77.9	41.2	80.9	73.5	8.8	22.1
138	JASWANTPURA	74	48.6	95.9	97.3	100.0	66.2	36.5	64.9	71.6	6.8	14.9
139	RANIWARA	84	51.2	94.0	97.6	97.6	61.9	39.3	48.8	61.9	4.8	10.7
140	SANCHORE	204	33.8	82.8	96.6	75.5	55.4	26.5	40.7	59.3	6.9	21.6
141	SAYLA	77	55.8	97.4	97.4	96.1	74.0	41.6	84.4	87.0	10.4	40.3
	JALOR	**697**	**47.8**	**90.7**	**97.4**	**90.0**	**63.6**	**36.9**	**61.1**	**70.3**	**8.0**	**23.7**
142	BAKANI	289	14.9	96.2	63.3	70.2	24.6	9.7	17.6	14.9	3.1	3.8
143	DAG	221	15.4	99.1	86.4	73.8	23.1	17.2	24.0	20.4	3.6	10.9
144	JHALRAPATAN	285	15.1	96.8	83.5	91.6	37.9	14.4	43.2	18.2	4.2	10.9
145	KHANPUR	193	18.7	98.4	79.3	93.3	27.5	15.5	47.7	16.6	3.1	6.7
146	MANOHARTHANA	284	10.9	96.5	79.9	61.6	21.8	10.6	16.2	14.8	1.4	4.2
147	PIRAWA	205	13.2	98.0	88.8	99.5	23.4	22.0	29.8	20.0	4.4	11.7
	JHALAWAR	**1477**	**14.5**	**97.4**	**79.5**	**80.3**	**26.6**	**14.4**	**28.8**	**17.3**	**3.2**	**7.8**
148	ALSISAR	124	32.3	75.0	96.0	97.6	56.5	31.5	64.5	59.7	6.5	18.5
149	BUHANA	126	50.0	88.1	99.2	99.2	66.7	42.9	50.8	61.1	2.4	14.3
150	CHIRAWA	84	42.9	96.4	98.8	100.0	73.8	39.3	86.9	72.6	4.8	31.0
151	JHUNJHUNUN	145	40.7	93.1	97.9	99.3	65.5	33.1	87.6	68.3	2.1	10.3
152	KHETRI	85	56.5	97.6	100.0	98.8	70.6	54.1	52.9	64.7	4.7	17.6
153	NAWALGARH	88	45.5	100.0	100.0	100.0	76.1	51.1	90.9	79.5	6.8	33.0
154	SURAJGARH	122	32.8	82.0	100.0	100.0	64.8	39.3	78.7	58.2	4.1	16.4
155	UDAIPURWATI	81	64.2	98.8	100.0	98.8	76.5	53.1	75.3	75.3	7.4	17.3
	JHUNJHUNUN	**855**	**44.2**	**90.2**	**98.8**	**99.2**	**67.7**	**41.6**	**73.2**	**66.4**	**4.6**	**18.7**
156	BALESAR	125	38.4	92.0	86.4	79.2	52.8	29.6	47.2	55.2	4.0	8.0
157	BAP	125	24.8	52.8	82.4	68.8	54.4	26.4	29.6	56.0	6.4	22.4
158	BHOPALGARH	86	52.3	93.0	100.0	97.7	81.4	46.5	69.8	93.0	10.5	18.6
159	BILARA	89	69.7	98.9	97.8	100.0	78.7	37.1	75.3	73.0	10.1	33.7
160	LUNI	135	51.9	89.6	94.8	88.9	59.3	30.4	74.8	65.2	5.9	15.6
161	MANDOR	105	35.2	91.4	99.0	97.1	61.9	27.6	71.4	64.8	6.7	22.9
162	OSIAN	175	52.6	96.6	96.6	96.6	70.3	42.3	60.6	79.4	8.0	21.7
163	PHALODI	111	36.0	88.3	93.7	83.8	59.5	34.2	45.0	60.4	10.8	23.4
164	SHERGARH	107	34.6	82.2	89.7	65.4	42.1	27.1	30.8	37.4	4.7	10.3
	JODHPUR	**1058**	**43.7**	**87.1**	**93.1**	**86.2**	**61.7**	**33.5**	**55.6**	**64.8**	**7.3**	**19.3**
165	HINDAUN	121	50.4	100.0	99.2	99.2	81.8	37.2	71.1	43.0	4.1	20.7
166	KARAULI	195	35.4	92.8	93.8	69.2	52.3	28.7	14.4	40.0	4.1	4.6
167	NADOTI	85	35.3	94.1	95.3	78.8	55.3	30.6	18.8	40.0	9.4	30.6
168	SAPOTRA	210	31.0	93.3	87.6	51.9	48.1	24.3	14.3	28.1	4.8	8.6
169	TODABHIM	144	41.7	96.5	95.1	87.5	69.4	34.7	48.6	30.6	4.2	18.1
	KARAULI	**755**	**37.7**	**95.0**	**93.4**	**73.8**	**59.5**	**30.2**	**30.5**	**35.4**	**4.9**	**13.8**
170	CHECHAT	144	31.3	95.8	90.3	97.9	57.6	16.7	50.0	27.8	4.2	8.3
171	ITAWA	163	20.2	98.2	84.0	71.2	33.7	18.4	27.0	22.7	4.3	17.2
172	LADPURA	145	29.7	99.3	89.0	94.5	80.0	19.3	59.3	22.1	6.9	11.7
173	SANGOD	197	22.3	99.5	88.8	98.0	41.6	17.8	41.6	26.4	4.1	13.2
174	SULTANPUR	163	36.8	99.4	91.4	92.0	49.1	18.4	36.2	19.6	7.4	18.4
	KOTA	**812**	**27.7**	**98.5**	**88.7**	**90.8**	**51.2**	**18.1**	**42.2**	**23.8**	**5.3**	**13.9**
175	DEGANA	148	39.9	76.4	97.3	98.6	52.7	35.1	62.8	79.1	7.4	23.0
176	DIDWANA	170	38.2	90.0	98.2	97.6	58.2	41.8	46.5	66.5	7.1	17.1
177	JAYAL	136	39.7	65.4	97.1	93.4	47.8	34.6	76.5	69.9	5.1	30.9
178	KUCHAMAN	193	32.1	81.3	96.9	100.0	48.2	29.5	42.5	50.8	5.7	12.4
179	LADNU	97	45.4	95.9	92.8	93.8	61.9	39.2	44.3	86.6	6.2	32.0
180	MAKRANA	119	44.5	72.3	96.6	97.5	46.2	40.3	64.7	70.6	8.4	14.3

P. Code	Panchayat Samiti	Total Inhabited Villages	Percentage of Villages Having Amenity of									
			Medical	Improved Drinking Water#	Edu-cation	Power Supply	Approach by Pucca Road	Post Office##	Tele-phone	Transport Communi-cations###	Banks	Ag. Credit Societies
1	2	3	4	5	6	7	8	9	10	11	12	13
181	MERTA	111	35.1	91.9	92.8	98.2	68.5	32.4	56.8	64.0	9.9	21.6
182	MUNDWA	121	38.8	94.2	94.2	93.4	54.5	33.1	31.4	71.9	7.4	28.1
183	NAGAUR	150	39.3	70.0	94.7	84.7	55.3	28.7	53.3	68.7	4.7	14.7
184	PARBATSAR	110	45.5	98.2	98.2	100.0	60.9	41.8	59.1	67.3	7.3	13.6
185	RIYAN	125	38.4	88.0	93.6	96.8	68.0	35.2	38.4	60.8	6.4	25.6
	NAGAUR	**1480**	**39.2**	**83.1**	**95.9**	**95.9**	**55.9**	**35.3**	**52.2**	**67.7**	**6.8**	**20.5**
186	BALI	91	57.1	98.9	96.7	92.3	87.9	42.9	89.0	79.1	9.9	19.8
187	DESURI	78	43.6	98.7	93.6	94.9	56.4	34.6	76.9	70.5	10.3	12.8
188	JAITARAN	103	52.4	91.3	96.1	90.3	59.2	35.9	59.2	47.6	12.6	22.3
189	KHARCHI/MARWAR JUN.	142	42.3	96.5	96.5	93.7	57.0	35.9	84.5	59.9	12.7	21.8
190	PALI	80	40.0	92.5	96.3	97.5	67.5	28.8	87.5	78.8	17.5	27.5
191	RAIPUR	109	45.0	100.0	95.4	88.1	56.9	36.7	60.6	47.7	10.1	18.3
192	RANI STATION	76	59.2	100.0	98.7	98.7	69.7	50.0	88.2	89.5	15.8	19.7
193	ROHAT	79	35.4	93.7	98.7	98.7	60.8	25.3	72.2	72.2	10.1	20.3
194	SOJAT	115	50.4	91.3	100.0	95.7	60.9	34.8	85.2	77.4	12.2	27.8
195	SUMERPUR	63	61.9	92.1	98.4	100.0	98.4	50.8	93.7	84.1	12.7	30.2
	PALI	**936**	**48.2**	**95.5**	**97.0**	**94.4**	**65.7**	**37.1**	**79.0**	**68.7**	**12.3**	**22.0**
196	AMET	136	20.6	100.0	89.7	100.0	42.6	16.2	58.8	66.2	2.9	3.7
197	BHIM	132	27.3	98.5	97.0	90.2	65.9	25.0	41.7	51.5	4.5	4.5
198	DEOGARH	131	15.3	100.0	90.8	96.9	34.4	11.5	59.5	45.0	3.1	5.3
199	KHAMNOR	187	29.9	98.9	84.5	96.8	54.5	19.8	53.5	49.7	3.7	11.8
200	KUMBHALGARH	164	26.2	98.8	92.7	98.8	42.1	21.3	33.5	51.2	3.0	6.1
201	RAILMAGRA	91	39.6	98.9	96.7	100.0	63.7	26.4	61.5	60.4	5.5	14.3
202	RAJSAMAND	132	24.2	99.2	92.4	99.2	51.5	24.2	84.8	52.3	5.3	9.8
	RAJSAMAND	**973**	**25.8**	**99.2**	**91.4**	**97.3**	**50.1**	**20.3**	**55.1**	**53.2**	**3.9**	**7.8**
203	BAMANWAS	136	29.4	88.2	87.5	73.5	43.4	30.9	32.4	31.6	6.6	17.6
204	BONLI	159	27.0	95.6	91.8	86.8	40.3	24.5	55.3	25.8	6.3	16.4
205	GANGAPUR	113	46.9	94.7	94.7	93.8	54.0	29.2	42.5	36.3	10.6	19.5
206	KHANDAR	155	30.3	96.1	87.1	62.6	47.1	20.6	31.6	37.4	3.9	10.3
207	SAWAI MADHOPUR	156	35.9	98.7	94.9	78.8	34.6	28.8	64.7	23.7	8.3	19.2
	SAWAI MADHOPUR	**719**	**33.2**	**94.9**	**91.1**	**78.4**	**43.3**	**26.6**	**45.9**	**30.6**	**7.0**	**16.4**
208	DANTA RAMGARH	157	45.9	96.8	94.3	99.4	59.9	40.8	73.2	65.0	9.6	23.6
209	DHOND	109	61.5	99.1	100.0	100.0	73.4	52.3	87.2	89.0	10.1	14.7
210	FATEHPUR	143	44.1	100.0	97.9	100.0	49.7	44.8	85.3	73.4	4.2	15.4
211	KHANDELA	126	50.8	98.4	91.3	96.0	54.8	46.8	54.8	58.7	6.3	15.9
212	LACHHMANGARH	140	33.6	98.6	98.6	99.3	47.1	40.7	78.6	75.0	5.7	7.1
213	NEEM KA THANA	151	49.0	98.0	93.4	91.4	53.6	39.1	61.6	39.1	9.9	14.6
214	PIPRALI	94	50.0	96.8	96.8	98.9	73.4	44.7	71.3	59.6	10.6	16.0
215	SRI MADHOPUR	66	54.5	97.0	98.5	100.0	77.3	59.1	80.3	63.6	13.6	22.7
	SIKAR	**986**	**47.7**	**98.2**	**96.0**	**97.9**	**58.9**	**44.7**	**73.4**	**64.9**	**8.3**	**15.9**
216	ABU ROAD	78	34.6	94.9	98.7	73.1	65.4	38.5	48.7	41.0	9.0	14.1
217	PINDWARA	99	45.5	96.0	91.9	74.7	65.7	31.3	55.6	40.4	7.1	10.1
218	REODAR	126	35.7	97.6	91.3	97.6	54.8	31.0	64.3	45.2	5.6	16.7
219	SHEOGANJ	69	49.3	91.3	94.2	92.8	66.7	42.0	66.7	53.6	10.1	13.0
220	SIROHI	83	60.2	95.2	91.6	97.6	65.1	45.8	78.3	73.5	13.3	15.7
	SIROHI	**455**	**44.2**	**95.4**	**93.2**	**87.7**	**62.6**	**36.7**	**62.6**	**49.9**	**8.6**	**14.1**
221	DEOLI	165	27.3	98.8	84.8	64.2	32.1	21.2	46.1	21.8	4.8	12.7
222	MALPURA	130	24.6	96.9	97.7	84.6	49.2	23.1	38.5	33.8	9.2	13.1
223	NIWAI	191	20.9	96.3	86.9	89.5	41.9	17.3	46.1	19.9	4.7	13.6
224	TODARAISINGH	112	26.8	98.2	86.6	86.6	36.6	25.0	44.6	19.6	3.6	19.6
225	TONK	238	28.2	97.9	89.9	74.4	49.6	16.8	32.8	15.1	4.2	11.8
226	UNIARA	196	16.3	94.4	80.6	80.1	32.7	14.8	28.1	19.9	3.1	11.7
	TONK	**1032**	**23.8**	**97.0**	**87.4**	**79.3**	**40.7**	**18.9**	**38.5**	**20.8**	**4.7**	**13.3**
227	BARGAON	107	29.9	99.1	92.5	92.5	53.3	26.2	41.1	45.8	8.4	1.9
228	BHINDER	279	22.2	100.0	79.6	95.0	38.4	14.3	31.5	38.7	3.6	4.3
229	DHARIAWAD	249	18.1	98.0	86.3	71.9	44.6	14.5	25.3	38.6	2.0	2.4
230	GIRWA	179	32.4	96.6	92.7	86.0	51.4	23.5	45.3	48.6	6.7	6.7
231	GOGUNDA	147	31.3	95.9	96.6	85.0	47.6	27.9	40.8	50.3	4.1	4.1
232	JHADOL	258	25.6	97.7	86.4	55.4	31.4	14.7	15.1	40.3	2.7	3.9
233	KHERWARA	250	30.8	98.0	89.6	63.6	48.0	18.8	35.6	35.6	2.8	4.0
234	KOTRA	302	14.2	84.8	76.8	21.5	29.1	9.3	5.3	26.2	2.6	2.6
235	MAVLI	149	41.6	100.0	94.6	100.0	51.7	22.8	81.2	49.0	6.0	9.4
236	SALUMBAR	234	27.8	99.1	91.9	73.9	37.2	19.2	24.4	42.7	3.8	3.8
237	SARADA	185	34.1	99.5	94.1	75.1	56.8	28.1	37.8	51.9	7.0	5.9
	UDAIPUR	**2339**	**26.5**	**96.7**	**87.8**	**70.5**	**42.5**	**18.4**	**31.1**	**40.8**	**4.1**	**4.3**
	RAJASTHAN	**39753**	**29.2**	**91.7**	**86.3**	**81.2**	**52.3**	**23.3**	**43.6**	**42.7**	**5.3**	**12.6**

Note: * Dungargarh PS shifted from Churu to Bikaner district on 1st April 2001.
** Excluding data of Dungargarh PS; *** Including data of Dungargarh PS.
# Improved Drinking Water (See Terminology), ## Post office includes Post office, telegraph office and Post and telegraph office.,
Transport Communication includes bus service, rail facility and navigable waterways.
Source: Directorate of Census Operation, Jaipur.

GENERAL ANNEX-VIII

PANCHAYAT SAMITI-WISE NO. OF MEDICAL INSTITUTIONS: RAJASTHAN 2001

P. Code	Panchayat Samiti	Medical Institutions								Total No. Medical Institutions#	Total Rural Population (2001)	Population Served Per Medical Institution#	Area Served Per Medical Institution (sq. kms.)
		Hospital	Dispensary	PHC	SHC	MCWC	FWC	Community Health Workers	Other Instituions				
1	2	3	4	5	6	7	8	9	10	11	12	13	14
1	ARAIN	0	9	9	27	5	1	9	11	50	133386	2668	24.04
2	BHINAY	0	17	12	29	3	5	7	7	61	155111	2543	19.94
3	JAWAJA	0	6	6	39	9	3	9	13	60	157901	2632	11.03
4	KEKRI	0	18	10	28	1	5	18	9	57	140921	2472	17.43
5	KISHANGARH	0	20	9	28	0	0	9	18	57	153474	2693	19.42
6	MASOODA	1	19	8	23	1	1	3	11	52	159600	3069	16.83
7	PISANGAN	0	19	17	38	7	2	31	20	81	236459	2919	14.86
8	SRINAGAR	0	13	9	23	5	0	10	13	50	170142	3403	17.95
	AJMER DISTRICT	**1**	**121**	**80**	**235**	**31**	**17**	**96**	**102**	**468**	**1306994**	**2793**	**17.43**
9	BANSURE	0	24	6	12	5	5	12	24	47	214351	4561	14.14
10	BEHROR	1	18	8	11	1	2	22	18	39	139503	3577	8.63
11	KATHUMAR	4	21	8	12	7	3	32	7	52	211689	4071	10.87
12	KISHANGARH BAS	0	7	8	15	5	1	8	9	35	167495	4786	14.44
13	KOTKASIM	0	7	4	4	2	0	13	14	17	117687	6923	20.26
14	LACHHMANGARH	0	10	14	17	3	2	30	31	44	225836	5133	14.07
15	MANDAWAR	0	30	14	16	5	2	26	51	65	197582	3040	8.88
16	NIMRANA	0	17	8	8	1	2	22	36	34	143329	4216	11.13
17	RAJGARH	0	14	6	12	3	2	22	20	35	144726	4135	28.83
18	RAMGARH	0	11	7	14	4	1	29	40	36	220219	6117	17.14
19	RENI	0	17	11	16	1	1	15	11	45	136491	3033	8.71
20	THANAGAZI	0	21	8	18	7	3	31	23	54	189977	3518	19.64
21	TIJARA	0	22	5	14	3	1	12	43	44	226974	5159	14.63
22	UMREN	0	13	7	29	1	2	29	29	50	221794	4436	16.97
	ALWAR	**5**	**232**	**114**	**198**	**48**	**27**	**303**	**356**	**597**	**2557653**	**4284**	**14.34**
23	ANANDPURI	1	9	9	25	4	0	10	1	48	111206	2317	7.12
24	BAGIDORA	0	6	15	35	6	1	17	15	62	176729	2850	8.32
25	GARHI	0	29	20	55	7	2	29	12	111	237521	2140	6.34
26	GHATOL	0	26	14	36	10	4	14	4	86	230344	2678	9.11
27	KUSHALGARH	0	10	15	25	19	1	18	20	69	138970	2014	9.29
28	PEEPALKHOONT	1	11	19	25	17	6	27	8	73	151273	2072	12.5
29	SAJJANGARH	0	11	17	22	7	2	26	7	57	134456	2359	7.06
30	TALWARA	2	20	29	32	7	6	21	19	90	213727	2375	8.34
	BANSWARA	**4**	**122**	**138**	**255**	**77**	**22**	**162**	**86**	**596**	**1394226**	**2339**	**8.48**
31	ANTA	0	13	13	9	7	3	20	27	42	148759	3542	22.2
32	ATRU	1	15	5	17	0	3	14	32	38	127043	3343	22.62
33	BARAN	0	5	5	12	0	0	11	7	22	103142	4688	27.85
34	CHHABRA	0	4	1	6	3	0	3	2	14	99472	7105	55.98
35	CHHIPABAROD	0	14	3	11	1	0	5	12	29	127858	4409	28.43
36	KISHANGANJ	0	8	7	14	1	3	16	27	30	135218	4507	48.35
37	SHAHBAD	0	4	11	14	11	3	10	28	40	108146	2704	36.71
	BARAN	**1**	**63**	**45**	**83**	**23**	**12**	**79**	**135**	**215**	**849638**	**3952**	**32.24**
38	BALOTRA	0	8	16	42	4	3	8	1	70	265596	3794	55.5
39	BARMER	0	7	10	48	0	2	10	0	65	238075	3663	58.67
40	BAYTOO	0	8	16	45	0	2	12	0	69	210345	3048	46.78
41	CHOHTAN	0	7	18	28	1	1	22	1	54	225754	4181	60.49
42	DHORIMANNA	0	13	8	38	2	1	15	6	61	250929	4114	43.74
43	SHEO	0	10	6	31	0	0	11	0	47	178539	3799	140.77
44	SINDHARI	0	17	23	36	10	6	13	8	86	236545	2751	36.23
45	SIWANA	0	16	19	28	3	3	15	9	66	213648	3237	30.03
	BARMER	**0**	**86**	**116**	**296**	**20**	**18**	**106**	**25**	**518**	**1819431**	**3512**	**55.17**
46	BAYANA	0	11	3	16	0	1	27	11	30	191632	6388	26.66
47	DEEG	0	6	6	17	2	1	42	11	31	154862	4996	15.82
48	KAMAN	0	7	7	13	1	0	37	10	28	212139	7576	19.88
49	KUMHER	0	13	14	17	8	3	46	34	52	155122	2983	8.47
50	NADBAI	0	12	4	20	1	1	50	14	37	161111	4354	11.67
51	NAGAR PAHARI	0	9	11	15	3	4	43	40	38	236329	6219	16.36
52	RUPBAS	1	26	13	17	8	3	41	36	65	211147	3248	8.29
53	SEWAR	0	14	9	9	3	2	23	25	35	167641	4790	13.09
54	WEIR	1	33	11	6	1	0	22	14	52	202199	3888	11.08
	BHARATPUR	**2**	**131**	**78**	**130**	**27**	**15**	**331**	**195**	**368**	**1692182**	**4598**	**13.35**

P. Code	Panchayat Samiti	Medical Institutions								Total No. Medical Institutions#	Total Rural Population (2001)	Population Served Per Medical Institution#	Area Served Per Medical Institution (sq. kms.)
		Hospital	Dispensary	PHC	SHC	MCWC	FWC	Community Health Workers	Other Institutions				
1	*2*	*3*	*4*	*5*	*6*	*7*	*8*	*9*	*10*	*11*	*12*	*13*	*14*
55	ASIND	0	25	16	34	9	2	28	6	84	192346	2290	13.22
56	BANERA	0	13	6	34	2	0	9	3	55	106222	1931	12.3
57	HURDA	1	11	7	21	0	0	5	1	40	91088	2277	15.43
58	JAHAZPUR	0	24	15	30	12	3	30	4	81	167782	2071	12.76
59	KOTRI	0	10	15	19	5	2	14	6	49	148702	3035	19.39
60	MANDAL	0	17	10	27	3	4	17	0	57	197500	3465	20.27
61	MANDALGARH	2	23	29	41	14	8	13	9	109	199935	1834	12.77
62	RAIPUR	2	6	11	19	5	3	8	3	43	84354	1962	11.99
63	SAHARA	0	14	11	21	3	1	4	1	49	98050	2001	12.92
64	SHAHPURA	0	21	8	33	0	0	4	1	62	148955	2403	18.18
65	SUWANA	1	18	11	28	5	2	14	2	63	164004	2603	13.21
	BHILWARA	**6**	**182**	**139**	**307**	**58**	**25**	**146**	**36**	**692**	**1598938**	**2311**	**14.51**
66	BIKANER	0	17	21	24	2	7	18	13	64	374802	5856	139.76
67	DUNGARGARH *	0	18	15	35	3	3	20	7	71	182819	2575	42.29
68	KOLAYAT	0	11	8	23	1	3	12	18	43	207749	4831	170.2
69	LUNKARANSAR	0	15	12	22	5	4	12	25	54	217341	4025	115.07
70	NOKHA	0	10	5	25	3	0	7	2	43	279343	6496	87.62
	BIKANER **	**0**	**53**	**46**	**94**	**11**	**14**	**49**	**58**	**204**	**1079235**	**5290**	**143.37**
71	HINDOLI	2	11	18	21	8	4	28	20	60	189290	3155	22.32
72	KESHORAIPATAN	0	16	14	22	7	4	15	30	59	178625	3028	21.82
73	NAINWA	0	17	3	25	9	6	8	21	54	156227	2893	21.11
74	TALERA	0	16	13	27	4	2	18	35	60	258916	4315	31.38
	BUNDI	**2**	**60**	**48**	**95**	**28**	**16**	**69**	**106**	**233**	**783058**	**3361**	**24.24**
75	ARNOD	0	10	10	6	4	1	7	1	30	119837	3995	23.38
76	BARI SADRI	0	5	4	5	0	0	24	2	14	88841	6346	33.89
77	BEGUN	0	13	16	21	13	1	9	3	63	102011	1619	15.2
78	BHADESAR	0	6	5	11	1	3	8	4	23	107393	4669	23.5
79	BHAINSRORGARH	0	10	2	11	1	2	17	6	24	80379	3349	57.08
80	BHOPALSAGAR	0	5	9	11	3	1	0	0	28	72675	2596	14.22
81	CHHOTI SADRI	0	6	6	7	5	1	8	8	24	100067	4169	28.83
82	CHITTAURGARH	0	14	9	25	4	0	6	3	52	167960	3230	15.65
83	DUNGLA	0	7	5	18	4	1	21	5	34	89975	2646	14.52
84	GANGRAR	0	9	3	16	1	0	11	0	29	88640	3057	19.16
85	KAPASAN	0	6	3	5	0	0	1	0	14	84531	6038	34.47
86	NIMBAHERA	0	10	12	16	0	1	21	5	38	135391	3563	21.39
87	PRATAPGARH	0	16	15	37	12	5	20	5	80	201229	2515	17.85
88	RASHMI	0	15	6	16	1	1	8	1	38	75326	1982	11.83
	CHITTAURGARH	**0**	**132**	**105**	**205**	**49**	**17**	**161**	**43**	**491**	**1514255**	**3084**	**20.71**
89	CHURU	0	21	15	45	0	2	15	2	81	152178	1879	19.25
90	RAJGARH	0	22	15	44	4	6	59	46	85	267403	3146	25.85
91	RATANGARH	0	23	13	46	4	3	16	1	86	158090	1838	19.1
92	SARDARSHAHAR	0	28	7	29	0	2	20	14	64	222979	3484	59.6
93	SUJANGARH	0	16	15	39	5	1	13	6	75	253207	3376	34.61
94	TARANAGAR	2	29	10	27	1	0	8	6	69	151006	2188	25.84
	CHURU ***	**2**	**157**	**90**	**265**	**17**	**17**	**151**	**82**	**531**	**1387682**	**2613**	**25.6**
95	BANDIKUI	0	10	8	12	7	2	35	32	37	267016	7217	16.24
96	DAUSA	0	18	14	28	12	3	12	59	72	271907	3776	12.61
97	LALSOT	0	15	8	25	2	2	13	43	50	251370	5027	17.08
98	MAHWA	0	12	11	11	9	3	27	7	43	179173	4167	11.01
99	SIKRAI	0	10	8	14	6	3	26	16	38	211779	5573	13.23
	DAUSA	**0**	**65**	**49**	**90**	**36**	**13**	**113**	**157**	**240**	**1181245**	**4922**	**13.91**
100	BARI	0	11	17	22	6	1	72	3	56	150595	2689	14.18
101	BASERI	2	14	6	15	8	2	20	9	45	201777	4484	22.25
102	DHAULPUR	2	19	16	15	10	4	24	25	62	262456	4233	9.31
103	RAJAKHERA	0	6	7	11	1	3	20	3	25	191812	7672	22.88
	DHAULPUR	**4**	**50**	**46**	**63**	**25**	**10**	**136**	**40**	**188**	**806640**	**4291**	**15.66**
104	ASPUR	1	23	25	49	39	4	10	6	137	184508	1347	5.05
105	BICHHIWARA	2	15	15	54	11	4	21	4	97	236114	2434	7.69
106	DUNGARPUR	1	16	22	50	6	6	18	3	95	172385	1815	6.05
107	SAGWARA	3	30	16	57	7	1	25	5	113	192681	1705	5.41
108	SIMALWARA	1	31	13	51	11	3	38	7	107	241099	2253	8.54
	DUNGARPUR	**8**	**115**	**91**	**261**	**74**	**18**	**112**	**25**	**549**	**1026787**	**1870**	**6.44**
109	ANUPGARH	2	25	13	41	5	7	81	288	86	417746	4858	41.21
110	GANGANAGAR	0	18	12	36	3	5	32	68	69	176517	2558	12.39
111	KARANPUR	1	6	4	34	1	0	20	47	46	103094	2241	17.62
112	PADAMPUR	1	15	6	20	3	4	51	105	45	121362	2697	18.72
113	RAISINGHNAGAR	0	19	6	27	0	2	70	80	52	157334	3026	25.3
114	SADULSHAHAR	1	13	13	32	8	1	23	57	67	146629	2188	22.16
115	SURATGARH	2	29	10	19	4	4	24	76	64	213384	3334	59.24
	GANGANAGAR	**7**	**125**	**64**	**209**	**24**	**23**	**301**	**721**	**429**	**1336066**	**3114**	**29.47**
116	BHADRA	0	30	10	21	4	4	42	58	65	220582	3394	26.36
117	HANUMANGARH	0	47	29	53	8	7	128	335	137	628123	4585	14.85
118	NOHAR	4	44	17	40	2	4	28	71	107	365762	3418	40.23
	HANUMANGARH	**4**	**121**	**56**	**114**	**14**	**15**	**198**	**464**	**309**	**1214467**	**3930**	**26.06**

P. Code	Panchayat Samiti	Medical Institutions								Total No. Medical Institutions#	Total Rural Population (2001)	Population Served Per Medical Institution#	Area Served Per Medical Institution (sq. kms.)
		Hospi-tal	Dispen-sary	PHC	SHC	MCWC	FWC	Community Health Workers	Other Instituions				
1	2	3	4	5	6	7	8	9	10	11	12	13	14
119	AMBER	0	11	10	28	8	7	39	47	57	262029	4597	14.73
120	BASSI	0	17	14	26	12	4	50	38	69	229639	3328	9.14
121	CHAKSU	0	14	4	13	6	2	2	6	37	161140	4355	20.72
122	DUDU	2	25	17	22	18	2	24	22	84	272517	3244	22.09
123	GOVINDGARH	0	22	10	23	10	5	27	24	65	275780	4243	10.25
124	JAMWA RAMGARH	0	30	17	23	0	3	52	30	70	250132	3573	14.45
125	JHOTWARA	0	13	3	8	7	1	4	13	31	88946	2869	12.42
126	KOTPUTLI	0	28	12	15	6	2	14	15	61	228470	3745	10.87
127	PHAGI	0	14	7	15	3	2	19	9	39	161610	4144	28.55
128	SAMBHAR	0	21	9	25	8	1	33	19	63	209528	3326	13.21
129	SANGANER	0	16	4	20	11	0	10	13	51	131301	2575	11.45
130	SHAHPURA	0	33	4	21	6	5	9	18	64	181498	2836	6.38
131	VIRATNAGAR	0	19	7	24	1	1	10	23	51	206414	4047	12.73
	JAIPUR	**2**	**263**	**118**	**263**	**96**	**35**	**293**	**277**	**742**	**2659004**	**3584**	**14.02**
132	JAISALMER	0	10	14	34	2	0	12	2	60	127798	2130	214.16
133	SAM	0	10	8	44	1	1	16	2	63	138679	2201	335.1
134	SANKRA	1	18	12	31	2	3	27	7	64	165376	2584	85.73
	JAISALMER	**1**	**38**	**34**	**109**	**5**	**4**	**55**	**11**	**187**	**431853**	**2309**	**210.95**
135	AHORE	0	13	7	52	1	2	6	6	73	177342	2429	21.87
136	BHINMAL	0	6	9	22	1	1	8	1	38	184751	4862	35.2
137	JALOR	0	12	8	32	3	1	7	5	55	131827	2397	19.18
138	JASWANTPURA	0	12	11	27	0	2	5	2	50	128410	2568	21.38
139	RANIWARA	0	3	7	25	0	2	19	15	35	163349	4667	28.11
140	SANCHORE	0	13	19	51	2	1	10	5	85	342120	4025	35.39
141	SAYLA	0	13	13	26	1	2	12	9	53	211147	3984	27.54
	JALOR	**0**	**72**	**74**	**235**	**8**	**11**	**67**	**43**	**389**	**1338946**	**3442**	**27.02**
142	BAKANI	0	7	6	20	3	1	32	33	36	152329	4231	24.6
143	DAG	0	11	6	27	1	1	8	9	45	167192	3715	25.12
144	JHALRAPATAN	0	13	14	15	2	2	10	10	44	205868	4679	30.21
145	KHANPUR	0	16	7	23	9	3	13	12	55	153370	2789	17.09
146	MANOHARTHANA	0	5	1	13	0	1	16	12	19	161425	8496	48.56
147	PIRAWA	0	7	11	16	9	1	9	8	43	171897	3998	23.28
	JHALAWAR	**0**	**59**	**45**	**114**	**24**	**9**	**88**	**84**	**242**	**1012081**	**4182**	**25.66**
148	ALSISAR	1	17	7	23	17	6	12	6	65	141416	2176	11.49
149	BUHANA	0	31	18	40	7	9	5	31	96	204411	2129	6.81
150	CHIRAWA	1	17	12	21	1	2	16	20	52	152843	2939	9.4
151	JHUNJHUNUN	0	28	7	45	4	0	9	9	84	176693	2103	9.77
152	KHETRI	0	16	22	26	2	4	18	24	66	214474	3250	12.06
153	NAWALGARH	0	14	19	31	8	7	21	29	72	217636	3023	9.24
154	SURAJGARH	0	7	10	21	12	1	4	2	50	175820	3516	15.63
155	UDAIPURWATI	0	16	16	34	20	7	38	30	86	235280	2736	9.66
	JHUNJHUNUN	**2**	**146**	**111**	**241**	**71**	**36**	**123**	**151**	**571**	**1518573**	**2659**	**10.13**
156	BALESAR	0	13	13	32	7	4	16	2	65	174179	2680	28.52
157	BAP	0	3	7	21	0	1	5	0	31	157290	5074	142.94
158	BHOPALGARH	0	12	11	36	4	5	13	4	63	202321	3211	27.67
159	BILARA	1	10	27	41	3	2	11	1	82	180550	2202	18.29
160	LUNI	0	13	14	43	0	3	19	16	70	229097	3273	28.32
161	MANDOR	0	9	3	14	1	4	9	17	27	151257	5602	47.01
162	OSIAN	0	23	20	70	4	3	38	15	117	422181	3608	35.76
163	PHALODI	0	13	10	27	3	1	6	4	53	229892	4338	61.09
164	SHERGARH	0	9	8	21	0	4	17	5	38	162656	4280	51.97
	JODHPUR	**1**	**105**	**113**	**305**	**22**	**27**	**134**	**64**	**546**	**1909423**	**3497**	**40.62**
165	HINDAUN	2	19	11	16	13	2	42	40	61	262403	4302	10.35
166	KARAULI	0	17	11	27	4	3	45	21	59	222621	3773	20.67
167	NADOTI	0	16	7	11	10	4	12	28	44	126089	2866	14.68
168	SAPOTRA	2	20	12	37	9	6	53	36	80	232513	2906	24.53
169	TODABHIM	1	17	9	18	22	6	32	26	67	194094	2897	7.8
	KARAULI	**5**	**89**	**50**	**109**	**58**	**21**	**184**	**151**	**311**	**1037720**	**3337**	**16.02**
170	CHECHAT	0	11	2	16	5	6	25	34	34	132073	3885	22.67
171	ITAWA	1	20	5	11	6	1	22	28	43	155646	3620	20.63
172	LADPURA	0	10	8	23	5	2	15	39	46	144691	3145	28.42
173	SANGOD	0	14	8	31	4	0	9	18	57	146951	2578	18.35
174	SULTANPUR	0	5	8	30	1	2	38	58	44	150587	3422	20.72
	KOTA	**1**	**60**	**31**	**111**	**21**	**11**	**109**	**177**	**224**	**729948**	**3259**	**21.98**
175	DEGANA	3	15	12	48	12	5	16	12	90	190085	2112	16.19
176	DIDWANA	1	16	10	54	1	3	15	11	82	285031	3476	19.61
177	JAYAL	0	15	11	40	3	3	30	4	69	224944	3260	30.26
178	KUCHAMAN	1	27	17	35	6	7	27	12	86	268146	3118	16.7
179	LADNU	0	11	20	25	14	3	5	9	70	158026	2258	19.59
180	MAKRANA	0	10	13	30	6	4	33	10	59	199671	3384	18.75
181	MERTA	0	12	12	29	4	6	11	3	57	183429	3218	24.51
182	MUNDWA	1	10	14	31	1	0	11	4	57	197532	3465	38.32
183	NAGAUR	0	15	8	51	0	1	16	6	74	224815	3038	32.17
184	PARBATSAR	0	20	22	22	4	2	22	10	68	186413	2741	15.75
185	RIYAN	1	19	14	32	7	5	16	7	73	179629	2461	16.98

P. Code	Panchayat Samiti	Medical Institutions								Total No. Medical Institutions#	Total Rural Population (2001)	Population Served Per Medical Institution#	Area Served Per Medical Institution (sq. kms.)
		Hospital	Dispensary	PHC	SHC	MCWC	FWC	Community Health Workers	Other Instituions				
1	2	3	4	5	6	7	8	9	10	11	12	13	14
	NAGAUR	**7**	**170**	**153**	**397**	**58**	**39**	**202**	**88**	**785**	**2297721**	**2927**	**22.09**
186	BALI	1	25	10	40	4	4	17	28	80	183802	2298	17.12
187	DESURI	6	13	12	20	3	4	20	11	54	102245	1893	15.35
188	JAITARAN	1	10	19	36	3	2	12	9	69	186938	2709	18.69
189	KHARCHI/MARWAR JUN.	2	16	19	39	2	6	22	17	78	181445	2326	17.83
190	PALI	1	7	6	22	0	2	9	2	36	89939	2498	36.02
191	RAIPUR	1	17	8	24	7	6	31	11	57	182004	3193	17.31
192	RANI STATION	7	24	5	33	4	1	18	14	73	106504	1459	10.45
193	ROHAT	1	8	14	17	4	2	2	4	44	102599	2332	31.92
194	SOJAT	2	9	35	46	11	12	16	2	103	155889	1513	15.80
195	SUMERPUR	0	8	19	26	4	4	10	14	57	137999	2421	16.00
	PALI	**22**	**137**	**147**	**303**	**42**	**43**	**157**	**112**	**651**	**1429364**	**2196**	**13.23**
196	AMET	0	7	4	23	0	2	3	3	34	88162	2593	14.86
197	BHIM	0	8	13	23	8	8	4	7	52	137578	2646	13.03
198	DEOGARH	0	4	4	12	0	3	9	0	20	77865	3893	29.46
199	KHAMNOR	0	25	17	32	12	5	26	6	86	172395	2005	6.92
200	KUMBHALGARH	1	15	22	33	20	14	28	2	91	131346	1443	8.53
201	RAILMAGRA	0	21	13	32	6	3	10	3	72	110435	1534	7.56
202	RAJSAMAND	0	15	7	22	2	3	4	14	46	140520	3055	12.38
	RAJSAMAND	**1**	**95**	**80**	**177**	**48**	**38**	**84**	**35**	**401**	**858301**	**2140**	**10.61**
203	BAMANWAS	1	21	10	16	2	2	32	19	50	149429	2989	14.58
204	BONLI	0	20	10	21	12	5	11	16	63	209833	3331	16.02
205	GANGAPUR	0	18	6	16	12	7	37	17	52	179209	3446	12.40
206	KHANDAR	0	21	7	21	2	3	38	14	51	150136	2944	26.52
207	SAWAI MADHOPUR	0	21	15	36	7	6	19	19	79	215810	2732	15.60
	SAWAI MADHOPUR	**1**	**101**	**48**	**110**	**35**	**23**	**137**	**85**	**295**	**904417**	**3066**	**16.84**
208	DANTA RAMGARH	3	30	29	46	13	2	26	22	121	262183	2167	9.22
209	DHOND	0	29	14	45	9	5	18	11	97	209919	2164	9.41
210	FATEHPUR	1	21	12	46	4	0	10	27	84	193473	2303	14.73
211	KHANDELA	2	13	28	37	0	3	20	21	80	218560	2732	9.80
212	LACHHMANGARH	0	18	10	31	0	5	7	11	59	197022	3339	17.41
213	NEEM KA THANA	1	30	12	50	8	4	44	53	101	317049	3139	11.75
214	PIPRALI	1	16	21	36	11	5	15	18	85	206064	2424	9.38
215	SRI MADHOPUR	0	12	10	22	3	0	14	21	47	210980	4489	12.06
	SIKAR	**8**	**169**	**136**	**313**	**48**	**24**	**154**	**184**	**674**	**1815250**	**2693**	**11.32**
216	ABU ROAD	0	9	5	16	3	2	4	3	33	114818	3479	26.00
217	PINDWARA	0	13	9	34	2	4	16	11	58	184803	3186	19.63
218	REODAR	1	11	16	29	18	7	24	13	75	175344	2338	14.49
219	SHEOGANJ	0	8	16	21	10	4	9	5	55	99663	1812	16.22
220	SIROHI	1	19	16	39	22	7	27	4	97	125589	1295	11.24
	SIROHI	**2**	**60**	**62**	**139**	**55**	**24**	**80**	**36**	**318**	**700217**	**2202**	**15.93**
221	DEOLI	1	18	14	20	2	2	21	14	55	169271	3078	22.46
222	MALPURA	0	26	11	13	1	2	15	21	51	176932	3469	28.22
223	NIWAI	0	30	6	19	6	2	17	13	61	165298	2710	16.89
224	TODARAISINGH	0	13	12	13	1	1	12	4	39	110131	2824	25.27
225	TONK	0	21	28	43	2	4	18	6	94	204362	2174	15.06
226	UNIARA	0	12	7	13	0	1	28	5	32	132509	4141	30.83
	TONK	**1**	**120**	**78**	**121**	**12**	**12**	**111**	**63**	**332**	**958503**	**2887**	**21.36**
227	BARGAON	2	15	10	14	11	5	10	12	52	123802	2381	12.46
228	BHINDER	0	21	12	33	22	2	10	6	88	201832	2294	11.19
229	DHARIAWAD	0	14	10	33	16	3	17	7	73	203605	2789	16.13
230	GIRWA	0	19	22	37	17	8	24	16	95	227623	2396	14.20
231	GOGUNDA	1	11	8	26	19	1	21	10	65	151575	2332	13.41
232	JHADOL	3	18	16	45	25	2	33	11	107	193810	1811	13.35
233	KHERWARA	0	13	23	48	12	6	23	2	96	254301	2649	11.22
234	KOTRA	1	12	10	36	1	3	5	7	60	183504	3058	19.86
235	MAVLI	0	22	12	43	5	3	15	8	82	194148	2368	9.74
236	SALUMBAR	0	29	14	47	16	3	9	4	106	196614	1855	8.70
237	SARADA	2	33	24	44	8	3	30	6	111	212181	1912	9.71
	UDAIPUR	**9**	**207**	**161**	**406**	**152**	**39**	**197**	**89**	**935**	**2142995**	**2292**	**12.33**
	RAJASTHAN	**109**	**3706**	**2746**	**6353**	**1317**	**675**	**4688**	**4281**	**14231**	**43292813**	**3042**	**23.58**

Note: # Include dispensary, hospital, MCWC, PHC and SHC, * Dungargarh PS shifted from Churu to Bikaner district on 1st April 2001.
** Excluding data of Dungargarh PS; *** Including data of Dungargarh PS.
Source: Directorate of Census Operation, Jaipur.

GENERAL ANNEX-IX

PANCHAYAT SAMITI-WISE NO. OF DOCTORS, BEDS AND PATIENTS TREATED (2001)

P. Code	Panchayat Samiti	No. of Doctors			No. of Beds	Patients Treated		Population Served Per Doctor	Population Served Per Bed
		Male	Female	Total		Allopathy	Ayurvedic, Homeopathic and Unani		
1	2	3	4	5	6	7	8	9	10
1	ARAIN	10	1	11	66	53120	56150	12126	2021
2	BHINAY	12	—	12	66	74003	230910	12926	2350
3	JAWAJA	15	—	15	78	75693	75008	10527	2024
4	KEKRI	16	3	19	112	97805	190710	7417	1258
5	KISHANGARH	6	—	6	30	6712	225450	25579	5116
6	MASOODA	8	2	10	62	83959	150801	15960	2574
7	PISANGAN	15	3	18	120	96508	200350	13137	1970
8	SRINAGAR	3	—	3	26	88865	101739	56714	6544
	AJMER DISTRICT	**85**	**9**	**94**	**560**	**449542**	**944058**	**13904**	**2334**
9	BANSURE	10	2	12	80	75472	155447	17863	2679
10	BEHROR	18	2	20	130	49342	182287	6975	1073
11	KATHUMAR	13	—	13	66	34758	94193	16284	3207
12	KISHANGARH BAS	9	1	10	74	60152	93265	16750	2263
13	KOTKASIM	5	—	5	48	43259	71846	23537	2452
14	LACHHMANGARH	10	4	14	110	114891	112207	16131	2053
15	MANDAWAR	11	2	13	84	62328	167177	15199	2352
16	NIMRANA	9	1	10	60	26737	134552	14333	2389
17	RAJGARH	16	2	18	86	57346	135245	8040	1683
18	RAMGARH	9	—	9	54	67626	126627	24469	4078
19	RENI	8	—	8	54	47535	126516	17061	2528
20	THANAGAZI	10	4	14	60	51081	143973	13570	3166
21	TIJARA	13	—	13	88	98184	149850	17460	2579
22	UMREN	7	3	10	54	54112	170143	22179	4107
	ALWAR	**148**	**21**	**169**	**1048**	**842823**	**1863328**	**15134**	**2441**
23	ANANDPURI	4	—	4	48	20869	55487	27802	2317
24	BAGIDORA	8	1	9	72	59079	116070	19637	2455
25	GARHI	13	5	18	128	111458	351766	13196	1856
26	GHATOL	10	1	11	102	68611	229340	20940	2258
27	KUSHALGARH	8	1	9	74	56448	59587	15441	1878
28	PEEPALKHOONT	6	—	6	60	34948	74134	25212	2521
29	SAJJANGARH	8	1	9	48	45397	67322	14940	2801
30	TALWARA	9	2	11	72	55490	328481	19430	2968
	BANSWARA	**66**	**11**	**77**	**604**	**452300**	**1282187**	**18107**	**2308**
31	ANTA	20	3	23	120	NA	96166	6468	1240
32	ATRU	7	1	8	54	NA	96875	15880	2353
33	BARAN	5	1	6	24	NA	94603	17190	4298
34	CHHABRA	12	1	13	68	NA	30790	7652	1463
35	CHHIPABAROD	6	2	8	48	NA	97621	15982	2664
36	KISHANGANJ	6	2	8	54	NA	68512	16902	2504
37	SHAHBAD	9	3	12	92	NA	43592	9012	1176
	BARAN #	**65**	**13**	**78**	**460**	**NA**	**431993**	**10893**	**1847**
38	BALOTRA	10	3	13	60	NA	NA	20430	4427
39	BARMER	10	—	10	48	NA	NA	23808	4960
40	BAYTOO	8	1	9	66	NA	NA	23372	3187
41	CHOHTAN	13	—	13	78	NA	NA	17366	2894
42	DHORIMANNA	16	1	17	122	NA	NA	14761	2057
43	SHEO	10	—	10	60	NA	NA	17854	2976
44	SINDHARI	7	1	8	72	NA	NA	29568	3285
45	SIWANA	12	3	15	96	NA	NA	14243	2226
	BARMER	**86**	**9**	**95**	**602**	**NA**	**NA**	**19152**	**3022**
46	BAYANA	12	1	13	80	74460	148410	14741	2395
47	DEEG	11	—	11	80	52169	133125	14078	1936
48	KAMAN	7	—	7	60	15252	85258	30306	3536
49	KUMHER	11	—	11	60	41134	138151	14102	2585
50	NADBAI	7	1	8	48	29266	132045	20139	3356
51	NAGAR PAHARI	7	1	8	60	43120	118443	29541	3939
52	RUPBAS	10	1	11	66	22790	264482	19195	3199
53	SEWAR	2	2	4	24	9529	265951	41910	6985
54	WEIR	19	1	20	108	11847	607050	10110	1872
	BHARATPUR	**86**	**7**	**93**	**586**	**299567**	**1892915**	**18196**	**2888**

P. Code	Panchayat Samiti	No. of Doctors			No. of Beds	Patients Treated		Population Served Per Doctor	Population Served Per Bed
		Male	Female	Total		Allopathy	Ayurvedic, Homeopathic and Unani		
1	2	3	4	5	6	7	8	9	10
55	ASIND	5	3	8	66	NA	NA	24043	2914
56	BANERA	7	1	8	48	NA	NA	13278	2213
57	HURDA	6	4	10	79	NA	NA	9109	1153
58	JAHAZPUR	16	5	21	147	NA	NA	7990	1141
59	KOTRI	8	2	10	84	NA	NA	14870	1770
60	MANDAL	7	4	11	66	NA	NA	17955	2992
61	MANDALGARH	8	6	14	131	NA	NA	14281	1526
62	RAIPUR	5	3	8	54	NA	NA	10544	1562
63	SAHARA	7	2	9	110	NA	NA	10894	891
64	SHAHPURA	3	2	5	34	NA	NA	29791	4381
65	SUWANA	9	2	11	54	NA	NA	14909	3037
	BHILWARA	**81**	**34**	**115**	**873**	**NA**	**NA**	**13904**	**1832**
66	BIKANER	18	4	22	146	NA	NA	17036	2567
67	DUNGARGARH *	12	3	15	78	NA	NA	12188	2344
68	KOLAYAT	6	5	11	76	NA	NA	18886	2734
69	LUNKARANSAR	10	3	13	78	NA	NA	16719	2786
70	NOKHA	15	1	16	104	NA	NA	17459	2686
	BIKANER **	**61**	**16**	**77**	**482**	**NA**	**NA**	**14016**	**2239**
71	HINDOLI	10	—	10	60	35450	99932	18929	3155
72	KESHORAIPATAN	17	2	19	84	30035	107853	9401	2126
73	NAINWA	11	1	12	92	49320	152998	13019	1698
74	TALERA	10	2	12	84	161109	129522	21576	3082
	BUNDI	**48**	**5**	**53**	**320**	**275914**	**490305**	**14775**	**2447**
75	ARNOD	8	—	8	54	19762	78094	14980	2219
76	BARI SADRI	6	1	7	74	20521	87016	12692	1201
77	BEGUN	13	—	13	92	29386	85017	7847	1109
78	BHADESAR	3	4	7	48	30257	122937	15342	2237
79	BHAINSRORGARH	3	2	5	48	13967	58964	16076	1675
80	BHOPALSAGAR	4	1	5	48	39265	77432	14535	1514
81	CHHOTI SADRI	6	1	7	42	6479	60913	14295	2383
82	CHITTAURGARH	8	2	10	36	52399	88530	16796	4666
83	DUNGLA	4	2	6	42	29897	69592	14996	2142
84	GANGRAR	6	—	6	42	28062	147131	14773	2110
85	KAPASAN	6	2	8	68	16849	57286	10566	1243
86	NIMBAHERA	14	3	17	80	25486	70521	7964	1692
87	PRATAPGARH	8	2	10	52	40493	197843	20123	3870
88	RASHMI	4	—	4	42	25329	98634	18832	1793
	CHITTAURGARH	**93**	**20**	**113**	**768**	**378152**	**1299910**	**13400**	**1972**
89	CHURU	14	5	19	96	40311	250436	8009	1585
90	RAJGARH	21	3	24	140	64911	142879	11142	1910
91	RATANGARH	19	1	20	90	49273	209284	7905	1757
92	SARDARSHAHAR	8	2	10	54	41679	145184	22298	4129
93	SUJANGARH	16	3	19	114	72358	260448	13327	2221
94	TARANAGAR	13	2	15	72	38084	151006	10067	2097
	CHURU ***	**91**	**16**	**107**	**566**	**306616**	**1271446**	**12969**	**2452**
95	BANDIKUI	13	1	14	86	148259	98554	19073	3105
96	DAUSA	26	1	27	166	126497	124618	10071	1638
97	LALSOT	11	2	13	66	105794	103435	19336	3809
98	MAHWA	16	2	18	96	105125	122413	9954	1866
99	SIKRAI	8	3	11	54	71668	122852	19253	3922
	DAUSA #	**74**	**9**	**83**	**468**	**409084**	**473318**	**14232**	**2524**
100	BARI	7	3	10	68	NA	NA	15060	2215
101	BASERI	7	—	7	60	NA	NA	28825	3363
102	DHAULPUR	9	1	10	66	NA	NA	26246	3977
103	RAJAKHERA	8	1	9	54	NA	NA	21312	3552
	DHAULPUR	**31**	**5**	**36**	**248**	**NA**	**NA**	**22407**	**3253**
104	ASPUR	14	1	15	96	47326	206140	12301	1922
105	BICHHIWARA	13	—	13	78	29611	183133	18163	3027
106	DUNGARPUR	7	4	11	66	23678	174945	15671	2612
107	SAGWARA	21	4	25	147	21452	473209	7707	1311
108	SIMALWARA	19	1	20	128	67332	259680	12055	1884
	DUNGARPUR	**74**	**10**	**84**	**515**	**189399**	**1297107**	**12224**	**1994**
109	ANUPGARH	17	6	23	104	NA	NA	18163	4017
110	GANGANAGAR	6	5	11	60	NA	NA	16047	2942
111	KARANPUR	9	2	11	68	NA	NA	9372	1516
112	PADAMPUR	9	1	10	66	NA	NA	12136	1839
113	RAISINGHNAGAR	11	3	14	80	NA	NA	11238	1967
114	SADULSHAHAR	5	2	7	66	NA	NA	20947	2222
115	SURATGARH	8	4	12	80	NA	NA	17782	2667
	GANGANAGAR	**65**	**23**	**88**	**524**	**NA**	**NA**	**15183**	**2550**
116	BHADRA	14	1	15	78	74870	149291	14705	2828
117	HANUMANGARH	20	5	25	176	123001	226027	25125	3569
118	NOHAR	23	2	25	158	93375	199776	14630	2315
	HANUMANGARH ##	**57**	**8**	**65**	**412**	**291246**	**575094**	**18684**	**2948**

P. Code	Panchayat Samiti	No. of Doctors			No. of Beds	Patients Treated		Population Served Per Doctor	Population Served Per Bed
		Male	Female	Total		Allopathy	Ayurvedic, Homeopathic and Unani		
1	2	3	4	5	6	7	8	9	10
119	AMBER	6	4	10	104	NA	NA	26203	2520
120	BASSI	11	2	13	54	NA	NA	17665	4253
121	CHAKSU	5	—	5	54	NA	NA	32228	2984
122	DUDU	10	3	13	78	NA	NA	20963	3494
123	GOVINDGARH	10	4	14	90	NA	NA	19699	3064
124	JAMWA RAMGARH	16	3	19	116	NA	NA	13165	2156
125	JHOTWARA	2	1	3	18	NA	NA	29649	4941
126	KOTPUTLI	7	4	11	60	NA	NA	20770	3808
127	PHAGI	8	—	8	54	NA	NA	20201	2993
128	SAMBHAR	8	2	10	66	NA	NA	20953	3175
129	SANGANER	2	5	7	66	NA	NA	18757	1989
130	SHAHPURA	6	4	10	64	NA	NA	18150	2836
131	VIRATNAGAR	9	2	11	116	NA	NA	18765	1779
	JAIPUR	**100**	**34**	**134**	**940**	**NA**	**NA**	**19843**	**2829**
132	JAISALMER	6	—	6	24	55371	36984	21300	5325
133	SAM	6	—	6	60	21811	34891	23113	2311
134	SANKRA	4	1	5	80	35825	58081	33075	2067
	JAISALMER	**16**	**1**	**17**	**164**	**113007**	**129956**	**25403**	**2633**
135	AHORE	10	1	11	66	47566	114805	16122	2687
136	BHINMAL	11	3	14	116	41103	44693	13197	1593
137	JALOR	7	2	9	49	23777	72118	14647	2690
138	JASWANTPURA	9	1	10	66	20361	71643	12841	1946
139	RANIWARA	12	—	12	72	28750	21552	13612	2269
140	SANCHORE	16	3	19	136	34326	43494	18006	2516
141	SAYLA	10	2	12	72	49180	60489	17596	2933
	JALOR	**75**	**12**	**87**	**577**	**245063**	**428794**	**15390**	**2321**
142	BAKANI	8	—	8	60	38929	58124	19041	2539
143	DAG	22	2	24	104	50048	132464	6966	1608
144	JHALRAPATAN	7	1	8	42	72981	103127	25734	4902
145	KHANPUR	8	2	10	60	90863	115614	15337	2556
146	MANOHARTHANA	11	2	13	92	45382	96923	12417	1755
147	PIRAWA	11	2	13	72	67209	146570	13223	2387
	JHALAWAR	**67**	**9**	**76**	**430**	**365412**	**652822**	**13317**	**2354**
148	ALSISAR	9	1	10	60	242898	140992	14142	2357
149	BUHANA	14	1	15	84	262255	154973	13627	2433
150	CHIRAWA	10	1	11	72	257191	135197	13895	2123
151	JHUNJHUNUN	11	1	12	96	296060	260742	14724	1841
152	KHETRI	8	1	9	54	244963	155076	23830	3972
153	NAWALGARH	21	5	26	116	268945	125570	8371	1876
154	SURAJGARH	12	1	13	78	260311	146934	13525	2254
155	UDAIPURWATI	18	2	20	96	247072	127458	11764	2451
	JHUNJHUNUN	**103**	**13**	**116**	**656**	**2079695**	**1246942**	**13091**	**2315**
156	BALESAR	9	—	9	80	20109	16255	19353	2177
157	BAP	4	2	6	60	23068	20623	26215	2622
158	BHOPALGARH	9	3	12	78	39622	37254	16860	2594
159	BILARA	23	11	34	164	43773	61103	5310	1101
160	LUNI	14	2	16	102	1804	34537	14319	2246
161	MANDOR	6	1	7	36	63275	36563	21608	4202
162	OSIAN	17	5	22	144	38883	82519	19190	2932
163	PHALODI	6	1	7	48	97688	50653	32842	4789
164	SHERGARH	9	1	10	60	8225	39452	16266	2711
	JODHPUR	**84**	**24**	**108**	**632**	**253648**	**304827**	**17680**	**3021**
165	HINDAUN	14	1	15	80	54182	156215	17494	3280
166	KARAULI	15	—	15	60	49466	120000	14841	3710
167	NADOTI	10	—	10	48	44570	97252	12609	2627
168	SAPOTRA	8	—	8	66	55823	91212	29064	3523
169	TODABHIM	8	—	8	60	44030	94000	24262	3235
	KARAULI ###	**55**	**1**	**56**	**314**	**248071**	**558679**	**18531**	**3305**
170	CHECHAT	9	5	14	104	97280	75908	9434	1270
171	ITAWA	11	1	12	60	87306	97821	12971	2594
172	LADPURA	18	10	28	170	124807	44630	5168	851
173	SANGOD	9	2	11	60	119215	145909	13359	2449
174	SULTANPUR	9	4	13	72	153425	78735	11584	2091
	KOTA	**56**	**22**	**78**	**466**	**582033**	**443003**	**9358**	**1566**
175	DEGANA	13	2	15	72	71161	16307	12672	2640
176	DIDWANA	17	2	19	114	50075	82781	15002	2500
177	JAYAL	9	5	14	84	47715	99743	16067	2678
178	KUCHAMAN	20	4	24	119	72921	170471	11173	2253
179	LADNU	10	—	10	63	32897	91897	15803	2508
180	MAKRANA	16	3	19	81	40979	102655	10509	2465
181	MERTA	13	2	15	101	75832	99886	12229	1816
182	MUNDWA	12	2	14	81	50042	83328	14109	2439
183	NAGAUR	9	1	10	51	59181	127904	22482	4408
184	PARBATSAR	5	2	7	45	41902	148421	26630	4143

P. Code	Panchayat Samiti	No. of Doctors			No. of Beds	Patients Treated		Population Served Per Doctor	Population Served Per Bed
		Male	Female	Total		Allopathy	Ayurvedic, Homeopathic and Unani		
1	2	3	4	5	6	7	8	9	10
185	RIYAN	12	2	14	72	60698	105507	12831	2495
	NAGAUR	**136**	**25**	**161**	**883**	**482167**	**1029812**	**14272**	**2602**
186	BALI	17	5	22	120	NA	NA	8355	1532
187	DESURI	14	1	15	86	NA	NA	6816	1189
188	JAITARAN	20	4	24	128	NA	NA	7789	1460
189	KHARCHI/MARWAR JUN.	16	1	17	84	NA	NA	10673	2160
190	PALI	6	—	6	24	NA	NA	14990	3747
191	RAIPUR	13	1	14	84	NA	NA	13000	2167
192	RANI STATION	11	—	11	54	NA	NA	9682	1972
193	ROHAT	8	1	9	48	NA	NA	11400	2137
194	SOJAT	13	2	15	78	NA	NA	10393	1999
195	SUMERPUR	14	2	16	84	NA	NA	8625	1643
	PALI	**132**	**17**	**149**	**790**	**NA**	**NA**	**9593**	**1809**
196	AMET	6	1	7	48	14632	163331	12595	1837
197	BHIM	11	2	13	74	44062	126270	10583	1859
198	DEOGARH	15	1	16	54	19369	252000	4867	1442
199	KHAMNOR	23	4	27	90	62525	161103	6385	1916
200	KUMBHALGARH	10	1	11	72	45917	168331	11941	1824
201	RAILMAGRA	11	1	12	60	42848	99673	9203	1841
202	RAJSAMAND	24	—	24	141	52508	108053	5855	997
	RAJSAMAND #	**100**	**10**	**110**	**539**	**267229**	**915430**	**7803**	**1592**
203	BAMANWAS	6	1	7	54	45053	103362	21347	2767
204	BONLI	9	—	9	54	71858	139057	23315	3886
205	GANGAPUR	11	2	13	74	50750	192346	13785	2422
206	KHANDAR	8	2	10	54	77251	124884	15014	2780
207	SAWAI MADHOPUR	3	1	4	50	44122	239235	53953	4316
	SAWAI MADHOPUR	**37**	**6**	**43**	**286**	**289034**	**798884**	**21033**	**3162**
208	DANTA RAMGARH	21	5	26	156	NA	NA	10084	1681
209	DHOND	13	—	13	84	NA	NA	16148	2499
210	FATEHPUR	22	6	28	128	NA	NA	6910	1512
211	KHANDELA	14	—	14	90	NA	NA	15611	2428
212	LACHHMANGARH	13	—	13	72	NA	NA	15156	2736
213	NEEM KA THANA	28	—	28	176	NA	NA	11323	1801
214	PIPRALI	13	1	14	78	NA	NA	14719	2642
215	SRI MADHOPUR	25	2	27	128	NA	NA	7814	1648
	SIKAR	**149**	**14**	**163**	**912**	**NA**	**NA**	**11137**	**1990**
216	ABU ROAD	11	2	13	98	11710	115015	8832	1172
217	PINDWARA	7	2	9	54	46325	76791	20534	3422
218	REODAR	9	1	10	67	74783	90735	17534	2617
219	SHEOGANJ	9	1	10	48	38299	89446	9966	2076
220	SIROHI	11	1	12	72	75324	116568	10466	1744
	SIROHI	**47**	**7**	**54**	**339**	**188406**	**296749**	**12967**	**2066**
221	DEOLI	5	1	6	66	56722	103573	28212	2565
222	MALPURA	13	2	15	92	61408	122367	11795	1923
223	NIWAI	11	2	13	86	39525	119636	12715	1922
224	TODARAISINGH	10	—	10	54	21974	59342	11013	2039
225	TONK	15	2	17	138	94735	144132	12021	1481
226	UNIARA	6	3	9	48	21968	63522	14723	2761
	TONK	**60**	**10**	**70**	**484**	**296332**	**612572**	**13693**	**1980**
227	BARGAON	5	2	7	48	NA	NA	17686	2579
228	BHINDER	12	6	18	160	NA	NA	11213	1261
229	DHARIAWAD	12	2	14	102	NA	NA	14543	1996
230	GIRWA	14	5	19	90	NA	NA	11980	2529
231	GOGUNDA	9	1	10	54	NA	NA	15158	2807
232	JHADOL	11	3	14	98	NA	NA	13844	1978
233	KHERWARA	11	3	14	108	NA	NA	18164	2355
234	KOTRA	4	2	6	66	NA	NA	30584	2780
235	MAVLI	12	4	16	108	NA	NA	12134	1798
236	SALUMBAR	12	2	14	92	NA	NA	14044	2137
237	SARADA	13	3	16	108	NA	NA	13261	1965
	UDAIPUR	**115**	**33**	**148**	**1034**	**NA**	**NA**	**14480**	**2073**
	RAJASTHAN	**2543**	**454**	**2997**	**18482**	**9304740**	**19240131**	**14445**	**2342**

Note: * Dungargarh PS shifted from Churu to Bikaner district on 1st April 2001; ** Excluding data of Dungargarh PS; *** Including data of Dungargarh PS.
Came in force from April, 1991; ## Came in force from July 1994; ### Came in force from July 1997.

Source: 1. Data related to No. of doctors and beds are compiled through *Assembly Questions*.

2. Data related to patients treated are compiled from District Statistical Abstract, 2002 (All Districts), DES, Jaipur.

GENERAL ANNEX-X

PANCHAYAT SAMITI-WISE NO. OF REGISTERED BIRTHS AND DEATHS: RAJASTHAN 2001

P. Code	Panchayat Samiti (Concerning Tehsil)	Births			Deaths			Child Deaths		
		M	F	T	M	F	T	M	F	T
1	2	3	4	5	6	7	8	9	10	11
1	ARAIN (Sarwar)	338	264	602	415	259	674	7	2	9
2	BHINAY (Bhinay)	731	776	1507	416	319	735	12	9	21
3	JAWAJA* (Beawar)	899	729	1628	524	314	838	10	10	20
4	KEKRI* (Kekri)	531	466	997	441	287	728	6	5	11
5	KISHANGARH (Kishangarh)	664	450	1114	747	259	1006	2	1	3
6	MASOODA* (Masooda)	767	677	1444	663	349	1012	17	25	42
7	PISANGAN (Pisangan)	1049	830	1879	912	551	1463	11	9	20
8	SRINAGAR (Ajmer)	573	451	1024	553	287	840	5	5	10
	AJMER DISTRICT	**5552**	**4643**	**10195**	**4671**	**2625**	**7296**	**70**	**66**	**136**
9	BANSURE* (Bansure)	NA	NA	1604	NA	NA	894	NA	NA	6
10	BEHROR (Behror)	NA	NA	1159	NA	NA	731	NA	NA	11
11	KATHUMAR (Kathumar)	NA	NA	747	NA	NA	726	NA	NA	4
12	KISHANGARH BAS (Kishangarh Bas)	NA	NA	1069	NA	NA	607	NA	NA	14
13	KOTKASIM* (Kotkasim)	NA	NA	1297	NA	NA	577	NA	NA	2
14	LACHHMANGARH (Lachmangarh)	NA	NA	1226	NA	NA	1077	NA	NA	9
15	MANDAWAR* (Mandawar)	NA	NA	1388	NA	NA	885	NA	NA	11
16	NIMRANA (Behror)	NA	NA	1586	NA	NA	761	NA	NA	2
17	RAJGARH (Rajgarh)	NA	NA	444	NA	NA	476	NA	NA	0
18	RAMGARH (Ramgarh)	NA	NA	1300	NA	NA	745	NA	NA	6
19	RENI (Rajgarh)	NA	NA	1208	NA	NA	684	NA	NA	4
20	THANAGAZI* (Thanagazi)	NA	NA	616	NA	NA	395	NA	NA	3
21	TIJARA* (Tijara)	NA	NA	1391	NA	NA	808	NA	NA	1
22	UMREN (Alwar)	NA	NA	1688	NA	NA	604	NA	NA	3
	ALWAR	**NA**	**NA**	**16723**	**NA**	**NA**	**9970**	**NA**	**NA**	**76**
23	ANANDPURI (Bagidora)	771	482	1253	458	308	766	27	23	50
24	BAGIDORA (Bagidora)	1176	1143	2319	482	354	836	20	15	35
25	GARHI* (Garhi)	860	858	1718	423	339	762	4	7	11
26	GHATOL (Ghatol)	1079	2472	3551	1535	502	2037	22	19	41
27	KUSHALGARH (Kushalgarh)	877	664	1541	558	378	936	23	26	49
28	PEEPALKHOONT (Banswara)	484	519	1003	265	197	462	20	11	31
29	SAJJANGARH (Kushalgarh)	802	869	1671	289	185	474	9	14	23
30	TALWARA (Banswara)	1075	885	1960	504	391	895	38	29	67
	BANSWARA	**7124**	**7892**	**15016**	**4514**	**2654**	**7168**	**163**	**144**	**307**
31	ANTA (Mangrol & Anta)	275	267	542	139	115	254	1	1	2
32	ATRU* (Atru)	160	157	317	141	99	240	0	0	0
33	BARAN* (Baran)	201	86	287	118	103	221	1	0	1
34	CHHABRA* (Chhabra)	167	124	291	48	66	114	0	0	0
35	CHHIPABAROD* (Chhipabarod)	924	794	1718	263	226	489	5	2	7
36	KISHANGANJ* (Kishanganj)	247	215	462	88	51	139	0	0	0
37	SHAHBAD* (Shahbad)	216	212	428	81	76	157	1	2	3
	BARAN	**2190**	**1855**	**4045**	**878**	**736**	**1614**	**8**	**5**	**13**
38	BALOTRA* (Panchpadra)	533	437	970	318	242	560	0	4	4
39	BARMER (Ramsar)	1742	1548	3290	213	35	248	0	0	0
40	BAYTOO (Baytoo)	855	846	1701	256	198	454	2	3	5
41	CHOHTAN (Chohtan)	2158	1610	3768	455	209	664	15	15	30
42	DHORIMANNA (Gudha Malani)	946	680	1626	295	152	447	0	0	0
43	SHEO* (Sheo)	380	311	691	173	49	222	1	0	1
44	SINDHARI (Gudha Malani)	933	833	1766	386	191	577	0	0	0
45	SIWANA* (Siwana)	1153	748	1901	392	314	706	0	0	0
	BARMER	**8700**	**7013**	**15713**	**2488**	**1390**	**3878**	**18**	**22**	**40**
46	BAYANA* (Bayana)	533	409	942	601	262	863	1	3	4
47	DEEG* (Deeg)	1248	982	2230	720	363	1083	21	20	41
48	KAMAN (Kaman)	1316	1070	2386	597	338	935	14	9	23
49	KUMHER* (Kumher)	564	490	1054	382	227	609	3	1	4
50	NADBAI* (Nadbai)	711	682	1393	569	258	827	5	5	10
51	NAGAR PAHARI (Nagar)	902	804	1706	305	181	486	8	10	18
52	RUPBAS* (Rupbas)	913	817	1730	682	277	959	16	10	26
53	SEWAR* (Bharatpur)	401	329	730	410	216	626	5	2	7
54	WEIR* (Weir)	564	384	948	665	238	903	5	0	5
	BHARATPUR	**7152**	**5967**	**13119**	**4931**	**2360**	**7291**	**78**	**60**	**138**

P. Code	*Panchayat Samiti (Concerning Tehsil)*	*Births*			*Deaths*			*Child Deaths*		
		M	*F*	*T*	*M*	*F*	*T*	*M*	*F*	*T*
1	*2*	*3*	*4*	*5*	*6*	*7*	*8*	*9*	*10*	*11*
55	ASIND* (Asind)	988	1002	1990	672	326	998	0	0	0
56	BANERA* (Banera)	883	663	1546	396	383	779	23	30	53
57	HURDA* (Hurda)	533	396	929	588	247	835	18	24	42
58	JAHAZPUR* (Jahazpur)	509	547	1056	822	294	1116	2	2	4
59	KOTRI* (Kotri)	420	408	828	400	139	539	5	4	9
60	MANDAL* (Mandal)	564	384	948	818	370	1188	6	4	10
61	MANDALGARH (Mandalgarh)	598	340	938	438	256	694	5	3	8
62	RAIPUR* (Raipur)	481	467	948	349	164	513	4	0	4
63	SAHARA* (Sahara)	465	373	838	303	196	499	9	6	15
64	SHAHPURA* (Sahahpura)	731	578	1309	480	246	726	10	8	18
65	SUWANA* (Bhilwara)	400	360	760	670	121	791	5	3	8
	BHILWARA	**6572**	**5518**	**12090**	**5936**	**2742**	**8678**	**87**	**84**	**171**
66	BIKANER (Bikaner)	1662	1367	3029	845	701	1546	3	4	7
67	DUNGARGARH* (Dungargarh)#	503	433	936	524	334	858	8	10	18
68	KOLAYAT* (Kolayat)	969	771	1740	747	386	1133	2	3	5
69	LUNKARANSAR (Lunkaransar)	1701	1335	3036	951	536	1487	2	2	4
70	NOKHA* (Nokha)	1382	1302	2684	745	415	1160	5	1	6
	BIKANER ##	**5714**	**4775**	**10489**	**3288**	**2038**	**5326**	**12**	**10**	**22**
71	HINDOLI* (Hindoli)	1178	949	2127	456	233	689	6	2	8
72	KESHORAIPATAN (Indragarh)	926	646	1572	632	366	998			
73	NAINWA* (Nainwa)	370	252	622	241	89	330	7	5	12
74	TALERA* (Bundi)	747	608	1355	585	355	940	4	5	9
	BUNDI	**3221**	**2455**	**5676**	**1914**	**1043**	**2957**	**17**	**12**	**29**
75	ARNOD* (Arnod)	406	342	748	357	221	578	7	6	13
76	BARI SADRI* (Bari Sadri)	309	255	564	320	236	556	2	3	5
77	BEGUN (Begun)	470	405	875	336	253	589	13	15	28
78	BHADESAR* (Bhadesar)	435	371	806	347	267	614	2	3	5
79	BHAINSRORGARH (Rawatbhata)	605	534	1139	246	179	425	16	11	27
80	BHOPALSAGAR (Kapasan)	346	302	648	245	179	424	6	8	14
81	CHHOTI SADRI * (Chhoti Sadri)	533	457	990	284	199	483	3	5	8
82	CHITTAURGARH* (Chittaurgarh)	880	720	1600	507	364	871	16	8	24
83	DUNGLA* (Dungla)	367	285	652	215	172	387	3	9	12
84	GANGRAR* (Gangrar)	507	444	951	303	232	535	9	5	14
85	KAPASAN (Kapasan)	390	325	715	301	238	539	6	10	16
86	NIMBAHERA* (Nimbahera)	535	443	978	394	307	701	12	9	21
87	PRATAPGARH* (Pratapgarh)	780	602	1382	463	369	832	5	2	7
88	RASHMI* (Rashmi)	425	347	772	265	204	469	7	11	18
	CHITTAURGARH	**6988**	**5832**	**12820**	**4583**	**3420**	**8003**	**107**	**105**	**212**
89	CHURU* (Churu)	312	333	645	247	125	372	0	0	0
90	RAJGARH* (Rajgarh)	1634	1229	2863	926	723	1649	0	0	0
91	RATANGARH* (Ratangarh)	463	407	870	435	328	763	0	1	1
92	SARDARSHAHAR* (Sardarshahar)	1930	1594	3524	591	437	1028	95	100	195
93	SUJANGARH* (Sujangarh)	1106	806	1912	987	830	1817	0	0	0
94	TARANAGAR* (Taranagar)	623	447	1070	369	196	565	15	10	25
	CHURU ###	**6571**	**5249**	**11820**	**4079**	**2973**	**7052**	**118**	**111**	**221**
95	BANDIKUI* (Baswa)	689	484	1173	554	209	763	6	5	11
96	DAUSA* (Dausa)	555	462	1017	482	286	768	0	0	0
97	LALSOT* (Lalsot)	947	801	1748	454	216	670	5	3	8
98	MAHWA* (Mahwa)	897	749	1646	449	141	590	2	1	3
99	SIKRAI* (Sikrai)	766	549	1315	443	239	682	17	8	25
	DAUSA	**3854**	**3045**	**6899**	**2382**	**1091**	**3473**	**30**	**17**	**47**
100	BARI* (Bari)	989	906	1895	394	336	730	6	11	17
101	BASERI* (Baseri)	434	230	664	515	154	669	0	1	1
102	DHAULPUR (Sepau)	598	433	1031	496	284	780	7	4	11
103	RAJAKHERA (Rajakhera)	466	290	756	162	140	302	13	20	33
	DHAULPUR	**2487**	**1859**	**4346**	**1567**	**914**	**2481**	**26**	**36**	**62**
104	ASPUR* (Aspur)	2324	1674	3998	809	649	1458	26	48	74
105	BICHHIWARA (Dungarpur)	2843	2539	5382	982	650	1632	30	17	47
106	DUNGARPUR (Dungarpur)	1785	1548	3333	973	593	1566	60	39	99
107	SAGWARA (Sagwara)	1690	1604	3294	708	645	1353	1	0	1
108	SIMALWARA (Simalwara)	1687	1442	3129	695	475	1170	18	11	29
	DUNGARPUR	**10329**	**8807**	**19136**	**4167**	**3012**	**7179**	**135**	**115**	**250**
109	ANUPGARH (Garsana)	650	345	995	930	286	1216	4	3	7
110	GANGANAGAR (Ganganagar)	289	197	486	399	217	616	0	0	0
111	KARANPUR* (Karanpur)	604	422	1026	458	226	684	0	0	0
112	PADAMPUR* (Padampur)	339	213	552	441	172	613	0	0	0
113	RAISINGHNAGAR* (Raisinghnagar)	175	143	318	282	164	446	0	0	0
114	SADULSHAHAR (Sadulshahar)	754	541	1295	495	282	777	8	8	16
115	SURATGARH* (Suratgarh)	282	315	597	438	213	651	1	1	
	GANGANAGAR	**3093**	**2176**	**5269**	**3443**	**1560**	**5003**	**13**	**11**	**24**
116	BHADRA* (Bhadra)	606	455	1061	919	342	1261	2	0	2
117	HANUMANGARH (Hanumangarh)	1358	977	2335	2083	1128	3211	0	0	0
118	NOHAR (Rawatsar)	583	528	1111	985	413	1398	4	0	4
	HANUMANGARH	**2547**	**1960**	**4507**	**3987**	**1883**	**5870**	**6**	**0**	**6**
119	AMBER* (Amber)	1631	1099	2730	289	115	404	9	3	12
120	BASSI* (Bassi)	683	576	1259	585	268	853	7	3	10

P. Code	Panchayat Samiti (Concerning Tehsil)	Births			Deaths			Child Deaths		
		M	F	T	M	F	T	M	F	T
1	2	3	4	5	6	7	8	9	10	11
121	CHAKSU* (Chaksu)	408	344	752	532	165	697	9	5	14
122	DUDU (Dudu)	346	302	648	499	214	713	3	4	7
123	GOVINDGARH* (Chomu)	537	791	1328	759	308	1067	6	8	14
124	JAMWA RAMGARH*(Jamwa Ramgarh)	373	234	607	1044	321	1365	5	4	9
125	JHOTWARA* (Jaipur)	377	325	702	205	97	302	4	7	11
126	KOTPUTLI (Kotputli)	564	251	815	667	244	911	0	0	0
127	PHAGI* (Phagi)	462	378	840	413	182	595	6	3	9
128	SAMBHAR (Phulara)	462	435	897	640	262	902	3	3	6
129	SANGANER* (Sanganer)	290	334	624	327	73	400	1	3	4
130	SHAHPURA (Shahpura)	254	211	465	404	120	524	0	2	2
131	VIRATNAGAR (Viratnagar)	370	302	672	397	203	600	8	1	9
	JAIPUR	**6757**	**5582**	**12339**	**6761**	**2572**	**9333**	**61**	**46**	**107**
132	JAISALMER (Jaisalmer)	3049	2341	5390	212	134	346	NA	NA	NA
133	SAM (Jaisalmer)	631	291	922	72	36	108	NA	NA	NA
134	SANKRA (Pokaran)	556	451	1007	230	181	411	NA	NA	NA
	JAISALMER	**4236**	**3083**	**7319**	**514**	**351.**	**865**	**NA**	**NA**	**NA**
135	AHORE (Ahore)	4115	3060	7175	691	448	1139	8	24	32
136	BHINMAL (Bagora)	3725	2170	5895	820	409	1229	22	10	32
137	JALOR (Jalor)	2237	2019	4256	604	563	1167	68	72	140
138	JASWANTPURA (Bhinmal)	3594	1902	5496	1198	602	1800	22	31	53
139	RANIWARA* (Raniwara)	3728	2644	6372	838	548	1386	8	5	13
140	SANCHORE* (Sanchore)	6091	3098	9189	1370	712	2082	43	11	54
141	SAYLA (Sayla)	3772	3314	7086	1119	679	1798	78	101	179
	JALOR	**27262**	**18207**	**45469**	**6640**	**3961**	**10601**	**249**	**254**	**503**
142	BAKANI (Jhalrapatan)	409	315	724	203	122	325	6	3	9
143	DAG (Gangdhar)	668	584	1252	278	224	502	4	2	6
144	JHALRAPATAN (Jhalrapatan)	1165	1048	2213	456	388	844	11	9	20
145	KHANPUR* (Khanpur)	1256	1131	2387	127	86	213	3	2	5
146	MANOHARTHANA (Manoharthana)	817	756	1573	326	200	526	15	13	28
147	PIRAWA* (Pirwa)	1160	945	2105	450	308	758	28	22	50
	JHALAWAR	**5475**	**4779**	**10254**	**1840**	**1328**	**3168**	**67**	**51**	**118**
148	ALSISAR (Jhunjhunun)	NA	NA	NA	NA	NA	NA	NA	NA	NA
149	BUHANA* (Buhana)	NA	NA	NA	NA	NA	NA	NA	NA	NA
150	CHIRAWA (Chirawa)	NA	NA	NA	NA	NA	NA	NA	NA	NA
151	JHUNJHUNUN (Jhunjhunun)	NA	NA	NA	NA	NA	NA	NA	NA	NA
152	KHETRI* (Khetri)	NA	NA	NA	NA	NA	NA	NA	NA	NA
153	NAWALGARH* (Nawalgarh)	NA	NA	NA	NA	NA	NA	NA	NA	NA
154	SURAJGARH (Chirawa)	NA	NA	NA	NA	NA	NA	NA	NA	NA
155	UDAIPURWATI* (Udaipurwati)	NA	NA	NA	NA	NA	NA	NA	NA	NA
	JHUNJHUNUN	**3113**	**2356**	**5469**	**1374**	**903**	**2277**	**2**	**0**	**2**
156	BALESAR (Shergarh)	1852	1551	3403	1034	299	1333	17	13	30
157	BAP (Phalodi)	1448	1041	2489	502	221	723	2	1	3
158	BHOPALGARH (Bhopalgarh)	730	627	1357	432	241	673	0	0	0
159	BILARA* (Bilara)	1799	1336	3135	685	441	1126	65	48	113
160	LUNI (Luni)	1046	835	1881	529	337	866	10	14	24
161	MANDOR (Jodhpur)	1236	984	2220	387	221	608	4	1	5
162	OSIAN (Osian)	3050	2483	5533	733	356	1089	32	25	57
163	PHALODI (Phalodi)	455	373	828	189	140	329	6	6	12
164	SHERGARH (Shergarh)	1641	1429	3070	352	216	568	1	1	2
	JODHPUR	**13257**	**10659**	**23916**	**4843**	**2472**	**7315**	**137**	**109**	**246**
165	HINDAUN* (Hindaun)	85	78	163	461	165	626	2	2	4
166	KARAULI* (Karauli)	537	493	1030	393	119	512	3	0	3
167	NADOTI* (Nadoti)	400	610	1010	345	156	501	0	0	0
168	SAPOTRA (Sapotra)	296	207	503	389	131	520	0	0	0
169	TODABHIM* (Todabhim)	596	392	988	337	182	519	6	10	16
	KARAULI	**1914**	**1780**	**3694**	**1925**	**753**	**2678**	**11**	**12**	**23**
170	CHECHAT* (Ranganjmandi)	552	507	1059	393	217	610	4	4	8
171	ITAWA* (Pipalda)	245	261	506	426	185	611	0	0	0
172	LADPURA* (Ladpura)	778	792	1570	392	364	756	0	0	0
173	SANGOD* (Sangod)	555	511	1066	236	218	454	3	2	5
174	SULTANPUR* (Digod)	595	545	1140	383	173	556	2	5	7
	KOTA	**2725**	**2616**	**5341**	**1830**	**1157**	**2987**	**9**	**11**	**20**
175	DEGANA (Degana)	904	831	1735	418	340	758	6	3	9
176	DIDWANA* (Didwana)	862	738	1600	779	650	1429	0	0	0
177	JAYAL* (Jayal)	851	824	1675	308	273	581	5	1	6
178	KUCHAMAN* (Nawa)	1057	1046	2103	878	866	1744	4	3	7
179	LADNU* (Ladnu)	529	441	970	292	279	571	0	0	0
180	MAKRANA* (Makrana)	1797	1093	2890	535	466	1001	37	19	56
181	MERTA (Merta)	357	310	667	478	412	890	0	0	0
182	MUNDWA (Nagaur)	822	655	1477	407	337	744	4	4	8
183	NAGAUR (Nagaur)	778	773	1551	477	503	980	0	3	3
184	PARBATSAR* (Parbatsar)	383	332	715	448	400	848	0	0	0
185	RIYAN (Merta)	931	722	1653	681	511	1192	1	1	2
	NAGAUR	**9271**	**7765**	**17036**	**5701**	**5037**	**10738**	**57**	**34**	**91**

P. Code	Panchayat Samiti (Concerning Tehsil)	Births			Deaths			Child Deaths		
		M	F	T	M	F	T	M	F	T
1	2	3	4	5	6	7	8	9	10	11
186	BALI* (Bali)	321	242	563	191	124	315	4	3	7
187	DESURI (Desuri)	580	405	985	171	147	318	0	2	2
188	JAITARAN* (Jaitaran)	622	600	1222	233	206	439	5	3	8
189	KHARCHI/MARWAR JUN.	440	328	768	262	102	364	1	0	1
190	PALI (Pali)	528	299	827	161	90	251	0	0	0
191	RAIPUR* (Raipur)	348	293	641	222	131	353	0	0	0
192	RANI STATION (Desuri)	1892	1768	3660	695	640	1335	20	15	35
193	ROHAT* (Rohat)	182	1141	1323	101	113	214	5	4	9
194	SOJAT* (Sojat)	291	260	551	210	173	383	6	6	12
195	SUMERPUR* (Sumerpur)	314	255	569	145	121	266	0	0	0
	PALI	**5518**	**5591**	**11109**	**2391**	**1847**	**4238**	**41**	**33**	**74**
196	AMET* (Amet)	514	383	897	270	189	459	0	0	0
197	BHIM* (Bhim)	889	728	1617	476	349	825	21	31	52
198	DEOGARH* (Deogarh)	241	190	431	227	98	325	5	2	7
199	KHAMNOR* (Nathdwara)	768	663	1431	517	242	759	46	38	84
200	KUMBHALGARH* (Kumbhalgarh)	341	253	594	208	111	319	8	6	14
201	RAILMAGRA* (Railmagra)	428	351	779	410	190	600	7	5	12
202	RAJSAMAND* (Rajsamand)	450	392	842	348	160	508	0	0	0
	RAJSAMAND	**3631**	**2960**	**6591**	**2456**	**1339**	**3795**	**87**	**82**	**169**
203	BAMANWAS* (Bamanwas)	329	275	604	150	102	252	2	0	2
204	BONLI (Bonli)	690	693	1383	400	384	784	10	12	22
205	GANGAPUR* (Gangapur)	718	510	1228	634	384	1018	0	0	0
206	KHANDAR (Khandar)	731	680	1411	368	194	562	18	18	36
207	SAWAI MADHOPUR (S. Madhopur)	915	737	1652	657	363	1020	6	4	10
	S. MADHOPUR	**3383**	**2895**	**6278**	**2209**	**1427**	**3636**	**36**	**34**	**70**
208	DANTA RAMGARH (Danta Ramgarh)	882	648	1530	575	303	878	3	2	5
209	DHOND (Sikar)	1394	1331	2725	549	440	989	0	0	0
210	FATEHPUR (Fatehpur)	891	779	1670	447	328	775	0	0	0
211	KHANDELA (Sri Madhopur)	751	508	1259	634	301	935	1	0	1
212	LACHHMANGARH (Lachhmangarh)	1031	640	1671	580	291	871	0	1	1
213	NEEM KA THANA* (Neem Ka Thana)	1235	838	2073	880	388	1268	0	0	0
214	PIPRALI (Sikar)	698	604	1302	462	325	787	0	0	0
215	SRI MADHOPUR (Sri Madhopur)	1231	900	2131	664	287	951	0	0	0
	SIKAR	**8113**	**6248**	**14361**	**4791**	**2663**	**7454**	**4**	**3**	**7**
216	ABU ROAD* (Abu Road)	127	94	221	71	34	105	1	1	2
217	PINDWARA* (Pindwara)	259	271	530	142	122	264	3	3	6
218	REODAR* (Reodar)	271	288	559	183	122	305	4	3	7
219	SHEOGANJ* (Sheoganj)	148	120	268	77	55	132	0	0	0
220	SIROHI* (Sirohi)	258	207	465	117	105	222	3	5	8
	SIROHI	**1063**	**980**	**2043**	**590**	**438**	**1028**	**11**	**12**	**23**
221	DEOLI* (Deoli)	672	686	1358	701	342	1043	5	3	8
222	MALPURA* (Malpura)	456	377	833	273	194	467	3	3	6
223	NIWAI* (Niwai)	595	480	1075	516	369	885	0	0	0
224	TODARAISINGH* (Todaraisingh)	566	506	1072	390	234	624	3	7	10
225	TONK (Tonk)	888	742	1630	808	337	1145	7	8	15
226	UNIARA* (Uniara)	629	491	1120	314	179	493	10	10	20
	TONK	**3806**	**3282**	**7088**	**3002**	**1655**	**4657**	**28**	**31**	**59**
227	BARGAON (Girwa)	269	249	518	490	185	681	3	5	8
228	BHINDER* (Vallabhnagar)	820	839	1659	860	336	1196	11	6	17
229	DHARIAWAD* (Dhariawad)	933	799	1732	756	490	1246	23	16	39
230	GIRWA (Girwa)	148	139	287	716	120	836	2	1	3
231	GOGUNDA* (Gogunda)	645	631	1276	575	169	744	2	0	2
232	JHADOL* (Jhadol)	238	225	463	360	166	526	2	1	3
233	KHERWARA* (Kherwara)	547	553	1100	614	352	966	9	3	12
234	KOTRA* (Kotra)	434	486	920	819	209	1028	22	29	51
235	MAVLI* (Mavli)	397	387	784	589	195	784	13	8	21
236	SALUMBAR* (Salumbar)	750	643	1393	414	311	725	12	17	29
237	SARADA* (Sarada)	361	300	661	327	235	562	31	32	63
	UDAIPUR	**5542**	**5251**	**10793**	**6520**	**2768**	**9294**	**130**	**118**	**248**
	RAJASTHAN	**187160**	**153080**	**356963**	**106215**	**61112**	**177303**	**1818**	**1628**	**3514**

Note: * Co-terminus Panchayat Samiti.
Dungargarh PS shifted from Churu to Bikaner district on 1st April 2001
Excluding data of Dungargarh PS; ### Including data of Dungargarh PS.
Source: District Statistical Abstract (All Districts), 2003, DES, Jaipur.

GENERAL ANNEX-XI

PANCHAYAT SAMITI-WISE PROGRESS OF FAMILY WELFARE PROGRAMME (2001)

(Nos)

P.Code	Panchayat Samiti /District	Progress of Family Welfare				
		Sterilization	I.U.D.	C.C.Users	Oral Pill Users	Total Accepted
1	2	3	4	5	6	7
1	ARAIN	624	640	2100	2348	5712
2	BHINAY	517	756	2413	2416	6102
3	JAWAJA	550	675	3378	3410	8013
4	KEKRI	768	714	2957	2976	7415
5	KISHANGARH	857	672	2785	2557	6871
6	MASOODA	522	566	2167	2336	5591
7	PISANGAN	1002	868	3289	3326	8485
8	SRINAGAR	711	389	1571	1581	4252
	AJMER DISTRICT	**5551**	**5280**	**20660**	**20950**	**52441**
9	BANSURE	1387	536	1822	1205	4950
10	BEHROR	845	495	994	582	2916
11	KATHUMAR	1058	442	1150	852	3502
12	KISHANGARH BAS	647	456	1240	735	3078
13	KOTKASIM	712	454	855	581	2602
14	LACHHMANGARH	1105	645	2050	972	4772
15	MANDAWAR	840	716	1945	1119	4620
16	NIMRANA	705	431	943	629	2708
17	RAJGARH	716	312	1406	926	3360
18	RAMGARH	701	446	1846	845	3838
19	RENI	722	301	1477	866	3366
20	THANAGAZI	1164	620	979	1011	3774
21	TIJARA	816	640	1734	1261	4451
22	UMREN	718	516	1735	988	3957
	ALWAR	**12136**	**7010**	**20176**	**12572**	**51894**
23	ANANDPURI	183	622	482	627	1914
24	BAGIDORA	687	929	999	1506	4121
25	GARHI	1228	1911	1956	2005	7100
26	GHATOL	739	1804	1212	1376	5131
27	KUSHALGARH	370	672	805	1164	3011
28	PEEPALKHOONT	464	1029	1218	1290	4001
29	SAJJANGARH	356	1216	418	763	2753
30	TALWARA	1208	1198	935	1057	4398
	BANSWARA	**5235**	**9381**	**8025**	**9788**	**32429**
31	ANTA	1337	1262	3115	2599	8313
32	ATRU	804	469	1225	995	3493
33	BARAN	1525	729	3021	2463	7738
34	CHHABRA	820	789	1829	1383	4821
35	CHHIPABAROD	875	665	2414	1738	5692
36	KISHANGANJ	848	856	1627	1586	4917
37	SHAHBAD	879	920	1463	1261	4523
	BARAN #	**7088**	**5690**	**14694**	**12025**	**39497**
38	BALOTRA	1094	963	7755	6455	16267
39	BARMER	488	808	5321	4905	11522
40	BAYTOO	429	616	3714	3434	8193
41	CHOHTAN	256	438	3521	3776	7991
42	DHORIMANNA	649	379	3825	3625	8478
43	SHEO	277	440	4350	4215	9282
44	SINDHARI	419	758	7763	5449	14389
45	SIWANA	897	650	3999	3564	8950
	BARMER	**4509**	**5052**	**40248**	**35423**	**85072**
46	BAYANA	822	690	2373	1597	5482
47	DEEG	1040	627	1427	1095	4189
48	KAMAN	687	889	1736	1404	4716
49	KUMHER	877	471	1423	1081	3852
50	NADBAI	1004	669	1476	1229	4378
51	NAGAR PAHARI	1023	745	1943	1483	5194
52	RUPBAS	924	618	1888	1401	4831
53	SEWAR	744	576	1781	1345	4446
54	WEIR	1214	694	1457	1222	4587
	BHARATPUR	**8335**	**5979**	**15504**	**11857**	**41675**

P.Code	Panchayat Samiti /District	Progress of Family Welfare				
		Sterilization	I.U.D.	C.C.Users	Oral Pill Users	Total Accepted
1	2	3	4	5	6	7
55	ASIND	505	1286	3434	3025	8250
56	BANERA	474	715	1760	1734	4683
57	HURDA	318	605	1538	1378	3839
58	JAHAZPUR	943	994	2367	2444	6748
59	KOTRI	673	854	3066	2315	6908
60	MANDAL	602	1210	2560	3098	7470
61	MANDALGARH	1218	1288	3108	3302	8916
62	RAIPUR	232	484	1184	1074	2974
63	SAHARA	371	588	1428	1856	4243
64	SHAHPURA	665	1022	2231	2117	6035
65	SUWANA	819	953	2857	2984	7613
	BHILWARA	**6820**	**9999**	**25533**	**25327**	**67679**
66	BIKANER	1262	1545	4674	5102	12583
67	DUNGARGARH *	756	794	4803	4490	10843
68	KOLAYAT	720	871	2701	2533	6825
69	LUNKARANSAR	978	486	2391	2266	6121
70	NOKHA	816	1678	4443	4238	11175
	BIKANER **	**3776**	**4580**	**14209**	**14139**	**36704**
71	HINDOLI	1035	871	1525	1869	5300
72	KESHORAIPATAN	1231	1082	1926	2190	6429
73	NAINWA	819	818	1462	1425	4524
74	TALERA	1869	1489	2340	2764	8432
	BUNDI	**4954**	**4260**	**7253**	**8248**	**24685**
75	ARNOD	490	572	533	664	2259
76	BARI SADRI	277	563	293	406	1539
77	BEGUN	483	742	652	777	2654
78	BHADESAR	381	446	440	489	1756
79	BHAINSRORGARH	415	355	403	536	1709
80	BHOPALSAGAR	239	339	292	388	1258
81	CHHOTI SADRI	357	236	318	375	1286
82	CHITTAURGARH	605	730	623	805	2763
83	DUNGLA	680	1343	800	1067	3890
84	GANGRAR	356	474	458	442	1730
85	KAPASAN	256	661	452	603	1972
86	NIMBAHERA	633	640	827	755	2855
87	PRATAPGARH	768	958	1313	1367	4406
88	RASHMI	760	1532	1222	1563	5077
	CHITTAURGARH	**6700**	**9591**	**8626**	**10237**	**35154**
89	CHURU	1385	1049	6185	6009	13333
90	RAJGARH	1349	1240	4891	15060	11191
91	RATANGARH	1098	1269	3902	4163	9334
92	SARDARSHAHAR	1452	1087	7516	6964	15567
93	SUJANGARH	1697	1413	6956	6258	14627
94	TARANAGAR	994	849	3605	4277	8731
	CHURU ***	**8731**	**7701**	**37858**	**38241**	**83626**
95	BANDIKUI	1517	761	2236	1418	5922
96	DAUSA	1802	1080	2547	1783	7212
97	LALSOT	1332	878	3103	1997	7310
98	MAHWA	1066	931	1984	1586	5567
99	SIKRAI	1267	736	1941	1046	4990
	DAUSA #	**6984**	**4386**	**11811**	**7830**	**31001**
100	BARI	363	468	1645	902	3378
101	BASERI	538	391	2077	1098	4104
102	DHAULPUR	746	484	1892	1262	4384
103	RAJAKHERA	556	413	1957	1278	4204
	DHAULPUR	**2203**	**1756**	**7571**	**4540**	**16070**
104	ASPUR	530	1453	1631	1967	5581
105	BICHHIWARA	440	1903	2243	2627	7213
106	DUNGARPUR	348	1104	1366	1619	4437
107	SAGWARA	714	1704	1989	2108	6515
108	SIMALWARA	541	1492	1827	2037	5897
	DUNGARPUR	**2573**	**7656**	**9056**	**10358**	**29643**
109	ANUPGARH	2707	2103	11193	7531	23534
110	GANGANAGAR	796	668	3316	1399	6179
111	KARANPUR	711	645	1668	1209	4233
112	PADAMPUR	837	757	3985	2051	7630
113	RAISINGHNAGAR	865	664	3783	1816	7128
114	SADULSHAHAR	816	688	2308	1018	4830
115	SURATGARH	1514	820	2190	1733	6257
	GANGANAGAR	**8246**	**6345**	**28443**	**16757**	**59791**
116	BHADRA	1515	1266	3795	2448	9024
117	HANUMANGARH	3545	2036	5016	4946	15543
118	NOHAR	4497	2205	8725	7370	22797
	HANUMANGARH ##	**9557**	**5507**	**17536**	**14764**	**47364**
119	AMBER	1640	317	2188	2050	6195
120	BASSI	710	638	1519	2083	4950

P.Code	Panchayat Samiti /District	Progress of Family Welfare				
		Sterilization	I.U.D.	C.C.Users	Oral Pill Users	Total Accepted
1	2	3	4	5	6	7
121	CHAKSU	832	216	1113	1082	3243
122	DUDU	1380	647	2177	1937	6141
123	GOVINDGARH	1623	720	2702	2713	7758
124	JAMWA RAMGARH	1111	223	1415	1170	3919
125	JHOTWARA	883	174	492	453	2002
126	KOTPUTLI	4338	1614	4649	3942	14543
127	PHAGI	998	379	1394	1548	4319
128	SAMBHAR	1950	762	2544	2106	7362
129	SANGANER	1403	352	1872	1593	5220
130	SHAHPURA	1765	556	1512	1385	5218
131	VIRATNAGAR	1155	541	1377	1113	4186
	JAIPUR	**19788**	**7139**	**24954**	**23175**	**75056**
132	JAISALMER	350	516	1364	1706	3936
133	SAM	300	667	1759	1568	4294
134	SANKRA	334	600	1927	2155	5016
	JAISALMER	**984**	**1783**	**5050**	**5429**	**13246**
135	AHORE	522	1686	1553	1593	5354
136	BHINMAL	980	1166	2021	1824	5991
137	JALOR	502	1090	1143	1195	3930
138	JASWANTPURA	652	1012	1033	1067	3764
139	RANIWARA	944	881	1240	1386	4451
140	SANCHORE	1394	2054	3124	3063	9635
141	SAYLA	718	1610	2195	2176	6699
	JALOR	**5712**	**9499**	**12309**	**12304**	**39824**
142	BAKANI	799	799	4981	2375	8954
143	DAG	1106	598	3139	2136	6979
144	JHALRAPATAN	1283	906	5906	2554	10649
145	KHANPUR	817	726	3704	2612	7859
146	MANOHARTHANA	821	668	5098	3024	9611
147	PIRAWA	1057	725	4440	1380	7602
	JHALAWAR	**5883**	**4422**	**27268**	**14081**	**51654**
148	ALSISAR	848	722	770	739	2379
149	BUHANA	1060	644	906	878	3488
150	CHIRAWA	1020	818	749	822	3409
151	JHUNJHUNUN	898	817	1084	831	3630
152	KHETRI	1098	542	862	924	3426
153	NAWALGARH	911	853	920	823	3507
154	SURAJGARH	746	780	828	766	3120
155	UDAIPURWATI	1020	918	980	981	3899
	JHUNJHUNUN	**7601**	**6094**	**7099**	**6764**	**26858**
156	BALESAR	366	573	963	885	2787
157	BAP	152	347	717	652	1868
158	BHOPALGARH	867	1091	1074	1090	4122
159	BILARA	882	1025	1128	1173	4208
160	LUNI	1125	1008	1485	1587	5205
161	MANDOR	859	619	1111	1041	3630
162	OSIAN	1383	1493	2385	2450	7711
163	PHALODI	467	760	933	988	3148
164	SHERGARH	309	731	1058	1034	3132
	JODHPUR	**6410**	**7647**	**10854**	**10900**	**35811**
165	HINDAUN	1758	1255	7538	5510	16061
166	KARAULI	1412	798	7367	5417	14994
167	NADOTI	759	658	3821	3362	8600
168	SAPOTRA	1360	873	5787	4598	12618
169	TODABHIM	1158	708	4880	4007	10753
	KARAULI ###	**6447**	**4292**	**29393**	**22894**	**63026**
170	CHECHAT	1180	1002	1824	1687	5693
171	ITAWA	941	706	1138	1145	3930
172	LADPURA	859	584	1190	1246	3879
173	SANGOD	1142	893	1409	1266	4710
174	SULTANPUR	996	694	1151	1047	3888
	KOTA	**5118**	**3879**	**6712**	**6391**	**22100**
175	DEGANA	1239	1118	2829	2570	7756
176	DIDWANA	1318	1528	4945	5035	12826
177	JAYAL	862	930	3129	2869	7790
178	KUCHAMAN	973	734	2724	2545	6976
179	LADNU	738	811	3295	2931	7775
180	MAKRANA	903	1017	2455	2096	6471
181	MERTA	996	941	2875	2663	7475
182	MUNDWA	631	921	2544	2492	6588
183	NAGAUR	824	1387	3788	4507	10506
184	PARBATSAR	915	1023	2958	2895	7791
185	RIYAN	1113	1118	2603	2577	7411
	NAGAUR	**10512**	**11528**	**34145**	**33180**	**89365**

P.Code	Panchayat Samiti /District	Progress of Family Welfare				
		Sterilization	I.U.D.	C.C.Users	Oral Pill Users	Total Accepted
1	2	3	4	5	6	7
186	BALI	642	702	1174	1285	3803
187	DESURI	592	593	287	339	1811
188	JAITARAN	1034	698	413	518	2663
189	KHARCHI/MARWAR JUN.	662	615	796	865	2938
190	PALI	481	569	462	595	2107
191	RAIPUR	672	1275	742	881	3507
192	RANI STATION	660	1090	784	1002	3536
193	ROHAT	453	521	400	461	1835
194	SOJAT	800	754	618	762	2934
195	SUMERPUR	482	656	429	699	2266
	PALI	**6478**	**7473**	**6105**	**7407**	**27400**
196	AMET	453	881	700	874	2908
197	BHIM	417	896	802	771	2886
198	DEOGARH	328	687	764	816	2595
199	KHAMNOR	665	1165	2081	2149	6060
200	KUMBHALGARH	302	900	1153	1407	3762
201	RAILMAGRA	538	869	1358	1426	4191
202	RAJSAMAND	717	1107	1665	1733	5222
	RAJSAMAND #	**3420**	**6505**	**8523**	**9176**	**27624**
203	BAMANWAS	802	612	3434	2387	7235
204	BONLI	1093	735	4586	4019	10433
205	GANGAPUR	1459	883	4788	3727	10857
206	KHANDAR	986	595	3356	2589	7526
207	SAWAI MADHOPUR	1934	1580	8188	5470	17172
	SAWAI MADHOPUR	**6274**	**4405**	**24352**	**18192**	**53223**
208	DANTA RAMGARH	1417	1059	1663	1274	5413
209	DHOND	1186	1222	1148	1098	4654
210	FATEHPUR	703	916	1588	1495	4702
211	KHANDELA	1036	616	1427	1259	4338
212	LACHHMANGARH	661	967	1679	1574	4881
213	NEEM KA THANA	2253	1146	2193	1590	7182
214	PIPRALI	834	519	882	783	3018
215	SRI MADHOPUR	1268	630	1457	1167	4522
	SIKAR	**9358**	**7075**	**12037**	**10240**	**38710**
216	ABU ROAD	2855	6353	16656	18127	43991
217	PINDWARA	515	1449	4899	5148	12011
218	REODAR	933	1649	3873	4467	10922
219	SHEOGANJ	483	1023	2348	2675	6529
220	SIROHI	723	1366	2943	3104	8136
	SIROHI	**5509**	**11840**	**30719**	**33521**	**81589**
221	DEOLI	1200	853	4049	4636	10738
222	MALPURA	1418	1043	3595	3252	9308
223	NIWAI	1409	914	5096	4533	11952
224	TODARAISINGH	796	699	2402	1772	5669
225	TONK	1446	1144	4942	4729	12261
226	UNIARA	552	748	2363	1769	5432
	TONK	**6821**	**5401**	**22447**	**20691**	**55360**
227	BARGAON	1011	1258	3369	3416	9054
228	BHINDER	778	1125	1524	1483	4910
229	DHARIAWAD	494	1328	1597	1453	4872
230	GIRWA	2082	1660	1173	2034	6949
231	GOGUNDA	160	458	1405	1622	3645
232	JHADOL	521	611	1314	1342	3788
233	KHERWARA	515	1655	3177	3498	8845
234	KOTRA	46	701	2398	1479	4624
235	MAVLI	606	1368	2644	2034	6652
236	SALUMBAR	527	1749	2137	1805	6218
237	SARADA	461	1494	2058	2384	6397
	UDAIPUR	**7201**	**13407**	**22796**	**22550**	**65954**
	RAJASTHAN	**216914**	**212562**	**571966**	**518931**	**1501525**

Note: * Dungargarh PS shifted from Churu to Bikaner district on 1st April 2001
** Excluding data of Dungargarh PS; *** Including data of Dungargarh PS.
# Came in force from April, 1991; ## Came in force from July 1994
Came in force from July 1997.
Source: Department of Medical & Family Welfare, Rajasthan, Jaipur.

GENERAL ANNEX-XII

DISTRICT-WISE AREA AND POPULATION CHARACTERISTICS: RAJASTHAN, 1991

S.No.	Districts	Area				Population (000's)	Annual Exponential Growth Rate	Density (Persons Per sq. km.)	Female Sex Ratio (Female Per 1000 Male)	Urban Population (%)	Literacy Rate		Work Participation Rate		Percentage of Workers in Secondary and Teritiary Sectors		Female Mean Ageat Marriage
		Total ('000 sq km)	Rural ('000 sq km)	Percentage of Rural to Total Area %)	% share Total Rural of the State						Male	Female	Male	Female	Male	Female	
1	2	3	4	5	6	7	8	9	10	11	12	13	14	15	16	17	18
1	AJMER	8.48	8.16	96.23	2.42	1729	1.83	204	918	40.70	68.70	34.50	50.40	27.90	50.30	15.30	16.40
2	ALWAR	8.38	8.22	98.09	2.44	2297	2.69	274	880	13.90	61.00	22.50	47.80	32.00	31.30	8.10	16.90
3	BANSWARA	5.04	5.01	99.40	1.49	1156	2.65	229	969	7.70	38.20	13.40	51.90	40.70	15.30	7.70	17.70
4	BARAN	6.96	6.92	99.43	2.05	2031	2.80	163	887	36.40	64.00	29.50	49.30	21.40	41.00	20.90	16.30
5	BARMER	28.39	28.33	99.79	8.40	1435	2.49	51	891	10.00	36.60	7.70	51.50	36.40	18.60	4.80	18.10
6	BHARATPUR	5.07	4.94	97.44	1.46	1652	2.40	326	832	19.40	62.10	19.60	45.80	21.60	28.40	17.70	17.20
7	BHILWARA	10.46	10.10	96.56	2.99	1593	1.95	152	945	19.50	45.90	16.50	56.10	36.80	28.10	6.10	15.30
8	BIKANER	27.24	27.06	99.34	8.02	1211	3.56	44	885	39.70	54.60	27.00	49.10	20.90	41.10	20.10	16.50
9	BUNDI	5.55	5.38	96.94	1.59	770	2.30	139	889	17.40	47.40	16.10	51.70	27.20	23.50	9.30	15.30
10	CHITTAURGARH	10.86	10.70	98.53	3.17	1484	1.86	137	950	15.60	50.50	17.20	56.00	41.70	23.40	5.00	15.60
11	CHURU	16.83	16.64	98.87	4.93	1543	2.69	92	937	28.90	51.30	17.30	47.20	29.30	27.50	5.20	15.90
12	DAUSA	3.39	3.34	98.53	0.99	4723	3.18	336	891	39.50	64.80	28.70	46.80	20.00	52.70	18.90	16.40
13	DHOLPUR	3.03	2.97	98.02	0.88	749	2.48	247	795	17.20	50.50	15.20	47.90	6.60	19.70	22.00	16.80
14	DUNGARPUR	3.77	3.74	99.20	1.11	875	2.47	232	995	7.30	45.70	15.40	51.30	38.00	19.50	9.70	17.50
15	GANGANAGAR	10.93	11.08	101.37	3.28	2623	2.56	127	877	21.10	55.30	26.40	52.40	19.90	28.70	16.70	17.60
16	HANUMANGARH	9.70	9.64	99.38	2.84	2623	2.56	127	877	21.10	55.30	26.40	52.40	19.90	28.70	16.70	17.60
17	JAIPUR	10.68	10.40	97.38	3.08	4723	3.18	336	891	39.50	64.80	28.70	46.80	20.00	52.70	18.90	16.40
18	JAISALMER	38.40	38.27	99.66	11.34	345	3.49	9	807	15.60	45.00	11.30	50.10	20.50	36.70	25.20	17.80
19	JALORE	10.64	10.59	99.53	3.14	1143	2.35	107	942	7.30	39.00	7.80	50.40	31.60	17.90	5.00	18.30
20	JHALAWAR	6.22	6.14	98.71	1.82	957	1.98	154	918	15.80	48.20	16.20	54.10	32.30	19.80	5.00	15.70
21	JHUNJHUNUN	5.93	5.79	97.64	1.72	1582	2.67	267	931	20.50	68.30	25.50	42.70	23.40	35.40	11.00	16.40
22	JODHPUR	22.85	22.64	99.08	6.71	2153	2.56	94	891	35.50	56.70	22.60	47.90	23.60	42.40	12.80	17.50
23	KARAULI	5.48	5.39	98.36	1.48	1963	2.46	186	854	14.80	54.60	14.60	47.10	28.20	25.60	7.60	16.40
24	KOTA	5.48	4.92	89.78	1.46	2031	2.80	163	887	36.40	64.00	29.50	49.30	21.40	41.00	20.90	16.30
25	NAGAUR	17.72	17.45	98.48	5.17	2145	2.75	121	942	16.00	49.30	13.30	48.20	30.70	27.90	4.10	16.40
26	PALI	12.39	12.07	97.42	3.58	1486	1.54	120	956	21.80	54.40	17.00	48.30	27.50	34.40	8.40	17.40
27	RAJSAMAND	4.56	4.42	96.93	1.32	2889	2.04	167	965	17.10	49.30	19.00	53.10	33.10	30.40	12.80	16.80
28	SAWAI MADHOPUR	5.04	4.97	98.61	1.47	1963	2.46	186	854	14.80	54.60	14.60	47.10	28.20	25.60	7.60	16.40
29	SIKAR	7.73	7.54	97.54	2.23	1843	2.91	238	946	21.00	64.10	19.90	42.90	19.70	38.10	11.00	16.20
30	SIROHI	5.14	5.06	98.44	1.50	654	1.88	127	949	19.50	46.20	17.00	50.30	25.80	37.40	13.60	18.00
31	TONK	7.19	7.03	97.77	2.08	975	2.18	136	923	19.50	50.60	15.20	50.20	32.10	29.20	9.90	14.90
32	UDAIPUR	12.29	12.91	105.04	3.83	2889	2.04	167	965	17.10	49.30	19.00	53.10	33.10	30.40	12.80	16.80
	RAJASTHAN	**342.24**	**337.37**	**98.58**	**100.00**	**44006**	**2.50**	**129**	**910**	**22.90**	**55.00**	**20.40**	**49.30**	**27.40**	**32.70**	**10.50**	**16.70**

Source: 1. Computed from data given in Primary Census Abustract, Rajasthan, Series -21, Census of India, 1991.
2. Occasional Paper No. 1 of 1997, District Level Estimates of Fertility And Child Mortality for 1991 and Their Inter Relations With Other Variables

GENERAL ANNEX-XIII

DISTRICT-WISE ESTIMATES OF FERTILITY INDICATORS: RAJASTHAN, 1981 AND 1991

S.No.	*Districts*	*CBR*		*TFR*		*TMFR*		*GFR*		*GMFR*	
		1981	*1991*	*1981*	*1991*	*1981*	*1991*	*1981*	*1991*	*1981*	*1991*
1	*2*	*3*	*4*	*5*	*6*	*7*	*8*	*9*	*10*	*11*	*12*
1	AJMER	39.08	34.99	5.50	4.75	6.10	5.41	167.00	152.00	194.00	178.00
2	ALWAR	41.36	35.00	6.40	5.04	6.90	5.73	194.00	164.00	220.00	187.00
3	BANSWARA	42.39	38.41	6.10	5.13	6.80	6.04	187.00	167.00	223.00	196.00
4	BARAN	40.14	36.60	6.30	5.00	6.80	5.52	196.00	163.00	219.00	184.00
5	BARMER	39.75	36.03	6.20	5.57	6.90	6.11	194.00	174.00	225.00	201.00
6	BHARATPUR	44.02	34.96	7.00	5.30	7.60	6.03	214.00	169.00	240.00	194.00
7	BHILWARA	37.99	35.23	5.30	4.80	5.60	5.11	162.00	150.00	175.00	164.00
8	BIKANER	41.32	35.36	6.00	4.99	6.40	5.66	188.00	165.00	216.00	189.00
9	BUNDI	40.68	35.70	5.90	5.03	6.30	5.35	179.00	160.00	193.00	175.00
10	CHITTAURGARH	38.96	33.00	5.40	4.41	5.70	4.77	168.00	139.00	183.00	155.00
11	CHURU	42.08	28.53	6.10	4.14	6.60	4.57	193.00	133.00	214.00	148.00
12	DAUSA	41.62	35.26	6.20	4.88	6.70	5.55	188.00	158.00	212.00	183.00
13	DHOLPUR	44.02	40.38	7.00	6.36	7.60	7.04	214.00	204.00	240.00	229.00
14	DUNGARPUR	45.12	40.24	6.10	5.16	6.60	5.86	185.00	166.00	216.00	197.00
15	GANGANAGAR	39.15	32.75	5.70	4.22	6.40	5.11	183.00	150.00	218.00	176.00
16	HANUMANGARH	39.15	32.75	5.70	4.22	6.40	5.11	183.00	150.00	218.00	176.00
17	JAIPUR	41.62	35.26	6.20	4.88	6.70	5.55	188.00	158.00	212.00	183.00
18	JAISALMER	41.55	34.01	5.50	5.48	6.10	6.14	173.00	175.00	199.00	202.00
19	JALORE	37.99	34.95	6.50	5.23	7.10	5.95	198.00	165.00	228.00	193.00
20	JHALAWAR	40.16	32.62	6.10	4.47	6.40	4.82	184.00	143.00	200.00	158.00
21	JHUNJHUNUN	39.98	34.48	5.90	4.83	6.30	5.35	179.00	159.00	202.00	179.00
22	JODHPUR	41.46	34.67	6.10	5.05	6.60	5.79	186.00	162.00	216.00	190.00
23	KARAULI	43.34	40.01	6.70	5.95	7.10	6.37	200.00	187.00	218.00	206.00
24	KOTA	40.14	36.60	6.30	5.00	6.80	5.52	196.00	163.00	219.00	184.00
25	NAGAUR	40.14	34.68	6.10	4.78	6.50	5.14	184.00	157.00	201.00	172.00
26	PALI	41.45	33.84	6.00	4.88	6.50	5.55	181.00	153.00	205.00	176.00
27	RAJSAMAND	40.65	34.69	5.60	4.62	6.20	5.17	173.00	145.00	199.00	167.00
28	S. MADHOPUR	43.34	40.01	6.70	5.95	7.10	6.37	200.00	187.00	218.00	206.00
29	SIKAR	41.00	37.64	6.20	5.41	6.50	5.81	189.00	174.00	207.00	192.00
30	SIROHI	39.75	33.33	5.80	4.73	6.40	5.46	174.00	148.00	206.00	176.00
31	TONK	36.18	35.50	6.50	4.99	6.80	5.37	190.00	159.00	209.00	175.00
32	UDAIPUR	40.65	34.69	5.60	4.62	6.20	5.17	173.00	145.00	199.00	167.00
	RAJASTHAN	**41.01**	**35.75**	**6.10**	**5.01**	**6.50**	**5.59**	**185.00**	**162.00**	**209.00**	**184.00**

Source: Occasional Paper No. 1 of 1997, District Level Estimates of Fertility and Child Mortality for 1991 and Their Inter-relations with Other Variables.

GENERAL ANNEX-XIV

ESTIMATES OF CHILD MORTALITY INDICATORS BY SEX AT DISTRICT LEVEL, RAJASTHAN, 1981 AND 1991

S.No.	*District*	*Year*	*Person*				*Male*				*Female*			
			q(1)	*q(2)*	*q(3)*	*q(5)*	*q(1)*	*q(2)*	*q(3)*	*q(5)*	*q(1)*	*q(2)*	*q(3)*	*q(5)*
1	*2*	*3*	*4*	*5*	*6*	*7*	*8*	*9*	*10*	*11*	*12*	*13*	*14*	*15*
1	AJMER	***1991***	113	118	126	130	115	122	129	134	111	116	121	124
		1981	174	172	178	202	178	176	176	195	170	169	180	210
2	ALWAR	***1991***	101	106	115	124	99	103	112	119	103	112	119	128
		1981	160	170	181	204	165	172	173	188	154	168	190	221
3	BANSWARA	***1991***	92	135	143	148	97	140	144	149	87	130	143	147
		1981	150	165	153	167	170	184	167	172	126	145	138	161
4	BARAN	***1991***	84	95	99	140	76	90	97	121	91	96	101	124
		1981	141	142	155	178	148	144	152	168	133	141	159	188
5	BARMER	***1991***	99	121	138	143	82	124	136	141	102	118	142	147
		1981	115	129	140	157	117	122	134	146	113	136	147	170
6	BHARATPUR	***1991***	78	101	111	126	72	89	97	110	95	114	128	145
		1981	186	199	215	236	175	184	185	199	199	216	249	278
7	BHILWARA	***1991***	120	125	129	143	121	134	137	144	119	123	127	142
		1981	191	196	206	225	204	204	208	226	176	188	203	224
8	BIKANER	***1991***	60	69	76	82	60	69	75	81	59	69	76	82
		1981	69	74	78	89	72	75	74	87	66	73	82	92
9	BUNDI	***1991***	82	105	108	120	61	102	109	114	96	106	108	127
		1981	151	165	161	196	143	164	163	185	160	166	159	208
10	CHITTAURGARH	***1991***	99	134	142	149	103	141	148	151	83	127	136	145
		1981	180	197	196	218	192	210	204	217	166	183	187	220
11	CHURU	***1991***	64	75	79	83	59	72	76	79	69	77	82	91
		1981	84	98	111	116	88	95	104	112	79	102	118	121
12	DAUSA	***1991***	67	78	84	94	65	76	81	88	69	81	87	102
		1981	137	144	148	162	144	146	143	151	129	142	154	174
13	DHOLPUR	***1991***	107	127	133	150	109	110	125	142	105	147	166	183
		1981	186	199	215	236	175	184	185	199	199	216	249	278
14	DUNGARPUR	***1991***	98	129	134	140	97	131	136	141	99	127	131	139
		1981	171	160	160	169	178	171	170	177	163	150	150	161
15	GANGANAGAR	***1991***	54	64	68	73	57	60	69	71	50	68	72	74
		1981	107	102	110	119	125	108	110	115	89	95	110	124
16	HANUMANGARH	***1991***	54	64	68	73	57	60	69	71	50	68	72	74
		1981	107	102	110	119	125	108	110	115	89	95	110	124
17	JAIPUR	***1991***	67	78	84	94	65	76	81	88	69	81	87	102
		1981	137	144	148	162	144	146	143	151	129	142	154	174
18	JAISALMER	***1991***	87	97	111	124	87	96	109	119	86	99	113	134
		1981	112	118	114	134	124	119	103	113	100	117	128	158
19	JALORE	***1991***	91	112	124	129	90	104	117	125	96	120	132	139
		1981	145	137	142	156	142	135	141	146	149	139	144	167
20	JHALAWAR	***1991***	100	111	118	124	122	113	119	122	88	110	117	128
		1981	140	174	179	196	142	173	180	190	138	175	179	203
21	JHUNJHUNUN	***1991***	56	66	67	80	48	63	65	73	66	69	71	88
		1981	108	113	128	138	100	109	121	126	116	117	135	152
22	JODHPUR	***1991***	72	75	83	86	74	77	79	82	69	71	89	96
		1981	108	111	114	131	108	111	107	120	107	111	122	143
23	KARAULI	***1991***	79	106	116	122	74	95	97	101	102	122	135	144
		1981	175	189	206	227	185	182	191	203	164	197	222	254
24	KOTA	***1991***	84	95	99	140	76	90	97	121	91	96	101	124
		1981	141	142	155	178	148	144	152	168	133	141	159	188
25	NAGAUR	***1991***	82	89	96	102	91	92	96	99	71	87	96	105
		1981	99	118	131	147	104	120	123	142	105	126	144	163
26	PALI	***1991***	111	128	137	156	97	123	124	140	127	136	152	174
		1981	166	168	182	218	161	167	175	208	170	170	189	229
27	RAJSAMAND	***1991***	92	113	120	129	71	103	114	122	109	127	139	146
		1981	179	177	173	189	200	191	176	194	156	163	169	184
28	S. MADHOPUR	***1991***	79	106	116	122	74	95	97	101	102	122	135	144
		1981	175	189	206	227	185	182	191	203	164	197	222	254
29	SIKAR	***1991***	57	70	74	78	61	62	69	74	51	78	80	83
		1981	106	127	128	145	106	127	116	129	106	127	142	162
30	SIROHI	***1991***	118	126	129	139	119	130	128	132	117	125	129	147
		1981	160	157	174	186	136	159	170	175	190	155	179	198
31	TONK	***1991***	123	127	136	149	109	123	137	146	129	134	136	157
		1981	164	203	217	233	177	218	213	232	152	188	222	233
32	UDAIPUR	***1991***	92	113	120	129	71	103	114	122	109	127	139	146
		1981	179	177	173	189	200	191	176	194	156	163	169	184
	RAJASTHAN	1991	**87**	**97**	**100**	**110**	**94**	**95**	**98**	**103**	**79**	**99**	**106**	**117**
		1981	**141**	**149**	**157**	**176**	**146**	**151**	**153**	**166**	**135**	**148**	**163**	**186**

Source: Occasional Paper No. 1 of 1997, District Level Estimates of Fertility and Child Mortality for 1991 and Their Inter Relations with Other Variables.

GENERAL ANNEX-XV

DISTRICT-WISE POPULATION CHARACTERISTICS: RAJASTHAN (2001)

S.No.	Name of Districts	Population, 2001 ('000' Number)						Percentage of Rural Pop. to Total Pop.	Sex-Ratio (No. of females per 1000 males)	Density of Pop. per sq. km.	Literacy Rate		
		Male	Female	Total	(% Share)	S.C.	S.T.				Male	Female	Total
1	2	3	4	5		6	7	8	9	10	11	12	13
1	Ajmer	1130	1052	2182	(3.9)	386	53	60	932	257	79.96	49.10	65.06
2	Alwar	1587	1406	2993	(5.3)	539	240	85	887	357	78.91	43.95	62.48
3	Banswara	761	741	1502	(2.7)	64	1085	93	978	298	60.24	27.86	44.22
4	Baran	535	487	1022	(1.8)	181	217	83	909	146	76.86	42.18	60.37
5	Barmer	1038	927	1965	(3.5)	309	119	93	896	69	73.64	43.91	59.65
6	Bharatpur	1130	968	2098	(3.7)	456	47	81	857	414	81.39	44.12	64.24
7	Bhilwara	1027	987	2014	(3.6)	317	181	79	964	192	68.12	33.47	51.09
8	Bikaner	886	788	1674	(3.0)	334	6	64	889	61	70.78	42.55	57.54
9	Bundi	503	458	963	(1.7)	174	195	81	908	173	72.17	37.76	55.80
10	Chittaurgarh	918	885	1804	(3.2)	251	388	84	966	166	71.82	36.45	54.37
11	Churu	988	936	1924	(3.4)	407	10	72	948	114	79.52	53.87	66.97
12	Dausa	693	623	1317	(2.3)	279	353	90	899	384	80.37	43.15	62.75
13	Dhaulpur	538	445	983	(1.7)	198	48	82	828	324	75.85	42.36	60.77
14	Dungarpur	548	560	1108	(2.0)	46	721	93	1027	294	66.19	31.22	48.32
15	Ganganagar	955	834	1789	(3.2)	603	15	75	873	224	75.49	52.69	64.84
16	Hanumangarh	801	717	1518	(2.7)	397	10	80	895	120	77.41	52.71	65.72
17	Jaipur	2768	2483	5251	(9.3)	778	413	51	897	471	83.58	56.18	70.63
18	Jaisalmer	279	229	508	(0.9)	74	28	85	821	13	66.89	32.25	51.40
19	Jalore	738	711	1449	(2.6)	261	127	92	968	136	65.10	27.53	46.51
20	Jhalawar	612	568	1180	(2.1)	185	142	86	928	190	74.29	40.39	57.98
21	Jhunjhunun	984	930	1914	(3.4)	309	37	79	946	323	86.61	60.10	73.61
22	Jodhpur	1514	1373	2887	(5.1)	456	80	66	908	126	73.86	39.18	57.38
23	Karauli	652	558	1210	(2.1)	280	271	86	858	218	80.93	45.44	64.59
24	Kota	828	741	1569	(2.8)	301	152	47	895	288	86.25	61.25	74.45
25	Nagaur	1425	1350	2775	(4.9)	545	6	83	951	157	75.33	40.45	58.26
26	Pali	919	901	1820	(3.2)	323	106	79	983	147	73.06	36.70	54.92
27	Rajsamand	493	494	987	(1.7)	123	129	87	1002	256	74.05	37.89	55.82
28	Sawai Madhopur	591	526	1117	(2.0)	223	241	81	889	248	76.75	35.44	57.34
29	Sikar	1173	1115	2288	(4.0)	340	63	79	951	296	85.20	56.70	71.19
30	Sirohi	438	413	851	(1.5)	163	211	82	944	166	70.58	37.37	54.39
31	Tonk	627	585	1212	(2.1)	233	146	79	936	168	71.25	32.30	52.39
32	Udaipur	1336	1297	2633	(4.7)	158	1260	81	972	196	74.47	43.71	59.26
	Total	**29420**	**27087**	**56507**	**100**	**9694**	**7098**	**77**	**922**	**165**	**76.46**	**44.34**	**61.03**

Source: Directorate of Census Operations, Jaipur.

DISTRICT-WISE NO. OF MEDICAL INSTITUTIONS AND BEDS (AS ON 31ST DEC. 2004): RAJASTHAN

S.No.	Name of Districts	No. of Medical Institutions (As on 31st Dec. 2004)								No. of Beds.	Average Area Served Per Medical Institution	Average Population Served Per Medical Institution	Average Population Served Per Bed
		Hospitals	Dispensaries	MCWCs	PHCs Rural	PHCs Urban	Aids Posts (Urban)	SHCs	Total				
1	2	3	4	5	6	7	8	9	10	11	12	13	13
1	Ajmer	14 (5)	12	7	48 (5)	2	1	279	363	2100	23	6010	1039
2	Alwar	9 (5)	6	4	83 (12)	2	—	459	563	1548	15	5315	1933
3	Banswara	2	6	1	57 (10)	1	—	334	401	942	13	3745	1594
4	Baran	5 (4)	2	—	36 (4)	—	—	197	240	622	29	4257	1643
5	Barmer	3	3	3	66 (9)	—	—	443	518	916	55	3793	2145
6	Bharatpur	4 (1)	5	3	57 (7)	—	—	362	431	1023	12	4875	2054
7	Bhilwara	8 (5)	7	2	72 (9)	1	1	391	482	1343	22	4178	1499
8	Bikaner	9 (2)	12	4	45 (5)	3	—	297	370	1879	74	4525	891
9	Bundi	4 (2)	4	3	28 (3)	1	1	174	215	497	26	4477	1937
10	Chittaurgarh	5 (2)	6	3	64 (10)	1	—	391	470	1102	23	3837	1637
11	Churu	10 (5)	5	5	59 (3)	4	1	349	433	1082	39	4443	1778
12	Dausa	3 (2)	1	3	32 (4)	—	—	232	271	486	13	4860	2710
13	Dhaulpur	1	3	2	25 (3)	—	—	159	190	404	16	5175	2434
14	Dungarpur	2	5	—	43 (7)	—	—	306	356	691	11	3111	1603
15	Ganganagar	4 (3)	7	1	44 (5)	1	—	348	405	876	27	4418	2043
16	Hanumangarh	3 (2)	2	4	42 (5)	1	—	272	324	654	30	4685	2321
17	Jaipur	28 (8)	41	17	93 (7)	4	2	506	691	5669	16	7599	926
18	Jaisalmer	3 (1)	5	1	16 (2)	—	—	127	152	360	253	3344	1412
19	Jalore	2	2	4	56 (8)	—	—	354	418	767	25	3466	1889
20	Jhalawar	5 (3)	3	3	35 (8)	—	—	228	274	860	23	4308	1372
21	Jhunjhunun	11 (8)	6	10	76 (4)	—	1	423	527	1127	11	3631	1698
22	Jodhpur	15 (3)	15	4	75 (10)	4	5	493	611	3152	37	4934	916
23	Karauli	2 (1)	3	1	27 (4)	—	—	225	258	466	20	4689	2596
24	Kota	9 (5)	11	1	30 (4)	2	—	159	212	1120	26	7399	1400
25	Nagaur	10 (6)	4	7	94 (8)	—	1	600	716	1406	25	3076	1974
26	Pali	9 (6)	5	11	71 (6)	—	—	414	510	1276	24	3569	1427
27	Rajsamand	3 (1)	1	—	40 (6)	—	—	205	249	739	19	3964	1336
28	Sawai Madhopur	2	2	2	26 (4)	1	—	197	230	468	22	4857	2387
29	Sikar	9 (8)	6	9	74 (8)	—	—	490	588	1312	13	3891	1744
30	Sirohi	4 (2)	3	1	26 (4)	—	—	187	221	509	23	3851	1672
31	Tonk	7 (4)	6	2	47 (3)	—	—	246	308	723	23	3934	1676
32	Udaipur	10 (1)	10	—	90 (16)	1	—	540	651	2754	19	4045	956
	Total	**215 (95)**	**209**	**118**	**1677 (203)**	**29**	**13**	**10387**	**12648**	**38873**	**27**	**4468**	**1454**

Note: Figures in brackets show No. of CHCs.
Source: Pragati Prativedan, 2004-05, Directorate of Medical & Health, Jaipur.

GENERAL ANNEX-XVII

DISTRICT-WISE TOTAL NO. OF PATIENTS TREATED IN GOVT. HOSPITALS: RAJASTHAN (2003)

S.No.	*Name of Districts*	*Patients Treated in Govt. Hospitals (in '000 No.)*			*Deaths*
		Outdoor	*Indoor*	*Total*	
1	*2*	*3*	*4*	*5*	*6*
1	Ajmer	1067	90	1157	2915
2	Alwar	1623	65	1688	812
3	Banswara	678	67	745	644
4	Baran	957	42	999	550
5	Barmer	552	25	577	470
6	Bharatpur	948	52	1000	662
7	Bhilwara	1347	81	1428	1392
8	Bikaner	1333	89	1422	2152
9	Bundi	514	35	549	413
10	Chittaurgarh	921	71	992	871
11	Churu	919	35	954	360
12	Dausa	713	24	737	134
13	Dhaulpur	393	27	420	402
14	Dungarpur	428	41	469	504
15	Ganganagar	924	22	946	625
16	Hanumangarh	705	16	721	305
17	Jaipur	3925	261	4186	7381
18	Jaisalmer	429	22	451	166
19	Jalore	579	19	598	169
20	Jhalawar	639	51	690	887
21	Jhunjhunun	984	28	1012	282
22	Jodhpur	1626	102	1728	3741
23	Karauli	482	41	523	342
24	Kota	1494	74	1568	2315
25	Nagaur	1129	30	1159	228
26	Pali	1026	41	1067	596
27	Rajsamand	503	30	533	148
28	Sawai Madhopur	516	44	560	459
29	Sikar	1199	43	1242	501
30	Sirohi	490	19	509	236
31	Tonk	764	34	798	258
32	Udaipur	1523	123	1646	2767
	Total	**31329**	**1743**	**33072**	**33687**

Source: Pragati Prativedan, 2004-05, Directorate of Medical & Health, Jaipur.

GENERAL ANNEX-XVIII

DISTRICT-WISE DETAILES OF BPL FAMILIES: RAJASTHAN

S. No.	Name of Districts	Detailes of BPL Families																	
		Total Rural Families	No. of Familes Below Poverty	Selected Families				Details of Families As Per Occupation						Other	Out of Total Families				
				S.C.	S.T.	Back Ward	Other	Self Employment							Widow	Handi-capped	Ceiling Surplus Land	Minority	Bonded Labour
								Agricultural Worker	Other Rural	Small Farmer	Marginal Farmer	Under Non Agri.	Rural Artisians						
1	2	3	4	5	6	7	8	9	10	11	12	13	14	15	16	17	18	19	20
1	Ajmer	237514	62932	16064	4003	33782	9083	26129	15204	4379	9086	2778	604	4752	4129	590	475	2268	—
2	Alwar	358627	78911	27168	6503	21120	24120	20395	14623	11110	20961	3592	2281	5949	5013	350	335	7193	20
3	Banswara	232657	169792	8875	149242	4914	6761	39612	12825	37741	64489	8939	750	5436	3436	917	11458	713	—
4	Baran	140172	45684	12934	13177	15805	3768	15420	9552	5249	10497	1944	539	2483	1382	360	1215	1087	136
5	Barmer	273750	78603	20082	9050	16745	32726	8471	4574	19768	39802	1925	613	3450	3771	261	557	6935	8
6	Bharatpur	249257	45869	17200	1327	12405	14937	15157	12206	3317	9332	1866	934	3057	3001	193	37	4521	3
7	Bhilwara	301451	104663	27253	21727	44025	11658	28922	19352	31149	33080	3258	920	6618	3733	46	5793	1450	1464
8	Bikaner	151505	55811	19426	621	10754	25010	15118	5318	9089	18886	2614	2737	2049	1602	225	897	2001	—
9	Bundi	121938	43918	12958	9993	17015	3952	9578	8874	6839	11644	3240	1640	2103	1146	436	346	662	—
10	Chittaurgarh	271184	133253	28411	48016	36650	20176	34658	17225	28020	39990	7183	1911	4266	4515	683	1926	1557	5459
11	Churu	224261	64191	30646	402	11499	21644	22021	6252	13568	16409	2187	1343	2411	3271	929	362	1321	158
12	Dausa	172585	40345	12983	9818	13016	4528	11803	8659	5744	10584	1602	898	1055	2385	—	2741	706	—
13	Dhaulpur	89060	31047	9697	1815	13899	5636	11715	7250	2580	5151	1648	232	2471	1481	10	2188	303	7840
14	Dungarpur	182900	130459	7249	106457	6380	10373	46600	14179	18795	36536	8896	1862	3591	4137	1681	11289	166	1938
15	Ganganagar	189467	40281	26023	63	8058	6137	25033	6997	2191	2105	1132	719	2104	1970	226	307	195	917
16	Hanumangarh	173138	37878	20099	151	8671	8957	23295	3509	5904	3472	596	370	732	1595	161	6	730	1
17	Jaipur	396800	61631	18671	9321	21108	13431	18521	24483	3575	3285	2390	1328	8849	1116	134	2433	5103	7
18	Jaisalmer	72217	18857	3332	1607	3367	10551	7194	6737	1235	1021	1241	148	1281	1396	160	773	5582	—
19	Jalore	179058	67150	21889	10664	20224	14373	16857	11375	17457	13326	3077	1633	3425	2416	353	959	1725	—
20	Jhalawar	166203	55190	16203	9671	18071	11245	19961	8607	8191	15480	1190	479	1282	2687	149	10	1766	1
21	Jhunjhunun	238401	25202	10675	1034	7430	6063	8592	7005	2066	4818	471	541	1709	2190	103	79	724	13
22	Jodhpur	255480	34744	10492	3577	7596	13079	7205	5560	9376	7781	1425	496	2901	2205	367	236	1059	86
23	Karauli	148473	60599	18520	14707	16906	10466	12530	13110	12085	15667	3324	567	3316	589	1	4223	1293	—
24	Kota	117934	37867	13134	4921	15682	4130	10945	16221	2377	2081	1650	580	4013	485	20	141	1805	45
25	Nagaur	339825	56157	27820	297	13597	15058	12861	8357	7221	20871	2584	1571	4699	2801	93	16	1588	110
26	Pali	268280	64414	22443	10439	23979	7553	20124	19317	6845	9201	3212	984	4731	4210	432	1178	1208	160
27	Rajsamand	162062	57961	10037	15355	24055	8514	15618	8677	6520	19399	3239	989	3598	2794	262	27	297	1
28	Sawai Madhopur	138336	51840	15306	9666	19002	7866	10425	8790	13419	12065	2061	1043	4037	2121	343	117	2637	—
29	Sikar	248931	28460	12281	1636	6937	7606	7267	5431	4231	7722	1142	422	2245	2328	105	19	646	—
30	Sirohi	116265	36060	10176	17940	5894	2050	7304	6932	5028	13106	1142	298	2250	705	20	679	419	—
31	Tonk	166625	54876	16316	10857	19404	8299	11102	9884	12046	13651	2916	1315	3962	1808	629	107	1431	—
32	Udaipur	384185	222915	13578	157539	22409	29388	50842	34459	38482	72546	12563	4233	9790	6445	1571	459	868	—
	Total	**6768541**	**2097560**	**537941**	**661596**	**520399**	**379138**	**591275**	**361544**	**355597**	**564044**	**97027**	**34980**	**114615**	**82863**	**11810**	**51388**	**59959**	**18367**

Source: BPL Census Survey, 1997, GoR, Jaipur.

GENERAL ANNEX-XIX

RANKING OF PSS BY TOTAL POPULATION: RAJASTHAN, 2001

(Descending Order)

RANK	P.CODE	PANCHAYAT SAMITIES NAME	TOTAL RURAL POP.
1	2	3	4
		VERY HIGH (>=160,000)	
1	117	**HANUMANGARH**	628123
2	162	**OSIAN**	422181
3	109	**ANUPGARH**	417746
4	66	**BIKANER**	374802
5	118	**NOHAR**	365762
6	140	**SANCHORE**	342120
7	213	**NEEM KA THANA**	317049
8	176	**DIDWANA**	285031
9	70	**NOKHA**	279343
10	123	**GOVINDGARH**	275780
11	122	**DUDU**	272517
12	96	**DAUSA**	271907
13	178	**KUCHAMAN**	268146
14	90	**RAJGARH**	267403
15	95	**BANDIKUI**	267016
16	38	**BALOTRA**	265596
17	102	**DHAULPUR**	262456
18	165	**HINDAUN**	262403
19	208	**DANTA RAMGARH**	262183
20	119	**AMBER**	262029
21	74	**TALERA**	258916
22	233	**KHERWARA**	254301
23	93	**SUJANGARH**	253207
24	97	**LALSOT**	251370
25	42	**DHORIMANNA**	250929
26	124	**JAMWA RAMGARH**	250132
27	108	**SIMALWARA**	241099
28	39	**BARMER**	238075
29	25	**GARHI**	237521
30	44	**SINDHARI**	236545
31	7	**PISANGAN**	236459
32	51	**NAGAR PAHARI**	236329
33	105	**BICHHIWARA**	236114
34	155	**UDAIPURWATI**	235280
35	168	**SAPOTRA**	232513
36	26	**GHATOL**	230344
37	163	**PHALODI**	229892
38	120	**BASSI**	229639
39	160	**LUNI**	229097
40	126	**KOTPUTLI**	228470
41	230	**GIRWA**	227623
42	21	**TIJARA**	226974
43	14	**LACHHMANGARH**	225836
44	41	**CHOHTAN**	225754
45	177	**JAYAL**	224944
46	183	**NAGAUR**	224815
47	92	**SARDARSHAHAR**	222979
48	166	**KARAULI**	222621
49	22	**UMREN**	221794
50	116	**BHADRA**	220582
51	18	**RAMGARH**	220219
52	211	**KHANDELA**	218560
53	153	**NAWALGARH**	217636
54	69	**LUNKARANSAR**	217341
55	207	**SAWAI MADHOPUR**	215810
56	152	**KHETRI**	214474
57	9	**BANSURE**	214351
58	30	**TALWARA**	213727
59	45	**SIWANA**	213648
60	115	**SURATGARH**	213384
61	237	**SARADA**	212181
62	48	**KAMAN**	212139
63	99	**SIKRAI**	211779
64	11	**KATHUMAR**	211689
65	52	**RUPBAS**	211147
65	141	**SAYLA**	211147
67	215	**SRI MADHOPUR**	210980
68	40	**BAYTOO**	210345
69	209	**DHOND**	209919
70	204	**BONLI**	209833
71	128	**SAMBHAR**	209528
72	68	**KOLAYAT**	207749
73	131	**VIRATNAGAR**	206414
74	214	**PIPRALI**	206064
75	144	**JHALRAPATAN**	205868
76	149	**BUHANA**	204411
77	225	**TONK**	204362
78	229	**DHARIAWAD**	203605
79	158	**BHOPALGARH**	202321
80	54	**WEIR**	202199
81	228	**BHINDER**	201832
82	101	**BASERI**	201777
83	87	**PRATAPGARH**	201229
84	61	**MANDALGARH**	199935
85	180	**MAKRANA**	199671
86	15	**MANDAWAR**	197582
87	182	**MUNDWA**	197532
88	60	**MANDAL**	197500
89	212	**LACHHMANGARH**	197022
90	236	**SALUMBAR**	196614
91	235	**MAVLI**	194148
92	169	**TODABHIM**	194094
93	232	**JHADOL**	193810
94	210	**FATEHPUR**	193473
95	107	**SAGWARA**	192681
96	55	**ASIND**	192346
97	103	**RAJAKHERA**	191812
98	46	**BAYANA**	191632
99	175	**DEGANA**	190085
100	20	**THANAGAZI**	189977
101	71	**HINDOLI**	189290
102	188	**JAITARAN**	186938
103	184	**PARBATSAR**	186413
104	217	**PINDWARA**	184803
105	136	**BHINMAL**	184751
106	104	**ASPUR**	184508
107	186	**BALI**	183802
108	234	**KOTRA**	183504
109	181	**MERTA**	183429
110	67	**DUNGARGARH**	182819
111	191	RAIPUR	182004
112	130	SHAHPURA	181498
113	189	KHARCHI/MARWAR JUN.	181445
114	159	BILARA	180550
115	185	RIYAN	179629
116	205	GANGAPUR	179209
117	98	MAHWA	179173
118	72	KESHORAIPATAN	178625
119	43	SHEO	178539
120	135	AHORE	177342
121	222	MALPURA	176932
122	24	BAGIDORA	176729
123	151	JHUNJHUNUN	176693
124	110	GANGANAGAR	176517
125	154	SURAJGARH	175820
126	218	REODAR	175344
127	156	BALESAR	174179
128	199	KHAMNOR	172395
129	106	DUNGARPUR	172385
130	147	PIRAWA	171897
131	8	SRINAGAR	170142
132	221	DEOLI	169271
133	82	CHITTAURGARH	167960
134	58	JAHAZPUR	167782
135	53	SEWAR	167641
136	12	KISHANGARH BAS	167495
137	143	DAG	167192
138	134	SANKRA	165376
139	223	NIWAI	165298
140	65	SUWANA	164004
141	139	RANIWARA	163349
142	164	SHERGARH	162656
143	127	PHAGI	161610
144	146	MANOHARTHANA	161425
145	121	CHAKSU	161140
146	50	NADBAI	161111
		HIGH (140,000-160,000)	
147	6	MASOODA	159600
148	91	RATANGARH	158090
149	179	LADNU	158026
150	3	JAWAJA	157901
151	113	RAISINGHNAGAR	157334
152	157	BAP	157290
153	73	NAINWA	156227
154	194	SOJAT	155889
155	171	ITAWA	155646
156	49	KUMHER	155122
157	2	BHINAY	155111
158	47	DEEG	154862
159	5	KISHANGARH	153474
160	145	KHANPUR	153370
161	150	CHIRAWA	152843
162	142	BAKANI	152329
163	89	CHURU	152178
164	231	GOGUNDA	151575
165	28	PEEPALKHOONT	151273
166	161	MANDOR	151257
167	94	TARANAGAR	151006
168	100	BARI	150595
169	174	SULTANPUR	150587
170	206	KHANDAR	150136
171	203	BAMANWAS	149429
172	64	SHAHPURA	148955
173	31	ANTA	148759
174	59	KOTRI	148702
175	173	SANGOD	146951
176	114	SADULSHAHAR	146629
177	17	RAJGARH	144726
178	172	LADPURA	144691
179	16	NIMRANA	143329
180	148	ALSISAR	141416
181	4	KEKRI	140921
182	202	RAJSAMAND	140520
		MEDIUM (120,000-140,000)	
183	10	BEHROR	139503
184	27	KUSHALGARH	138970
185	133	SAM	138679
186	195	SUMERPUR	137999
187	197	BHIM	137578
188	19	RENI	136491
189	86	NIMBAHERA	135391
190	36	KISHANGANJ	135218
191	29	SAJJANGARH	134456
192	1	ARAIN	133386
193	226	UNIARA	132509
194	170	CHECHAT	132073
195	137	JALOR	131827
196	200	KUMBHALGARH	131346
197	129	SANGANER	131301
198	138	JASWANTPURA	128410
199	35	CHHIPABAROD	127858
200	132	JAISALMER	127798
201	32	ATRU	127043
202	167	NADOTI	126089
203	220	SIROHI	125589
204	227	BARGAON	123802
205	112	PADAMPUR	121362
		LOW (100,000-120,000)	
206	75	ARNOD	119837
207	13	KOTKASIM	117687
208	216	ABU ROAD	114818
209	23	ANANDPURI	111206
210	201	RAILMAGRA	110435
211	224	TODARAISINGH	110131
212	37	SHAHBAD	108146
213	78	BHADESAR	107393
214	192	RANI STATION	106504
215	56	BANERA	106222
216	33	BARAN	103142
217	111	KARANPUR	103094
218	193	ROHAT	102599
219	187	DESURI	102245
220	77	BEGUN	102011
221	81	CHHOTI SADRI	100067
		VERY LOW (<100,000)	
222	219	SHEOGANJ	99663
223	34	CHHABRA	99472
224	63	SAHARA	98050
225	57	HURDA	91088
226	83	DUNGLA	89975
227	190	PALI	89939
228	125	JHOTWARA	88946
229	76	BARI SADRI	88841
230	84	GANGRAR	88640
231	196	AMET	88162
232	85	KAPASAN	84531
233	62	RAIPUR	84354
234	79	BHAINSRORGARH	80379
235	198	DEOGARH	77865
236	88	RASHMI	75326
237	80	BHOPALSAGAR	72675
RAJASTHAN		**TOTAL**	**43,292,813**
		AVERAGE	**182,670**
		% AGE OF AAPs	**46.41**

BOLD: Equal/Above Average Panchayat Samities (AAPs)

Source : General Annex V.

ANNEX-8.1

RANKING OF PSS BY PERCENTAGE OF RURAL POPULATION SERVED BY MEDICAL AMENITIES: RAJASTHAN, 1991

(Descending Order)

RANK	PANCHAYAT SAMITIES P.CODE	PANCHAYAT SAMITIES NAME	%
1	2	3	4
		VERY HIGH (>60)	
1	123	**GOVINDGARH**	78.48
2	159	**BILARA**	75.35
3	56	**BANERA**	74.52
4	186	**BALI**	73.69
5	153	**NAWALGARH**	73.61
6	192	**RANI STATION**	72.90
7	57	**HURDA**	72.82
8	195	**SUMERPUR**	71.11
9	209	**DHOND**	70.61
10	187	**DESURI**	69.91
11	4	**KEKRI**	66.66
12	7	**PISANGAN**	66.45
13	156	**BALESAR**	65.93
14	152	**KHETRI**	64.87
15	63	**SAHARA**	64.86
16	208	**DANTA RAMGARH**	64.52
17	107	**SAGWARA**	64.03
18	137	**JALOR**	63.83
19	66	**BIKANER**	62.59
20	141	**SAYLA**	62.45
21	155	**UDAIPURWATI**	62.41
22	219	**SHEOGANJ**	62.27
23	67	**DUNGARGARH**	61.86
24	117	**HANUMANGARH**	61.81
25	135	**AHORE**	61.62
25	214	**PIPRALI**	61.62
27	5	**KISHANGARH**	61.56
28	230	**GIRWA**	61.35
29	213	**NEEM KA THANA**	61.28
30	2	**BHINAY**	61.21
31	199	**KHAMNOR**	61.20
32	60	**MANDAL**	60.90
33	181	**MERTA**	60.84
34	188	**JAITARAN**	60.77
35	58	**JAHAZPUR**	60.42
36	201	**RAILMAGRA**	60.35
		HIGH (50-60)	
37	221	**DEOLI**	59.57
38	237	**SARADA**	59.24
39	62	**RAIPUR**	58.84
40	49	**KUMHER**	58.39
41	235	**MAVLI**	58.29
42	116	**BHADRA**	58.13
43	158	**BHOPALGARH**	57.94
44	25	**GARHI**	57.70
45	130	**SHAHPURA**	57.66
46	222	**MALPURA**	57.64
47	211	**KHANDELA**	57.41
48	205	**GANGAPUR**	57.32
49	88	**RASHMI**	57.13
50	183	**NAGAUR**	56.47
51	189	**KHARCHI/MARWAR**	56.45
52	164	**SHERGARH**	56.34
53	131	**VIRATNAGAR**	55.76
54	55	**ASIND**	55.33
55	150	**CHIRAWA**	55.30
56	102	**DHAULPUR**	54.95
57	148	**ALSISAR**	54.82
58	94	**TARANAGAR**	54.77
59	160	**LUNI**	54.43
60	217	**PINDWARA**	54.31
61	64	**SHAHPURA**	54.26
62	20	**THANAGAZI**	54.16
63	91	**RATANGARH**	54.03
64	6	**MASOODA**	53.89
65	179	**LADNU**	53.60
66	118	**NOHAR**	53.42
67	110	**GANGANAGAR**	53.05
68	65	**SUWANA**	52.81
69	194	**SOJAT**	52.75
70	215	**SRI MADHOPUR**	52.56
71	80	**BHOPALSAGAR**	52.38
72	190	**PALI**	52.13
73	70	**NOKHA**	51.78
74	10	**BEHROR**	51.70
74	185	**RIYAN**	51.70
76	220	**SIROHI**	51.63
77	61	**MANDALGARH**	51.48
78	114	**SADULSHAHAR**	51.17
79	59	**KOTRI**	51.05
80	203	**BAMANWAS**	50.75

RANK	PANCHAYAT SAMITIES P.CODE	PANCHAYAT SAMITIES NAME	%
1	2	3	4
81	167	**NADOTI**	50.63
82	178	**KUCHAMAN**	50.62
83	30	**TALWARA**	50.26
		MEDIUM (40-50)	
84	104	**ASPUR**	49.97
85	16	**NIMRANA**	49.90
86	165	**HINDAUN**	49.73
87	1	**ARAIN**	49.69
88	32	**ATRU**	49.63
89	24	**BAGIDORA**	49.32
90	177	**JAYAL**	49.20
91	101	**BASERI**	48.81
92	105	**BICHHIWARA**	48.60
93	224	**TODARAISINGH**	48.57
94	170	**CHECHAT**	48.55
95	93	**SUJANGARH**	48.32
96	8	**SRINAGAR**	48.26
97	197	**BHIM**	47.94
98	175	**DEGANA**	47.79
99	210	**FATEHPUR**	47.62
100	17	**RAJGARH**	47.48
101	126	**KOTPUTLI**	47.34
102	207	**SAWAI MADHOPUR**	47.33
103	54	**WEIR**	47.23
103	180	**MAKRANA**	47.23
105	212	**LACHHMANGARH**	47.16
106	182	**MUNDWA**	46.95
107	206	**KHANDAR**	46.80
108	228	**BHINDER**	46.70
109	151	**JHUNJHUNUN**	46.68
110	127	**PHAGI**	46.57
111	128	**SAMBHAR**	46.52
112	124	**JAMWA RAMGARH**	46.40
113	138	**JASWANTPURA**	46.36
114	236	**SALUMBAR**	46.31
115	202	RAJSAMAND	45.94
116	232	JHADOL	45.76
117	45	SIWANA	45.72
118	168	SAPOTRA	45.68
119	184	PARBATSAR	45.59
120	122	DUDU	45.57
121	120	BASSI	45.36
122	31	ANTA	45.34
123	171	ITAWA	45.23
124	69	LUNKARANSAR	44.96
125	169	TODABHIM	44.80
126	28	PEEPALKHOONT	44.79
127	15	MANDAWAR	44.44
128	68	KOLAYAT	44.43
129	227	BARGAON	44.27
130	172	LADPURA	44.19
131	11	KATHUMAR	44.10
132	46	BAYANA	44.02
133	9	BANSURE	43.66
134	176	DIDWANA	43.15
135	225	TONK	43.08
136	174	SULTANPUR	42.97
137	204	BONLI	42.81
138	99	SIKRAI	42.43
139	26	GHATOL	42.31
140	162	OSIAN	42.29
141	52	RUPBAS	42.28
142	73	NAINWA	42.07
143	96	DAUSA	41.91
144	149	BUHANA	41.81
145	233	KHERWARA	41.44
146	108	SIMALWARA	41.42
147	115	SURATGARH	41.22
148	196	AMET	41.18
149	13	KOTKASIM	40.96
150	19	RENI	40.87
151	106	DUNGARPUR	40.56
152	22	UMREN	40.52
153	112	PADAMPUR	40.47
154	85	KAPASAN	40.30
155	119	AMBER	40.10
156	223	NIWAI	40.04
157	132	JAISALMER	40.03
		LOW (30-40)	
158	200	KUMBHALGARH	39.80
159	75	ARNOD	39.79
160	113	RAISINGHNAGAR	39.53

RANK	PANCHAYAT SAMITIES P.CODE	PANCHAYAT SAMITIES NAME	%
1	2	3	4
161	12	KISHANGARH BAS	39.46
161	23	ANANDPURI	39.46
163	84	GANGRAR	39.45
164	145	KHANPUR	39.25
165	98	MAHWA	39.16
166	129	SANGANER	39.08
167	218	REODAR	38.66
168	226	UNIARA	38.55
169	72	KESHORAIPATAN	38.22
170	173	SANGOD	38.03
171	166	KARAULI	37.77
172	142	BAKANI	37.62
173	36	KISHANGANJ	37.27
173	136	BHINMAL	37.27
175	121	CHAKSU	37.06
176	89	CHURU	37.04
177	125	JHOTWARA	37.02
177	143	DAG	37.02
179	231	GOGUNDA	36.94
180	18	RAMGARH	36.72
181	78	BHADESAR	36.66
182	163	PHALODI	36.59
183	83	DUNGLA	36.47
184	41	CHOHTAN	36.45
185	100	BARI	36.22
186	191	RAIPUR	36.11
187	140	SANCHORE	35.96
188	139	RANIWARA	35.35
189	154	SURAJGARH	35.21
190	95	BANDIKUI	35.14
190	147	PIRAWA	35.14
192	74	TALERA	34.98
193	77	BEGUN	34.91
194	229	DHARIAWAD	34.79
195	38	BALOTRA	34.77
196	193	ROHAT	34.73
197	50	NADBAI	34.37
198	111	KARANPUR	34.03
199	53	SEWAR	33.86
200	14	LACHHMANGARH	33.66
201	90	RAJGARH	33.61
202	3	JAWAJA	33.60
203	76	BARI SADRI	33.53
204	82	CHITTAURGARH	33.39
205	144	JHALRAPATAN	33.21
206	87	PRATAPGARH	33.18
207	47	DEEG	33.08
208	92	SARDARSHAHAR	33.05
209	134	SANKRA	32.92
210	33	BARAN	31.62
211	97	LALSOT	31.00
212	133	SAM	30.42
213	21	TIJARA	30.22
		VERY LOW (<30)	
214	48	KAMAN	29.99
215	35	CHHIPABAROD	29.30
216	37	SHAHBAD	29.04
217	198	DEOGARH	28.25
218	146	MANOHARTHANA	28.21
219	103	RAJAKHERA	28.16
220	161	MANDOR	27.67
221	71	HINDOLI	26.47
222	157	BAP	26.40
223	86	NIMBAHERA	25.09
224	44	SINDHARI	25.07
225	51	NAGAR PAHARI	24.36
226	34	CHHABRA	24.20
227	234	KOTRA	23.73
228	79	BHAINSRORGARH	23.52
229	29	SAJJANGARH	23.46
230	109	ANUPGARH	23.07
231	43	SHEO	21.26
232	42	DHORIMANNA	20.23
233	39	BARMER	20.21
234	81	CHHOTI SADRI	20.08
235	27	KUSHALGARH	16.90
236	40	BAYTOO	15.49
237	216	ABU ROAD	4.41
		RAJASTHAN	**46.17**
		% AGE OF AAPs	**48.10**

BOLD: Equal/Above Average Panchayat Samities (AAPs)

Source : General Annex III.

ANNEX-8.2

RANKING OF PSS BY PERCENTAGE OF INHABITED VILLAGES HAVING MEDICAL AMENITIES: RAJASTHAN, 1991

(Descending Order)

RANK	PANCHAYAT SAMITIES P.CODE	NAME	%
1	2	3	4
		<u>**VERY HIGH (>50)**</u>	
1	153	**NAWALGARH**	54.29
2	209	**DHOND**	50.93
		<u>**HIGH (40-50)**</u>	
3	159	**BILARA**	48.10
4	123	**GOVINDGARH**	47.37
5	195	**SUMERPUR**	46.03
6	164	**SHERGARH**	46.00
7	137	**JALOR**	45.45
8	7	**PISANGAN**	44.74
9	192	**RANI STATION**	43.84
10	56	**BANERA**	42.68
11	156	**BALESAR**	42.65
12	186	**BALI**	41.57
13	213	**NEEM KA THANA**	41.26
14	152	**KHETRI**	41.25
15	57	**HURDA**	41.18
16	102	**DHAULPUR**	40.38
		<u>**MEDIUM (30-40)**</u>	
17	67	**DUNGARGARH**	40.00
18	187	**DESURI**	39.47
19	215	**SRI MADHOPUR**	39.34
20	130	**SHAHPURA**	39.24
21	2	**BHINAY**	39.17
22	141	**SAYLA**	38.96
23	25	**GARHI**	38.04
24	4	**KEKRI**	37.23
25	155	**UDAIPURWATI**	37.04
25	208	**DANTA RAMGARH**	37.04
27	91	**RATANGARH**	34.37
28	188	**JAITARAN**	33.70
29	199	**KHAMNOR**	33.33
30	235	**MAVLI**	33.11
31	5	**KISHANGARH**	32.73
32	107	**SAGWARA**	32.68
33	8	**SRINAGAR**	32.63
34	49	**KUMHER**	32.43
35	135	**AHORE**	32.41
36	158	**BHOPALGARH**	32.14
37	165	**HINDAUN**	31.93
38	211	**KHANDELA**	31.90
39	63	**SAHARA**	31.87
39	214	**PIPRALI**	31.87
41	205	**GANGAPUR**	31.30
42	194	**SOJAT**	31.25
43	237	**SARADA**	31.12
44	126	**KOTPUTLI**	31.09
45	58	**JAHAZPUR**	30.94
46	45	**SIWANA**	30.93
47	222	**MALPURA**	30.89
48	150	**CHIRAWA**	30.49
49	219	**SHEOGANJ**	30.30
50	104	**ASPUR**	30.28
51	179	**LADNU**	30.21
		<u>**LOW (20-30)**</u>	
52	210	**FATEHPUR**	29.79
53	217	**PINDWARA**	29.59
54	178	**KUCHAMAN**	29.45
55	16	**NIMRANA**	29.41
56	62	**RAIPUR**	29.07
57	10	**BEHROR**	28.89
57	201	**RAILMAGRA**	28.89
59	221	**DEOLI**	28.66
60	183	**NAGAUR**	28.57
61	66	**BIKANER**	28.39
62	64	**SHAHPURA**	28.19
63	60	**MANDAL**	27.85
63	106	**DUNGARPUR**	27.85
65	70	**NOKHA**	27.78
65	138	**JASWANTPURA**	27.78
65	184	**PARBATSAR**	27.78
68	230	**GIRWA**	27.67
69	93	**SUJANGARH**	27.45
70	167	**NADOTI**	27.38
71	191	**RAIPUR**	27.18
72	6	**MASOODA**	27.01
73	110	**GANGANAGAR**	26.97
74	54	**WEIR**	26.76
74	169	**TODABHIM**	26.76
76	55	**ASIND**	26.60
77	160	**LUNI**	26.56
78	212	**LACHHMANGARH**	26.47
79	24	**BAGIDORA**	26.28
79	189	**KHARCHI/MARWAR JUN.**	26.28
81	131	**VIRATNAGAR**	26.27
82	190	**PALI**	26.25
83	15	**MANDAWAR**	26.06
84	181	**MERTA**	26.04
85	185	**RIYAN**	25.83
86	162	**OSIAN**	25.75
87	220	**SIROHI**	25.61
88	163	**PHALODI**	25.58
89	88	**RASHMI**	25.32
90	89	**CHURU**	24.75
91	105	**BICHHIWARA**	24.71
92	59	**KOTRI**	24.66
92	175	**DEGANA**	24.66
94	149	**BUHANA**	24.59
95	182	**MUNDWA**	24.55
96	65	**SUWANA**	24.43
97	120	**BASSI**	24.40
98	151	**JHUNJHUNUN**	24.36
99	30	**TALWARA**	24.30
100	46	**BAYANA**	23.90
101	224	**TODARAISINGH**	23.85
102	232	**JHADOL**	23.83
103	1	**ARAIN**	23.77
104	177	**JAYAL**	23.48
105	94	**TARANAGAR**	23.42
106	52	**RUPBAS**	23.40
107	236	**SALUMBAR**	23.38
108	154	**SURAJGARH**	23.33
109	128	**SAMBHAR**	23.08
109	216	**ABU ROAD**	23.08
111	100	**BARI**	23.02
112	148	**ALSISAR**	23.01
113	101	**BASERI**	22.95
114	140	**SANCHORE**	22.78
115	176	**DIDWANA**	22.75
116	28	**PEEPALKHOONT**	22.58
117	32	**ATRU**	22.22
118	197	**BHIM**	22.02
119	233	**KHERWARA**	21.99
120	113	**RAISINGHNAGAR**	21.81
121	124	**JAMWA RAMGARH**	21.65
122	20	**THANAGAZI**	21.62
123	134	**SANKRA**	21.54
124	136	**BHINMAL**	21.52
125	85	**KAPASAN**	21.50
126	92	**SARDARSHAHAR**	21.18
127	23	**ANANDPURI**	21.14
128	119	**AMBER**	21.13
129	200	**KUMBHALGARH**	21.12
130	50	**NADBAI**	21.05
131	227	**BARGAON**	20.98
132	11	**KATHUMAR**	20.89
133	180	**MAKRANA**	20.83
134	53	SEWAR	20.13
134	207	SAWAI MADHOPUR	20.13
136	12	KISHANGARH BAS	20.00
136	13	KOTKASIM	20.00
136	22	UMREN	20.00
136	202	RAJSAMAND	20.00
		<u>**VERY LOW (<20)**</u>	
140	170	CHECHAT	19.86
141	9	BANSURE	19.85
142	203	BAMANWAS	19.70
143	3	JAWAJA	19.69
144	61	MANDALGARH	19.63
145	90	RAJGARH	19.51
146	116	BHADRA	19.47
147	166	KARAULI	19.39
148	139	RANIWARA	19.28
149	69	LUNKARANSAR	19.23
150	196	AMET	19.12
151	193	ROHAT	18.99
152	99	SIKRAI	18.84
153	48	KAMAN	18.72
154	168	SAPOTRA	18.66
155	112	PADAMPUR	18.64
156	41	CHOHTAN	18.56
157	172	LADPURA	18.49
157	231	GOGUNDA	18.49
159	127	PHAGI	18.45
160	225	TONK	18.15
161	18	RAMGARH	18.13
162	122	DUDU	18.10
163	80	BHOPALSAGAR	18.07
164	206	KHANDAR	17.95
165	121	CHAKSU	17.83
165	204	BONLI	17.83
167	31	ANTA	17.69
168	118	NOHAR	17.68
169	108	SIMALWARA	17.35
170	218	REODAR	17.21
171	68	KOLAYAT	17.16
172	147	PIRAWA	17.00
173	174	SULTANPUR	16.87
174	74	TALERA	16.86
175	125	JHOTWARA	16.67
176	17	RAJGARH	16.18
177	171	ITAWA	16.15
178	157	BAP	16.13
179	129	SANGANER	16.10
180	26	GHATOL	16.06
180	132	JAISALMER	16.06
182	96	DAUSA	15.84
183	72	KESHORAIPATAN	15.74
184	19	RENI	15.69
185	103	RAJAKHERA	15.65
186	143	DAG	15.45
187	98	MAHWA	15.33
188	33	BARAN	15.31
189	117	HANUMANGARH	15.30
190	161	MANDOR	15.24
191	47	DEEG	15.00
192	73	NAINWA	14.86
193	114	SADULSHAHAR	14.85
194	38	BALOTRA	14.81
195	228	BHINDER	14.77
196	146	MANOHARTHANA	14.60
197	144	JHALRAPATAN	14.54
198	111	KARANPUR	14.50
199	95	BANDIKUI	14.49
200	145	KHANPUR	14.21
201	29	SAJJANGARH	13.74
202	14	LACHHMANGARH	13.69
203	115	SURATGARH	13.68
204	173	SANGOD	13.64
205	142	BAKANI	13.48
206	87	PRATAPGARH	13.44
207	42	DHORIMANNA	13.10
208	226	UNIARA	13.09
209	21	TIJARA	13.07
210	75	ARNOD	12.87
211	83	DUNGLA	12.75
212	84	GANGRAR	12.60
213	223	NIWAI	12.57
214	44	SINDHARI	12.50
215	35	CHHIPABAROD	12.02
216	51	NAGAR PAHARI	11.98
217	36	KISHANGANJ	11.93
218	77	BEGUN	11.87
219	71	HINDOLI	11.49
220	198	DEOGARH	11.45
221	39	BARMER	11.32
222	34	CHHABRA	11.05
223	229	DHARIAWAD	10.98
224	43	SHEO	10.78
225	78	BHADESAR	10.56
226	76	BARI SADRI	10.42
227	133	SAM	9.96
228	97	LALSOT	9.90
229	27	KUSHALGARH	9.62
230	37	SHAHBAD	8.80
231	82	CHITTAURGARH	7.80
232	234	KOTRA	7.62
233	109	ANUPGARH	7.61
234	79	BHAINSRORGARH	7.33
234	86	NIMBAHERA	7.33
236	40	BAYTOO	6.85
237	81	CHHOTI SADRI	6.38
		RAJASTHAN	**20.68**
		% AGE OF AAPs	**56.11**

BOLD: Equal/Above Average Panchayat Samities (AAPs)
Source: General Annex IV.

ANNEX-8.3

RANKING OF PSS BY TOTAL NO. OF MEDICAL INSTITUTIONS.: RAJASTHAN, 1991

(Descending Order)

RANK	P.CODE	PANCHAYAT SAMITIES NAME	MEDICAL INSTITUTIONS
1	2	3	4
		VERY HIGH (>80)	
1	25	GARHI	104
2	61	MANDALGARH	100
3	104	ASPUR	88
4	208	DANTA RAMGARH	81
		HIGH (60-80)	
5	232	JHADOL	79
5	233	KHERWARA	79
7	7	PISANGAN	78
8	107	SAGWARA	74
9	60	MANDAL	72
9	30	TALWARA	72
11	237	SARADA	71
12	105	BICHHIWARA	68
13	26	GHATOL	66
14	209	DHOND	65
14	213	NEEM KA THANA	65
16	228	BHINDER	64
16	143	DAG	64
16	58	JAHAZPUR	64
16	235	MAVLI	64
20	24	BAGIDORA	62
20	106	DUNGARPUR	62
20	5	KISHANGARH	62
23	123	GOVINDGARH	61
23	52	RUPBAS	61
25	178	KUCHAMAN	60
25	113	RAISINGHNAGAR	60
		MEDIUM (40-60)	
27	32	ATRU	59
27	186	BALI	59
27	2	BHINAY	59
27	199	KHAMNOR	59
27	189	KHARCHI/MARWAR JUN.	59
27	59	KOTRI	59
27	98	MAHWA	59
27	207	SAWAI MADHOPUR	59
27	115	SURATGARH	59
36	162	OSIAN	58
36	87	PRATAPGARH	58
36	54	WEIR	58
39	176	DIDWANA	57
39	57	HURDA	57
39	144	JHALRAPATAN	57
39	74	TALERA	57
43	175	DEGANA	56
43	236	SALUMBAR	56
43	64	SHAHPURA	56
43	93	SUJANGARH	56
47	230	GIRWA	55
47	4	KEKRI	55
47	118	NOHAR	55
50	135	AHORE	54
50	187	DESURI	54
50	205	GANGAPUR	54
50	117	HANUMANGARH	54
54	177	JAYAL	53
54	191	RAIPUR	53
56	221	DEOLI	52
56	90	RAJGARH	52
56	192	RANI STATION	52
56	128	SAMBHAR	52
56	225	TONK	52
61	66	BIKANER	51
61	159	BILARA	51
61	124	JAMWA RAMGARH	51
61	108	SIMALWARA	51
65	122	DUDU	50
65	151	JHUNJHUNUN	50
65	126	KOTPUTLI	50
65	147	PIRAWA	50
69	56	BANERA	49
69	89	CHURU	49
69	231	GOGUNDA	49
69	141	SAYLA	49
73	102	DHAULPUR	48
73	152	KHETRI	48
73	153	NAWALGARH	48
76	171	ITAWA	47
76	137	JALOR	47
76	163	PHALODI	47
76	140	SANCHORE	47
80	200	KUMBHALGARH	46
80	217	PINDWARA	46
82	212	LACHHMANGARH	45
82	160	LUNI	45
82	51	NAGAR PAHARI	45
82	134	SANKRA	45
82	130	SHAHPURA	45
82	45	SIWANA	45
88	121	CHAKSU	44
88	71	HINDOLI	44
88	166	KARAULI	44
88	11	KATHUMAR	44
88	202	RAJSAMAND	44
88	63	SAHARA	44
94	75	ARNOD	43
94	77	BEGUN	43
94	188	JAITARAN	43
94	72	KESHORAIPATAN	43
94	181	MERTA	43
94	73	NAINWA	43
94	70	NOKHA	43
94	184	PARBATSAR	43
94	168	SAPOTRA	43
94	194	SOJAT	43
94	195	SUMERPUR	43
105	55	ASIND	42
105	42	DHORIMANNA	42
105	206	KHANDAR	42
105	222	MALPURA	42
105	214	PIPRALI	42
105	114	SADULSHAHAR	42
105	65	SUWANA	42
105	169	TODABHIM	42
113	156	BALESAR	41
113	3	JAWAJA	41
113	183	NAGAUR	41
113	129	SANGANER	41
113	155	UDAIPURWATI	41
118	31	ANTA	40
118	38	BALOTRA	40
118	116	BHADRA	40
118	197	BHIM	40
118	204	BONLI	40
118	96	DAUSA	40
118	210	FATEHPUR	40
118	179	LADNU	40
118	180	MAKRANA	40
118	164	SHERGARH	40
118	20	THANAGAZI	40
		LOW (20-40)	
129	120	BASSI	39
129	10	BEHROR	39
129	170	CHECHAT	39
129	229	DHARIAWAD	39
129	36	KISHANGANJ	39
129	68	KOLAYAT	39
129	15	MANDAWAR	39
129	6	MASOODA	39
129	44	SINDHARI	39
138	148	ALSISAR	38
138	62	RAIPUR	38
138	17	RAJGARH	38
138	218	REODAR	38
138	99	SIKRAI	38
143	80	BHOPALSAGAR	37
143	138	JASWANTPURA	37
143	69	LUNKARANSAR	37
143	88	RASHMI	37
143	185	RIYAN	37
143	215	SRI MADHOPUR	37
149	9	BANSURE	36
149	158	BHOPALGARH	36
149	110	GANGANAGAR	36
149	167	NADOTI	36
149	91	RATANGARH	36
149	133	SAM	36
149	174	SULTANPUR	36
149	131	VIRATNAGAR	36
157	227	BARGAON	35
157	39	BARMER	35
157	49	KUMHER	35
157	146	MANOHARTHANA	35
157	223	NIWAI	35
157	127	PHAGI	35
157	201	RAILMAGRA	35
157	18	RAMGARH	35
157	8	SRINAGAR	35
166	23	ANANDPURI	34
166	1	ARAIN	34
166	100	BARI	34
166	149	BUHANA	34
166	150	CHIRAWA	34
166	165	HINDAUN	34
166	182	MUNDWA	34
166	173	SANGOD	34
174	119	AMBER	33
174	203	BAMANWAS	33
174	14	LACHHMANGARH	33
174	28	PEEPALKHOONT	33
174	94	TARANAGAR	33
174	22	UMREN	33
180	46	BAYANA	32
180	211	KHANDELA	32
180	234	KOTRA	32
180	27	KUSHALGARH	32
180	112	PADAMPUR	32
185	196	AMET	31
185	142	BAKANI	31
185	95	BANDIKUI	31
185	172	LADPURA	31
189	101	BASERI	30
189	41	CHOHTAN	30
189	132	JAISALMER	30
189	97	LALSOT	30
189	220	SIROHI	30
194	34	CHHABRA	29
194	35	CHHIPABAROD	29
194	85	KAPASAN	29
194	145	KHANPUR	29
194	190	PALI	29
199	109	ANUPGARH	28
199	67	DUNGARGARH	28
199	16	NIMRANA	28
199	29	SAJJANGARH	28
199	154	SURAJGARH	28
199	21	TIJARA	28
199	226	UNIARA	28
206	33	BARAN	26
206	76	BARI SADRI	26
206	78	BHADESAR	26
206	84	GANGRAR	26
206	13	KOTKASIM	26
206	53	SEWAR	26
206	219	SHEOGANJ	26
213	40	BAYTOO	25
213	92	SARDARSHAHAR	25
215	50	NADBAI	24
215	19	RENI	24
217	216	ABU ROAD	23
217	136	BHINMAL	23
217	82	CHITTAURGARH	23
217	47	DEEG	23
217	103	RAJAKHERA	23
222	125	JHOTWARA	22
223	83	DUNGLA	21
223	37	SHAHBAD	21
223	224	TODARAISINGH	21
226	193	ROHAT	20
226	43	SHEO	20
		VERY LOW (< 20)	
228	81	CHHOTI SADRI	18
228	12	KISHANGARH BAS	18
228	161	MANDOR	18
231	48	KAMAN	17
232	79	BHAINSRORGARH	16
232	86	NIMBAHERA	16
232	139	RANIWARA	16
235	157	BAP	13
235	198	DEOGARH	13
237	111	KARANPUR	12
RAJASTHAN		TOTAL	10050
		AVERAGE	42.41
		% AGE OF AAPs	43.88

BOLD: Equal/Above Average Panchayat Samities (AAPs)
Source : General Annex II.

ANNEX-8.4

RANKING OF PSS BY NO. OF HOSPITALS: RAJASTHAN, 1991

(Descending Order)

RANK	PANCHAYAT SAMITIES P.CODE	NAME	HOSPITALS
1	2	3	4
		VERY HIGH (>=8)	**73**
1	24	**BAGIDORA**	20
2	178	**KUCHAMAN**	18
3	186	**BALI**	17
3	54	**WEIR**	17
5	143	**DAG**	16
6	187	**DESURI**	15
6	189	**KHARCHI/MARWAR JUN.**	15
6	118	**NOHAR**	15
6	147	**PIRAWA**	15
10	32	**ATRU**	13
10	208	**DANTA RAMGARH**	13
10	176	**DIDWANA**	13
10	171	**ITAWA**	13
10	72	**KESHORAIPATAN**	13
10	152	**KHETRI**	13
16	105	**BICHHIWARA**	12
16	61	**MANDALGARH**	12
16	213	**NEEM KA THANA**	12
16	7	**PISANGAN**	12
16	52	**RUPBAS**	12
16	107	**SAGWARA**	12
16	207	**SAWAI MADHOPUR**	12
16	74	**TALERA**	12
24	10	**BEHROR**	11
24	228	**BHINDER**	11
24	71	**HINDOLI**	11
24	144	**JHALRAPATAN**	11
24	59	**KOTRI**	11
24	194	**SOJAT**	11
30	75	**ARNOD**	10
30	156	**BALESAR**	10
30	204	**BONLI**	10
30	221	**DEOLI**	10
30	102	**DHAULPUR**	10
30	138	**JASWANTPURA**	10
30	151	**JHUNJHUNUN**	10
30	233	**KHERWARA**	10
30	5	**KISHANGARH**	10
30	98	**MAHWA**	10
30	70	**NOKHA**	10
41	135	**AHORE**	9
41	148	**ALSISAR**	9
41	33	**BARAN**	9
41	100	**BARI**	9
41	76	**BARI SADRI**	9
41	80	**BHOPALSAGAR**	9
41	170	**CHECHAT**	9
41	210	**FATEHPUR**	9
41	205	**GANGAPUR**	9
41	188	**JAITARAN**	9
41	4	**KEKRI**	9
41	69	**LUNKARANSAR**	9
41	162	**OSIAN**	9
41	63	**SAHARA**	9
41	134	**SANKRA**	9
41	237	**SARADA**	9
41	45	**SIWANA**	9
41	195	**SUMERPUR**	9
41	155	**UDAIPURWATI**	9
60	104	**ASPUR**	8
60	106	**DUNGARPUR**	8
60	231	**GOGUNDA**	8
60	177	**JAYAL**	8
60	68	**KOLAYAT**	8
60	60	**MANDAL**	8
60	184	**PARBATSAR**	8
60	217	**PINDWARA**	8
60	62	**RAIPUR**	8
60	191	**RAIPUR**	8
60	173	**SANGOD**	8
60	53	**SEWAR**	8
60	22	**UMREN**	8
		HIGH (6-8)	
73	1	**ARAIN**	7
73	38	**BALOTRA**	7
73	77	**BEGUN**	7
73	116	**BHADRA**	7
73	66	**BIKANER**	7
73	159	**BILARA**	7
73	89	**CHURU**	7
73	137	**JALOR**	7
73	3	**JAWAJA**	7
73	166	**KARAULI**	7
73	211	**KHANDELA**	7
73	145	**KHANPUR**	7
73	160	**LUNI**	7
73	146	**MANOHARTHANA**	7
73	16	**NIMRANA**	7
73	163	**PHALODI**	7
73	90	**RAJGARH**	7
73	114	**SADULSHAHAR**	7
73	130	**SHAHPURA**	7
73	215	**SRI MADHOPUR**	7
73	93	**SUJANGARH**	7
73	174	**SULTANPUR**	7
95	216	ABU ROAD	6
95	31	ANTA	6
95	142	BAKANI	6
95	203	BAMANWAS	6
95	197	BHIM	6
95	2	BHINAY	6
95	25	GARHI	6
95	232	JHADOL	6
95	48	KAMAN	6
95	11	KATHUMAR	6
95	36	KISHANGANJ	6
95	126	KOTPUTLI	6
95	14	LACHHMANGARH	6
95	179	LADNU	6
95	15	MANDAWAR	6
95	235	MAVLI	6
95	181	MERTA	6
95	73	NAINWA	6
95	153	NAWALGARH	6
95	168	SAPOTRA	6
95	219	SHEOGANJ	6
95	115	SURATGARH	6
95	30	TALWARA	6
		MEDIUM (4-6)	
118	101	BASERI	5
118	120	BASSI	5
118	46	BAYANA	5
118	78	BHADESAR	5
118	158	BHOPALGARH	5
118	35	CHHIPABAROD	5
118	175	DEGANA	5
118	83	DUNGLA	5
118	26	GHATOL	5
118	230	GIRWA	5
118	123	GOVINDGARH	5
118	117	HANUMANGARH	5
118	165	HINDAUN	5
118	57	HURDA	5
118	13	KOTKASIM	5
118	180	MAKRANA	5
118	51	NAGAR PAHARI	5
118	183	NAGAUR	5
118	86	NIMBAHERA	5
118	190	PALI	5
118	17	RAJGARH	5
118	192	RANI STATION	5
118	185	RIYAN	5
118	140	SANCHORE	5
118	141	SAYLA	5
118	37	SHAHBAD	5
118	94	TARANAGAR	5
118	169	TODABHIM	5
146	79	BHAINSRORGARH	4
146	149	BUHANA	4
146	34	CHHABRA	4
146	82	CHITTAURGARH	4
146	41	CHOHTAN	4
146	96	DAUSA	4
146	42	DHORIMANNA	4
146	122	DUDU	4
146	110	GANGANAGAR	4
146	84	GANGRAR	4
146	199	KHAMNOR	4
146	206	KHANDAR	4
146	234	KOTRA	4
146	212	LACHHMANGARH	4
146	172	LADPURA	4
146	6	MASOODA	4
146	50	NADBAI	4
146	167	NADOTI	4
146	28	PEEPALKHOONT	4
146	201	RAILMAGRA	4
146	113	RAISINGHNAGAR	4
146	218	REODAR	4
146	164	SHERGARH	4
146	108	SIMALWARA	4
146	8	SRINAGAR	4
146	65	SUWANA	4
146	20	THANAGAZI	4
146	225	TONK	4
146	131	VIRATNAGAR	4
		LOW (2-4)	
175	55	ASIND	3
175	157	BAP	3
175	81	CHHOTI SADRI	3
175	150	CHIRAWA	3
175	49	KUMHER	3
175	214	PIPRALI	3
175	87	PRATAPGARH	3
175	139	RANIWARA	3
175	91	RATANGARH	3
175	19	RENI	3
175	193	ROHAT	3
175	236	SALUMBAR	3
175	129	SANGANER	3
175	99	SIKRAI	3
175	44	SINDHARI	3
175	220	SIROHI	3
175	154	SURAJGARH	3
192	109	ANUPGARH	2
192	227	BARGAON	2
192	39	BARMER	2
192	136	BHINMAL	2
192	47	DEEG	2
192	198	DEOGARH	2
192	209	DHOND	2
192	67	DUNGARGARH	2
192	58	JAHAZPUR	2
192	132	JAISALMER	2
192	124	JAMWA RAMGARH	2
192	85	KAPASAN	2
192	111	KARANPUR	2
192	222	MALPURA	2
192	182	MUNDWA	2
192	112	PADAMPUR	2
192	127	PHAGI	2
192	103	RAJAKHERA	2
192	202	RAJSAMAND	2
192	18	RAMGARH	2
192	88	RASHMI	2
192	29	SAJJANGARH	2
192	133	SAM	2
192	92	SARDARSHAHAR	2
192	226	UNIARA	2
		VERY LOW (<2)	
217	119	AMBER	1
217	23	ANANDPURI	1
217	56	BANERA	1
217	9	BANSURE	1
217	125	JHOTWARA	1
217	200	KUMBHALGARH	1
217	27	KUSHALGARH	1
217	97	LALSOT	1
217	128	SAMBHAR	1
217	64	SHAHPURA	1
217	43	SHEO	1
		NIL (0)	
228	196	AMET	
228	95	BANDIKUI	
228	40	BAYTOO	
228	121	CHAKSU	
228	229	DHARIAWAD	
228	12	KISHANGARH BAS	
228	161	MANDOR	
228	223	NIWAI	
228	21	TIJARA	
228	224	TODARAISINGH	
RAJASTHAN		**TOTAL**	**1433**
		AVERAGE	**6.05**
		% AGE OF AAPs	**39.66**

BOLD: Equal/Above Average Panchayat Samities (AAPs)

Source : General Annex II.

ANNEX-8.5

RANKING OF PSS BY NO. OF DISPENSARIES: RAJASTHAN, 1991

(Descending Order)

RANK	PANCHAYAT SAMITIES P.CODE	NAME	DISPENSARIES
1	2	3	4
		VERY HIGH (>=20)	
1	118	**NOHAR**	35
2	123	**GOVINDGARH**	34
2	61	**MANDALGARH**	34
4	115	**SURATGARH**	33
5	124	**JAMWA RAMGARH**	30
6	54	**WEIR**	29
7	107	**SAGWARA**	28
7	128	**SAMBHAR**	28
9	151	**JHUNJHUNUN**	27
9	126	**KOTPUTLI**	27
9	7	**PISANGAN**	27
12	208	**DANTA RAMGARH**	26
12	237	**SARADA**	26
14	116	**BHADRA**	25
14	25	**GARHI**	25
14	26	**GHATOL**	25
14	117	**HANUMANGARH**	25
14	58	**JAHAZPUR**	25
14	207	**SAWAI MADHOPUR**	25
14	130	**SHAHPURA**	25
21	186	**BALI**	24
21	66	**BIKANER**	24
21	122	**DUDU**	24
21	64	**SHAHPURA**	24
25	209	**DHOND**	23
25	205	**GANGAPUR**	23
25	232	**JHADOL**	23
25	4	**KEKRI**	23
25	93	**SUJANGARH**	23
30	104	**ASPUR**	22
30	57	**HURDA**	22
30	108	**SIMALWARA**	22
33	9	**BANSURE**	21
33	96	**DAUSA**	21
33	98	**MAHWA**	21
33	162	**OSIAN**	21
33	74	**TALERA**	21
38	2	**BHINAY**	20
38	228	**BHINDER**	20
38	150	**CHIRAWA**	20
38	60	**MANDAL**	20
38	90	**RAJGARH**	20
38	52	**RUPBAS**	20
38	164	**SHERGARH**	20
		HIGH (15-20)	
45	95	**BANDIKUI**	19
45	89	**CHURU**	19
45	221	**DEOLI**	19
45	206	**KHANDAR**	19
45	5	**KISHANGARH**	19
45	69	**LUNKARANSAR**	19
45	235	**MAVLI**	19
45	153	**NAWALGARH**	19
45	213	**NEEM KA THANA**	19
45	112	**PADAMPUR**	19
45	202	**RAJSAMAND**	19
45	99	**SIKRAI**	19
45	155	**UDAIPURWATI**	19
45	131	**VIRATNAGAR**	19
59	55	**ASIND**	18
59	149	**BUHANA**	18
59	102	**DHAULPUR**	18
59	230	**GIRWA**	18
59	222	**MALPURA**	18
59	15	**MANDAWAR**	18
59	73	**NAINWA**	18
59	70	**NOKHA**	18
59	92	**SARDARSHAHAR**	18
59	20	**THANAGAZI**	18
69	105	**BICHHIWARA**	17
69	143	**DAG**	17
69	187	**DESURI**	17
69	144	**JHALRAPATAN**	17
69	152	**KHETRI**	17
69	223	**NIWAI**	17
69	236	**SALUMBAR**	17
69	129	**SANGANER**	17
77	171	**ITAWA**	16
77	178	**KUCHAMAN**	16
77	49	**KUMHER**	16
77	212	**LACHHMANGARH**	16
77	17	**RAJGARH**	16
77	30	**TALWARA**	16
77	21	**TIJARA**	16
77	225	**TONK**	16
85	56	**BANERA**	15
85	227	**BARGAON**	15
85	204	**BONLI**	15
85	121	**CHAKSU**	15
85	176	**DIDWANA**	15
85	11	**KATHUMAR**	15
85	72	**KESHORAIPATAN**	15
85	233	**KHERWARA**	15
85	59	**KOTRI**	15
85	97	**LALSOT**	15
85	127	**PHAGI**	15
85	201	**RAILMAGRA**	15
85	192	**RANI STATION**	15
85	114	**SADULSHAHAR**	15
85	134	**SANKRA**	15
85	168	**SAPOTRA**	15
85	215	**SRI MADHOPUR**	15
85	94	**TARANAGAR**	15
85	169	**TODABHIM**	15
		MEDIUM (10-15)	
104	148	ALSISAR	14
104	32	ATRU	14
104	229	DHARIAWAD	14
104	67	DUNGARGARH	14
104	177	JAYAL	14
104	27	KUSHALGARH	14
104	6	MASOODA	14
104	50	NADBAI	14
104	167	NADOTI	14
104	184	PARBATSAR	14
104	91	RATANGARH	14
104	185	RIYAN	14
104	173	SANGOD	14
117	31	ANTA	13
117	120	BASSI	13
117	10	BEHROR	13
117	159	BILARA	13
117	34	CHHABRA	13
117	210	FATEHPUR	13
117	166	KARAULI	13
117	68	KOLAYAT	13
117	13	KOTKASIM	13
117	200	KUMBHALGARH	13
117	51	NAGAR PAHARI	13
117	183	NAGAUR	13
117	163	PHALODI	13
117	214	PIPRALI	13
117	147	PIRAWA	13
117	87	PRATAPGARH	13
117	191	RAIPUR	13
117	65	SUWANA	13
135	135	AHORE	12
135	119	AMBER	12
135	109	ANUPGARH	12
135	203	BAMANWAS	12
135	77	BEGUN	12
135	106	DUNGARPUR	12
135	199	KHAMNOR	12
135	189	KHARCHI/MARWAR JUN.	12
135	14	LACHHMANGARH	12
135	181	MERTA	12
135	16	NIMRANA	12
135	113	RAISINGHNAGAR	12
135	218	REODAR	12
135	63	SAHARA	12
135	141	SAYLA	12
135	22	UMREN	12
151	75	ARNOD	11
151	38	BALOTRA	11
151	46	BAYANA	11
151	197	BHIM	11
151	41	CHOHTAN	11
151	231	GOGUNDA	11
151	165	HINDAUN	11
151	137	JALOR	11
151	36	KISHANGANJ	11
151	180	MAKRANA	11
151	18	RAMGARH	11
151	44	SINDHARI	11
151	220	SIROHI	11
151	45	SIWANA	11
165	24	BAGIDORA	10
165	100	BARI	10
165	80	BHOPALSAGAR	10
165	47	DEEG	10
165	110	GANGANAGAR	10
165	188	JAITARAN	10
165	125	JHOTWARA	10
165	145	KHANPUR	10
165	234	KOTRA	10
165	179	LADNU	10
165	182	MUNDWA	10
165	88	RASHMI	10
165	19	RENI	10
165	43	SHEO	10
165	174	SULTANPUR	10
165	195	SUMERPUR	10
165	224	TODARAISINGH	10
		LOW (5-10)	
182	156	BALESAR	9
182	39	BARMER	9
182	101	BASERI	9
182	158	BHOPALGARH	9
182	42	DHORIMANNA	9
182	84	GANGRAR	9
182	71	HINDOLI	9
182	138	JASWANTPURA	9
182	133	SAM	9
182	8	SRINAGAR	9
182	154	SURAJGARH	9
193	76	BARI SADRI	8
193	78	BHADESAR	8
193	170	CHECHAT	8
193	82	CHITTAURGARH	8
193	175	DEGANA	8
193	132	JAISALMER	8
193	211	KHANDELA	8
193	12	KISHANGARH BAS	8
193	172	LADPURA	8
193	146	MANOHARTHANA	8
193	28	PEEPALKHOONT	8
193	37	SHAHBAD	8
193	226	UNIARA	8
206	216	ABU ROAD	7
206	196	AMET	7
206	142	BAKANI	7
206	40	BAYTOO	7
206	35	CHHIPABAROD	7
206	83	DUNGLA	7
206	160	LUNI	7
206	62	RAIPUR	7
206	103	RAJAKHERA	7
206	29	SAJJANGARH	7
206	140	SANCHORE	7
206	53	SEWAR	7
206	194	SOJAT	7
219	48	KAMAN	6
219	139	RANIWARA	6
219	190	PALI	6
222	23	ANANDPURI	5
222	1	ARAIN	5
222	3	JAWAJA	5
222	217	PINDWARA	5
		VERY LOW (<5)	
226	33	BARAN	4
226	136	BHINMAL	4
226	85	KAPASAN	4
226	193	ROHAT	4
231	198	DEOGARH	3
231	111	KARANPUR	3
231	161	MANDOR	3
231	86	NIMBAHERA	3
235	157	BAP	2
235	219	SHEOGANJ	2
237	79	BHAINSRORGARH	1
RAJASTHAN		TOTAL	3377
		AVERAGE	14.25
		% AGE OF AAPs	43.46

BOLD: Equal/Above Average Panchayat Samities (AAPs)
Source : General Annex-II.

ANNEX-8.6

RANKING OF PSS BY NO. OF PHCS: RAJASTHAN, 1991

(Descending Order)

RANK	P.CODE	PANCHAYAT SAMITIES NAME	PHC
1	*2*	*3*	*4*
		VERY HIGH (>=8)	
1	**25**	**GARHI**	**22**
2	**232**	**JHADOL**	**21**
3	**233**	**KHERWARA**	**19**
4	**208**	**DANTA RAMGARH**	**18**
4	**59**	**KOTRI**	**18**
6	**87**	**PRATAPGARH**	**17**
6	**218**	**REODAR**	**17**
6	**30**	**TALWARA**	**17**
9	**209**	**DHOND**	**16**
10	**105**	**BICHHIWARA**	**15**
10	**60**	**MANDAL**	**15**
10	**61**	**MANDALGARH**	**15**
10	**237**	**SARADA**	**15**
14	**104**	**ASPUR**	**14**
14	**5**	**KISHANGARH**	**14**
16	**58**	**JAHAZPUR**	**13**
16	**74**	**TALERA**	**13**
16	**225**	**TONK**	**13**
19	**26**	**GHATOL**	**12**
19	**189**	**KHARCHI/MARWAR JUN.**	**12**
19	**162**	**OSIAN**	**12**
19	**45**	**SIWANA**	**12**
23	**24**	**BAGIDORA**	**11**
23	**228**	**BHINDER**	**11**
23	**110**	**GANGANAGAR**	**11**
23	**137**	**JALOR**	**11**
23	**124**	**JAMWA RAMGARH**	**11**
23	**36**	**KISHANGANJ**	**11**
29	**42**	**DHORIMANNA**	**10**
29	**68**	**KOLAYAT**	**10**
29	**160**	**LUNI**	**10**
29	**181**	**MERTA**	**10**
29	**213**	**NEEM KA THANA**	**10**
29	**28**	**PEEPALKHOONT**	**10**
29	**62**	**RAIPUR**	**10**
29	**88**	**RASHMI**	**10**
29	**236**	**SALUMBAR**	**10**
29	**140**	**SANCHORE**	**10**
39	**75**	**ARNOD**	**9**
39	**156**	**BALESAR**	**9**
39	**2**	**BHINAY**	**9**
39	**221**	**DEOLI**	**9**
39	**106**	**DUNGARPUR**	**9**
39	**71**	**HINDOLI**	**9**
39	**57**	**HURDA**	**9**
39	**132**	**JAISALMER**	**9**
39	**3**	**JAWAJA**	**9**
39	**27**	**KUSHALGARH**	**9**
39	**179**	**LADNU**	**9**
39	**98**	**MAHWA**	**9**
39	**180**	**MAKRANA**	**9**
39	**184**	**PARBATSAR**	**9**
39	**133**	**SAM**	**9**
39	**134**	**SANKRA**	**9**
39	**115**	**SURATGARH**	**9**
39	**65**	**SUWANA**	**9**
57	**119**	**AMBER**	**8**
57	**109**	**ANUPGARH**	**8**
57	**1**	**ARAIN**	**8**
57	**170**	**CHECHAT**	**8**
57	**175**	**DEGANA**	**8**
57	**117**	**HANUMANGARH**	**8**
57	**144**	**JHALRAPATAN**	**8**
57	**11**	**KATHUMAR**	**8**
57	**14**	**LACHHMANGARH**	**8**
57	**235**	**MAVLI**	**8**
57	**51**	**NAGAR PAHARI**	**8**
57	**112**	**PADAMPUR**	**8**
57	**163**	**PHALODI**	**8**
57	**147**	**PIRAWA**	**8**
57	**7**	**PISANGAN**	**8**
57	**201**	**RAILMAGRA**	**8**
57	**103**	**RAJAKHERA**	**8**
57	**18**	**RAMGARH**	**8**
57	**52**	**RUPBAS**	**8**
57	**107**	**SAGWARA**	**8**
57	**168**	**SAPOTRA**	**8**
57	**141**	**SAYLA**	**8**
57	**93**	**SUJANGARH**	**8**
		HIGH (6-8)	
80	**135**	**AHORE**	7
80	**23**	**ANANDPURI**	7
80	**31**	**ANTA**	7
80	**55**	**ASIND**	7
80	**38**	**BALOTRA**	7
80	**39**	**BARMER**	7
80	**158**	**BHOPALGARH**	7
80	**80**	**BHOPALSAGAR**	7
80	**159**	**BILARA**	7
80	**149**	**BUHANA**	7
80	**35**	**CHHIPABAROD**	7
80	**143**	**DAG**	7
80	**230**	**GIRWA**	7
80	**231**	**GOGUNDA**	7
80	**188**	**JAITARAN**	7
80	**199**	**KHAMNOR**	7
80	**200**	**KUMBHALGARH**	7
80	**90**	**RAJGARH**	7
80	**114**	**SADULSHAHAR**	7
80	**29**	**SAJJANGARH**	7
80	**164**	**SHERGARH**	7
80	**44**	**SINDHARI**	7
80	**174**	**SULTANPUR**	7
80	**195**	**SUMERPUR**	7
80	**155**	**UDAIPURWATI**	7
105	32	ATRU	6
105	203	BAMANWAS	6
105	56	BANERA	6
105	40	BAYTOO	6
105	78	BHADESAR	6
105	197	BHIM	6
105	204	BONLI	6
105	96	DAUSA	6
105	176	DIDWANA	6
105	210	FATEHPUR	6
105	171	ITAWA	6
105	85	KAPASAN	6
105	126	KOTPUTLI	6
105	161	MANDOR	6
105	153	NAWALGARH	6
105	191	RAIPUR	6
105	63	SAHARA	6
105	64	SHAHPURA	6
105	108	SIMALWARA	6
105	8	SRINAGAR	6
105	154	SURAJGARH	6
105	20	THANAGAZI	6
105	131	VIRATNAGAR	6
		MEDIUM (4-6)	
128	148	ALSISAR	5
128	142	BAKANI	5
128	101	BASERI	5
128	10	BEHROR	5
128	136	BHINMAL	5
128	150	CHIRAWA	5
128	41	CHOHTAN	5
128	177	JAYAL	5
128	4	KEKRI	5
128	234	KOTRA	5
128	178	KUCHAMAN	5
128	49	KUMHER	5
128	222	MALPURA	5
128	183	NAGAUR	5
128	86	NIMBAHERA	5
128	214	PIPRALI	5
128	91	RATANGARH	5
128	128	SAMBHAR	5
128	207	SAWAI MADHOPUR	5
128	53	SEWAR	5
128	99	SIKRAI	5
128	194	SOJAT	5
128	94	TARANAGAR	5
128	21	TIJARA	5
152	196	AMET	4
152	9	BANSURE	4
152	33	BARAN	4
152	227	BARGAON	4
152	77	BEGUN	4
152	66	BIKANER	4
152	82	CHITTAURGARH	4
152	229	DHARIAWAD	4
152	122	DUDU	4
152	165	HINDAUN	4
152	138	JASWANTPURA	4
152	151	JHUNJHUNUN	4
152	72	KESHORAIPATAN	4
152	212	LACHHMANGARH	4
152	146	MANOHARTHANA	4
152	167	NADOTI	4
152	223	NIWAI	4
152	70	NOKHA	4
152	190	PALI	4
152	217	PINDWARA	4
152	192	RANI STATION	4
152	19	RENI	4
152	185	RIYAN	4
152	130	SHAHPURA	4
152	219	SHEOGANJ	4
152	215	SRI MADHOPUR	4
152	169	TODABHIM	4
		LOW (2-4)	
179	186	BALI	3
179	95	BANDIKUI	3
179	157	BAP	3
179	79	BHAINSRORGARH	3
179	34	CHHABRA	3
179	47	DEEG	3
179	102	DHAULPUR	3
179	123	GOVINDGARH	3
179	125	JHOTWARA	3
179	166	KARAULI	3
179	211	KHANDELA	3
179	145	KHANPUR	3
179	152	KHETRI	3
179	6	MASOODA	3
179	73	NAINWA	3
179	127	PHAGI	3
179	113	RAISINGHNAGAR	3
179	139	RANIWARA	3
179	129	SANGANER	3
179	92	SARDARSHAHAR	3
179	43	SHEO	3
179	22	UMREN	3
179	226	UNIARA	3
179	54	WEIR	3
203	216	ABU ROAD	2
203	120	BASSI	2
203	121	CHAKSU	2
203	81	CHHOTI SADRI	2
203	187	DESURI	2
203	67	DUNGARGARH	2
203	205	GANGAPUR	2
203	111	KARANPUR	2
203	206	KHANDAR	2
203	12	KISHANGARH BAS	2
203	13	KOTKASIM	2
203	15	MANDAWAR	2
203	118	NOHAR	2
203	17	RAJGARH	2
203	202	RAJSAMAND	2
203	173	SANGOD	2
203	37	SHAHBAD	2
203	220	SIROHI	2
203	224	TODARAISINGH	2
		VERY LOW (<2)	
222	100	BARI	1
222	116	BHADRA	1
222	89	CHURU	1
222	198	DEOGARH	1
222	83	DUNGLA	1
222	84	GANGRAR	1
222	48	KAMAN	1
222	97	LALSOT	1
222	69	LUNKARANSAR	1
222	182	MUNDWA	1
222	50	NADBAI	1
222	16	NIMRANA	1
222	193	ROHAT	1
		NIL (0)	
235	76	BARI SADRI	
235	46	BAYANA	
235	172	LADPURA	
RAJASTHAN		**TOTAL**	**1516**
		AVERAGE	**6.40**
		% AGE OF AAPs	**43.88**

BOLD: Equal/Above Average Panchayat Samities (AAPs)

Source : General Annex II.

ANNEX-8.7

RANKING OF PSS BY NO. OF SHCS: RAJASTHAN, 1991

(Descending Order)

RANK	P.CODE	PANCHAYAT SAMITIES NAME	SHC
1	2	3	4
		VERY HIGH (>=20)	
1	61	MANDALGARH	31
2	199	KHAMNOR	27
3	175	DEGANA	26
4	106	DUNGARPUR	25
4	25	GARHI	25
4	177	JAYAL	25
4	232	JHADOL	25
4	7	PISANGAN	25
4	140	SANCHORE	25
10	159	BILARA	24
10	209	DHOND	24
10	233	KHERWARA	24
13	56	BANERA	23
13	60	MANDAL	23
13	107	SAGWARA	23
13	64	SHAHPURA	23
13	30	TALWARA	23
18	135	AHORE	22
18	121	CHAKSU	22
18	58	JAHAZPUR	22
18	235	MAVLI	22
18	192	RANI STATION	22
18	141	SAYLA	22
24	2	BHINAY	21
24	89	CHURU	21
24	178	KUCHAMAN	21
24	212	LACHHMANGARH	21
24	213	NEEM KA THANA	21
29	196	AMET	20
29	23	ANANDPURI	20
29	143	DAG	20
29	26	GHATOL	20
29	57	HURDA	20
		HIGH (15-20)	
34	208	DANTA RAMGARH	19
34	176	DIDWANA	19
34	182	MUNDWA	19
34	217	PINDWARA	19
34	214	PIPRALI	19
39	187	DESURI	18
39	230	GIRWA	18
39	166	KARAULI	18
39	189	KHARCHI/MARWAR JUN.	18
39	183	NAGAUR	18
39	225	TONK	18
45	104	ASPUR	17
45	137	JALOR	17
45	172	LADPURA	17
45	87	PRATAPGARH	17
45	44	SINDHARI	17
45	93	SUJANGARH	17
51	66	BIKANER	16
51	42	DHORIMANNA	16
51	4	KEKRI	16
51	191	RAIPUR	16
51	90	RAJGARH	16
51	202	RAJSAMAND	16
51	63	SAHARA	16
51	236	SALUMBAR	16
51	207	SAWAI MADHOPUR	16
51	108	SIMALWARA	16
51	194	SOJAT	16
51	169	TODABHIM	16
63	24	BAGIDORA	15
63	186	BALI	15
63	120	BASSI	15
63	46	BAYANA	15
63	117	HANUMANGARH	15
63	3	JAWAJA	15
63	144	JHALRAPATAN	15
63	85	KAPASAN	15
63	5	KISHANGARH	15
63	179	LADNU	15
63	160	LUNI	15
63	180	MAKRANA	15
63	128	SAMBHAR	15
63	226	UNIARA	15
		MEDIUM (10-15)	
77	32	ATRU	14
77	38	BALOTRA	14
77	39	BARMER	14
77	77	BEGUN	14
77	158	BHOPALGARH	14
77	123	GOVINDGARH	14
77	188	JAITARAN	14
77	138	JASWANTPURA	14
77	211	KHANDELA	14
77	152	KHETRI	14
77	6	MASOODA	14
77	181	MERTA	14
77	190	PALI	14
77	147	PIRAWA	14
77	17	RAJGARH	14
77	91	RATANGARH	14
77	133	SAM	14
77	219	SHEOGANJ	14
77	65	SUWANA	14
96	1	ARAIN	13
96	55	ASIND	13
96	100	BARI	13
96	228	BHINDER	13
96	105	BICHHIWARA	13
96	221	DEOLI	13
96	122	DUDU	13
96	234	KOTRA	13
96	73	NAINWA	13
96	223	NIWAI	13
96	162	OSIAN	13
96	113	RAISINGHNAGAR	13
96	88	RASHMI	13
96	195	SUMERPUR	13
110	40	BAYTOO	12
110	210	FATEHPUR	12
110	71	HINDOLI	12
110	15	MANDAWAR	12
110	146	MANOHARTHANA	12
110	127	PHAGI	12
110	134	SANKRA	12
110	220	SIROHI	12
118	142	BAKANI	11
118	136	BHINMAL	11
118	80	BHOPALSAGAR	11
118	84	GANGRAR	11
118	132	JAISALMER	11
118	126	KOTPUTLI	11
118	59	KOTRI	11
118	200	KUMBHALGARH	11
118	97	LALSOT	11
118	98	MAHWA	11
118	222	MALPURA	11
118	184	PARBATSAR	11
118	28	PEEPALKHOONT	11
118	163	PHALODI	11
118	18	RAMGARH	11
118	185	RIYAN	11
118	114	SADULSHAHAR	11
118	168	SAPOTRA	11
118	45	SIWANA	11
118	8	SRINAGAR	11
118	115	SURATGARH	11
139	119	AMBER	10
139	156	BALESAR	10
139	197	BHIM	10
139	170	CHECHAT	10
139	41	CHOHTAN	10
139	205	GANGAPUR	10
139	231	GOGUNDA	10
139	153	NAWALGARH	10
139	70	NOKHA	10
139	29	SAJJANGARH	10
139	129	SANGANER	10
139	173	SANGOD	10
139	237	SARADA	10
139	174	SULTANPUR	10
		LOW (5-10)	
153	31	ANTA	9
153	227	BARGAON	9
153	229	DHARIAWAD	9
153	102	DHAULPUR	9
153	67	DUNGARGARH	9
153	110	GANGANAGAR	9
153	171	ITAWA	9
153	151	JHUNJHUNUN	9
153	206	KHANDAR	9
153	145	KHANPUR	9
153	62	RAIPUR	9
153	193	ROHAT	9
153	52	RUPBAS	9
153	164	SHERGARH	9
153	74	TALERA	9
153	20	THANAGAZI	9
153	224	TODARAISINGH	9
153	22	UMREN	9
171	75	ARNOD	8
171	76	BARI SADRI	8
171	101	BASERI	8
171	79	BHAINSRORGARH	8
171	34	CHHABRA	8
171	35	CHHIPABAROD	8
171	83	DUNGLA	8
171	72	KESHORAIPATAN	8
171	36	KISHANGANJ	8
171	27	KUSHALGARH	8
171	69	LUNKARANSAR	8
171	161	MANDOR	8
171	167	NADOTI	8
171	51	NAGAR PAHARI	8
171	16	NIMRANA	8
171	130	SHAHPURA	8
171	215	SRI MADHOPUR	8
188	203	BAMANWAS	7
188	95	BANDIKUI	7
188	33	BARAN	7
188	78	BHADESAR	7
188	204	BONLI	7
188	82	CHITTAURGARH	7
188	198	DEOGARH	7
188	124	JAMWA RAMGARH	7
188	125	JHOTWARA	7
188	11	KATHUMAR	7
188	12	KISHANGARH BAS	7
188	68	KOLAYAT	7
188	99	SIKRAI	7
188	94	TARANAGAR	7
202	216	ABU ROAD	6
202	148	ALSISAR	6
202	109	ANUPGARH	6
202	10	BEHROR	6
202	96	DAUSA	6
202	165	HINDAUN	6
202	13	KOTKASIM	6
202	49	KUMHER	6
202	201	RAILMAGRA	6
202	103	RAJAKHERA	6
202	19	RENI	6
202	53	SEWAR	6
202	21	TIJARA	6
215	157	BAP	5
215	116	BHADRA	5
215	149	BUHANA	5
215	47	DEEG	5
215	111	KARANPUR	5
215	14	LACHHMANGARH	5
215	43	SHEO	5
215	131	VIRATNAGAR	5
215	54	WEIR	5
		VERY LOW (<5)	
224	9	BANSURE	4
224	150	CHIRAWA	4
224	48	KAMAN	4
224	50	NADBAI	4
228	81	CHHOTI SADRI	3
228	86	NIMBAHERA	3
228	118	NOHAR	3
228	112	PADAMPUR	3
228	139	RANIWARA	3
228	37	SHAHBAD	3
228	155	UDAIPURWATI	3
235	218	REODAR	2
235	92	SARDARSHAHAR	2
235	154	SURAJGARH	2
RAJASTHAN		TOTAL	2942
		AVERAGE	12.41
		% AGE OF AAPs	45.99

BOLD: Equal/Above Average Panchayat Samities (AAPs)

Source : General Annex II.

ANNEX-8.8

RANKING OF PSS BY NO. OF MCW CENTRES: RAJASTHAN, 1991

(Descending Order)

RANK	P.CODE	PANCHAYAT SAMITIES NAME	MCWC
1	2	3	4
		VERY HIGH (>=8)	
1	113	**RAISINGHNAGAR**	28
2	104	**ASPUR**	27
3	25	**GARHI**	26
4	200	**KUMBHALGARH**	14
5	231	**GOGUNDA**	13
6	32	**ATRU**	12
6	229	**DHARIAWAD**	12
6	52	**RUPBAS**	12
9	105	**BICHHIWARA**	11
9	233	**KHERWARA**	11
9	51	**NAGAR PAHARI**	11
9	237	**SARADA**	11
13	205	**GANGAPUR**	10
13	217	**PINDWARA**	10
13	191	**RAIPUR**	10
13	236	**SALUMBAR**	10
13	30	**TALWARA**	10
18	228	**BHINDER**	9
18	175	**DEGANA**	9
18	199	**KHAMNOR**	9
18	235	**MAVLI**	9
22	102	**DHAULPUR**	8
22	106	**DUNGARPUR**	8
22	165	**HINDAUN**	8
22	11	**KATHUMAR**	8
22	206	**KHANDAR**	8
22	98	**MAHWA**	8
22	61	**MANDALGARH**	8
22	163	**PHALODI**	8
22	87	**PRATAPGARH**	8
22	129	**SANGANER**	8
22	154	**SURAJGARH**	8
		HIGH (6-8)	
33	197	**BHIM**	7
33	230	**GIRWA**	7
33	153	**NAWALGARH**	7
36	24	**BAGIDORA**	6
36	9	**BANSURE**	6
36	77	**BEGUN**	6
36	81	**CHHOTI SADRI**	6
36	144	**JHALRAPATAN**	6
36	160	**LUNI**	6
36	222	**MALPURA**	6
36	60	**MANDAL**	6
36	167	**NADOTI**	6
36	7	**PISANGAN**	6
36	192	**RANI STATION**	6
		MEDIUM (4-6)	
47	31	**ANTA**	5
47	75	**ARNOD**	5
47	227	**BARGAON**	5
47	121	**CHAKSU**	5
47	208	**DANTA RAMGARH**	5
47	122	**DUDU**	5
47	123	**GOVINDGARH**	5
47	3	**JAWAJA**	5
47	49	**KUMHER**	5
47	202	**RAJSAMAND**	5
47	8	**SRINAGAR**	5
58	5	**KISHANGARH**	4
58	135	**AHORE**	4
58	148	**ALSISAR**	4
58	56	**BANERA**	4
58	120	**BASSI**	4
58	10	**BEHROR**	4
58	170	**CHECHAT**	4
58	143	**DAG**	4
58	176	**DIDWANA**	4
58	26	**GHATOL**	4
58	232	**JHADOL**	4
58	59	**KOTRI**	4
58	146	**MANOHARTHANA**	4
58	6	**MASOODA**	4
58	62	**RAIPUR**	4
58	99	**SIKRAI**	4
58	194	**SOJAT**	4
58	195	**SUMERPUR**	4
58	54	**WEIR**	4
		LOW (2-4)	
77	156	BALESAR	3
77	39	BARMER	3
77	101	BASERI	3
77	2	BHINAY	3
77	96	DAUSA	3
77	47	DEEG	3
77	42	DHORIMANNA	3
77	71	HINDOLI	3
77	171	ITAWA	3
77	188	JAITARAN	3
77	166	KARAULI	3
77	72	KESHORAIPATAN	3
77	36	KISHANGANJ	3
77	73	NAINWA	3
77	213	NEEM KA THANA	3
77	162	OSIAN	3
77	127	PHAGI	3
77	18	RAMGARH	3
77	218	REODAR	3
77	185	RIYAN	3
77	193	ROHAT	3
77	107	SAGWARA	3
77	128	SAMBHAR	3
77	168	SAPOTRA	3
77	37	SHAHBAD	3
77	108	SIMALWARA	3
77	215	SRI MADHOPUR	3
77	20	THANAGAZI	3
77	155	UDAIPURWATI	3
106	216	ABU ROAD	2
106	119	AMBER	2
106	142	BAKANI	2
106	203	BAMANWAS	2
106	95	BANDIKUI	2
106	33	BARAN	2
106	116	BHADRA	2
106	204	BONLI	2
106	35	CHHIPABAROD	2
106	150	CHIRAWA	2
106	187	DESURI	2
106	110	GANGANAGAR	2
106	58	JAHAZPUR	2
106	85	KAPASAN	2
106	4	KEKRI	2
106	189	KHARCHI/MARWAR JUN.	2
106	14	LACHHMANGARH	2
106	172	LADPURA	2
106	97	LALSOT	2
106	182	MUNDWA	2
106	214	PIPRALI	2
106	201	RAILMAGRA	2
106	90	RAJGARH	2
106	88	RASHMI	2
106	114	SADULSHAHAR	2
106	29	SAJJANGARH	2
106	133	SAM	2
106	141	SAYLA	2
106	64	SHAHPURA	2
106	220	SIROHI	2
106	45	SIWANA	2
106	174	SULTANPUR	2
106	65	SUWANA	2
106	74	TALERA	2
106	169	TODABHIM	2
106	131	VIRATNAGAR	2
		LOW (<2)	
142	23	ANANDPURI	1
142	1	ARAIN	1
142	55	ASIND	1
142	38	BALOTRA	1
142	100	BARI	1
142	76	BARI SADRI	1
142	46	BAYANA	1
142	136	BHINMAL	1
142	158	BHOPALGARH	1
142	34	CHHABRA	1
142	89	CHURU	1
142	221	DEOLI	1
142	67	DUNGARGARH	1
142	84	GANGRAR	1
142	117	HANUMANGARH	1
142	57	HURDA	1
142	137	JALOR	1
142	124	JAMWA RAMGARH	1
142	177	JAYAL	1
142	125	JHOTWARA	1
142	152	KHETRI	1
142	12	KISHANGARH BAS	1
142	68	KOLAYAT	1
142	15	MANDAWAR	1
142	161	MANDOR	1
142	181	MERTA	1
142	50	NADBAI	1
142	223	NIWAI	1
142	70	NOKHA	1
142	184	PARBATSAR	1
142	17	RAJGARH	1
142	139	RANIWARA	1
142	19	RENI	1
142	63	SAHARA	1
142	207	SAWAI MADHOPUR	1
142	130	SHAHPURA	1
142	43	SHEO	1
142	44	SINDHARI	1
142	93	SUJANGARH	1
142	94	TARANAGAR	1
142	21	TIJARA	1
142	225	TONK	1
142	22	UMREN	1
		NIL (0)	
185	196	AMET	
185	109	ANUPGARH	
185	186	BALI	
185	157	BAP	
185	40	BAYTOO	
185	78	BHADESAR	
185	79	BHAINSRORGARH	
185	80	BHOPALSAGAR	
185	66	BIKANER	
185	159	BILARA	
185	149	BUHANA	
185	82	CHITTAURGARH	
185	41	CHOHTAN	
185	198	DEOGARH	
185	209	DHOND	
185	83	DUNGLA	
185	210	FATEHPUR	
185	132	JAISALMER	
185	138	JASWANTPURA	
185	151	JHUNJHUNUN	
185	48	KAMAN	
185	111	KARANPUR	
185	211	KHANDELA	
185	145	KHANPUR	
185	13	KOTKASIM	
185	126	KOTPUTLI	
185	234	KOTRA	
185	178	KUCHAMAN	
185	27	KUSHALGARH	
185	212	LACHHMANGARH	
185	179	LADNU	
185	69	LUNKARANSAR	
185	180	MAKRANA	
185	183	NAGAUR	
185	86	NIMBAHERA	
185	16	NIMRANA	
185	118	NOHAR	
185	112	PADAMPUR	
185	190	PALI	
185	28	PEEPALKHOONT	
185	147	PIRAWA	
185	103	RAJAKHERA	
185	91	RATANGARH	
185	140	SANCHORE	
185	173	SANGOD	
185	134	SANKRA	
185	92	SARDARSHAHAR	
185	53	SEWAR	
185	219	SHEOGANJ	
185	164	SHERGARH	
185	115	SURATGARH	
185	224	TODARAISINGH	
185	226	UNIARA	
RAJASTHAN		**TOTAL**	**782**
		AVERAGE	**3.30**
		% AGE OF AAPs	**32.07**

BOLD: Equal/Above Average Panchayat Samities (AAPs)

Source : General Annex II.

ANNEX-8.9

RANKING OF PSS BY NO. OF FPCS: RAJASTHAN, 1991

(Descending Order)

RANK	P.CODE	PANCHAYAT SAMITIES NAME	FPC
1	2	3	4
		VERY HIGH (>=5)	
1	158	**BHOPALGARH**	7
1	233	**KHERWARA**	7
3	185	**RIYAN**	6
4	228	**BHINDER**	5
4	204	**BONLI**	5
4	177	**JAYAL**	5
4	160	**LUNI**	5
4	163	**PHALODI**	5
4	20	**THANAGAZI**	5
		HIGH (4)	
10	148	**ALSISAR**	
10	55	**ASIND**	
10	142	**BAKANI**	
10	208	**DANTA RAMGARH**	
10	187	**DESURI**	
10	176	**DIDWANA**	
10	51	**NAGAR PAHARI**	
10	162	**OSIAN**	
10	218	**REODAR**	
10	207	**SAWAI MADHOPUR**	
10	30	**TALWARA**	
10	225	**TONK**	
		MEDIUM (3)	
22	135	**AHORE**	
22	119	**AMBER**	
22	209	**DHOND**	
22	123	**GOVINDGARH**	
22	188	**JAITARAN**	
22	151	**JHUNJHUNUN**	
22	11	**KATHUMAR**	
22	4	**KEKRI**	
22	126	**KOTPUTLI**	
22	235	**MAVLI**	
22	153	**NAWALGARH**	
22	213	**NEEM KA THANA**	
22	112	**PADAMPUR**	
22	62	**RAIPUR**	
22	168	**SAPOTRA**	
22	194	**SOJAT**	
22	174	**SULTANPUR**	
22	65	**SUWANA**	
		LOW (2)	
40	196	**AMET**	
40	1	**ARAIN**	
40	32	**ATRU**	
40	24	**BAGIDORA**	
40	156	**BALESAR**	
40	77	**BEGUN**	
40	197	**BHIM**	
40	80	**BHOPALSAGAR**	
40	105	**BICHHIWARA**	
40	66	**BIKANER**	
40	159	**BILARA**	
40	149	**BUHANA**	
40	110	**GANGANAGAR**	
40	230	**GIRWA**	
40	117	**HANUMANGARH**	
40	71	**HINDOLI**	
40	58	**JAHAZPUR**	
40	132	**JAISALMER**	
40	206	**KHANDAR**	
40	211	**KHANDELA**	
40	189	**KHARCHI/MARWAR JUN.**	
40	152	**KHETRI**	
40	36	**KISHANGANJ**	
40	68	**KOLAYAT**	
40	200	**KUMBHALGARH**	
40	69	**LUNKARANSAR**	
40	61	**MANDALGARH**	
40	183	**NAGAUR**	
40	73	**NAINWA**	
40	70	**NOKHA**	
40	28	**PEEPALKHOONT**	
40	147	**PIRAWA**	
40	7	**PISANGAN**	
40	18	**RAMGARH**	
40	192	**RANI STATION**	
40	88	**RASHMI**	
40	19	**RENI**	
40	193	**ROHAT**	
40	52	**RUPBAS**	
40	114	**SADULSHAHAR**	
40	63	**SAHARA**	
40	129	**SANGANER**	
40	130	**SHAHPURA**	
40	99	**SIKRAI**	
40	45	**SIWANA**	
40	215	**SRI MADHOPUR**	
40	8	**SRINAGAR**	
40	195	**SUMERPUR**	
40	169	**TODABHIM**	
40	224	**TODARAISINGH**	
40	155	**UDAIPURWATI**	
40	22	**UMREN**	
		VERY LOW (1)	
92	31	ANTA	
92	109	ANUPGARH	
92	75	ARNOD	
92	104	ASPUR	
92	186	BALI	
92	38	BALOTRA	
92	203	BAMANWAS	
92	95	BANDIKUI	
92	56	BANERA	
92	9	BANSURE	
92	33	BARAN	
92	227	BARGAON	
92	76	BARI SADRI	
92	46	BAYANA	
92	10	BEHROR	
92	116	BHADRA	
92	79	BHAINSRORGARH	
92	2	BHINAY	
92	121	CHAKSU	
92	34	CHHABRA	
92	35	CHHIPABAROD	
92	150	CHIRAWA	
92	82	CHITTAURGARH	
92	41	CHOHTAN	
92	143	DAG	
92	175	DEGANA	
92	221	DEOLI	
92	102	DHAULPUR	
92	122	DUDU	
92	67	DUNGARGARH	
92	83	DUNGLA	
92	210	FATEHPUR	
92	25	GARHI	
92	26	GHATOL	
92	231	GOGUNDA	
92	165	HINDAUN	
92	171	ITAWA	
92	137	JALOR	
92	124	JAMWA RAMGARH	
92	138	JASWANTPURA	
92	3	JAWAJA	
92	232	JHADOL	
92	144	JHALRAPATAN	
92	125	JHOTWARA	
92	85	KAPASAN	
92	72	KESHORAIPATAN	
92	199	KHAMNOR	
92	145	KHANPUR	
92	5	KISHANGARH	
92	13	KOTKASIM	
92	234	KOTRA	
92	59	KOTRI	
92	178	KUCHAMAN	
92	49	KUMHER	
92	172	LADPURA	
92	97	LALSOT	
92	180	MAKRANA	
92	222	MALPURA	
92	60	MANDAL	
92	6	MASOODA	
92	181	MERTA	
92	167	NADOTI	
92	16	NIMRANA	
92	190	PALI	
92	184	PARBATSAR	
92	127	PHAGI	
92	217	PINDWARA	
92	214	PIPRALI	
92	87	PRATAPGARH	
92	201	RAILMAGRA	
92	191	RAIPUR	
92	113	RAISINGHNAGAR	
92	103	RAJAKHERA	
92	17	RAJGARH	
92	90	RAJGARH	
92	202	RAJSAMAND	
92	91	RATANGARH	
92	107	SAGWARA	
92	29	SAJJANGARH	
92	236	SALUMBAR	
92	128	SAMBHAR	
92	140	SANCHORE	
92	237	SARADA	
92	92	SARDARSHAHAR	
92	37	SHAHBAD	
92	64	SHAHPURA	
92	164	SHERGARH	
92	108	SIMALWARA	
92	93	SUJANGARH	
92	154	SURAJGARH	
92	74	TALERA	
92	94	TARANAGAR	
92	226	UNIARA	
92	131	VIRATNAGAR	
		NIL (0)	
186	216	ABU ROAD	
186	23	ANANDPURI	
186	157	BAP	
186	100	BARI	
186	39	BARMER	
186	101	BASERI	
186	120	BASSI	
186	40	BAYTOO	
186	78	BHADESAR	
186	136	BHINMAL	
186	170	CHECHAT	
186	81	CHHOTI SADRI	
186	89	CHURU	
186	96	DAUSA	
186	47	DEEG	
186	198	DEOGARH	
186	229	DHARIAWAD	
186	42	DHORIMANNA	
186	106	DUNGARPUR	
186	205	GANGAPUR	
186	84	GANGRAR	
186	57	HURDA	
186	48	KAMAN	
186	111	KARANPUR	
186	166	KARAULI	
186	12	KISHANGARH BAS	
186	27	KUSHALGARH	
186	14	LACHHMANGARH	
186	212	LACHHMANGARH	
186	179	LADNU	
186	98	MAHWA	
186	15	MANDAWAR	
186	161	MANDOR	
186	146	MANOHARTHANA	
186	182	MUNDWA	
186	50	NADBAI	
186	86	NIMBAHERA	
186	223	NIWAI	
186	118	NOHAR	
186	139	RANIWARA	
186	133	SAM	
186	173	SANGOD	
186	134	SANKRA	
186	141	SAYLA	
186	53	SEWAR	
186	43	SHEO	
186	219	SHEOGANJ	
186	44	SINDHARI	
186	220	SIROHI	
186	115	SURATGARH	
186	21	TIJARA	
186	54	WEIR	
RAJASTHAN		TOTAL	350
		AVERAGE	1.48
		% AGE OF AAPs	38.40

BOLD: Equal/Above Average Panchayat Samities (AAPs)

Source : General Annex II.

ANNEX-8.10

RANKING OF PSS BY PERCENTAGE OF RURAL POPULATION SERVED BY DRINKING WATER AMENITIES: RAJASTHAN, 1991

(Descending Order)

RANK	P.CODE	PANCHAYAT SAMITIES NAME	%
1	2	3	4
		PERFECT (100)	
1	23	**ANANDPURI**	100.00
1	31	**ANTA**	100.00
1	1	**ARAIN**	100.00
1	75	**ARNOD**	100.00
1	55	**ASIND**	100.00
1	32	**ATRU**	100.00
1	24	**BAGIDORA**	100.00
1	95	**BANDIKUI**	100.00
1	56	**BANERA**	100.00
1	9	**BANSURE**	100.00
1	33	**BARAN**	100.00
1	100	**BARI**	100.00
1	76	**BARI SADRI**	100.00
1	101	**BASERI**	100.00
1	46	**BAYANA**	100.00
1	77	**BEGUN**	100.00
1	10	**BEHROR**	100.00
1	78	**BHADESAR**	100.00
1	79	**BHAINSRORGARH**	100.00
1	2	**BHINAY**	100.00
1	80	**BHOPALSAGAR**	100.00
1	105	**BICHHIWARA**	100.00
1	34	**CHHABRA**	100.00
1	35	**CHHIPABAROD**	100.00
1	81	**CHHOTI SADRI**	100.00
1	82	**CHITTAURGARH**	100.00
1	41	**CHOHTAN**	100.00
1	96	**DAUSA**	100.00
1	47	**DEEG**	100.00
1	102	**DHAULPUR**	100.00
1	42	**DHORIMANNA**	100.00
1	83	**DUNGLA**	100.00
1	84	**GANGRAR**	100.00
1	25	**GARHI**	100.00
1	26	**GHATOL**	100.00
1	71	**HINDOLI**	100.00
1	57	**HURDA**	100.00
1	58	**JAHAZPUR**	100.00
1	85	**KAPASAN**	100.00
1	11	**KATHUMAR**	100.00
1	4	**KEKRI**	100.00
1	72	**KESHORAIPATAN**	100.00
1	5	**KISHANGARH**	100.00
1	12	**KISHANGARH BAS**	100.00
1	13	**KOTKASIM**	100.00
1	59	**KOTRI**	100.00
1	14	**LACHHMANGARH**	100.00
1	97	**LALSOT**	100.00
1	98	**MAHWA**	100.00
1	60	**MANDAL**	100.00
1	61	**MANDALGARH**	100.00
1	15	**MANDAWAR**	100.00
1	6	**MASOODA**	100.00
1	50	**NADBAI**	100.00
1	51	**NAGAR PAHARI**	100.00
1	73	**NAINWA**	100.00
1	16	**NIMRANA**	100.00
1	28	**PEEPALKHOONT**	100.00
1	7	**PISANGAN**	100.00
1	87	**PRATAPGARH**	100.00
1	62	**RAIPUR**	100.00
1	103	**RAJAKHERA**	100.00
1	17	**RAJGARH**	100.00
1	18	**RAMGARH**	100.00
1	88	**RASHMI**	100.00
1	19	**RENI**	100.00
1	52	**RUPBAS**	100.00
1	63	**SAHARA**	100.00
1	29	**SAJJANGARH**	100.00
1	64	**SHAHPURA**	100.00
1	99	**SIKRAI**	100.00
1	45	**SIWANA**	100.00
1	8	**SRINAGAR**	100.00
1	65	**SUWANA**	100.00
1	74	**TALERA**	100.00
1	30	**TALWARA**	100.00
1	94	**TARANAGAR**	100.00
1	20	**THANAGAZI**	100.00
1	21	**TIJARA**	100.00
1	22	**UMREN**	100.00
1	54	**WEIR**	100.00
1	216	**ABU ROAD**	100.00
1	135	**AHORE**	100.00
1	148	**ALSISAR**	100.00
1	196	**AMET**	100.00
1	109	**ANUPGARH**	100.00
1	142	**BAKANI**	100.00
1	186	**BALI**	100.00
1	203	**BAMANWAS**	100.00
1	120	**BASSI**	100.00
1	116	**BHADRA**	100.00
1	197	**BHIM**	100.00
1	136	**BHINMAL**	100.00
1	159	**BILARA**	100.00
1	149	**BUHANA**	100.00
1	143	**DAG**	100.00
1	208	**DANTA RAMGARH**	100.00
1	175	**DEGANA**	100.00
1	198	**DEOGARH**	100.00
1	187	**DESURI**	100.00
1	176	**DIDWANA**	100.00
1	106	**DUNGARPUR**	100.00
1	210	**FATEHPUR**	100.00
1	110	**GANGANAGAR**	100.00
1	205	**GANGAPUR**	100.00
1	123	**GOVINDGARH**	100.00
1	117	**HANUMANGARH**	100.00
1	165	**HINDAUN**	100.00
1	171	**ITAWA**	100.00
1	188	**JAITARAN**	100.00
1	137	**JALOR**	100.00
1	124	**JAMWA RAMGARH**	100.00
1	138	**JASWANTPURA**	100.00
1	177	**JAYAL**	100.00
1	144	**JHALRAPATAN**	100.00
1	125	**JHOTWARA**	100.00
1	111	**KARANPUR**	100.00
1	166	**KARAULI**	100.00
1	199	**KHAMNOR**	100.00
1	206	**KHANDAR**	100.00
1	211	**KHANDELA**	100.00
1	145	**KHANPUR**	100.00
1	189	**KHARCHI/MARWAR JUN.**	100.00
1	152	**KHETRI**	100.00
1	126	**KOTPUTLI**	100.00
1	200	**KUMBHALGARH**	100.00
1	179	**LADNU**	100.00
1	172	**LADPURA**	100.00
1	160	**LUNI**	100.00
1	180	**MAKRANA**	100.00
1	146	**MANOHARTHANA**	100.00
1	181	**MERTA**	100.00
1	182	**MUNDWA**	100.00
1	167	**NADOTI**	100.00
1	183	**NAGAUR**	100.00
1	153	**NAWALGARH**	100.00
1	112	**PADAMPUR**	100.00
1	190	**PALI**	100.00
1	214	**PIPRALI**	100.00
1	147	**PIRAWA**	100.00
1	201	**RAILMAGRA**	100.00
1	191	**RAIPUR**	100.00
1	113	**RAISINGHNAGAR**	100.00
1	202	**RAJSAMAND**	100.00
1	192	**RANI STATION**	100.00
1	139	**RANIWARA**	100.00
1	218	**REODAR**	100.00
1	193	**ROHAT**	100.00
1	107	**SAGWARA**	100.00
1	129	**SANGANER**	100.00
1	173	**SANGOD**	100.00
1	134	**SANKRA**	100.00
1	207	**SAWAI MADHOPUR**	100.00
1	219	**SHEOGANJ**	100.00
1	108	**SIMALWARA**	100.00
1	220	**SIROHI**	100.00
1	194	**SOJAT**	100.00
1	215	**SRI MADHOPUR**	100.00
1	174	**SULTANPUR**	100.00
1	195	**SUMERPUR**	100.00
1	115	**SURATGARH**	100.00
1	169	**TODABHIM**	100.00
1	155	**UDAIPURWATI**	100.00
1	227	**BARGAON**	100.00
1	228	**BHINDER**	100.00
1	221	**DEOLI**	100.00
1	229	**DHARIAWAD**	100.00
1	230	**GIRWA**	100.00
1	231	**GOGUNDA**	100.00
1	232	**JHADOL**	100.00
1	233	**KHERWARA**	100.00
1	234	**KOTRA**	100.00
1	222	**MALPURA**	100.00
1	235	**MAVLI**	100.00
1	223	**NIWAI**	100.00
1	236	**SALUMBAR**	100.00
1	237	**SARADA**	100.00
1	224	**TODARAISINGH**	100.00
1	225	**TONK**	100.00
1	226	**UNIARA**	100.00
		VERY HIGH (98-100)	
181	121	**CHAKSU**	99.98
182	104	**ASPUR**	99.97
183	130	**SHAHPURA**	99.96
184	91	**RATANGARH**	99.94
185	141	**SAYLA**	99.92
186	133	**SAM**	99.91
187	36	**KISHANGANJ**	99.90
188	170	**CHECHAT**	99.89
188	53	**SEWAR**	99.89
190	86	**NIMBAHERA**	99.88
191	162	**OSIAN**	99.86
191	128	**SAMBHAR**	99.86
191	48	**KAMAN**	99.86
194	119	**AMBER**	99.85
195	204	**BONLI**	99.83
195	178	**KUCHAMAN**	99.83
197	69	**LUNKARANSAR**	99.81
198	157	**BAP**	99.79
199	209	**DHOND**	99.76
200	131	**VIRATNAGAR**	99.75
200	27	**KUSHALGARH**	99.75
202	212	**LACHHMANGARH**	99.73
202	122	**DUDU**	99.73
202	118	**NOHAR**	99.73
202	114	**SADULSHAHAR**	99.73
206	44	**SINDHARI**	99.71
207	127	**PHAGI**	99.70
208	151	**JHUNJHUNUN**	99.68
208	38	**BALOTRA**	99.68
210	92	SARDARSHAHAR	99.67
211	150	CHIRAWA	99.65
212	185	RIYAN	99.58
213	168	SAPOTRA	99.54
214	156	BALESAR	99.52
215	37	SHAHBAD	99.45
216	70	NOKHA	99.43
216	49	KUMHER	99.43
218	217	PINDWARA	99.42
219	213	NEEM KA THANA	99.34
219	158	BHOPALGARH	99.34
221	184	PARBATSAR	99.27
222	43	SHEO	99.24
223	93	SUJANGARH	99.18
223	67	DUNGARGARH	99.18
225	3	JAWAJA	99.08
226	154	SURAJGARH	98.87
227	132	JAISALMER	98.50
228	66	BIKANER	98.42
229	161	MANDOR	98.37
230	140	SANCHORE	98.29
231	89	CHURU	98.21
		HIGH (96-98)	
232	68	KOLAYAT	97.53
233	39	BARMER	97.29
234	40	BAYTOO	96.39
		MEDIUM (94-96)	
235	90	RAJGARH	95.52
236	164	SHERGARH	95.15
		LOW (<94)	
237	163	PHALODI	93.03
		RAJASTHAN	**99.68**
		% AGE OF AAPs	**88.19**

BOLD: Equal/Above Average Panchayat Samities (AAPs)
Source : General Annex III.

ANNEX-8.11

RANKING OF PSS BY PERCENTAGE OF RURAL POPULATION SERVED BY EDUCATION AMENITIES: RAJASTHAN, 1991

(Descending Order)

RANK	PANCHAYAT SAMITIES P.CODE	PANCHAYAT SAMITIES NAME	%
1	2	3	4
		PERFECT (100)	
1	153	NAWALGARH	100.00
1	164	SHERGARH	100.00
		VERY HIGH (95-100)	
3	139	RANIWARA	99.98
4	130	SHAHPURA	99.96
5	215	SRI MADHOPUR	99.93
6	141	SAYLA	99.91
7	186	BALI	99.86
8	8	SRINAGAR	99.84
9	210	FATEHPUR	99.76
10	7	PISANGAN	99.74
11	159	BILARA	99.73
12	216	ABU ROAD	99.71
13	154	SURAJGARH	99.67
14	137	JALOR	99.66
15	102	DHAULPUR	99.64
16	4	KEKRI	99.60
17	194	SOJAT	99.51
18	156	BALESAR	99.43
19	49	KUMHER	99.42
20	192	RANI STATION	99.39
21	155	UDAIPURWATI	99.38
22	2	BHINAY	99.35
23	123	GOVINDGARH	99.34
24	175	DEGANA	99.32
25	57	HURDA	99.29
26	89	CHURU	99.24
27	214	PIPRALI	99.23
28	193	ROHAT	99.17
29	190	PALI	99.15
29	212	LACHHMANGARH	99.15
31	10	BEHROR	99.14
32	217	PINDWARA	99.13
33	1	ARAIN	99.06
33	33	BARAN	99.06
35	160	LUNI	99.04
36	149	BUHANA	99.00
37	107	SAGWARA	98.99
38	15	MANDAWAR	98.94
38	135	AHORE	98.94
38	158	BHOPALGARH	98.94
41	185	RIYAN	98.92
42	148	ALSISAR	98.87
42	205	GANGAPUR	98.87
44	54	WEIR	98.86
44	138	JASWANTPURA	98.86
46	220	SIROHI	98.84
47	161	MANDOR	98.81
48	219	SHEOGANJ	98.80
49	182	MUNDWA	98.76
49	211	KHANDELA	98.76
51	179	LADNU	98.74
52	235	MAVLI	98.60
53	50	NADBAI	98.55
54	70	NOKHA	98.50
55	66	BIKANER	98.48
56	16	NIMRANA	98.47
56	209	DHOND	98.47
58	150	CHIRAWA	98.43
59	195	SUMERPUR	98.36
60	52	RUPBAS	98.35
61	208	DANTA RAMGARH	98.34
62	140	SANCHORE	98.33
63	180	MAKRANA	98.30
64	88	RASHMI	98.29
65	62	RAIPUR	98.27
66	178	KUCHAMAN	98.26
67	136	BHINMAL	98.24
68	152	KHETRI	98.21
69	53	SEWAR	98.18
70	11	KATHUMAR	98.16
71	65	SUWANA	98.14
72	187	DESURI	98.10
73	218	REODAR	98.09
74	64	SHAHPURA	98.07
75	151	JHUNJHUNUN	98.06
76	9	BANSURE	98.03
76	184	PARBATSAR	98.03
78	45	SIWANA	98.01
79	177	JAYAL	97.99
80	69	LUNKARANSAR	97.98
81	46	BAYANA	97.91
82	126	KOTPUTLI	97.87
83	25	GARHI	97.85
84	165	HINDAUN	97.83
85	63	SAHARA	97.82
86	213	NEEM KA THANA	97.70
87	93	SUJANGARH	97.69
88	207	SAWAI MADHOPUR	97.68
89	91	RATANGARH	97.66
90	47	DEEG	97.64
91	67	DUNGARGARH	97.62
91	222	MALPURA	97.62
93	176	DIDWANA	97.60
94	188	JAITARAN	97.54
95	202	RAJSAMAND	97.51
96	183	NAGAUR	97.38
97	181	MERTA	97.35
98	56	BANERA	97.32
99	203	BAMANWAS	97.30
100	128	SAMBHAR	97.29
101	163	PHALODI	97.26
102	231	GOGUNDA	97.17
103	94	TARANAGAR	97.08
104	201	RAILMAGRA	97.04
105	105	BICHHIWARA	97.03
106	20	THANAGAZI	96.97
107	199	KHAMNOR	96.90
108	90	RAJGARH	96.82
108	147	PIRAWA	96.82
110	106	DUNGARPUR	96.75
111	60	MANDAL	96.74
112	23	ANANDPURI	96.69
113	92	SARDARSHAHAR	96.60
114	227	BARGAON	96.55
115	59	KOTRI	96.26
116	101	BASERI	96.25
117	5	KISHANGARH	96.24
117	71	HINDOLI	96.24
117	169	TODABHIM	96.24
120	103	RAJAKHERA	96.21
121	230	GIRWA	95.96
122	99	SIKRAI	95.87
123	204	BONLI	95.86
124	98	MAHWA	95.78
125	58	JAHAZPUR	95.72
126	237	SARADA	95.70
127	26	GHATOL	95.51
128	172	LADPURA	95.43
129	221	DEOLI	95.39
130	14	LACHHMANGARH	95.38
131	189	KHARCHI/MARWAR JUN.	95.37
132	6	MASOODA	95.36
133	31	ANTA	95.29
134	191	RAIPUR	95.25
135	13	KOTKASIM	95.15
136	197	BHIM	95.03
		HIGH (90-95)	
137	122	DUDU	94.97
138	233	KHERWARA	94.95
139	12	KISHANGARH BAS	94.84
140	125	JHOTWARA	94.81
141	83	DUNGLA	94.79
142	124	JAMWA RAMGARH	94.75
143	134	SANKRA	94.69
144	167	NADOTI	94.53
145	73	NAINWA	94.52
146	132	JAISALMER	94.45
147	116	BHADRA	94.23
148	68	KOLAYAT	94.12
149	17	RAJGARH	94.10
150	80	BHOPALSAGAR	94.01
151	51	NAGAR PAHARI	93.95
152	19	RENI	93.94
153	55	ASIND	93.89
154	22	UMREN	93.88
155	223	NIWAI	93.73
156	24	BAGIDORA	93.58
157	168	SAPOTRA	93.49
158	18	RAMGARH	93.48
159	127	PHAGI	93.40
160	108	SIMALWARA	93.24
161	85	KAPASAN	93.20
162	86	NIMBAHERA	93.17
163	120	BASSI	93.16
164	72	KESHORAIPATAN	93.11
165	3	JAWAJA	93.02
166	100	BARI	92.99
167	200	KUMBHALGARH	92.88
168	21	TIJARA	92.70
169	112	PADAMPUR	92.63
170	131	VIRATNAGAR	92.62
171	174	SULTANPUR	92.60
172	119	AMBER	92.59
173	111	KARANPUR	92.46
174	170	CHECHAT	92.39
175	30	TALWARA	92.30
176	104	ASPUR	92.25
177	48	KAMAN	92.16
178	96	DAUSA	91.84
179	38	BALOTRA	91.72
180	43	SHEO	91.67
181	32	ATRU	91.66
182	224	TODARAISINGH	91.58
183	225	TONK	91.48
184	84	GANGRAR	91.41
185	166	KARAULI	91.38
186	81	CHHOTI SADRI	91.21
187	228	BHINDER	91.20
188	171	ITAWA	91.19
189	74	TALERA	90.99
190	133	SAM	90.78
191	82	CHITTAURGARH	90.65
192	232	JHADOL	90.58
193	41	CHOHTAN	90.54
194	157	BAP	90.26
195	196	AMET	90.05
196	162	OSIAN	90.02
		MEDIUM (85-90)	
197	129	SANGANER	89.88
198	145	KHANPUR	89.75
199	97	LALSOT	89.73
200	143	DAG	89.62
201	206	KHANDAR	89.45
202	75	ARNOD	89.30
203	34	CHHABRA	89.27
204	35	CHHIPABAROD	88.85
205	118	NOHAR	88.34
206	110	GANGANAGAR	87.95
207	95	BANDIKUI	87.60
208	226	UNIARA	87.49
209	61	MANDALGARH	87.08
210	229	DHARIAWAD	86.99
211	76	BARI SADRI	86.91
212	78	BHADESAR	86.85
213	27	KUSHALGARH	85.70
214	37	SHAHBAD	85.51
214	114	SADULSHAHAR	85.51
216	144	JHALRAPATAN	85.26
217	29	SAJJANGARH	85.12
218	28	PEEPALKHOONT	85.08
		LOW (<85)	
219	236	SALUMBAR	84.64
220	87	PRATAPGARH	84.47
221	77	BEGUN	83.91
222	36	KISHANGANJ	83.73
223	173	SANGOD	83.71
224	39	BARMER	83.65
225	113	RAISINGHNAGAR	82.59
226	79	BHAINSRORGARH	81.15
227	142	BAKANI	80.66
228	198	DEOGARH	80.52
229	44	SINDHARI	79.53
230	121	CHAKSU	78.13
231	42	DHORIMANNA	77.69
232	117	HANUMANGARH	76.20
233	40	BAYTOO	74.35
234	146	MANOHARTHANA	74.31
235	115	SURATGARH	74.25
236	234	KOTRA	72.73
237	109	ANUPGARH	56.53
RAJASTHAN			93.90
		% AGE OF AAPs	64.13

BOLD: Equal/Above Average Panchayat Samities (AAPs)
Source: General Annex III

ANNEX- 8.12

RANKING OF PSS BY PERCENTAGE OF RURAL POPULATION SERVED BY POWER AMENITIES: RAJASTHAN, 1991

(Descending Order)

RANK	P.CODE	PANCHAYAT SAMITIES NAME	%
1	2	3	4
		PERFECT (100)	
1	57	**HURDA**	100.00
1	123	**GOVINDGARH**	100.00
1	150	**CHIRAWA**	100.00
1	153	**NAWALGARH**	100.00
1	195	**SUMERPUR**	100.00
1	201	**RAILMAGRA**	100.00
1	209	**DHOND**	100.00
		VERY HIGH (75-100)	
8	16	**NIMRANA**	99.99
9	129	**SANGANER**	99.94
10	125	**JHOTWARA**	99.92
11	12	**KISHANGARH BAS**	99.82
12	10	**BEHROR**	99.77
13	215	**SRI MADHOPUR**	99.76
14	139	**RANIWARA**	99.74
15	220	**SIROHI**	99.68
16	159	**BILARA**	99.59
16	192	**RANI STATION**	99.59
16	211	**KHANDELA**	99.59
19	178	**KUCHAMAN**	99.58
20	130	**SHAHPURA**	99.54
21	9	**BANSURE**	99.32
22	212	**LACHHMANGARH**	99.30
23	131	**VIRATNAGAR**	99.18
24	155	**UDAIPURWATI**	99.11
25	54	**WEIR**	99.09
26	7	**PISANGAN**	99.02
27	124	**JAMWA RAMGARH**	99.01
28	137	**JALOR**	98.77
29	128	**SAMBHAR**	98.71
30	184	**PARBATSAR**	98.68
31	85	**KAPASAN**	98.59
32	80	**BHOPALSAGAR**	98.43
33	135	**AHORE**	98.30
34	119	**AMBER**	98.01
35	181	**MERTA**	97.96
36	170	**CHECHAT**	97.92
37	111	**KARANPUR**	97.91
38	56	**BANERA**	97.74
38	138	**JASWANTPURA**	97.74
40	210	**FATEHPUR**	97.62
41	151	**JHUNJHUNUN**	97.59
42	65	**SUWANA**	97.57
43	63	**SAHARA**	97.50
44	141	**SAYLA**	97.38
45	190	**PALI**	97.32
46	218	**REODAR**	97.24
47	15	**MANDAWAR**	97.08
48	187	**DESURI**	96.47
49	91	**RATANGARH**	96.21
50	95	**BANDIKUI**	96.02
51	154	**SURAJGARH**	95.91
52	185	**RIYAN**	95.87
53	22	**UMREN**	95.59
54	193	**ROHAT**	94.98
55	165	**HINDAUN**	94.97
56	188	**JAITARAN**	94.95
57	49	**KUMHER**	94.74
58	86	**NIMBAHERA**	94.73
59	4	**KEKRI**	94.58
60	8	**SRINAGAR**	94.48
61	208	**DANTA RAMGARH**	94.24
62	199	**KHAMNOR**	94.22
63	152	**KHETRI**	94.15
64	227	**BARGAON**	93.85
65	64	**SHAHPURA**	93.70
66	186	**BALI**	93.69
67	126	**KOTPUTLI**	93.58
68	213	**NEEM KA THANA**	93.39
69	81	**CHHOTI SADRI**	93.32
70	158	**BHOPALGARH**	93.15
71	110	**GANGANAGAR**	93.11
72	156	**BALESAR**	93.05
73	33	**BARAN**	92.87
74	60	**MANDAL**	92.72
75	62	**RAIPUR**	92.67
76	149	**BUHANA**	92.29
77	5	**KISHANGARH**	92.28
78	189	**KHARCHI/MARWAR JUN.**	91.71
79	70	**NOKHA**	91.41
80	180	**MAKRANA**	90.66
81	205	**GANGAPUR**	90.65
82	161	**MANDOR**	90.45
83	67	**DUNGARGARH**	90.27
84	144	**JHALRAPATAN**	90.24
85	45	**SIWANA**	90.23
86	194	**SOJAT**	90.21
87	25	**GARHI**	90.16
88	89	**CHURU**	89.99
89	235	**MAVLI**	89.54
90	167	**NADOTI**	89.21
91	228	**BHINDER**	89.10
92	6	**MASOODA**	88.78
93	18	**RAMGARH**	88.68
94	136	**BHINMAL**	88.50
95	61	**MANDALGARH**	88.47
96	147	**PIRAWA**	88.43
97	223	**NIWAI**	88.31
98	204	**BONLI**	88.02
99	176	**DIDWANA**	87.87
100	58	**JAHAZPUR**	87.71
101	50	**NADBAI**	87.60
102	55	**ASIND**	87.27
103	82	**CHITTAURGARH**	86.91
104	32	**ATRU**	86.89
105	77	**BEGUN**	86.83
106	69	**LUNKARANSAR**	86.80
107	114	**SADULSHAHAR**	86.71
108	172	**LADPURA**	86.66
109	71	**HINDOLI**	86.26
110	96	**DAUSA**	86.02
111	196	**AMET**	86.00
112	73	**NAINWA**	85.91
113	53	**SEWAR**	85.68
114	173	**SANGOD**	85.45
115	59	**KOTRI**	85.41
116	120	**BASSI**	85.38
117	13	**KOTKASIM**	84.95
118	175	**DEGANA**	83.96
119	36	**KISHANGANJ**	83.90
120	217	**PINDWARA**	83.82
121	148	**ALSISAR**	83.48
122	2	**BHINAY**	83.15
123	145	**KHANPUR**	83.13
124	84	**GANGRAR**	83.01
124	160	**LUNI**	83.01
126	222	**MALPURA**	82.89
127	162	**OSIAN**	82.44
128	20	**THANAGAZI**	82.39
129	117	**HANUMANGARH**	82.33
130	88	**RASHMI**	81.47
131	93	**SUJANGARH**	81.40
132	174	**SULTANPUR**	81.21
133	230	**GIRWA**	81.16
134	19	**RENI**	80.84
135	83	**DUNGLA**	80.62
136	182	**MUNDWA**	80.57
137	21	**TIJARA**	80.50
138	197	**BHIM**	80.18
139	66	**BIKANER**	80.10
140	76	**BARI SADRI**	79.58
141	74	**TALERA**	79.43
142	17	**RAJGARH**	79.08
143	31	**ANTA**	78.99
144	94	**TARANAGAR**	78.86
145	104	**ASPUR**	78.67
146	105	**BICHHIWARA**	78.26
147	203	**BAMANWAS**	77.86
148	164	**SHERGARH**	77.72
149	191	**RAIPUR**	77.13
150	231	GOGUNDA	76.94
151	68	KOLAYAT	76.59
152	79	BHAINSRORGARH	76.44
153	216	ABU ROAD	76.11
154	112	PADAMPUR	75.74
155	179	LADNU	75.53
156	163	PHALODI	75.41
157	237	SARADA	75.39
158	1	ARAIN	75.23
		HIGH (50-75)	
159	207	SAWAI MADHOPUR	74.47
160	198	DEOGARH	73.96
161	127	PHAGI	73.50
162	47	DEEG	72.50
163	103	RAJAKHERA	72.47
164	46	BAYANA	72.19
165	75	ARNOD	72.13
166	226	UNIARA	70.80
167	34	CHHABRA	70.79
168	97	LALSOT	70.32
169	99	SIKRAI	70.09
170	169	TODABHIM	69.77
171	183	NAGAUR	68.65
172	78	BHADESAR	68.60
173	26	GHATOL	68.35
174	142	BAKANI	68.18
175	107	SAGWARA	68.11
176	121	CHAKSU	67.92
177	11	KATHUMAR	67.66
178	92	SARDARSHAHAR	65.90
179	229	DHARIAWAD	65.53
180	37	SHAHBAD	65.45
181	219	SHEOGANJ	65.25
182	30	TALWARA	63.92
183	236	SALUMBAR	63.88
184	14	LACHHMANGARH	63.11
185	225	TONK	62.37
186	113	RAISINGHNAGAR	62.02
187	221	DEOLI	61.79
188	177	JAYAL	61.73
189	52	RUPBAS	61.63
190	38	BALOTRA	61.52
191	3	JAWAJA	61.43
192	108	SIMALWARA	61.29
193	140	SANCHORE	60.02
194	98	MAHWA	59.28
195	24	BAGIDORA	58.17
196	72	KESHORAIPATAN	58.07
197	87	PRATAPGARH	57.96
197	168	SAPOTRA	57.96
199	106	DUNGARPUR	57.59
200	166	KARAULI	55.68
201	116	BHADRA	54.97
202	48	KAMAN	54.12
203	233	KHERWARA	50.08
		MEDIUM (25-50)	
204	42	DHORIMANNA	49.91
205	224	TODARAISINGH	49.23
206	118	NOHAR	48.94
207	102	DHAULPUR	48.88
208	23	ANANDPURI	48.42
209	90	RAJGARH	48.25
210	143	DAG	46.85
211	232	JHADOL	46.34
212	35	CHHIPABAROD	46.26
213	171	ITAWA	44.90
214	51	NAGAR PAHARI	44.80
215	206	KHANDAR	43.50
216	115	SURATGARH	43.31
217	27	KUSHALGARH	41.36
218	146	MANOHARTHANA	40.79
219	122	DUDU	40.58
220	132	JAISALMER	38.59
221	214	PIPRALI	38.37
222	101	BASERI	37.45
223	29	SAJJANGARH	35.33
224	44	SINDHARI	34.02
225	157	BAP	33.77
226	43	SHEO	33.15
227	234	KOTRA	29.21
228	28	PEEPALKHOONT	28.32
229	41	CHOHTAN	28.30
230	200	KUMBHALGARH	26.08
231	202	RAJSAMAND	26.00
		LOW (<25)	
232	40	BAYTOO	25.00
233	109	ANUPGARH	23.09
234	100	BARI	22.36
235	39	BARMER	21.99
236	134	SANKRA	19.51
237	133	SAM	1.51
		RAJASTHAN	**77.09**
		% AGE OF AAPs	**62.90**

BOLD: Equal/Above Average Panchayat Samities (AAPs)
Source : General Annex III.

ANNEX- 8.13

RANKING OF PSS BY PERCENTAGE OF RURAL POPULATION SERVED BY PUCCA ROAD AMENITIES: RAJASTHAN, 1991

(Descending Order)

RANK	P.CODE	PANCHAYAT SAMITIES NAME	%	RANK	P.CODE	PANCHAYAT SAMITIES NAME	%	RANK	P.CODE	PANCHAYAT SAMITIES NAME	%
1	2	3	4	1	2	3	4	1	2	3	4
		VERY HIGH (>80)		80	47	**DEEG**	53.77	162	198	DEOGARH	40.34
1	219	**SHEOGANJ**	98.01	81	194	**SOJAT**	53.56	163	231	GOGUNDA	40.13
2	195	**SUMERPUR**	87.74	82	211	**KHANDELA**	53.51			LOW (20-40)	
3	155	**UDAIPURWATI**	83.25	83	126	**KOTPUTLI**	53.49	164	51	NAGAR PAHARI	39.78
		HIGH (60-80)		84	12	**KISHANGARH BAS**	53.29	165	79	BHAINSRORGARH	39.55
4	158	**BHOPALGARH**	79.73	84	56	**BANERA**	53.29	166	173	SANGOD	38.99
5	159	**BILARA**	77.71	84	64	**SHAHPURA**	53.29	167	103	RAJAKHERA	38.87
6	117	**HANUMANGARH**	75.79	87	52	**RUPBAS**	53.20	167	142	BAKANI	38.87
7	125	**JHOTWARA**	75.19	88	106	**DUNGARPUR**	53.17	169	21	TIJARA	38.57
8	7	**PISANGAN**	75.18	89	167	**NADOTI**	52.95	170	33	BARAN	38.47
9	172	**LADPURA**	74.97	90	43	**SHEO**	52.70	171	62	RAIPUR	38.20
10	216	**ABU ROAD**	73.83	91	209	**DHOND**	52.68	172	140	SANCHORE	38.18
11	8	**SRINAGAR**	71.81	92	102	**DHAULPUR**	52.65	173	229	DHARIAWAD	37.89
12	160	**LUNI**	71.73	93	18	**RAMGARH**	52.36	174	171	ITAWA	37.61
13	110	**GANGANAGAR**	71.40	94	70	**NOKHA**	52.29	175	168	SAPOTRA	37.54
14	114	**SADULSHAHAR**	70.57	95	16	**NIMRANA**	52.25	176	212	LACHHMANGARH	37.38
15	151	**JHUNJHUNUN**	70.30	96	237	**SARADA**	51.71	177	118	NOHAR	37.22
16	130	**SHAHPURA**	69.72	97	113	**RAISINGHNAGAR**	51.38	178	44	SINDHARI	37.19
17	153	**NAWALGARH**	69.44	98	104	**ASPUR**	51.20	179	221	DEOLI	37.15
18	217	**PINDWARA**	68.95	99	112	**PADAMPUR**	51.18	180	31	ANTA	37.02
19	214	**PIPRALI**	68.81	100	124	**JAMWA RAMGARH**	50.93	181	144	JHALRAPATAN	36.92
20	123	**GOVINDGARH**	67.16	101	156	**BALESAR**	50.89	182	28	PEEPALKHOONT	36.75
21	150	**CHIRAWA**	66.65	102	122	**DUDU**	50.46	183	97	LALSOT	36.70
22	186	**BALI**	66.07	103	163	**PHALODI**	50.31	184	85	KAPASAN	36.67
23	220	**SIROHI**	66.05	104	203	**BAMANWAS**	50.14	185	174	SULTANPUR	36.39
24	80	**BHOPALSAGAR**	65.40	105	9	**BANSURE**	49.59	186	204	BONLI	36.28
25	137	**JALOR**	64.94	106	169	**TODABHIM**	49.57	187	193	ROHAT	36.26
26	218	**REODAR**	64.81	107	170	**CHECHAT**	49.46	188	233	KHERWARA	36.09
27	161	**MANDOR**	64.26	108	154	**SURAJGARH**	49.19	189	73	NAINWA	35.42
28	181	**MERTA**	63.84	109	54	**WEIR**	49.05	190	207	SAWAI MADHOPUR	35.37
29	49	**KUMHER**	63.22	110	134	**SANKRA**	48.92	191	100	BARI	35.05
30	164	**SHERGARH**	62.89	111	149	**BUHANA**	48.81	192	37	SHAHBAD	34.95
31	190	**PALI**	62.32	112	15	**MANDAWAR**	48.61	193	32	ATRU	34.85
32	152	**KHETRI**	62.31	113	38	**BALOTRA**	48.60	194	41	CHOHTAN	34.84
33	57	**HURDA**	62.07	114	26	**GHATOL**	48.55	195	224	TODARAISINGH	34.54
34	65	**SUWANA**	61.51	115	199	**KHAMNOR**	48.45	196	84	GANGRAR	34.50
34	120	**BASSI**	61.51	116	202	**RAJSAMAND**	48.26	197	196	AMET	34.17
36	230	**GIRWA**	61.28	117	182	MUNDWA	47.85	198	83	DUNGLA	33.99
37	129	**SANGANER**	61.05	118	213	NEEM KA THANA	47.73	199	92	SARDARSHAHAR	33.71
38	53	**SEWAR**	60.67	119	94	TARANAGAR	47.70	200	36	KISHANGANJ	33.70
39	101	**BASERI**	60.56	120	14	LACHHMANGARH	47.48	201	91	RATANGARH	33.55
40	201	**RAILMAGRA**	60.30	121	116	BHADRA	47.44	202	226	UNIARA	33.35
41	107	**SAGWARA**	60.25	122	63	SAHARA	47.41	203	145	KHANPUR	33.22
42	197	**BHIM**	60.06	123	60	MANDAL	46.93	204	184	PARBATSAR	33.20
43	66	**BIKANER**	60.00	124	50	NADBAI	46.51	205	179	LADNU	33.19
		MEDIUM (40-60)		125	127	PHAGI	46.47	206	1	ARAIN	33.04
44	30	**TALWARA**	59.56	126	10	BEHROR	46.41	207	232	JHADOL	33.00
45	6	**MASOODA**	59.51	127	175	DEGANA	46.16	208	183	NAGAUR	32.85
46	25	**GARHI**	59.48	128	61	MANDALGARH	46.04	209	71	HINDOLI	32.55
47	235	**MAVLI**	59.18	129	39	BARMER	46.00	210	81	CHHOTI SADRI	32.39
48	24	**BAGIDORA**	59.05	130	74	TALERA	45.82	211	188	JAITARAN	32.30
49	131	**VIRATNAGAR**	58.97	131	108	SIMALWARA	45.52	212	143	DAG	32.18
50	215	**SRI MADHOPUR**	58.77	132	11	KATHUMAR	45.42	213	166	KARAULI	32.14
51	105	**BICHHIWARA**	58.76	133	82	CHITTAURGARH	45.17	214	75	ARNOD	31.82
52	139	**RANIWARA**	58.53	134	222	MALPURA	45.15	215	29	SAJJANGARH	31.53
53	185	**RIYAN**	58.40	135	205	GANGAPUR	45.02	216	93	SUJANGARH	31.30
54	141	**SAYLA**	58.32	136	192	RANI STATION	44.43	217	48	KAMAN	30.99
55	162	**OSIAN**	57.89	137	23	ANANDPURI	44.38	218	225	TONK	30.92
56	119	**AMBER**	57.57	138	77	BEGUN	44.37	219	234	KOTRA	30.72
57	208	**DANTA RAMGARH**	57.35	139	135	AHORE	44.36	220	133	SAM	30.11
58	115	**SURATGARH**	57.34	140	99	SIKRAI	44.26	221	42	DHORIMANNA	29.64
59	187	**DESURI**	57.32	141	58	JAHAZPUR	44.23	222	72	KESHORAIPATAN	29.43
60	68	**KOLAYAT**	56.99	142	13	KOTKASIM	44.12	223	223	NIWAI	29.38
61	3	**JAWAJA**	56.92	143	96	DAUSA	43.96	224	178	KUCHAMAN	28.74
62	111	**KARANPUR**	56.84	144	236	SALUMBAR	43.91	225	121	CHAKSU	28.30
63	5	**KISHANGARH**	56.80	145	55	ASIND	43.62	226	87	PRATAPGARH	27.99
64	20	**THANAGAZI**	56.25	146	22	UMREN	43.41	227	95	BANDIKUI	27.56
65	4	**KEKRI**	56.23	147	46	BAYANA	43.22	228	210	FATEHPUR	24.68
66	109	**ANUPGARH**	55.68	148	98	MAHWA	43.14	229	146	MANOHARTHANA	23.14
67	17	**RAJGARH**	55.58	149	78	BHADESAR	43.04	230	27	KUSHALGARH	21.96
68	165	**HINDAUN**	55.31	150	86	NIMBAHERA	42.87	231	35	CHHIPABAROD	21.67
69	228	**BHINDER**	54.96	151	191	RAIPUR	42.68	232	157	BAP	20.79
70	148	**ALSISAR**	54.93	152	59	KOTRI	42.57			VERY LOW (<20)	
71	88	**RASHMI**	54.92	153	200	KUMBHALGARH	42.14	233	180	MAKRANA	19.99
72	132	**JAISALMER**	54.67	154	19	RENI	42.11	234	40	BAYTOO	19.60
73	67	**DUNGARGARH**	54.62	155	89	CHURU	41.65	235	34	CHHABRA	13.71
74	227	**BARGAON**	54.57	156	177	JAYAL	41.60	236	147	PIRAWA	12.43
75	189	**KHARCHI/MARWAR JUN.**	54.49	157	90	RAJGARH	41.20	237	176	DIDWANA	4.84
76	138	**JASWANTPURA**	54.35	158	76	BARI SADRI	41.15				
77	2	**BHINAY**	54.30	159	45	SIWANA	40.98			**RAJASTHAN**	**48.21**
78	128	**SAMBHAR**	54.29	160	206	KHANDAR	40.69				
79	69	**LUNKARANSAR**	54.02	161	136	BHINMAL	40.64			**% AGE OF AAPs**	**48.95**

BOLD: Equal/Above Average Panchayat Samities (AAPs)
Source: General Annex III.

ANNEX-9.1

RANKING OF PSS BY PERCENTAGE OF RURAL POP. SERVED BY MEDICAL AMENITIES: RAJASTHAN, 2001

(Descending Order)

RANK	P.CODE	PANCHAYAT SAMITIES NAME	%
1	2	3	4
		VERY HIGH (>60)	
1	**220**	**SIROHI**	**88.10**
2	**159**	**BILARA**	**86.10**
3	**91**	**RATANGARH**	**85.90**
4	**135**	**AHORE**	**83.20**
5	**186**	**BALI**	**82.70**
6	**195**	**SUMERPUR**	**82.10**
6	**192**	**RANI STATION**	**82.10**
8	**67**	**DUNGARGARH**	**80.70**
9	**155**	**UDAIPURWATI**	**80.10**
10	**123**	**GOVINDGARH**	**79.40**
11	**152**	**KHETRI**	**78.80**
12	**160**	**LUNI**	**78.70**
13	**209**	**DHOND**	**78.20**
14	**141**	**SAYLA**	**77.80**
15	**188**	**JAITARAN**	**77.70**
16	**114**	**SADULSHAHAR**	**77.20**
17	**158**	**BHOPALGARH**	**77.10**
18	**56**	**BANERA**	**76.70**
19	**214**	**PIPRALI**	**76.60**
20	**89**	**CHURU**	**76.40**
21	**116**	**BHADRA**	**76.30**
22	**50**	**NADBAI**	**76.20**
23	**217**	**PINDWARA**	**76.10**
24	**49**	**KUMHER**	**75.50**
25	**219**	**SHEOGANJ**	**74.50**
25	**211**	**KHANDELA**	**74.50**
27	**179**	**LADNU**	**73.40**
28	**137**	**JALOR**	**73.20**
29	**4**	**KEKRI**	**73.10**
30	**107**	**SAGWARA**	**72.90**
31	**191**	**RAIPUR**	**72.80**
32	**194**	**SOJAT**	**72.60**
32	**130**	**SHAHPURA**	**72.60**
34	**7**	**PISANGAN**	**72.40**
34	**181**	**MERTA**	**72.40**
36	**187**	**DESURI**	**72.10**
37	**208**	**DANTA RAMGARH**	**72.00**
38	**162**	**OSIAN**	**71.60**
38	**213**	**NEEM KA THANA**	**71.60**
40	**205**	**GANGAPUR**	**71.10**
41	**139**	**RANIWARA**	**71.00**
41	**201**	**RAILMAGRA**	**71.00**
41	**189**	**KHARCHI/MARWAR JUN.**	**71.00**
44	**215**	**SRI MADHOPUR**	**70.90**
45	**57**	**HURDA**	**70.70**
46	**45**	**SIWANA**	**70.30**
47	**138**	**JASWANTPURA**	**70.10**
48	**235**	**MAVLI**	**69.80**
49	**149**	**BUHANA**	**69.40**
50	**25**	**GARHI**	**68.90**
51	**185**	**RIYAN**	**68.60**
51	**177**	**JAYAL**	**68.60**
53	**5**	**KISHANGARH**	**68.40**
53	**105**	**BICHHIWARA**	**68.40**
55	**94**	**TARANAGAR**	**68.00**
55	**16**	**NIMRANA**	**68.00**
57	**104**	**ASPUR**	**67.50**
58	**10**	**BEHROR**	**67.30**
59	**47**	**DEEG**	**67.00**
60	**93**	**SUJANGARH**	**66.90**
61	**150**	**CHIRAWA**	**66.80**
62	**182**	**MUNDWA**	**66.50**
63	**218**	**REODAR**	**66.20**
64	**153**	**NAWALGARH**	**66.10**
64	**180**	**MAKRANA**	**66.10**
66	**190**	**PALI**	**66.00**
67	**184**	**PARBATSAR**	**65.60**
68	**88**	**RASHMI**	**65.20**
69	**175**	**DEGANA**	**65.00**
70	**174**	**SULTANPUR**	**64.80**
70	**165**	**HINDAUN**	**64.80**
72	**207**	**SAWAI MADHOPUR**	**64.50**
73	**230**	**GIRWA**	**64.00**
74	**63**	**SAHARA**	**63.90**
74	**110**	**GANGANAGAR**	**63.90**
76	**136**	**BHINMAL**	**63.80**
77	**128**	**SAMBHAR**	**63.60**
78	**210**	**FATEHPUR**	**63.40**
79	**169**	**TODABHIM**	**63.30**
80	**156**	**BALESAR**	**62.90**
81	**183**	**NAGAUR**	**62.10**
81	**151**	**JHUNJHUNUN**	**62.10**
83	**8**	**SRINAGAR**	**61.90**
83	**83**	**DUNGLA**	**61.90**
85	**117**	**HANUMANGARH**	**61.80**
86	**28**	**PEEPALKHOONT**	**61.50**
87	**100**	**BARI**	**61.10**
88	**20**	**THANAGAZI**	**61.00**
88	**176**	**DIDWANA**	**61.00**
90	**237**	**SARADA**	**60.60**
91	**106**	**DUNGARPUR**	**60.50**
		HIGH (50-60)	
92	**112**	**PADAMPUR**	**59.60**
92	**167**	**NADOTI**	**59.60**
94	**225**	**TONK**	**59.20**
95	**65**	**SUWANA**	**59.10**
96	**119**	**AMBER**	**59.00**
97	**19**	**RENI**	**58.60**
97	**148**	**ALSISAR**	**58.60**
99	**108**	**SIMALWARA**	**58.50**
100	**221**	**DEOLI**	**58.20**
101	**172**	**LADPURA**	**58.10**
102	**164**	**SHERGARH**	**58.00**
102	**122**	**DUDU**	**58.00**
104	**2**	**BHINAY**	**57.90**
105	**168**	**SAPOTRA**	**57.80**
105	**132**	**JAISALMER**	**57.80**
107	**203**	**BAMANWAS**	**57.30**
108	**62**	**RAIPUR**	**57.00**
108	**1**	**ARAIN**	**57.00**
110	**131**	**VIRATNAGAR**	**56.70**
110	**224**	**TODARAISINGH**	**56.70**
112	212	LACHHMANGARH	56.50
113	170	CHECHAT	56.30
113	120	BASSI	56.30
115	199	KHAMNOR	56.20
115	124	JAMWA RAMGARH	56.20
117	58	JAHAZPUR	56.10
118	30	TALWARA	55.90
118	161	MANDOR	55.90
120	52	RUPBAS	55.60
121	206	KHANDAR	55.50
122	64	SHAHPURA	55.10
122	166	KARAULI	55.10
124	90	RAJGARH	55.00
125	163	PHALODI	54.80
126	22	UMREN	54.70
127	178	KUCHAMAN	54.50
128	111	KARANPUR	54.30
129	14	LACHHMANGARH	54.20
130	53	SEWAR	54.10
130	228	BHINDER	54.10
130	38	BALOTRA	54.10
133	26	GHATOL	54.00
133	204	BONLI	54.00
135	70	NOKHA	53.90
136	69	LUNKARANSAR	53.70
137	171	ITAWA	53.40
138	193	ROHAT	53.10
139	129	SANGANER	53.00
140	54	WEIR	52.80
140	55	ASIND	52.80
142	60	MANDAL	52.70
142	71	HINDOLI	52.70
142	96	DAUSA	52.70
145	6	MASOODA	52.50
146	15	MANDAWAR	52.10
147	222	MALPURA	51.90
148	125	JHOTWARA	51.70
149	24	BAGIDORA	51.50
150	11	KATHUMAR	51.40
151	202	RAJSAMAND	51.30
152	95	BANDIKUI	51.00
153	236	SALUMBAR	50.90
153	9	BANSURE	50.90
155	61	MANDALGARH	50.50
156	80	BHOPALSAGAR	50.00
		MEDIUM (40-50)	
157	231	GOGUNDA	49.70
157	216	ABU ROAD	49.70
159	134	SANKRA	49.50
160	68	KOLAYAT	49.20
161	32	ATRU	49.10
162	59	KOTRI	49.00
163	31	ANTA	48.90
164	233	KHERWARA	48.80
165	140	SANCHORE	48.40
165	86	NIMBAHERA	48.40
167	197	BHIM	48.30
168	232	JHADOL	48.20
169	226	UNIARA	48.10
169	23	ANANDPURI	48.10
171	154	SURAJGARH	47.80
171	98	MAHWA	47.80
171	200	KUMBHALGARH	47.80
174	66	BIKANER	47.70
175	92	SARDARSHAHAR	47.60
176	133	SAM	47.30
176	223	NIWAI	47.30
178	41	CHOHTAN	47.10
179	126	KOTPUTLI	46.90
179	145	KHANPUR	46.90
179	84	GANGRAR	46.90
179	227	BARGAON	46.90
183	29	SAJJANGARH	46.60
184	18	RAMGARH	46.40
185	173	SANGOD	46.30
186	17	RAJGARH	46.10
186	48	KAMAN	46.10
186	46	BAYANA	46.10
189	118	NOHAR	45.80
190	76	BARI SADRI	45.70
191	33	BARAN	45.40
192	157	BAP	45.00
193	36	KISHANGANJ	44.90
194	196	AMET	44.80
195	113	RAISINGHNAGAR	44.70
196	82	CHITTAURGARH	43.60
197	127	PHAGI	43.50
198	74	TALERA	43.40
199	73	NAINWA	43.30
199	229	DHARIAWAD	43.30
201	115	SURATGARH	42.40
202	87	PRATAPGARH	42.20
202	101	BASERI	42.20
204	3	JAWAJA	41.90
205	77	BEGUN	41.60
206	99	SIKRAI	41.40
207	72	KESHORAIPATAN	41.30
208	51	NAGAR PAHARI	41.20
209	97	LALSOT	40.50
210	13	KOTKASIM	40.30
		LOW (30-40)	
211	102	DHAULPUR	37.90
211	109	ANUPGARH	37.90
213	78	BHADESAR	37.30
214	234	KOTRA	36.70
215	21	TIJARA	36.60
216	37	SHAHBAD	36.30
217	44	SINDHARI	36.20
217	12	KISHANGARH BAS	36.20
219	198	DEOGARH	35.20
220	143	DAG	34.90
221	27	KUSHALGARH	34.70
222	79	BHAINSRORGARH	34.10
222	142	BAKANI	34.10
224	75	ARNOD	33.80
225	147	PIRAWA	33.20
225	144	JHALRAPATAN	33.20
227	121	CHAKSU	31.40
227	39	BARMER	31.40
229	42	DHORIMANNA	30.80
230	43	SHEO	30.30
231	81	CHHOTI SADRI	30.20
		VERY LOW (<30)	
232	35	CHHIPABAROD	28.80
233	103	RAJAKHERA	28.10
234	40	BAYTOO	27.40
235	85	KAPASAN	24.30
236	146	MANOHARTHANA	21.10
237	34	CHHABRA	14.80
		RAJASTHAN	**56.64**
		% AGE OF AAPs	**46.84**

BOLD: Equal/Above Average Panchayat Samities (AAPs)

Source : General Annex VI.

ANNEX-9.2

RANKING OF PSS BY PERCENTAGE OF INHABITED VILLAGES HAVING MEDICAL AMENITIES: RAJASTHAN, 2001

(Descending Order)

RANK	P.CODE	PANCHAYAT SAMITIES NAME	%
1	2	3	4
		VERY HIGH (>=50)	
1	159	**BILARA**	69.7
2	91	**RATANGARH**	65.3
3	155	**UDAIPURWATI**	64.2
4	195	**SUMERPUR**	61.9
4	89	**CHURU**	61.9
6	209	**DHOND**	61.5
7	67	**DUNGARGARH**	60.9
8	137	**JALOR**	60.3
9	220	**SIROHI**	60.2
10	192	**RANI STATION**	59.2
11	135	**AHORE**	57.3
12	186	**BALI**	57.1
13	50	**NADBAI**	57.0
14	152	**KHETRI**	56.5
15	141	**SAYLA**	55.8
16	49	**KUMHER**	54.7
17	215	**SRI MADHOPUR**	54.5
18	162	**OSIAN**	52.6
19	188	**JAITARAN**	52.4
20	158	**BHOPALGARH**	52.3
21	160	**LUNI**	51.9
22	100	**BARI**	51.8
23	139	**RANIWARA**	51.2
24	211	**KHANDELA**	50.8
25	194	**SOJAT**	50.4
25	165	**HINDAUN**	50.4
27	149	**BUHANA**	50.0
27	214	**PIPRALI**	50.0
		HIGH (40-50)	
29	219	**SHEOGANJ**	49.3
30	213	**NEEM KA THANA**	49.0
30	107	**SAGWARA**	49.0
30	123	**GOVINDGARH**	49.0
33	25	**GARHI**	48.8
34	138	**JASWANTPURA**	48.6
35	104	**ASPUR**	48.3
36	16	**NIMRANA**	48.2
37	7	**PISANGAN**	47.7
37	130	**SHAHPURA**	47.7
39	4	**KEKRI**	47.5
39	136	**BHINMAL**	47.5
41	56	**BANERA**	47.0
42	205	**GANGAPUR**	46.9
43	106	**DUNGARPUR**	46.5
44	208	**DANTA RAMGARH**	45.9
45	153	**NAWALGARH**	45.5
45	184	**PARBATSAR**	45.5
45	217	**PINDWARA**	45.5
48	47	**DEEG**	45.4
48	179	**LADNU**	45.4
50	191	**RAIPUR**	45.0
51	180	**MAKRANA**	44.5
52	210	**FATEHPUR**	44.1
53	105	**BICHHIWARA**	44.0
54	187	**DESURI**	43.6
55	150	**CHIRAWA**	42.9
56	189	**KHARCHI/MARWAR JUN.**	42.3
57	8	**SRINAGAR**	41.7
57	169	**TODABHIM**	41.7
59	235	**MAVLI**	41.6
60	57	**HURDA**	41.4
61	93	**SUJANGARH**	41.3
62	128	**SAMBHAR**	41.0
63	45	**SIWANA**	40.9
64	151	**JHUNJHUNUN**	40.7
65	10	**BEHROR**	40.0
65	190	**PALI**	40.0
		MEDIUM (30-40)	
67	175	**DEGANA**	39.9
68	177	**JAYAL**	39.7
69	201	**RAILMAGRA**	39.6
70	183	**NAGAUR**	39.3
71	112	**PADAMPUR**	38.9
72	182	**MUNDWA**	38.8
73	52	**RUPBAS**	38.7
74	156	**BALESAR**	38.4
74	185	**RIYAN**	38.4
76	176	**DIDWANA**	38.2
77	5	**KISHANGARH**	37.8
78	119	**AMBER**	37.5
79	174	**SULTANPUR**	36.8
80	131	**VIRATNAGAR**	36.7
81	163	**PHALODI**	36.0
82	116	**BHADRA**	35.9
82	207	**SAWAI MADHOPUR**	35.9
84	218	**REODAR**	35.7
85	90	**RAJGARH**	35.7
86	124	**JAMWA RAMGARH**	35.6
87	193	**ROHAT**	35.4
87	166	**KARAULI**	35.4
89	167	**NADOTI**	35.3
90	15	**MANDAWAR**	35.2
90	161	**MANDOR**	35.2
92	181	**MERTA**	35.1
93	92	**SARDARSHAHAR**	34.7
94	216	**ABU ROAD**	34.6
94	164	**SHERGARH**	34.6
96	237	**SARADA**	34.1
97	140	**SANCHORE**	33.8
98	94	**TARANAGAR**	33.6
98	212	**LACHHMANGARH**	33.6
100	83	**DUNGLA**	33.3
101	154	**SURAJGARH**	32.8
102	28	**PEEPALKHOONT**	32.6
103	230	**GIRWA**	32.4
104	108	**SIMALWARA**	32.3
104	148	**ALSISAR**	32.3
106	126	**KOTPUTLI**	32.2
107	178	**KUCHAMAN**	32.1
108	2	**BHINAY**	32.0
109	120	**BASSI**	31.9
110	22	**UMREN**	31.5
111	19	**RENI**	31.4
112	63	**SAHARA**	31.3
112	170	**CHECHAT**	31.3
114	231	**GOGUNDA**	31.3
115	110	**GANGANAGAR**	31.1
116	14	**LACHHMANGARH**	31.0
116	168	**SAPOTRA**	31.0
118	88	**RASHMI**	30.9
119	233	**KHERWARA**	30.8
120	1	**ARAIN**	30.4
120	11	**KATHUMAR**	30.4
122	206	**KHANDAR**	30.3
122	24	**BAGIDORA**	30.3
122	62	**RAIPUR**	30.3
125	65	**SUWANA**	30.1
125	132	**JAISALMER**	30.1
125	134	**SANKRA**	30.1
		LOW (20-30)	
128	199	**KHAMNOR**	29.9
129	227	**BARGAON**	29.9
130	9	**BANSURE**	29.8
130	46	**BAYANA**	29.8
130	64	**SHAHPURA**	29.8
133	172	**LADPURA**	29.7
134	98	**MAHWA**	29.6
135	54	**WEIR**	29.5
136	203	**BAMANWAS**	29.4
137	53	**SEWAR**	29.3
138	70	**NOKHA**	29.2
139	20	THANAGAZI	29.1
140	71	HINDOLI	28.7
141	29	SAJJANGARH	28.6
141	30	TALWARA	28.6
143	225	TONK	28.2
144	69	LUNKARANSAR	28.1
145	236	SALUMBAR	27.8
146	58	JAHAZPUR	27.6
147	41	CHOHTAN	27.3
147	48	KAMAN	27.3
149	197	BHIM	27.3
149	221	DEOLI	27.3
151	23	ANANDPURI	27.1
152	204	BONLI	27.0
152	114	SADULSHAHAR	27.0
154	38	BALOTRA	26.8
154	224	TODARAISINGH	26.8
156	111	KARANPUR	26.6
157	113	RAISINGHNAGAR	26.4
158	33	BARAN	26.3
159	200	KUMBHALGARH	26.2
160	125	JHOTWARA	26.0
161	32	ATRU	25.7
162	3	JAWAJA	25.6
162	122	DUDU	25.6
162	232	JHADOL	25.6
165	27	KUSHALGARH	25.4
166	95	BANDIKUI	25.1
167	26	GHATOL	25.0
167	55	ASIND	25.0
169	18	RAMGARH	24.9
170	157	BAP	24.8
171	222	MALPURA	24.6
172	51	NAGAR PAHARI	24.5
173	202	RAJSAMAND	24.2
174	61	MANDALGARH	23.8
174	129	SANGANER	23.8
176	6	MASOODA	23.0
177	59	KOTRI	22.9
177	60	MANDAL	22.9
179	66	BIKANER	22.8
180	96	DAUSA	22.4
181	102	DHAULPUR	22.3
181	173	SANGOD	22.3
183	228	BHINDER	22.2
184	42	DHORIMANNA	21.5
185	44	SINDHARI	21.2
186	86	NIMBAHERA	21.1
187	223	NIWAI	20.9
188	21	TIJARA	20.8
189	196	AMET	20.6
190	74	TALERA	20.2
190	171	ITAWA	20.2
		VERY LOW (<20)	
192	39	BARMER	19.9
193	84	GANGRAR	19.7
194	31	ANTA	19.6
195	68	KOLAYAT	19.4
196	12	KISHANGARH BAS	19.3
196	17	RAJGARH	19.3
196	72	KESHORAIPATAN	19.3
196	80	BHOPALSAGAR	19.3
200	13	KOTKASIM	19.1
201	36	KISHANGANJ	18.9
201	76	BARI SADRI	18.9
201	115	SURATGARH	18.9
201	117	HANUMANGARH	18.9
201	127	PHAGI	18.9
206	87	PRATAPGARH	18.8
207	99	SIKRAI	18.7
207	145	KHANPUR	18.7
209	101	BASERI	18.4
210	229	DHARIAWAD	18.1
211	40	BAYTOO	18.0
212	73	NAINWA	17.8
213	43	SHEO	17.2
214	103	RAJAKHERA	17.1
214	133	SAM	17.1
216	109	ANUPGARH	16.8
217	77	BEGUN	16.7
218	226	UNIARA	16.3
219	118	NOHAR	16.2
220	79	BHAINSRORGARH	15.6
220	82	CHITTAURGARH	15.6
222	143	DAG	15.4
223	198	DEOGARH	15.3
224	144	JHALRAPATAN	15.1
225	142	BAKANI	14.9
226	97	LALSOT	14.3
227	234	KOTRA	14.2
228	147	PIRAWA	13.2
229	37	SHAHBAD	12.6
230	75	ARNOD	12.4
231	78	BHADESAR	11.7
232	81	CHHOTI SADRI	11.3
233	35	CHHIPABAROD	11.0
234	146	MANOHARTHANA	10.9
235	85	KAPASAN	10.3
236	121	CHAKSU	10.1
237	34	CHHABRA	7.5
		RAJASTHAN	**29.20**
		% AGE OF AAPs	**58.23**

BOLD: Equal/Above Average Panchayat Samities (AAPs)

Source : General Annex VII.

ANNEX-9.3

RANKING OF PSS BY TOTAL NO. OF MEDICAL INSTITUTIONS: RAJASTHAN, 2001

(Descending Order)

RANK	P.CODE	PANCHAYAT SAMITIES NAME	No.
1	2	3	4
		VERY HIGH (>=80)	
1	104	ASPUR	137
1	117	HANUMANGARH	137
3	208	DANTA RAMGARH	121
4	162	OSIAN	117
5	107	SAGWARA	113
6	25	GARHI	111
6	237	SARADA	111
8	61	MANDALGARH	109
9	232	JHADOL	107
9	118	NOHAR	107
9	108	SIMALWARA	107
12	236	SALUMBAR	106
13	194	SOJAT	103
14	213	NEEM KA THANA	101
15	105	BICHHIWARA	97
15	209	DHOND	97
15	220	SIROHI	97
18	149	BUHANA	96
18	233	KHERWARA	96
20	106	DUNGARPUR	95
20	230	GIRWA	95
22	225	TONK	94
23	200	KUMBHALGARH	91
24	175	DEGANA	90
24	30	TALWARA	90
26	228	BHINDER	88
27	109	ANUPGARH	86
27	26	GHATOL	86
27	199	KHAMNOR	86
27	178	KUCHAMAN	86
27	91	RATANGARH	86
27	44	SINDHARI	86
27	155	UDAIPURWATI	86
34	214	PIPRALI	85
34	90	RAJGARH	85
34	140	SANCHORE	85
37	55	ASIND	84
37	122	DUDU	84
37	210	FATEHPUR	84
37	151	JHUNJHUNUN	84
41	159	BILARA	82
41	176	DIDWANA	82
41	235	MAVLI	82
44	89	CHURU	81
44	58	JAHAZPUR	81
44	7	PISANGAN	81
47	186	BALI	80
47	211	KHANDELA	80
47	87	PRATAPGARH	80
47	168	SAPOTRA	80
		HIGH (60-80)	
51	207	SAWAI MADHOPUR	79
52	189	KHARCHI/MARWAR JUN.	78
53	218	REODAR	75
53	93	SUJANGARH	75
55	183	NAGAUR	74
56	135	AHORE	73
56	229	DHARIAWAD	73
56	28	PEEPALKHOONT	73
56	192	RANI STATION	73
56	185	RIYAN	73
61	96	DAUSA	72
61	153	NAWALGARH	72
61	201	RAILMAGRA	72
64	67	DUNGARGARH	71
65	38	BALOTRA	70
65	124	JAMWA RAMGARH	70
65	179	LADNU	70
65	160	LUNI	70
69	120	BASSI	69
69	40	BAYTOO	69
69	110	GANGANAGAR	69
69	188	JAITARAN	69
69	177	JAYAL	69
69	27	KUSHALGARH	69
69	94	TARANAGAR	69
76	184	PARBATSAR	68
77	114	SADULSHAHAR	67
77	169	TODABHIM	67
79	152	KHETRI	66
79	45	SIWANA	66
81	148	ALSISAR	65
81	156	BALESAR	65
81	39	BARMER	65
81	116	BHADRA	65
81	231	GOGUNDA	65
81	123	GOVINDGARH	65
81	15	MANDAWAR	65
81	52	RUPBAS	65
89	66	BIKANER	64
89	134	SANKRA	64
89	92	SARDARSHAHAR	64
89	130	SHAHPURA	64
89	115	SURATGARH	64
94	77	BEGUN	63
94	158	BHOPALGARH	63
94	204	BONLI	63
94	133	SAM	63
94	128	SAMBHAR	63
94	65	SUWANA	63
100	24	BAGIDORA	62
100	102	DHAULPUR	62
100	64	SHAHPURA	62
103	2	BHINAY	61
103	42	DHORIMANNA	61
103	165	HINDAUN	61
103	126	KOTPUTLI	61
103	223	NIWAI	61
108	71	HINDOLI	60
108	132	JAISALMER	60
108	3	JAWAJA	60
108	234	KOTRA	60
108	74	TALERA	60
		MEDIUM (40-60)	
113	166	KARAULI	59
113	72	KESHORAIPATAN	59
113	212	LACHHMANGARH	59
113	180	MAKRANA	59
117	217	PINDWARA	58
118	119	AMBER	57
118	4	KEKRI	57
118	5	KISHANGARH	57
118	60	MANDAL	57
118	181	MERTA	57
118	182	MUNDWA	57
118	191	RAIPUR	57
118	29	SAJJANGARH	57
118	173	SANGOD	57
118	195	SUMERPUR	57
128	100	BARI	56
129	56	BANERA	55
129	221	DEOLI	55
129	137	JALOR	55
129	145	KHANPUR	55
129	219	SHEOGANJ	55
134	41	CHOHTAN	54
134	187	DESURI	54
134	69	LUNKARANSAR	54
134	73	NAINWA	54
134	20	THANAGAZI	54
139	163	PHALODI	53
139	141	SAYLA	53
141	227	BARGAON	52
141	197	BHIM	52
141	150	CHIRAWA	52
141	82	CHITTAURGARH	52
141	205	GANGAPUR	52
141	11	KATHUMAR	52
141	49	KUMHER	52
141	6	MASOODA	52
141	113	RAISINGHNAGAR	52
141	54	WEIR	52
151	206	KHANDAR	51
151	222	MALPURA	51
151	129	SANGANER	51
151	131	VIRATNAGAR	51
155	1	ARAIN	50
155	203	BAMANWAS	50
155	138	JASWANTPURA	50
155	97	LALSOT	50
155	8	SRINAGAR	50
155	154	SURAJGARH	50
155	22	UMREN	50
162	59	KOTRI	49
162	63	SAHARA	49
164	23	ANANDPURI	48
165	9	BANSURE	47
165	43	SHEO	47
165	215	SRI MADHOPUR	47
168	111	KARANPUR	46
168	172	LADPURA	46
168	202	RAJSAMAND	46
171	101	BASERI	45
171	143	DAG	45
171	112	PADAMPUR	45
171	19	RENI	45
175	144	JHALRAPATAN	44
175	14	LACHHMANGARH	44
175	167	NADOTI	44
175	193	ROHAT	44
175	174	SULTANPUR	44
175	21	TIJARA	44
181	171	ITAWA	43
181	68	KOLAYAT	43
181	98	MAHWA	43
181	70	NOKHA	43
181	147	PIRAWA	43
181	62	RAIPUR	43
187	31	ANTA	42
188	57	HURDA	40
188	37	SHAHBAD	40
		LOW (20-40)	
190	10	BEHROR	39
190	127	PHAGI	39
190	224	TODARAISINGH	39
193	32	ATRU	38
193	136	BHINMAL	38
193	51	NAGAR PAHARI	38
193	86	NIMBAHERA	38
193	88	RASHMI	38
193	164	SHERGARH	38
193	99	SIKRAI	38
200	95	BANDIKUI	37
200	121	CHAKSU	37
200	50	NADBAI	37
203	142	BAKANI	36
203	190	PALI	36
203	18	RAMGARH	36
206	12	KISHANGARH BAS	35
206	17	RAJGARH	35
206	139	RANIWARA	35
206	53	SEWAR	35
210	196	AMET	34
210	170	CHECHAT	34
210	83	DUNGLA	34
210	16	NIMRANA	34
214	216	ABU ROAD	33
215	226	UNIARA	32
216	157	BAP	31
216	47	DEEG	31
216	125	JHOTWARA	31
219	75	ARNOD	30
219	46	BAYANA	30
219	36	KISHANGANJ	30
222	35	CHHIPABAROD	29
222	84	GANGRAR	29
224	80	BHOPALSAGAR	28
224	48	KAMAN	28
226	161	MANDOR	27
227	103	RAJAKHERA	25
228	79	BHAINSRORGARH	24
228	81	CHHOTI SADRI	24
230	78	BHADESAR	23
231	33	BARAN	22
232	198	DEOGARH	20
		VERY LOW (<20)	
233	146	MANOHARTHANA	19
234	13	KOTKASIM	17
235	76	BARI SADRI	14
235	34	CHHABRA	14
235	85	KAPASAN	14
RAJASTHAN		TOTAL	14231
		AVERAGE	60
		% AGE OF AAPs	45.15

BOLD: Equal/Above Average Panchayat Samities (AAPs)
Source: General Annex VIII.

ANNEX-9.4

RANKING OF PSS BY NO. OF HOSPITALS: RAJASTHAN, 2001

(*Descending Order*)

RANK	P.CODE	PANCHAYAT SAMITIES NAME	HOSPITALS
1	2	3	4
		HIGH (>=4)	
1	**192**	**RANI STATION**	**7**
2	**187**	**DESURI**	**6**
3	**11**	**KATHUMAR**	**4**
3	**118**	**NOHAR**	**4**
		MEDIUM (3)	
5	**107**	**SAGWARA**	**3**
5	**175**	**DEGANA**	**3**
5	**208**	**DANTA RAMGARH**	**3**
5	**232**	**JHADOL**	**3**
		LOW (2)	
9	**30**	**TALWARA**	**2**
9	**61**	**MANDALGARH**	**2**
9	**62**	**RAIPUR**	**2**
9	**71**	**HINDOLI**	**2**
9	**94**	**TARANAGAR**	**2**
9	**101**	**BASERI**	**2**
9	**102**	**DHAULPUR**	**2**
9	**105**	**BICHHIWARA**	**2**
9	**109**	**ANUPGARH**	**2**
9	**115**	**SURATGARH**	**2**
9	**122**	**DUDU**	**2**
9	**165**	**HINDAUN**	**2**
9	**168**	**SAPOTRA**	**2**
9	**189**	**KHARCHI/MARWAR JUN.**	**2**
9	**194**	**SOJAT**	**2**
9	**211**	**KHANDELA**	**2**
9	**227**	**BARGAON**	**2**
9	**237**	**SARADA**	**2**
		VERY LOW (1)	
27	**6**	**MASOODA**	**1**
27	**10**	**BEHROR**	**1**
27	**23**	**ANANDPURI**	**1**
27	**28**	**PEEPALKHOONT**	**1**
27	**32**	**ATRU**	**1**
27	**52**	**RUPBAS**	**1**
27	**54**	**WEIR**	**1**
27	**57**	**HURDA**	**1**
27	**65**	**SUWANA**	**1**
27	**104**	**ASPUR**	**1**
27	**106**	**DUNGARPUR**	**1**
27	**108**	**SIMALWARA**	**1**
27	**111**	**KARANPUR**	**1**
27	**112**	**PADAMPUR**	**1**
27	**114**	**SADULSHAHAR**	**1**
27	**134**	**SANKRA**	**1**
27	**148**	**ALSISAR**	**1**
27	**150**	**CHIRAWA**	**1**
27	**159**	**BILARA**	**1**
27	**169**	**TODABHIM**	**1**
27	**171**	**ITAWA**	**1**
27	**176**	**DIDWANA**	**1**
27	**178**	**KUCHAMAN**	**1**
27	**182**	**MUNDWA**	**1**
27	**185**	**RIYAN**	**1**
27	**186**	**BALI**	**1**
27	**188**	**JAITARAN**	**1**
27	**190**	**PALI**	**1**
27	**191**	**RAIPUR**	**1**
27	**193**	**ROHAT**	**1**
27	**200**	**KUMBHALGARH**	**1**
27	**203**	**BAMANWAS**	**1**
27	**210**	**FATEHPUR**	**1**
27	**213**	**NEEM KA THANA**	**1**
27	**214**	**PIPRALI**	**1**
27	**218**	**REODAR**	**1**
27	**220**	**SIROHI**	**1**
27	**221**	**DEOLI**	**1**
27	**231**	**GOGUNDA**	**1**
27	**234**	**KOTRA**	**1**
		NIL (0)	
67	1	ARAIN	
67	2	BHINAY	
67	3	JAWAJA	
67	4	KEKRI	
67	5	KISHANGARH	
67	7	PISANGAN	
67	8	SRINAGAR	
67	9	BANSURE	
67	12	KISHANGARH BAS	
67	13	KOTKASIM	
67	14	LACHHMANGARH	
67	15	MANDAWAR	
67	16	NIMRANA	
67	17	RAJGARH	
67	18	RAMGARH	
67	19	RENI	
67	20	THANAGAZI	
67	21	TIJARA	
67	22	UMREN	
67	24	BAGIDORA	
67	25	GARHI	
67	26	GHATOL	
67	27	KUSHALGARH	
67	29	SAJJANGARH	
67	31	ANTA	
67	33	BARAN	
67	34	CHHABRA	
67	35	CHHIPABAROD	
67	36	KISHANGANJ	
67	37	SHAHBAD	
67	38	BALOTRA	
67	39	BARMER	
67	40	BAYTOO	
67	41	CHOHTAN	
67	42	DHORIMANNA	
67	43	SHEO	
67	44	SINDHARI	
67	45	SIWANA	
67	46	BAYANA	
67	47	DEEG	
67	48	KAMAN	
67	49	KUMHER	
67	50	NADBAI	
67	51	NAGAR PAHARI	
67	53	SEWAR	
67	55	ASIND	
67	56	BANERA	
67	58	JAHAZPUR	
67	59	KOTRI	
67	60	MANDAL	
67	63	SAHARA	
67	64	SHAHPURA	
67	66	BIKANER	
67	67	DUNGARGARH	
67	68	KOLAYAT	
67	69	LUNKARANSAR	
67	70	NOKHA	
67	72	KESHORAIPATAN	
67	73	NAINWA	
67	74	TALERA	
67	75	ARNOD	
67	76	BARI SADRI	
67	77	BEGUN	
67	78	BHADESAR	
67	79	BHAINSRORGARH	
67	80	BHOPALSAGAR	
67	81	CHHOTI SADRI	
67	82	CHITTAURGARH	
67	83	DUNGLA	
67	84	GANGRAR	
67	85	KAPASAN	
67	86	NIMBAHERA	
67	87	PRATAPGARH	
67	88	RASHMI	
67	89	CHURU	
67	90	RAJGARH	
67	91	RATANGARH	
67	92	SARDARSHAHAR	
67	93	SUJANGARH	
67	95	BANDIKUI	
67	96	DAUSA	
67	97	LALSOT	
67	98	MAHWA	
67	99	SIKRAI	
67	100	BARI	
67	103	RAJAKHERA	
67	110	GANGANAGAR	
67	113	RAISINGHNAGAR	
67	116	BHADRA	
67	117	HANUMANGARH	
67	119	AMBER	
67	120	BASSI	
67	121	CHAKSU	
67	123	GOVINDGARH	
67	124	JAMWA RAMGARH	
67	125	JHOTWARA	
67	126	KOTPUTLI	
67	127	PHAGI	
67	128	SAMBHAR	
67	129	SANGANER	
67	130	SHAHPURA	
67	131	VIRATNAGAR	
67	132	JAISALMER	
67	133	SAM	
67	135	AHORE	
67	136	BHINMAL	
67	137	JALOR	
67	138	JASWANTPURA	
67	139	RANIWARA	
67	140	SANCHORE	
67	141	SAYLA	
67	142	BAKANI	
67	143	DAG	
67	144	JHALRAPATAN	
67	145	KHANPUR	
67	146	MANOHARTHANA	
67	147	PIRAWA	
67	149	BUHANA	
67	151	JHUNJHUNUN	
67	152	KHETRI	
67	153	NAWALGARH	
67	154	SURAJGARH	
67	155	UDAIPURWATI	
67	156	BALESAR	
67	157	BAP	
67	158	BHOPALGARH	
67	160	LUNI	
67	161	MANDOR	
67	162	OSIAN	
67	163	PHALODI	
67	164	SHERGARH	
67	166	KARAULI	
67	167	NADOTI	
67	170	CHECHAT	
67	172	LADPURA	
67	173	SANGOD	
67	174	SULTANPUR	
67	177	JAYAL	
67	179	LADNU	
67	180	MAKRANA	
67	181	MERTA	
67	183	NAGAUR	
67	184	PARBATSAR	
67	195	SUMERPUR	
67	196	AMET	
67	197	BHIM	
67	198	DEOGARH	
67	199	KHAMNOR	
67	201	RAILMAGRA	
67	202	RAJSAMAND	
67	204	BONLI	
67	205	GANGAPUR	
67	206	KHANDAR	
67	207	SAWAI MADHOPUR	
67	209	DHOND	
67	212	LACHHMANGARH	
67	215	SRI MADHOPUR	
67	216	ABU ROAD	
67	217	PINDWARA	
67	219	SHEOGANJ	
67	222	MALPURA	
67	223	NIWAI	
67	224	TODARAISINGH	
67	225	TONK	
67	226	UNIARA	
67	228	BHINDER	
67	229	DHARIAWAD	
67	230	GIRWA	
67	233	KHERWARA	
67	235	MAVLI	
67	236	SALUMBAR	
RAJASTHAN		**TOTAL**	**109**
		AVERAGE	**0.46**
		% AGE OF AAPs	**27.85**

BOLD: Equal/Above Average Panchayat Samities (AAPs)
Source: General Annex VIII.

ANNEX-9.5

RANKING OF PSS BY NO. OF DISPENSARIES: RAJASTHAN, 2001

(Descending Order)

RANK	PANCHAYAT SAMITIES P.CODE	NAME	DISPEN-SARIES
1	2	3	4
		VERY HIGH (>=8)	
1	**117**	**HANUMANGARH**	**47**
2	**118**	**NOHAR**	**44**
3	**54**	**WEIR**	**33**
3	**130**	**SHAHPURA**	**33**
3	**237**	**SARADA**	**33**
6	**108**	**SIMALWARA**	**31**
6	**149**	**BUHANA**	**31**
8	**15**	**MANDAWAR**	**30**
8	**107**	**SAGWARA**	**30**
8	**116**	**BHADRA**	**30**
8	**124**	**JAMWA RAMGARH**	**30**
8	**208**	**DANTA RAMGARH**	**30**
8	**213**	**NEEM KA THANA**	**30**
8	**223**	**NIWAI**	**30**
15	**25**	**GARHI**	**29**
15	**94**	**TARANAGAR**	**29**
15	**115**	**SURATGARH**	**29**
15	**209**	**DHOND**	**29**
15	**236**	**SALUMBAR**	**29**
20	**92**	**SARDARSHAHAR**	**28**
20	**126**	**KOTPUTLI**	**28**
20	**151**	**JHUNJHUNUN**	**28**
23	**178**	**KUCHAMAN**	**27**
24	**26**	**GHATOL**	**26**
24	**52**	**RUPBAS**	**26**
24	**222**	**MALPURA**	**26**
27	**55**	**ASIND**	**25**
27	**109**	**ANUPGARH**	**25**
27	**122**	**DUDU**	**25**
27	**186**	**BALI**	**25**
27	**199**	**KHAMNOR**	**25**
32	**9**	**BANSURE**	**24**
32	**58**	**JAHAZPUR**	**24**
32	**192**	**RANI STATION**	**24**
35	**61**	**MANDALGARH**	**23**
35	**91**	**RATANGARH**	**23**
35	**104**	**ASPUR**	**23**
35	**162**	**OSIAN**	**23**
39	**21**	**TIJARA**	**22**
39	**90**	**RAJGARH**	**22**
39	**123**	**GOVINDGARH**	**22**
39	**235**	**MAVLI**	**22**
43	**11**	**KATHUMAR**	**21**
43	**20**	**THANAGAZI**	**21**
43	**64**	**SHAHPURA**	**21**
43	**89**	**CHURU**	**21**
43	**128**	**SAMBHAR**	**21**
43	**201**	**RAILMAGRA**	**21**
43	**203**	**BAMANWAS**	**21**
43	**206**	**KHANDAR**	**21**
43	**207**	**SAWAI MADHOPUR**	**21**
43	**210**	**FATEHPUR**	**21**
43	**225**	**TONK**	**21**
43	**228**	**BHINDER**	**21**
55	**5**	**KISHANGARH**	**20**
55	**30**	**TALWARA**	**20**
55	**168**	**SAPOTRA**	**20**
55	**171**	**ITAWA**	**20**
55	**184**	**PARBATSAR**	**20**
55	**204**	**BONLI**	**20**
61	**6**	**MASOODA**	**19**
61	**7**	**PISANGAN**	**19**
61	**102**	**DHAULPUR**	**19**
61	**113**	**RAISINGHNAGAR**	**19**
61	**131**	**VIRATNAGAR**	**19**
61	**165**	**HINDAUN**	**19**
61	**185**	**RIYAN**	**19**
61	**220**	**SIROHI**	**19**
61	**230**	**GIRWA**	**19**
70	**4**	**KEKRI**	**18**
70	**10**	**BEHROR**	**18**
70	**65**	**SUWANA**	**18**
70	**67**	**DUNGARGARH**	**18**
70	**96**	**DAUSA**	**18**
70	**110**	**GANGANAGAR**	**18**
70	**134**	**SANKRA**	**18**
70	**205**	**GANGAPUR**	**18**
70	**212**	**LACHHMANGARH**	**18**
70	**221**	**DEOLI**	**18**
70	**232**	**JHADOL**	**18**
81	**2**	**BHINAY**	**17**
81	**16**	**NIMRANA**	**17**
81	**19**	**RENI**	**17**
81	**44**	**SINDHARI**	**17**
81	**60**	**MANDAL**	**17**
81	**66**	**BIKANER**	**17**
81	**73**	**NAINWA**	**17**
81	**120**	**BASSI**	**17**
81	**148**	**ALSISAR**	**17**
81	**150**	**CHIRAWA**	**17**
81	**166**	**KARAULI**	**17**
81	**169**	**TODABHIM**	**17**
81	**191**	**RAIPUR**	**17**
94	**45**	**SIWANA**	**16**
94	**72**	**KESHORAIPATAN**	**16**
94	**74**	**TALERA**	**16**
94	**87**	**PRATAPGARH**	**16**
94	**93**	**SUJANGARH**	**16**
94	**106**	**DUNGARPUR**	**16**
94	**129**	**SANGANER**	**16**
94	**145**	**KHANPUR**	**16**
94	**152**	**KHETRI**	**16**
94	**155**	**UDAIPURWATI**	**16**
94	**167**	**NADOTI**	**16**
94	**176**	**DIDWANA**	**16**
94	**189**	**KHARCHI/MARWAR JUN.**	**16**
94	**214**	**PIPRALI**	**16**
108	32	ATRU	15
108	69	LUNKARANSAR	15
108	88	RASHMI	15
108	97	LALSOT	15
108	105	BICHHIWARA	15
108	112	PADAMPUR	15
108	175	DEGANA	15
108	177	JAYAL	15
108	183	NAGAUR	15
108	200	KUMBHALGARH	15
108	202	RAJSAMAND	15
108	227	BARGAON	15
120	17	RAJGARH	14
120	35	CHHIPABAROD	14
120	53	SEWAR	14
120	63	SAHARA	14
120	82	CHITTAURGARH	14
120	101	BASERI	14
120	121	CHAKSU	14
120	127	PHAGI	14
120	153	NAWALGARH	14
120	173	SANGOD	14
120	229	DHARIAWAD	14
131	8	SRINAGAR	13
131	22	UMREN	13
131	31	ANTA	13
131	42	DHORIMANNA	13
131	49	KUMHER	13
131	56	BANERA	13
131	77	BEGUN	13
131	114	SADULSHAHAR	13
131	125	JHOTWARA	13
131	135	AHORE	13
131	140	SANCHORE	13
131	141	SAYLA	13
131	144	JHALRAPATAN	13
131	156	BALESAR	13
131	160	LUNI	13
131	163	PHALODI	13
131	187	DESURI	13
131	211	KHANDELA	13
131	217	PINDWARA	13
131	224	TODARAISINGH	13
131	233	KHERWARA	13
152	50	NADBAI	12
152	98	MAHWA	12
152	137	JALOR	12
152	138	JASWANTPURA	12
152	158	BHOPALGARH	12
152	181	MERTA	12
152	215	SRI MADHOPUR	12
152	226	UNIARA	12
152	234	KOTRA	12
161	18	RAMGARH	11
161	28	PEEPALKHOONT	11
161	29	SAJJANGARH	11
161	46	BAYANA	11
161	57	HURDA	11
161	68	KOLAYAT	11
161	71	HINDOLI	11
161	100	BARI	11
161	119	AMBER	11
161	143	DAG	11
161	170	CHECHAT	11
161	179	LADNU	11
161	218	REODAR	11
161	231	GOGUNDA	11
175	14	LACHHMANGARH	10
175	27	KUSHALGARH	10
175	43	SHEO	10
175	59	KOTRI	10
175	70	NOKHA	10
175	75	ARNOD	10
175	79	BHAINSRORGARH	10
175	86	NIMBAHERA	10
175	95	BANDIKUI	10
175	99	SIKRAI	10
175	132	JAISALMER	10
175	133	SAM	10
175	159	BILARA	10
175	172	LADPURA	10
175	180	MAKRANA	10
175	182	MUNDWA	10
175	188	JAITARAN	10
192	1	ARAIN	9
192	23	ANANDPURI	9
192	51	NAGAR PAHARI	9
192	84	GANGRAR	9
192	161	MANDOR	9
192	164	SHERGARH	9
192	194	SOJAT	9
192	216	ABU ROAD	9
200	36	KISHANGANJ	8
200	38	BALOTRA	8
200	40	BAYTOO	8
200	193	ROHAT	8
200	195	SUMERPUR	8
200	197	BHIM	8
200	219	SHEOGANJ	8
		HIGH (6-8)	
207	12	KISHANGARH BAS	7
207	13	KOTKASIM	7
207	39	BARMER	7
207	41	CHOHTAN	7
207	48	KAMAN	7
207	83	DUNGLA	7
207	142	BAKANI	7
207	147	PIRAWA	7
207	154	SURAJGARH	7
207	190	PALI	7
207	196	AMET	7
218	3	JAWAJA	6
218	24	BAGIDORA	6
218	47	DEEG	6
218	62	RAIPUR	6
218	78	BHADESAR	6
218	81	CHHOTI SADRI	6
218	85	KAPASAN	6
218	103	RAJAKHERA	6
218	111	KARANPUR	6
218	136	BHINMAL	6
		MEDIUM (4-6)	
228	33	BARAN	5
228	76	BARI SADRI	5
228	80	BHOPALSAGAR	5
228	146	MANOHARTHANA	5
228	174	SULTANPUR	5
233	34	CHHABRA	4
233	37	SHAHBAD	4
233	198	DEOGARH	4
		LOW (<4)	
236	139	RANIWARA	3
236	157	BAP	3
RAJASTHAN		**TOTAL**	**3706**
		AVERAGE	**15.64**
		% AGE OF AAPs	**45.15**

BOLD: Equal/Above Average Panchayat Samities (AAPs)

Source: General Annex VIII.

ANNEX-9.6

RANKING OF PSS BY NO. OF PHCS: RAJASTHAN, 2001

(Descending Order)

RANK	P.CODE	PANCHAYAT SAMITIES NAME	PHC
1	2	3	4
		VERY HIGH (>=5)	
1	194	**SOJAT**	35
2	30	**TALWARA**	29
2	61	**MANDALGARH**	29
2	117	**HANUMANGARH**	29
2	208	**DANTA RAMGARH**	29
6	211	**KHANDELA**	28
6	225	**TONK**	28
8	159	**BILARA**	27
9	104	**ASPUR**	25
10	237	**SARADA**	24
11	44	**SINDHARI**	23
11	233	**KHERWARA**	23
13	106	**DUNGARPUR**	22
13	152	**KHETRI**	22
13	184	**PARBATSAR**	22
13	200	**KUMBHALGARH**	22
13	230	**GIRWA**	22
18	66	**BIKANER**	21
18	214	**PIPRALI**	21
20	25	**GARHI**	20
20	162	**OSIAN**	20
20	179	**LADNU**	20
23	28	**PEEPALKHOONT**	19
23	45	**SIWANA**	19
23	140	**SANCHORE**	19
23	153	**NAWALGARH**	19
23	188	**JAITARAN**	19
23	189	**KHARCHI/MARWAR JUN.**	19
23	195	**SUMERPUR**	19
30	41	**CHOHTAN**	18
30	71	**HINDOLI**	18
30	149	**BUHANA**	18
33	7	**PISANGAN**	17
33	29	**SAJJANGARH**	17
33	100	**BARI**	17
33	118	**NOHAR**	17
33	122	**DUDU**	17
33	124	**JAMWA RAMGARH**	17
33	178	**KUCHAMAN**	17
33	199	**KHAMNOR**	17
41	38	**BALOTRA**	16
41	40	**BAYTOO**	16
41	55	**ASIND**	16
41	77	**BEGUN**	16
41	102	**DHAULPUR**	16
41	107	**SAGWARA**	16
41	155	**UDAIPURWATI**	16
41	218	**REODAR**	16
41	219	**SHEOGANJ**	16
41	220	**SIROHI**	16
41	232	**JHADOL**	16
52	24	**BAGIDORA**	15
52	27	**KUSHALGARH**	15
52	58	**JAHAZPUR**	15
52	59	**KOTRI**	15
52	67	**DUNGARGARH**	15
52	87	**PRATAPGARH**	15
52	89	**CHURU**	15
52	90	**RAJGARH**	15
52	93	**SUJANGARH**	15
52	105	**BICHHIWARA**	15
52	207	**SAWAI MADHOPUR**	15
63	14	**LACHHMANGARH**	14
63	15	**MANDAWAR**	14
63	26	**GHATOL**	14
63	49	**KUMHER**	14
63	72	**KESHORAIPATAN**	14
63	96	**DAUSA**	14
63	120	**BASSI**	14
63	132	**JAISALMER**	14
63	144	**JHALRAPATAN**	14
63	160	**LUNI**	14
63	182	**MUNDWA**	14
63	185	**RIYAN**	14
63	193	**ROHAT**	14
63	209	**DHOND**	14
63	221	**DEOLI**	14
63	236	**SALUMBAR**	14
79	31	**ANTA**	13
79	52	**RUPBAS**	13
79	74	**TALERA**	13
79	91	**RATANGARH**	13
79	108	**SIMALWARA**	13
79	109	**ANUPGARH**	13
79	114	**SADULSHAHAR**	13
79	141	**SAYLA**	13
79	156	**BALESAR**	13
79	180	**MAKRANA**	13
79	197	**BHIM**	13
79	201	**RAILMAGRA**	13
91	2	**BHINAY**	12
91	69	**LUNKARANSAR**	12
91	86	**NIMBAHERA**	12
91	110	**GANGANAGAR**	12
91	126	**KOTPUTLI**	12
91	134	**SANKRA**	12
91	150	**CHIRAWA**	12
91	168	**SAPOTRA**	12
91	175	**DEGANA**	12
91	181	**MERTA**	12
91	187	**DESURI**	12
91	210	**FATEHPUR**	12
91	213	**NEEM KA THANA**	12
91	224	**TODARAISINGH**	12
91	228	**BHINDER**	12
91	235	**MAVLI**	12
107	19	RENI	11
107	37	SHAHBAD	11
107	51	NAGAR PAHARI	11
107	54	WEIR	11
107	62	RAIPUR	11
107	63	SAHARA	11
107	65	SUWANA	11
107	98	MAHWA	11
107	138	JASWANTPURA	11
107	147	PIRAWA	11
107	158	BHOPALGARH	11
107	165	HINDAUN	11
107	166	KARAULI	11
107	177	JAYAL	11
107	222	MALPURA	11
122	4	KEKRI	10
122	39	BARMER	10
122	60	MANDAL	10
122	75	ARNOD	10
122	94	TARANAGAR	10
122	115	SURATGARH	10
122	116	BHADRA	10
122	119	AMBER	10
122	123	GOVINDGARH	10
122	154	SURAJGARH	10
122	163	PHALODI	10
122	176	DIDWANA	10
122	186	BALI	10
122	203	BAMANWAS	10
122	204	BONLI	10
122	212	LACHHMANGARH	10
122	215	SRI MADHOPUR	10
122	227	BARGAON	10
122	229	DHARIAWAD	10
122	234	KOTRA	10
142	1	ARAIN	9
142	5	KISHANGARH	9
142	8	SRINAGAR	9
142	23	ANANDPURI	9
142	53	SEWAR	9
142	80	BHOPALSAGAR	9
142	82	CHITTAURGARH	9
142	128	SAMBHAR	9
142	136	BHINMAL	9
142	169	TODABHIM	9
142	217	PINDWARA	9
153	6	MASOODA	8
153	10	BEHROR	8
153	11	KATHUMAR	8
153	12	KISHANGARH BAS	8
153	16	NIMRANA	8
153	20	THANAGAZI	8
153	42	DHORIMANNA	8
153	64	SHAHPURA	8
153	68	KOLAYAT	8
153	95	BANDIKUI	8
153	97	LALSOT	8
153	99	SIKRAI	8
153	133	SAM	8
153	137	JALOR	8
153	164	SHERGARH	8
153	172	LADPURA	8
153	173	SANGOD	8
153	174	SULTANPUR	8
153	183	NAGAUR	8
153	191	RAIPUR	8
153	231	GOGUNDA	8
174	18	RAMGARH	7
174	22	UMREN	7
174	36	KISHANGANJ	7
174	48	KAMAN	7
174	57	HURDA	7
174	92	SARDARSHAHAR	7
174	103	RAJAKHERA	7
174	127	PHAGI	7
174	131	VIRATNAGAR	7
174	135	AHORE	7
174	139	RANIWARA	7
174	145	KHANPUR	7
174	148	ALSISAR	7
174	151	JHUNJHUNUN	7
174	157	BAP	7
174	167	NADOTI	7
174	202	RAJSAMAND	7
174	206	KHANDAR	7
174	226	UNIARA	7
193	3	JAWAJA	6
193	9	BANSURE	6
193	17	RAJGARH	6
193	43	SHEO	6
193	47	DEEG	6
193	56	BANERA	6
193	81	CHHOTI SADRI	6
193	88	RASHMI	6
193	101	BASERI	6
193	112	PADAMPUR	6
193	113	RAISINGHNAGAR	6
193	142	BAKANI	6
193	143	DAG	6
193	190	PALI	6
193	205	GANGAPUR	6
193	223	NIWAI	6
209	21	TIJARA	5
209	32	ATRU	5
209	33	BARAN	5
209	70	NOKHA	5
209	78	BHADESAR	5
209	83	DUNGLA	5
209	171	ITAWA	5
209	192	RANI STATION	5
209	216	ABU ROAD	5
		HIGH (4)	
218	13	KOTKASIM	
218	50	NADBAI	
218	76	BARI SADRI	
218	111	KARANPUR	
218	121	CHAKSU	
218	129	SANGANER	
218	130	SHAHPURA	
218	196	AMET	
218	198	DEOGARH	
		MEDIUM (3)	
227	35	CHHIPABAROD	
227	46	BAYANA	
227	73	NAINWA	
227	84	GANGRAR	
227	85	KAPASAN	
227	125	JHOTWARA	
227	161	MANDOR	
		LOW (2)	
234	79	BHAINSRORGARH	
234	170	CHECHAT	
		VERY LOW (1)	
236	34	CHHABRA	
236	146	MANOHARTHANA	
RAJASTHAN		**TOTAL**	**2746**
		AVERAGE	**11.59**
		% AGE OF AAPs	**44.73**

BOLD: Equal/Above Average Panchayat Samities (AAPs)
Source: General Annex VIII.

ANNEX-9.7

RANKING OF PSS BY NO. OF SHCS: RAJASTHAN, 2001

(Descending Order)

RANK	P.CODE	PANCHAYAT SAMITIES NAME	SHC
1	2	3	4
		VERY HIGH (>=20)	
1	**162**	**OSIAN**	**70**
2	**107**	**SAGWARA**	**57**
3	**25**	**GARHI**	**55**
4	**105**	**BICHHIWARA**	**54**
4	**176**	**DIDWANA**	**54**
6	**117**	**HANUMANGARH**	**53**
7	**135**	**AHORE**	**52**
8	**108**	**SIMALWARA**	**51**
8	**140**	**SANCHORE**	**51**
8	**183**	**NAGAUR**	**51**
11	**106**	**DUNGARPUR**	**50**
11	**213**	**NEEM KA THANA**	**50**
13	**104**	**ASPUR**	**49**
14	**39**	**BARMER**	**48**
14	**175**	**DEGANA**	**48**
14	**233**	**KHERWARA**	**48**
17	**236**	**SALUMBAR**	**47**
18	**91**	**RATANGARH**	**46**
18	**194**	**SOJAT**	**46**
18	**208**	**DANTA RAMGARH**	**46**
18	**210**	**FATEHPUR**	**46**
22	**40**	**BAYTOO**	**45**
22	**89**	**CHURU**	**45**
22	**151**	**JHUNJHUNUN**	**45**
22	**209**	**DHOND**	**45**
22	**232**	**JHADOL**	**45**
27	**90**	**RAJGARH**	**44**
27	**133**	**SAM**	**44**
27	**237**	**SARADA**	**44**
30	**160**	**LUNI**	**43**
30	**225**	**TONK**	**43**
30	**235**	**MAVLI**	**43**
33	**38**	**BALOTRA**	**42**
34	**61**	**MANDALGARH**	**41**
34	**109**	**ANUPGARH**	**41**
34	**159**	**BILARA**	**41**
37	**118**	**NOHAR**	**40**
37	**149**	**BUHANA**	**40**
37	**177**	**JAYAL**	**40**
37	**186**	**BALI**	**40**
41	**3**	**JAWAJA**	**39**
41	**93**	**SUJANGARH**	**39**
41	**189**	**KHARCHI/MARWAR JUN.**	**39**
41	**220**	**SIROHI**	**39**
45	**7**	**PISANGAN**	**38**
45	**42**	**DHORIMANNA**	**38**
47	**87**	**PRATAPGARH**	**37**
47	**168**	**SAPOTRA**	**37**
47	**211**	**KHANDELA**	**37**
47	**230**	**GIRWA**	**37**
51	**26**	**GHATOL**	**36**
51	**44**	**SINDHARI**	**36**
51	**110**	**GANGANAGAR**	**36**
51	**158**	**BHOPALGARH**	**36**
51	**188**	**JAITARAN**	**36**
51	**207**	**SAWAI MADHOPUR**	**36**
51	**214**	**PIPRALI**	**36**
51	**234**	**KOTRA**	**36**
59	**24**	**BAGIDORA**	**35**
59	**67**	**DUNGARGARH ***	**35**
59	**178**	**KUCHAMAN**	**35**
62	**55**	**ASIND**	**34**
62	**56**	**BANERA**	**34**
62	**111**	**KARANPUR**	**34**
62	**132**	**JAISALMER**	**34**
62	**155**	**UDAIPURWATI**	**34**
62	**217**	**PINDWARA**	**34**
68	**64**	**SHAHPURA**	**33**
68	**192**	**RANI STATION**	**33**
68	**200**	**KUMBHALGARH**	**33**
68	**228**	**BHINDER**	**33**
68	**229**	**DHARIAWAD**	**33**
73	**30**	**TALWARA**	**32**
73	**114**	**SADULSHAHAR**	**32**
73	**137**	**JALOR**	**32**
73	**156**	**BALESAR**	**32**
73	**185**	**RIYAN**	**32**
73	**199**	**KHAMNOR**	**32**
73	**201**	**RAILMAGRA**	**32**
80	**43**	**SHEO**	**31**
80	**134**	**SANKRA**	**31**
80	**153**	**NAWALGARH**	**31**
80	**173**	**SANGOD**	**31**
80	**182**	**MUNDWA**	**31**
80	**212**	**LACHHMANGARH**	**31**
86	**58**	**JAHAZPUR**	**30**
86	**174**	**SULTANPUR**	**30**
86	**180**	**MAKRANA**	**30**
89	**2**	**BHINAY**	**29**
89	**22**	**UMREN**	**29**
89	**92**	**SARDARSHAHAR**	**29**
89	**181**	**MERTA**	**29**
89	**218**	**REODAR**	**29**
94	**4**	**KEKRI**	**28**
94	**5**	**KISHANGARH**	**28**
94	**41**	**CHOHTAN**	**28**
94	**45**	**SIWANA**	**28**
94	**65**	**SUWANA**	**28**
94	**96**	**DAUSA**	**28**
94	**119**	**AMBER**	**28**
101	**1**	**ARAIN**	**27**
101	**60**	**MANDAL**	**27**
101	**74**	**TALERA**	**27**
101	**94**	**TARANAGAR**	**27**
101	**113**	**RAISINGHNAGAR**	**27**
101	**138**	**JASWANTPURA**	**27**
101	**143**	**DAG**	**27**
101	**163**	**PHALODI**	**27**
101	**166**	**KARAULI**	**27**
110	120	BASSI	26
110	141	SAYLA	26
110	152	KHETRI	26
110	195	SUMERPUR	26
110	231	GOGUNDA	26
115	23	ANANDPURI	25
115	27	KUSHALGARH	25
115	28	PEEPALKHOONT	25
115	70	NOKHA	25
115	73	NAINWA	25
115	82	CHITTAURGARH	25
115	97	LALSOT	25
115	128	SAMBHAR	25
115	139	RANIWARA	25
115	179	LADNU	25
125	66	BIKANER	24
125	131	VIRATNAGAR	24
125	191	RAIPUR	24
128	6	MASOODA	23
128	8	SRINAGAR	23
128	68	KOLAYAT	23
128	123	GOVINDGARH	23
128	124	JAMWA RAMGARH	23
128	145	KHANPUR	23
128	148	ALSISAR	23
128	172	LADPURA	23
128	196	AMET	23
128	197	BHIM	23
138	29	SAJJANGARH	22
138	69	LUNKARANSAR	22
138	72	KESHORAIPATAN	22
138	100	BARI	22
138	122	DUDU	22
138	136	BHINMAL	22
138	184	PARBATSAR	22
138	190	PALI	22
138	202	RAJSAMAND	22
138	215	SRI MADHOPUR	22
148	57	HURDA	21
148	63	SAHARA	21
148	71	HINDOLI	21
148	77	BEGUN	21
148	116	BHADRA	21
148	130	SHAHPURA	21
148	150	CHIRAWA	21
148	154	SURAJGARH	21
148	157	BAP	21
148	164	SHERGARH	21
148	204	BONLI	21
148	206	KHANDAR	21
148	219	SHEOGANJ	21
161	50	NADBAI	20
161	112	PADAMPUR	20
161	129	SANGANER	20
161	142	BAKANI	20
161	187	DESURI	20
161	221	DEOLI	20
		HIGH (15-20)	
167	59	KOTRI	19
167	62	RAIPUR	19
167	115	SURATGARH	19
167	223	NIWAI	19
171	20	THANAGAZI	18
171	83	DUNGLA	18
171	169	TODABHIM	18
174	14	LACHHMANGARH	17
174	32	ATRU	17
174	47	DEEG	17
174	49	KUMHER	17
174	52	RUPBAS	17
174	193	ROHAT	17
180	15	MANDAWAR	16
180	19	RENI	16
180	46	BAYANA	16
180	84	GANGRAR	16
180	86	NIMBAHERA	16
180	88	RASHMI	16
180	147	PIRAWA	16
180	165	HINDAUN	16
180	170	CHECHAT	16
180	203	BAMANWAS	16
180	205	GANGAPUR	16
180	216	ABU ROAD	16
192	12	KISHANGARH BAS	15
192	51	NAGAR PAHARI	15
192	101	BASERI	15
192	102	DHAULPUR	15
192	126	KOTPUTLI	15
192	127	PHAGI	15
192	144	JHALRAPATAN	15
		MEDIUM (10-15)	
199	18	RAMGARH	14
199	21	TIJARA	14
199	36	KISHANGANJ	14
199	37	SHAHBAD	14
199	99	SIKRAI	14
199	161	MANDOR	14
199	227	BARGAON	14
206	48	KAMAN	13
206	121	CHAKSU	13
206	146	MANOHARTHANA	13
206	222	MALPURA	13
206	224	TODARAISINGH	13
206	226	UNIARA	13
212	9	BANSURE	12
212	11	KATHUMAR	12
212	17	RAJGARH	12
212	33	BARAN	12
212	95	BANDIKUI	12
212	198	DEOGARH	12
218	10	BEHROR	11
218	35	CHHIPABAROD	11
218	78	BHADESAR	11
218	79	BHAINSRORGARH	11
218	80	BHOPALSAGAR	11
218	98	MAHWA	11
218	103	RAJAKHERA	11
218	167	NADOTI	11
218	171	ITAWA	11
		LOW (5-10)	
227	31	ANTA	9
227	53	SEWAR	9
229	16	NIMRANA	8
229	125	JHOTWARA	8
231	81	CHHOTI SADRI	7
232	34	CHHABRA	6
232	54	WEIR	6
232	75	ARNOD	6
235	76	BARI SADRI	5
235	85	KAPASAN	5
		VERY LOW (<5)	
237	13	KOTKASIM	4
RAJASTHAN		**TOTAL**	**6353**
		AVERAGE	**26.81**
		% AGE OF AAPs	**45.99**

BOLD: Equal/Above Average Panchayat Samities (AAPs)
Source: General Annex VIII

ANNEX-9.8

RANKING OF PSS BY NO. OF MCWCS: RAJASTHAN, 2001

(Descending Order)

RANK	P.CODE	PANCHAYAT SAMITIES NAME	MCWC
1	2	3	4
		VERY HIGH (>=8)	
1	104	**ASPUR**	39
2	232	**JHADOL**	25
3	169	**TODABHIM**	22
3	220	**SIROHI**	22
3	228	**BHINDER**	22
6	155	**UDAIPURWATI**	20
6	200	**KUMBHALGARH**	20
8	27	**KUSHALGARH**	19
8	231	**GOGUNDA**	19
10	122	**DUDU**	18
10	218	**REODAR**	18
12	28	**PEEPALKHOONT**	17
12	148	**ALSISAR**	17
12	230	**GIRWA**	17
15	229	**DHARIAWAD**	16
15	236	**SALUMBAR**	16
17	61	**MANDALGARH**	14
17	179	**LADNU**	14
19	77	**BEGUN**	13
19	165	**HINDAUN**	13
19	208	**DANTA RAMGARH**	13
22	58	**JAHAZPUR**	12
22	87	**PRATAPGARH**	12
22	96	**DAUSA**	12
22	120	**BASSI**	12
22	154	**SURAJGARH**	12
22	175	**DEGANA**	12
22	199	**KHAMNOR**	12
22	204	**BONLI**	12
22	205	**GANGAPUR**	12
22	233	**KHERWARA**	12
32	37	**SHAHBAD**	11
32	105	**BICHHIWARA**	11
32	108	**SIMALWARA**	11
32	129	**SANGANER**	11
32	194	**SOJAT**	11
32	214	**PIPRALI**	11
32	227	**BARGAON**	11
39	26	**GHATOL**	10
39	44	**SINDHARI**	10
39	102	**DHAULPUR**	10
39	123	**GOVINDGARH**	10
39	167	**NADOTI**	10
39	219	**SHEOGANJ**	10
45	3	**JAWAJA**	9
45	55	**ASIND**	9
45	73	**NAINWA**	9
45	98	**MAHWA**	9
45	145	**KHANPUR**	9
45	147	**PIRAWA**	9
45	168	**SAPOTRA**	9
45	209	**DHOND**	9
53	49	**KUMHER**	8
53	52	**RUPBAS**	8
53	71	**HINDOLI**	8
53	101	**BASERI**	8
53	114	**SADULSHAHAR**	8
53	117	**HANUMANGARH**	8
53	119	**AMBER**	8
53	128	**SAMBHAR**	8
53	153	**NAWALGARH**	8
53	197	**BHIM**	8
53	213	**NEEM KA THANA**	8
53	237	**SARADA**	8
		HIGH (6-8)	
65	7	**PISANGAN**	7
65	11	**KATHUMAR**	7
65	20	**THANAGAZI**	7
65	25	**GARHI**	7
65	29	**SAJJANGARH**	7
65	30	**TALWARA**	7
65	31	**ANTA**	7
65	72	**KESHORAIPATAN**	7
65	95	**BANDIKUI**	7
65	107	**SAGWARA**	7
65	125	**JHOTWARA**	7
65	149	**BUHANA**	7
65	156	**BALESAR**	7
65	185	**RIYAN**	7
65	191	**RAIPUR**	7
65	207	**SAWAI MADHOPUR**	7
81	24	**BAGIDORA**	6
81	99	**SIKRAI**	6
81	100	**BARI**	6
81	106	**DUNGARPUR**	6
81	121	**CHAKSU**	6
81	126	**KOTPUTLI**	6
81	130	**SHAHPURA**	6
81	171	**ITAWA**	6
81	178	**KUCHAMAN**	6
81	180	**MAKRANA**	6
81	201	**RAILMAGRA**	6
81	223	**NIWAI**	6
		MEDIUM (4-6)	
93	1	ARAIN	5
93	8	SRINAGAR	5
93	9	BANSURE	5
93	12	KISHANGARH BAS	5
93	15	MANDAWAR	5
93	59	KOTRI	5
93	62	RAIPUR	5
93	65	SUWANA	5
93	69	LUNKARANSAR	5
93	81	CHHOTI SADRI	5
93	93	SUJANGARH	5
93	109	ANUPGARH	5
93	170	CHECHAT	5
93	172	LADPURA	5
93	235	MAVLI	5
108	18	RAMGARH	4
108	23	ANANDPURI	4
108	38	BALOTRA	4
108	74	TALERA	4
108	75	ARNOD	4
108	82	CHITTAURGARH	4
108	83	DUNGLA	4
108	90	RAJGARH	4
108	91	RATANGARH	4
108	115	SURATGARH	4
108	116	BHADRA	4
108	151	JHUNJHUNUN	4
108	158	BHOPALGARH	4
108	162	OSIAN	4
108	166	KARAULI	4
108	173	SANGOD	4
108	181	MERTA	4
108	184	PARBATSAR	4
108	186	BALI	4
108	192	RANI STATION	4
108	193	ROHAT	4
108	195	SUMERPUR	4
108	210	FATEHPUR	4
		LOW (2-4)	
131	2	BHINAY	3
131	14	LACHHMANGARH	3
131	17	RAJGARH	3
131	21	TIJARA	3
131	34	CHHABRA	3
131	45	SIWANA	3
131	51	NAGAR PAHARI	3
131	53	SEWAR	3
131	60	MANDAL	3
131	63	SAHARA	3
131	67	DUNGARGARH	3
131	70	NOKHA	3
131	80	BHOPALSAGAR	3
131	110	GANGANAGAR	3
131	112	PADAMPUR	3
131	127	PHAGI	3
131	137	JALOR	3
131	142	BAKANI	3
131	159	BILARA	3
131	163	PHALODI	3
131	177	JAYAL	3
131	187	DESURI	3
131	188	JAITARAN	3
131	215	SRI MADHOPUR	3
131	216	ABU ROAD	3
156	13	KOTKASIM	2
156	42	DHORIMANNA	2
156	47	DEEG	2
156	56	BANERA	2
156	66	BIKANER	2
156	97	LALSOT	2
156	118	NOHAR	2
156	132	JAISALMER	2
156	134	SANKRA	2
156	140	SANCHORE	2
156	144	JHALRAPATAN	2
156	152	KHETRI	2
156	189	KHARCHI/MARWAR JUN.	2
156	202	RAJSAMAND	2
156	203	BAMANWAS	2
156	206	KHANDAR	2
156	217	PINDWARA	2
156	221	DEOLI	2
156	225	TONK	2
		VERY LOW (<2)	
175	4	KEKRI	
175	6	MASOODA	
175	10	BEHROR	
175	16	NIMRANA	
175	19	RENI	
175	22	UMREN	
175	35	CHHIPABAROD	
175	36	KISHANGANJ	
175	41	CHOHTAN	
175	48	KAMAN	
175	50	NADBAI	
175	54	WEIR	
175	68	KOLAYAT	
175	78	BHADESAR	
175	79	BHAINSRORGARH	
175	84	GANGRAR	
175	88	RASHMI	
175	94	TARANAGAR	
175	103	RAJAKHERA	
175	111	KARANPUR	
175	131	VIRATNAGAR	
175	133	SAM	
175	135	AHORE	
175	136	BHINMAL	
175	141	SAYLA	
175	143	DAG	
175	150	CHIRAWA	
175	161	MANDOR	
175	174	SULTANPUR	
175	176	DIDWANA	
175	182	MUNDWA	
175	222	MALPURA	
175	224	TODARAISINGH	
175	234	KOTRA	
		NIL (0)	
209	5	KISHANGARH	
209	32	ATRU	
209	33	BARAN	
209	39	BARMER	
209	40	BAYTOO	
209	43	SHEO	
209	46	BAYANA	
209	57	HURDA	
209	64	SHAHPURA	
209	76	BARI SADRI	
209	85	KAPASAN	
209	86	NIMBAHERA	
209	89	CHURU	
209	92	SARDARSHAHAR	
209	113	RAISINGHNAGAR	
209	124	JAMWA RAMGARH	
209	138	JASWANTPURA	
209	139	RANIWARA	
209	146	MANOHARTHANA	
209	157	BAP	
209	160	LUNI	
209	164	SHERGARH	
209	183	NAGAUR	
209	190	PALI	
209	196	AMET	
209	198	DEOGARH	
209	211	KHANDELA	
209	212	LACHHMANGARH	
209	226	UNIARA	
RAJASTHAN		**TOTAL**	**1317**
		AVERAGE	**5.56**
		% AGE OF AAPs	**38.82**

BOLD: Equal/Above Average Panchayat Samities (AAPs)

Source: General Annex VIII.

ANNEX-9.9

RANKING OF PSS BY NO. OF FWCS: RAJASTHAN, 2001

(Descending Order)

RANK	P.CODE	PANCHAYAT SAMITIES NAME	FWC
1	*2*	*3*	*4*
		VERY HIGH (>=5)	
1	**200**	**KUMBHALGARH**	**14**
2	**194**	**SOJAT**	**12**
3	**149**	**BUHANA**	**9**
4	**61**	**MANDALGARH**	**8**
4	**197**	**BHIM**	**8**
4	**230**	**GIRWA**	**8**
7	**66**	**BIKANER**	**7**
7	**109**	**ANUPGARH**	**7**
7	**117**	**HANUMANGARH**	**7**
7	**119**	**AMBER**	**7**
7	**153**	**NAWALGARH**	**7**
7	**155**	**UDAIPURWATI**	**7**
7	**178**	**KUCHAMAN**	**7**
7	**205**	**GANGAPUR**	**7**
7	**218**	**REODAR**	**7**
7	**220**	**SIROHI**	**7**
17	**28**	**PEEPALKHOONT**	**6**
17	**30**	**TALWARA**	**6**
17	**44**	**SINDHARI**	**6**
17	**73**	**NAINWA**	**6**
17	**90**	**RAJGARH**	**6**
17	**106**	**DUNGARPUR**	**6**
17	**148**	**ALSISAR**	**6**
17	**168**	**SAPOTRA**	**6**
17	**169**	**TODABHIM**	**6**
17	**170**	**CHECHAT**	**6**
17	**181**	**MERTA**	**6**
17	**189**	**KHARCHI/MARWAR JUN.**	**6**
17	**191**	**RAIPUR**	**6**
17	**207**	**SAWAI MADHOPUR**	**6**
17	**233**	**KHERWARA**	**6**
32	**2**	**BHINAY**	**5**
32	**4**	**KEKRI**	**5**
32	**9**	**BANSURE**	**5**
32	**87**	**PRATAPGARH**	**5**
32	**110**	**GANGANAGAR**	**5**
32	**123**	**GOVINDGARH**	**5**
32	**130**	**SHAHPURA**	**5**
32	**158**	**BHOPALGARH**	**5**
32	**175**	**DEGANA**	**5**
32	**185**	**RIYAN**	**5**
32	**199**	**KHAMNOR**	**5**
32	**204**	**BONLI**	**5**
32	**209**	**DHOND**	**5**
32	**212**	**LACHHMANGARH**	**5**
32	**214**	**PIPRALI**	**5**
32	**227**	**BARGAON**	**5**
		HIGH (4)	
48	**26**	**GHATOL**	
48	**51**	**NAGAR PAHARI**	
48	**60**	**MANDAL**	
48	**69**	**LUNKARANSAR**	
48	**71**	**HINDOLI**	
48	**72**	**KESHORAIPATAN**	
48	**102**	**DHAULPUR**	
48	**104**	**ASPUR**	
48	**105**	**BICHHIWARA**	
48	**112**	**PADAMPUR**	
48	**115**	**SURATGARH**	
48	**116**	**BHADRA**	
48	**118**	**NOHAR**	
48	**120**	**BASSI**	
48	**152**	**KHETRI**	
48	**156**	**BALESAR**	
48	**161**	**MANDOR**	
48	**164**	**SHERGARH**	
48	**167**	**NADOTI**	
48	**180**	**MAKRANA**	
48	**186**	**BALI**	
48	**187**	**DESURI**	
48	**195**	**SUMERPUR**	
48	**213**	**NEEM KA THANA**	
48	**217**	**PINDWARA**	
48	**219**	**SHEOGANJ**	
48	**225**	**TONK**	
		MEDIUM (3)	
75	**3**	**JAWAJA**	
75	**11**	**KATHUMAR**	
75	**20**	**THANAGAZI**	
75	**31**	**ANTA**	
75	**32**	**ATRU**	
75	**36**	**KISHANGANJ**	
75	**37**	**SHAHBAD**	
75	**38**	**BALOTRA**	
75	**45**	**SIWANA**	
75	**49**	**KUMHER**	
75	**52**	**RUPBAS**	
75	**58**	**JAHAZPUR**	
75	**62**	**RAIPUR**	
75	**67**	**DUNGARGARH**	
75	**68**	**KOLAYAT**	
75	**78**	**BHADESAR**	
75	**91**	**RATANGARH**	
75	**96**	**DAUSA**	
75	**98**	**MAHWA**	
75	**99**	**SIKRAI**	
75	**103**	**RAJAKHERA**	
75	**108**	**SIMALWARA**	
75	**124**	**JAMWA RAMGARH**	
75	**134**	**SANKRA**	
75	**145**	**KHANPUR**	
75	**160**	**LUNI**	
75	**162**	**OSIAN**	
75	**166**	**KARAULI**	
75	**176**	**DIDWANA**	
75	**177**	**JAYAL**	
75	**179**	**LADNU**	
75	**198**	**DEOGARH**	
75	**201**	**RAILMAGRA**	
75	**202**	**RAJSAMAND**	
75	**206**	**KHANDAR**	
75	**211**	**KHANDELA**	
75	**229**	**DHARIAWAD**	
75	**234**	**KOTRA**	
75	**235**	**MAVLI**	
75	**236**	**SALUMBAR**	
75	**237**	**SARADA**	
		LOW (2)	
116	7	PISANGAN	
116	10	BEHROR	
116	14	LACHHMANGARH	
116	15	MANDAWAR	
116	16	NIMRANA	
116	17	RAJGARH	
116	22	UMREN	
116	25	GARHI	
116	29	SAJJANGARH	
116	39	BARMER	
116	40	BAYTOO	
116	53	SEWAR	
116	55	ASIND	
116	59	KOTRI	
116	65	SUWANA	
116	74	TALERA	
116	79	BHAINSRORGARH	
116	89	CHURU	
116	92	SARDARSHAHAR	
116	95	BANDIKUI	
116	97	LALSOT	
116	101	BASERI	
116	113	RAISINGHNAGAR	
116	121	CHAKSU	
116	122	DUDU	
116	126	KOTPUTLI	
116	127	PHAGI	
116	135	AHORE	
116	138	JASWANTPURA	
116	139	RANIWARA	
116	141	SAYLA	
116	144	JHALRAPATAN	
116	150	CHIRAWA	
116	159	BILARA	
116	165	HINDAUN	
116	172	LADPURA	
116	174	SULTANPUR	
116	184	PARBATSAR	
116	188	JAITARAN	
116	190	PALI	
116	193	ROHAT	
116	196	AMET	
116	203	BAMANWAS	
116	208	DANTA RAMGARH	
116	216	ABU ROAD	
116	221	DEOLI	
116	222	MALPURA	
116	223	NIWAI	
116	228	BHINDER	
116	232	JHADOL	
		VERY LOW (1)	
166	1	ARAIN	
166	6	MASOODA	
166	12	KISHANGARH BAS	
166	18	RAMGARH	
166	19	RENI	
166	21	TIJARA	
166	24	BAGIDORA	
166	27	KUSHALGARH	
166	41	CHOHTAN	
166	42	DHORIMANNA	
166	46	BAYANA	
166	47	DEEG	
166	50	NADBAI	
166	63	SAHARA	
166	75	ARNOD	
166	77	BEGUN	
166	80	BHOPALSAGAR	
166	81	CHHOTI SADRI	
166	83	DUNGLA	
166	86	NIMBAHERA	
166	88	RASHMI	
166	93	SUJANGARH	
166	100	BARI	
166	107	SAGWARA	
166	114	SADULSHAHAR	
166	125	JHOTWARA	
166	128	SAMBHAR	
166	131	VIRATNAGAR	
166	133	SAM	
166	136	BHINMAL	
166	137	JALOR	
166	140	SANCHORE	
166	142	BAKANI	
166	143	DAG	
166	146	MANOHARTHANA	
166	147	PIRAWA	
166	154	SURAJGARH	
166	157	BAP	
166	163	PHALODI	
166	171	ITAWA	
166	183	NAGAUR	
166	192	RANI STATION	
166	224	TODARAISINGH	
166	226	UNIARA	
166	231	GOGUNDA	
		NIL (0)	
211	5	KISHANGARH	
211	8	SRINAGAR	
211	13	KOTKASIM	
211	23	ANANDPURI	
211	33	BARAN	
211	34	CHHABRA	
211	35	CHHIPABAROD	
211	43	SHEO	
211	48	KAMAN	
211	54	WEIR	
211	56	BANERA	
211	57	HURDA	
211	64	SHAHPURA	
211	70	NOKHA	
211	76	BARI SADRI	
211	82	CHITTAURGARH	
211	84	GANGRAR	
211	85	KAPASAN	
211	94	TARANAGAR	
211	111	KARANPUR	
211	129	SANGANER	
211	132	JAISALMER	
211	151	JHUNJHUNUN	
211	173	SANGOD	
211	182	MUNDWA	
211	210	FATEHPUR	
211	215	SRI MADHOPUR	
RAJASTHAN		**TOTAL**	**675**
		AVERAGE	**2.85**
		% AGE OF AAPs	**48.52**

BOLD: Equal/Above Average Panchayat Samities (AAPs)
Source: General Annex VIII.

ANNEX-9.10

RANKING OF PSS BY PERCENTAGE OF RURAL POP. SERVED BY DRINKING WATER AMENITIES: RAJASTHAN, 2001

(Descending Order)

RANK	P.CODE	PANCHAYAT SAMITIES NAME	%
1	2	3	4
		PERFECT (100)	
1	3	**JAWAJA**	100.00
1	4	**KEKRI**	100.00
1	6	**MASOODA**	100.00
1	7	**PISANGAN**	100.00
1	8	**SRINAGAR**	100.00
1	13	**KOTKASIM**	100.00
1	14	**LACHHMANGARH**	100.00
1	15	**MANDAWAR**	100.00
1	18	**RAMGARH**	100.00
1	25	**GARHI**	100.00
1	29	**SAJJANGARH**	100.00
1	31	**ANTA**	100.00
1	32	**ATRU**	100.00
1	33	**BARAN**	100.00
1	47	**DEEG**	100.00
1	50	**NADBAI**	100.00
1	65	**SUWANA**	100.00
1	77	**BEGUN**	100.00
1	78	**BHADESAR**	100.00
1	83	**DUNGLA**	100.00
1	84	**GANGRAR**	100.00
1	85	**KAPASAN**	100.00
1	86	**NIMBAHERA**	100.00
1	88	**RASHMI**	100.00
1	99	**SIKRAI**	100.00
1	104	**ASPUR**	100.00
1	107	**SAGWARA**	100.00
1	119	**AMBER**	100.00
1	123	**GOVINDGARH**	100.00
1	126	**KOTPUTLI**	100.00
1	130	**SHAHPURA**	100.00
1	153	**NAWALGARH**	100.00
1	165	**HINDAUN**	100.00
1	173	**SANGOD**	100.00
1	174	**SULTANPUR**	100.00
1	186	**BALI**	100.00
1	191	**RAIPUR**	100.00
1	192	**RANI STATION**	100.00
1	196	**AMET**	100.00
1	198	**DEOGARH**	100.00
1	202	**RAJSAMAND**	100.00
1	207	**SAWAI MADHOPUR**	100.00
1	210	**FATEHPUR**	100.00
1	213	**NEEM KA THANA**	100.00
1	228	**BHINDER**	100.00
1	235	**MAVLI**	100.00
1	237	**SARADA**	100.00
		VERY HIGH (98-100)	
48	9	**BANSURE**	99.90
48	10	**BEHROR**	99.90
48	21	**TIJARA**	99.90
48	26	**GHATOL**	99.90
48	49	**KUMHER**	99.90
48	76	**BARI SADRI**	99.90
48	98	**MAHWA**	99.90
48	120	**BASSI**	99.90
48	218	**REODAR**	99.90
57	16	**NIMRANA**	99.80
57	52	**RUPBAS**	99.80
57	56	**BANERA**	99.80
57	60	**MANDAL**	99.80
57	81	**CHHOTI SADRI**	99.80
57	137	**JALOR**	99.80
57	155	**UDAIPURWATI**	99.80
57	171	**ITAWA**	99.80
57	201	**RAILMAGRA**	99.80
57	224	**TODARAISINGH**	99.80
67	20	**THANAGAZI**	99.70
67	36	**KISHANGANJ**	99.70
67	80	**BHOPALSAGAR**	99.70
67	97	**LALSOT**	99.70
67	108	**SIMALWARA**	99.70
67	124	**JAMWA RAMGARH**	99.70
67	127	**PHAGI**	99.70
67	131	**VIRATNAGAR**	99.70
67	147	**PIRAWA**	99.70
67	179	**LADNU**	99.70
67	199	**KHAMNOR**	99.70
67	221	**DEOLI**	99.70
79	1	**ARAIN**	99.60
79	5	**KISHANGARH**	99.60
79	12	**KISHANGARH BAS**	99.60
79	54	**WEIR**	99.60
79	61	**MANDALGARH**	99.60
79	74	**TALERA**	99.60
79	79	**BHAINSRORGARH**	99.60
79	220	**SIROHI**	99.60
79	236	**SALUMBAR**	99.60
88	82	**CHITTAURGARH**	99.50
88	129	**SANGANER**	99.50
88	172	**LADPURA**	99.50
88	215	**SRI MADHOPUR**	99.50
88	222	**MALPURA**	99.50
93	37	**SHAHBAD**	99.40
93	105	**BICHHIWARA**	99.40
93	145	**KHANPUR**	99.40
93	159	**BILARA**	99.40
93	214	**PIPRALI**	99.40
98	55	**ASIND**	99.30
98	170	**CHECHAT**	99.30
98	206	**KHANDAR**	99.30
98	209	**DHOND**	99.30
98	211	**KHANDELA**	99.30
98	227	**BARGAON**	99.30
104	2	**BHINAY**	99.20
104	63	**SAHARA**	99.20
104	87	**PRATAPGARH**	99.20
104	141	**SAYLA**	99.20
104	152	**KHETRI**	99.20
104	200	**KUMBHALGARH**	99.20
110	162	**OSIAN**	99.10
110	212	**LACHHMANGARH**	99.10
112	22	**UMREN**	99.00
112	59	**KOTRI**	99.00
112	102	**DHAULPUR**	99.00
112	121	**CHAKSU**	99.00
112	197	**BHIM**	99.00
112	217	**PINDWARA**	99.00
118	28	**PEEPALKHOONT**	98.90
118	46	**BAYANA**	98.90
118	53	**SEWAR**	98.90
118	57	**HURDA**	98.90
118	95	**BANDIKUI**	98.90
118	208	**DANTA RAMGARH**	98.90
124	51	**NAGAR PAHARI**	98.80
124	135	**AHORE**	98.80
124	225	**TONK**	98.80
127	58	**JAHAZPUR**	98.70
127	71	**HINDOLI**	98.70
127	233	**KHERWARA**	98.70
130	19	**RENI**	98.60
130	96	**DAUSA**	98.60
130	110	**GANGANAGAR**	98.60
130	143	**DAG**	98.60
130	150	**CHIRAWA**	98.60
130	216	**ABU ROAD**	98.60
130	223	**NIWAI**	98.60
137	138	**JASWANTPURA**	98.50
137	204	**BONLI**	98.50
139	62	**RAIPUR**	98.40
139	232	**JHADOL**	98.40
141	30	**TALWARA**	98.30
141	103	**RAJAKHERA**	98.30
141	187	**DESURI**	98.30
141	205	**GANGAPUR**	98.30
145	27	**KUSHALGARH**	98.20
145	169	**TODABHIM**	98.20
145	226	**UNIARA**	98.20
148	11	**KATHUMAR**	98.10
148	35	**CHHIPABAROD**	98.10
148	101	**BASERI**	98.10
148	146	**MANOHARTHANA**	98.10
152	230	**GIRWA**	98.00
		HIGH (96-98)	
153	24	**BAGIDORA**	97.90
153	144	**JHALRAPATAN**	97.90
153	189	**KHARCHI/MARWAR JUN.**	97.90
156	75	**ARNOD**	97.80
156	142	**BAKANI**	97.80
156	229	**DHARIAWAD**	97.80
159	23	**ANANDPURI**	97.70
159	45	**SIWANA**	97.70
159	167	**NADOTI**	97.70
159	188	**JAITARAN**	97.70
163	231	**GOGUNDA**	97.60
164	73	**NAINWA**	97.50
164	156	**BALESAR**	97.50
166	72	**KESHORAIPATAN**	97.40
167	106	**DUNGARPUR**	97.10
167	122	**DUDU**	97.10
169	64	**SHAHPURA**	97.00
170	168	**SAPOTRA**	96.90
170	219	**SHEOGANJ**	96.90
172	184	**PARBATSAR**	96.70
173	100	**BARI**	96.50
174	34	**CHHABRA**	96.40
175	182	**MUNDWA**	96.30
176	193	**ROHAT**	96.10
		MEDIUM (94-96)	
177	17	**RAJGARH**	95.90
178	166	**KARAULI**	95.80
179	70	**NOKHA**	95.70
179	158	**BHOPALGARH**	95.70
181	128	**SAMBHAR**	95.60
181	163	**PHALODI**	95.60
183	194	**SOJAT**	95.50
184	139	RANIWARA	95.30
185	181	MERTA	95.10
186	117	HANUMANGARH	94.90
187	111	KARANPUR	94.80
187	151	JHUNJHUNUN	94.80
189	160	LUNI	94.50
190	125	JHOTWARA	94.40
191	195	SUMERPUR	94.30
192	112	PADAMPUR	94.20
193	185	RIYAN	94.10
194	190	PALI	94.00
		LOW (<94)	
195	176	DIDWANA	93.70
196	48	KAMAN	93.40
196	149	BUHANA	93.40
198	203	BAMANWAS	93.20
199	91	RATANGARH	93.00
199	161	MANDOR	93.00
201	113	RAISINGHNAGAR	92.80
202	234	KOTRA	92.40
203	40	BAYTOO	91.20
204	42	DHORIMANNA	90.90
205	178	KUCHAMAN	89.90
206	93	SUJANGARH	89.60
207	154	SURAJGARH	88.80
208	164	SHERGARH	88.70
209	67	DUNGARGARH	88.30
210	175	DEGANA	86.70
211	148	ALSISAR	86.20
212	140	SANCHORE	85.90
213	116	BHADRA	85.60
214	136	BHINMAL	85.40
215	41	CHOHTAN	85.30
216	90	RAJGARH	85.20
217	134	SANKRA	84.10
218	109	ANUPGARH	83.90
219	133	SAM	83.50
220	4[illegible]	SINDHARI	83.40
221	94	TARANAGAR	82.40
222	38	BALOTRA	82.00
223	43	SHEO	81.00
224	114	SADULSHAHAR	79.50
225	115	SURATGARH	78.70
226	183	NAGAUR	78.30
227	180	MAKRANA	77.50
228	39	BARMER	77.00
229	69	LUNKARANSAR	76.20
230	89	CHURU	75.90
231	66	BIKANER	74.30
232	118	NOHAR	73.50
233	68	KOLAYAT	73.20
234	177	JAYAL	73.00
235	132	JAISALMER	70.80
236	157	BAP	66.40
237	92	SARDARSHAHAR	52.50
		RAJASTHAN	**95.40**
		% AGE OF AAPs	**77.22**

BOLD: Equal/Above Average Panchayat Samities (AAPs)

Source : General Annex VI.

ANNEX-9.11

RANKING OF PSS BY PERCENTAGE OF RURAL POP. SERVED BY EDUCATION AMENITIES: RAJASTHAN, 2001

(Descending Order)

RANK	P.CODE	PANCHAYAT SAMITIES NAME	%
1	2	3	4
		PERFECT (100)	
1	216	**ABU ROAD**	100.00
1	2	**BHINAY**	100.00
1	136	**BHINMAL**	100.00
1	158	**BHOPALGARH**	100.00
1	150	**CHIRAWA**	100.00
1	47	**DEEG**	100.00
1	209	**DHOND**	100.00
1	106	**DUNGARPUR**	100.00
1	137	**JALOR**	100.00
1	11	**KATHUMAR**	100.00
1	152	**KHETRI**	100.00
1	126	**KOTPUTLI**	100.00
1	153	**NAWALGARH**	100.00
1	16	**NIMRANA**	100.00
1	7	**PISANGAN**	100.00
1	139	**RANIWARA**	100.00
1	130	**SHAHPURA**	100.00
1	194	**SOJAT**	100.00
1	215	**SRI MADHOPUR**	100.00
1	154	**SURAJGARH**	100.00
1	155	**UDAIPURWATI**	100.00
		HIGH (95-100)	
22	186	**BALI**	99.90
22	56	**BANERA**	99.90
22	9	**BANSURE**	99.90
22	175	**DEGANA**	99.90
22	67	**DUNGARGARH**	99.90
22	25	**GARHI**	99.90
22	188	**JAITARAN**	99.90
22	138	**JASWANTPURA**	99.90
22	151	**JHUNJHUNUN**	99.90
22	5	**KISHANGARH**	99.90
22	49	**KUMHER**	99.90
22	214	**PIPRALI**	99.90
22	192	**RANI STATION**	99.90
22	193	**ROHAT**	99.90
22	8	**SRINAGAR**	99.90
37	1	**ARAIN**	99.80
37	4	**KEKRI**	99.80
37	52	**RUPBAS**	99.80
37	94	**TARANAGAR**	99.80
37	105	**BICHHIWARA**	99.80
37	107	**SAGWARA**	99.80
37	141	**SAYLA**	99.80
37	149	**BUHANA**	99.80
37	180	**MAKRANA**	99.80
37	184	**PARBATSAR**	99.80
37	219	**SHEOGANJ**	99.80
37	222	**MALPURA**	99.80
49	33	**BARAN**	99.70
49	50	**NADBAI**	99.70
49	51	**NAGAR PAHARI**	99.70
49	63	**SAHARA**	99.70
49	65	**SUWANA**	99.70
49	90	**RAJGARH**	99.70
49	128	**SAMBHAR**	99.70
49	160	**LUNI**	99.70
49	162	**OSIAN**	99.70
49	197	**BHIM**	99.70
49	208	**DANTA RAMGARH**	99.70
49	212	**LACHHMANGARH**	99.70
61	13	**KOTKASIM**	99.60
61	44	**SINDHARI**	99.60
61	54	**WEIR**	99.60
61	108	**SIMALWARA**	99.60
61	135	**AHORE**	99.60
61	176	**DIDWANA**	99.60
61	201	**RAILMAGRA**	99.60
61	210	**FATEHPUR**	99.60
69	14	**LACHHMANGARH**	99.50
69	15	**MANDAWAR**	99.50
69	62	**RAIPUR**	99.50
69	80	**BHOPALSAGAR**	99.50
69	123	**GOVINDGARH**	99.50
69	131	**VIRATNAGAR**	99.50
69	159	**BILARA**	99.50
69	177	**JAYAL**	99.50
69	205	**GANGAPUR**	99.50
69	231	**GOGUNDA**	99.50
79	26	**GHATOL**	99.40
79	45	**SIWANA**	99.40
79	48	**KAMAN**	99.40
79	64	**SHAHPURA**	99.40
79	207	**SAWAI MADHOPUR**	99.40
79	211	**KHANDELA**	99.40
79	217	**PINDWARA**	99.40
79	220	**SIROHI**	99.40
87	10	**BEHROR**	99.30
87	140	**SANCHORE**	99.30
87	169	**TODABHIM**	99.30
87	187	**DESURI**	99.30
87	191	**RAIPUR**	99.30
92	24	**BAGIDORA**	99.20
92	46	**BAYANA**	99.20
92	104	**ASPUR**	99.20
92	161	**MANDOR**	99.20
92	167	**NADOTI**	99.20
92	189	**KHARCHI/MARWAR JUN.**	99.20
98	32	**ATRU**	99.10
98	41	**CHOHTAN**	99.10
98	53	**SEWAR**	99.10
98	74	**TALERA**	99.10
98	86	**NIMBAHERA**	99.10
98	91	**RATANGARH**	99.10
98	127	**PHAGI**	99.10
98	195	**SUMERPUR**	99.10
106	27	**KUSHALGARH**	99.00
106	31	**ANTA**	99.00
106	60	**MANDAL**	99.00
106	99	**SIKRAI**	99.00
106	165	**HINDAUN**	99.00
106	179	**LADNU**	99.00
106	183	**NAGAUR**	99.00
106	213	**NEEM KA THANA**	99.00
106	218	**REODAR**	99.00
115	29	**SAJJANGARH**	98.90
115	83	**DUNGLA**	98.90
115	95	**BANDIKUI**	98.90
115	178	**KUCHAMAN**	98.90
115	190	**PALI**	98.90
115	202	**RAJSAMAND**	98.90
115	203	**BAMANWAS**	98.90
115	230	**GIRWA**	98.90
115	237	**SARADA**	98.90
124	19	**RENI**	98.80
124	73	**NAINWA**	98.80
126	55	**ASIND**	98.70
126	57	**HURDA**	98.70
126	148	**ALSISAR**	98.70
126	166	**KARAULI**	98.70
126	181	**MERTA**	98.70
126	182	**MUNDWA**	98.70
126	185	**RIYAN**	98.70
126	204	**BONLI**	98.70
126	235	**MAVLI**	98.70
135	30	**TALWARA**	98.60
136	12	**KISHANGARH BAS**	98.50
136	89	**CHURU**	98.50
136	93	**SUJANGARH**	98.50
136	119	**AMBER**	98.50
136	122	**DUDU**	98.50
136	200	**KUMBHALGARH**	98.50
136	224	**TODARAISINGH**	98.50
143	18	**RAMGARH**	98.40
143	163	**PHALODI**	98.40
143	170	**CHECHAT**	98.40
143	174	**SULTANPUR**	98.40
147	6	**MASOODA**	98.30
147	20	**THANAGAZI**	98.30
147	92	**SARDARSHAHAR**	98.30
147	120	**BASSI**	98.30
147	199	**KHAMNOR**	98.30
152	23	**ANANDPURI**	98.20
152	72	**KESHORAIPATAN**	98.20
154	68	**KOLAYAT**	98.10
154	88	**RASHMI**	98.10
154	125	**JHOTWARA**	98.10
157	59	**KOTRI**	98.00
157	70	**NOKHA**	98.00
157	168	**SAPOTRA**	98.00
160	134	**SANKRA**	97.90
160	172	**LADPURA**	97.90
162	42	**DHORIMANNA**	97.80
162	102	**DHAULPUR**	97.80
162	225	**TONK**	97.80
165	132	**JAISALMER**	97.70
165	206	**KHANDAR**	97.70
165	227	**BARGAON**	97.70
165	236	**SALUMBAR**	97.70
169	103	RAJAKHERA	97.60
169	173	SANGOD	97.60
171	71	HINDOLI	97.50
172	101	BASERI	97.40
172	196	AMET	97.40
174	22	UMREN	97.30
174	85	KAPASAN	97.30
174	147	PIRAWA	97.30
174	221	DEOLI	97.30
178	232	JHADOL	97.20
179	3	JAWAJA	97.10
179	38	BALOTRA	97.10
179	84	GANGRAR	97.10
179	96	DAUSA	97.10
179	229	DHARIAWAD	97.10
184	28	PEEPALKHOONT	97.00
184	223	NIWAI	97.00
186	124	JAMWA RAMGARH	96.90
187	82	CHITTAURGARH	96.60
187	198	DEOGARH	96.60
187	233	KHERWARA	96.60
190	97	LALSOT	96.30
190	143	DAG	96.30
190	171	ITAWA	96.30
193	21	TIJARA	96.20
193	98	MAHWA	96.20
193	111	KARANPUR	96.20
196	37	SHAHBAD	96.10
196	66	BIKANER	96.10
196	69	LUNKARANSAR	96.10
196	129	SANGANER	96.10
200	17	RAJGARH	95.90
200	43	SHEO	95.90
202	144	JHALRAPATAN	95.60
203	78	BHADESAR	95.50
203	100	BARI	95.50
205	81	CHHOTI SADRI	95.40
206	58	JAHAZPUR	95.30
206	61	MANDALGARH	95.30
206	164	SHERGARH	95.30
209	133	SAM	95.10
210	156	BALESAR	95.00
		HIGH (90-95)	
211	87	PRATAPGARH	94.80
211	228	BHINDER	94.80
213	75	ARNOD	94.70
214	36	KISHANGANJ	94.60
215	35	CHHIPABAROD	94.30
215	226	UNIARA	94.30
217	76	BARI SADRI	94.10
217	114	SADULSHAHAR	94.10
219	34	CHHABRA	93.70
219	112	PADAMPUR	93.70
221	121	CHAKSU	93.50
222	110	GANGANAGAR	93.20
222	116	BHADRA	93.20
224	234	KOTRA	93.10
225	146	MANOHARTHANA	92.80
226	145	KHANPUR	92.60
227	40	BAYTOO	92.30
227	113	RAISINGHNAGAR	92.30
229	39	BARMER	92.10
230	157	BAP	91.70
231	77	BEGUN	91.40
		MEDIUM (85-90)	
232	79	BHAINSRORGARH	88.80
233	118	NOHAR	87.90
234	142	BAKANI	87.00
235	117	HANUMANGARH	85.50
		LOW (<85)	
236	115	SURATGARH	78.90
237	109	ANUPGARH	78.10
RAJASTHAN		**TOTAL**	**97.65**
		% AGE OF AAPs	**70.89**

BOLD: Equal/Above Average Panchayat Samities (AAPs)
Source: General Annex VI.

ANNEX-9.12

RANKING OF PSS BY PERCENTAGE OF RURAL POP. SERVED BY POWER AMENITIES: RAJASTHAN, 2001

(Descending Order)

RANK	P.CODE	PANCHAYAT SAMITIES NAME	%
1	2	3	4
		PERFECT (100)	
1	**9**	**BANSURE**	**100.00**
1	**16**	**NIMRANA**	**100.00**
1	**19**	**RENI**	**100.00**
1	**33**	**BARAN**	**100.00**
1	**56**	**BANERA**	**100.00**
1	**63**	**SAHARA**	**100.00**
1	**78**	**BHADESAR**	**100.00**
1	**89**	**CHURU**	**100.00**
1	**95**	**BANDIKUI**	**100.00**
1	**124**	**JAMWA RAMGARH**	**100.00**
1	**129**	**SANGANER**	**100.00**
1	**131**	**VIRATNAGAR**	**100.00**
1	**138**	**JASWANTPURA**	**100.00**
1	**150**	**CHIRAWA**	**100.00**
1	**153**	**NAWALGARH**	**100.00**
1	**154**	**SURAJGARH**	**100.00**
1	**159**	**BILARA**	**100.00**
1	**178**	**KUCHAMAN**	**100.00**
1	**181**	**MERTA**	**100.00**
1	**184**	**PARBATSAR**	**100.00**
1	**195**	**SUMERPUR**	**100.00**
1	**196**	**AMET**	**100.00**
1	**201**	**RAILMAGRA**	**100.00**
1	**202**	**RAJSAMAND**	**100.00**
1	**208**	**DANTA RAMGARH**	**100.00**
1	**209**	**DHOND**	**100.00**
1	**210**	**FATEHPUR**	**100.00**
1	**215**	**SRI MADHOPUR**	**100.00**
1	**235**	**MAVLI**	**100.00**
		VERY HIGH (75-100)	
30	**10**	**BEHROR**	**99.90**
30	**62**	**RAIPUR**	**99.90**
30	**81**	**CHHOTI SADRI**	**99.90**
30	**86**	**NIMBAHERA**	**99.90**
30	**91**	**RATANGARH**	**99.90**
30	**128**	**SAMBHAR**	**99.90**
30	**147**	**PIRAWA**	**99.90**
30	**151**	**JHUNJHUNUN**	**99.90**
30	**170**	**CHECHAT**	**99.90**
30	**175**	**DEGANA**	**99.90**
30	**192**	**RANI STATION**	**99.90**
30	**211**	**KHANDELA**	**99.90**
42	**53**	**SEWAR**	**99.80**
42	**83**	**DUNGLA**	**99.80**
42	**88**	**RASHMI**	**99.80**
42	**93**	**SUJANGARH**	**99.80**
42	**193**	**ROHAT**	**99.80**
42	**212**	**LACHHMANGARH**	**99.80**
42	**214**	**PIPRALI**	**99.80**
42	**218**	**REODAR**	**99.80**
50	**18**	**RAMGARH**	**99.70**
50	**67**	**DUNGARGARH**	**99.70**
50	**84**	**GANGRAR**	**99.70**
50	**120**	**BASSI**	**99.70**
50	**137**	**JALOR**	**99.70**
50	**139**	**RANIWARA**	**99.70**
50	**152**	**KHETRI**	**99.70**
50	**165**	**HINDAUN**	**99.70**
50	**220**	**SIROHI**	**99.70**
59	**32**	**ATRU**	**99.60**
59	**65**	**SUWANA**	**99.60**
59	**119**	**AMBER**	**99.60**
59	**190**	**PALI**	**99.60**
63	**110**	**GANGANAGAR**	**99.50**
63	**123**	**GOVINDGARH**	**99.50**
63	**130**	**SHAHPURA**	**99.50**
63	**135**	**AHORE**	**99.50**
67	**6**	**MASOODA**	**99.40**
67	**125**	**JHOTWARA**	**99.40**
67	**158**	**BHOPALGARH**	**99.40**
67	**176**	**DIDWANA**	**99.40**
71	**5**	**KISHANGARH**	**99.30**
71	**173**	**SANGOD**	**99.30**
71	**180**	**MAKRANA**	**99.30**
74	**76**	**BARI SADRI**	**99.20**
74	**80**	**BHOPALSAGAR**	**99.20**
74	**185**	**RIYAN**	**99.20**
74	**187**	**DESURI**	**99.20**
78	**50**	**NADBAI**	**99.10**
78	**54**	**WEIR**	**99.10**
78	**155**	**UDAIPURWATI**	**99.10**
78	**162**	**OSIAN**	**99.10**
78	**198**	**DEOGARH**	**99.10**
78	**200**	**KUMBHALGARH**	**99.10**
84	**13**	**KOTKASIM**	**98.90**
84	**49**	**KUMHER**	**98.90**
84	**57**	**HURDA**	**98.90**
87	**85**	**KAPASAN**	**98.80**
87	**149**	**BUHANA**	**98.80**
87	**194**	**SOJAT**	**98.80**
87	**199**	**KHAMNOR**	**98.80**
91	**105**	**BICHHIWARA**	**98.70**
91	**114**	**SADULSHAHAR**	**98.70**
91	**148**	**ALSISAR**	**98.70**
94	**11**	**KATHUMAR**	**98.60**
94	**82**	**CHITTAURGARH**	**98.60**
94	**219**	**SHEOGANJ**	**98.60**
97	**111**	**KARANPUR**	**98.50**
97	**172**	**LADPURA**	**98.50**
97	**228**	**BHINDER**	**98.50**
100	**22**	**UMREN**	**98.40**
101	**14**	**LACHHMANGARH**	**98.30**
101	**141**	**SAYLA**	**98.30**
101	**161**	**MANDOR**	**98.30**
104	**7**	**PISANGAN**	**98.20**
104	**12**	**KISHANGARH BAS**	**98.20**
104	**213**	**NEEM KA THANA**	**98.20**
107	**15**	**MANDAWAR**	**98.10**
107	**179**	**LADNU**	**98.10**
107	**205**	**GANGAPUR**	**98.10**
110	**45**	**SIWANA**	**98.00**
111	**21**	**TIJARA**	**97.90**
111	**70**	**NOKHA**	**97.90**
113	**4**	**KEKRI**	**97.80**
113	**112**	**PADAMPUR**	**97.80**
113	**188**	**JAITARAN**	**97.80**
116	**8**	**SRINAGAR**	**97.60**
116	**145**	**KHANPUR**	**97.60**
116	**174**	**SULTANPUR**	**97.60**
116	**189**	**KHARCHI/MARWAR JUN.**	**97.60**
120	**47**	**DEEG**	**97.40**
120	**177**	**JAYAL**	**97.40**
122	**2**	**BHINAY**	**97.30**
122	**31**	**ANTA**	**97.30**
122	**55**	**ASIND**	**97.30**
122	**116**	**BHADRA**	**97.30**
126	**227**	**BARGAON**	**97.20**
127	**77**	**BEGUN**	**97.10**
127	**94**	**TARANAGAR**	**97.10**
129	**25**	**GARHI**	**97.00**
129	**73**	**NAINWA**	**97.00**
129	**224**	**TODARAISINGH**	**97.00**
132	**1**	**ARAIN**	**96.90**
133	**96**	**DAUSA**	**96.80**
134	**144**	**JHALRAPATAN**	**96.70**
135	**127**	**PHAGI**	**96.60**
136	**186**	**BALI**	**96.50**
137	**182**	**MUNDWA**	**96.40**
138	**126**	**KOTPUTLI**	**96.20**
139	**3**	**JAWAJA**	**96.10**
140	**61**	**MANDALGARH**	**96.00**
141	**223**	**NIWAI**	**95.90**
142	**20**	**THANAGAZI**	**95.50**
143	**64**	**SHAHPURA**	**95.20**
143	**99**	**SIKRAI**	**95.20**
145	**58**	**JAHAZPUR**	**95.10**
145	**117**	**HANUMANGARH**	**95.10**
145	**160**	**LUNI**	**95.10**
145	**222**	**MALPURA**	**95.10**
149	**17**	**RAJGARH**	**95.00**
149	**60**	**MANDAL**	**95.00**
149	**197**	**BHIM**	**95.00**
152	**122**	**DUDU**	**94.90**
153	**71**	**HINDOLI**	**94.70**
153	**98**	**MAHWA**	**94.70**
153	**191**	**RAIPUR**	**94.70**
156	**226**	**UNIARA**	**94.50**
157	**92**	**SARDARSHAHAR**	**94.40**
158	**36**	**KISHANGANJ**	**94.30**
159	**103**	**RAJAKHERA**	**94.10**
160	**51**	**NAGAR PAHARI**	**93.90**
161	**34**	**CHHABRA**	**93.80**
161	**204**	**BONLI**	**93.80**
163	**136**	**BHINMAL**	**93.70**
164	**106**	**DUNGARPUR**	**93.60**
165	**59**	**KOTRI**	**93.40**
165	**74**	**TALERA**	**93.40**
167	**52**	**RUPBAS**	**92.80**
168	**104**	**ASPUR**	**92.60**
169	**107**	**SAGWARA**	**92.50**
170	**79**	**BHAINSRORGARH**	**92.30**
171	**183**	**NAGAUR**	**91.90**
171	**230**	**GIRWA**	**91.90**
173	**35**	**CHHIPABAROD**	**91.80**
173	**169**	**TODABHIM**	**91.80**
175	72	KESHORAIPATAN	91.40
176	46	BAYANA	91.00
176	167	NADOTI	91.00
178	156	BALESAR	90.80
179	171	ITAWA	90.30
180	97	LALSOT	90.20
181	163	PHALODI	90.10
182	90	RAJGARH	90.00
183	69	LUNKARANSAR	89.60
184	231	GOGUNDA	89.20
185	217	PINDWARA	89.00
186	48	KAMAN	88.40
186	121	CHAKSU	88.40
188	207	SAWAI MADHOPUR	88.20
189	108	SIMALWARA	87.80
190	225	TONK	87.60
191	229	DHARIAWAD	86.90
192	37	SHAHBAD	86.40
193	113	RAISINGHNAGAR	86.30
194	140	SANCHORE	86.00
194	142	BAKANI	86.00
196	203	BAMANWAS	85.90
197	30	TALWARA	85.80
198	143	DAG	85.10
199	166	KARAULI	84.60
200	216	ABU ROAD	84.50
201	26	GHATOL	84.40
201	221	DEOLI	84.40
203	237	SARADA	83.10
204	87	PRATAPGARH	82.60
204	236	SALUMBAR	82.60
206	102	DHAULPUR	82.30
207	75	ARNOD	81.60
208	157	BAP	81.40
209	68	KOLAYAT	80.10
210	206	KHANDAR	79.80
211	164	SHERGARH	79.50
212	38	BALOTRA	77.70
212	42	DHORIMANNA	77.70
214	23	ANANDPURI	75.40
		HIGH (50-75)	
215	146	MANOHARTHANA	74.30
216	41	CHOHTAN	73.10
217	232	JHADOL	72.30
218	168	SAPOTRA	72.10
219	118	NOHAR	72.00
220	66	BIKANER	71.90
221	109	ANUPGARH	69.00
222	233	KHERWARA	68.90
223	29	SAJJANGARH	66.90
224	24	BAGIDORA	64.60
225	101	BASERI	63.60
226	132	JAISALMER	62.90
227	27	KUSHALGARH	57.80
228	100	BARI	57.20
229	44	SINDHARI	56.90
230	115	SURATGARH	56.50
231	134	SANKRA	55.20
232	43	SHEO	54.30
233	39	BARMER	51.50
		MEDIUM (<50)	
234	28	PEEPALKHOONT	41.00
235	133	SAM	39.50
236	40	BAYTOO	35.00
237	234	KOTRA	33.30
		RAJASTHAN	**91.57**
		% AGE OF AAPs	**73.41**

BOLD: Equal/Above Average Panchayat Samities (AAPs)

Source: General Annex VI.

ANNEX-9.13

RANKING OF PSS BY PERCENTAGE OF RURAL POP. SERVED BY PUCCA ROAD AMENITIES: RAJASTHAN, 2001

(Descending Order)

RANK	P.CODE	PANCHAYAT SAMITIES NAME	%
1	2	3	4
		VERY HIGH (> 80)	
1	**195**	**SUMERPUR**	**99.80**
2	**186**	**BALI**	**95.10**
3	**110**	**GANGANAGAR**	**94.80**
4	**53**	**SEWAR**	**94.00**
5	**158**	**BHOPALGARH**	**93.20**
6	**114**	**SADULSHAHAR**	**92.20**
7	**137**	**JALOR**	**91.80**
8	**172**	**LADPURA**	**91.60**
9	**111**	**KARANPUR**	**91.10**
10	**117**	**HANUMANGARH**	**91.00**
11	**91**	**RATANGARH**	**90.90**
12	**215**	**SRI MADHOPUR**	**90.40**
13	**123**	**GOVINDGARH**	**90.10**
13	**150**	**CHIRAWA**	**90.10**
15	**66**	**BIKANER**	**90.00**
16	**155**	**UDAIPURWATI**	**89.90**
16	**159**	**BILARA**	**89.90**
18	**181**	**MERTA**	**89.80**
19	**8**	**SRINAGAR**	**89.60**
20	**89**	**CHURU**	**89.50**
20	**116**	**BHADRA**	**89.50**
22	**153**	**NAWALGARH**	**88.90**
23	**165**	**HINDAUN**	**88.40**
24	**16**	**NIMRANA**	**88.30**
25	**130**	**SHAHPURA**	**88.10**
25	**220**	**SIROHI**	**88.10**
27	**214**	**PIPRALI**	**88.00**
28	**141**	**SAYLA**	**87.90**
29	**219**	**SHEOGANJ**	**87.50**
30	**22**	**UMREN**	**87.40**
31	**3**	**JAWAJA**	**86.90**
32	**17**	**RAJGARH**	**86.80**
32	**192**	**RANI STATION**	**86.80**
34	**7**	**PISANGAN**	**86.30**
35	**131**	**VIRATNAGAR**	**86.00**
36	**49**	**KUMHER**	**85.90**
37	**152**	**KHETRI**	**85.30**
38	**126**	**KOTPUTLI**	**85.20**
39	**217**	**PINDWARA**	**85.00**
40	**160**	**LUNI**	**84.70**
41	**162**	**OSIAN**	**84.50**
42	**185**	**RIYAN**	**84.30**
42	**201**	**RAILMAGRA**	**84.30**
44	**138**	**JASWANTPURA**	**84.00**
44	**209**	**DHOND**	**84.00**
46	**20**	**THANAGAZI**	**83.90**
47	**190**	**PALI**	**83.30**
48	**99**	**SIKRAI**	**83.20**
48	**125**	**JHOTWARA**	**83.20**
50	**169**	**TODABHIM**	**82.80**
51	**11**	**KATHUMAR**	**82.60**
52	**4**	**KEKRI**	**82.50**
53	**120**	**BASSI**	**82.40**
54	**19**	**RENI**	**82.10**
55	**189**	**KHARCHI/MARWAR JUN.**	**81.70**
56	**10**	**BEHROR**	**81.50**
57	**18**	**RAMGARH**	**81.30**
57	**194**	**SOJAT**	**81.30**
59	**47**	**DEEG**	**81.20**
59	**69**	**LUNKARANSAR**	**81.20**
61	**216**	**ABU ROAD**	**80.90**
62	**187**	**DESURI**	**80.80**
63	**135**	**AHORE**	**80.60**
64	**191**	**RAIPUR**	**80.50**
65	**25**	**GARHI**	**80.40**
66	**132**	**JAISALMER**	**80.30**
67	**5**	**KISHANGARH**	**80.20**
67	**6**	**MASOODA**	**80.20**
69	**149**	**BUHANA**	**80.10**
69	**188**	**JAITARAN**	**80.10**
		HIGH (60-80)	
71	**57**	**HURDA**	**79.70**
71	**124**	**JAMWA RAMGARH**	**79.70**
73	**21**	**TIJARA**	**79.50**
73	**70**	**NOKHA**	**79.50**
73	**136**	**BHINMAL**	**79.50**
73	**151**	**JHUNJHUNUN**	**79.50**
77	**67**	**DUNGARGARH**	**79.30**
78	**50**	**NADBAI**	**79.10**
79	**68**	**KOLAYAT**	**79.00**
80	**65**	**SUWANA**	**78.80**
81	**139**	**RANIWARA**	**78.60**
81	**199**	**KHAMNOR**	**78.60**
83	**88**	**RASHMI**	**78.20**
83	**104**	**ASPUR**	**78.20**
83	**107**	**SAGWARA**	**78.20**
83	**122**	**DUDU**	**78.20**
87	**161**	**MANDOR**	**77.70**
87	**218**	**REODAR**	**77.70**
89	**148**	**ALSISAR**	**77.50**
90	**184**	**PARBATSAR**	**77.40**
91	**33**	**BARAN**	**77.30**
91	**176**	**DIDWANA**	**77.30**
93	**112**	**PADAMPUR**	**77.00**
93	**179**	**LADNU**	**77.00**
95	**109**	**ANUPGARH**	**76.60**
96	**9**	**BANSURE**	**76.50**
96	**208**	**DANTA RAMGARH**	**76.50**
98	**15**	**MANDAWAR**	**76.30**
98	**222**	**MALPURA**	**76.30**
98	**230**	**GIRWA**	**76.30**
101	**46**	**BAYANA**	**76.20**
101	**163**	**PHALODI**	**76.20**
103	**52**	**RUPBAS**	**76.00**
103	**197**	**BHIM**	**76.00**
105	**95**	**BANDIKUI**	**75.90**
106	**86**	**NIMBAHERA**	**75.80**
106	**154**	**SURAJGARH**	**75.80**
108	**237**	**SARADA**	**75.70**
109	**129**	**SANGANER**	**75.30**
110	**45**	**SIWANA**	**75.20**
110	**96**	**DAUSA**	**75.20**
112	**128**	**SAMBHAR**	**75.10**
112	**167**	**NADOTI**	**75.10**
112	**205**	**GANGAPUR**	**75.10**
112	**235**	**MAVLI**	**75.10**
116	**14**	**LACHHMANGARH**	**75.00**
116	**213**	**NEEM KA THANA**	**75.00**
118	**170**	**CHECHAT**	**74.70**
118	**227**	**BARGAON**	**74.70**
120	**119**	**AMBER**	**74.50**
121	**63**	**SAHARA**	**74.30**
122	**90**	**RAJGARH**	**74.00**
123	**102**	**DHAULPUR**	**73.60**
123	**182**	**MUNDWA**	**73.60**
123	**193**	**ROHAT**	**73.60**
123	**202**	**RAJSAMAND**	**73.60**
127	**94**	**TARANAGAR**	**73.50**
128	12	KISHANGARH BAS	73.30
129	174	SULTANPUR	73.00
130	177	JAYAL	72.70
131	13	KOTKASIM	72.60
132	30	TALWARA	72.50
133	60	MANDAL	72.40
133	108	SIMALWARA	72.40
135	56	BANERA	72.10
135	103	RAJAKHERA	72.10
135	118	NOHAR	72.10
138	140	SANCHORE	72.00
139	2	BHINAY	71.90
140	115	SURATGARH	71.80
141	48	KAMAN	71.70
142	51	NAGAR PAHARI	71.60
143	211	KHANDELA	71.50
144	183	NAGAUR	71.30
145	225	TONK	71.20
146	166	KARAULI	71.00
147	98	MAHWA	70.40
148	175	DEGANA	70.30
149	101	BASERI	70.20
150	113	RAISINGHNAGAR	70.10
151	156	BALESAR	69.90
152	74	TALERA	69.70
152	168	SAPOTRA	69.70
154	38	BALOTRA	69.60
154	157	BAP	69.60
156	31	ANTA	69.40
156	93	SUJANGARH	69.40
158	206	KHANDAR	69.30
159	26	GHATOL	68.40
160	41	CHOHTAN	68.30
161	105	BICHHIWARA	67.80
162	233	KHERWARA	67.30
163	180	MAKRANA	67.00
164	32	ATRU	66.90
165	106	DUNGARPUR	66.80
166	82	CHITTAURGARH	66.50
167	223	NIWAI	66.10
168	61	MANDALGARH	66.00
168	71	HINDOLI	66.00
168	178	KUCHAMAN	66.00
171	224	TODARAISINGH	65.90
172	97	LALSOT	65.00
172	133	SAM	65.00
174	171	ITAWA	64.70
175	55	ASIND	64.50
176	127	PHAGI	64.30
177	1	ARAIN	64.10
177	231	GOGUNDA	64.10
179	54	WEIR	63.80
180	203	BAMANWAS	63.70
181	228	BHINDER	63.50
182	24	BAGIDORA	62.90
183	92	SARDARSHAHAR	62.60
184	79	BHAINSRORGARH	62.50
185	80	BHOPALSAGAR	62.40
186	212	LACHHMANGARH	62.10
187	36	KISHANGANJ	62.00
188	204	BONLI	61.90
189	229	DHARIAWAD	61.60
190	164	SHERGARH	61.20
191	173	SANGOD	60.60
192	78	BHADESAR	60.30
192	210	FATEHPUR	60.30
194	221	DEOLI	60.10
		MEDIUM (40-60)	
195	200	KUMBHALGARH	59.90
196	87	PRATAPGARH	59.80
197	23	ANANDPURI	59.10
198	73	NAINWA	58.80
198	84	GANGRAR	58.80
200	236	SALUMBAR	58.50
201	83	DUNGLA	58.30
201	207	SAWAI MADHOPUR	58.30
203	72	KESHORAIPATAN	57.90
204	226	UNIARA	57.80
205	42	DHORIMANNA	57.60
206	37	SHAHBAD	57.40
206	100	BARI	57.40
208	58	JAHAZPUR	57.00
208	81	CHHOTI SADRI	57.00
210	39	BARMER	56.90
211	59	KOTRI	56.70
212	75	ARNOD	56.60
212	76	BARI SADRI	56.60
214	64	SHAHPURA	56.30
214	196	AMET	56.30
216	62	RAIPUR	56.10
217	134	SANKRA	55.90
218	77	BEGUN	55.40
219	145	KHANPUR	54.20
220	44	SINDHARI	53.90
221	35	CHHIPABAROD	53.50
222	29	SAJJANGARH	53.00
223	85	KAPASAN	52.80
224	198	DEOGARH	52.30
225	232	JHADOL	51.50
226	43	SHEO	50.90
227	144	JHALRAPATAN	50.70
228	121	CHAKSU	50.10
229	28	PEEPALKHOONT	47.20
230	234	KOTRA	46.80
231	27	KUSHALGARH	46.50
232	142	BAKANI	46.10
233	40	BAYTOO	44.20
234	147	PIRAWA	44.00
235	143	DAG	40.90
		LOW (<40)	
236	34	CHHABRA	36.40
237	146	MANOHARTHANA	31.10
RAJASTHAN		**TOTAL**	**73.48**
		% AGE OF AAPs	**53.59**

BOLD: Equal/Above Average Panchayat Samities (AAPs)
Source: General Annex VI.

ANNEX-10.1

PANCHAYAT SAMITI-WISE HEALTH STATUS INDEX: RAJASTHAN, 1991

P. Code	Panchayat Samiti	%age of Rural Pop. Served by Medical Amenity (V1)	%age of Rural Pop. Served by Drinking Water Amenity (V2)	Sex Ratio (V3)	Female LR (%) (V4)	%age of Villages Having Medical Amenity (V5)	%age of Pop. Served by Education Amenity (V6)	%age of Rural Pop. Approached by Pucca Road (V7)	%age of Rural Pop. Served by Power Amenity (V8)	Health Status Index
1	2	3	4	5	6	7	8	9	10	11
1	ARAIN	49.7	100.0	941	11.7	23.8	99.1	33.0	75.2	0.5614
2	BHINAY	61.2	100.0	937	13.3	39.2	99.4	54.3	83.2	0.6324
3	JAWAJA	33.6	99.1	986	12.3	19.7	93.0	56.9	61.4	0.5583
4	KEKRI	66.7	100.0	943	19.9	37.2	99.6	56.2	94.6	0.6643
5	KISHANGARH	61.6	100.0	913	12.7	32.7	96.2	56.8	92.3	0.6251
6	MASOODA	53.9	100.0	919	12.1	27.0	95.4	59.5	88.8	0.6080
7	PISANGAN	66.5	100.0	924	16.2	44.7	99.7	75.2	99.0	0.6908
8	SRINAGAR	48.3	100.0	924	12.8	32.6	99.8	71.8	94.5	0.6389
	AJMER DISTRICT	**55.7**	**99.9**	**935**	**14.0**	**30.9**	**97.9**	**59.3**	**87.0**	**0.6243**
9	BANSURE	43.7	100.0	881	12.7	19.9	98.0	49.6	99.3	0.5763
10	BEHROR	51.7	100.0	933	28.6	28.9	99.1	46.4	99.8	0.6358
11	KATHUMAR	44.1	100.0	837	11.4	20.9	98.2	45.4	67.7	0.5148
12	KISHANGARH BAS	39.5	100.0	902	18.9	20.0	94.8	53.3	99.8	0.5884
13	KOTKASIM	41.0	100.0	896	26.3	20.0	95.2	44.1	85.0	0.5676
14	LACHHMANGARH	33.7	100.0	882	12.2	13.7	95.4	47.5	63.1	0.5046
15	MANDAWAR	44.4	100.0	917	25.3	26.1	98.9	48.6	97.1	0.6119
16	NIMRANA	49.9	100.0	944	32.0	29.4	98.5	52.3	100.0	0.6495
17	RAJGARH	47.5	100.0	882	12.2	16.2	94.1	55.6	79.1	0.5535
18	RAMGARH	36.7	100.0	879	14.4	18.1	93.5	52.4	88.7	0.5513
19	RENI	40.9	100.0	875	11.2	15.7	93.9	42.1	80.8	0.5256
20	THANAGAZI	54.2	100.0	889	8.9	21.6	97.0	56.3	82.4	0.5759
21	TIJARA	30.2	100.0	886	14.3	13.1	92.7	38.6	80.5	0.5110
22	UMREN	40.5	100.0	867	11.9	20.0	93.9	43.4	95.6	0.5484
	ALWAR	**42.3**	**100.0**	**888**	**16.7**	**19.5**	**96.0**	**48.2**	**86.6**	**0.5616**
23	ANANDPURI	39.5	100.0	963	7.1	21.1	96.7	44.4	48.4	0.5258
24	BAGIDORA	49.3	100.0	971	10.6	26.3	93.6	59.1	58.2	0.5788
25	GARHI	57.7	100.0	973	16.1	38.0	97.9	59.5	90.2	0.6575
26	GHATOL	42.3	100.0	986	8.1	16.1	95.5	48.6	68.4	0.5620
27	KUSHALGARH	16.9	99.8	966	3.9	9.6	85.7	22.0	41.4	0.4296
28	PEEPALKHOONT	44.8	100.0	966	3.0	22.6	85.1	36.8	28.3	0.4813
29	SAJJANGARH	23.5	100.0	957	6.6	13.7	85.1	31.5	35.3	0.4466
30	TALWARA	50.3	100.0	988	8.9	24.3	92.3	59.6	63.9	0.5883
	BANSWARA	**42.9**	**100.0**	**973**	**8.9**	**20.8**	**92.3**	**47.8**	**58.7**	**0.5475**
31	ANTA	45.3	100.0	909	16.8	17.7	95.3	37.0	79.0	0.5471
32	ATRU	49.6	100.0	893	15.8	22.2	91.7	34.9	86.9	0.5534
33	BARAN	31.6	100.0	904	15.7	15.3	99.1	38.5	92.9	0.5476
34	CHHABRA	24.2	100.0	884	6.4	11.1	89.3	13.7	70.8	0.4429
35	CHHIPABAROD	29.3	100.0	905	7.1	12.0	88.9	21.7	46.3	0.4383
36	KISHANGANJ	37.3	99.9	902	11.1	11.9	83.7	33.7	83.9	0.5074
37	SHAHBAD	29.0	99.5	877	10.9	8.8	85.5	35.0	65.5	0.4635
	BARAN	**36.1**	**99.9**	**897**	**12.3**	**13.7**	**90.5**	**30.8**	**75.9**	**0.5025**
38	BALOTRA	34.8	99.7	919	6.9	14.8	91.7	48.6	61.5	0.5096
39	BARMER	20.2	97.3	857	3.4	11.3	83.7	46.0	22.0	0.3928
40	BAYTOO	15.5	96.4	920	4.7	6.9	74.4	19.6	25.0	0.3656
41	CHOHTAN	36.5	100.0	873	2.2	18.6	90.5	34.8	28.3	0.4328
42	DHORIMANNA	20.2	100.0	912	3.0	13.1	77.7	29.6	49.9	0.4263
43	SHEO	21.3	99.2	826	3.3	10.8	91.7	52.7	33.2	0.4160
44	SINDHARI	25.1	99.7	914	2.9	12.5	79.5	37.2	34.0	0.4238
45	SIWANA	45.7	100.0	938	7.1	30.9	98.0	41.0	90.2	0.5856
	BARMER	**27.4**	**99.1**	**896**	**4.2**	**13.4**	**85.6**	**38.5**	**42.7**	**0.4418**
46	BAYANA	44.0	100.0	787	9.7	23.9	97.9	43.2	72.2	0.4991
47	DEEG	33.1	100.0	818	12.0	15.0	97.6	53.8	72.5	0.5026
48	KAMAN	30.0	99.9	864	6.1	18.7	92.2	31.0	54.1	0.4556
49	KUMHER	58.4	99.4	826	16.4	32.4	99.4	63.2	94.7	0.6056
50	NADBAI	34.4	100.0	820	14.2	21.1	98.6	46.5	87.6	0.5265
51	NAGAR PAHARI	24.4	100.0	849	9.8	12.0	94.0	39.8	44.8	0.4408
52	RUPBAS	42.3	100.0	818	17.0	23.4	98.4	53.2	61.6	0.5175
53	SEWAR	33.9	99.9	823	14.4	20.1	98.2	60.7	85.7	0.5408
54	WEIR	47.2	100.0	824	13.9	26.8	98.9	49.1	99.1	0.5688
	BHARATPUR	**38.3**	**99.9**	**826**	**12.5**	**20.7**	**97.1**	**48.3**	**73.3**	**0.5134**
55	ASIND	55.3	100.0	989	8.4	26.6	93.9	43.6	87.3	0.6084
56	BANERA	74.5	100.0	954	10.2	42.7	97.3	53.3	97.7	0.6704
57	HURDA	72.8	100.0	930	18.5	41.2	99.3	62.1	100.0	0.6838
58	JAHAZPUR	60.4	100.0	916	8.8	30.9	95.7	44.2	87.7	0.5956
59	**KOTRI**	**51.1**	**100.0**	**931**	**13.2**	**24.7**	**96.3**	**42.6**	**85.4**	**0.5834**

P. Code	*Panchayat Samiti*	*%age of Rural Pop. Served by Medical Amenity (V1)*	*%age of Rural Pop. Served by Drinking Water Amenity (V2)*	*Sex Ratio (V3)*	*Female LR (%) (V4)*	*%age of Villages Having Medical Amenity (V5)*	*%age of Pop. Served by Education Amenity (V6)*	*%age of Rural Pop. Approached by Pucca Road (V7)*	*%age of Rural Pop. Served by Power Amenity (V8)*	*Health Status Index*
1	*2*	*3*	*4*	*5*	*6*	*7*	*8*	*9*	*10*	*11*
60	MANDAL	60.9	100.0	996	9.1	27.9	96.7	46.9	92.7	0.6350
61	MANDALGARH	51.5	100.0	901	9.0	19.6	87.1	46.0	88.5	0.5573
62	RAIPUR	58.8	100.0	1018	9.8	29.1	98.3	38.2	92.7	0.6344
63	SAHARA	64.9	100.0	1039	10.1	31.9	97.8	47.4	97.5	0.6710
64	SHAHPURA	54.3	100.0	941	7.7	28.2	98.1	53.3	93.7	0.6149
65	SUWANA	52.8	100.0	959	9.3	24.4	98.1	61.5	97.6	0.6324
	BHILWARA	**58.4**	**100.0**	**957**	**10.0**	**27.7**	**95.7**	**48.6**	**92.0**	**0.6175**
66	BIKANER	62.6	98.4	871	10.0	28.4	98.5	60.0	80.1	0.5909
67	DUNGARGARH *	61.9	99.2	933	8.0	40.0	97.6	54.6	90.3	0.6321
68	KOLAYAT	44.4	97.5	876	8.7	17.2	94.1	57.0	76.6	0.5398
69	LUNKARANSAR	45.0	99.8	904	10.3	19.2	98.0	54.0	86.8	0.5726
70	NOKHA	51.8	99.4	926	6.6	27.8	98.5	52.3	91.4	0.5996
	BIKANER **	**52.4**	**98.9**	**894**	**8.8**	**22.9**	**97.5**	**56.0**	**84.1**	**0.5781**
71	HINDOLI	26.5	100.0	891	7.9	11.5	96.2	32.6	86.3	0.5024
72	KESHORAIPATAN	38.2	100.0	897	10.9	15.7	93.1	29.4	58.1	0.4853
73	NAINWA	42.1	100.0	885	7.7	14.9	94.5	35.4	85.9	0.5245
74	TALERA	35.0	100.0	878	10.4	16.9	91.0	45.8	79.4	0.5193
	BUNDI	**35.1**	**100.0**	**887**	**9.4**	**15.0**	**93.4**	**36.8**	**68.0**	**0.4968**
75	ARNOD	39.8	100.0	968	12.8	12.9	89.3	31.8	72.1	0.5296
76	BARI SADRI	33.5	100.0	979	9.5	10.4	86.9	41.2	79.6	0.5369
77	BEGUN	34.9	100.0	948	8.6	11.9	83.9	44.4	86.8	0.5366
78	BHADESAR	36.7	100.0	954	9.8	10.6	86.9	43.0	68.6	0.5203
79	BHAINSRORGARH	23.5	100.0	890	9.3	7.3	81.2	39.6	76.4	0.4724
80	BHOPALSAGAR	52.4	100.0	970	11.8	18.1	94.0	65.4	98.4	0.6321
81	CHHOTI SADRI	20.1	100.0	957	12.0	6.4	91.2	32.4	93.3	0.5213
82	CHITTAURGARH	33.4	100.0	960	11.2	7.8	90.7	45.2	86.9	0.5471
83	DUNGLA	36.5	100.0	977	9.8	12.8	94.8	34.0	80.6	0.5454
84	GANGRAR	39.5	100.0	937	10.0	12.6	91.4	34.5	83.0	0.5329
85	KAPASAN	40.3	100.0	979	7.1	21.5	93.2	36.7	98.6	0.5823
86	NIMBAHERA	25.1	99.9	959	12.2	7.3	93.2	42.9	94.7	0.5469
87	PRATAPGARH	33.2	100.0	953	10.9	13.4	84.5	28.0	58.0	0.4854
88	RASHMI	57.1	100.0	1003	11.0	25.3	98.3	54.9	81.5	0.6300
	CHITTAURGARH	**35.2**	**100.0**	**959**	**10.6**	**11.9**	**89.6**	**39.9**	**81.9**	**0.5391**
89	CHURU	37.0	98.2	957	10.6	24.8	99.2	41.7	90.0	0.5789
90	RAJGARH	33.6	95.5	943	13.7	19.5	96.8	41.2	48.3	0.5073
91	RATANGARH	54.0	99.9	937	8.9	34.4	97.7	33.6	96.2	0.6000
92	SARDARSHAHAR	33.1	99.7	935	6.1	21.2	96.6	33.7	65.9	0.5138
93	SUJANGARH	48.3	99.2	942	7.5	27.5	97.7	31.3	81.4	0.5623
94	TARANAGAR	54.8	100.0	948	9.0	23.4	97.1	47.7	78.9	0.5871
	CHURU ***	**44.7**	**99.4**	**942**	**9.3**	**25.7**	**97.4**	**39.8**	**75.7**	**0.5611**
95	BANDIKUI	35.1	100.0	889	12.9	14.5	87.6	27.6	96.0	0.5175
96	DAUSA	41.9	100.0	888	9.8	15.8	91.8	44.0	86.0	0.5366
97	LALSOT	31.0	100.0	896	9.4	9.9	89.7	36.7	70.3	0.4869
98	MAHWA	39.2	100.0	854	13.9	15.3	95.8	43.1	59.3	0.4950
99	SIKRAI	42.4	100.0	894	9.1	18.8	95.9	44.3	70.1	0.5281
	DAUSA	**37.8**	**100.0**	**885**	**10.9**	**14.2**	**91.9**	**38.9**	**77.5**	**0.5129**
100	BARI	36.2	100.0	763	6.7	23.0	93.0	35.1	22.4	0.3966
101	BASERI	48.8	100.0	789	12.0	23.0	96.3	60.6	37.5	0.4841
102	DHAULPUR	55.0	100.0	798	11.5	40.4	99.6	52.7	48.9	0.5250
103	RAJAKHERA	28.2	100.0	785	8.0	15.7	96.2	38.9	72.5	0.4591
	DHAULPUR	**43.4**	**100.0**	**786**	**9.9**	**26.0**	**96.7**	**47.9**	**46.8**	**0.4735**
104	ASPUR	50.0	100.0	1053	12.9	30.3	92.3	51.2	78.7	0.6338
105	BICHHIWARA	48.6	100.0	976	9.7	24.7	97.0	58.8	78.3	0.6058
106	DUNGARPUR	40.6	100.0	1022	10.3	27.9	96.8	53.2	57.6	0.5854
107	SAGWARA	64.0	100.0	1021	16.6	32.7	99.0	60.3	68.1	0.6529
108	SIMALWARA	41.4	100.0	965	10.3	17.4	93.2	45.5	61.3	0.5415
	DUNGARPUR	**48.9**	**100.0**	**1003**	**11.9**	**25.8**	**96.6**	**53.7**	**65.2**	**0.5975**
109	ANUPGARH	23.1	100.0	870	17.5	7.6	56.5	55.7	23.1	0.3974
110	GANGANAGAR	53.1	100.0	858	28.5	27.0	88.0	71.4	93.1	0.6146
111	KARANPUR	34.0	100.0	905	27.8	14.5	92.5	56.8	97.9	0.5860
112	PADAMPUR	40.5	100.0	905	28.3	18.6	92.6	51.2	75.7	0.5653
113	RAISINGHNAGAR	39.5	100.0	915	23.3	21.8	82.6	51.4	62.0	0.5363
114	SADULSHAHAR	51.2	99.7	862	22.8	14.9	85.5	70.6	86.7	0.5791
115	SURATGARH	41.2	100.0	852	16.3	13.7	74.3	57.3	43.3	0.4686
	GANGANAGAR	**39.4**	**100.0**	**873**	**21.9**	**14.1**	**77.5**	**59.8**	**60.7**	**0.5109**
116	BHADRA	58.1	100.0	905	16.8	19.5	94.2	47.4	55.0	0.5454
117	HANUMANGARH	61.8	100.0	890	18.6	15.3	76.2	75.8	82.3	0.5883
118	NOHAR	53.4	99.7	908	12.1	17.7	88.3	37.2	48.9	0.5045
	HANUMANGARH	**58.0**	**99.9**	**900**	**15.8**	**16.8**	**84.6**	**55.5**	**64.2**	**0.5483**

P. Code	Panchayat Samiti	%age of Rural Pop. Served by Medical Amenity (V1)	%age of Rural Pop. Served by Drinking Water Amenity (V2)	Sex Ratio (V3)	Female LR (%) (V4)	%age of Villages Having Medical Amenity (V5)	%age of Pop. Served by Education Amenity (V6)	%age of Rural Pop. Approached by Pucca Road (V7)	%age of Rural Pop. Served by Power Amenity (V8)	Health Status Index
1	2	3	4	5	6	7	8	9	10	11
119	AMBER	40.1	99.9	909	11.1	21.1	92.6	57.6	98.0	0.5838
120	BASSI	45.4	100.0	903	9.7	24.4	93.2	61.5	85.4	0.5804
121	CHAKSU	37.1	100.0	908	8.0	17.8	78.1	28.3	67.9	0.4794
122	DUDU	45.6	99.7	914	12.6	18.1	95.0	50.5	40.6	0.5128
123	GOVINDGARH	78.5	100.0	915	15.7	47.4	99.3	67.2	100.0	0.6956
124	JAMWA RAMGARH	46.4	100.0	903	9.2	21.7	94.8	50.9	99.0	0.5834
125	JHOTWARA	37.0	100.0	884	15.6	16.7	94.8	75.2	99.9	0.5975
126	KOTPUTLI	47.3	100.0	911	13.9	31.1	97.9	53.5	93.6	0.6056
127	PHAGI	46.6	99.7	905	10.9	18.5	93.4	46.5	73.5	0.5430
128	SAMBHAR	46.5	99.9	930	12.6	23.1	97.3	54.3	98.7	0.6069
129	SANGANER	39.1	100.0	893	14.6	16.1	89.9	61.1	99.9	0.5779
130	SHAHPURA	57.7	100.0	909	13.9	39.2	100.0	69.7	99.5	0.6583
131	VIRATNAGAR	55.8	99.8	901	12.5	26.3	92.6	59.0	99.2	0.6116
	JAIPUR	**48.7**	**99.9**	**908**	**12.3**	**22.7**	**94.1**	**56.4**	**88.4**	**0.5860**
132	JAISALMER	40.0	98.5	780	6.4	16.1	94.5	54.7	38.6	0.4439
133	SAM	30.4	99.9	794	3.5	10.0	90.8	30.1	1.5	0.3460
134	SANKRA	32.9	100.0	858	4.6	21.5	94.7	48.9	19.5	0.4409
	JAISALMER	**34.1**	**99.6**	**815**	**4.7**	**14.5**	**93.4**	**44.4**	**18.9**	**0.4085**
135	AHORE	61.6	100.0	986	10.9	32.4	98.9	44.4	98.3	0.6464
136	BHINMAL	37.3	100.0	931	3.2	21.5	98.2	40.6	88.5	0.5534
137	JALOR	63.8	100.0	969	9.4	45.5	99.7	64.9	98.8	0.6843
138	JASWANTPURA	46.4	100.0	962	5.5	27.8	98.9	54.4	97.7	0.6173
139	RANIWARA	35.4	100.0	921	4.8	19.3	100.0	58.5	99.7	0.5850
140	SANCHORE	36.0	98.3	924	3.0	22.8	98.3	38.2	60.0	0.5099
141	SAYLA	62.5	99.9	956	6.4	39.0	99.9	58.3	97.4	0.6559
	JALOR	**47.7**	**99.6**	**947**	**5.9**	**28.4**	**99.0**	**49.2**	**87.6**	**0.5948**
142	BAKANI	37.6	100.0	921	8.8	13.5	80.7	38.9	68.2	0.4975
143	DAG	37.0	100.0	939	8.4	15.5	89.6	32.2	46.9	0.4819
144	JHALRAPATAN	33.2	100.0	919	10.3	14.5	85.3	36.9	90.2	0.5251
145	KHANPUR	39.3	100.0	896	14.9	14.2	89.8	33.2	83.1	0.5213
146	MANOHARTHANA	28.2	100.0	916	3.2	14.6	74.3	23.1	40.8	0.4163
147	PIRAWA	35.1	100.0	930	10.3	17.0	96.8	12.4	88.4	0.5164
	JHALAWAR	**35.0**	**100.0**	**921**	**9.3**	**14.8**	**86.1**	**29.8**	**70.2**	**0.4944**
148	ALSISAR	54.8	100.0	981	21.6	23.0	98.9	54.9	83.5	0.6323
149	BUHANA	41.8	100.0	936	25.3	24.6	99.0	48.8	92.3	0.6085
150	CHIRAWA	55.3	99.7	948	23.3	30.5	98.4	66.7	100.0	0.6659
151	JHUNJHUNUN	46.7	99.7	966	25.3	24.4	98.1	70.3	97.6	0.6581
152	KHETRI	64.9	100.0	898	18.9	41.3	98.2	62.3	94.2	0.6536
153	NAWALGARH	73.6	100.0	959	21.9	54.3	100.0	69.4	100.0	0.7268
154	SURAJGARH	35.2	98.9	917	21.7	23.3	99.7	49.2	95.9	0.5913
155	UDAIPURWATI	62.4	100.0	949	18.9	37.0	99.4	83.3	99.1	0.6990
	JHUNJHUNUN	**55.1**	**99.8**	**942**	**22.0**	**30.1**	**99.0**	**63.9**	**95.7**	**0.6531**
156	BALESAR	65.9	99.5	924	4.9	42.7	99.4	50.9	93.1	0.6346
157	BAP	26.4	99.8	885	5.3	16.1	90.3	20.8	33.8	0.4145
158	BHOPALGARH	57.9	99.3	930	7.0	32.1	98.9	79.7	93.2	0.6515
159	BILARA	75.4	100.0	920	8.8	48.1	99.7	77.7	99.6	0.6991
160	LUNI	54.4	100.0	918	9.4	26.6	99.0	71.7	83.0	0.6169
161	MANDOR	27.7	98.4	906	7.5	15.2	98.8	64.3	90.5	0.5600
162	OSIAN	42.3	99.9	914	5.9	25.8	90.0	57.9	82.4	0.5654
163	PHALODI	36.6	93.0	916	5.8	25.6	97.3	50.3	75.4	0.5410
164	SHERGARH	56.3	95.2	895	4.3	46.0	100.0	62.9	77.7	0.6058
	JODHPUR	**46.9**	**95.6**	**914**	**6.6**	**28.7**	**94.7**	**58.0**	**78.6**	**0.5715**
165	HINDAUN	49.7	100.0	833	9.8	31.9	97.8	55.3	95.0	0.5779
166	KARAULI	37.8	100.0	818	7.0	19.4	91.4	32.1	55.7	0.4519
167	NADOTI	50.6	100.0	864	11.0	27.4	94.5	53.0	89.2	0.5728
168	SAPOTRA	45.7	99.5	828	9.7	18.7	93.5	37.5	58.0	0.4799
169	TODABHIM	44.8	100.0	843	8.9	26.8	96.2	49.6	69.8	0.5275
	KARAULI	**45.5**	**99.9**	**834**	**9.2**	**23.5**	**94.8**	**45.1**	**72.8**	**0.5174**
170	CHECHAT	48.6	99.9	883	16.3	19.9	92.4	49.5	97.9	0.5786
171	ITAWA	45.2	100.0	889	13.8	16.2	91.2	37.6	44.9	0.4865
172	LADPURA	44.2	100.0	896	16.8	18.5	95.4	75.0	86.7	0.5989
173	SANGOD	38.0	100.0	906	17.2	13.6	83.7	39.0	85.5	0.5283
174	SULTANPUR	43.0	100.0	892	18.0	16.9	92.6	36.4	81.2	0.5368
	KOTA	**43.8**	**100.0**	**893**	**16.4**	**16.8**	**91.0**	**46.8**	**78.8**	**0.5440**
175	DEGANA	47.8	100.0	961	9.4	24.7	99.3	46.2	84.0	0.5928
176	DIDWANA	43.2	100.0	982	10.9	22.8	97.6	4.8	87.9	0.5458
177	JAYAL	49.2	100.0	954	7.3	23.5	98.0	41.6	61.7	0.5524
178	KUCHAMAN	50.6	99.8	944	11.3	29.5	98.3	28.7	99.6	0.5941
179	LADNU	53.6	100.0	977	12.4	30.2	98.7	33.2	75.5	0.5893
180	MAKRANA	47.2	100.0	955	12.0	20.8	98.3	20.0	90.7	0.5624
181	MERTA	60.8	100.0	919	11.2	26.0	97.4	63.8	98.0	0.6336
182	MUNDWA	47.0	100.0	930	6.3	24.6	98.8	47.9	80.6	0.5729

P. Code	Panchayat Samiti	%age of Rural Pop. Served by Medical Amenity (V1)	%age of Rural Pop. Served by Drinking Water Amenity (V2)	Sex Ratio (V3)	Female LR (%) (V4)	%age of Villages Having Medical Amenity (V5)	%age of Pop. Served by Education Amenity (V6)	%age of Rural Pop. Approached by Pucca Road (V7)	%age of Rural Pop. Served by Power Amenity (V8)	Health Status Index
1	2	3	4	5	6	7	8	9	10	11
183	NAGAUR	56.5	100.0	935	7.1	28.6	97.4	32.9	68.7	0.5574
184	PARBATSAR	45.6	99.3	942	10.5	27.8	98.0	33.2	98.7	0.5875
185	RIYAN	51.7	99.6	940	9.5	25.8	98.9	58.4	95.9	0.6201
	NAGAUR	**50.0**	**99.9**	**949**	**9.8**	**25.7**	**98.2**	**35.6**	**85.4**	**0.5796**
186	BALI	73.7	100.0	987	15.4	41.6	99.9	66.1	93.7	0.7016
187	DESURI	69.9	100.0	1007	13.6	39.5	98.1	57.3	96.5	0.6901
188	JAITARAN	60.8	100.0	948	7.8	33.7	97.5	32.3	95.0	0.6074
189	KHARCHI/MARWAR JUN.	56.5	100.0	983	11.2	26.3	95.4	54.5	91.7	0.6316
190	PALI	52.1	100.0	933	8.7	26.3	99.2	62.3	97.3	0.6250
191	RAIPUR	36.1	100.0	961	8.9	27.2	95.3	42.7	77.1	0.5626
192	RANI STATION	72.9	100.0	1004	15.8	43.8	99.4	44.4	99.6	0.6903
193	ROHAT	34.7	100.0	944	7.5	19.0	99.2	36.3	95.0	0.5615
194	SOJAT	52.8	100.0	975	11.1	31.3	99.5	53.6	90.2	0.6321
195	SUMERPUR	71.1	100.0	972	13.8	46.0	98.4	87.7	100.0	0.7291
	PALI	**60.7**	**100.0**	**972**	**11.5**	**32.5**	**98.1**	**54.0**	**93.0**	**0.6448**
196	AMET	41.2	100.0	972	7.8	19.1	90.1	34.2	86.0	0.5557
197	BHIM	47.9	100.0	1045	9.6	22.0	95.0	60.1	80.2	0.6298
198	DEOGARH	28.3	100.0	1013	6.6	11.5	80.5	40.3	74.0	0.5253
199	KHAMNOR	61.2	100.0	1014	13.7	33.3	96.9	48.5	94.2	0.6589
200	KUMBHALGARH	39.8	100.0	993	8.3	21.1	92.9	42.1	26.1	0.5039
201	RAILMAGRA	60.4	100.0	986	14.7	28.9	97.0	60.3	100.0	0.6649
202	RAJSAMAND	45.9	100.0	984	13.3	20.0	97.5	48.3	26.0	0.5263
	RAJSAMAND	**47.7**	**100.0**	**1001**	**10.9**	**21.9**	**93.8**	**48.6**	**67.7**	**0.5825**
203	BAMANWAS	50.8	100.0	867	9.9	19.7	97.3	50.1	77.9	0.5488
204	BONLI	42.8	99.8	882	10.4	17.8	95.9	36.3	88.0	0.5364
205	GANGAPUR	57.3	100.0	857	11.1	31.3	98.9	45.0	90.7	0.5807
206	KHANDAR	46.8	100.0	858	7.3	18.0	89.5	40.7	43.5	0.4703
207	SAWAI MADHOPUR	47.3	100.0	888	9.0	20.1	97.7	35.4	74.5	0.5300
	SAWAI MADHOPUR	**48.8**	**100.0**	**872**	**9.6**	**20.9**	**96.1**	**40.9**	**76.3**	**0.5343**
208	DANTA RAMGARH	64.5	100.0	949	15.2	37.0	98.3	57.4	94.2	0.6572
209	DHOND	70.6	99.8	968	14.7	50.9	98.5	52.7	100.0	0.6902
210	FATEHPUR	47.6	100.0	996	15.2	29.8	99.8	24.7	97.6	0.6105
211	KHANDELA	57.4	100.0	944	14.5	31.9	98.8	53.5	99.6	0.6414
212	LACHHMANGARH	47.2	99.7	986	15.5	26.5	99.2	37.4	99.3	0.6191
213	NEEM KA THANA	61.3	99.3	914	15.7	41.3	97.7	47.7	93.4	0.6307
214	PIPRALI	61.6	100.0	946	15.9	31.9	99.2	68.8	38.4	0.5924
215	SRI MADHOPUR	52.6	100.0	937	16.8	39.3	99.9	58.8	99.8	0.6531
	SIKAR	**58.4**	**99.8**	**952**	**15.4**	**35.7**	**98.8**	**49.0**	**90.7**	**0.6347**
216	ABU ROAD	4.4	100.0	941	7.4	23.1	99.7	73.8	76.1	0.5513
217	PINDWARA	54.3	99.4	964	10.6	29.6	99.1	69.0	83.8	0.6370
218	REODAR	38.7	100.0	947	8.2	17.2	98.1	64.8	97.2	0.6033
219	SHEOGANJ	62.3	100.0	961	8.4	30.3	98.8	98.0	65.3	0.6573
220	SIROHI	51.6	100.0	1010	10.7	25.6	98.8	66.1	99.7	0.6633
	SIROHI	**43.4**	**99.9**	**965**	**9.2**	**24.4**	**98.9**	**72.5**	**86.4**	**0.6234**
221	DEOLI	59.6	100.0	919	11.1	28.7	95.4	37.2	61.8	0.5542
222	MALPURA	57.6	100.0	932	10.1	30.9	97.6	45.2	82.9	0.5976
223	NIWAI	40.0	100.0	939	12.5	12.6	93.7	29.4	88.3	0.5405
224	TODARAISINGH	48.6	100.0	944	8.7	23.9	91.6	34.5	49.2	0.5175
225	TONK	43.1	100.0	914	6.7	18.2	91.5	30.9	62.4	0.5010
226	UNIARA	38.6	100.0	911	7.6	13.1	87.5	33.4	70.8	0.4976
	TONK	**48.2**	**100.0**	**926**	**9.5**	**19.9**	**93.2**	**35.2**	**70.3**	**0.5351**
227	BARGAON	44.3	100.0	936	14.8	21.0	96.6	54.6	93.9	0.6000
228	BHINDER	46.7	100.0	973	11.2	14.8	91.2	55.0	89.1	0.5931
229	DHARIAWAD	34.8	100.0	962	4.9	11.0	87.0	37.9	65.5	0.5053
230	GIRWA	61.4	100.0	942	11.7	27.7	96.0	61.3	81.2	0.6200
231	GOGUNDA	36.9	100.0	975	8.9	18.5	97.2	40.1	76.9	0.5571
232	JHADOL	45.8	100.0	955	7.2	23.8	90.6	33.0	46.3	0.5095
233	KHERWARA	41.4	100.0	1023	13.1	22.0	95.0	36.1	50.1	0.5497
234	KOTRA	23.7	100.0	954	2.6	7.6	72.7	30.7	29.2	0.4090
235	MAVLI	58.3	100.0	960	13.9	33.1	98.6	59.2	89.5	0.6439
236	SALUMBAR	46.3	100.0	1002	8.5	23.4	84.6	43.9	63.9	0.5577
237	SARADA	59.2	100.0	1011	11.6	31.1	95.7	51.7	75.4	0.6290
	UDAIPUR	**46.2**	**100.0**	**974**	**10.1**	**19.9**	**91.6**	**46.1**	**69.2**	**0.5625**
	RAJASTHAN	**46.2**	**99.7**	**919**	**11.6**	**20.7**	**93.9**	**48.2**	**77.1**	**0.5588**

Note: For Calculation of HSI Please See Methodology (Chapter I).
* Dungargarh PS shifted from Churu to Bikaner district on 1st April 2001
** Excluding data of Dungargarh PS; *** Including data of Dungargarh PS.
Source: General Annex- I, III & IV.

ANNEX-10.2

RANKING OF PANCHAYAT SAMITIES BY HEALTH STATUS INDEX, 1991

(Descending Order)

RANK	PANCHAYAT SAMITIES P.CODE	PANCHAYAT SAMITIES NAME	HEALTH STATUS INDEX
1	2	3	4
		HIGH (0.7-0.8)	
1	195	**SUMERPUR**	**0.7291**
2	153	**NAWALGARH**	**0.7268**
3	186	**BALI**	**0.7016**
		MEDIUM (0.6-0.7)	
4	159	**BILARA**	**0.6991**
5	155	**UDAIPURWATI**	**0.6990**
6	123	**GOVINDGARH**	**0.6956**
7	7	**PISANGAN**	**0.6908**
8	192	**RANI STATION**	**0.6903**
9	209	**DHOND**	**0.6902**
10	187	**DESURI**	**0.6901**
11	137	**JALOR**	**0.6843**
12	57	**HURDA**	**0.6838**
13	63	**SAHARA**	**0.6710**
14	56	**BANERA**	**0.6704**
15	150	**CHIRAWA**	**0.6659**
16	201	**RAILMAGRA**	**0.6649**
17	4	**KEKRI**	**0.6643**
18	220	**SIROHI**	**0.6633**
19	199	**KHAMNOR**	**0.6589**
20	130	**SHAHPURA**	**0.6583**
21	151	**JHUNJHUNUN**	**0.6581**
22	25	**GARHI**	**0.6575**
23	219	**SHEOGANJ**	**0.6573**
24	208	**DANTA RAMGARH**	**0.6572**
25	141	**SAYLA**	**0.6559**
26	152	**KHETRI**	**0.6536**
27	215	**SRI MADHOPUR**	**0.6531**
28	107	**SAGWARA**	**0.6529**
29	158	**BHOPALGARH**	**0.6515**
30	16	**NIMRANA**	**0.6495**
31	135	**AHORE**	**0.6464**
32	235	**MAVLI**	**0.6439**
33	211	**KHANDELA**	**0.6414**
34	8	**SRINAGAR**	**0.6389**
35	217	**PINDWARA**	**0.6370**
36	10	**BEHROR**	**0.6358**
37	60	**MANDAL**	**0.6350**
38	156	**BALESAR**	**0.6346**
39	62	**RAIPUR**	**0.6344**
40	104	**ASPUR**	**0.6338**
41	181	**MERTA**	**0.6336**
42	2	**BHINAY**	**0.6324**
42	65	**SUWANA**	**0.6324**
44	148	**ALSISAR**	**0.6323**
45	194	**SOJAT**	**0.6321**
45	67	**DUNGARGARH**	**0.6321**
45	80	**BHOPALSAGAR**	**0.6321**
48	189	**KHARCHI/MARWAR JUN.**	**0.6316**
49	213	**NEEM KA THANA**	**0.6307**
50	88	**RASHMI**	**0.6300**
51	197	**BHIM**	**0.6298**
52	237	**SARADA**	**0.6290**
53	5	**KISHANGARH**	**0.6251**
54	190	**PALI**	**0.6250**
55	185	**RIYAN**	**0.6201**
56	230	**GIRWA**	**0.6200**
57	212	**LACHHMANGARH**	**0.6191**
58	138	**JASWANTPURA**	**0.6173**
59	160	**LUNI**	**0.6169**
60	64	**SHAHPURA**	**0.6149**
61	110	**GANGANAGAR**	**0.6146**
62	15	**MANDAWAR**	**0.6119**
63	131	**VIRATNAGAR**	**0.6116**
64	210	**FATEHPUR**	**0.6105**
65	149	**BUHANA**	**0.6085**
66	55	**ASIND**	**0.6084**
67	6	**MASOODA**	**0.6080**
68	188	**JAITARAN**	**0.6074**
69	128	**SAMBHAR**	**0.6069**
70	105	**BICHHIWARA**	**0.6058**
70	164	**SHERGARH**	**0.6058**
72	49	**KUMHER**	**0.6056**
72	126	**KOTPUTLI**	**0.6056**
74	218	**REODAR**	**0.6033**
75	227	**BARGAON**	**0.6000**
75	91	**RATANGARH**	**0.6000**
		LOW (0.5-0.6)	
77	70	**NOKHA**	**0.5996**
78	172	**LADPURA**	**0.5989**
79	222	**MALPURA**	**0.5976**
80	125	**JHOTWARA**	**0.5975**
81	58	**JAHAZPUR**	**0.5956**
82	178	**KUCHAMAN**	**0.5941**
83	228	**BHINDER**	**0.5931**
84	175	**DEGANA**	**0.5928**
85	214	**PIPRALI**	**0.5924**
86	154	**SURAJGARH**	**0.5913**
87	66	**BIKANER**	**0.5909**
88	179	**LADNU**	**0.5893**
89	12	**KISHANGARH BAS**	**0.5884**
90	30	**TALWARA**	**0.5883**
90	117	**HANUMANGARH**	**0.5883**
92	184	**PARBATSAR**	**0.5875**
93	94	**TARANAGAR**	**0.5871**
94	111	**KARANPUR**	**0.5860**
95	45	**SIWANA**	**0.5856**
96	106	**DUNGARPUR**	**0.5854**
97	139	**RANIWARA**	**0.5850**
98	119	**AMBER**	**0.5838**
99	59	**KOTRI**	**0.5834**
99	124	**JAMWA RAMGARH**	**0.5834**
101	85	**KAPASAN**	**0.5823**
102	205	**GANGAPUR**	**0.5807**
103	120	**BASSI**	**0.5804**
104	114	**SADULSHAHAR**	**0.5791**
105	89	**CHURU**	**0.5789**
106	24	**BAGIDORA**	**0.5788**
107	170	**CHECHAT**	**0.5786**
108	165	**HINDAUN**	**0.5779**
108	129	**SANGANER**	**0.5779**
110	9	**BANSURE**	**0.5763**
111	20	**THANAGAZI**	**0.5759**
112	182	**MUNDWA**	**0.5729**
113	167	**NADOTI**	**0.5728**
114	69	**LUNKARANSAR**	**0.5726**
115	54	**WEIR**	**0.5688**
116	13	**KOTKASIM**	**0.5676**
117	162	**OSIAN**	**0.5654**
118	112	**PADAMPUR**	**0.5653**
119	191	**RAIPUR**	**0.5626**
120	180	**MAKRANA**	**0.5624**
121	93	**SUJANGARH**	**0.5623**
122	26	**GHATOL**	**0.5620**
123	193	**ROHAT**	**0.5615**
124	1	**ARAIN**	**0.5614**
125	161	**MANDOR**	**0.5600**
126	3	JAWAJA	0.5583
127	236	SALUMBAR	0.5577
128	183	NAGAUR	0.5574
129	61	MANDALGARH	0.5573
130	231	GOGUNDA	0.5571
131	196	AMET	0.5557
132	221	DEOLI	0.5542
133	17	RAJGARH	0.5535
134	136	BHINMAL	0.5534
134	32	ATRU	0.5534
136	177	JAYAL	0.5524
137	216	ABU ROAD	0.5513
138	18	RAMGARH	0.5513
139	233	KHERWARA	0.5497
140	203	BAMANWAS	0.5488
141	22	UMREN	0.5484
142	33	BARAN	0.5476
143	31	ANTA	0.5471
143	82	CHITTAURGARH	0.5471
145	86	NIMBAHERA	0.5469
146	176	DIDWANA	0.5458
147	83	DUNGLA	0.5454
147	116	BHADRA	0.5454
149	127	PHAGI	0.5430
150	108	SIMALWARA	0.5415
151	163	PHALODI	0.5410
152	53	SEWAR	0.5408
153	223	NIWAI	0.5405
154	68	KOLAYAT	0.5398
155	76	BARI SADRI	0.5369
156	174	SULTANPUR	0.5368
157	96	DAUSA	0.5366
157	77	BEGUN	0.5366
159	204	BONLI	0.5364
160	113	RAISINGHNAGAR	0.5363
161	84	GANGRAR	0.5329
162	207	SAWAI MADHOPUR	0.5300
163	75	ARNOD	0.5296
164	173	SANGOD	0.5283
165	99	SIKRAI	0.5281
166	169	TODABHIM	0.5275
167	50	NADBAI	0.5265
168	202	RAJSAMAND	0.5263
169	23	ANANDPURI	0.5258
170	19	RENI	0.5256
171	198	DEOGARH	0.5253
172	144	JHALRAPATAN	0.5251
173	102	DHAULPUR	0.5250
174	73	NAINWA	0.5245
175	81	CHHOTI SADRI	0.5213
175	145	KHANPUR	0.5213
177	78	BHADESAR	0.5203
178	74	TALERA	0.5193
179	52	RUPBAS	0.5175
179	95	BANDIKUI	0.5175
181	224	TODARAISINGH	0.5175
182	147	PIRAWA	0.5164
183	11	KATHUMAR	0.5148
184	92	SARDARSHAHAR	0.5138
185	122	DUDU	0.5128
186	21	TIJARA	0.5110
187	140	SANCHORE	0.5099
188	38	BALOTRA	0.5096
189	232	JHADOL	0.5095
190	36	KISHANGANJ	0.5074
191	90	RAJGARH	0.5073
192	229	DHARIAWAD	0.5053
193	14	LACHHMANGARH	0.5046
194	118	NOHAR	0.5045
195	200	KUMBHALGARH	0.5039
196	47	DEEG	0.5026
197	71	HINDOLI	0.5024
198	225	TONK	0.5010
		VERY LOW (< 0.5)	
199	46	BAYANA	0.4991
200	226	UNIARA	0.4976
201	142	BAKANI	0.4975
202	98	MAHWA	0.4950
203	97	LALSOT	0.4869
204	171	ITAWA	0.4865
205	87	PRATAPGARH	0.4854
206	72	KESHORAIPATAN	0.4853
207	101	BASERI	0.4841
208	143	DAG	0.4819
209	28	PEEPALKHOONT	0.4813
210	168	SAPOTRA	0.4799
211	121	CHAKSU	0.4794
212	79	BHAINSRORGARH	0.4724
213	206	KHANDAR	0.4703
214	115	SURATGARH	0.4686
215	37	SHAHBAD	0.4635
216	103	RAJAKHERA	0.4591
217	48	KAMAN	0.4556
218	166	KARAULI	0.4519
219	29	SAJJANGARH	0.4466
220	132	JAISALMER	0.4439
221	34	CHHABRA	0.4429
222	134	SANKRA	0.4409
223	51	NAGAR PAHARI	0.4408
224	35	CHHIPABAROD	0.4383
225	41	CHOHTAN	0.4328
226	27	KUSHALGARH	0.4296
227	42	DHORIMANNA	0.4263
228	44	SINDHARI	0.4238
229	146	MANOHARTHANA	0.4163
230	43	SHEO	0.4160
231	157	BAP	0.4145
232	234	KOTRA	0.4090
233	109	ANUPGARH	0.3974
234	100	BARI	0.3966
235	39	BARMER	0.3928
236	40	BAYTOO	0.3656
237	133	SAM	0.3460
		RAJASTHAN	**0.5588**
		% AGE OF AAPs	**52.74**

BOLD: Equal/Above Average Panchayat Samities (AAPs)

Source: Annex 10.1

ANNEX-11.1

PANCHAYAT SAMITI-WISE HEALTH STATUS INDEX: RAJ., 2001

P. Code	Panchayat Samiti	%age of Rural Pop. Served by Medical Amenity (V1)	%age of Rural Pop. Served by Drinking Water Amenity (V2)	Sex Ratio (V3)	Female LR (%) (V4)	%age of Villages Having Medical Amenity (V5)	%age of Pop. Served by Education Amenity (V6)	%age of Rural Pop. Approached by Pucca Road (V7)	%age of Rural Pop. Served by Power Amenity (V8)	Health Status Index
1	2	3	4	5	6	7	8	9	10	11
1	ARAIN	57.0	99.6	961	28.3	30.4	99.8	64.1	96.9	0.6736
2	BHINAY	57.9	99.2	959	21.2	32.0	100.0	71.9	97.3	0.6771
3	JAWAJA	41.9	100.0	983	58.0	25.6	97.1	86.9	96.1	0.7191
4	KEKRI	73.1	100.0	957	25.6	47.5	99.8	82.5	97.8	0.7348
5	KISHANGARH	68.4	99.6	935	33.9	37.8	99.9	80.2	99.3	0.7172
6	MASOODA	52.5	100.0	954	31.9	23.0	98.3	80.2	99.4	0.6824
7	PISANGAN	72.4	100.0	943	31.6	47.7	100.0	86.3	98.2	0.7417
8	SRINAGAR	61.9	100.0	925	30.3	41.7	99.9	89.6	97.6	0.7157
	AJMER DISTRICT	**61.2**	**99.8**	**951**	**32.7**	**34.3**	**99.4**	**81.0**	**97.9**	**0.7075**
9	BANSURE	50.9	99.9	904	39.5	29.8	99.9	76.5	100.0	0.6769
10	BEHROR	67.3	99.9	917	72.2	40.0	99.3	81.5	99.9	0.7615
11	KATHUMAR	51.4	98.1	868	36.8	30.4	100.0	82.6	98.6	0.6646
12	KISHANGARH BAS	36.2	99.6	909	36.2	19.3	98.5	73.3	98.2	0.6348
13	KOTKASIM	40.3	100.0	907	52.7	19.1	99.6	72.6	98.9	0.6614
14	LACHHMANGARH	54.2	100.0	892	34.5	31.0	99.5	75.0	98.3	0.6672
15	MANDAWAR	52.1	100.0	918	52.4	35.2	99.5	76.3	98.1	0.7037
16	NIMRANA	68.0	99.8	926	45.4	48.2	100.0	88.3	100.0	0.7520
17	RAJGARH	46.1	95.9	890	32.7	19.3	95.9	86.8	95.0	0.6404
18	RAMGARH	46.4	100.0	895	32.6	24.9	98.4	81.3	99.7	0.6569
19	RENI	58.6	98.6	882	35.2	31.4	98.8	82.1	100.0	0.6785
20	THANAGAZI	61.0	99.7	902	26.2	29.1	98.3	83.9	95.5	0.6726
21	TIJARA	36.6	99.9	860	32.8	20.8	96.2	79.5	97.9	0.6187
22	UMREN	54.7	99.0	886	32.4	31.5	97.3	87.4	98.4	0.6751
	ALWAR	**51.3**	**99.4**	**895**	**39.2**	**28.3**	**98.6**	**80.5**	**98.5**	**0.6725**
23	ANANDPURI	48.1	97.7	964	24.0	27.1	98.2	59.1	75.4	0.6167
24	BAGIDORA	51.5	97.9	983	24.0	30.3	99.2	62.9	64.6	0.6251
25	GARHI	68.9	100.0	976	34.7	48.8	99.9	80.4	97.0	0.7465
26	GHATOL	54.0	99.9	989	21.7	25.0	99.4	68.4	84.4	0.6555
27	KUSHALGARH	34.7	98.2	987	18.1	25.4	99.0	46.5	57.8	0.5633
28	PEEPALKHOONT	61.5	98.9	967	11.9	32.6	97.0	47.2	41.0	0.5685
29	SAJJANGARH	46.6	100.0	973	21.1	28.6	98.9	53.0	66.9	0.6021
30	TALWARA	55.9	98.3	973	26.5	28.6	98.6	72.5	85.8	0.6660
	BANSWARA	**54.2**	**99.0**	**977**	**23.8**	**30.5**	**98.9**	**63.7**	**74.5**	**0.6405**
31	ANTA	48.9	100.0	917	45.0	19.6	99.0	69.4	97.3	0.6603
32	ATRU	49.1	100.0	905	43.8	25.7	99.1	66.9	99.6	0.6619
33	BARAN	45.4	100.0	904	46.5	26.3	99.7	77.3	100.0	0.6753
34	CHHABRA	14.8	96.4	894	32.8	7.5	93.7	36.4	93.8	0.5216
35	CHHIPABAROD	28.8	98.1	916	27.7	11.0	94.3	53.5	91.8	0.5674
36	KISHANGANJ	44.9	99.7	919	35.8	18.9	94.6	62.0	94.3	0.6249
37	SHAHBAD	36.3	99.4	896	34.0	12.6	96.1	57.4	86.4	0.5809
	BARAN	**39.3**	**99.2**	**908**	**38.2**	**16.3**	**96.7**	**61.0**	**94.9**	**0.6148**
38	BALOTRA	54.1	82.0	924	37.0	26.8	97.1	69.6	77.7	0.6194
39	BARMER	31.4	77.0	853	36.5	19.9	92.1	56.9	51.5	0.4930
40	BAYTOO	27.4	91.2	904	42.9	18.0	92.3	44.2	35.0	0.4950
41	CHOHTAN	47.1	85.3	872	35.2	27.3	99.1	68.3	73.1	0.5880
42	DHORIMANNA	30.8	90.9	912	56.7	21.5	97.8	57.6	77.7	0.6006
43	SHEO	30.3	81.0	842	39.8	17.2	95.9	50.9	54.3	0.4938
44	SINDHARI	36.2	83.4	924	46.4	21.2	99.6	53.9	56.9	0.5611
45	SIWANA	70.3	97.7	922	43.6	40.9	99.4	75.2	98.0	0.7197
	BARMER	**41.2**	**86.0**	**896**	**42.4**	**22.4**	**96.7**	**59.9**	**66.1**	**0.5715**
46	BAYANA	46.1	98.9	807	33.7	29.8	99.2	76.2	91.0	0.6120
47	DEEG	67.0	100.0	849	36.3	45.4	100.0	81.2	97.4	0.6939
48	KAMAN	46.1	93.4	883	26.2	27.3	99.4	71.7	88.4	0.6137
49	KUMHER	75.5	99.9	857	46.1	54.7	99.9	85.9	98.9	0.7390
50	NADBAI	76.2	100.0	840	46.8	57.0	99.7	79.1	99.1	0.7286
51	NAGAR PAHARI	41.2	98.8	876	38.1	24.5	99.7	71.6	93.9	0.6301
52	RUPBAS	55.6	99.8	843	47.3	38.7	99.8	76.0	92.8	0.6699
53	SEWAR	54.1	98.9	855	46.7	29.3	99.1	94.0	99.8	0.6895
54	WEIR	52.8	99.6	847	38.3	29.5	99.6	63.8	99.1	0.6374
	BHARATPUR	**55.7**	**98.7**	**851**	**39.6**	**35.2**	**99.6**	**76.9**	**95.2**	**0.6617**
55	ASIND	52.8	99.3	1018	22.9	25.0	98.7	64.5	97.3	0.6764
56	BANERA	76.7	99.8	983	31.9	47.0	99.9	72.1	100.0	0.7464
57	HURDA	70.7	98.9	949	32.1	41.4	98.7	79.7	98.9	0.7243
58	JAHAZPUR	56.1	98.7	929	29.7	27.6	95.3	57.0	95.1	0.6404
59	KOTRI	49.0	99.0	955	22.5	22.9	98.0	56.7	93.4	0.6281
60	MANDAL	52.7	99.8	1033	24.6	22.9	99.0	72.4	95.0	0.6896
61	MANDALGARH	50.5	99.6	929	25.9	23.8	95.3	66.0	96.0	0.6374

P. Code	Panchayat Samiti	%age of Rural Pop. Served by Medical Amenity (V1)	%age of Rural Pop. Served by Drinking Water Amenity (V2)	Sex Ratio (V3)	Female LR (%) (V4)	%age of Villages Having Medical Amenity (V5)	%age of Pop. Served by Education Amenity (V6)	%age of Rural Pop. Approached by Pucca Road (V7)	%age of Rural Pop. Served by Power Amenity (V8)	Health Status Index
1	2	3	4	5	6	7	8	9	10	11
62	RAIPUR	57.0	98.4	1042	24.2	30.3	99.5	56.1	99.9	0.6919
63	SAHARA	63.9	99.2	1070	26.4	31.3	99.7	74.3	100.0	0.7396
64	SHAHPURA	55.1	97.0	951	24.6	29.8	99.4	56.3	95.2	0.6464
65	SUWANA	59.1	100.0	965	26.4	30.1	99.7	78.8	99.6	0.6972
	BHILWARA	**56.9**	**99.1**	**979**	**26.1**	**27.9**	**98.2**	**66.4**	**96.9**	**0.6749**
66	BIKANER	47.7	74.3	888	30.2	22.8	96.1	90.0	71.9	0.5913
67	DUNGARGARH *	80.7	88.3	947	41.7	60.9	99.9	79.3	99.7	0.7612
68	KOLAYAT	49.2	73.2	877	24.6	19.4	98.1	79.0	80.1	0.5752
69	LUNKARANSAR	53.7	76.2	912	30.3	28.1	96.1	81.2	89.6	0.6284
70	NOKHA	53.9	95.7	913	28.8	29.2	98.0	79.5	97.9	0.6635
	BIKANER **	**50.8**	**80.0**	**897**	**28.8**	**24.3**	**97.0**	**83.4**	**83.8**	**0.6136**
71	HINDOLI	52.7	98.7	901	27.6	28.7	97.5	66.0	94.7	0.6375
72	KESHORAIPATAN	41.3	97.4	915	36.9	19.3	98.2	57.9	91.4	0.6136
73	NAINWA	43.3	97.5	910	29.7	17.8	98.8	58.8	97.0	0.6122
74	TALERA	43.4	99.6	906	34.4	20.2	99.1	69.7	93.4	0.6318
	BUNDI	**45.1**	**98.5**	**908**	**32.4**	**21.2**	**98.4**	**63.9**	**94.0**	**0.6247**
75	ARNOD	33.8	97.8	970	29.7	12.4	94.7	56.6	81.6	0.5903
76	BARI SADRI	45.7	99.9	999	25.1	18.9	94.1	56.6	99.2	0.6427
77	BEGUN	41.6	100.0	965	28.8	16.7	91.4	55.4	97.1	0.6188
78	BHADESAR	37.3	100.0	979	28.3	11.7	95.5	60.3	100.0	0.6269
79	BHAINSRORGARH	34.1	99.6	903	27.9	15.6	88.8	62.5	92.3	0.5819
80	BHOPALSAGAR	50.0	99.7	1003	32.4	19.3	99.5	62.4	99.2	0.6731
81	CHHOTI SADRI	30.2	99.8	966	31.9	11.3	95.4	57.0	99.9	0.6124
82	CHITTAURGARH	43.6	99.5	963	31.6	15.6	96.6	66.5	98.6	0.6443
83	DUNGLA	61.9	100.0	1003	28.6	33.3	98.9	58.3	99.8	0.6959
84	GANGRAR	46.9	100.0	971	28.2	19.7	97.1	58.8	99.7	0.6454
85	KAPASAN	24.3	100.0	992	25.3	10.3	97.3	52.8	98.8	0.6016
86	NIMBAHERA	48.4	100.0	969	32.4	21.1	99.1	75.8	99.9	0.6775
87	PRATAPGARH	42.2	99.2	958	35.5	18.8	94.8	59.8	82.6	0.6185
88	RASHMI	65.2	100.0	1020	24.6	30.9	98.1	78.2	99.8	0.7226
	CHITTAURGARH	**42.8**	**99.6**	**973**	**30.0**	**17.4**	**95.8**	**61.7**	**95.3**	**0.6365**
89	CHURU	76.4	75.9	959	52.9	61.9	98.5	89.5	100.0	0.7716
90	RAJGARH	55.0	85.2	933	59.8	35.7	99.7	74.0	90.0	0.6918
91	RATANGARH	85.9	93.0	975	51.8	65.3	99.1	90.9	99.9	0.8164
92	SARDARSHAHAR	47.6	52.5	953	43.6	34.7	98.3	62.6	94.4	0.6175
93	SUJANGARH	66.9	89.6	968	48.7	41.3	98.5	69.4	99.8	0.7240
94	TARANAGAR	68.0	82.4	940	61.7	33.6	99.8	73.5	97.1	0.7154
	CHURU ***	**66.6**	**80.7**	**953**	**51.5**	**44.7**	**99.1**	**75.6**	**96.8**	**0.7191**
95	BANDIKUI	51.0	98.9	899	48.4	25.1	98.9	75.9	100.0	0.6771
96	DAUSA	52.7	98.6	907	36.1	22.4	97.1	75.2	96.8	0.6561
97	LALSOT	40.5	99.7	916	32.3	14.3	96.3	65.0	90.2	0.6088
98	MAHWA	47.8	99.9	872	45.2	29.6	96.2	70.4	94.7	0.6485
99	SIKRAI	41.4	100.0	899	43.6	18.7	99.0	83.2	95.2	0.6557
	DAUSA	**47.0**	**99.3**	**900**	**40.8**	**21.2**	**97.5**	**73.9**	**95.5**	**0.6487**
100	BARI	61.1	96.5	796	36.8	51.8	95.5	57.4	57.2	0.5844
101	BASERI	42.2	98.1	825	42.8	18.4	97.4	70.2	63.6	0.5663
102	DHAULPUR	37.9	99.0	836	39.1	22.3	97.8	73.6	82.3	0.5947
103	RAJAKHERA	28.1	98.3	816	38.0	17.1	97.6	72.1	94.1	0.5785
	DHAULPUR	**41.0**	**98.1**	**821**	**39.4**	**26.3**	**97.2**	**69.4**	**75.7**	**0.5827**
104	ASPUR	67.5	100.0	1071	27.6	48.3	99.2	78.2	92.6	0.7632
105	BICHHIWARA	68.4	99.4	1001	27.9	44.0	99.8	67.8	98.7	0.7266
106	DUNGARPUR	60.5	97.1	1032	27.6	46.5	100.0	66.8	93.6	0.7214
107	SAGWARA	72.9	100.0	1074	33.6	49.0	99.8	78.2	92.5	0.7802
108	SIMALWARA	58.5	99.7	996	24.6	32.3	99.6	72.4	87.8	0.6858
	DUNGARPUR	**65.4**	**99.3**	**1031**	**28.2**	**43.1**	**99.7**	**72.5**	**93.0**	**0.7324**
109	ANUPGARH	37.9	83.9	894	44.6	16.8	78.1	76.6	69.0	0.5610
110	GANGANAGAR	63.9	98.6	886	51.6	31.1	93.2	94.8	99.5	0.7151
111	KARANPUR	54.3	94.8	897	49.9	26.6	96.2	91.1	98.5	0.6928
112	PADAMPUR	59.6	94.2	906	50.6	38.9	93.7	77.0	97.8	0.6968
113	RAISINGHNAGAR	44.7	92.8	913	53.1	26.4	92.3	70.1	86.3	0.6419
114	SADULSHAHAR	77.2	79.5	851	48.2	27.0	94.1	92.2	98.7	0.6817
115	SURATGARH	42.4	78.7	839	40.1	18.9	78.9	71.8	56.5	0.5150
	GANGANAGAR	**50.4**	**87.4**	**883**	**47.3**	**23.1**	**86.5**	**80.3**	**81.2**	**0.6183**
116	BHADRA	76.3	85.6	898	52.9	35.9	93.2	89.5	97.3	0.7173
117	HANUMANGARH	61.8	94.9	895	48.7	18.9	85.5	91.0	95.1	0.6726
118	NOHAR	45.8	73.5	903	50.6	16.2	87.9	72.1	72.0	0.5785
	HANUMANGARH	**59.6**	**86.8**	**898**	**50.0**	**20.0**	**87.6**	**85.1**	**88.6**	**0.6510**
119	AMBER	59.0	100.0	906	38.1	37.5	98.5	74.5	99.6	0.6910
120	BASSI	56.3	99.9	910	37.0	31.9	98.3	82.4	99.7	0.6905
121	CHAKSU	31.4	99.0	915	29.7	10.1	93.5	50.1	88.4	0.5633
122	DUDU	58.0	97.1	927	36.8	25.6	98.5	78.2	94.9	0.6766

P. Code	Panchayat Samiti	%age of Rural Pop. Served by Medical Amenity (V1)	%age of Rural Pop. Served by Drinking Water Amenity (V2)	Sex Ratio (V3)	Female LR (%) (V4)	%age of Villages Having Medical Amenity (V5)	%age of Pop. Served by Education Amenity (V6)	%age of Rural Pop. Approached by Pucca Road (V7)	%age of Rural Pop. Served by Power Amenity (V8)	Health Status Index
1	2	3	4	5	6	7	8	9	10	11
123	GOVINDGARH	79.4	100.0	919	47.4	49.0	99.5	90.1	99.5	0.7682
124	JAMWA RAMGARH	56.2	99.7	908	43.9	35.6	96.9	79.7	100.0	0.6978
125	JHOTWARA	51.7	94.4	915	49.7	26.0	98.1	83.2	99.4	0.6887
126	KOTPUTLI	46.9	100.0	906	59.7	32.2	100.0	85.2	96.2	0.7073
127	PHAGI	43.5	99.7	918	43.8	18.9	99.1	64.3	96.6	0.6441
128	SAMBHAR	63.6	95.6	933	50.3	41.0	99.7	75.1	99.9	0.7241
129	SANGANER	53.0	99.5	914	43.4	23.8	96.1	75.3	100.0	0.6740
130	SHAHPURA	72.6	100.0	902	46.7	47.7	100.0	88.1	99.5	0.7487
131	VIRATNAGAR	56.7	99.7	909	52.8	36.7	99.5	86.0	100.0	0.7225
	JAIPUR	**57.4**	**99.0**	**914**	**44.4**	**29.9**	**98.4**	**78.7**	**98.1**	**0.6925**
132	JAISALMER	57.8	70.8	811	27.7	30.1	97.7	80.3	62.9	0.5541
133	SAM	47.3	83.5	787	24.0	17.1	95.1	65.0	39.5	0.4749
134	SANKRA	49.5	84.1	876	30.0	30.1	97.9	55.9	55.2	0.5487
	JAISALMER	**51.3**	**80.0**	**827**	**27.4**	**24.0**	**97.0**	**66.0**	**52.4**	**0.5238**
135	AHORE	83.2	98.8	1019	35.3	57.3	99.6	80.6	99.5	0.7941
136	BHINMAL	63.8	85.4	974	19.5	47.5	100.0	79.5	93.7	0.6954
137	JALOR	73.2	99.8	997	27.2	60.3	100.0	91.8	99.7	0.7826
138	JASWANTPURA	70.1	98.5	995	20.7	48.6	99.9	84.0	100.0	0.7441
139	RANIWARA	71.0	95.3	933	28.4	51.2	100.0	78.6	99.7	0.7228
140	SANCHORE	48.4	85.9	938	26.1	33.8	99.3	72.0	86.0	0.6339
141	SAYLA	77.8	99.2	977	23.1	55.8	99.8	87.9	98.3	0.7621
	JALOR	**67.1**	**93.4**	**970**	**25.9**	**47.8**	**99.7**	**80.6**	**95.1**	**0.7190**
142	BAKANI	34.1	97.8	927	23.9	14.9	87.0	46.1	86.0	0.5525
143	DAG	34.9	98.6	949	27.6	15.4	96.3	40.9	85.1	0.5723
144	JHALRAPATAN	33.2	97.9	926	37.7	15.1	95.6	50.7	96.7	0.5985
145	KHANPUR	46.9	99.4	914	47.2	18.7	92.6	54.2	97.6	0.6309
146	MANOHARTHANA	21.1	98.1	924	28.2	10.9	92.8	31.1	74.3	0.5097
147	PIRAWA	33.2	99.7	939	49.0	13.2	97.3	44.0	99.9	0.6153
	JHALAWAR	**33.8**	**98.6**	**930**	**35.5**	**14.5**	**93.8**	**44.7**	**90.3**	**0.5804**
148	ALSISAR	58.6	86.2	989	61.7	32.3	98.7	77.5	98.7	0.7316
149	BUHANA	69.4	93.4	944	64.5	50.0	99.8	80.1	98.8	0.7669
150	CHIRAWA	66.8	98.6	958	61.3	42.9	100.0	90.1	100.0	0.7770
151	JHUNJHUNUN	62.1	94.8	977	63.0	40.7	99.9	79.5	99.9	0.7596
152	KHETRI	78.8	99.2	940	50.4	56.5	100.0	85.3	99.7	0.7827
153	NAWALGARH	66.1	100.0	968	53.8	45.5	100.0	88.9	100.0	0.7741
154	SURAJGARH	47.8	88.8	930	55.9	32.8	100.0	75.8	100.0	0.6928
155	UDAIPURWATI	80.1	99.8	963	68.0	64.2	100.0	89.9	99.1	0.8307
	JHUNJHUNUN	**67.3**	**95.6**	**957**	**59.8**	**44.2**	**99.8**	**83.8**	**99.5**	**0.7645**
156	BALESAR	62.9	97.5	914	19.8	38.4	95.0	69.9	90.8	0.6530
157	BAP	45.0	66.4	899	24.7	24.8	91.7	69.6	81.4	0.5588
158	BHOPALGARH	77.1	95.7	943	23.4	52.3	100.0	93.2	99.4	0.7479
159	BILARA	86.1	99.4	931	28.2	69.7	99.5	89.9	100.0	0.7828
160	LUNI	78.7	94.5	928	34.1	51.9	99.7	84.7	95.1	0.7390
161	MANDOR	55.9	93.0	909	22.1	35.2	99.2	77.7	98.3	0.6600
162	OSIAN	71.6	99.1	923	27.5	52.6	99.7	84.5	99.1	0.7313
163	PHALODI	54.8	95.6	914	27.5	36.0	98.4	76.2	90.1	0.6584
164	SHERGARH	58.0	88.7	911	19.5	34.6	95.3	61.2	79.5	0.6050
	JODHPUR	67.0	93.6	**921**	**25.1**	**43.7**	98.0	79.9	93.7	0.6891
165	HINDAUN	64.8	100.0	843	57.8	50.4	99.0	88.4	99.7	0.7326
166	KARAULI	55.1	95.8	839	35.9	35.4	98.7	71.0	84.6	0.6265
167	NADOTI	59.6	97.7	889	46.1	35.3	99.2	75.1	91.0	0.6804
168	SAPOTRA	57.8	96.9	849	37.9	31.0	98.0	69.7	72.1	0.6140
169	TODABHIM	63.3	98.2	858	39.7	41.7	99.3	82.8	91.8	0.6843
	KARAULI	**60.2**	**97.8**	**852**	**43.8**	**37.7**	**98.8**	**77.8**	**87.8**	**0.6658**
170	CHECHAT	56.3	99.3	905	52.4	31.3	98.4	74.7	99.9	0.6970
171	ITAWA	53.4	99.8	906	44.6	20.2	96.3	64.7	90.3	0.6437
172	LADPURA	58.1	99.5	903	49.1	29.7	97.9	91.6	98.5	0.7114
173	SANGOD	46.3	100.0	916	53.1	22.3	97.6	60.6	99.3	0.6599
174	SULTANPUR	64.8	100.0	913	54.3	36.8	98.4	73.0	97.6	0.7159
	KOTA	**55.8**	**99.7**	**908**	**50.6**	**27.7**	**97.7**	**72.8**	**97.0**	**0.6844**
175	DEGANA	65.0	86.7	980	35.3	39.9	99.9	70.3	99.9	0.7072
176	DIDWANA	61.0	93.7	985	46.5	38.2	99.6	77.3	99.4	0.7325
177	JAYAL	68.6	73.0	958	32.2	39.7	99.5	72.7	97.4	0.6812
178	KUCHAMAN	54.5	89.9	933	45.5	32.1	98.9	66.0	100.0	0.6762
179	LADNU	73.4	99.7	979	42.4	45.4	99.0	77.0	98.1	0.7543
180	MAKRANA	66.1	77.5	957	44.9	44.5	99.8	67.0	99.3	0.7008
181	MERTA	72.4	95.1	924	34.4	35.1	98.7	89.8	100.0	0.7209
182	MUNDWA	66.5	96.3	947	24.4	38.8	98.7	73.6	96.4	0.6914
183	NAGAUR	62.1	78.3	945	30.8	39.3	99.0	71.3	91.9	0.6631
184	PARBATSAR	65.6	96.7	940	39.1	45.5	99.8	77.4	100.0	0.7254
185	RIYAN	68.6	94.1	943	32.3	38.4	98.7	84.3	99.2	0.7160
	NAGAUR	**65.1**	**88.8**	**954**	**37.6**	**39.2**	**99.2**	**74.7**	**98.3**	**0.7044**

P. Code	Panchayat Samiti	%age of Rural Pop. Served by Medical Amenity (V1)	%age of Rural Pop. Served by Drinking Water Amenity (V2)	Sex Ratio (V3)	Female LR (%) (V4)	%age of Villages Having Medical Amenity (V5)	%age of Pop. Served by Education Amenity (V6)	%age of Rural Pop. Approached by Pucca Road (V7)	%age of Rural Pop. Served by Power Amenity (V8)	Health Status Index
1	2	3	4	5	6	7	8	9	10	11
186	BALI	82.7	100.0	1012	34.5	57.1	99.9	95.1	96.5	0.8057
187	DESURI	72.1	98.3	1054	34.4	43.6	99.3	80.8	99.2	0.7745
188	JAITARAN	77.7	97.7	968	26.7	52.4	99.9	80.1	97.8	0.7466
189	KHARCHI/MARWAR JUN.	71.0	97.9	1011	30.7	42.3	99.2	81.7	97.6	0.7486
190	PALI	66.0	94.0	979	29.4	40.0	98.9	83.3	99.6	0.7246
191	RAIPUR	72.8	100.0	985	29.7	45.0	99.3	80.5	94.7	0.7404
192	RANI STATION	82.1	100.0	1040	36.4	59.2	99.9	86.8	99.9	0.8148
193	ROHAT	53.1	96.1	965	30.9	35.4	99.9	73.6	99.8	0.6911
194	SOJAT	72.6	95.5	1009	31.8	50.4	100.0	81.3	98.8	0.7603
195	SUMERPUR	82.1	94.3	995	35.4	61.9	99.1	99.8	100.0	0.8076
	PALI	**74.2**	**97.6**	**1000**	**31.8**	**48.2**	**99.6**	**84.6**	**98.0**	**0.7612**
196	AMET	44.8	100.0	1000	30.9	20.6	97.4	56.3	100.0	0.6562
197	BHIM	48.3	99.0	1024	33.1	27.3	99.7	76.0	95.0	0.7011
198	DEOGARH	35.2	100.0	1042	31.4	15.3	96.6	52.3	99.1	0.6475
199	KHAMNOR	56.2	99.7	1005	34.3	29.9	98.3	78.6	98.8	0.7155
200	KUMBHALGARH	47.8	99.2	1033	28.2	26.2	98.5	59.9	99.1	0.6803
201	RAILMAGRA	71.0	99.8	1019	36.8	39.6	99.6	84.3	100.0	0.7650
202	RAJSAMAND	51.3	100.0	974	36.3	24.2	98.9	73.6	100.0	0.6890
	RAJSAMAND	**51.7**	**99.6**	**1012**	**33.2**	**25.8**	**98.6**	**70.6**	**98.7**	**0.6962**
203	BAMANWAS	57.3	93.2	882	38.7	29.4	98.9	63.7	85.9	0.6316
204	BONLI	54.0	98.5	905	30.8	27.0	98.7	61.9	93.8	0.6376
205	GANGAPUR	71.1	98.3	875	34.4	46.9	99.5	75.1	98.1	0.6992
206	KHANDAR	55.5	99.3	871	20.5	30.3	97.7	69.3	79.8	0.6089
207	SAWAI MADHOPUR	64.5	100.0	904	24.7	35.9	99.4	58.3	88.2	0.6450
	SAWAI MADHOPUR	**60.7**	**98.1**	**889**	**29.7**	**33.2**	**98.9**	**65.2**	**89.7**	**0.6448**
208	DANTA RAMGARH	72.0	98.9	967	55.7	45.9	99.7	76.5	100.0	0.7667
209	DHOND	78.2	99.3	961	52.5	61.5	100.0	84.0	100.0	0.7978
210	FATEHPUR	63.4	100.0	994	62.2	44.1	99.6	60.3	100.0	0.7534
211	KHANDELA	74.5	99.3	965	59.4	50.8	99.4	71.5	99.9	0.7736
212	LACHHMANGARH	56.5	99.1	972	61.6	33.6	99.7	62.1	99.8	0.7233
213	NEEM KA THANA	71.6	100.0	924	51.5	49.0	99.0	75.0	98.2	0.7444
214	PIPRALI	76.6	99.4	950	54.2	50.0	99.9	88.0	99.8	0.7841
215	SRI MADHOPUR	70.9	99.5	950	51.3	54.5	100.0	90.4	100.0	0.7825
	SIKAR	**70.7**	**99.4**	**958**	**55.7**	**47.7**	**99.6**	**76.1**	**99.6**	**0.7633**
216	ABU ROAD	49.7	98.6	935	26.4	34.6	100.0	80.9	84.5	0.6618
217	PINDWARA	76.1	99.0	954	35.7	45.5	99.4	85.0	89.0	0.7379
218	REODAR	66.2	99.9	945	30.2	35.7	99.0	77.7	99.8	0.7079
219	SHEOGANJ	74.5	96.9	964	32.7	49.3	99.8	87.5	98.6	0.7538
220	SIROHI	88.1	99.6	1013	30.5	60.2	99.4	88.1	99.7	0.8059
	SIROHI	**71.2**	**99.0**	**960**	**31.5**	**44.2**	**99.5**	**83.4**	**94.3**	**0.7320**
221	DEOLI	58.2	99.7	932	23.4	27.3	97.3	60.1	84.4	0.6302
222	MALPURA	51.9	99.5	944	26.5	24.6	99.8	76.3	95.1	0.6640
223	NIWAI	47.3	98.6	919	29.2	20.9	97.0	66.1	95.9	0.6309
224	TODARAISINGH	56.7	99.8	951	32.7	26.8	98.5	65.9	97.0	0.6713
225	TONK	59.2	98.8	932	21.9	28.2	97.8	71.2	87.6	0.6480
226	UNIARA	48.1	98.2	916	22.6	16.3	94.3	57.8	94.5	0.6007
	TONK	**53.8**	**99.1**	**932**	**25.6**	**23.8**	**97.5**	**66.8**	**91.9**	**0.6404**
227	BARGAON	46.9	99.3	943	50.7	29.9	97.7	74.7	97.2	0.6920
228	BHINDER	54.1	100.0	983	44.5	22.2	94.8	63.5	98.5	0.6841
229	DHARIAWAD	43.3	97.8	995	18.2	18.1	97.1	61.6	86.9	0.6205
230	GIRWA	64.0	98.0	960	40.5	32.4	98.9	76.3	91.9	0.7056
231	GOGUNDA	49.7	97.6	981	32.3	31.3	99.5	64.1	89.2	0.6659
232	JHADOL	48.2	98.4	978	43.4	25.6	97.2	51.5	72.3	0.6309
233	KHERWARA	48.8	98.7	1003	36.2	30.8	96.6	67.3	68.9	0.6541
234	KOTRA	36.7	92.4	979	11.1	14.2	93.1	46.8	33.3	0.4951
235	MAVLI	69.8	100.0	975	35.4	41.6	98.7	75.1	100.0	0.7348
236	SALUMBAR	50.9	99.6	1025	41.4	27.8	97.7	58.5	82.6	0.6766
237	SARADA	60.6	100.0	1018	36.8	34.1	98.9	75.7	83.1	0.7122
	UDAIPUR	**52.5**	**98.4**	**987**	**35.5**	**26.5**	**97.3**	**65.1**	**81.7**	**0.6599**
	RAJASTHAN	**56.6**	**95.4**	**930**	**37.7**	**29.2**	**97.7**	**73.5**	**91.6**	**0.6684**

Note: For Calculation of HSI Please See Methodology (Chapter I).
* Dungargarh PS shifted from Churu to Bikaner district on 1st April 2001
** Excluding data of Dungargarh PS; *** Including data of Dungargarh PS.
Source: 1. Directorate of Census Operation, Jaipur.
2. General Annex- V, VI & VII.

ANNEX-11.2

RANKING OF PANCHAYAT SAMITIES BY HEALTH STATUS INDEX, 2001

(Descending Order)

RANK	PANCHAYAT SAMITIES P.CODE	NAME	HEALTH STATUS INDEX
1	2	3	4
		VERY HIGH (>0.8)	
1	155	**UDAIPURWATI**	**0.8307**
2	91	**RATANGARH**	**0.8164**
3	192	**RANI STATION**	**0.8148**
4	195	**SUMERPUR**	**0.8076**
5	220	**SIROHI**	**0.8059**
6	186	**BALI**	**0.8057**
		HIGH (0.7-0.8)	
7	209	**DHOND**	**0.7978**
8	135	**AHORE**	**0.7941**
9	214	**PIPRALI**	**0.7841**
10	159	**BILARA**	**0.7828**
11	152	**KHETRI**	**0.7827**
12	137	**JALOR**	**0.7826**
13	215	**SRI MADHOPUR**	**0.7825**
14	107	**SAGWARA**	**0.7802**
15	150	**CHIRAWA**	**0.7770**
16	187	**DESURI**	**0.7745**
17	153	**NAWALGARH**	**0.7741**
18	211	**KHANDELA**	**0.7736**
19	89	**CHURU**	**0.7716**
20	123	**GOVINDGARH**	**0.7682**
21	149	**BUHANA**	**0.7669**
22	208	**DANTA RAMGARH**	**0.7667**
23	201	**RAILMAGRA**	**0.7650**
24	104	**ASPUR**	**0.7632**
25	141	**SAYLA**	**0.7621**
26	10	**BEHROR**	**0.7615**
27	67	**DUNGARGARH ***	**0.7612**
28	194	**SOJAT**	**0.7603**
29	151	**JHUNJHUNUN**	**0.7596**
30	179	**LADNU**	**0.7543**
31	219	**SHEOGANJ**	**0.7538**
32	210	**FATEHPUR**	**0.7534**
33	16	**NIMRANA**	**0.7520**
34	130	**SHAHPURA**	**0.7487**
35	189	**KHARCHI/MARWAR JUN.**	**0.7486**
36	158	**BHOPALGARH**	**0.7479**
37	188	**JAITARAN**	**0.7466**
38	25	**GARHI**	**0.7465**
39	56	**BANERA**	**0.7464**
40	213	**NEEM KA THANA**	**0.7444**
41	138	**JASWANTPURA**	**0.7441**
42	7	**PISANGAN**	**0.7417**
43	191	**RAIPUR**	**0.7404**
44	63	**SAHARA**	**0.7396**
45	49	**KUMHER**	**0.7390**
46	160	**LUNI**	**0.7390**
47	217	**PINDWARA**	**0.7379**
48	4	**KEKRI**	**0.7348**
49	235	**MAVLI**	**0.7348**
50	165	**HINDAUN**	**0.7326**
51	176	**DIDWANA**	**0.7325**
52	148	**ALSISAR**	**0.7316**
53	162	**OSIAN**	**0.7313**
54	50	**NADBAI**	**0.7286**
55	105	**BICHHIWARA**	**0.7266**
56	184	**PARBATSAR**	**0.7254**
57	190	**PALI**	**0.7246**
58	57	**HURDA**	**0.7243**
59	128	**SAMBHAR**	**0.7241**
60	93	**SUJANGARH**	**0.7240**
61	212	**LACHHMANGARH**	**0.7233**
62	139	**RANIWARA**	**0.7228**
63	88	**RASHMI**	**0.7226**
64	131	**VIRATNAGAR**	**0.7225**
65	106	**DUNGARPUR**	**0.7214**
66	181	**MERTA**	**0.7209**
67	45	**SIWANA**	**0.7197**
68	3	**JAWAJA**	**0.7191**
69	116	**BHADRA**	**0.7173**
70	5	**KISHANGARH**	**0.7172**
71	185	**RIYAN**	**0.7160**
72	174	**SULTANPUR**	**0.7159**
73	8	**SRINAGAR**	**0.7157**
74	199	**KHAMNOR**	**0.7155**
75	94	**TARANAGAR**	**0.7154**
76	110	**GANGANAGAR**	**0.7151**
77	237	**SARADA**	**0.7122**
78	172	**LADPURA**	**0.7114**
79	218	**REODAR**	**0.7079**
80	126	**KOTPUTLI**	**0.7073**
81	175	**DEGANA**	**0.7072**
82	230	**GIRWA**	**0.7056**
83	15	**MANDAWAR**	**0.7037**
84	197	**BHIM**	**0.7011**
85	180	**MAKRANA**	**0.7008**
		MEDIUM (0.6-0.7)	
86	205	**GANGAPUR**	**0.6992**
87	124	**JAMWA RAMGARH**	**0.6978**
88	65	**SUWANA**	**0.6972**
89	170	**CHECHAT**	**0.6970**
90	112	**PADAMPUR**	**0.6968**
91	83	**DUNGLA**	**0.6959**
92	136	**BHINMAL**	**0.6954**
93	47	**DEEG**	**0.6939**
94	154	**SURAJGARH**	**0.6928**
95	111	**KARANPUR**	**0.6928**
96	227	**BARGAON**	**0.6920**
97	62	**RAIPUR**	**0.6919**
98	90	**RAJGARH**	**0.6918**
99	182	**MUNDWA**	**0.6914**
100	193	**ROHAT**	**0.6911**
101	119	**AMBER**	**0.6910**
102	120	**BASSI**	**0.6905**
103	60	**MANDAL**	**0.6896**
104	53	**SEWAR**	**0.6895**
105	202	**RAJSAMAND**	**0.6890**
106	125	**JHOTWARA**	**0.6887**
107	108	**SIMALWARA**	**0.6858**
108	169	**TODABHIM**	**0.6843**
109	228	**BHINDER**	**0.6841**
110	6	**MASOODA**	**0.6824**
111	114	**SADULSHAHAR**	**0.6817**
112	177	**JAYAL**	**0.6812**
113	167	**NADOTI**	**0.6804**
114	200	**KUMBHALGARH**	**0.6803**
115	19	**RENI**	**0.6785**
116	86	**NIMBAHERA**	**0.6775**
117	2	**BHINAY**	**0.6771**
118	95	**BANDIKUI**	**0.6771**
119	9	**BANSURE**	**0.6769**
120	122	**DUDU**	**0.6766**
121	236	**SALUMBAR**	**0.6766**
122	55	**ASIND**	**0.6764**
123	178	**KUCHAMAN**	**0.6762**
124	33	**BARAN**	**0.6753**
125	22	**UMREN**	**0.6751**
126	129	**SANGANER**	**0.6740**
127	1	**ARAIN**	**0.6736**
128	80	**BHOPALSAGAR**	**0.6731**
129	117	**HANUMANGARH**	**0.6726**
130	20	**THANAGAZI**	**0.6726**
131	224	**TODARAISINGH**	**0.6713**
132	52	**RUPBAS**	**0.6699**
133	14	LACHHMANGARH	0.6672
134	30	TALWARA	0.6660
135	231	GOGUNDA	0.6659
136	11	KATHUMAR	0.6646
137	222	MALPURA	0.6640
138	70	NOKHA	0.6635
139	183	NAGAUR	0.6631
140	32	ATRU	0.6619
141	216	ABU ROAD	0.6618
142	13	KOTKASIM	0.6614
143	31	ANTA	0.6603
144	161	MANDOR	0.6600
145	173	SANGOD	0.6599
146	163	PHALODI	0.6584
147	18	RAMGARH	0.6569
148	196	AMET	0.6562
149	96	DAUSA	0.6561
150	99	SIKRAI	0.6557
151	26	GHATOL	0.6555
152	233	KHERWARA	0.6541
153	156	BALESAR	0.6530
154	98	MAHWA	0.6485
155	225	TONK	0.6480
156	198	DEOGARH	0.6475
157	64	SHAHPURA	0.6464
158	84	GANGRAR	0.6454
159	207	SAWAI MADHOPUR	0.6450
160	82	CHITTAURGARH	0.6443
161	127	PHAGI	0.6441
162	171	ITAWA	0.6437
163	76	BARI SADRI	0.6427
164	113	RAISINGHNAGAR	0.6419
165	17	RAJGARH	0.6404
166	58	JAHAZPUR	0.6404
167	204	BONLI	0.6376
168	71	HINDOLI	0.6375
169	61	MANDALGARH	0.6374
170	54	WEIR	0.6374
171	12	KISHANGARH BAS	0.6348
172	140	SANCHORE	0.6339
173	74	TALERA	0.6318
174	203	BAMANWAS	0.6316
175	223	NIWAI	0.6309
176	145	KHANPUR	0.6309
177	232	JHADOL	0.6309
178	221	DEOLI	0.6302
179	51	NAGAR PAHARI	0.6301
180	69	LUNKARANSAR	0.6284
181	59	KOTRI	0.6281
182	78	BHADESAR	0.6269
183	166	KARAULI	0.6265
184	24	BAGIDORA	0.6251
185	36	KISHANGANJ	0.6249
186	229	DHARIAWAD	0.6205
187	38	BALOTRA	0.6194
188	77	BEGUN	0.6188
189	21	TIJARA	0.6187
190	87	PRATAPGARH	0.6185
191	92	SARDARSHAHAR	0.6175
192	23	ANANDPURI	0.6167
193	147	PIRAWA	0.6153
194	168	SAPOTRA	0.6140
195	48	KAMAN	0.6137
196	72	KESHORAIPATAN	0.6136
197	81	CHHOTI SADRI	0.6124
198	73	NAINWA	0.6122
199	46	BAYANA	0.6120
200	206	KHANDAR	0.6089
201	97	LALSOT	0.6088
202	164	SHERGARH	0.6050
203	29	SAJJANGARH	0.6021
204	85	KAPASAN	0.6016
205	226	UNIARA	0.6007
206	42	DHORIMANNA	0.6006
		LOW (0.5-0.6)	
207	144	JHALRAPATAN	0.5985
208	102	DHAULPUR	0.5947
209	66	BIKANER	0.5913
210	75	ARNOD	0.5903
211	41	CHOHTAN	0.5880
212	100	BARI	0.5844
213	79	BHAINSRORGARH	0.5819
214	37	SHAHBAD	0.5809
215	103	RAJAKHERA	0.5785
216	118	NOHAR	0.5785
217	68	KOLAYAT	0.5752
218	143	DAG	0.5723
219	28	PEEPALKHOONT	0.5685
220	35	CHHIPABAROD	0.5674
221	101	BASERI	0.5663
222	27	KUSHALGARH	0.5633
222	121	CHAKSU	0.5633
224	44	SINDHARI	0.5611
225	109	ANUPGARH	0.5610
226	157	BAP	0.5588
227	132	JAISALMER	0.5541
228	142	BAKANI	0.5525
229	134	SANKRA	0.5487
230	34	CHHABRA	0.5216
231	115	SURATGARH	0.5150
232	146	MANOHARTHANA	0.5097
		VERY LOW (< 0.5)	
233	234	KOTRA	0.4951
234	40	BAYTOO	0.4950
235	43	SHEO	0.4938
236	39	BARMER	0.4930
237	133	SAM	0.4749
		RAJASTHAN	**0.6684**
		% AGE OF AAPs	**55.70**

BOLD: Above Average Panchayat Samities (AAPs)
Source: Annex 11.1

ANNEX-12.1

PANCHAYAT SAMITI-WISE CHANGED PATTERN OF HEALTH STATUS INDEX (1991-01)

P. CODE	PANCHAYAT SAMITI	HEALTH STATUS INDEX 1991 RANK	1991 VALUE	2001 RANK	2001 VALUE	DIFFERENCES (1991-01) RANK	DIFFERENCES (1991-01) VALUE	% INCREASE IN HSI VALUE	REMARKS
1	2	3	4	5	6	7	8	9	10
1	ARAIN	124	0.5614	127	0.6736	-3	0.1122	20	B
2	BHINAY	42	0.6324	117	0.6771	-75	0.0447	7	B
3	JAWAJA	126	0.5583	68	0.7191	58	0.1608	29	A
4	KEKRI	17	0.6643	48	0.7348	-31	0.0705	11	B
5	KISHANGARH	53	0.6251	70	0.7172	-17	0.0921	15	B
6	MASOODA	67	0.6080	110	0.6824	-43	0.0744	12	B
7	PISANGAN	7	0.6908	42	0.7417	-35	0.0509	7	B
8	SRINAGAR	34	0.6389	73	0.7157	-39	0.0768	12	B
	AJMER DISTRICT		**0.6243**		**0.7075**		**0.0832**	**13**	
9	BANSURE	110	0.5763	119	0.6769	-9	0.1006	17	B
10	BEHROR	36	0.6358	26	0.7615	10	0.1257	20	A
11	KATHUMAR	183	0.5148	136	0.6646	47	0.1498	29	A
12	KISHANGARH BAS	89	0.5884	171	0.6348	-82	0.0464	8	B
13	KOTKASIM	116	0.5676	142	0.6614	-26	0.0938	17	B
14	LACHHMANGARH	193	0.5046	133	0.6672	60	0.1626	32	A
15	MANDAWAR	62	0.6119	83	0.7037	-21	0.0918	15	B
16	NIMRANA	30	0.6495	33	0.7520	-3	0.1025	16	B
17	RAJGARH	133	0.5535	165	0.6404	-32	0.0869	16	B
18	RAMGARH	138	0.5513	147	0.6569	-9	0.1056	19	B
19	RENI	170	0.5256	115	0.6785	55	0.1529	29	A
20	THANAGAZI	111	0.5759	130	0.6726	-19	0.0967	17	B
21	TIJARA	186	0.5110	189	0.6187	-3	0.1077	21	B
22	UMREN	141	0.5484	125	0.6751	16	0.1267	23	A
	ALWAR		**0.5616**		**0.6725**		**0.1109**	**20**	
23	ANANDPURI	169	0.5258	192	0.6167	-23	0.0909	17	B
24	BAGIDORA	106	0.5788	184	0.6251	-78	0.0463	8	B
25	GARHI	22	0.6575	38	0.7465	-16	0.0890	14	B
26	GHATOL	122	0.5620	151	0.6555	-29	0.0935	17	B
27	KUSHALGARH	226	0.4296	222	0.5633	4	0.1337	31	A
28	PEEPALKHOONT	209	0.4813	219	0.5685	-10	0.0872	18	B
29	SAJJANGARH	219	0.4466	203	0.6021	16	0.1555	35	A
30	TALWARA	90	0.5883	134	0.6660	-44	0.0777	13	B
	BANSWARA		**0.5475**		**0.6405**		**0.0930**	**17**	
31	ANTA	143	0.5471	143	0.6603	0	0.1132	21	C
32	ATRU	134	0.5534	140	0.6619	-6	0.1085	20	B
33	BARAN	142	0.5476	124	0.6753	18	0.1277	23	A
34	CHHABRA	221	0.4429	230	0.5216	-9	0.0787	18	B
35	CHHIPABAROD	224	0.4383	220	0.5674	4	0.1291	29	A
36	KISHANGANJ	190	0.5074	185	0.6249	5	0.1175	23	A
37	SHAHBAD	215	0.4635	214	0.5809	1	0.1174	25	A
	BARAN		**0.5025**		**0.6148**		**0.1123**	**22**	
38	BALOTRA	188	0.5096	187	0.6194	1	0.1098	22	A
39	BARMER	235	0.3928	236	0.4930	-1	0.1002	26	B
40	BAYTOO	236	0.3656	234	0.4950	2	0.1294	35	A
41	CHOHTAN	225	0.4328	211	0.5880	14	0.1552	36	A
42	DHORIMANNA	227	0.4263	206	0.6006	21	0.1743	41	A
43	SHEO	230	0.4160	235	0.4938	-5	0.0778	19	B
44	SINDHARI	228	0.4238	224	0.5611	4	0.1373	32	A
45	SIWANA	95	0.5856	67	0.7197	28	0.1341	23	A
	BARMER		**0.4418**		**0.5715**		**0.1297**	**29**	
46	BAYANA	199	0.4991	199	0.6120	0	0.1129	23	C
47	DEEG	196	0.5026	93	0.6939	103	0.1913	38	A
48	KAMAN	217	0.4556	195	0.6137	22	0.1581	35	A
49	KUMHER	72	0.6056	45	0.7390	27	0.1334	22	A
50	NADBAI	167	0.5265	54	0.7286	113	0.2021	38	A
51	NAGAR PAHARI	223	0.4408	179	0.6301	44	0.1893	43	A
52	RUPBAS	179	0.5175	132	0.6699	47	0.1524	29	A
53	SEWAR	152	0.5408	104	0.6895	48	0.1487	27	A
54	WEIR	115	0.5688	170	0.6374	-55	0.0686	12	B
	BHARATPUR		**0.5134**		**0.6617**		**0.1483**	**29**	
55	ASIND	66	0.6084	122	0.6764	-56	0.0680	11	B
56	BANERA	14	0.6704	39	0.7464	-25	0.0760	11	B
57	HURDA	12	0.6838	58	0.7243	-46	0.0405	6	B
58	JAHAZPUR	81	0.5956	166	0.6404	-85	0.0448	8	B
59	KOTRI	99	0.5834	181	0.6281	-82	0.0447	8	B

P. CODE	*PANCHAYAT SAMITI*	*HEALTH STATUS INDEX 1991 RANK*	*1991 VALUE*	*2001 RANK*	*2001 VALUE*	*DIFFERENCES (1991-01) RANK*	*DIFFERENCES (1991-01) VALUE*	*% INCRE-ASE IN HSI VALUE*	*REMARKS*
1	*2*	*3*	*4*	*5*	*6*	*7*	*8*	*9*	*10*
60	MANDAL	37	0.6350	103	0.6896	-66	0.0546	9	B
61	MANDALGARH	129	0.5573	169	0.6374	-40	0.0801	14	B
62	RAIPUR	39	0.6344	97	0.6919	-58	0.0575	9	B
63	SAHARA	13	0.6710	44	0.7396	-31	0.0686	10	B
64	SHAHPURA	60	0.6149	157	0.6464	-97	0.0315	5	B
65	SUWANA	42	0.6324	88	0.6972	-46	0.0648	10	B
	BHILWARA		**0.6175**		**0.6749**		**0.0574**	**9**	
66	BIKANER	87	0.5909	209	0.5913	-122	0.0004	0	B
67	DUNGARGARH *	45	0.6321	27	0.7612	18	0.1291	20	A
68	KOLAYAT	154	0.5398	217	0.5752	-63	0.0354	7	B
69	LUNKARANSAR	114	0.5726	180	0.6284	-66	0.0558	10	B
70	NOKHA	77	0.5996	138	0.6635	-61	0.0639	11	B
	BIKANER **		**0.5781**		**0.6136**		**0.0355**	**6**	
71	HINDOLI	197	0.5024	168	0.6375	29	0.1351	27	A
72	KESHORAIPATAN	206	0.4853	196	0.6136	10	0.1283	26	A
73	NAINWA	174	0.5245	198	0.6122	-24	0.0877	17	B
74	TALERA	178	0.5193	173	0.6318	5	0.1125	22	A
	BUNDI		**0.4968**		**0.6247**		**0.1279**	**26**	
75	ARNOD	163	0.5296	210	0.5903	-47	0.0607	11	B
76	BARI SADRI	155	0.5369	163	0.6427	-8	0.1058	20	B
77	BEGUN	157	0.5366	188	0.6188	-31	0.0822	15	B
78	BHADESAR	177	0.5203	182	0.6269	-5	0.1066	20	B
79	BHAINSRORGARH	212	0.4724	213	0.5819	-1	0.1095	23	B
80	BHOPALSAGAR	45	0.6321	128	0.6731	-83	0.0410	6	B
81	CHHOTI SADRI	175	0.5213	197	0.6124	-22	0.0911	17	B
82	CHITTAURGARH	143	0.5471	160	0.6443	-17	0.0972	18	B
83	DUNGLA	147	0.5454	91	0.6959	56	0.1505	28	A
84	GANGRAR	161	0.5329	158	0.6454	3	0.1125	21	A
85	KAPASAN	101	0.5823	204	0.6016	-103	0.0193	3	B
86	NIMBAHERA	145	0.5469	116	0.6775	29	0.1306	24	A
87	PRATAPGARH	205	0.4854	190	0.6185	15	0.1331	27	A
88	RASHMI	50	0.6300	63	0.7226	-13	0.0926	15	B
	CHITTAURGARH		**0.5391**		**0.6365**		**0.0974**	**18**	
89	CHURU	105	0.5789	19	0.7716	86	0.1927	33	A
90	RAJGARH	191	0.5073	98	0.6918	93	0.1845	36	A
91	RATANGARH	76	0.6000	2	0.8164	74	0.2164	36	A
92	SARDARSHAHAR	184	0.5138	191	0.6175	-7	0.1037	20	B
93	SUJANGARH	121	0.5623	60	0.7240	61	0.1617	29	A
94	TARANAGAR	93	0.5871	75	0.7154	18	0.1283	22	A
	CHURU ***		**0.5611**		**0.7191**		**0.1580**	**28**	
95	BANDIKUI	179	0.5175	118	0.6771	61	0.1596	31	A
96	DAUSA	157	0.5366	149	0.6561	8	0.1195	22	A
97	LALSOT	203	0.4869	201	0.6088	2	0.1219	25	A
98	MAHWA	202	0.4950	154	0.6485	48	0.1535	31	A
99	SIKRAI	165	0.5281	150	0.6557	15	0.1276	24	A
	DAUSA		**0.5129**		**0.6487**		**0.1358**	**26**	
100	BARI	234	0.3966	212	0.5844	22	0.1878	47	A
101	BASERI	207	0.4841	221	0.5663	-14	0.0822	17	B
102	DHAULPUR	173	0.5250	208	0.5947	-35	0.0697	13	B
103	RAJAKHERA	216	0.4591	215	0.5785	1	0.1194	26	A
	DHAULPUR		**0.4735**		**0.5827**		**0.1092**	**23**	
104	ASPUR	40	0.6338	24	0.7632	16	0.1294	20	A
105	BICHHIWARA	70	0.6058	55	0.7266	15	0.1208	20	A
106	DUNGARPUR	96	0.5854	65	0.7214	31	0.1360	23	A
107	SAGWARA	28	0.6529	14	0.7802	14	0.1273	19	A
108	SIMALWARA	150	0.5415	107	0.6858	43	0.1443	27	A
	DUNGARPUR		**0.5975**		**0.7324**		**0.1349**	**23**	
109	ANUPGARH	233	0.3974	225	0.5610	8	0.1636	41	A
110	GANGANAGAR	61	0.6146	76	0.7151	-15	0.1005	16	B
111	KARANPUR	94	0.5860	95	0.6928	-1	0.1068	18	B
112	PADAMPUR	118	0.5653	90	0.6968	28	0.1315	23	A
113	RAISINGHNAGAR	160	0.5363	164	0.6419	-4	0.1056	20	B
114	SADULSHAHAR	104	0.5791	111	0.6817	-7	0.1026	18	B
115	SURATGARH	214	0.4686	231	0.5150	-17	0.0464	10	B
	GANGANAGAR		**0.5109**		**0.6183**		**0.1074**	**21**	
116	BHADRA	147	0.5454	69	0.7173	78	0.1719	32	A
117	HANUMANGARH	90	0.5883	129	0.6726	-39	0.0843	14	D
118	NOHAR	194	0.5045	216	0.5785	-22	0.0740	15	B
	HANUMANGARH		**0.5483**		**0.6510**		**0.1027**	**19**	
119	AMBER	98	0.5838	101	0.6910	-3	0.1072	18	B
120	BASSI	103	0.5804	102	0.6905	1	0.1101	19	A
121	CHAKSU	211	0.4794	222	0.5633	-11	0.0839	18	B
122	DUDU	185	0.5128	120	0.6766	65	0.1638	32	A

P. CODE	PANCHAYAT SAMITI	HEALTH STATUS INDEX 1991 RANK	1991 VALUE	2001 RANK	2001 VALUE	DIFFERENCES (1991-01) RANK	DIFFERENCES VALUE	% INCRE-ASE IN HSI VALUE	REMARKS
1	2	3	4	5	6	7	8	9	10
123	GOVINDGARH	6	0.6956	20	0.7682	-14	0.0726	10	B
124	JAMWA RAMGARH	99	0.5834	87	0.6978	12	0.1144	20	A
125	JHOTWARA	80	0.5975	106	0.6887	-26	0.0912	15	B
126	KOTPUTLI	72	0.6056	80	0.7073	-8	0.1017	17	B
127	PHAGI	149	0.5430	161	0.6441	-12	0.1011	19	B
128	SAMBHAR	69	0.6069	59	0.7241	10	0.1172	19	A
129	SANGANER	108	0.5779	126	0.6740	-18	0.0961	17	B
130	SHAHPURA	20	0.6583	34	0.7487	-14	0.0904	14	B
131	VIRATNAGAR	63	0.6116	64	0.7225	-1	0.1109	18	B
	JAIPUR		**0.5860**		**0.6925**		**0.1065**	**18**	
132	JAISALMER	220	0.4439	227	0.5541	-7	0.1102	25	B
133	SAM	237	0.3460	237	0.4749	0	0.1289	37	C
134	SANKRA	222	0.4409	229	0.5487	-7	0.1078	24	B
	JAISALMER		**0.4085**		**0.5238**		**0.1153**	**28**	
135	AHORE	31	0.6464	8	0.7941	23	0.1477	23	A
136	BHINMAL	134	0.5534	92	0.6954	42	0.1420	26	A
137	JALOR	11	0.6843	12	0.7826	-1	0.0983	14	B
138	JASWANTPURA	58	0.6173	41	0.7441	17	0.1268	21	A
139	RANIWARA	97	0.5850	62	0.7228	35	0.1378	24	A
140	SANCHORE	187	0.5099	172	0.6339	15	0.1240	24	A
141	SAYLA	25	0.6559	25	0.7621	0	0.1062	16	C
	JALOR		**0.5948**		**0.7190**		**0.1242**	**21**	
142	BAKANI	201	0.4975	228	0.5525	-27	0.0550	11	B
143	DAG	208	0.4819	218	0.5723	-10	0.0904	19	B
144	JHALRAPATAN	172	0.5251	207	0.5985	-35	0.0734	14	B
145	KHANPUR	175	0.5213	176	0.6309	-1	0.1096	21	B
146	MANOHARTHANA	229	0.4163	232	0.5097	-3	0.0934	22	B
147	PIRAWA	182	0.5164	193	0.6153	-11	0.0989	19	B
	JHALAWAR		**0.4944**		**0.5804**		**0.0860**	**17**	
148	ALSISAR	44	0.6323	52	0.7316	-8	0.0993	16	B
149	BUHANA	65	0.6085	21	0.7669	44	0.1584	26	A
150	CHIRAWA	15	0.6659	15	0.7770	0	0.1111	17	C
151	JHUNJHUNUN	21	0.6581	29	0.7596	-8	0.1015	15	B
152	KHETRI	26	0.6536	11	0.7827	15	0.1291	20	A
153	NAWALGARH	2	0.7268	17	0.7741	-15	0.0473	7	B
154	SURAJGARH	86	0.5913	94	0.6928	-8	0.1015	17	B
155	UDAIPURWATI	5	0.6990	1	0.8307	4	0.1317	19	A
	JHUNJHUNUN		**0.6531**		**0.7645**		**0.1114**	**17**	
156	BALESAR	38	0.6346	153	0.6530	-115	0.0184	3	B
157	BAP	231	0.4145	226	0.5588	5	0.1443	35	A
158	BHOPALGARH	29	0.6515	36	0.7479	-7	0.0964	15	B
159	BILARA	4	0.6991	10	0.7828	-6	0.0837	12	B
160	LUNI	59	0.6169	46	0.7390	13	0.1221	20	A
161	MANDOR	125	0.5600	144	0.6600	-19	0.1000	18	B
162	OSIAN	117	0.5654	53	0.7313	64	0.1659	29	A
163	PHALODI	151	0.5410	146	0.6584	5	0.1174	22	A
164	SHERGARH	70	0.6058	202	0.6050	-132	-0.0008	0	B
	JODHPUR		**0.5715**		**0.6891**		**0.1176**	**21**	
165	HINDAUN	108	0.5779	50	0.7326	58	0.1547	27	A
166	KARAULI	218	0.4519	183	0.6265	35	0.1746	39	A
167	NADOTI	113	0.5728	113	0.6804	0	0.1076	19	C
168	SAPOTRA	210	0.4799	194	0.6140	16	0.1341	28	A
169	TODABHIM	166	0.5275	108	0.6843	58	0.1568	30	A
	KARAULI		**0.5174**		**0.6658**		**0.1484**	**29**	
170	CHECHAT	107	0.5786	89	0.6970	18	0.1184	20	A
171	ITAWA	204	0.4865	162	0.6437	42	0.1572	32	A
172	LADPURA	78	0.5989	78	0.7114	0	0.1125	19	C
173	SANGOD	164	0.5283	145	0.6599	19	0.1316	25	A
174	SULTANPUR	156	0.5368	72	0.7159	84	0.1791	33	A
	KOTA		**0.5440**		**0.6844**		**0.1404**	**26**	
175	DEGANA	84	0.5928	81	0.7072	3	0.1144	19	A
176	DIDWANA	146	0.5458	51	0.7325	95	0.1867	34	A
177	JAYAL	136	0.5524	112	0.6812	24	0.1288	23	A
178	KUCHAMAN	82	0.5941	123	0.6762	-41	0.0821	14	B
179	LADNU	88	0.5893	30	0.7543	58	0.1650	28	A
180	MAKRANA	120	0.5624	85	0.7008	35	0.1384	25	A
181	MERTA	41	0.6336	66	0.7209	-25	0.0873	14	B
182	MUNDWA	112	0.5729	99	0.6914	13	0.1185	21	A
183	NAGAUR	128	0.5574	139	0.6631	-11	0.1057	19	B
184	PARBATSAR	92	0.5875	56	0.7254	36	0.1379	23	A
185	RIYAN	55	0.6201	71	0.7160	-16	0.0959	15	B
	NAGAUR		**0.5796**		**0.7044**		**0.1248**	**22**	
186	BALI	3	0.7016	6	0.8057	-3	0.1041	15	B
187	DESURI	10	0.6901	16	0.7745	-6	0.0844	12	B

P. CODE	PANCHAYAT SAMITI	HEALTH STATUS INDEX 1991 RANK	1991 VALUE	2001 RANK	2001 VALUE	DIFFERENCES (1991-01) RANK	VALUE	% INCREASE IN HSI VALUE	REMARKS
1	2	3	4	5	6	7	8	9	10
188	JAITARAN	68	0.6074	37	0.7466	31	0.1392	23	A
189	KHARCHI/MARWAR JUN.	48	0.6316	35	0.7486	13	0.1170	19	A
190	PALI	54	0.6250	57	0.7246	-3	0.0996	16	B
191	RAIPUR	119	0.5626	43	0.7404	76	0.1778	32	A
192	RANI STATION	8	0.6903	3	0.8148	5	0.1245	18	A
193	ROHAT	123	0.5615	100	0.6911	23	0.1296	23	A
194	SOJAT	45	0.6321	28	0.7603	17	0.1282	20	A
195	SUMERPUR	1	0.7291	4	0.8076	-3	0.0785	11	B
	PALI		**0.6448**		**0.7612**		**0.1164**	**18**	
196	AMET	131	0.5557	148	0.6562	-17	0.1005	18	B
197	BHIM	51	0.6298	84	0.7011	-33	0.0713	11	B
198	DEOGARH	171	0.5253	156	0.6475	15	0.1222	23	A
199	KHAMNOR	19	0.6589	74	0.7155	-55	0.0566	9	B
200	KUMBHALGARH	195	0.5039	114	0.6803	81	0.1764	35	A
201	RAILMAGRA	16	0.6649	23	0.7650	-7	0.1001	15	B
202	RAJSAMAND	168	0.5263	105	0.6890	63	0.1627	31	A
	RAJSAMAND		**0.5825**		**0.6962**		**0.1137**	**20**	
203	BAMANWAS	140	0.5488	174	0.6316	-34	0.0828	15	B
204	BONLI	159	0.5364	167	0.6376	-8	0.1012	19	B
205	GANGAPUR	102	0.5807	86	0.6992	16	0.1185	20	A
206	KHANDAR	213	0.4703	200	0.6089	13	0.1386	29	A
207	SAWAI MADHOPUR	162	0.5300	159	0.6450	3	0.1150	22	A
	SAWAI MADHOPUR		**0.5343**		**0.6448**		**0.1105**	**21**	
208	DANTA RAMGARH	24	0.6572	22	0.7667	2	0.1095	17	A
209	DHOND	9	0.6902	7	0.7978	2	0.1076	16	A
210	FATEHPUR	64	0.6105	32	0.7534	32	0.1429	23	A
211	KHANDELA	33	0.6414	18	0.7736	15	0.1322	21	A
212	LACHHMANGARH	57	0.6191	61	0.7233	-4	0.1042	17	B
213	NEEM KA THANA	49	0.6307	40	0.7444	9	0.1137	18	A
214	PIPRALI	85	0.5924	9	0.7841	76	0.1917	32	A
215	SRI MADHOPUR	27	0.6531	13	0.7825	14	0.1294	20	A
	SIKAR		**0.6347**		**0.7633**		**0.1286**	**20**	
216	ABU ROAD	137	0.5513	141	0.6618	-4	0.1105	20	B
217	PINDWARA	35	0.6370	47	0.7379	-12	0.1009	16	B
218	REODAR	74	0.6033	79	0.7079	-5	0.1046	17	B
219	SHEOGANJ	23	0.6573	31	0.7538	-8	0.0965	15	B
220	SIROHI	18	0.6633	5	0.8059	13	0.1426	21	A
	SIROHI		**0.6234**		**0.7320**		**0.1086**	**17**	
221	DEOLI	132	0.5542	178	0.6302	-46	0.0760	14	B
222	MALPURA	79	0.5976	137	0.6640	-58	0.0664	11	B
223	NIWAI	153	0.5405	175	0.6309	-22	0.0904	17	B
224	TODARAISINGH	181	0.5175	131	0.6713	50	0.1538	30	A
225	TONK	198	0.5010	155	0.6480	43	0.1470	29	A
226	UNIARA	200	0.4976	205	0.6007	-5	0.1031	21	B
	TONK		**0.5351**		**0.6404**		**0.1053**	**20**	
227	BARGAON	75	0.6000	96	0.6920	-21	0.0920	15	B
228	BHINDER	83	0.5931	109	0.6841	-26	0.0910	15	B
229	DHARIAWAD	192	0.5053	186	0.6205	6	0.1152	23	A
230	GIRWA	56	0.6200	82	0.7056	-26	0.0856	14	B
231	GOGUNDA	130	0.5571	135	0.6659	-5	0.1088	20	B
232	JHADOL	189	0.5095	177	0.6309	12	0.1214	24	A
233	KHERWARA	139	0.5497	152	0.6541	-13	0.1044	19	B
234	KOTRA	232	0.4090	233	0.4951	-1	0.0861	21	B
235	MAVLI	32	0.6439	49	0.7348	-17	0.0909	14	B
236	SALUMBAR	127	0.5577	121	0.6766	6	0.1189	21	A
237	SARADA	52	0.6290	77	0.7122	-25	0.0832	13	B
	UDAIPUR		**0.5625**		**0.6599**		**0.0974**	**17**	
	RAJASTHAN		**0.5588**		**0.6684**		**0.1096**	**20**	

Note: A. Improvement In Both HSI Value and Rank C. Increase In HSI Value But Rank Remained Constant
B. Increase In HSI Value But Rank Deteriorated D. Decrease In Both HSI Value and Rank

* Dungargarh PS shifted from Churu to Bikaner District on 1st April 2001

** Excluding data of Dungargarh PS

*** Including data of Dungargarh PS

Source: Annex 10.1 & 11.1.

ANNEX-12.2

RANKING OF PSS BY PERCENTAGE INCREASE / DECREASE IN HEALTH STATUS INDEX: RAJASTHAN (1991-01)

(Descending Order)

RANK	P.CODE	PANCHAYAT SAMITIES NAME	%
1	2	3	4
		VERY HIGH (>40)	
1	100	**BARI**	47
2	51	**NAGAR PAHARI**	43
3	42	**DHORIMANNA**	41
3	109	**ANUPGARH**	41
		HIGH (30-40)	
5	166	**KARAULI**	39
6	47	**DEEG**	38
6	50	**NADBAI**	38
8	133	**SAM**	37
9	41	**CHOHTAN**	36
9	90	**RAJGARH**	36
9	91	**RATANGARH**	36
12	29	**SAJJANGARH**	35
12	40	**BAYTOO**	35
12	48	**KAMAN**	35
12	157	**BAP**	35
12	200	**KUMBHALGARH**	35
17	176	**DIDWANA**	34
18	89	**CHURU**	33
18	174	**SULTANPUR**	33
20	14	**LACHHMANGARH**	32
20	44	**SINDHARI**	32
20	116	**BHADRA**	32
20	122	**DUDU**	32
20	171	**ITAWA**	32
20	191	**RAIPUR**	32
20	214	**PIPRALI**	32
27	27	**KUSHALGARH**	31
27	95	**BANDIKUI**	31
27	98	**MAHWA**	31
27	202	**RAJSAMAND**	31
31	169	**TODABHIM**	30
31	224	**TODARAISINGH**	30
		MEDIUM (20-30)	
33	3	**JAWAJA**	29
33	11	**KATHUMAR**	29
33	19	**RENI**	29
33	35	**CHHIPABAROD**	29
33	52	**RUPBAS**	29
33	93	**SUJANGARH**	29
33	162	**OSIAN**	29
33	206	**KHANDAR**	29
33	225	**TONK**	29
42	53	**SEWAR**	28
42	83	**DUNGLA**	28
42	168	**SAPOTRA**	28
42	179	**LADNU**	28
46	71	**HINDOLI**	27
46	87	**PRATAPGARH**	27
46	108	**SIMALWARA**	27
46	165	**HINDAUN**	27
50	39	**BARMER**	26
50	72	**KESHORAIPATAN**	26
50	103	**RAJAKHERA**	26
50	136	**BHINMAL**	26
50	149	**BUHANA**	26
55	37	**SHAHBAD**	25
55	97	**LALSOT**	25
55	132	**JAISALMER**	25
55	173	**SANGOD**	25
55	180	**MAKRANA**	25
60	86	**NIMBAHERA**	24
60	99	**SIKRAI**	24
60	134	**SANKRA**	24
60	139	**RANIWARA**	24
60	140	**SANCHORE**	24
60	232	**JHADOL**	24
66	22	**UMREN**	23
66	33	**BARAN**	23
66	36	**KISHANGANJ**	23
66	45	**SIWANA**	23
66	46	**BAYANA**	23
66	79	**BHAINSRORGARH**	23
66	106	**DUNGARPUR**	23
66	112	**PADAMPUR**	23
66	135	**AHORE**	23
66	177	**JAYAL**	23
66	184	**PARBATSAR**	23
66	188	**JAITARAN**	23
66	193	**ROHAT**	23
66	198	**DEOGARH**	23

RANK	P.CODE	PANCHAYAT SAMITIES NAME	%
1	2	3	4
66	210	**FATEHPUR**	23
66	229	**DHARIAWAD**	23
82	38	**BALOTRA**	22
82	49	**KUMHER**	22
82	74	**TALERA**	22
82	94	**TARANAGAR**	22
82	96	**DAUSA**	22
82	146	**MANOHARTHANA**	22
82	163	**PHALODI**	22
82	207	**SAWAI MADHOPUR**	22
90	21	**TIJARA**	21
90	31	**ANTA**	21
90	78	**BHADESAR**	21
90	84	**GANGRAR**	21
90	138	**JASWANTPURA**	21
90	145	**KHANPUR**	21
90	182	**MUNDWA**	21
90	211	**KHANDELA**	21
90	220	**SIROHI**	21
90	226	**UNIARA**	21
90	234	**KOTRA**	21
90	236	**SALUMBAR**	21
102	1	**ARAIN**	20
102	10	**BEHROR**	20
102	32	**ATRU**	20
102	67	**DUNGARGARH**	20
102	76	**BARI SADRI**	20
102	92	**SARDARSHAHAR**	20
102	104	**ASPUR**	20
102	105	**BICHHIWARA**	20
102	113	**RAISINGHNAGAR**	20
102	124	**JAMWA RAMGARH**	20
102	152	**KHETRI**	20
102	160	**LUNI**	20
102	170	**CHECHAT**	20
102	194	**SOJAT**	20
102	205	**GANGAPUR**	20
102	215	**SRI MADHOPUR**	20
102	216	**ABU ROAD**	20
102	231	**GOGUNDA**	20
		LOW (10-20)	
120	18	RAMGARH	19
120	43	SHEO	19
120	107	SAGWARA	19
120	120	BASSI	19
120	127	PHAGI	19
120	128	SAMBHAR	19
120	143	DAG	19
120	147	PIRAWA	19
120	155	UDAIPURWATI	19
120	167	NADOTI	19
120	172	LADPURA	19
120	175	DEGANA	19
120	183	NAGAUR	19
120	189	KHARCHI/MARWAR JUN.	19
120	204	BONLI	19
120	233	KHERWARA	19
136	28	PEEPALKHOONT	18
136	34	CHHABRA	18
136	82	CHITTAURGARH	18
136	111	KARANPUR	18
136	114	SADULSHAHAR	18
136	119	AMBER	18
136	121	CHAKSU	18
136	131	VIRATNAGAR	18
136	161	MANDOR	18
136	192	RANI STATION	18
136	196	AMET	18
136	213	NEEM KA THANA	18
148	9	BANSURE	17
148	13	KOTKASIM	17
148	20	THANAGAZI	17
148	23	ANANDPURI	17
148	26	GHATOL	17
148	73	NAINWA	17
148	81	CHHOTI SADRI	17
148	101	BASERI	17
148	126	KOTPUTLI	17
148	129	SANGANER	17
148	150	CHIRAWA	17
148	154	SURAJGARH	17
148	208	DANTA RAMGARH	17

RANK	P.CODE	PANCHAYAT SAMITIES NAME	%
1	2	3	4
148	212	LACHHMANGARH	17
148	218	REODAR	17
148	223	NIWAI	17
164	16	NIMRANA	16
164	17	RAJGARH	16
164	110	GANGANAGAR	16
164	141	SAYLA	16
164	148	ALSISAR	16
164	190	PALI	16
164	209	DHOND	16
164	217	PINDWARA	16
172	5	KISHANGARH	15
172	15	MANDAWAR	15
172	77	BEGUN	15
172	88	RASHMI	15
172	118	NOHAR	15
172	125	JHOTWARA	15
172	151	JHUNJHUNUN	15
172	158	BHOPALGARH	15
172	185	RIYAN	15
172	186	BALI	15
172	201	RAILMAGRA	15
172	203	BAMANWAS	15
172	219	SHEOGANJ	15
172	227	BARGAON	15
172	228	BHINDER	15
187	25	GARHI	14
187	61	MANDALGARH	14
187	117	HANUMANGARH	14
187	130	SHAHPURA	14
187	137	JALOR	14
187	144	JHALRAPATAN	14
187	178	KUCHAMAN	14
187	181	MERTA	14
187	221	DEOLI	14
187	230	GIRWA	14
187	235	MAVLI	14
198	30	TALWARA	13
198	102	DHAULPUR	13
198	237	SARADA	13
201	6	MASOODA	12
201	8	SRINAGAR	12
201	54	WEIR	12
201	159	BILARA	12
201	187	DESURI	12
206	4	KEKRI	11
206	55	ASIND	11
206	56	BANERA	11
206	70	NOKHA	11
206	75	ARNOD	11
206	142	BAKANI	11
206	195	SUMERPUR	11
206	197	BHIM	11
206	222	MALPURA	11
215	63	SAHARA	10
215	65	SUWANA	10
215	69	LUNKARANSAR	10
215	115	SURATGARH	10
215	123	GOVINDGARH	10
		VERY LOW (<10)	
220	60	MANDAL	9
220	62	RAIPUR	9
220	199	KHAMNOR	9
223	12	KISHANGARH BAS	8
223	24	BAGIDORA	8
223	58	JAHAZPUR	8
223	59	KOTRI	8
227	2	BHINAY	7
227	7	PISANGAN	7
227	68	KOLAYAT	7
227	153	NAWALGARH	7
231	57	HURDA	6
231	80	BHOPALSAGAR	6
233	64	SHAHPURA	5
234	85	KAPASAN	3
234	156	BALESAR	3
236	66	BIKANER *	0
		DECREASE (-)	
236	164	SHERGARH **	0
		RAJASTHAN	**20**
		% AGE OF AAPs	**50.21**

BOLD: Equal/Above Average Panchayat Samities (AAPs)
** Shergarh PS of Jodhpur District is the only PS which Regisered Decrease (-0.13%) in HSI.

Note: * Bikaner PS Registered the Lowest 0.07% Increase in HSI.
Source : Annex 12.1.

ANNEX-12.3

RANKING OF PSS BY DIFFERENCE IN HEALTH STATUS INDEX VALUE: RAJASTHAN (1991-01)

(Descending Order)

RANK	P.CODE	PANCHAYAT SAMITIES NAME	VALUE
1	2	3	4
		VERY HIGH (>0.20)	
1	91	**RATANGARH**	0.2164
2	50	**NADBAI**	0.2021
		HIGH (0.15-0.20)	
3	89	**CHURU**	0.1927
4	214	**PIPRALI**	0.1917
5	47	**DEEG**	0.1913
6	51	**NAGAR PAHARI**	0.1893
7	100	**BARI**	0.1878
8	176	**DIDWANA**	0.1867
9	90	**RAJGARH**	0.1845
10	174	**SULTANPUR**	0.1791
11	191	**RAIPUR**	0.1778
12	200	**KUMBHALGARH**	0.1764
13	166	**KARAULI**	0.1746
14	42	**DHORIMANNA**	0.1743
15	116	**BHADRA**	0.1719
16	162	**OSIAN**	0.1659
17	179	**LADNU**	0.1650
18	122	**DUDU**	0.1638
19	109	**ANUPGARH**	0.1636
20	202	**RAJSAMAND**	0.1627
21	14	**LACHHMANGARH**	0.1626
22	93	**SUJANGARH**	0.1617
23	3	**JAWAJA**	0.1608
24	95	**BANDIKUI**	0.1596
25	149	**BUHANA**	0.1584
26	48	**KAMAN**	0.1581
27	171	**ITAWA**	0.1572
28	169	**TODABHIM**	0.1568
29	29	**SAJJANGARH**	0.1555
30	41	**CHOHTAN**	0.1552
31	165	**HINDAUN**	0.1547
32	224	**TODARAISINGH**	0.1538
33	98	**MAHWA**	0.1535
34	19	**RENI**	0.1529
35	52	**RUPBAS**	0.1524
36	83	**DUNGLA**	0.1505
		MEDIUM (0.10-0.15)	
37	11	**KATHUMAR**	0.1498
38	53	**SEWAR**	0.1487
39	135	**AHORE**	0.1477
40	225	**TONK**	0.1470
41	108	**SIMALWARA**	0.1443
41	157	**BAP**	0.1443
43	210	**FATEHPUR**	0.1429
44	220	**SIROHI**	0.1426
45	136	**BHINMAL**	0.1420
46	188	**JAITARAN**	0.1392
47	206	**KHANDAR**	0.1386
48	180	**MAKRANA**	0.1384
49	184	**PARBATSAR**	0.1379
50	139	**RANIWARA**	0.1378
51	44	**SINDHARI**	0.1373
52	106	**DUNGARPUR**	0.1360
53	71	**HINDOLI**	0.1351
54	45	**SIWANA**	0.1341
54	168	**SAPOTRA**	0.1341
56	27	**KUSHALGARH**	0.1337
57	49	**KUMHER**	0.1334
58	87	**PRATAPGARH**	0.1331
59	211	**KHANDELA**	0.1322
60	155	**UDAIPURWATI**	0.1317
61	173	**SANGOD**	0.1316
62	112	**PADAMPUR**	0.1315
63	86	**NIMBAHERA**	0.1306
64	193	**ROHAT**	0.1296
65	40	**BAYTOO**	0.1294
65	104	**ASPUR**	0.1294
65	215	**SRI MADHOPUR**	0.1294
68	35	**CHHIPABAROD**	0.1291
68	67	**DUNGARGARH ***	0.1291
68	152	**KHETRI**	0.1291
71	133	**SAM**	0.1289
72	177	**JAYAL**	0.1288
73	72	**KESHORAIPATAN**	0.1283
73	94	**TARANAGAR**	0.1283
75	194	**SOJAT**	0.1282
76	33	**BARAN**	0.1277
77	99	**SIKRAI**	0.1276
78	107	**SAGWARA**	0.1273
79	138	**JASWANTPURA**	0.1268

RANK	P.CODE	PANCHAYAT SAMITIES NAME	VALUE
1	2	3	4
80	22	**UMREN**	0.1267
81	10	**BEHROR**	0.1257
82	192	**RANI STATION**	0.1245
83	140	**SANCHORE**	0.1240
84	198	**DEOGARH**	0.1222
85	160	**LUNI**	0.1221
86	97	**LALSOT**	0.1219
87	232	**JHADOL**	0.1214
88	105	**BICHHIWARA**	0.1208
89	96	**DAUSA**	0.1195
90	103	**RAJAKHERA**	0.1194
91	236	**SALUMBAR**	0.1189
92	182	**MUNDWA**	0.1185
92	205	**GANGAPUR**	0.1185
94	170	**CHECHAT**	0.1184
95	36	**KISHANGANJ**	0.1175
96	37	**SHAHBAD**	0.1174
96	163	**PHALODI**	0.1174
98	128	**SAMBHAR**	0.1172
99	189	**KHARCHI/MARWAR JUN.**	0.1170
100	229	**DHARIAWAD**	0.1152
101	207	**SAWAI MADHOPUR**	0.1150
102	124	**JAMWA RAMGARH**	0.1144
102	175	**DEGANA**	0.1144
104	213	**NEEM KA THANA**	0.1137
105	31	**ANTA**	0.1132
106	46	**BAYANA**	0.1129
107	74	**TALERA**	0.1125
107	84	**GANGRAR**	0.1125
107	172	**LADPURA**	0.1125
110	1	**ARAIN**	0.1122
111	150	**CHIRAWA**	0.1111
112	131	**VIRATNAGAR**	0.1109
113	216	**ABU ROAD**	0.1105
114	132	**JAISALMER**	0.1102
115	120	**BASSI**	0.1101
116	38	**BALOTRA**	0.1098
117	145	**KHANPUR**	0.1096
118	79	BHAINSRORGARH	0.1095
118	208	DANTA RAMGARH	0.1095
120	231	GOGUNDA	0.1088
121	32	ATRU	0.1085
122	134	SANKRA	0.1078
123	21	TIJARA	0.1077
124	167	NADOTI	0.1076
124	209	DHOND	0.1076
126	119	AMBER	0.1072
127	111	KARANPUR	0.1068
128	78	BHADESAR	0.1066
129	141	SAYLA	0.1062
130	76	BARI SADRI	0.1058
131	183	NAGAUR	0.1057
132	18	RAMGARH	0.1056
132	113	RAISINGHNAGAR	0.1056
134	218	REODAR	0.1046
135	233	KHERWARA	0.1044
136	212	LACHHMANGARH	0.1042
137	186	BALI	0.1041
138	92	SARDARSHAHAR	0.1037
139	226	UNIARA	0.1031
140	114	SADULSHAHAR	0.1026
141	16	NIMRANA	0.1025
142	126	KOTPUTLI	0.1017
143	151	JHUNJHUNUN	0.1015
143	154	SURAJGARH	0.1015
145	204	BONLI	0.1012
146	127	PHAGI	0.1011
147	217	PINDWARA	0.1009
148	9	BANSURE	0.1006
149	110	GANGANAGAR	0.1005
149	196	AMET	0.1005
151	39	BARMER	0.1002
152	201	RAILMAGRA	0.1001
153	161	MANDOR	0.1000
		LOW (0.05-0.10)	
154	190	PALI	0.0996
155	148	ALSISAR	0.0993
156	147	PIRAWA	0.0989
157	137	JALOR	0.0983
158	82	CHITTAURGARH	0.0972
159	20	THANAGAZI	0.0967
160	219	SHEOGANJ	0.0965

RANK	P.CODE	PANCHAYAT SAMITIES NAME	VALUE
1	2	3	4
161	158	BHOPALGARH	0.0964
162	129	SANGANER	0.0961
163	185	RIYAN	0.0959
164	13	KOTKASIM	0.0938
165	26	GHATOL	0.0935
166	146	MANOHARTHANA	0.0934
167	88	RASHMI	0.0926
168	5	KISHANGARH	0.0921
169	227	BARGAON	0.0920
170	15	MANDAWAR	0.0918
171	125	JHOTWARA	0.0912
172	81	CHHOTI SADRI	0.0911
173	228	BHINDER	0.0910
174	23	ANANDPURI	0.0909
174	235	MAVLI	0.0909
176	130	SHAHPURA	0.0904
176	143	DAG	0.0904
176	223	NIWAI	0.0904
179	25	GARHI	0.0890
180	73	NAINWA	0.0877
181	181	MERTA	0.0873
182	28	PEEPALKHOONT	0.0872
183	17	RAJGARH	0.0869
184	234	KOTRA	0.0861
185	230	GIRWA	0.0856
186	187	DESURI	0.0844
187	117	HANUMANGARH	0.0843
188	121	CHAKSU	0.0839
189	159	BILARA	0.0837
190	237	SARADA	0.0832
191	203	BAMANWAS	0.0828
192	77	BEGUN	0.0822
192	101	BASERI	0.0822
194	178	KUCHAMAN	0.0821
195	61	MANDALGARH	0.0801
196	34	CHHABRA	0.0787
197	195	SUMERPUR	0.0785
198	43	SHEO	0.0778
199	30	TALWARA	0.0777
200	8	SRINAGAR	0.0768
201	56	BANERA	0.0760
201	221	DEOLI	0.0760
203	6	MASOODA	0.0744
204	118	NOHAR	0.0740
205	144	JHALRAPATAN	0.0734
206	123	GOVINDGARH	0.0726
207	197	BHIM	0.0713
208	4	KEKRI	0.0705
209	102	DHAULPUR	0.0697
210	54	WEIR	0.0686
210	63	SAHARA	0.0686
212	55	ASIND	0.0680
213	222	MALPURA	0.0664
214	65	SUWANA	0.0648
215	70	NOKHA	0.0639
216	75	ARNOD	0.0607
217	62	RAIPUR	0.0575
218	199	KHAMNOR	0.0566
219	69	LUNKARANSAR	0.0558
220	142	BAKANI	0.0550
221	60	MANDAL	0.0546
222	7	PISANGAN	0.0509
		VERY LOW (<0.05)	
223	153	NAWALGARH	0.0473
224	12	KISHANGARH BAS	0.0464
224	115	SURATGARH	0.0464
226	24	BAGIDORA	0.0463
227	58	JAHAZPUR	0.0448
228	2	BHINAY	0.0447
228	59	KOTRI	0.0447
230	80	BHOPALSAGAR	0.0410
231	57	HURDA	0.0405
232	68	KOLAYAT	0.0354
233	64	SHAHPURA	0.0315
234	85	KAPASAN	0.0193
235	156	BALESAR	0.0184
236	66	BIKANER	0.0004
237	164	SHERGARH	-0.0008
		RAJASTHAN	**0.1096**
		% AGE OF AAPs	**49.37**

BOLD: Equal/Above Average Panchayat Samities (AAPs)

Source : Annex 12.1

ANNEX-12.4

RANKING OF PANCHAYAT SAMITIES BY HSI RANK DIFFERENCE, 1991-01

(Descending Order)

RANK	P.CODE	PANCHAYAT SAMITIES NAME	RANK DIFFERENCE	RANK	P.CODE	PANCHAYAT SAMITIES NAME	RANK DIFFERENCE	RANK	P.CODE	PANCHAYAT SAMITIES NAME	RANK DIFFERENCE
1	2	3	4	1	2	3	4	1	2	3	4
		VERY HIGH (>=50)		80	124	JAMWA RAMGARH	12	161	121	CHAKSU	-11
1	50	NADBAI	113	80	232	JHADOL	12	161	147	PIRAWA	-11
2	47	DEEG	103	82	10	BEHROR	10	161	183	NAGAUR	-11
3	176	DIDWANA	95	82	72	KESHORAIPATAN	10	164	127	PHAGI	-12
4	90	RAJGARH	93	82	128	SAMBHAR	10	164	217	PINDWARA	-12
5	89	CHURU	86	85	213	NEEM KA THANA	9	166	88	RASHMI	-13
6	174	SULTANPUR	84	86	96	DAUSA	8	166	233	KHERWARA	-13
7	200	KUMBHALGARH	81	86	109	ANUPGARH	8	168	101	BASERI	-14
8	116	BHADRA	78	88	229	DHARIAWAD	6	168	123	GOVINDGARH	-14
9	191	RAIPUR	76	88	236	SALUMBAR	6	168	130	SHAHPURA	-14
9	214	PIPRALI	76	90	36	KISHANGANJ	5	171	110	GANGANAGAR	-15
11	91	RATANGARH	74	90	74	TALERA	5	171	153	NAWALGARH	-15
12	122	DUDU	65	90	157	BAP	5	173	25	GARHI	-16
13	162	OSIAN	64	90	163	PHALODI	5	173	185	RIYAN	-16
14	202	RAJSAMAND	63	90	192	RANI STATION	5	175	5	KISHANGARH	-17
15	93	SUJANGARH	61	95	27	KUSHALGARH	4	175	82	CHITTAURGARH	-17
15	95	BANDIKUI	61	95	35	CHHIPABAROD	4	175	115	SURATGARH	-17
17	14	LACHHMANGARH	60	95	44	SINDHARI	4	175	196	AMET	-17
18	3	JAWAJA	58	95	155	UDAIPURWATI	4	175	235	MAVLI	-17
18	165	HINDAUN	58	99	84	GANGRAR	3	180	129	SANGANER	-18
18	169	TODABHIM	58	99	175	DEGANA	3	181	20	THANAGAZI	-19
18	179	LADNU	58	99	207	SAWAI MADHOPUR	3	181	161	MANDOR	-19
22	83	DUNGLA	56	102	40	BAYTOO	2	183	15	MANDAWAR	-21
23	19	RENI	55	102	97	LALSOT	2	183	227	BARGAON	-21
24	224	TODARAISINGH	50	102	208	DANTA RAMGARH	2	185	81	CHHOTI SADRI	-22
		HIGH (25-50)		102	209	DHOND	2	185	118	NOHAR	-22
25	53	SEWAR	48	106	37	SHAHBAD	1	185	223	NIWAI	-22
25	98	MAHWA	48	106	38	BALOTRA	1	188	23	ANANDPURI	-23
27	11	KATHUMAR	47	106	103	RAJAKHERA	1	189	73	NAINWA	-24
27	52	RUPBAS	47	106	120	BASSI	1	190	56	BANERA	-25
29	51	NAGAR PAHARI	44	110	31	ANTA	0	190	181	MERTA	-25
29	149	BUHANA	44	110	46	BAYANA	0	190	237	SARADA	-25
31	108	SIMALWARA	43	110	133	SAM	0			**VERY LOW (-25 to -50)**	
31	225	TONK	43	110	141	SAYLA	0	193	13	KOTKASIM	-26
33	136	BHINMAL	42	110	150	CHIRAWA	0	193	125	JHOTWARA	-26
33	171	ITAWA	42	110	167	NADOTI	0	193	228	BHINDER	-26
35	184	PARBATSAR	36	110	172	LADPURA	0	193	230	GIRWA	-26
36	139	RANIWARA	35			**LOW (0 to -25)**		197	142	BAKANI	-27
36	166	KARAULI	35	117	39	BARMER	-1	198	26	GHATOL	-29
36	180	MAKRANA	35	117	79	BHAINSRORGARH	-1	199	4	KEKRI	-31
39	210	FATEHPUR	32	117	111	KARANPUR	-1	199	63	SAHARA	-31
40	106	DUNGARPUR	31	117	131	VIRATNAGAR	-1	199	77	BEGUN	-31
40	188	JAITARAN	31	117	137	JALOR	-1	202	17	RAJGARH	-32
42	71	HINDOLI	29	117	145	KHANPUR	-1	203	197	BHIM	-33
42	86	NIMBAHERA	29	117	234	KOTRA	-1	204	203	BAMANWAS	-34
44	45	SIWANA	28	124	1	ARAIN	-3	205	7	PISANGAN	-35
44	112	PADAMPUR	28	124	16	NIMRANA	-3	205	102	DHAULPUR	-35
46	49	KUMHER	27	124	21	TIJARA	-3	205	144	JHALRAPATAN	-35
		MEDIUM (0-25)		124	119	AMBER	-3	208	8	SRINAGAR	-39
47	177	JAYAL	24	124	146	MANOHARTHANA	-3	208	117	HANUMANGARH	-39
48	135	AHORE	23	124	186	BALI	-3	210	61	MANDALGARH	-40
48	193	ROHAT	23	124	190	PALI	-3	211	178	KUCHAMAN	-41
50	48	KAMAN	22	124	195	SUMERPUR	-3	212	6	MASOODA	-43
50	100	BARI	22	132	113	RAISINGHNAGAR	-4	213	30	TALWARA	-44
52	42	DHORIMANNA	21	132	212	LACHHMANGARH	-4	214	57	HURDA	-46
53	173	SANGOD	19	132	216	ABU ROAD	-4	214	65	SUWANA	-46
54	33	BARAN	18	135	43	SHEO	-5	214	221	DEOLI	-46
54	67	DUNGARGARH	18	135	78	BHADESAR	-5	217	75	ARNOD	-47
54	94	TARANAGAR	18	135	218	REODAR	-5			**EXTREMELY LOW (< - 50)**	
54	170	CHECHAT	18	135	226	UNIARA	-5	218	54	WEIR	-55
58	138	JASWANTPURA	17	135	231	GOGUNDA	-5	218	199	KHAMNOR	-55
58	194	SOJAT	17	140	32	ATRU	-6	220	55	ASIND	-56
60	22	UMREN	16	140	159	BILARA	-6	221	62	RAIPUR	-58
60	29	SAJJANGARH	16	140	187	DESURI	-6	221	222	MALPURA	-58
60	104	ASPUR	16	143	92	SARDARSHAHAR	-7	223	70	NOKHA	-61
60	168	SAPOTRA	16	143	114	SADULSHAHAR	-7	224	68	KOLAYAT	-63
60	205	GANGAPUR	16	143	132	JAISALMER	-7	225	60	MANDAL	-66
65	87	PRATAPGARH	15	143	134	SANKRA	-7	225	69	LUNKARANSAR	-66
65	99	SIKRAI	15	143	158	BHOPALGARH	-7	227	2	BHINAY	-75
65	105	BICHHIWARA	15	143	201	RAILMAGRA	-7	228	24	BAGIDORA	-78
65	140	SANCHORE	15	149	76	BARI SADRI	-8	229	12	KISHANGARH BAS	-82
65	152	KHETRI	15	149	126	KOTPUTLI	-8	229	59	KOTRI	-82
65	198	DEOGARH	15	149	148	ALSISAR	-8	231	80	BHOPALSAGAR	-83
65	211	KHANDELA	15	149	151	JHUNJHUNUN	-8	232	58	JAHAZPUR	-85
72	41	CHOHTAN	14	149	154	SURAJGARH	-8	233	64	SHAHPURA	-97
72	107	SAGWARA	14	149	204	BONLI	-8	234	85	KAPASAN	-103
72	215	SRI MADHOPUR	14	149	219	SHEOGANJ	-8	235	156	BALESAR	-115
75	160	LUNI	13	156	9	BANSURE	-9	236	66	BIKANER	-122
75	182	MUNDWA	13	156	18	RAMGARH	-9	237	164	SHERGARH	-132
75	189	KHARCHI/MARWAR JUN	13	156	34	CHHABRA	-9				
75	206	KHANDAR	13	159	28	PEEPALKHOONT	-10				
75	220	SIROHI	13	159	143	DAG	-10				

BOLD: Equal/Above Average Panchayat Samities (AAPs)

Source: Annex 12.1

ANNEX-12.5

RANKING OF PSS BY POPULATION SERVED PER MEDICAL INSTITUTION: RAJASTHAN 1991

(Descending Order)

RANK	PANCHAYAT SAMITIES P.CODE	PANCHAYAT SAMITIES NAME	POP. SERVED PER MEDICAL INSTITUTION
1	2	3	4
		VERY HIGH/WORST (>5000)	
1	**109**	**ANUPGARH**	**10503**
2	**48**	**KAMAN**	**9076**
3	**157**	**BAP**	**7973**
4	**139**	**RANIWARA**	**7695**
5	**111**	**KARANPUR**	**7682**
6	**12**	**KISHANGARH BAS**	**7560**
7	**92**	**SARDARSHAHAR**	**6998**
8	**86**	**NIMBAHERA**	**6893**
9	**103**	**RAJAKHERA**	**6566**
10	**136**	**BHINMAL**	**6356**
11	**97**	**LALSOT**	**6248**
12	**119**	**AMBER**	**6223**
13	**161**	**MANDOR**	**6218**
14	**117**	**HANUMANGARH**	**6184**
15	**43**	**SHEO**	**6078**
16	**40**	**BAYTOO**	**6071**
17	**95**	**BANDIKUI**	**6015**
18	**82**	**CHITTAURGARH**	**5901**
19	**165**	**HINDAUN**	**5774**
20	**41**	**CHOHTAN**	**5704**
21	**140**	**SANCHORE**	**5539**
22	**211**	**KHANDELA**	**5518**
23	**47**	**DEEG**	**5462**
24	**21**	**TIJARA**	**5400**
25	**14**	**LACHHMANGARH**	**5343**
26	**50**	**NADBAI**	**5320**
27	**162**	**OSIAN**	**5283**
28	**118**	**NOHAR**	**5270**
29	**96**	**DAUSA**	**5199**
30	**53**	**SEWAR**	**5137**
31	**149**	**BUHANA**	**5084**
32	**154**	**SURAJGARH**	**5044**
33	**101**	**BASERI**	**5040**
		HIGH/WORSE (4000-5000)	
34	**114**	**SADULSHAHAR**	**4961**
35	**22**	**UMREN**	**4931**
36	**198**	**DEOGARH**	**4908**
37	**39**	**BARMER**	**4890**
38	**70**	**NOKHA**	**4858**
39	**38**	**BALOTRA**	**4803**
40	**67**	**DUNGARGARH**	**4771**
41	**46**	**BAYANA**	**4744**
42	**81**	**CHHOTI SADRI**	**4717**
43	**125**	**JHOTWARA**	**4685**
44	**115**	**SURATGARH**	**4650**
45	**18**	**RAMGARH**	**4619**
46	**155**	**UDAIPURWATI**	**4574**
47	**66**	**BIKANER**	**4550**
48	**9**	**BANSURE**	**4544**
49	**215**	**SRI MADHOPUR**	**4533**
50	**116**	**BHADRA**	**4519**
51	**110**	**GANGANAGAR**	**4511**
52	**182**	**MUNDWA**	**4492**
53	**183**	**NAGAUR**	**4424**
54	**19**	**RENI**	**4406**
55	**158**	**BHOPALGARH**	**4348**
56	**224**	**TODARAISINGH**	**4323**
57	**131**	**VIRATNAGAR**	**4313**
58	**42**	**DHORIMANNA**	**4310**
59	**44**	**SINDHARI**	**4303**
60	**16**	**NIMRANA**	**4298**
61	**90**	**RAJGARH**	**4257**
62	**168**	**SAPOTRA**	**4241**
63	**69**	**LUNKARANSAR**	**4227**
64	**99**	**SIKRAI**	**4227**
65	**122**	**DUDU**	**4213**
66	**102**	**DHAULPUR**	**4189**
67	**142**	**BAKANI**	**4188**
68	**15**	**MANDAWAR**	**4154**
69	**204**	**BONLI**	**4113**
70	**120**	**BASSI**	**4096**
71	**145**	**KHANPUR**	**4087**
72	**234**	**KOTRA**	**4077**
73	**193**	**ROHAT**	**4065**
74	**51**	**NAGAR PAHARI**	**4037**
75	**229**	**DHARIAWAD**	**4001**
		MEDIUM/NORMAL (3000-4000)	
76	**79**	**BHAINSRORGARH**	**3996**
77	**37**	**SHAHBAD**	**3954**
78	**210**	**FATEHPUR**	**3934**
79	**176**	**DIDWANA**	**3933**
80	**223**	**NIWAI**	**3928**
81	**214**	**PIPRALI**	**3908**
82	**180**	**MAKRANA**	**3907**
83	**213**	**NEEM KA THANA**	**3890**
84	**185**	**RIYAN**	**3863**
85	**11**	**KATHUMAR**	**3854**
86	**166**	**KARAULI**	**3783**
87	**8**	**SRINAGAR**	**3782**
88	**153**	**NAWALGARH**	**3777**
89	**94**	**TARANAGAR**	**3761**
90	**74**	**TALERA**	**3755**
91	**129**	**SANGANER**	**3753**
92	**152**	**KHETRI**	**3746**
93	**124**	**JAMWA RAMGARH**	**3742**
94	**127**	**PHAGI**	**3727**
95	**108**	**SIMALWARA**	**3718**
96	**55**	**ASIND**	**3715**
97	**160**	**LUNI**	**3705**
98	**226**	**UNIARA**	**3694**
99	**49**	**KUMHER**	**3687**
100	**29**	**SAJJANGARH**	**3685**
101	**169**	**TODABHIM**	**3676**
102	**83**	**DUNGLA**	**3669**
103	**13**	**KOTKASIM**	**3668**
104	**150**	**CHIRAWA**	**3665**
105	**203**	**BAMANWAS**	**3644**
106	**173**	**SANGOD**	**3605**
107	**20**	**THANAGAZI**	**3603**
108	**146**	**MANOHARTHANA**	**3601**
109	**126**	**KOTPUTLI**	**3552**
110	**34**	**CHHABRA**	**3536**
111	**172**	**LADPURA**	**3536**
112	**212**	**LACHHMANGARH**	**3533**
113	**222**	**MALPURA**	**3533**
114	**227**	**BARGAON**	**3528**
115	**220**	**SIROHI**	**3527**
116	**216**	**ABU ROAD**	**3505**
117	**91**	**RATANGARH**	**3485**
118	**218**	**REODAR**	**3477**
119	**93**	**SUJANGARH**	**3471**
120	**72**	**KESHORAIPATAN**	**3469**
121	**100**	**BARI**	**3452**
122	**123**	**GOVINDGARH**	**3450**
123	**71**	**HINDOLI**	**3447**
124	**78**	**BHADESAR**	**3444**
125	**174**	**SULTANPUR**	**3440**
126	**163**	**PHALODI**	**3435**
127	**178**	**KUCHAMAN**	**3418**
128	**68**	**KOLAYAT**	**3401**
129	141	SAYLA	3373
130	28	PEEPALKHOONT	3352
131	177	JAYAL	3334
132	184	PARBATSAR	3322
133	181	MERTA	3315
134	112	PADAMPUR	3308
135	6	MASOODA	3266
136	225	TONK	3249
137	1	ARAIN	3226
138	230	GIRWA	3221
139	27	KUSHALGARH	3184
140	151	JHUNJHUNUN	3146
141	188	JAITARAN	3136
142	128	SAMBHAR	3120
143	33	BARAN	3110
144	156	BALESAR	3110
145	170	CHECHAT	3093
146	65	SUWANA	3089
147	31	ANTA	3086
148	179	LADNU	3079
149	219	SHEOGANJ	3072
150	194	SOJAT	3055
		LOW/BETTER (2000-3000)	
151	45	SIWANA	2989
152	148	ALSISAR	2966
153	17	RAJGARH	2962
154	76	BARI SADRI	2958
155	10	BEHROR	2950
156	207	SAWAI MADHOPUR	2937
157	3	JAWAJA	2928
158	190	PALI	2915
159	84	GANGRAR	2886
160	236	SALUMBAR	2886
161	138	JASWANTPURA	2874
162	201	RAILMAGRA	2866
163	144	JHALRAPATAN	2860
164	121	CHAKSU	2857
165	130	SHAHPURA	2848
166	206	KHANDAR	2842
167	73	NAINWA	2829
168	164	SHERGARH	2827
169	167	NADOTI	2824
170	35	CHHIPABAROD	2814
171	217	PINDWARA	2783
172	135	AHORE	2781
173	36	KISHANGANJ	2778
174	159	BILARA	2777
175	54	WEIR	2768
176	175	DEGANA	2756
177	87	PRATAPGARH	2745
178	52	RUPBAS	2731
179	205	GANGAPUR	2716
180	171	ITAWA	2705
181	195	SUMERPUR	2682
182	132	JAISALMER	2677
183	26	GHATOL	2667
184	105	BICHHIWARA	2659
185	228	BHINDER	2647
186	133	SAM	2637
187	209	DHOND	2635
188	189	KHARCHI/MARWAR JUN.	2625
189	221	DEOLI	2607
190	197	BHIM	2602
191	147	PIRAWA	2599
192	134	SANKRA	2571
193	235	MAVLI	2570
194	208	DANTA RAMGARH	2549
195	186	BALI	2529
196	233	KHERWARA	2520
197	89	CHURU	2516
198	85	KAPASAN	2513
199	23	ANANDPURI	2497
200	191	RAIPUR	2493
201	98	MAHWA	2486
202	231	GOGUNDA	2484
203	200	KUMBHALGARH	2467
204	202	RAJSAMAND	2467
205	237	SARADA	2409
206	196	AMET	2308
207	137	JALOR	2297
208	30	TALWARA	2280
209	7	PISANGAN	2227
210	24	BAGIDORA	2214
211	107	SAGWARA	2170
212	143	DAG	2167
213	64	SHAHPURA	2154
214	106	DUNGARPUR	2149
215	113	RAISINGHNAGAR	2147
216	75	ARNOD	2126
217	2	BHINAY	2123
218	4	KEKRI	2091
219	58	JAHAZPUR	2076
220	59	KOTRI	2065
221	60	MANDAL	2041
		VERY LOW/BEST (<2000)	
222	77	BEGUN	1996
223	5	KISHANGARH	1970
224	63	SAHARA	1935
225	199	KHAMNOR	1900
226	62	RAIPUR	1878
227	232	JHADOL	1861
228	32	ATRU	1821
229	25	GARHI	1812
230	192	RANI STATION	1810
231	56	BANERA	1797
232	88	RASHMI	1778
233	80	BHOPALSAGAR	1732
234	104	ASPUR	1665
235	187	DESURI	1581
236	61	MANDALGARH	1564
237	57	HURDA	1280
		RAJASTHAN	**3377**
		% AGE OF AAPs	**54.00**

BOLD: Equal/Above Average Panchayat Samities (AAPs)

Source: General Annex II.

ANNEX-12.6

RANKING OF PSS BY POPULATION SERVED PER MEDICAL INSTITUTION: RAJASTHAN, 2001

(Descending Order)

RANK	PANCHAYAT SAMITIES P.CODE	PANCHAYAT SAMITIES NAME	POP. SERVED PER MEDICAL INSTITUTION
1	2	3	4
		VERY HIGH/WORST (>=5000)	
1	146	MANOHARTHANA	8496
2	103	RAJAKHERA	7672
3	48	KAMAN	7576
4	95	BANDIKUI	7217
5	34	CHHABRA	7105
6	13	KOTKASIM	6923
7	70	NOKHA	6496
8	46	BAYANA	6388
9	76	BARI SADRI	6346
10	51	NAGAR PAHARI	6219
11	18	RAMGARH	6117
12	85	KAPASAN	6038
13	66	BIKANER	5856
14	161	MANDOR	5602
15	99	SIKRAI	5573
16	21	TIJARA	5159
17	14	LACHHMANGARH	5133
18	157	BAP	5074
19	97	LALSOT	5027
		HIGH/WORSE (4000-5000)	
20	47	DEEG	4996
21	136	BHINMAL	4862
22	109	ANUPGARH	4858
23	68	KOLAYAT	4831
24	53	SEWAR	4790
25	12	KISHANGARH BAS	4786
26	33	BARAN	4688
27	144	JHALRAPATAN	4679
28	78	BHADESAR	4669
29	139	RANIWARA	4667
30	119	AMBER	4597
31	117	HANUMANGARH	4585
32	9	BANSURE	4561
33	36	KISHANGANJ	4507
34	215	SRI MADHOPUR	4489
35	101	BASERI	4484
36	22	UMREN	4436
37	35	CHHIPABAROD	4409
38	121	CHAKSU	4355
39	50	NADBAI	4354
40	163	PHALODI	4338
41	74	TALERA	4315
42	165	HINDAUN	4302
43	164	SHERGARH	4280
44	123	GOVINDGARH	4243
45	102	DHAULPUR	4233
46	142	BAKANI	4231
47	16	NIMRANA	4216
48	41	CHOHTAN	4181
49	81	CHHOTI SADRI	4169
50	98	MAHWA	4167
51	127	PHAGI	4144
52	226	UNIARA	4141
53	17	RAJGARH	4135
54	42	DHORIMANNA	4114
55	11	KATHUMAR	4071
56	131	VIRATNAGAR	4047
57	69	LUNKARANSAR	4025
57	140	SANCHORE	4025
		MEDIUM/NORMAL (3000-4000)	
59	147	PIRAWA	3998
60	75	ARNOD	3995
61	141	SAYLA	3984
62	198	DEOGARH	3893
63	54	WEIR	3888
64	170	CHECHAT	3885
65	43	SHEO	3799
66	38	BALOTRA	3794
67	96	DAUSA	3776
68	166	KARAULI	3773
69	126	KOTPUTLI	3745
70	143	DAG	3715
71	39	BARMER	3663
72	171	ITAWA	3620
73	162	OSIAN	3608
74	10	BEHROR	3577
75	124	JAMWA RAMGARH	3573
76	86	NIMBAHERA	3563
77	31	ANTA	3542
78	20	THANAGAZI	3518
79	154*	SURAJGARH	3516

RANK	PANCHAYAT SAMITIES P.CODE	PANCHAYAT SAMITIES NAME	POP. SERVED PER MEDICAL INSTITUTION
1	2	3	4
80	92	SARDARSHAHAR	3484
81	216	ABU ROAD	3479
82	176	DIDWANA	3476
83	222	MALPURA	3469
84	60	MANDAL	3465
84	182	MUNDWA	3465
86	205	GANGAPUR	3446
87	174	SULTANPUR	3422
88	118	NOHAR	3418
89	8	SRINAGAR	3403
90	116	BHADRA	3394
91	180	MAKRANA	3384
92	93	SUJANGARH	3376
93	79	BHAINSRORGARH	3349
94	32	ATRU	3343
95	212	LACHHMANGARH	3339
96	115	SURATGARH	3334
97	204	BONLI	3331
98	120	BASSI	3328
99	128	SAMBHAR	3326
100	160	LUNI	3273
101	177	JAYAL	3260
102	152	KHETRI	3250
103	52	RUPBAS	3248
104	122	DUDU	3244
105	45	SIWANA	3237
106	82	CHITTAURGARH	3230
107	181	MERTA	3218
108	158	BHOPALGARH	3211
109	191	RAIPUR	3193
110	217	PINDWARA	3186
111	71	HINDOLI	3155
112	90	RAJGARH	3146
113	172	LADPURA	3145
114	213	NEEM KA THANA	3139
115	178	KUCHAMAN	3118
116	221	DEOLI	3078
117	6	MASOODA	3069
118	234	KOTRA	3058
119	84	GANGRAR	3057
120	202	RAJSAMAND	3055
121	40	BAYTOO	3048
122	15	MANDAWAR	3040
123	183	NAGAUR	3038
124	59	KOTRI	3035
125	19	RENI	3033
126	72	KESHORAIPATAN	3028
127	113	RAISINGHNAGAR	3026
128	153	NAWALGARH	3023
		LOW/BETTER (2000-3000)	
129	203	BAMANWAS	2989
130	49	KUMHER	2983
131	206	KHANDAR	2944
132	150	CHIRAWA	2939
133	7	PISANGAN	2919
134	168	SAPOTRA	2906
135	169	TODABHIM	2897
136	73	NAINWA	2893
137	125	JHOTWARA	2869
138	167	NADOTI	2866
139	24	BAGIDORA	2850
140	130	SHAHPURA	2836
141	224	TODARAISINGH	2824
142	145	KHANPUR	2789
142	229	DHARIAWAD	2789
144	44	SINDHARI	2751
145	184	PARBATSAR	2741
146	155	UDAIPURWATI	2736
147	207	SAWAI MADHOPUR	2732
148	211	KHANDELA	2732
149	223	NIWAI	2710
150	188	JAITARAN	2709
151	37	SHAHBAD	2704
152	112	PADAMPUR	2697
153	5	KISHANGARH	2693
154	100	BARI	2689
155	156	BALESAR	2680
156	26	GHATOL	2678
157	1	ARAIN	2668
158	233	KHERWARA	2649
159	83	DUNGLA	2646
159	197	BHIM	2646

RANK	PANCHAYAT SAMITIES P.CODE	PANCHAYAT SAMITIES NAME	POP. SERVED PER MEDICAL INSTITUTION
1	2	3	4
161	3	JAWAJA	2632
162	65	SUWANA	2603
163	80	BHOPALSAGAR	2596
164	196	AMET	2593
165	134	SANKRA	2584
166	173	SANGOD	2578
167	67	DUNGARGARH	2575
167	129	SANGANER	2575
169	138	JASWANTPURA	2568
170	110	GANGANAGAR	2558
171	2	BHINAY	2543
172	87	PRATAPGARH	2515
173	190	PALI	2498
174	4	KEKRI	2472
175	185	RIYAN	2461
176	105	BICHHIWARA	2434
177	135	AHORE	2429
178	214	PIPRALI	2424
179	195	SUMERPUR	2421
180	64	SHAHPURA	2403
181	137	JALOR	2397
182	230	GIRWA	2396
183	227	BARGAON	2381
184	30	TALWARA	2375
185	235	MAVLI	2368
186	29	SAJJANGARH	2359
187	218	REODAR	2338
188	193	ROHAT	2332
188	231	GOGUNDA	2332
190	189	KHARCHI/MARWAR JUN.	2326
191	23	ANANDPURI	2317
192	210	FATEHPUR	2303
193	186	BALI	2298
194	228	BHINDER	2294
195	55	ASIND	2290
196	57	HURDA	2277
197	179	LADNU	2258
198	108	SIMALWARA	2253
199	111	KARANPUR	2241
200	159	BILARA	2202
201	133	SAM	2201
202	94	TARANAGAR	2188
202	114	SADULSHAHAR	2188
204	148	ALSISAR	2176
205	225	TONK	2174
206	208	DANTA RAMGARH	2167
207	209	DHOND	2164
208	25	GARHI	2140
209	132	JAISALMER	2130
210	149	BUHANA	2129
211	175	DEGANA	2112
212	151	JHUNJHUNUN	2103
213	28	PEEPALKHOONT	2072
214	58	JAHAZPUR	2071
215	27	KUSHALGARH	2014
216	199	KHAMNOR	2005
217	63	SAHARA	2001
		VERY LOW/BEST (<2000)	
218	88	RASHMI	1982
219	62	RAIPUR	1962
220	56	BANERA	1931
221	237	SARADA	1912
222	187	DESURI	1893
223	89	CHURU	1879
224	236	SALUMBAR	1855
225	91	RATANGARH	1838
226	61	MANDALGARH	1834
227	106	DUNGARPUR	1815
228	219	SHEOGANJ	1812
229	232	JHADOL	1811
230	107	SAGWARA	1705
231	77	BEGUN	1619
232	201	RAILMAGRA	1534
233	194	SOJAT	1513
234	192	RANI STATION	1459
235	200	KUMBHALGARH	1443
236	104	ASPUR	1347
237	220	SIROHI	1295
		RAJASTHAN	3042
		% AGE OF AAPs	51.05

BOLD: Equal Above Average Panchayat Samities (AAPs)
Source: General Annex VIII

ANNEX-12.7

RANKING OF PSS BY AREA SERVED PER MEDICAL INSTITUTION: RAJASTHAN 1991

(Descending Order)

RANK	PANCHAYAT SAMITIES P.CODE	PANCHAYAT SAMITIES NAME	AREA SERVED PER MEDICAL INSTITUTION (sq. kms)
1	2	3	4
		VERY HIGH / WORST (>40)	
1	**133**	**SAM**	**586.42**
2	**132**	**JAISALMER**	**428.32**
3	**157**	**BAP**	**340.86**
4	**43**	**SHEO**	**330.82**
5	**68**	**KOLAYAT**	**187.66**
6	**66**	**BIKANER**	**175.39**
7	**69**	**LUNKARANSAR**	**167.95**
8	**92**	**SARDARSHAHAR**	**152.58**
9	**40**	**BAYTOO**	**129.12**
10	**109**	**ANUPGARH**	**126.56**
11	**134**	**SANKRA**	**121.92**
12	**39**	**BARMER**	**108.95**
13	**41**	**CHOHTAN**	**108.88**
14	**67**	**DUNGARGARH**	**107.24**
15	**38**	**BALOTRA**	**97.13**
16	**70**	**NOKHA**	**87.62**
17	**79**	**BHAINSRORGARH**	**85.61**
18	**44**	**SINDHARI**	**79.89**
19	**118**	**NOHAR**	**78.27**
20	**162**	**OSIAN**	**72.15**
21	**161**	**MANDOR**	**70.51**
22	**193**	**ROHAT**	**70.22**
23	**37**	**SHAHBAD**	**69.91**
24	**163**	**PHALODI**	**68.89**
25	**111**	**KARANPUR**	**67.54**
26	**115**	**SURATGARH**	**64.26**
27	**182**	**MUNDWA**	**64.24**
28	**140**	**SANCHORE**	**64.01**
29	**42**	**DHORIMANNA**	**63.53**
30	**139**	**RANIWARA**	**61.50**
31	**136**	**BHINMAL**	**58.16**
32	**183**	**NAGAUR**	**58.06**
33	**94**	**TARANAGAR**	**54.03**
34	**86**	**NIMBAHERA**	**50.79**
35	**164**	**SHERGARH**	**49.38**
36	**158**	**BHOPALGARH**	**48.43**
37	**224**	**TODARAISINGH**	**46.93**
38	**93**	**SUJANGARH**	**46.36**
39	**168**	**SAPOTRA**	**45.63**
40	**91**	**RATANGARH**	**45.62**
41	**198**	**DEOGARH**	**45.32**
42	**156**	**BALESAR**	**45.22**
43	**190**	**PALI**	**44.71**
44	**160**	**LUNI**	**44.06**
45	**45**	**SIWANA**	**44.05**
46	**116**	**BHADRA**	**42.83**
47	**90**	**RAJGARH**	**42.26**
48	**172**	**LADPURA**	**42.18**
		HIGH / WORSE (30-40)	
49	**177**	**JAYAL**	**39.40**
50	**81**	**CHHOTI SADRI**	**38.44**
51	**194**	**SOJAT**	**37.84**
52	**117**	**HANUMANGARH**	**37.69**
53	**216**	**ABU ROAD**	**37.31**
54	**234**	**KOTRA**	**37.23**
55	**36**	**KISHANGANJ**	**37.19**
56	**122**	**DUDU**	**37.10**
57	**220**	**SIROHI**	**36.35**
58	**82**	**CHITTAURGARH**	**35.39**
59	**1**	**ARAIN**	**35.35**
60	**114**	**SADULSHAHAR**	**35.35**
61	**226**	**UNIARA**	**35.23**
62	**219**	**SHEOGANJ**	**34.32**
63	**179**	**LADNU**	**34.28**
64	**222**	**MALPURA**	**34.26**
65	**185**	**RIYAN**	**33.50**
66	101	BASERI	33.38
67	74	TALERA	33.03
68	48	KAMAN	32.74
69	181	MERTA	32.49
70	145	KHANPUR	32.42
71	206	KHANDAR	32.20
72	89	CHURU	31.83
73	127	PHAGI	31.81
74	210	FATEHPUR	30.92
75	173	SANGOD	30.77
76	71	HINDOLI	30.43
77	229	DHARIAWAD	30.19
		MEDIUM / NORMAL (20-30)	
78	188	JAITARAN	30.00
79	72	KESHORAIPATAN	29.93
80	141	SAYLA	29.78
81	135	AHORE	29.56
82	223	NIWAI	29.43
83	159	BILARA	29.40
84	138	JASWANTPURA	28.89
85	218	REODAR	28.60
86	142	BAKANI	28.56
87	97	LALSOT	28.47
88	35	CHHIPABAROD	28.43
89	176	DIDWANA	28.21
90	12	KISHANGARH BAS	28.08
91	154	SURAJGARH	27.91
92	166	KARAULI	27.72
93	28	PEEPALKHOONT	27.66
94	180	MAKRANA	27.66
95	225	TONK	27.22
96	34	CHHABRA	27.02
97	17	RAJGARH	26.56
98	20	THANAGAZI	26.51
99	73	NAINWA	26.51
100	55	ASIND	26.43
101	146	MANOHARTHANA	26.36
102	112	PADAMPUR	26.33
103	175	DEGANA	26.03
104	22	UMREN	25.71
105	8	SRINAGAR	25.65
106	119	AMBER	25.44
107	174	SULTANPUR	25.33
108	204	BONLI	25.24
109	46	BAYANA	24.99
110	184	PARBATSAR	24.90
111	103	RAJAKHERA	24.87
112	217	PINDWARA	24.75
113	87	PRATAPGARH	24.62
114	230	GIRWA	24.53
115	211	KHANDELA	24.49
116	178	KUCHAMAN	23.94
117	221	DEOLI	23.76
118	110	GANGANAGAR	23.75
119	189	KHARCHI/MARWAR JUN.	23.57
120	33	BARAN	23.56
121	83	DUNGLA	23.50
122	100	BARI	23.35
123	144	JHALRAPATAN	23.32
124	31	ANTA	23.31
125	186	BALI	23.22
126	21	TIJARA	22.98
127	212	LACHHMANGARH	22.82
128	96	DAUSA	22.70
129	6	MASOODA	22.44
130	137	JALOR	22.44
131	77	BEGUN	22.27
132	203	BAMANWAS	22.08
133	113	RAISINGHNAGAR	21.92
134	84	GANGRAR	21.37
135	47	DEEG	21.32
136	195	SUMERPUR	21.21
137	207	SAWAI MADHOPUR	20.89
138	78	BHADESAR	20.79
139	2	BHINAY	20.61
140	155	UDAIPURWATI	20.27
141	64	SHAHPURA	20.13
142	27	KUSHALGARH	20.03
143	147	PIRAWA	20.02
		LOW / BETTER (10-20)	
144	124	JAMWA RAMGARH	19.83
145	65	SUWANA	19.82
146	170	CHECHAT	19.77
147	148	ALSISAR	19.66
148	95	BANDIKUI	19.38
149	149	BUHANA	19.22
150	214	PIPRALI	18.99
151	171	ITAWA	18.87
152	14	LACHHMANGARH	18.75
153	191	RAIPUR	18.61
154	165	HINDAUN	18.57
155	227	BARGAON	18.51
156	9	BANSURE	18.46
157	213	NEEM KA THANA	18.26
158	76	BARI SADRI	18.25
159	232	JHADOL	18.08
160	4	KEKRI	18.06
161	131	VIRATNAGAR	18.03
162	50	NADBAI	17.99
163	167	NADOTI	17.94
164	108	SIMALWARA	17.91
165	5	KISHANGARH	17.85
166	231	GOGUNDA	17.79
167	143	DAG	17.66
168	18	RAMGARH	17.63
169	53	SEWAR	17.62
170	125	JHOTWARA	17.50
171	121	CHAKSU	17.43
172	197	BHIM	16.94
173	200	KUMBHALGARH	16.87
174	85	KAPASAN	16.64
175	152	KHETRI	16.59
176	236	SALUMBAR	16.46
177	151	JHUNJHUNUN	16.41
178	19	RENI	16.33
179	75	ARNOD	16.31
180	196	AMET	16.30
181	120	BASSI	16.18
182	3	JAWAJA	16.15
183	58	JAHAZPUR	16.15
184	59	KOTRI	16.10
185	60	MANDAL	16.04
186	128	SAMBHAR	16.01
187	201	RAILMAGRA	15.55
188	7	PISANGAN	15.43
189	228	BHINDER	15.39
190	187	DESURI	15.35
191	215	SRI MADHOPUR	15.31
192	237	SARADA	15.19
193	15	MANDAWAR	14.80
194	192	RANI STATION	14.67
195	32	ATRU	14.57
196	63	SAHARA	14.39
197	29	SAJJANGARH	14.38
198	150	CHIRAWA	14.38
199	129	SANGANER	14.24
200	209	DHOND	14.04
201	61	MANDALGARH	13.92
202	153	NAWALGARH	13.86
203	51	NAGAR PAHARI	13.82
204	56	BANERA	13.81
205	208	DANTA RAMGARH	13.77
206	233	KHERWARA	13.63
207	62	RAIPUR	13.56
208	16	NIMRANA	13.51
209	126	KOTPUTLI	13.27
210	13	KOTKASIM	13.25
211	99	SIKRAI	13.23
212	202	RAJSAMAND	12.94
213	11	KATHUMAR	12.84
214	49	KUMHER	12.58
215	235	MAVLI	12.48
216	169	TODABHIM	12.44
217	88	RASHMI	12.15
218	102	DHAULPUR	12.03
219	205	GANGAPUR	11.94
220	26	GHATOL	11.87
221	105	BICHHIWARA	10.97
222	123	GOVINDGARH	10.92
223	57	HURDA	10.83
224	80	BHOPALSAGAR	10.76
225	30	TALWARA	10.42
226	199	KHAMNOR	10.08
227	23	ANANDPURI	10.05
		VERY LOW / BEST (<10)	
228	54	WEIR	9.93
229	106	DUNGARPUR	9.28
230	130	SHAHPURA	9.07
231	52	RUPBAS	8.84
232	10	BEHROR	8.63
233	24	BAGIDORA	8.32
234	107	SAGWARA	8.27
235	98	MAHWA	8.03
236	104	ASPUR	7.86
237	25	GARHI	6.77
RAJASTHAN			**33.39**
		% AGE OF AAPs	**27.40**

BOLD: Equal/Above Average Panchayat Samities (AAPs)

Source: General Annex II.

ANNEX-12.8

RANKING OF PSS BY AREA SERVED PER MEDICAL INSTITUTION: RAJASTHAN, 2001

(Descending Order)

RANK	PANCHAYAT SAMITIES P.CODE	PANCHAYAT SAMITIES NAME	AREA SERVED PER MEDICAL INSTITUTION (sq. kms.)
1	2	3	4
		VERY HIGH/WORST (>40)	
1	133	SAM	335.10
2	132	JAISALMER	214.16
3	68	KOLAYAT	170.20
4	157	BAP	142.94
5	43	SHEO	140.77
6	66	BIKANER	139.76
7	69	LUNKARANSAR	115.07
8	70	NOKHA	87.62
9	134	SANKRA	85.73
10	163	PHALODI	61.09
11	41	CHOHTAN	60.49
12	92	SARDARSHAHAR	59.60
13	115	SURATGARH	59.24
14	39	BARMER	58.67
15	79	BHAINSRORGARH	57.08
16	34	CHHABRA	55.98
17	38	BALOTRA	55.50
18	164	SHERGARH	51.97
19	146	MANOHARTHANA	48.56
20	36	KISHANGANJ	48.35
21	161	MANDOR	47.01
22	40	BAYTOO	46.78
23	42	DHORIMANNA	43.74
24	67	DUNGARGARH	42.29
25	109	ANUPGARH	41.21
26	118	NOHAR	40.23
		HIGH/WORSE (30-40)	
27	182	MUNDWA	38.32
28	37	SHAHBAD	36.71
29	44	SINDHARI	36.23
30	190	PALI	36.02
31	162	OSIAN	35.76
32	140	SANCHORE	35.39
33	136	BHINMAL	35.20
34	93	SUJANGARH	34.61
35	85	KAPASAN	34.47
36	76	BARI SADRI	33.89
37	183	NAGAUR	32.17
38	193	ROHAT	31.92
39	74	TALERA	31.38
40	226	UNIARA	30.83
41	177	JAYAL	30.26
42	144	JHALRAPATAN	30.21
43	45	SIWANA	30.03
		MEDIUM/NORMAL (20-30)	
44	198	DEOGARH	29.46
45	17	RAJGARH	28.83
45	81	CHHOTI SADRI	28.83
47	127	PHAGI	28.55
48	156	BALESAR	28.52
49	35	CHHIPABAROD	28.43
50	172	LADPURA	28.42
51	160	LUNI	28.32
52	222	MALPURA	28.22
53	139	RANIWARA	28.11
54	33	BARAN	27.85
55	158	BHOPALGARH	27.67
56	141	SAYLA	27.54
57	46	BAYANA	26.66
58	206	KHANDAR	26.52
59	116	BHADRA	26.36
60	216	ABU ROAD	26.00
61	90	RAJGARH	25.85
62	94	TARANAGAR	25.84
63	113	RAISINGHNAGAR	25.30
64	224	TODARAISINGH	25.27
65	143	DAG	25.12
66	142	BAKANI	24.60
67	168	SAPOTRA	24.53
68	181	MERTA	24.51
69	1	ARAIN	24.04
70	78	BHADESAR	23.50
71	75	ARNOD	23.38
72	147	PIRAWA	23.28
73	103	RAJAKHERA	22.88
74	170	CHECHAT	22.67
75	32	ATRU	22.62
76	221	DEOLI	22.46
77	71	HINDOLI	22.32
78	191	BASERI	22.25
79	31	ANTA	22.20
80	114	SADULSHAHAR	22.16
81	122	DUDU	22.09
82	135	AHORE	21.87
83	72	KESHORAIPATAN	21.82
84	86	NIMBAHERA	21.39
85	138	JASWANTPURA	21.38
86	73	NAINWA	21.11
87	121	CHAKSU	20.72
87	174	SULTANPUR	20.72
89	166	KARAULI	20.67
90	171	ITAWA	20.63
91	60	MANDAL	20.27
92	13	KOTKASIM	20.26
		LOW/BETTER (10-20)	
93	2	BHINAY	19.94
94	48	KAMAN	19.88
95	234	KOTRA	19.86
96	20	THANAGAZI	19.64
97	217	PINDWARA	19.63
98	176	DIDWANA	19.61
99	179	LADNU	19.59
100	5	KISHANGARH	19.42
101	59	KOTRI	19.39
102	89	CHURU	19.25
103	137	JALOR	19.18
104	84	GANGRAR	19.16
105	91	RATANGARH	19.10
106	180	MAKRANA	18.75
107	112	PADAMPUR	18.72
108	188	JAITARAN	18.69
109	173	SANGOD	18.35
110	159	BILARA	18.29
111	64	SHAHPURA	18.18
112	8	SRINAGAR	17.95
113	87	PRATAPGARH	17.85
114	189	KHARCHI/MARWAR JUN.	17.83
115	111	KARANPUR	17.62
116	4	KEKRI	17.43
117	212	LACHHMANGARH	17.41
118	191	RAIPUR	17.31
119	18	RAMGARH	17.14
120	186	BALI	17.12
121	145	KHANPUR	17.09
122	97	LALSOT	17.08
123	185	RIYAN	16.98
124	22	UMREN	16.97
125	223	NIWAI	16.89
126	6	MASOODA	16.83
127	178	KUCHAMAN	16.70
128	51	NAGAR PAHARI	16.36
129	95	BANDIKUI	16.24
130	219	SHEOGANJ	16.22
131	175	DEGANA	16.19
132	229	DHARIAWAD	16.13
133	204	BONLI	16.02
134	195	SUMERPUR	16.00
135	47	DEEG	15.82
136	194	SOJAT	15.80
137	184	PARBATSAR	15.75
138	82	CHITTAURGARH	15.65
139	154	SURAJGARH	15.63
140	207	SAWAI MADHOPUR	15.60
141	57	HURDA	15.43
142	187	DESURI	15.35
143	77	BEGUN	15.20
144	225	TONK	15.06
145	7	PISANGAN	14.86
145	196	AMET	14.86
147	117	HANUMANGARH	14.85
148	119	AMBER	14.73
148	210	FATEHPUR	14.73
150	167	NADOTI	14.68
151	21	TIJARA	14.63
152	203	BAMANWAS	14.58
153	83	DUNGLA	14.52
154	218	REODAR	14.49
155	124	JAMWA RAMGARH	14.45
156	12	KISHANGARH BAS	14.44
157	80	BHOPALSAGAR	14.22
158	230	GIRWA	14.20
159	100	BARI	14.18
160	9	BANSURE	14.14
161	14	LACHHMANGARH	14.07
162	231	GOGUNDA	13.41
163	232	JHADOL	13.35
164	99	SIKRAI	13.23
165	55	ASIND	13.22
166	65	SUWANA	13.21
166	128	SAMBHAR	13.21
168	53	SEWAR	13.09
169	197	BHIM	13.03
170	63	SAHARA	12.92
171	61	MANDALGARH	12.77
172	58	JAHAZPUR	12.76
173	131	VIRATNAGAR	12.73
174	96	DAUSA	12.61
175	28	PEEPALKHOONT	12.50
176	227	BARGAON	12.46
177	125	JHOTWARA	12.42
178	205	GANGAPUR	12.40
179	110	GANGANAGAR	12.39
180	202	RAJSAMAND	12.38
181	56	BANERA	12.30
182	152	KHETRI	12.06
182	215	SRI MADHOPUR	12.06
184	62	RAIPUR	11.99
185	88	RASHMI	11.83
186	213	NEEM KA THANA	11.75
187	50	NADBAI	11.67
188	148	ALSISAR	11.49
189	129	SANGANER	11.45
190	220	SIROHI	11.24
191	233	KHERWARA	11.22
192	228	BHINDER	11.19
193	16	NIMRANA	11.13
194	54	WEIR	11.08
195	3	JAWAJA	11.03
196	98	MAHWA	11.01
197	11	KATHUMAR	10.87
197	126	KOTPUTLI	10.87
199	192	RANI STATION	10.45
200	165	HINDAUN	10.35
201	123	GOVINDGARH	10.25
		VERY LOW/BEST (<10)	
202	211	KHANDELA	9.80
203	151	JHUNJHUNUN	9.77
204	235	MAVLI	9.74
205	237	SARADA	9.71
206	155	UDAIPURWATI	9.66
207	209	DHOND	9.41
208	150	CHIRAWA	9.40
209	214	PIPRALI	9.38
210	102	DHAULPUR	9.31
211	27	KUSHALGARH	9.29
212	153	NAWALGARH	9.24
213	208	DANTA RAMGARH	9.22
214	120	BASSI	9.14
215	26	GHATOL	9.11
216	15	MANDAWAR	8.88
217	19	RENI	8.71
218	236	SALUMBAR	8.70
219	10	BEHROR	8.63
220	108	SIMALWARA	8.54
221	200	KUMBHALGARH	8.53
222	49	KUMHER	8.47
223	30	TALWARA	8.34
224	24	BAGIDORA	8.32
225	52	RUPBAS	8.29
226	169	TODABHIM	7.80
227	105	BICHHIWARA	7.69
228	201	RAILMAGRA	7.56
229	23	ANANDPURI	7.12
230	29	SAJJANGARH	7.06
231	199	KHAMNOR	6.92
232	149	BUHANA	6.81
233	130	SHAHPURA	6.38
234	25	GARHI	6.34
235	106	DUNGARPUR	6.05
236	107	SAGWARA	5.41
237	104	ASPUR	5.05
		RAJASTHAN	23.6
		% AGE OF AAPs	29.11

BOLD: Equal/Above Average Panchayat Samities (AAPs)
Source: General Annex VIII.

ANNEX-12.9

RANKING OF PSS BY POPULATION SERVED PER BED: RAJASTHAN, 2001

(Descending Order)

RANK	PANCHAYAT SAMITIES P.CODE	PANCHAYAT SAMITIES NAME	POPULATION SERVED PER BED
1	2	3	4
		VERY HIGH/WORST (>4000)	
1	53	**SEWAR**	6985
2	8	**SRINAGAR**	6544
3	132	**JAISALMER**	5325
4	5	**KISHANGARH**	5116
5	39	**BARMER**	4960
6	125	**JHOTWARA**	4941
7	144	**JHALRAPATAN**	4902
8	163	**PHALODI**	4789
9	82	**CHITTAURGARH**	4666
10	38	**BALOTRA**	4427
11	183	**NAGAUR**	4408
12	64	**SHAHPURA**	4381
13	207	**SAWAI MADHOPUR**	4316
14	33	**BARAN**	4298
15	120	**BASSI**	4253
16	161	**MANDOR**	4202
17	184	**PARBATSAR**	4143
18	92	**SARDARSHAHAR**	4129
19	22	**UMREN**	4107
20	18	**RAMGARH**	4078
21	109	**ANUPGARH**	4017
		HIGH/WORSE (3000-4000)	
22	102	**DHAULPUR**	3977
23	152	**KHETRI**	3972
24	51	**NAGAR PAHARI**	3939
25	99	**SIKRAI**	3922
26	204	**BONLI**	3886
27	87	**PRATAPGARH**	3870
28	97	**LALSOT**	3809
29	126	**KOTPUTLI**	3808
30	190	**PALI**	3747
31	166	**KARAULI**	3710
32	117	**HANUMANGARH**	3569
33	103	**RAJAKHERA**	3552
34	48	**KAMAN**	3536
35	168	**SAPOTRA**	3523
36	122	**DUDU**	3494
37	217	**PINDWARA**	3422
38	101	**BASERI**	3363
39	50	**NADBAI**	3356
40	44	**SINDHARI**	3285
41	165	**HINDAUN**	3280
42	169	**TODABHIM**	3235
43	11	**KATHUMAR**	3207
44	52	**RUPBAS**	3199
45	40	**BAYTOO**	3187
46	128	**SAMBHAR**	3175
47	20	**THANAGAZI**	3166
48	71	**HINDOLI**	3155
49	95	**BANDIKUI**	3105
50	74	**TALERA**	3082
51	123	**GOVINDGARH**	3064
52	65	**SUWANA**	3037
53	105	**BICHHIWARA**	3027
		MEDIUM/NORMAL (2000-3000)	
54	127	**PHAGI**	2993
55	60	**MANDAL**	2992
56	121	**CHAKSU**	2984
57	43	**SHEO**	2976
58	30	**TALWARA**	2968
59	110	**GANGANAGAR**	2942
60	141	**SAYLA**	2933
61	162	**OSIAN**	2932
62	55	**ASIND**	2914
63	41	**CHOHTAN**	2894
64	130	**SHAHPURA**	2836
65	116	**BHADRA**	2828
66	231	**GOGUNDA**	2807
67	29	**SAJJANGARH**	2801
68	69	**LUNKARANSAR**	2786
69	206	**KHANDAR**	2780
70	234	**KOTRA**	2780
71	203	**BAMANWAS**	2767
72	226	**UNIARA**	2761
73	212	**LACHHMANGARH**	2736
74	68	**KOLAYAT**	2734
75	164	**SHERGARH**	2711
76	137	**JALOR**	2690
77	135	**AHORE**	2687
78	70	**NOKHA**	2686
79	9	**BANSURE**	2679
80	177	**JAYAL**	2678
81	115	**SURATGARH**	2667
82	35	**CHHIPABAROD**	2664
83	214	**PIPRALI**	2642
84	175	**DEGANA**	2640
85	167	**NADOTI**	2627
86	157	**BAP**	2622
87	218	**REODAR**	2617
88	106	**DUNGARPUR**	2612
89	158	**BHOPALGARH**	2594
90	171	**ITAWA**	2594
91	49	**KUMHER**	2585
92	21	**TIJARA**	2579
93	227	**BARGAON**	2579
94	6	**MASOODA**	2574
95	66	**BIKANER**	2567
96	221	**DEOLI**	2565
97	145	**KHANPUR**	2556
98	142	**BAKANI**	2539
99	230	**GIRWA**	2529
100	19	**RENI**	2528
101	28	**PEEPALKHOONT**	2521
102	119	**AMBER**	2520
103	140	**SANCHORE**	2516
104	179	**LADNU**	2508
105	36	**KISHANGANJ**	2504
106	176	**DIDWANA**	2500
107	209	**DHOND**	2499
108	185	**RIYAN**	2495
109	180	**MAKRANA**	2465
110	24	**BAGIDORA**	2455
111	13	**KOTKASIM**	2452
112	155	**UDAIPURWATI**	2451
113	173	**SANGOD**	2449
114	182	**MUNDWA**	2439
115	149	**BUHANA**	2433
116	211	**KHANDELA**	2428
117	205	**GANGAPUR**	2422
118	46	**BAYANA**	2395
119	16	**NIMRANA**	2389
120	147	**PIRAWA**	2387
121	81	**CHHOTI SADRI**	2383
122	148	**ALSISAR**	2357
123	233	**KHERWARA**	2355
124	32	**ATRU**	2353
125	15	**MANDAWAR**	2352
126	2	**BHINAY**	2350
127	67	**DUNGARGARH**	2344
128	23	ANANDPURI	2317
129	118	NOHAR	2315
130	133	SAM	2311
131	139	RANIWARA	2269
132	12	KISHANGARH BAS	2263
133	26	GHATOL	2258
134	154	SURAJGARH	2254
135	178	KUCHAMAN	2253
136	160	LUNI	2246
137	78	BHADESAR	2237
138	45	SIWANA	2226
139	114	SADULSHAHAR	2222
140	93	SUJANGARH	2221
141	75	ARNOD	2219
142	100	BARI	2215
143	56	BANERA	2213
144	156	BALESAR	2177
145	191	RAIPUR	2167
146	189	KHARCHI/MARWAR JUN.	2160
147	124	JAMWA RAMGARH	2156
148	83	DUNGLA	2142
149	193	ROHAT	2137
150	236	SALUMBAR	2137
151	72	KESHORAIPATAN	2126
152	150	CHIRAWA	2123
153	84	GANGRAR	2110
154	94	TARANAGAR	2097
155	174	SULTANPUR	2091
156	219	SHEOGANJ	2076
157	134	SANKRA	2067
158	42	DHORIMANNA	2057
159	14	LACHHMANGARH	2053
160	224	TODARAISINGH	2039
161	3	JAWAJA	2024
162	1	ARAIN	2021
		LOW/BETTER (1000-2000)	
163	194	SOJAT	1999
164	229	DHARIAWAD	1996
165	129	SANGANER	1989
166	232	JHADOL	1978
167	192	RANI STATION	1972
168	7	PISANGAN	1970
169	113	RAISINGHNAGAR	1967
170	237	SARADA	1965
171	138	JASWANTPURA	1946
172	47	DEEG	1936
173	222	MALPURA	1923
174	104	ASPUR	1922
175	223	NIWAI	1922
176	199	KHAMNOR	1916
177	90	RAJGARH	1910
178	108	SIMALWARA	1884
179	27	KUSHALGARH	1878
180	153	NAWALGARH	1876
181	54	WEIR	1872
182	98	MAHWA	1866
183	197	BHIM	1859
184	25	GARHI	1856
185	151	JHUNJHUNUN	1841
186	201	RAILMAGRA	1841
187	112	PADAMPUR	1839
188	196	AMET	1837
189	200	KUMBHALGARH	1824
190	181	MERTA	1816
191	213	NEEM KA THANA	1801
192	235	MAVLI	1798
193	88	RASHMI	1793
194	131	VIRATNAGAR	1779
195	59	KOTRI	1770
196	91	RATANGARH	1757
197	146	MANOHARTHANA	1755
198	220	SIROHI	1744
199	73	NAINWA	1698
200	86	NIMBAHERA	1692
201	17	RAJGARH	1683
202	208	DANTA RAMGARH	1681
203	79	BHAINSRORGARH	1675
204	215	SRI MADHOPUR	1648
205	195	SUMERPUR	1643
206	96	DAUSA	1638
207	143	DAG	1608
208	136	BHINMAL	1593
209	89	CHURU	1585
210	62	RAIPUR	1562
211	186	BALI	1532
212	61	MANDALGARH	1526
213	111	KARANPUR	1516
214	80	BHOPALSAGAR	1514
215	210	FATEHPUR	1512
216	225	TONK	1481
217	34	CHHABRA	1463
218	188	JAITARAN	1460
219	198	DEOGARH	1442
220	107	SAGWARA	1311
221	170	CHECHAT	1270
222	228	BHINDER	1261
223	4	KEKRI	1258
224	85	KAPASAN	1243
225	31	ANTA	1240
226	76	BARI SADRI	1201
227	187	DESURI	1189
228	37	SHAHBAD	1176
229	216	ABU ROAD	1172
230	57	HURDA	1153
231	58	JAHAZPUR	1141
232	77	BEGUN	1109
233	159	BILARA	1101
234	10	BEHROR	1073
		VERY LOW/BEST (<1000)	
235	202	RAJSAMAND	997
236	63	SAHARA	891
237	172	LADPURA	851
		RAJASTHAN	**2342**
		%AGE OF AAPs	**53.59**

BOLD: Equal/Above Average Panchayat Samities (AAPs)

Source: General Annex IX.

ANNEX-12.10

RANKING OF PSS BY POPULATION SERVED PER DOCTOR: RAJASTHAN, 2001

(Descending Order)

RANK	PANCHAYAT SAMITIES P.CODE	PANCHAYAT SAMITIES NAME	POPULATION SERVED PER DOCTOR
1	2	3	4
		VERY HIGH/WORST (>25,000)	
1	8	**SRINAGAR**	56714
2	207	**SAWAI MADHOPUR**	53953
3	53	**SEWAR**	41910
4	134	**SANKRA**	33075
5	163	**PHALODI**	32842
6	121	**CHAKSU**	32228
7	234	**KOTRA**	30584
8	48	**KAMAN**	30306
9	64	**SHAHPURA**	29791
10	125	**JHOTWARA**	29649
11	44	**SINDHARI**	29568
12	51	**NAGAR PAHARI**	29541
13	168	**SAPOTRA**	29064
14	101	**BASERI**	28825
15	221	**DEOLI**	28212
16	23	**ANANDPURI**	27802
17	184	**PARBATSAR**	26630
18	102	**DHAULPUR**	26246
19	157	**BAP**	26215
20	119	**AMBER**	26203
21	144	**JHALRAPATAN**	25734
22	5	**KISHANGARH**	25579
23	28	**PEEPALKHOONT**	25212
24	117	**HANUMANGARH**	25125
		HIGH/WORSE (20,000-25,000)	
25	18	**RAMGARH**	24469
26	169	**TODABHIM**	24262
27	55	**ASIND**	24043
28	152	**KHETRI**	23830
29	39	**BARMER**	23808
30	13	**KOTKASIM**	23537
31	40	**BAYTOO**	23372
32	204	**BONLI**	23315
33	133	**SAM**	23113
34	183	**NAGAUR**	22482
35	92	**SARDARSHAHAR**	22298
36	22	**UMREN**	22179
37	161	**MANDOR**	21608
38	74	**TALERA**	21576
39	203	**BAMANWAS**	21347
40	103	**RAJAKHERA**	21312
41	132	**JAISALMER**	21300
42	122	**DUDU**	20963
43	128	**SAMBHAR**	20953
44	114	**SADULSHAHAR**	20947
45	26	**GHATOL**	20940
46	126	**KOTPUTLI**	20770
47	217	**PINDWARA**	20534
48	38	**BALOTRA**	20430
49	127	**PHAGI**	20201
50	50	**NADBAI**	20139
51	87	**PRATAPGARH**	20123
		MEDIUM/NORMAL (15,000-20,000)	
52	123	**GOVINDGARH**	19699
53	24	**BAGIDORA**	19637
54	30	**TALWARA**	19430
55	156	**BALESAR**	19353
56	97	**LALSOT**	19336
57	99	**SIKRAI**	19253
58	52	**RUPBAS**	19195
59	162	**OSIAN**	19190
60	95	**BANDIKUI**	19073
61	142	**BAKANI**	19041
62	71	**HINDOLI**	18929
63	68	**KOLAYAT**	18886
64	88	**RASHMI**	18832
65	131	**VIRATNAGAR**	18765
66	129	**SANGANER**	18757
67	233	**KHERWARA**	18164
68	105	**BICHHIWARA**	18163
68	109	**ANUPGARH**	18163
70	130	**SHAHPURA**	18150
71	140	**SANCHORE**	18006
72	60	**MANDAL**	17955
73	9	**BANSURE**	17863
74	43	**SHEO**	17854
75	115	**SURATGARH**	17782
76	227	**BARGAON**	17686
77	120	**BASSI**	17665
78	141	**SAYLA**	17596
79	218	**REODAR**	17534
80	165	**HINDAUN**	17494
81	21	**TIJARA**	17460
82	70	**NOKHA**	17459
83	41	**CHOHTAN**	17366
84	33	**BARAN**	17190
85	19	**RENI**	17061
86	66	**BIKANER**	17036
87	36	**KISHANGANJ**	16902
88	158	**BHOPALGARH**	16860
89	82	**CHITTAURGARH**	16796
90	12	**KISHANGARH BAS**	16750
91	69	**LUNKARANSAR**	16719
92	11	**KATHUMAR**	16284
93	164	**SHERGARH**	16266
94	209	**DHOND**	16148
95	14	**LACHHMANGARH**	16131
96	135	**AHORE**	16122
97	79	**BHAINSRORGARH**	16076
98	177	**JAYAL**	16067
99	110	**GANGANAGAR**	16047
100	35	**CHHIPABAROD**	15982
101	6	**MASOODA**	15960
102	32	**ATRU**	15880
103	179	**LADNU**	15803
104	106	**DUNGARPUR**	15671
105	211	**KHANDELA**	15611
106	27	**KUSHALGARH**	15441
107	78	**BHADESAR**	15342
108	145	**KHANPUR**	15337
109	15	**MANDAWAR**	15199
110	231	**GOGUNDA**	15158
111	212	**LACHHMANGARH**	15156
112	100	**BARI**	15060
113	206	**KHANDAR**	15014
114	176	**DIDWANA**	15002
		LOW/BETTER (10,000-15,000)	
115	83	**DUNGLA**	14996
116	190	**PALI**	14990
117	75	**ARNOD**	14980
118	29	**SAJJANGARH**	14940
119	65	**SUWANA**	14909
120	59	**KOTRI**	14870
121	166	**KARAULI**	14841
122	84	**GANGRAR**	14773
123	42	**DHORIMANNA**	14761
124	46	**BAYANA**	14741
125	151	**JHUNJHUNUN**	14724
126	226	**UNIARA**	14723
127	214	**PIPRALI**	14719
128	116	**BHADRA**	14705
129	137	**JALOR**	14647
130	118	**NOHAR**	14630
131	229	**DHARIAWAD**	14543
132	80	**BHOPALSAGAR**	14535
133	16	NIMRANA	14333
134	160	LUNI	14319
135	81	CHHOTI SADRI	14295
136	61	MANDALGARH	14281
137	45	SIWANA	14243
138	148	ALSISAR	14142
139	182	MUNDWA	14109
140	49	KUMHER	14102
141	47	DEEG	14078
142	236	SALUMBAR	14044
143	150	CHIRAWA	13895
144	232	JHADOL	13844
145	205	GANGAPUR	13785
146	149	BUHANA	13627
147	139	RANIWARA	13612
148	20	THANAGAZI	13570
149	154	SURAJGARH	13525
150	173	SANGOD	13359
151	93	SUJANGARH	13327
152	56	BANERA	13278
153	237	SARADA	13261
154	147	PIRAWA	13223
155	136	BHINMAL	13197
156	25	GARHI	13196
157	124	JAMWA RAMGARH	13165
158	7	PISANGAN	13137
159	73	NAINWA	13019
160	191	RAIPUR	13000
161	171	ITAWA	12971
162	2	BHINAY	12926
163	138	JASWANTPURA	12841
164	185	RIYAN	12831
165	223	NIWAI	12715
166	76	BARI SADRI	12692
167	175	DEGANA	12672
168	167	NADOTI	12609
169	196	AMET	12595
170	146	MANOHARTHANA	12417
171	104	ASPUR	12301
172	181	MERTA	12229
173	67	DUNGARGARH	12188
174	112	PADAMPUR	12136
175	235	MAVLI	12134
176	1	ARAIN	12126
177	108	SIMALWARA	12055
178	225	TONK	12021
179	230	GIRWA	11980
180	200	KUMBHALGARH	11941
181	222	MALPURA	11795
182	155	UDAIPURWATI	11764
183	174	SULTANPUR	11584
184	193	ROHAT	11400
185	213	NEEM KA THANA	11323
186	113	RAISINGHNAGAR	11238
187	228	BHINDER	11213
188	178	KUCHAMAN	11173
189	90	RAJGARH	11142
190	224	TODARAISINGH	11013
191	63	SAHARA	10894
192	189	KHARCHI/MARWAR JUN.	10673
193	197	BHIM	10583
194	85	KAPASAN	10566
195	62	RAIPUR	10544
196	3	JAWAJA	10527
197	180	MAKRANA	10509
198	220	SIROHI	10466
199	194	SOJAT	10393
200	54	WEIR	10110
201	208	DANTA RAMGARH	10084
202	96	DAUSA	10071
203	94	TARANAGAR	10067
		VERY LOW/BEST (<10,000)	
204	219	SHEOGANJ	9966
205	98	MAHWA	9954
206	192	RANI STATION	9682
207	170	CHECHAT	9434
208	72	KESHORAIPATAN	9401
209	111	KARANPUR	9372
210	201	RAILMAGRA	9203
211	57	HURDA	9109
212	37	SHAHBAD	9012
213	216	ABU ROAD	8832
214	195	SUMERPUR	8625
215	153	NAWALGARH	8371
216	186	BALI	8355
217	17	RAJGARH	8040
218	89	CHURU	8009
219	58	JAHAZPUR	7990
220	86	NIMBAHERA	7964
221	91	RATANGARH	7905
222	77	BEGUN	7847
223	215	SRI MADHOPUR	7814
224	188	JAITARAN	7789
225	107	SAGWARA	7707
226	34	CHHABRA	7652
227	4	KEKRI	7417
228	10	BEHROR	6975
229	143	DAG	6966
230	210	FATEHPUR	6910
231	187	DESURI	6816
232	31	ANTA	6468
233	199	KHAMNOR	6385
234	202	RAJSAMAND	5855
235	159	BILARA	5310
236	172	LADPURA	5168
237	198	DEOGARH	4867
		RAJASTHAN	**14445**
		% AGE OF AAPs	**55.70**

BOLD: Equal/Above Average Panchayat Samities (AAPs)

Source: General Annex IX

ANNEX - 12.11

RANKING OF PSS BY SEX-RATIO (0-6 POPULATION): RAJASTHAN, 2001

(Descending Order)

RANK	P.CODE	PANCHAYAT SAMITIES NAME	SEX-RATIO
1	2	3	4
		VERY HIGH (>1000)	
1	27	**KUSHALGARH**	1007
		HIGH (950-1000)	
2	56	**BANERA**	996
2	234	**KOTRA**	996
4	23	**ANANDPURI**	990
4	232	**JHADOL**	990
6	28	**PEEPALKHOONT**	987
7	29	**SAJJANGARH**	983
8	105	**BICHHIWARA**	978
8	108	**SIMALWARA**	978
10	229	**DHARIAWAD**	972
11	61	**MANDALGARH**	970
11	216	**ABU ROAD**	970
13	60	**MANDAL**	969
14	24	**BAGIDORA**	968
14	63	**SAHARA**	968
16	164	**SHERGARH**	966
16	231	**GOGUNDA**	966
18	62	**RAIPUR**	965
19	55	**ASIND**	964
20	233	**KHERWARA**	963
21	196	**AMET**	962
22	64	**SHAHPURA**	961
23	59	**KOTRI**	960
23	75	**ARNOD**	960
25	143	**DAG**	958
26	30	**TALWARA**	955
27	36	**KISHANGANJ**	954
27	106	**DUNGARPUR**	954
27	230	**GIRWA**	954
30	26	**GHATOL**	953
31	77	**BEGUN**	951
32	1	**ARAIN**	950
32	6	**MASOODA**	950
32	146	**MANOHARTHANA**	950
		MEDIUM (900-950)	
35	85	**KAPASAN**	949
35	237	**SARADA**	949
37	222	**MALPURA**	948
38	179	**LADNU**	947
38	197	**BHIM**	947
38	202	**RAJSAMAND**	947
41	2	**BHINAY**	946
41	76	**BARI SADRI**	946
41	147	**PIRAWA**	946
41	217	**PINDWARA**	946
45	88	**RASHMI**	945
45	186	**BALI**	945
47	42	**DHORIMANNA**	944
47	107	**SAGWARA**	944
47	200	**KUMBHALGARH**	944
47	201	**RAILMAGRA**	944
51	65	**SUWANA**	943
52	171	**ITAWA**	942
52	191	**RAIPUR**	942
54	25	**GARHI**	941
54	78	**BHADESAR**	941
54	87	**PRATAPGARH**	941
54	218	**REODAR**	941
54	236	**SALUMBAR**	941
59	96	**DAUSA**	940
60	125	**JHOTWARA**	938
61	92	**SARDARSHAHAR**	937
62	38	**BALOTRA**	936
62	81	**CHHOTI SADRI**	936
62	189	**KHARCHI/MARWAR JUN.**	936
62	224	**TODARAISINGH**	936
66	145	**KHANPUR**	935
67	4	**KEKRI**	934
68	41	**CHOHTAN**	933
68	67	**DUNGARGARH**	933
68	142	**BAKANI**	933
68	170	**CHECHAT**	933
68	225	**TONK**	933
73	82	**CHITTAURGARH**	932
73	160	**LUNI**	932
73	221	**DEOLI**	932
76	137	**JALOR**	931
76	194	**SOJAT**	931
78	57	**HURDA**	930
78	198	**DEOGARH**	930

RANK	P.CODE	PANCHAYAT SAMITIES NAME	SEX-RATIO
1	2	3	4
80	97	**LALSOT**	929
80	228	**BHINDER**	929
82	70	**NOKHA**	928
82	72	**KESHORAIPATAN**	928
82	104	**ASPUR**	928
82	136	**BHINMAL**	928
82	141	**SAYLA**	928
82	144	**JHALRAPATAN**	928
82	227	**BARGAON**	928
89	5	**KISHANGARH**	927
89	80	**BHOPALSAGAR**	927
89	128	**SAMBHAR**	927
89	162	**OSIAN**	927
93	177	**JAYAL**	926
93	183	**NAGAUR**	926
95	58	**JAHAZPUR**	925
95	140	**SANCHORE**	925
95	163	**PHALODI**	925
98	44	**SINDHARI**	924
98	190	**PALI**	924
100	7	**PISANGAN**	923
100	45	**SIWANA**	923
100	93	**SUJANGARH**	923
100	131	**VIRATNAGAR**	923
100	182	**MUNDWA**	923
105	159	**BILARA**	922
105	188	**JAITARAN**	922
105	235	**MAVLI**	922
108	69	**LUNKARANSAR**	921
108	124	**JAMWA RAMGARH**	921
108	127	**PHAGI**	921
108	156	**BALESAR**	921
112	39	**BARMER**	920
112	172	**LADPURA**	920
112	176	**DIDWANA**	920
112	192	**RANI STATION**	920
112	223	**NIWAI**	920
117	34	**CHHABRA**	919
117	37	**SHAHBAD**	919
117	66	**BIKANER**	919
117	74	**TALERA**	919
117	203	**BAMANWAS**	919
122	83	**DUNGLA**	918
122	135	**AHORE**	918
122	158	**BHOPALGARH**	918
125	84	**GANGRAR**	917
125	175	**DEGANA**	917
127	20	**THANAGAZI**	916
127	94	**TARANAGAR**	916
127	119	**AMBER**	916
127	157	**BAP**	916
131	12	**KISHANGARH BAS**	915
131	32	**ATRU**	915
131	35	**CHHIPABAROD**	915
131	40	**BAYTOO**	915
131	187	**DESURI**	915
136	120	**BASSI**	914
136	180	**MAKRANA**	914
136	193	**ROHAT**	914
139	79	BHAINSRORGARH	912
139	122	DUDU	912
139	199	KHAMNOR	912
142	3	JAWAJA	911
142	71	HINDOLI	911
142	138	JASWANTPURA	911
142	204	BONLI	911
146	33	BARAN	910
147	18	RAMGARH	909
147	22	UMREN	909
147	48	KAMAN	909
150	8	SRINAGAR	908
150	174	SULTANPUR	908
152	31	ANTA	907
153	73	NAINWA	906
153	121	CHAKSU	906
153	129	SANGANER	906
153	139	RANIWARA	906
153	161	MANDOR	906
153	173	SANGOD	906
159	123	GOVINDGARH	905
160	68	KOLAYAT	904
160	86	NIMBAHERA	904

RANK	P.CODE	PANCHAYAT SAMITIES NAME	SEX-RATIO
1	2	3	4
160	130	SHAHPURA	904
163	21	TIJARA	903
163	184	PARBATSAR	903
163	195	SUMERPUR	903
166	178	KUCHAMAN	902
166	207	SAWAI MADHOPUR	902
168	14	LACHHMANGARH	901
168	226	UNIARA	901
170	95	BANDIKUI	900
170	118	NOHAR	900
		LOW (850-900)	
172	9	BANSURE	899
172	17	RAJGARH	899
172	91	RATANGARH	899
172	185	RIYAN	899
172	219	SHEOGANJ	899
177	168	SAPOTRA	898
178	155	UDAIPURWATI	897
179	19	RENI	896
180	115	SURATGARH	895
180	213	NEEM KA THANA	895
182	181	MERTA	893
183	89	CHURU	892
183	211	KHANDELA	892
185	11	KATHUMAR	891
185	53	SEWAR	891
185	215	SRI MADHOPUR	891
188	51	NAGAR PAHARI	890
188	134	SANKRA	890
188	206	KHANDAR	890
191	208	DANTA RAMGARH	888
192	50	NADBAI	886
192	99	SIKRAI	886
192	109	ANUPGARH	886
192	205	GANGAPUR	886
196	90	RAJGARH	883
197	132	JAISALMER	880
198	47	DEEG	879
199	49	KUMHER	878
199	54	WEIR	878
201	148	ALSISAR	877
201	166	KARAULI	877
203	210	FATEHPUR	875
204	116	BHADRA	874
204	152	KHETRI	874
204	167	NADOTI	874
204	220	SIROHI	874
208	214	PIPRALI	873
209	98	MAHWA	871
209	102	DHAULPUR	871
211	212	LACHHMANGARH	867
212	126	KOTPUTLI	866
213	209	DHOND	865
214	101	BASERI	864
214	103	RAJAKHERA	864
216	117	HANUMANGARH	861
216	153	NAWALGARH	861
218	13	KOTKASIM	860
219	15	MANDAWAR	859
219	151	JHUNJHUNUN	859
221	46	BAYANA	858
221	52	RUPBAS	858
223	165	HINDAUN	856
224	150	CHIRAWA	854
225	113	RAISINGHNAGAR	853
226	43	SHEO	851
		VERY LOW (<850)	
227	16	NIMRANA	849
227	100	BARI	849
227	154	SURAJGARH	849
227	169	TODABHIM	849
231	10	BEHROR	842
232	112	PADAMPUR	841
233	149	BUHANA	840
234	133	SAM	837
235	111	KARANPUR	831
236	110	GANGANAGAR	823
237	114	SADULSHAHAR	814
		RAJASTHAN	**914**
		% AGE OF AAPs	**58.23**

BOLD: Equal/Above Average Panchayat Samities (AAPs)
Source : General Annex V.

ANNEX - 12.12

RANKING OF PSS BY SEX-RATIO (TOTAL POPULATION): RAJASTHAN, 2001

(Descending Order)

RANK	P.CODE	PANCHAYAT SAMITIES NAME	SEX-RATIO
1	2	3	4
		VERY HIGH (>1000)	
1	107	SAGWARA	1074
2	104	ASPUR	1071
3	63	SAHARA	1070
4	187	DESURI	1054
5	62	RAIPUR	1042
5	198	DEOGARH	1042
7	192	RANI STATION	1040
8	60	MANDAL	1033
8	200	KUMBHALGARH	1033
10	106	DUNGARPUR	1032
11	236	SALUMBAR	1025
12	197	BHIM	1024
13	88	RASHMI	1020
14	135	AHORE	1019
14	201	RAILMAGRA	1019
16	55	ASIND	1018
16	237	SARADA	1018
18	220	SIROHI	1013
19	186	BALI	1012
20	189	KHARCHI/MARWAR JUN.	1011
21	194	SOJAT	1009
22	199	KHAMNOR	1005
23	80	BHOPALSAGAR	1003
23	83	DUNGLA	1003
23	233	KHERWARA	1003
26	105	BICHHIWARA	1001
27	196	AMET	1000
		HIGH (950-1000)	
28	76	BARI SADRI	999
29	137	JALOR	997
30	108	SIMALWARA	996
31	138	JASWANTPURA	995
31	195	SUMERPUR	995
31	229	DHARIAWAD	995
34	210	FATEHPUR	994
35	85	KAPASAN	992
36	26	GHATOL	989
36	148	ALSISAR	989
38	27	KUSHALGARH	987
39	176	DIDWANA	985
39	191	RAIPUR	985
41	3	JAWAJA	983
41	24	BAGIDORA	983
41	56	BANERA	983
41	228	BHINDER	983
45	231	GOGUNDA	981
46	175	DEGANA	980
47	78	BHADESAR	979
47	179	LADNU	979
47	190	PALI	979
47	234	KOTRA	979
51	232	JHADOL	978
52	141	SAYLA	977
52	151	JHUNJHUNUN	977
54	25	GARHI	976
55	91	RATANGARH	975
55	235	MAVLI	975
57	136	BHINMAL	974
57	202	RAJSAMAND	974
59	29	SAJJANGARH	973
59	30	TALWARA	973
61	212	LACHHMANGARH	972
62	84	GANGRAR	971
63	75	ARNOD	970
64	86	NIMBAHERA	969
65	93	SUJANGARH	968
65	153	NAWALGARH	968
65	188	JAITARAN	968
68	28	PEEPALKHOONT	967
68	208	DANTA RAMGARH	967
70	81	CHHOTI SADRI	966
71	65	SUWANA	965
71	77	BEGUN	965
71	193	ROHAT	965
71	211	KHANDELA	965
75	23	ANANDPURI	964
75	219	SHEOGANJ	964
77	82	CHITTAURGARH	963
77	155	UDAIPURWATI	963
79	1	ARAIN	961
79	209	DHOND	961
81	230	GIRWA	960
82	2	BHINAY	959
82	89	CHURU	959
84	87	PRATAPGARH	958
84	150	CHIRAWA	958
84	177	JAYAL	958
87	4	KEKRI	957
87	180	MAKRANA	957
89	59	KOTRI	955
90	6	MASOODA	954
90	217	PINDWARA	954
92	92	SARDARSHAHAR	953
93	64	SHAHPURA	951
93	224	TODARAISINGH	951
95	214	PIPRALI	950
95	215	SRI MADHOPUR	950
		MEDIUM (900-950)	
97	57	HURDA	949
97	143	DAG	949
99	67	DUNGARGARH	947
99	182	MUNDWA	947
101	183	NAGAUR	945
101	218	REODAR	945
103	149	BUHANA	944
103	222	MALPURA	944
105	7	PISANGAN	943
105	158	BHOPALGARH	943
105	185	RIYAN	943
105	227	BARGAON	943
109	94	TARANAGAR	940
109	152	KHETRI	940
109	184	PARBATSAR	940
112	147	PIRAWA	939
113	140	SANCHORE	938
114	5	KISHANGARH	935
114	216	ABU ROAD	935
116	90	RAJGARH	933
116	128	SAMBHAR	933
116	139	RANIWARA	933
116	178	KUCHAMAN	933
120	221	DEOLI	932
120	225	TONK	932
122	159	BILARA	931
123	154	SURAJGARH	930
124	58	JAHAZPUR	929
124	61	MANDALGARH	929
126	160	LUNI	928
127	122	DUDU	927
127	142	BAKANI	927
129	16	NIMRANA	926
129	144	JHALRAPATAN	926
131	8	SRINAGAR	925
132	38	BALOTRA	924
132	44	SINDHARI	924
132	146	MANOHARTHANA	924
132	181	MERTA	924
132	213	NEEM KA THANA	924
137	162	OSIAN	923
138	45	SIWANA	922
139	36	KISHANGANJ	919
139	123	GOVINDGARH	919
139	223	NIWAI	919
142	15	MANDAWAR	918
142	127	PHAGI	918
144	10	BEHROR	917
144	31	ANTA	917
146	35	CHHIPABAROD	916
146	97	LALSOT	916
146	173	SANGOD	916
146	226	UNIARA	916
150	72	KESHORAIPATAN	915
150	121	CHAKSU	915
150	125	JHOTWARA	915
153	129	SANGANER	914
153	145	KHANPUR	914
153	156	BALESAR	914
153	163	PHALODI	914
157	70	NOKHA	913
157	113	RAISINGHNAGAR	913
157	174	SULTANPUR	913
160	42	DHORIMANNA	912
160	69	LUNKARANSAR	912
162	164	SHERGARH	911
163	73	NAINWA	910
163	120	BASSI	910
165	12	KISHANGARH BAS	909
165	131	VIRATNAGAR	909
165	161	MANDOR	909
168	124	JAMWA RAMGARH	908
169	13	KOTKASIM	907
169	96	DAUSA	907
171	74	TALERA	906
171	112	PADAMPUR	906
171	119	AMBER	906
171	126	KOTPUTLI	906
171	171	ITAWA	906
176	32	ATRU	905
176	170	CHECHAT	905
176	204	BONLI	905
179	9	BANSURE	904
179	33	BARAN	904
179	40	BAYTOO	904
179	207	SAWAI MADHOPUR	904
183	79	BHAINSRORGARH	903
183	118	NOHAR	903
183	172	LADPURA	903
186	20	THANAGAZI	902
186	130	SHAHPURA	902
188	71	HINDOLI	901
		LOW (850-900)	
189	95	BANDIKUI	899
189	99	SIKRAI	899
189	157	BAP	899
192	116	BHADRA	898
193	111	KARANPUR	897
194	37	SHAHBAD	896
195	18	RAMGARH	895
195	117	HANUMANGARH	895
197	34	CHHABRA	894
197	109	ANUPGARH	894
199	14	LACHHMANGARH	892
200	17	RAJGARH	890
201	167	NADOTI	889
202	66	BIKANER	888
203	22	UMREN	886
203	110	GANGANAGAR	886
205	48	KAMAN	883
206	19	RENI	882
206	203	BAMANWAS	882
208	68	KOLAYAT	877
209	51	NAGAR PAHARI	876
209	134	SANKRA	876
211	205	GANGAPUR	875
212	41	CHOHTAN	872
212	98	MAHWA	872
214	206	KHANDAR	871
215	11	KATHUMAR	868
216	21	TIJARA	860
217	169	TODABHIM	858
218	49	KUMHER	857
219	53	SEWAR	855
220	39	BARMER	853
221	114	SADULSHAHAR	851
		VERY LOW (<850)	
222	47	DEEG	849
222	168	SAPOTRA	849
224	54	WEIR	847
225	52	RUPBAS	843
225	165	HINDAUN	843
227	43	SHEO	842
228	50	NADBAI	840
229	115	SURATGARH	839
229	166	KARAULI	839
231	102	DHAULPUR	836
232	101	BASERI	825
233	103	RAJAKHERA	816
234	132	JAISALMER	811
235	46	BAYANA	807
236	100	BARI	796
237	133	SAM	787
		RAJASTHAN	930
		% AGE OF AAPs	51.90

BOLD: Equal/Above Average Panchayat Samities (AAPs)

Source: General Annex V.

ANNEX - 12.13

RANKING OF PSS BY FEMALE LITERACY RATE: RAJASTHAN, 2001

(Descending Order)

RANK	PANCHAYAT SAMITIES P.CODE	NAME	FLR
1	2	3	4
		VERY HIGH (>60)	
1	**10**	**BEHROR**	**72.18**
2	**155**	**UDAIPURWATI**	**67.95**
3	**149**	**BUHANA**	**64.48**
4	**151**	**JHUNJHUNUN**	**63.03**
5	**210**	**FATEHPUR**	**62.22**
6	**148**	**ALSISAR**	**61.72**
7	**94**	**TARANAGAR**	**61.68**
8	**212**	**LACHHMANGARH**	**61.57**
9	**150**	**CHIRAWA**	**61.32**
		HIGH (45-60)	
10	**90**	**RAJGARH**	**59.75**
11	**126**	**KOTPUTLI**	**59.70**
12	**211**	**KHANDELA**	**59.38**
13	**3**	**JAWAJA**	**58.02**
14	**165**	**HINDAUN**	**57.83**
15	**42**	**DHORIMANNA**	**56.72**
16	**154**	**SURAJGARH**	**55.94**
17	**208**	**DANTA RAMGARH**	**55.74**
18	**174**	**SULTANPUR**	**54.27**
19	**214**	**PIPRALI**	**54.18**
20	**153**	**NAWALGARH**	**53.78**
21	**173**	**SANGOD**	**53.14**
22	**113**	**RAISINGHNAGAR**	**53.13**
23	**89**	**CHURU**	**52.87**
23	**116**	**BHADRA**	**52.87**
25	**131**	**VIRATNAGAR**	**52.78**
26	**13**	**KOTKASIM**	**52.73**
27	**209**	**DHOND**	**52.47**
28	**15**	**MANDAWAR**	**52.37**
29	**170**	**CHECHAT**	**52.35**
30	**91**	**RATANGARH**	**51.80**
31	**110**	**GANGANAGAR**	**51.58**
32	**213**	**NEEM KA THANA**	**51.47**
33	**215**	**SRI MADHOPUR**	**51.28**
34	**227**	**BARGAON**	**50.66**
35	**118**	**NOHAR**	**50.61**
36	**112**	**PADAMPUR**	**50.58**
37	**152**	**KHETRI**	**50.40**
38	**128**	**SAMBHAR**	**50.35**
39	**111**	**KARANPUR**	**49.94**
40	**125**	**JHOTWARA**	**49.73**
41	**172**	**LADPURA**	**49.08**
42	**147**	**PIRAWA**	**49.01**
43	**93**	**SUJANGARH**	**48.74**
44	**117**	**HANUMANGARH**	**48.67**
45	**95**	**BANDIKUI**	**48.43**
46	**114**	**SADULSHAHAR**	**48.16**
47	**123**	**GOVINDGARH**	**47.39**
48	**52**	**RUPBAS**	**47.27**
49	**145**	**KHANPUR**	**47.17**
50	**50**	**NADBAI**	**46.83**
51	**130**	**SHAHPURA**	**46.69**
52	**53**	**SEWAR**	**46.66**
53	**176**	**DIDWANA**	**46.46**
54	**33**	**BARAN**	**46.45**
55	**44**	**SINDHARI**	**46.42**
56	**167**	**NADOTI**	**46.14**
57	**49**	**KUMHER**	**46.09**
58	**178**	**KUCHAMAN**	**45.52**
59	**16**	**NIMRANA**	**45.39**
60	**98**	**MAHWA**	**45.15**
61	**31**	**ANTA**	**45.01**
		MEDIUM (30-45)	
62	**180**	**MAKRANA**	**44.92**
63	**109**	**ANUPGARH**	**44.63**
64	**171**	**ITAWA**	**44.58**
65	**228**	**BHINDER**	**44.49**
66	**124**	**JAMWA RAMGARH**	**43.93**
67	**127**	**PHAGI**	**43.83**
68	**32**	**ATRU**	**43.82**
69	**99**	**SIKRAI**	**43.63**
70	**92**	**SARDARSHAHAR**	**43.60**
71	**45**	**SIWANA**	**43.56**
72	**232**	**JHADOL**	**43.43**
73	**129**	**SANGANER**	**43.38**
74	**40**	**BAYTOO**	**42.93**
75	**101**	**BASERI**	**42.82**
76	**179**	**LADNU**	**42.38**
77	**67**	**DUNGARGARH**	**41.71**
78	**236**	**SALUMBAR**	**41.44**
79	**230**	**GIRWA**	**40.48**
80	**115**	**SURATGARH**	**40.06**
81	**43**	**SHEO**	**39.80**
82	**169**	**TODABHIM**	**39.72**
83	**9**	**BANSURE**	**39.51**
84	**102**	**DHAULPUR**	**39.12**
85	**184**	**PARBATSAR**	**39.08**
86	**203**	**BAMANWAS**	**38.71**
87	**54**	**WEIR**	**38.31**
88	**51**	**NAGAR PAHARI**	**38.12**
89	**119**	**AMBER**	**38.11**
90	**103**	**RAJAKHERA**	**38.01**
91	**168**	**SAPOTRA**	**37.87**
92	144	JHALRAPATAN	37.66
93	38	BALOTRA	36.97
94	120	BASSI	36.96
95	72	KESHORAIPATAN	36.89
96	100	BARI	36.84
97	237	SARADA	36.82
98	122	DUDU	36.78
99	11	KATHUMAR	36.76
100	201	RAILMAGRA	36.75
101	39	BARMER	36.53
102	192	RANI STATION	36.43
103	47	DEEG	36.34
104	202	RAJSAMAND	36.25
105	12	KISHANGARH BAS	36.23
106	233	KHERWARA	36.17
107	96	DAUSA	36.15
108	166	KARAULI	35.89
109	36	KISHANGANJ	35.83
110	217	PINDWARA	35.65
111	87	PRATAPGARH	35.45
112	235	MAVLI	35.43
113	195	SUMERPUR	35.36
114	175	DEGANA	35.32
115	135	AHORE	35.28
116	19	RENI	35.18
117	41	CHOHTAN	35.17
118	25	GARHI	34.71
119	186	BALI	34.53
120	14	LACHHMANGARH	34.48
121	181	MERTA	34.44
122	74	TALERA	34.39
123	187	DESURI	34.37
123	205	GANGAPUR	34.37
125	199	KHAMNOR	34.30
126	160	LUNI	34.07
127	37	SHAHBAD	34.03
128	5	KISHANGARH	33.86
129	46	BAYANA	33.74
130	107	SAGWARA	33.61
131	197	BHIM	33.15
132	21	TIJARA	32.81
133	34	CHHABRA	32.77
134	219	SHEOGANJ	32.75
135	17	RAJGARH	32.72
136	224	TODARAISINGH	32.67
137	18	RAMGARH	32.60
138	86	NIMBAHERA	32.44
139	22	UMREN	32.40
140	'80	BHOPALSAGAR	32.38
141	231	GOGUNDA	32.32
142	97	LALSOT	32.30
142	185	RIYAN	32.30
144	177	JAYAL	32.19
145	57	HURDA	32.11
146	6	MASOODA	31.93
147	81	CHHOTI SADRI	31.89
148	56	BANERA	31.87
149	194	SOJAT	31.78
150	7	PISANGAN	31.64
151	82	CHITTAURGARH	31.58
152	198	DEOGARH	31.44
153	193	ROHAT	30.91
154	196	AMET	30.90
155	183	NAGAUR	30.80
156	204	BONLI	30.75
157	189	KHARCHI/MARWAR JUN.	30.73
158	220	SIROHI	30.51
159	69	LUNKARANSAR	30.34
160	8	SRINAGAR	30.31
161	218	REODAR	30.24
162	66	BIKANER	30.23
163	134	SANKRA	30.03
		LOW (15-30)	
164	75	ARNOD	29.72
165	73	NAINWA	29.68
166	58	JAHAZPUR	29.67
167	121	CHAKSU	29.66
167	191	RAIPUR	29.66
169	190	PALI	29.38
170	223	NIWAI	29.16
171	70	NOKHA	28.78
172	77	BEGUN	28.76
173	83	DUNGLA	28.62
174	139	RANIWARA	28.45
175	78	BHADESAR	28.33
176	1	ARAIN	28.30
177	84	GANGRAR	28.23
178	200	KUMBHALGARH	28.21
179	146	MANOHARTHANA	28.18
179	159	BILARA	28.18
181	79	BHAINSRORGARH	27.93
182	105	BICHHIWARA	27.92
183	132	JAISALMER	27.72
184	35	CHHIPABAROD	27.71
185	104	ASPUR	27.61
186	71	HINDOLI	27.60
187	143	DAG	27.58
188	106	DUNGARPUR	27.56
189	162	OSIAN	27.45
189	163	PHALODI	27.45
191	137	JALOR	27.19
192	188	JAITARAN	26.68
193	222	MALPURA	26.49
194	30	TALWARA	26.47
195	63	SAHARA	26.44
196	65	SUWANA	26.41
196	216	ABU ROAD	26.41
198	20	THANAGAZI	26.20
198	48	KAMAN	26.20
200	140	SANCHORE	26.09
201	61	MANDALGARH	25.94
202	4	KEKRI	25.57
203	85	KAPASAN	25.30
204	76	BARI SADRI	25.13
205	207	SAWAI MADHOPUR	24.74
206	157	BAP	24.67
207	68	KOLAYAT	24.64
207	88	RASHMI	24.64
207	108	SIMALWARA	24.64
210	60	MANDAL	24.62
211	64	SHAHPURA	24.59
212	182	MUNDWA	24.44
213	62	RAIPUR	24.21
214	24	BAGIDORA	24.03
215	23	ANANDPURI	24.02
216	133	SAM	23.98
217	142	BAKANI	23.85
218	221	DEOLI	23.45
219	158	BHOPALGARH	23.41
220	141	SAYLA	23.10
221	55	ASIND	22.93
222	226	UNIARA	22.56
223	59	KOTRI	22.53
224	161	MANDOR	22.08
225	225	TONK	21.93
226	26	GHATOL	21.70
227	2	BHINAY	21.23
228	29	SAJJANGARH	21.12
229	138	JASWANTPURA	20.68
230	206	KHANDAR	20.53
231	156	BALESAR	19.80
232	136	BHINMAL	19.50
233	164	SHERGARH	19.48
234	229	DHARIAWAD	18.21
235	27	KUSHALGARH	18.10
		VERY LOW (<15)	
236	28	PEEPALKHOONT	11.87
237	234	KOTRA	11.14
		RAJASTHAN	**37.74**
		% AGE OF AAPs	**38.40**

BOLD: Equal/Above Average Panchayat Samities (AAPs)
Source: General Annex V.

ANNEX-12.14

PANCHAYAT SAMITIES OF RAJASTHAN: CODE NUMBERS

PANCHAYAT SAMITIES		
P.CODE *	Census Code	NAME
		AJMER DISTRICT
1	2102	ARAIN
2	2107	BHINAY
3	2105	JAWAJA
4	2108	KEKRI
5	2101	KISHANGARH
6	2106	MASOODA
7	2104	PISANGAN
8	2103	SRINAGAR
		ALWAR
9	0609	BANSURE
10	0601	BEHROR
11	0614	KATHUMAR
12	0604	KISHANGARH BAS
13	0605	KOTKASIM
14	0613	LACHHMANGARH
15	0603	MANDAWAR
16	0602	NIMRANA
17	0611	RAJGARH
18	0607	RAMGARH
19	0612	RENI
20	0610	THANAGAZI
21	0606	TIJARA
22	0608	UMREN
		BANSWARA
23	2805	ANANDPURI
24	2806	BAGIDORA
25	2804	GARHI
26	2801	GHATOL
27	2808	KUSHALGARH
28	2802	PEEPALKHOONT
29	2807	SAJJANGARH
30	2803	TALWARA
		BARAN
31	3101	ANTA
32	3105	ATRU
33	3102	BARAN
34	3107	CHHABRA
35	3106	CHHIPABAROD
36	3103	KISHANGANJ
37	3104	SHAHBAD
		BARMER
38	1703	BALOTRA
39	1706	BARMER
40	1702	BAYTOO
41	1707	CHOHTAN
42	1708	DHORIMANNA
43	1701	SHEO
44	1705	SINDHARI
45	1704	SIWANA
		BHARATPUR
46	0708	BAYANA
47	0703	DEEG
48	0701	KAMAN
49	0704	KUMHER
50	0706	NADBAI
51	0702	NAGAR PAHARI
52	0709	RUPBAS
53	0705	SEWAR
54	0707	WEIR
		BHILWARA
55	2401	ASIND
56	2404	BANERA
57	2402	HURDA
58	2410	JAHAZPUR
59	2409	KOTRI
60	2405	MANDAL
61	2411	MANDALGARH
62	2406	RAIPUR
63	2407	SAHARA
64	2403	SHAHPURA
65	2408	SUWANA
		BIKANER
66	0301	BIKANER
67	0405	DUNGARGARH #
68	0303	KOLAYAT
69	0302	LUNKARANSAR
70	0304	NOKHA
		BUNDI
71	2301	HINDOLI
72	2303	KESHORAIPATAN
73	2302	NAINWA
74	2304	TALERA
		CHITTAURGARH
75	2914	ARNOD
76	2912	BARI SADRI
77	2903	BEGUN
78	2909	BHADESAR
79	2904	BHAINSRORGARH
80	2907	BHOPALSAGAR
81	2911	CHHOTI SADRI
82	2905	CHITTAURGARH
83	2908	DUNGLA
84	2902	GANGRAR
85	2906	KAPASAN
86	2910	NIMBAHERA
87	2913	PRATAPGARH
88	2901	RASHMI
		CHURU
89	0404	CHURU
90	0402	RAJGARH
91	0406	RATANGARH
92	0403	SARDARSHAHAR
93	0407	SUJANGARH
94	0401	TARANAGAR
		DAUSA
95	1101	BANDIKUI
96	1104	DAUSA
97	1105	LALSOT
98	1102	MAHWA
99	1103	SIKRAI
		DHAULPUR
100	0802	BARI
101	0801	BASERI
102	0803	DHAULPUR
103	0804	RAJAKHERA
		DUNGARPUR
104	2703	ASPUR
105	2701	BICHHIWARA
106	2702	DUNGARPUR
107	2704	SAGWARA
108	2705	SIMALWARA
		GANGANAGAR
109	0106	ANUPGARH
110	0102	GANGANAGAR
111	0101	KARANPUR
112	0104	PADAMPUR
113	0105	RAISINGHNAGAR
114	0103	SADULSHAHAR
115	0107	SURATGARH
		HANUMANGARH
116	0203	BHADRA
117	0201	HANUMANGARH
118	0202	NOHAR
		JAIPUR
119	1206	AMBER
120	1208	BASSI
121	1213	CHAKSU
122	1210	DUDU
123	1204	GOVINDGARH
124	1207	JAMWA RAMGARH
125	1209	JHOTWARA
126	1201	KOTPUTLI
127	1211	PHAGI
128	1205	SAMBHAR
129	1212	SANGANER
130	1203	SHAHPURA
131	1202	VIRATNAGAR
		JAISALMER
132	1601	JAISALMER
133	1602	SAM
134	1603	SANKRA
		JALOR
135	1801	AHORE
136	1804	BHINMAL
137	1802	JALOR
138	1807	JASWANTPURA
139	1806	RANIWARA
140	1805	SANCHORE
141	1803	SAYLA
		JHALAWAR
142	3204	BAKANI
143	3206	DAG
144	3202	JHALRAPATAN
145	3201	KHANPUR
146	3203	MANOHARTHANA
147	3205	PIRAWA
		JHUNJHUNUN
148	0502	ALSISAR
149	0505	BUHANA
150	0503	CHIRAWA
151	0501	JHUNJHUNUN
152	0506	KHETRI
153	0507	NAWALGARH
154	0504	SURAJGARH
155	0508	UDAIPURWATI
		JODHPUR
156	1504	BALESAR
157	1501	BAP
158	1506	BHOPALGARH
159	1509	BILARA
160	1508	LUNI
161	1507	MANDOR
162	1505	OSIAN
163	1502	PHALODI
164	1503	SHERGARH
		KARAULI
165	0903	HINDAUN
166	0904	KARAULI
167	0901	NADOTI
168	0905	SAPOTRA
169	0902	TODABHIM
		KOTA
170	3004	CHECHAT
171	3001	ITAWA
172	3003	LADPURA
173	3005	SANGOD
174	3002	SULTANPUR
		NAGAUR
175	1408	DEGANA
176	1402	DIDWANA
177	1405	JAYAL
178	1403	KUCHAMAN
179	1401	LADNU
180	1404	MAKRANA
181	1409	MERTA
182	1407	MUNDWA
183	1406	NAGAUR
184	1411	PARBATSAR
185	1410	RIYAN
		PALI
186	2009	BALI
187	2010	DESURI
188	2001	JAITARAN
189	2006	KHARCHI/MARWAR JUN.
190	2005	PALI
191	2002	RAIPUR
192	2007	RANI STATION
193	2004	ROHAT
194	2003	SOJAT
195	2008	SUMERPUR
		RAJSAMAND
196	2503	AMET
197	2501	BHIM
198	2502	DEOGARH
199	2505	KHAMNOR
200	2504	KUMBHALGARH
201	2507	RAILMAGRA
202	2506	RAJSAMAND
		SAWAI MADHOPUR
203	1001	BAMANWAS
204	1003	BONLI
205	1002	GANGAPUR
206	1005	KHANDAR
207	1004	SAWAI MADHOPUR
		SIKAR
208	1304	DANTA RAMGARH
209	1303	DHOND
210	1301	FATEHPUR
211	1306	KHANDELA
212	1302	LACHHMANGARH
213	1307	NEEM KA THANA
214	1305	PIPRALI
215	1308	SRI MADHOPUR
		SIROHI
216	1904	ABU ROAD
217	1905	PINDWARA
218	1903	REODAR
219	1901	SHEOGANJ
220	1902	SIROHI
		TONK
221	2205	DEOLI
222	2201	MALPURA
223	2203	NIWAI
224	2204	TODARAISINGH
225	2202	TONK
226	2206	UNIARA
		UDAIPUR
227	2602	BARGAON
228	2604	BHINDER
229	2611	DHARIAWAD
230	2605	GIRWA
231	2601	GOGUNDA
232	2607	JHADOL
233	2608	KHERWARA
234	2606	KOTRA
235	2603	MAVLI
236	2610	SALUMBAR
237	2609	SARADA

Note:* Panchayat samiti code number used in the research, # Dungargarh PS shifted from Churu to Bikaner district on 1st April 2001.

ANNEX- 12.15

KEY TO PANCHAYAT SAMITIES

(Alphabetical Order)

HSI RANK, 2001	PANCHAYAT SAMITIES P CODE	NAME	HEALTH STATUS INDEX	HSI RANK, 2001	PANCHAYAT SAMITIES P.CODE	NAME	HEALTH STATUS INDEX	HSI RANK, 2001	PANCHAYAT SAMITIES P.CODE	NAME	HEALTH STATUS INDEX
1	2	3	4	1	2	3	4	1	2	3	4
141	216	ABU ROAD	0.6618	151	26	GHATOL	0.6555	90	112	PADAMPUR	0.6968
8	135	AHORE	0.7941	82	230	GIRWA	0.7056	57	190	PALI	0.7246
52	148	ALSISAR	0.7316	135	231	GOGUNDA	0.6659	56	184	PARBATSAR	0.7254
101	119	AMBER	0.6910	20	123	GOVINDGARH	0.7682	219	28	PEEPALKHOONT	0.5685
148	196	AMET	0.6562	129	117	HANUMANGARH	0.6726	161	127	PHAGI	0.6441
192	23	ANANDPURI	0.6167	50	165	HINDAUN	0.7326	146	163	PHALODI	0.6584
143	31	ANTA	0.6603	168	71	HINDOLI	0.6375	47	217	PINDWARA	0.7379
225	109	ANUPGARH	0.5610	58	57	HURDA	0.7243	9	214	PIPRALI	0.7841
127	1	ARAIN	0.6736	162	171	ITAWA	0.6437	193	147	PIRAWA	0.6153
210	75	ARNOD	0.5903	166	58	JAHAZPUR	0.6404	42	7	PISANGAN	0.7417
122	55	ASIND	0.6764	227	132	JAISALMER	0.5541	190	87	PRATAPGARH	0.6185
24	104	ASPUR	0.7632	37	188	JAITARAN	0.7466	23	201	RAILMAGRA	0.7650
140	32	ATRU	0.6619	12	137	JALOR	0.7826	43	191	RAIPUR	0.7404
184	24	BAGIDORA	0.6251	87	124	JAMWA RAMGARH	0.6978	97	62	RAIPUR	0.6919
228	142	BAKANI	0.5525	41	138	JASWANTPURA	0.7441	164	113	RAISINGHNAGAR	0.6419
153	156	BALESAR	0.6530	68	3	JAWAJA	0.7191	215	103	RAJAKHERA	0.5785
6	186	BALI	0.8057	112	177	JAYAL	0.6812	98	90	RAJGARH	0.6918
187	38	BALOTRA	0.6194	177	232	JHADOL	0.6309	165	17	RAJGARH	0.6404
174	203	BAMANWAS	0.6316	207	144	JHALRAPATAN	0.5985	105	202	RAJSAMAND	0.6890
118	95	BANDIKUI	0.6771	106	125	JHOTWARA	0.6887	147	18	RAMGARH	0.6569
39	56	BANERA	0.7464	29	151	JHUNJHUNUN	0.7596	3	192	RANI STATION	0.8148
119	9	BANSURE	0.6769	195	48	KAMAN	0.6137	62	139	RANIWARA	0.7228
226	157	BAP	0.5588	204	85	KAPASAN	0.6016	63	88	RASHMI	0.7226
124	33	BARAN	0.6753	95	111	KARANPUR	0.6928	2	91	RATANGARH	0.8164
96	227	BARGAON	0.6920	183	166	KARAULI	0.6265	115	19	RENI	0.6785
212	100	BARI	0.5844	136	11	KATHUMAR	0.6646	79	218	REODAR	0.7079
163	76	BARI SADRI	0.6427	48	4	KEKRI	0.7348	71	185	RIYAN	0.7160
236	39	BARMER	0.4930	196	72	KESHORAIPATAN	0.6136	100	193	ROHAT	0.6911
221	101	BASERI	0.5663	74	199	KHAMNOR	0.7155	132	52	RUPBAS	0.6699
102	120	BASSI	0.6905	200	206	KHANDAR	0.6089	111	114	SADULSHAHAR	0.6817
199	46	BAYANA	0.6120	18	211	KHANDELA	0.7736	14	107	SAGWARA	0.7802
234	40	BAYTOO	0.4950	176	145	KHANPUR	0.6309	44	63	SAHARA	0.7396
188	77	BEGUN	0.6188	35	189	KHARCHI/MARWAR JUN.	0.7486	203	29	SAJJANGARH	0.6021
26	10	BEHROR	0.7615	152	233	KHERWARA	0.6541	121	236	SALUMBAR	0.6766
182	78	BHADESAR	0.6269	11	152	KHETRI	0.7827	237	133	SAM	0.4749
69	116	BHADRA	0.7173	185	36	KISHANGANJ	0.6249	59	128	SAMBHAR	0.7241
213	79	BHAINSRORGARH	0.5819	70	5	KISHANGARH	0.7172	172	140	SANCHORE	0.6339
84	197	BHIM	0.7011	171	12	KISHANGARH BAS	0.6348	126	129	SANGANER	0.6740
117	2	BHINAY	0.6771	217	68	KOLAYAT	0.5752	145	173	SANGOD	0.6599
109	228	BHINDER	0.6841	142	13	KOTKASIM	0.6614	229	134	SANKRA	0.5487
92	136	BHINMAL	0.6954	80	126	KOTPUTLI	0.7073	194	168	SAPOTRA	0.6140
36	158	BHOPALGARH	0.7479	233	234	KOTRA	0.4951	77	237	SARADA	0.7122
128	80	BHOPALSAGAR	0.6731	181	59	KOTRI	0.6281	191	92	SARDARSHAHAR	0.6175
55	105	BICHHIWARA	0.7266	123	178	KUCHAMAN	0.6762	159	207	SAWAI MADHOPUR	0.6450
209	66	BIKANER	0.5913	114	200	KUMBHALGARH	0.6803	25	141	SAYLA	0.7621
10	159	BILARA	0.7828	45	49	KUMHER	0.7390	104	53	SEWAR	0.6895
167	204	BONLI	0.6376	222	27	KUSHALGARH	0.5633	214	37	SHAHBAD	0.5809
21	149	BUHANA	0.7669	61	212	LACHHMANGARH	0.7233	34	130	SHAHPURA	0.7487
222	121	CHAKSU	0.5633	133	14	LACHHMANGARH	0.6672	157	64	SHAHPURA	0.6464
89	170	CHECHAT	0.6970	30	179	LADNU	0.7543	235	43	SHEO	0.4938
230	34	CHHABRA	0.5216	78	172	LADPURA	0.7114	31	219	SHEOGANJ	0.7538
220	35	CHHIPABAROD	0.5674	201	97	LALSOT	0.6088	202	164	SHERGARH	0.6050
197	81	CHHOTI SADRI	0.6124	46	160	LUNI	0.7390	150	99	SIKRAI	0.6557
15	150	CHIRAWA	0.7770	180	69	LUNKARANSAR	0.6284	107	108	SIMALWARA	0.6858
160	82	CHITTAURGARH	0.6443	154	98	MAHWA	0.6485	224	44	SINDHARI	0.5611
211	41	CHOHTAN	0.5880	85	180	MAKRANA	0.7008	5	220	SIROHI	0.8059
19	89	CHURU	0.7716	137	222	MALPURA	0.6640	67	45	SIWANA	0.7197
218	143	DAG	0.5723	103	60	MANDAL	0.6896	28	194	SOJAT	0.7603
22	208	DANTA RAMGARH	0.7667	169	61	MANDALGARH	0.6374	13	215	SRI MADHOPUR	0.7825
149	96	DAUSA	0.6561	83	15	MANDAWAR	0.7037	73	8	SRINAGAR	0.7157
93	47	DEEG	0.6939	144	161	MANDOR	0.6600	60	93	SUJANGARH	0.7240
81	175	DEGANA	0.7072	232	146	MANOHARTHANA	0.5097	72	174	SULTANPUR	0.7159
156	198	DEOGARH	0.6475	110	6	MASOODA	0.6824	4	195	SUMERPUR	0.8076
178	221	DEOLI	0.6302	49	235	MAVLI	0.7348	94	154	SURAJGARH	0.6928
16	187	DESURI	0.7745	66	181	MERTA	0.7209	231	115	SURATGARH	0.5150
186	229	DHARIAWAD	0.6205	99	182	MUNDWA	0.6914	88	65	SUWANA	0.6972
208	102	DHAULPUR	0.5947	54	50	NADBAI	0.7286	173	74	TALERA	0.6318
7	209	DHOND	0.7978	113	167	NADOTI	0.6804	134	30	TALWARA	0.6660
206	42	DHORIMANNA	0.6006	179	51	NAGAR PAHARI	0.6301	75	94	TARANAGAR	0.7154
51	176	DIDWANA	0.7325	139	183	NAGAUR	0.6631	130	20	THANAGAZI	0.6726
120	122	DUDU	0.6766	198	73	NAINWA	0.6122	189	21	TIJARA	0.6187
27	67	DUNGARGARH *	0.7612	17	153	NAWALGARH	0.7741	108	169	TODABHIM	0.6843
65	106	DUNGARPUR	0.7214	40	213	NEEM KA THANA	0.7444	131	224	TODARAISINGH	0.6713
91	83	DUNGLA	0.6959	116	86	NIMBAHERA	0.6775	155	225	TONK	0.6480
32	210	FATEHPUR	0.7534	33	16	NIMRANA	0.7520	1	155	UDAIPURWATI	0.8307
76	110	GANGANAGAR	0.7151	175	223	NIWAI	0.6309	125	22	UMREN	0.6751
86	205	GANGAPUR	0.6992	216	118	NOHAR	0.5785	205	226	UNIARA	0.6007
158	84	GANGRAR	0.6454	138	70	NOKHA	0.6635	64	131	VIRATNAGAR	0.7225
38	25	GARHI	0.7465	53	162	OSIAN	0.7313	170	54	WEIR	0.6374

Source: Annex 11.2.

BIBLIOGRAPHY

Anand, Sudhir. and Amartya Sen. 1994. "Human Development Index: Methodology and Measurement". Occasional Paper 12. United Nations Development Programme, Human Development Report Office, New York.

Anand, Sudhir. and Amartya Sen. 1995. "Gender Inequality in Human Development: Theories and Measurement". Occasional Paper 15. United Nations Development Programme. Human Development Report Office. New York.

Anand, Sudhir. and Amartya Sen. 1997. "Concepts of Human Development and Poverty: A Multidimensional Perspective". United Nations Development Programme, Human Development Report 1997 Papers: Poverty and Human Development, New York.

Basu, A M and Basu K 1991 Women"s Economic Role and Child"s Survival: The Case of India, *Health Transition Review,* Volume 1, No. 1.

Bhargava, S.K. *et al.* 1991, "Current Status on Neonatal Care and Alternate Strategies for Reduction of Neonatal Mortality in the Decade of Nineties", *Indian Pediatrics,* 28 (12) .

Bhat, Ramesh 1993 . "The Public/Private Mix in Health Care in India", *International Journal of Health Policy and Planning,* 8 (1).

Bhatia, J. C. 1982 *'A Study of Maternal Mortality in Anantpur District, Andhra Pradesh',* Indian Institute of Management, Banglore.

Bose, Ashish. 2002. "Towards Population Stabilisation", *NFI Bulletin,* October, The Nutritional Foundation of India, New Delhi.

Buchert, Lene. Ed. 1998. "Education Reform in the South in the 1990s". UNESCO, Paris.

Caldwell, John C. 1986. Routes to Low Mortality in Poor Countries, *Population & Development Review,* Vol. 12, No. 2.

Caldwell, John C. 1992. Old and New Factors in Health Transition, *Health Transition Review,* Volume 2, Supplementary Issue.

Central, Bureau of Health, Intelligence, "Health Information India", Various Years, Directorate General of Health Services, Ministry of Health & Family Welfare, New Delhi.

Centre for Energy, 2001. "India: Raising the Sights-Better Health System for India's Poor", Health, Nutrition, Population Sector Unit, India, South Asia Region, Report No. 22304.

Centre for Policy Research. 2000. "The Report on the Restructuring of the Ministry of Health and Family Welfare", New Delhi.

Chaterjee, Meera. 1990. "Indian Women: Their Health and Productivity". Discussion paper No. 109, World Bank, Washington D.C.

Chaturwedi, A., Khanna A. and Kothari D. 2001. "Provision of Two-Child Norm in Panchayati Raj Act of Rajasthan: A Critical Review of Impact and Perception", FPA Working paper No 9, Forum for Population Action, Jaipur.

Chaudhary, Ranjit Roy 2001. "The Medicines Scenario in India", Background Paper, National Institute of Immunology, New Delhi.

Chiapah, Vinayagum. 1997. "Handbook on Monitoring Learning Achievement: Towards Capacity Building", United Nations Educational Scientific and Cultural Organization, Paris.

Chima, R.I. and A. Mills 1998. *"Estimating the Economic Impact of Malaria in Sub-Saharan Africa: A Review of the Empirical Evidence"*, Mimeo, London School of Hygiene and Tropical Medicine, June.

Colombini, Manuela. "Gender-based and Sexual Violence against Women during Armed Conflict". *Journal of Health Management,* 4, 2 (2002). "The case for Gender Equity in Health Research". Sage Publications New Delhi, Thousand Oaks, London.

Corbett, Jenny. 1998. *"Special Educational Needs in the Twentieth Century: A Cultural Analysis"*, Institute of Education Series, London, Cassell.

Cornia, Andrea and Julius Court. 2001. "Inequality, Growth and Poverty in the Era of Liberalisation and Globalisation". Policy Brief 4. United Nations University and World Institute for Development Economics Research, Helsinki, Finland.

Das Gupta, Monica, Chen, Lincoln C. and Krishana, T.N. eds. 1998. *"Health, Poverty and Development in India"*, Oxford University Press, Delhi.

Deaton, Angus. 2001. "Health, Ineqality and Economics Development", NBER Working Paper No. 8313, National Bureau of Economic Research, Cambridge, Mass.

Department of Family Welfare, 2000-01. *"Bulletin on Rural Health, Family Welfare Programme in India-Year Book"*, GoI, New Delhi.

Dev, S. Mahendra, Antony Piush, Gayathri, V. and Mamgain, R.P. 2001. *"Social and Economic Security in India"*, Institute of Human Development, New Delhi, Manohar Publishers.

DGHS. 1998. "Directory of Hospitals in India", Office of the Registrar General India, Ministry of Health and Family Welfare, GoI, New Delhi.

Directorate of Census Operation, 1991. "Primary Census Abstract of Rajasthan", Census of India-Rajasthan, Series-21, Jaipur.

Directorate of Census Operation, 1991. "District Census Handbook (All Districts)", Raj., Jaipur.

Directorate of Census Operations, Rajasthan, 2001 "Final Population Totals", Rajasthan.

Directorate of Census Operations, 1991 "Census Atlas-Rajasthan", Part-XI.

Directorate of Economics and Statistics. 2003. "District Statistical Abstract-All Districts", Jaipur.

Directorate of Economics and Statistics. 2005. "Economic Review, 2004-05", Jaipur.

Directorate of Medical and Health, 2005. "Pragati Prativedan 2004-05". GoR. Jaipur.

Directorate of Medical, Health and FP, "Pragati Prativedan 2004-05". GoR. Jaipur

Dubey, Amresh, Gangopadhyay, Shubhashis. 1999. "Counting the Poor: Where are the Poor in India", Servekshana Analtical Report No. 1, Department of Statistics, New Delhi.

Health Monitor, 2004. Foundation for Research in Health System, Ahmedabad.

GoI, "Tenth Five-Year Plan Document", Planning Commission, New Delhi.

GoI, 2004-05. "Economic Survey". Ministry of Finance & Economic Division. New Delhi.

GoI, 2000. National Population Policy, Department of Family Welfare, Government of India, 1954-55. New Delhi, p.71. New Delhi.

Gopalan, Sarala and Shiva Mira. 2000. *"National Profile on Women, Health and Development"*, Country Profile-India VHAI and WHO. New Delhi.

GoR, 1992. "Jan Mangal-Project Document". (Unpublished), Department of Medical & Health Services, Jaipur.

GoR, 1992. Report on the Mid-Term Evaluation of the UNFPA Assisted Area Project Phase-II (Jaipur: Department of Medical & Health).

GoR, 1997. "Population Policy for Rajasthan: Identification of Issues—*Proceedings of Workshop"*, Jointly Organised By the Indian Institute of Health Management Research, Jaipur and Government of Rajasthan.

GoR, 1998. "Draft Population Policy for Rajasthan". Developed By the Indian Institute of Health Management Research, Jaipur.

Goverenment of Madhya Pradesh, 1995 & 1998. "The Madhya Pradesh Human Development Report", Directorate of Institutional Finance, Project Office, Bhopal.

Guijt, Lrena and Shah, Meena Kaul. " The Myth of Community". *Journal of Health Management,* 4, 2 (2002). "The case for Gender Equity in Health Research". Sage Publications New Delhi, Thousand Oaks, London.

Gupta, R.N. 1988. "Health and Family Welfare Programme in Rajasthan-An Appraisal in M.E. Khan *et al.* (ed) *Performance of Health and Family Welfare Programme in India* (Bombay: Himalaya Publishing House.

Gupta, Indrani and Arup Mitra. 2001. *"Economic Growth, Health and Poverty: An Exploratory Study on India"*, Background Paper, ICRIER, New Delhi.

Haq, Mahbub Ul. 1998. *"Human Development in South Asia"*, Human Development Centre, Pakistan.

Harman, H. H. 1967. *"Modern Factor Analysis,"* University Press, Chicago, U.S.A.

Harvard Centre for Population and Development Studies 2000. "Neonatal Mortality in India: Emerging Paradoxes", *Working Paper Series,* 10 (13), Harvard University.

IIPS, 1993. "National Family Health Survey (NFHS-1)", International Institute of Population Sciences, Mumbai.

IIPS, 1998. "Infant and Child Mortality in India", Subject Report, International Institute of Population Sciences, Mumbai.

IIPS, 1998. "Mother's Employment and Infant and Child Mortality in India", NFHS Subject Report, December, Mumbai.

IIPS and ORC Macro. 2000. National Family Health Survey (NFHS-2), 1998-99: India International Institute for Population Sciences, Mumbai.

Indian Council of Social Service Research (ICSSR). 1981. "Health for All, An Alternative Strategy", ICSSR/ ICMR Report, Committee under the Chairmanship of Ramalingaswamy, New Delhi.

Indira Gandhi Institute of Development Research. 1997. "Indian Development Report", Mumbai.

International Fund for Agricultural Development. 2001. *"Rural Poverty Report 2001: The Challenge of Ending Rural Poverty".* Oxford University Press, New Delhi.

International Institute for Population Sciences, "National Family Health Survey 1992-93 and 1988-89" India and Various State Reports, Mumbai.

IPU Inter-Parliamentary Union. 1995. *"Women in Parliaments 1945-1995"*, A World Statistical Survey. Geneva.

Joshi, Hemlata, 2002. "Gender Related Educational Development Index-Raj. 2000, A Geographical Analysis at Panchayat Samiti Level", Transactions, *Institute of Indian Geographers,* Vol. 24, No. 1 & 2, pp. 41-52.

Joshi, Hemlata, 2003. "Educational Development Index-Rajasthan Spatio-Temporal Appraisal at Panchayat Samiti/Block Level, 1991-2000", Published Research Report, Institute of Development Studies, University Book House, Jaipur.

Joshi, Hemlata, 2005. "Economic Development Index (Spatio-Temporal Appraisal at Panchayat Samiti/Block Level), Published Research Report, Institute of Development Studies, University Book House, Jaipur.

Kalita, P., Choudhary, H. and Borha, M. 2004. "Factors Affecting the use of Contraception: A Case Study of Assam, based on a Multivariate Analysis", *Indian Journal of Regional Science,* Volume XXXVI, No. 2, pp 45.

Kanjilal, Barun and Sharma, Suneeta, 1999. *Journal of Health Management,* 1, 1.

"Sustainability of Private Voluntary Health Organisation (PVHO) in India: Some Methodology Issues". Sage Publications New Delhi, Thousand Oaks, London.

Kothari, Devendra, 1989. " Family Welfare Programme in Rajasthan: Beyond the Existing Apporach". Sponsored by the Department of Family Welfare, Ministry of Health and Family Welfare, Government of India, New Delhi. Indian Institute of Health Management Research, Jaipur.

Kothari, Devendra, 2001. "Rajasthan: Repoductive Health Needs of Women as Emerged from the Recent Findings", FPA Working Paper No. 14, Forum for Population Action, Jaipur.

Kothari, Devendra, Krishnaswamy, S., Maru, R.M., *et al.* 1997. "A Note on Recent Stagnation of Infant Mortality Rate in Rajasthan". Working Paper, Indian Institute of Health Management Research, Jaipur.

Kothari, Devendra, Maru R.M., Khanna, Anoop, *et al.* 1997. "Vikalp: Managing Family Planning Programme in the Post-ICPD Era: An Experiment in Rajasthan, India". IIHMR Occasional Paper No. 2, Indian Institute of Health Management Research, Jaipur.

Lubhaya, Ram, 1998. "Target-free Approach for Family Welfare: A Review of Expenditure in Rajasthan". In the Policy Project. Targets for Family Planning in India: An analysis of Policy Change, Consequences and Alternative Choices. The Futures Group International, New Delhi.

Lubhaya, Ram. *Innovative approaches to population programme management in Rajasthan.*

Malhotra, Rajeev, 1998. "An Interpretation of The Capability Approach for Constructing Development and Derivational Indices – A Comparison of Alternative Estimates at Regional Level for India", Mimeograph.

Measham, Anthony R. *et al.* 1999. "Reducing Infant Mortality and Fertility, 1975-90, Performance of all India and State Level", *EPW,* Sameeksha Trust, Mumbai.

Ministry of Health and Family Welfare. 1983. National Health Policy. GoI.

Ministry of Health and Family Welfare. 2000. National Population Policy, New Delhi.

Ministry of Human Resource Development "Annual Report". Various Years, New Delhi.

Ministry of Human Resource Development. 1997. "Women in India: A Statistical Profile", Department of Women and Child Development", Government of India, New Delhi.

Ministry of Human Resource Development, 1998. "India Nutrition Profile", Department of Women and Child Development, Government of India", New Delhi.

Morris, 1979. *"Measuring the Condition of the World"s Poor-The Physical Quality of Life Index",* Oxford Pergamon Press.

National Council of Applied Economic Research, 1996. "Human Development Profile of India: Inter-State and Inter-Group Differentials, Volume II, Statistical Tables", National Council of Applied Economic Research, New Delhi.

National Council of Applied Economic Research, 1999. "India Human Development Report", National Council of Applied Economic Research, Oxford University Press, New Delhi.

National Council of Applied Economic Research, 2002. "West and Central India Human Development Report", Oxford University Press

National Institute of Rural Development, 1999. "Rural Development Statistics", Hyderabad.

National Sample Survey Organiation, 1989. Morbidity and Utilisation of Medical Services 42nd Round, Department of Statistics, GoI, New Delhi.

National Sample Survey Organisation, 1992. "Morbidity and Utilisation of Medical Services", NSS 42nd Round 1986-87, *Sarvekshana,* 51st Issue, Volume-XV No. 4, Department of Statistics, New Delhi.

National Sample Survey Organisation, 1998. "The Aged in India: A Socio-Economic Profile", Department of Statistics, Ministry of Planning and Programme Implementation, New Delhi.

National Sample Survey Organistion, 1998. Morbidity and Treatment of Ailments, 52nd Round, July 1995-June 1996, Report No. 445, Department of Statistics, New Delhi.

National Sample Survey Organisation, 1999. "Drinking Water, Sanitation and Hygiene in India", 54th Round, January-June 1998, Report No. 449, Department of Statistics, New Delhi.

National Sample Survey Organiation, 2001. "Poverty Estimates, 2001". Department of Statistics, GoI, New Delhi.

National Sample Survey Organisation, 2001. "Employment and Unemployment Situation in India – 1999-2000", Part – I, NSS, 55th Round, July 1999-June 2000, Report No. 458, Ministry of Statistics and Programme Implementation, New Delhi.

NCERT, 2000. *"Fifth Survey of Educational Research 1988-92",* Vol. II, New Delhi.

NFHS-I. "Rajasthan: National Family Health Survey", 1992-93. International Institute of Population Sciences, Mumbai, 1991.

NFHS-II. "Rajasthan: National Family Health Survey", 1998-99. International Institute of Population Sciences, Mumbai, 2001.

OECD, 2000. "A New Economy-The Changing Roll of Innovation and Information Technology in Growth", Organization for Economic Co-operation and Development, Paris.

Office of the Registrar General India. 1987. "Child Mortality & Fertility, Rajasthan, "Occasional Paper-13, 1987, Based on 1981 Census, Demographic Division, Ministry of Home Affairs, New Delhi.

Office of the Registrar General India. 1988. "Child Mortality Estimates of India", Census of India, 1981, "Occasional paper No. 5 of 1988", Demographic Division, Ministry of Home Affairs, New Delhi.

Office of the Registrar General India. 1991. "Statistics in India for the Quarter Ending December 1991", Rural Health Division, Directorate General of Health Services, Ministry of Health & FW. GoI, New Delhi.

Office of the Registrar General India. 1992. "Sample Registration Bulletin", Volume XXII, No. 1. Ministry of Home Affairs, New Delhi.

Office of Registrar General, India. 1996. Population Projections for India and States, 1996-2016, Report of the Technical Group of Population Projections. GoI. New Delhi.

Office of the Registrar General India. 1998. "Sample Registration System-SRS, Annual Report". Vital Statistics Division, Ministry of Home Affairs, August, 1992.

Office of the Registrar General India. 1998. "Survey of Causes of Death-Rural, Series 3, No. 21, Annual Report", Ministry of Home Affairs, New Delhi, March, 1990.

Pahariya, S. *"Vikalp: An Innovative Strategy for Management of Family Welfare Programme"*.

Pandey, Arvind, Choe, M.K., Luther, N.Y., Sahu, D. and Chand, J. 1998. "Infant and Child Mortality in India", National Family Health Survey, Subject Reports No. 11, East-West-Center Honolulu, Hawaii.

Parikh, Kirit S. and R. Sudershana, Ed. 1993. *"Human Development and Structural Adjustment"*, Macmillan India Limited, Madras.

Planning Commission, GoI. 1951. "Recommendations of the Sub-Committee on Population Growth and Family Planning". New Delhi.

Pyle, David F. *Journal of Health Management,* 1, 1 (1999). "Community Driven Strategy to Reduce Malnutrition: Experience from Tanzania and Sri Lanka". Sage Publications New Delhi, Thousand Oaks, London.

Rajvanshi, Jyotsna. December 2004. "Existing System of Distribution of Nutrition its Quality Acceptability of beneficiaries and Need for Alternative Cost Effective System". Institute of Development Studies, Jaipur.

Rao, Hemlata, G.P. Mishra (Ed.) 1992. "Inter-State Disparities in Development in India," *op. cit.* 7.

Rao, Mohan. "Disinvesting in Health The World Bank's Prescription for Health". *Journal of Health Management,* 4, 2 (2002). "The case for Gender Equity in Health Research". Sage Publications New Delhi, Thousand Oaks, London.

RBI. 2000. *Reserve Bank of India Bulletin,* October 2000, IV (10).

Registrar General of India, SRS based Abridged Lief Tables, Various issues, New Delhi.

Registrar General of India, 1981. "Indirect Estimates of Fertility and Mortality at the District Level 1981 and Report of the Expert Committee on Population Projection, 1981-2001, Census of India-Occasional Paper No. 4 of 1994.

Registrar General of India, 1987. Fertility and Child Mortality, Estimates of Rajasthan, Census of India-Occasional Paper No. 5 of 1987.

Registrar General of India, 1997. District Level Estimates of Fertility and Child Mortality for 1991 and their Interrelations with other Variables, Occasional Paper No. 1, New Delhi.

Registrar General of India, 1998. "State Profile 1991 India", Census of India 1991, RGI, New Delhi.

Registrar General India, 1999. "Working Children in India, an Analysis of the 1991 Census Data", New Delhi.

Registrar General of India, 2001. "Census of India", Provisional Population Totals-India, Paper 1 of 2001, New Delhi.

Registrar General of India, 2002. *"SRS Bulletin"* New Delhi, Volume 36, No. 2, New Delhi.

Registrar General of India. 2001, *SRS Bulletin,* Sample Registration System, Volume 35, No. 1, Vital Statistics Division, New Delhi.

Sachdeva, Arvinder S. 2002. "Urbanisation in India: Past Trends and Future Projections", *The Asian Journal,* Vol. 9, No. 1 February, New Delhi.

Sangwana, Naveen and Maru, M. Rushikesh. *Journal of Health Management,* 1, 1 (1999). "The Target-Free Approach: An Overview". Sage Publications New Delhi, Thousand Oaks, London.

Sen, Amartya, 1995, Mortality as an Indicator of Economic Success and Failure, Discussion Paper, DEP No. 66, Development Economics Research Programme, Sti CERD, London School of Economics, London.

Sen, Amartya, 1996. "Radical Needs and Moderate Reforms", in Jean Dreze and Amartya Sen (ed.), *Indian Development: Selected Regional Perspectives,* pp. 1-32, UNI/WIDER.

Sen, Amartya, 1999, Health in Development, *Bulletin of the World Health Organisation,* 77 (8), pp. 619-623, World Health Organisation, Geneva.

Sen, Gita, George, Asha and Ostlin, Piroska. *Journal of Health Management,* 4, 2 (2002). "The case for Gender Equity in Health Research". Sage Publications New Delhi, Thousand Oaks, London.

Sen, A. K. 1981. *"Patterns of Regional Development–A Comparative Study",* Sterling, New Delhi.

Shankaranarayanan, R. 1997. "Health Care Auxiliaries in the Detection and Prevention of Oral Cancer". *Oral Oncology,* 149-54.

Shariff, Abusaleh, 1999. "India Human Development Report", NCAER, Oxford University Press, Delhi".

Sharma, R., Goyal, R. and Gupta, H. Rajlakshmi, 2002. "An initiative for improving the status of Girl Child in Rajasthan". FPA Working paper No. 13, Forum for population Action, Jaipur.

Shiva, Kumar. 1991. "Human Development Index for Indian States", *Economical and Political Weekly,* Vol. XXVI.

Singhi, N.K. 1999. "Development Debate and Human Development Index: Rajasthan", Institute of Development Studies-Jaipur.

Singhi, N.K. and Joshi Varsha. "Can ICDS do it: Health and Nutrition in Rajasthan". August 1996. Working Paper No. 072. Institute of Development Studies, Jaipur.

Sisodia, P. and RVHA. 1991. *"Expenditure Targets and Achievements of Selected National Health Programmes in Rajasthan",* Jaipur

Sisodia, P. 1991. "Public Expenditure on Health Care through the State Government of Rajasthan, Jaipur, IIHMR Mimeograph.

Sisodia, P. 1992. "Identification of Availability and Composition of Health Resources in Public Sector, Jaipur, IIHMR Mimeograph.

Society for International Development. 1999. "Human Development Report-Rajasthan", Jaipur.

Srinivasan, K. and Abusaleh Shariff. 1997. *"India Towards Population and Development Goals".* Delhi Oxford University Press, p. 11.

Srinivasan, Venkatesh. 2001.*"Health and Family Welfare Programmes in Developing Countries-Study of Innovations in an Indian State".* Aalekh Publishers, Jaipur.

Stuart, Gillespie and Geraldine McNeill. Food, Health and Survival in India and Developing Countries.

Sundaram, K. 2001. "Employment – Unemployment in the Nineties, Result From NSS 55th Round", *Economic and Political Weekly,* Volume XXXVI No. 11, March 17, 2001.

Sundaram, K. V. 1997. *"Decentralized Multilevel Planning: Principles and Practice: Asian and African Experiences",* New Delhi, Concept Pub. House, New Delhi.

Theobald, S., Elsey H. and R. Tolhurst, 2002."Gender Mainstreaming and Sector-Wide Apporaches in Health: Key Areas for Debate". *Journal of Health Management,* 4, 2. "The case for Gender Equity in Health Research". Sage Publications New Delhi, Thousand Oaks, London.

Tilak, Jandhyala B.G. 1999. "Investment in Human Capital in India: An Inter-State Analysis of Stock and Flow of Human Capital", *Journal of Indian School of Political Economy,* Volume XI, No. 1, pp. 39-75.

Tolhurst, R.K. de Koning, Price J., Kemp J., Theoblad S. and Squire S.B. 2002."The challenge of Infectious Disease: Time to Take Gender into Account". *Journal of Health Management,* 4, 2. "The case for Gender Equity in Health Research". Sage Publications New Delhi, Thousand Oaks, London.

United Nations. 2001. "World Population Prospects, 1950-2050: The 1998 Revision Database", Department of Economics and Social Affairs, Population Division, New York.

United Nations. 2002 a. "Correspondence on Time Use Survey", Department of Economics and Social Affairs, Statistical Division, February, New York.

United Nations. 2002 c. "United Nations Population Division Database on Contraceptive Use", Department of Economics and Social Affairs, Population Division, January, New York.

United Nations. 2002 d. "World Urbanisation Prospects: The 2001 Revision," Department of Economics and Social Affairs", Population Division, New York.

UNAIDS 2000. Report on the Global HIV/AIDS Epidemic, Geneva.

UNDP. 1990 to 2005. "Human Development Report", United Nations Development Programme, Oxford University Press, New York.

UNDP. 2001. "Correspondence on State-Level Communication, Education, Energy and Electricity Data for India", United Nations Development Programme, India Country Office, New Delhi.

UNDP and GoK. 1999. "Human Development in Karnataka", United Nations Development Programme and Government of Karnataka, Bangalore, India.

UNESCO. 2000. *"Statistical Yearbook",* United Nations Educational, Scientific and Cultural Organization, Paris.

UNICEF. 1994. "The Status of the World's Children", New Delhi: UNICEF. Pp, 23-31.

UNICEF, 1995. "The Progress of Indian States", Delhi.

UNICEF. 2001. "The State of the World"s Children 2001", New York: Oxford University Press.

UNICEF. 2002 a. "Correspondence on Infant and Under-Five Mortality Rates", January, New York.

UNICEF. 2002 b. "Official Summary: The State of the World Children 2002", New York, Oxford University Press.

WHO World Health Organisation. 2002 a. "Correspondence on Births Attended by Skilled Health Staff", Geneva.

WHO World Health Organisation. 2001 b. "Global Tuberculosis Control: WHO Report"

WHO World Health Organisation. 2002. "Report on the Global HIV/AIDS Epidemic", Geneva.

Williamson, J.G. 1965. "Regional Inequality and the Process of National Development", Economic Development and Cultural Change, 134.

World Bank, 2005. "World development Report. A Better Investment Climate for Everyone", Washington DC.

INDEX